D0759429

Capital Taxation

Capital Taxation

Martin Feldstein

Harvard University Press
Cambridge, Massachusetts
and London, England   1983

This book is printed on acid-free paper, and its binding
materials have been chosen for strength and durability.

Library of Congress Cataloging in Publication Data

Feldstein, Martin S.
  Capital taxation.

  Bibliography: p.
  Includes index.
  1. Saving and investment. 2. Taxation.
3. Tax incidence. 4. Capital levy. I. Title.
HC79.S3F42 1983   336.2   82-11819
ISBN 0-674-09482-4

Preface

The research presented in this volume examines the effects of capital taxation on the process of economic growth and the allocation of economic resources. The first seventeen chapters are theoretical and empirical studies of the ways in which taxation affects individual aspects of capital accumulation, including household and corporate saving, portfolio behavior, and business investment. In contrast, the final five chapters develop general equilibrium analyses of the impact of capital taxation in a growing economy. An introductory chapter provides a broad overview of the research and a summary of the principal conclusions.

Many of the chapters were written with coauthors: Louis Dicks-Mireaux, George Fane, John Flemming, Daniel Frisch, Jerry Green, James Poterba, Michael Rothschild, Eytan Sheshinski, Joel Slemrod, and Shlomo Yitzhaki. I am grateful for their collaboration in this research and for their permission to include our joint papers in this volume.

I have also been fortunate over the years to have the help of a very able group of research assistants. This group has included Virginia Ambrosini, Ann Black, Gary Chamberlain, Charles Horioka, Janet Hornby, Alicia Munnell, Harvey Rosen, and Amy Taylor, as well as some of those whose names appear as coauthors of other chapters. Douglas Bernheim and George Sofianos rechecked all of the theoretical derivations in the volume. Judy Frink prepared the manuscript and the bibliography for publication.

The chapters in the present volume were written between 1965 and 1980. I have benefited during these years from stimulating discussions with colleagues and students at Nuffield College in Oxford, at Harvard, and at the National Bureau of Economic Research. In addition to my coauthors and research assistants, I want to thank particularly Alan Auerbach, David Bradford, Kathleen Feldstein, Terence Gorman, John Helliwell, Mervyn King, Richard Musgrave, and Lawrence Summers. I am grateful also for the financial support of the National Science Foundation and the National Bureau of Economic Research. Several chapters were prepared as part of the NBER Special Study of Capital Formation.

Publication of this book does not indicate the end of my research on capital taxation. Much work remains to be done on this important subject. I plan to do some of that research myself, and I hope that this volume will encourage others to turn their attention to these crucial problems as well.

Contents

Capital Taxation

Introduction

The process of capital accumulation plays a central role in the growth of every economy. As a consequence, capital accumulation has been a major focus of economic theory and of empirical research throughout the history of modern economic analysis. In recent decades, the rate and form of capital accumulation have been substantially influenced by prevailing systems of taxation. The papers in this volume analyze the ways in which capital taxation alters the process of capital accumulation and affects the rewards to capital and labor.

The emphasis in these studies is on the behavioral response of households and businesses to changes in tax rules. Part One deals with the overall rate of saving and analyzes the separate effects of taxes on personal saving and on corporate saving as well as the interaction between the two types of saving. The papers in Part Two examine the effect of tax rules on the composition of household portfolios and on the process of portfolio adjustment. In Part Three I turn to corporate investment in plant and equipment and in inventories. The studies in these three sections focus on the individual components of the capital accumulation process rather than on the process as a whole. In contrast, Part Four presents general equilibrium analyses that look at the system as a whole in order to determine who bears the taxes levied on capital and capital income. The studies in this section differ from earlier treatments in the literature by emphasizing a growing economy and portfolio diversification.

A common theme throughout these chapters is that tax rules have a substantial effect on economic decisions. Both the theoretical analyses and the empirical research in the present volume support this theme. In contrast, much of the writing on taxation during the period since World War II implicitly assumed or explicitly asserted that the relative price changes implied by different types of capital taxation would have little or no impact on capital formation. The view that taxes do not influence capital formation followed from a general Keynesian presumption that the responses of individuals and businesses to price changes are small, and from the more specific beliefs that saving reflects income rather than the rate of return and that investment is determined by capacity utilization or anticipated sales rather than by the relation between the net-of-tax cost of funds and the net-of-tax return that firms can earn on those funds. The studies in this volume contradict this presumption of low price elasticities and show that tax rules significantly alter economic behavior.

These behavioral responses imply that tax rules distort both the amount of capital formation and the distribution of capital and of risk bearing in the economy. Such distortions imply a loss of economic efficiency and thus a lower level of real economic income. I have, however, limited the papers in this volume to the positive analysis of the effects of capital taxation and have not included papers that discuss the efficiency costs of alternative tax rules or that prescribe systems of optimal taxation.

This volume is thus not a book about economic policy as such but an attempt to understand how an important aspect of government policy influences the functioning of a modern economy. Moreover, the individual papers do not represent a comprehensive treatment of all aspects of capital taxation but focus on those questions that have appeared to me to be both economically important and analytically tractable. Although the empirical studies deal almost exclusively with the United States, I believe that much of the empirical work as well as the analytic papers will be of more general relevance.

The papers that are collected here were published in a variety of academic journals during a period of more than a dozen years. Not surprisingly, I would no longer agree with everything that I wrote in all of them. More important, if I were doing the studies now I would in several cases use somewhat different theoretical models or statistical methods. I have nevertheless resisted the temptation to make substantial changes because, if I once started, there would be no natural place to stop. I do, moreover, still believe in the basic conclusions of each of the papers included here.

This introduction summarizes these specific conclusions and indicates the structure of the overall analysis that links the individual chapters.

Household and Corporate Saving

A nation's rate of capital accumulation is governed by the amount of saving that is done within its borders. Although international capital flows can supplement or reduce the funds available for investment, in practice net international capital flows have been quite small relative to domestic savings and investment. Moreover, long-run differences among industrial countries in the fraction of income that is saved are matched by approximately equal differences in the ratio of domestic investment to national income (Feldstein and Horioka 1980). The present study therefore focuses on domestic saving by individuals and businesses.

In the simplest textbook picture of national saving, all saving is done by individuals who save during their working lives for consumption during retirement. This life-cycle model has shown itself to be a powerful tool for thinking about saving and capital accumulation and provides the framework for the analysis in Chapter 1 of this volume. A more realistic picture, however, recognizes that not all individual saving is for retirement and that a very large part of saving is done by corporations. The subsequent chapters in Part One therefore look beyond the simple life-cycle model and consider explicitly the role of corporate saving and its interaction with personal saving.

An economy's tax rules can affect the process of saving in a variety of ways. Any tax that drives a wedge between the pretax marginal product of capital and the net-of-tax return that savers receive will distort the saving decisions. Chapter 2 shows that under existing law that tax wedge is very large, with federal, state, and local taxes taking more than two-thirds of the real pretax return on nonfinancial corporate capital. The effect of changing this wedge by increasing the taxation of consumption or labor income and decreasing the taxation of capital income is the subject of Chapter 1.

The tax laws also affect the extent of corporate saving by altering the return on corporate capital and by inducing companies to reduce dividends in favor of retained earnings. Chapters 3 through 5 examine the effect of tax rules on corporate dividend behavior. The theory suggests and the evidence confirms that existing tax rules significantly distort the corporate financial decisions in favor of a higher level of retained earnings. The effect of this increase in corporate savings on total private savings depends on the extent to which shareholders "see through the corporate veil" and reduce their own savings in response to the higher level of corporate saving. The reaction of shareholders and therefore of total saving is the subject of Chapters 6 and 7.

The final chapter of Part One uses the estimates of the earlier chapters to examine the effect of alternative corporate tax integration proposals on aggregate capital accumulation. The impact of integration depends on the effect of the resulting higher net rate of return to savers and on the effect of the increase in dividends on personal savings. The evidence suggests that although corporate tax integrations could do much to reduce the distortions in corporate finance and resource allocation that currently exist, the net impact of integration on aggregate savings is likely to be small.

I turn now to discussing each of the chapters in more detail. The first chapter, "The Rate of Return, Taxation, and Personal Savings," examines how the tax wedge between the pretax and after-tax rates of return affects the level of saving. The results are surprising and contrary to conventional wisdom. The analysis shows that replacing a tax on capital income with a tax on labor income can actually decrease private saving. However, even when this anomalous result is true, such a tax change will raise national saving, that is, the sum of private and public saving.

The analysis uses a simple life-cycle model in which an individual works in the first period of life and saves to finance consumption in the second period when no work is done. Substituting a payroll tax or consumption tax for an income tax of equal present value lowers the price of second-period consumption relative to present consumption (because capital income is not taxed) and therefore unambiguously causes an increase in future consumption and a decrease in current consumption.

The rise in future consumption does not, however, imply that first-period saving must rise. Future consumption can rise even if current saving falls because the change in tax rules raises the net rate of return that converts present saving into future consumption.

A fall in both current saving and current consumption appears at first to be inconsistent with the individual's budget constraint. In fact, a fall in both only implies that the individual's current taxes have risen, that is, that taxes have been moved forward from retirement years to working years. This obviously happens when a payroll tax is substituted for a tax on capital income, since none of the payroll tax is paid during retirement years. It also happens when a consumption tax is substituted for a tax on capital income.

The crucial implication of this analysis is that the substitution of a consumption tax or a payroll tax for the tax on capital income reduces current consumer expenditure and therefore frees resources for investment even if personal savings are not increased. Since current consumption falls, the sum of private saving and tax payments must rise. This in turn implies that if government spending does not change, national saving will rise even if private saving falls. The response of the government surplus or deficit to the tax change is therefore of substantial importance. Maintaining a balanced budget when substituting a payroll tax for an equal-present-value capital income tax must imply a rise in government spending and therefore may imply a fall in national saving.

The analysis of Chapter 1 also shows the importance of the transition from one tax regime to the next. In a simple two-period life-cycle model with overlapping generations, the older generation that already exists when the tax law changes (and that has paid tax under the old regime) must be treated differently from all future generations to avoid imposing a windfall tax loss or gain and a corresponding change in national saving.

Before turning to the empirical studies in subsequent chapters, it is useful to establish what has been happening to effective tax rates on capital income. Because of the complexity of the tax rules, the statutory tax rates are a very poor indication of actual effective tax rates. Moreover, in recent years the combination of high rates of inflation and the conventional accounting procedures have substantially exacerbated this problem.

The second chapter, "The Effective Tax Rate and the Pretax Rate of Return," (written with Louis Dicks-Mireaux and James Poterba), examines empirically the effective tax rate paid on the earnings of capital in the nonfinancial corporate sector of the United States in the quarter-century ending in 1979. The total tax paid by the corporations, their shareholders, and their creditors in 1979 to governments at all levels was 69 percent of the real capital income of the corporations, including both debt and equity income. This effective tax rate fluctuated between 53 percent and 85 percent during the previous quarter-century. It is clear that such high tax rates deserve careful attention in any attempt to understand the process of capital accumulation.

The analysis in Chapter 2 stresses the importance of looking beyond the tax paid by the corporations themselves to include also the taxes paid by shareholders and creditors. The evidence also shows that an important share of the total tax is paid to state and local governments; these taxes exceed 17 percent of real pretax capital income.

Failure to look at all the relevant taxes gives a misleading picture of the trend as well as of the level of capital taxation. The taxes paid directly by the corporations themselves, that is, corporate tax payments to all levels of government plus state and local property tax payments, fell from 59 percent of real capital income in the first five years of the sample period (1953 through 1957) to 47 percent in the five years ending in 1979. Much of this fall reflects the impact of inflation, which raised the nominal interest expenses that companies could deduct in calculating taxable income. But this reduction in corporate tax liabilities was offset by increases in the taxes paid by creditors and shareholders. The total tax rate paid by corporations, creditors, and shareholders was nearly as high in the five years from 1975 to 1979 (68 percent) as it had been from 1953 to 1957 (70 percent).

The total effective capital income tax rate remained high despite a series of reductions in the statutory tax rates paid by corporations and individuals and despite the introduction of the investment tax credit and the use of accelerated depreciation. The effective and statutory tax rates behaved so differently because the interaction of inflation with the historic cost methods of tax accounting caused an understatement of the costs of production and therefore an increasing ratio of taxable income to real income. This is particularly clear in the period since inflation began to accelerate in the mid-1960s. Between 1963 and 1967, the total effective tax rate was 55 percent; a decade later, it averaged 71 percent and ended the 1970s at 69 percent.

The analysis in Chapter 2 also provides estimates of the pretax rate of return to capital in the nonfinancial corporate sector for each year since 1948. For this calculation, the usual national income account measure of profits is adjusted by adding back in the property taxes paid by these corporations. Between 1948 and 1979, the total pretax return averaged 11.5 percent. The decade of the 1960s was one of greater than average profitability; even after cyclical fluctuations in profitability were adjusted for, profitability in the 1960s was about 1.5 percent higher than in the 1970s.

The combination of lower pretax profitability in the 1970s and a higher effective tax rate caused the net-of-tax rate of return to decline sharply between the 1960s and the 1970s. The average real net rate of return was 5.2 percent in the 1960s but only 3.1 percent in the 1970s. The statistical analysis shows no evidence that the broad fluctuations in the effective tax rate over the past twenty-five years induced offsetting changes in the opposite direction by the pretax rate of return. Changes in the effective tax rate were therefore associated with correspondingly large changes in the net rate of return.

These figures are indicative of the very substantial magnitude of capital income taxes as a share of real capital income. They do not, however, provide an estimate of the marginal tax rates on income from different types of capital or of the marginal tax rates that apply to individual savers in different situations. For example, to the extent that the depreciation rules for new investment are more generous than they had been at an earlier time, the effective marginal tax rate is below the average tax rate. Conversely, if the typical individual receives some capital income in an untaxed pension but does all marginal saving in forms that are taxed, the effective marginal tax rate will be above the average rate. The extent to which low tax options are and are not marginally available and attractive requires more study.

Corporate saving plays a major role in the process of capital accumulation. In 1979, for example, corporate retained earnings were $59 billion while personal saving was $86 billion; corporate saving thus accounted for 41 percent of total net private saving. Moreover, this figure substantially understates the relative size of corporate saving because it ignores the fall in the real value of the net debt of nonfinancial corporations caused by inflation. The 10 percent inflation in 1979 (as measured by the personal consumer expenditure deflator) reduced the value of corporate debt by $73 billion, thereby transferring that amount from personal saving to a corrected measure of corporate saving and raising corporate saving to 91 percent of total private saving.

The nearly universal policy of paying substantial dividends is the primary puzzle of corporate finance. During the past fifteen years, dividends have averaged 45 percent of real after-tax profits. Before 1982 dividends were taxed at rates varying up to 70 percent and averaging nearly 40 percent for individual shareholders. In contrast, retained earnings imply no concurrent tax liability; the rise in the share value that results from retained earnings is taxed only when the stock is sold, and then at least 60 percent of the gain is untaxed. Why then do corporations not eliminate or sharply reduce their dividends and increase their retained earnings? And how do alternative tax systems influence the way in which corporations divide their income between dividends and retained earnings? These questions are the subject of Chapters 3, 4, and 5.

In the third chapter, "Why Do Companies Pay Dividends?", Jerry Green and I develop a simple theoretical model in which firms choose to pay dividends in order to maximize the value of their shares. The analysis emphasizes the heterogeneity of shareholder tax rates and the desire of shareholders to diversify their investments. We consider an economy with two kinds of investors: taxable individuals and untaxed institutions (like pension funds and nonprofit organizations). Firms can distribute profits currently or retain them and thereby raise the value of the firm's capital stock. Shareholders can sell their shares and realize this increased value in the form of capital gains. In the absence of uncertainty, these assumptions would lead to a segmentation of the market and specialization of share ownership, with the share price per dollar of retained earnings less than one. In the equilibrium, the taxable individuals would invest only in firms that pay no dividends even though, ceteris paribus, they would prefer an immediate payment, while untaxed investors would buy only the shares of firms that paid all profits out immediately as dividends. If untaxed investors did otherwise, they would reduce the income they earned per dollar spent on purchasing shares. The taxable individuals, in contrast, willingly accept the lower pretax income because it corresponds to greater after-tax income. This type of segmented equilibrium is not observed because of uncertainty. Because investors regard each firm's return as both unique and uncertain, they wish to diversify their investments. Chapter 3 shows that each firm can, in general, maximize its share price by attracting both types of investors and that this requires a dividend policy of distributing some unique fraction of earnings as dividends. Only in the special cases of little or no uncertainty or of a limited ability to diversify risks (because of a high enough correlation among the returns of different companies) can the equilibrium be of the segmented form.

The simple model of Chapter 3 cannot be applied directly to an economy with a large number of firms. Since the riskiness of a portfolio decreases as the number of securities increases, a segmented equilibrium could be established with two groups of securities, one of which pays out all earnings and the other of which retains all of its earnings. We believe, however, that the simple model could be extended to prevent such segmentation and preserve the optimal dividend result by introducing some diversity of expectations among the two groups of shareholders with respect to the prospects for each firm.

Within the simple framework, the model of Chapter 3 can be used to examine the comparative statics of how the dividend payment rate would respond to changes in tax rules. The analysis shows that a rise in the tax rate on dividends unambiguously raises total retained earnings even though the dividends of any particular company may actually be decreased. This model thus provides an explicit rationale for the earlier empirical research for the United Kingdom that is reported in Chapters 4 and 5.

Between 1950 and 1958, the British government operated a corporate income tax system that taxed dividends more heavily than retained earnings. The relative rates of tax within this framework were changed several times. Beginning in 1959, the differential taxation was ended and a pound of retained earnings had an opportunity cost of a pound of dividends. Chapter 4, "Corporate Taxation and Dividend Behavior," uses quarterly financial data to estimate the effect of the changing tax rules on the dividend payout rate. Chapter 5 extends this analysis by considering more general functional specifications.

The evidence in these chapters indicates that increasing the opportunity cost of retained earnings (measured in terms of the foregone net dividend income to an individual shareholder who paid the "standard rate" of British personal income tax) raised dividends substantially. The elasticity of the equilibrium dividend-income ratio with respect to tax-induced changes in the opportunity cost of retained earnings is approximately 0.9, and the first year impact elasticity is approximately 0.4. The abolition of the differential tax in 1958 raised the opportunity cost of retained earnings by nearly 50 percent and therefore raised the equilibrium dividend payout rate by some 40 percent.

Although the parameter estimates are quite robust with respect to a variety of different specifications and estimation methods, the constant elasticity specification should be regarded as only an approximation. As the analysis of Chapter 3 implies, a tax system that penalized retained earnings for investors in all tax situations would lead to a 100 percent payout and not to the behavior implied by a constant elasticity relation. It is clear, however, that in the range of tax rates in which a 100 percent payout is preferred by some investors but not by others, the actual payment rate is quite sensitive to the structure of taxation.

The sensitivity of the dividend payout rate to relative tax rates implies that the current U.S. system of corporate income taxation substantially increases the retained earnings of existing corporations. The higher level of corporate saving does not, of course, imply an equal net increase in the total private saving of individuals and corporations. To the extent that shareholders "see through the corporate veil" and take the corporate saving into account in making their own saving decisions, the higher level of corporate saving need not change total private saving at all. Similarly, the greater retained earnings of existing corporations do not necessarily mean that they invest more or that new businesses have a harder time raising capital. The established corporations that retain more earnings may as a result borrow less and issue less equity, thereby leaving more external funds for new businesses and for other firms with a greater net demand for capital. Under an appropriate set of simplifying assumptions, the greater retained earnings would be exactly offset by reduced personal saving and a lower level of external finance, leaving all significant aspects of capital formation unchanged.

The economy may not, however, correspond to those simplifying assumptions. Individuals may not see through the corporate veil or may feel constrained by capital gains tax rules and estate taxes not to offset increased retained earnings by selling shares. Corporations may treat retained earnings differently from external funds. New businesses may have a harder (or easier) time raising money when other and more established firms are not raising equity capital. Moreover, to the extent that the greater retained earnings raise the total saving rate, those firms that are seeking external capital may find it easier to obtain. The impact of increased retained earnings on total capital accumulation and on its distribution among sectors and firms is thus an empirical issue.

Chapters 6 and 7 address one aspect of this issue, the effect of retained earnings on total private saving. Chapter 6 deals with the U.S. experience from 1929 through 1965, while Chapter 7 deals with the British postwar experience. Both studies examine the effect of corporate retained earnings on household consumer expenditure. The conventional Keynesian consumption function that relates consumer expenditure to disposable income implicitly assumes that reducing dividends by a dollar and increasing retained earnings by an equal amount will lower consumer expenditure by nearly one dollar, that is, by the marginal propensity to consume. In this common specification of behavior, households do not see through the corporate veil at all, and a tax-induced rise in retained earnings raises private saving nearly dollar for dollar. In contrast, the less common specification of consumer expenditure behavior associated with Irving Fisher that relates consumer spending to labor income and the real rate of interest implies that shifts of funds between retained earnings and dividends have no effect on consumer spending.

The analysis of Chapters 6 and 7 considers a more general specification of the consumer expenditure function that includes retained earnings as a separate variable and therefore one within which the impact of the dividend payment decision can be estimated. The specification extends the permanent income hypothesis by emphasizing that consumer spending responds to different components of observed income according to the relation between current observed income of that type and expected future income. Thus an increase in dividends has a substantial impact on consumer expenditures because shareholders believe that such changes are relatively permanent, a view that correctly corresponds to the distributed lag relation between dividends and corporate profits. In contrast, an increase in retained earnings that is caused by a transitory rise in profits does not induce a substantial rise in consumer spending. It would be wrong, however, to conclude (as the Keynesian specification implicitly does) that every increase in retained earnings would have a small impact on consumer spending. A rise in retained earnings that represents a tax-induced switch from dividends should be regarded as "permanent" and should therefore have a positive impact on consumer spending that is comparable to the negative impact of the reduced dividends. The implication is that, since observed changes in retained earnings reflect both temporary and permanent changes, the estimated effect of retained earnings on consumer spending will understate the effect of the relatively permanent changes in retained earnings that result from tax-induced changes in the dividend payout ratio.

The statistical evidence in both chapters shows that an extra dollar of retained earnings raises consumer spending substantially, although by less than an extra dollar of disposable income. For the United States in the period from 1929 through 1965,[1] the estimates indicate that an extra dollar of retained earnings raises consumer spending by 50 cents while an extra dollar of disposable income raises consumer spending by 75 cents. This difference can well be due to the future tax that must be paid when the retained earnings are eventually converted to spendable dividends and to the transitory component of variations in retained earnings. This evidence thus implies that households see through the corporate veil and adjust their personal savings to changes in corporate savings. The current system of corporate income taxation, although inducing corporations to retain a higher fraction of earnings than otherwise, therefore appears to have little if any effect on the total volume of private saving.

The estimates based on the British experience in the postwar period ("Taxes, Corporate Dividend Policy, and Personal Savings: The British Postwar Experience," written jointly with George Fane) is also contrary to the extreme Keynesian specification but does imply that the dividend payout rate may influence consumption. The long-run propensity to consume out of disposable income is estimated to be 0.77, while the long-run propensity to consume retained earnings is only 0.23. The British evidence thus suggests that a tax policy that reduces dividends by one pound and increases retained earnings by an equal amount may raise total private saving by as much as 0.5 pounds. It is not clear whether the difference between the U.S. and British estimates is the result of real differences in behavior or only reflects problems of measurement and estimation of such things as the foreign ownership of British shares. Subsequent studies with more recent U.S. data confirm the result for the United States; additional studies for the United Kingdom remain to be done.

The estimated effects of corporate tax rules on dividend behavior and of dividend behavior on aggregate private saving can be used to evaluate the effect of corporate tax integration proposals on capital formation. In Chapter 8, "Corporate Tax Integration: The Estimated Effects on Capital Accumulation and Tax Distribution of Two Integration Proposals," Daniel Frisch and I conclude that corporate tax integration could eliminate or reduce some of the distortions in the allocation of capital without significantly reducing overall private saving. The two alternative corporate tax integration proposals that we consider are complete integration by the partnership method and a partial integration method that keeps the

1. "Tax Incentives, Corporate Saving, and Capital Accumulation," presented in Chapter 6.

tax burden on corporate income unchanged. The chapter discusses how integration would reduce distortions in the allocation of resources between the corporate and the noncorporate sector, between present and future consumption, and among different types of corporate finance. The analysis then examines the claim of integration advocates that it would raise the aggregate rate of capital accumulation.

The evidence of Chapters 4 through 7 is used to assess the decrease in corporate saving that would be likely to result from integration and the extent of the offsetting increase in personal saving. Since the complete integration scheme represents a net reduction in the taxation of capital income, we also consider the implication of the increased net rate of return on aggregate saving. As the analysis of Chapter 1 emphasized, this effect is ambiguous. If other taxes are not increased, there is a positive income effect that may induce an increase in current private consumption as well as in future consumption. If other taxes are increased, the effect on national saving depends on the responses of both individual and government spending. In particular, if the present value of tax revenue is unchanged and government spending does not rise, the rate of return effect implies an increase in national saving. On balance, it seems best to give little weight to any possible change in aggregate saving in assessing the effect of corporate tax integration.

Portfolio Investment Behavior

The tax system affects not only the flow of saving and the size of the capital stock but also the allocation of capital among alternative activities. Several previous studies have examined how tax rules influence the demand for housing and the share of housing in the total capital stock.[2] The research presented in Part Two of this book focuses on the nonhousing portion of individual portfolio investment behavior. The analysis here shows that tax considerations substantially distort the portfolio investment decisions that individuals make under existing tax rules. Differences in the tax treatment of different kinds of capital income influence the composition of portfolios, and the realization method of taxing capital gains reduces investors' willingness to revise portfolios in response to new information.

These distortions in portfolio behavior imply that capital is misallocated among industries and firms. The result is that the wrong products are produced and that production occurs with inefficient ratios of capital to labor.

2. See, for example, Laidler (1969), Aaron (1972), and Feldstein (1982).

In addition, distorting the demand for portfolio assets alters the mix of financial assets that firms supply (for example, the ratio of debt to equity) and the allocation of risk bearing in the economy. A full evaluation of the welfare costs of taxes on portfolio income should evaluate the welfare losses that result from the misallocation of risk as well as from the distortion of production decisions.

Economists first became interested in the effects of taxes on portfolio behavior when individual income tax rates began rising during World War II. The very sharp increase in tax rates caused a widespread concern that the tax system would reduce the willingness of individual portfolio investors to take risks and that this in turn would raise the market price of risk and induce firms to make investments with lower risk and therefore lower expected return. In an important early article, Domar and Musgrave (1944) argued that the opposite was more likely to be true: because a tax implies that the government shares the risk as well as the return on investments, the tax need not change the net return per unit of net risk but does reduce both risk and income. In their particular parameterization, this implied that individuals would unambiguously increase their demand for the risky asset. Subsequent analysis by Tobin (1958) showed that the same conclusion could be obtained in a model with expected utility maximization.

By the mid-1960s (when I wrote the paper that appears as Chapter 9, "The Effects of Taxation on Risk Taking"), professional economists generally accepted the proposition that a proportional tax with full loss offset increases personal risk taking. My paper showed that previous demonstrations relied on a variety of restrictive and implausible assumptions and that, when these assumptions are relaxed, the previous conclusion is no longer true. The key point of the analysis is that even in a restricted world in which a mean-variance analysis is appropriate, the proportional tax can be shown to increase risk taking only when there is a riskless asset with zero yield. When all assets are risky, or even when the safe asset has a nonzero yield, the effect of a proportional tax on the demand for risky assets is ambiguous and can only be resolved by further restrictions on the utility function. Subsequent papers by Mossin (1968), Stiglitz (1969b), and others identified the restrictions on utility functions and asset structures that could produce different results but confirmed that no general theoretical conclusion about portfolio choice could be obtained.

The theory of portfolio choice thus identifies the basic ways in which taxation affects portfolio composition without providing any clear answer about its net effect. Moreover, the actual tax rules that affect portfolio investment in the United States are quite different from the simple proportional tax with full loss offset that has been the subject of the theoretical analyses. The United States taxes nominal capital gains, but only on realization and at a lower rate than other types of capital income. The law also exempts from taxation the income of state and local government bonds and the implicit income on owner-occupied housing. Because of the theoretical and institutional complexities, evaluating the likely effect of the actual progressive tax requires direct empirical research.

The study presented in Chapter 10, "Personal Taxation and Portfolio Composition: An Econometric Analysis," uses household survey data (the Federal Reserve Board's survey of income and assets) to study the effects of taxes on portfolio composition. The first stage of the analysis relates the composition of each individual's financial wealth to the individual's tax bracket, wealth, and other relevant variables. The parameter estimates from these equations are then used to assess the impact of tax rates on asset demand.

The evidence indicates that tax effects are quite important. The estimates imply that, with the special features of the U.S. tax system (like the method of taxing capital gains), higher marginal tax rates increase the demand for common stock and municipal bonds and decrease the demand for other types of financial assets. A simple model relating asset demand to the relative net-of-tax asset yields is capable of explaining why different income classes hold different fractions of their portfolios in each type of asset. The relative net yield differences can also account for much of the variation among asset proportions for each income class. By construction, the differences in relative net yields reflect only the tax rules and tax rates. The analysis thus provides strong evidence for the importance of taxes in determining portfolio composition and asset demand.

The basic question that originally motivated research on the effect of taxation on risk taking was whether the tax law discouraged high-income individuals from making investments with high pretax yields and high risks. To answer this question directly, I calculated an estimated mean pretax yield for the portfolio of each individual in the sample and a corresponding variance based on the historic covariance matrix of the individual asset yields. I then related these measures to the individuals' tax classes, wealth, and demographic characteristics. The results indicate that both pretax yield and risk rise with taxable income. The basic reason for this is the increasing share of equities in the portfolios of higher-income individuals, which in turn was a result of very progressive tax rates on ordinary income (reaching a maximum rate of more than 90 percent in the 1962 survey year) and a maximum capital gains tax rate of 25 percent. Thus the combination of very progressive tax rates on other income and low tax rates on capital gains encourages an allocation of portfolio wealth into investments with higher pretax yield than would otherwise have occurred.

Capital gains are not only taxed at a lower rate than ordinary income but are subject to tax only when an asset is sold. Moreover, the capital gains tax is avoided completely when an asset is bequeathed, since the recipient takes the asset's value at the time of transfer as a new basis for calculating subsequent taxable gains. The likely result of this method of taxing capital gains is to discourage the sale of assets and the realization of taxable gains. To the extent that investors are "locked into" previous investments in this way, the asset markets are less efficient at allocating risks and resources. The demand for shares of companies whose prices have risen in the past are artificially inflated, while new companies and those whose share prices have recently declined have a harder time attracting buyers.

This potential lock-in problem assumed growing importance in the 1970s as changes in tax rules raised the maximum tax rate on capital gains. The so-called "alternative tax" rule that limited the capital gains rate to 25 percent was modified to restrict its application to the first $50,000 of capital gains. Other rules governing the "minimum tax" and the "maximum tax" raised the total marginal rate on capital gains to more than 40 percent for many individuals before the 1978 reduction in the tax rates on capital gains.

Chapters 11, 12, and 13 report three studies that were designed to evaluate the effect of capital gains taxation on the selling of corporate stock and the realization of capital gains. All three studies indicate that investors are quite sensitive to tax considerations in their decisions to sell common stock.

An important feature of the first of these studies, "The Effects of the Capital Gains Tax on the Selling and Switching of Common Stock," which was done jointly with Shlomo Yitzhaki, was the use of survey data that permitted separating "switches" of stock (that is, stock sales followed by purchases of different stock or other financial assets) from "net sales" in which proceeds are not reinvested. The distinction is useful because the lock-in effect applies only to switch sellers. Although higher capital gains tax rates should unambiguously reduce switch selling, the effect of high tax rates on net selling is ambiguous. A higher tax rate may discourage an individual from selling stock in order to buy a consumer durable or to make some other large purchase, but an individual who wishes to sell in order to obtain some given net amount of after-tax cash will have to sell more if he is in a higher tax bracket than if he is in a lower tax bracket. The net balance of these two factors determines whether net selling is an increasing or decreasing function of the capital gains tax rate.

The survey data examined in Chapter 11 imply that 56 percent of those who sold stock during the year also purchased other stock and that 58 percent of the pretax value of common stock sale proceeds was reinvested in common stock by the end of the calendar year. The parameter estimates conform to the theoretical prediction and indicate that the portfolio reallocation decisions ("switches") are particularly sensitive to tax considerations, while net selling does not appear to be influenced by the tax rate on capital gains.

The second study, "The Effects of Taxation on the Selling of Corporate Stock and the Realization of Capital Gains," done jointly with Joel Slemrod and Shlomo Yitzhaki and reported in Chapter 12, extends the first analysis by examining a large sample of individual tax returns that report sales of corporate stock. With the tax return data, we were able to estimate the effect of taxation on the realization of gains as well as on the sale of stock. The evidence supports the earlier finding that corporate stock sales are quite sensitive to tax rates and then shows that the effect on the value of the net capital gains that are realized is even stronger. As an indication of the strength of these effects, the study reports a simulation of lowering the 1973 maximum tax rate on capital gains to 25 percent. The simulation indicates that, on the basis of the cross-section differences in realization at different tax rates, this change would cause nearly a doubling of stock sales and would increase realized gains by enough to increase tax revenue despite the lower tax rate. In practice, the actual effect of a lower capital gains tax rate would depend on the extent to which individuals had realizable gains. Since only a small fraction of accrued nominal capital gains is actually realized, a very substantial increase in stock sales and tax revenue is quite possible.

The analyses of Chapters 11 and 12 use cross-section data to estimate the likely effect of a change in tax rates. These samples permit studying large numbers of individual taxpayers and making quite precise estimates of their capital gains tax rates and their sales of corporate stock. Although cross-section data can in principle provide valid estimates of how individuals would respond to a change in rules, it is reassuring to have evidence based on a comparison of behavior under different tax regimes.

Chapter 13, "The Lock-in Effect of the Capital Gains Tax: Some Time-Series Evidence," written with Joel Slemrod, presents such a "before and after" comparison. Before 1969 all taxpayers were subject to a maximum capital gains rate of 25 percent. During the 1970s the capital gains tax rate remained essentially unchanged for moderate-income taxpayers but rose substantially for those with very high incomes and large potential gains. The evidence on capital gains by income class presented in Chapter 13 shows that the ratio of net capital gains to other income was actually higher in 1975–1976 than in 1967–1968 among taxpayers with incomes under $100,000, but fell substantially among higher-income groups. Although it is not possible to make precise parameter estimates on the basis of these data, they clearly support the sensitivity of capital gains to tax rules that is implied by the cross-section data.

Consideration of individual portfolio behavior suggests a significant modification of the conventional analysis of the corporate income tax and of other partial factor taxes. The conventional analysis follows Harberger (1962) and assumes that capital is allocated among alternative uses in a way that equalizes the after-tax rate of return on capital in all of its uses. The portfolio perspective implies that this conventional analysis should be modified to recognize that the net rates of return on capital in different uses are not generally equal but reflect the risk-return preferences of investors and their equilibrium portfolio compositions.

The portfolio approach explains why different types of taxpayers ranging from high-tax-rate individuals to untaxed pension funds all hold mixed portfolios despite the differences among taxpayer groups in the *relative* net rates of return on different types of assets. If risk considerations were irrelevant to these investors, each type of investor would specialize in the particular type of investment that had the highest net yield for his tax situation. The lack of specialization is significant because it implies that different groups of portfolio investors may respond differently to tax-induced changes in the net rates of return. In contrast, the conventional analysis assumes that there are no differences in response but that all capital owners respond with an "infinite" asset adjustment to any divergences of net rates of return.

Chapter 14, "Personal Taxation, Portfolio Choice, and the Effect of the Corporation Income Tax" (written with Joel Slemrod), shows that the portfolio approach can radically change the implied effect of the corporate income tax on the sectoral allocation of capital. Corporate income is subject to tax at a corporate rate of 46 percent; when some fraction of that income is paid as dividends, it is subject to an additional tax at the shareholder's rate of individual income tax. Before 1982 investment income from noncorporate activities was taxed at individual rates of up to 70 percent, and this same rate was applied to dividend income; since 1982 the maximum individual rate has been reduced to 50 percent.

Recognizing the differences in personal income tax rates significantly changes the appropriate analysis of the effect of the corporate income tax.

Although the corporate income tax represents an additional tax for lower-income individuals and untaxed institutions, the corporate tax system can also shelter retained earnings from high rates of personal taxation. When personal tax rates were as high as 70 percent and the corporate rate was 48 percent, the total taxation of corporate income could easily be below the tax rate applicable to the income of unincorporated businesses. In this situation, the corporate income tax induces investors with low individual tax rates to shift investments from the corporate to the noncorporate sector but induces investors with high marginal tax rates to shift resources into the corporate sector.

The net effect of the corporate tax system therefore depends on the distribution of wealth among investors in different tax classes and on the relative sensitivity of their adjustments to changes in yields. If the portfolios of high-income individuals are more responsive to yield differences than the portfolios of low-income individuals, the corporate tax system can actually result in a net flow of capital from the unincorporated sector to the corporate sector. Chapter 14 presents a two-sector model calibrated to U.S. data for 1973 and shows that the corporate tax system could increase the size of the corporate capital stock with feasible differences in the portfolio balance elasticities. More generally, with portfolio balance elasticities that are more realistic, the disaggregated portfolio analysis of the U.S. corporate tax system implies a very substantial reduction in the extent to which the corporate tax system shifts the capital stock.

The reduction of the maximum individual income tax rate to 50 percent as of 1982 makes it virtually impossible for anyone to pay a lower tax on corporate income (subject to a 46 percent rate plus a tax on dividends) than on unincorporated business income.[3] This implies that the corporate tax system unequivocally reduces the flow of capital to the corporate sector. The lower rate of individual income tax does not, however, change the general analytic point that only a disaggregated portfolio analysis can explain the absence of complete specialization and indicate the likely quantitative response of asset allocation to changes in tax rules.

Business Investment

Part Three of this book deals with business investment in plant and equipment. As in the previous sections, the research focuses on testing and measuring the incentive effects of alternative tax rules. The estimates

---

3. Very small corporations do pay tax rates below 46 percent, but these firms account for a minute fraction of all corporate capital and income.

show that tax rules have a powerful effect on the volume of business investment. In the 1960s, the changes in depreciation rules and the introduction of the investment tax credit provided a substantial stimulus to increased net nonresidential investment. But in the 1970s, the high rate of inflation interacted with the prevailing tax rules to reduce the investment incentive and to shrink the share of nonresidential investment in GNP back to the level that prevailed before the stimulating changes of the 1960s.

The importance of tax incentives stands in sharp contrast to the Keynesian tradition in macroeconomics that emphasized the importance of sales and capacity utilization as determinants of investment in plant and equipment and minimized the effect of changes in the cost of capital. In an influential series of papers written in the mid-1960s, Dale Jorgenson and his collaborators (for example, Jorgenson 1963; Hall and Jorgenson 1967) presented statistically estimated investment equations that gave a prominent role to the effects on investment of tax-induced changes in the cost of capital. More specifically, Jorgenson derived a desired capital stock, based on an assumed Cobb-Douglas technology, that is proportional to the ratio of current output to the user cost of capital. This user cost of capital reflects the tax depreciation rules, a rate of interest, and the corporate tax rate. Jorgenson and his collaborators found that a distributed lag of the changes in the desired capital stock can explain a significant fraction of the variance of net investment.

Although the Jorgenson framework implied a substantial sensitivity of investment to tax-induced changes in the cost of capital, this sensitivity was not estimated independently but was the result of the Cobb-Douglas specification that constrained the elasticity of the desired capital stock with respect to the cost of capital to be minus one. The statistical estimation only indicated the time path of the adjustment of investment to changes in the composite variable that reflected both output and the user cost of capital. Even after Jorgenson's pioneering work, skeptics could still easily believe that all of the explanatory power in his statistical model came from changes in sales and that tax policies have no effect on investment.

Only by relaxing the constraint implied by the Cobb-Douglas specification can the effect of the tax rules be estimated explicitly. In Chapter 15, "Tax Policy, Corporate Saving, and Investment Behavior in Britain," John Flemming and I estimated a more general specification in which the effect of tax policy can be examined directly. The natural generalization of the Cobb-Douglas specification is a constant elasticity of substitution technology in which the elasticity of substitution is not constrained to be one; this in turn implies that the elasticity of the desired capital stock with respect to the cost of capital may also be greater or less than minus one. We adopt this constant elasticity of substitution specification and then go even further and allow different responses to the different components of the cost of capital: the depreciation rules, the corporate tax rate, and the net rate of return. In principle, such response differences might be the result of differences in the extent to which firms understand these factors and take them into account or of differences between permanent and transitory effects.

During part of the sample period that we examined (1954 through 1967), the British government had used tax policy to encourage greater corporate saving. The evidence presented in Chapters 4 and 5 indicates that these policies were successful in achieving this particular aim. The purpose of encouraging increased retained earnings was, of course, to raise the rate of investment. Chapter 15 also examines the extent to which tax-induced changes in retention affect the rate of investment.

The statistical evidence implies that both the accelerated depreciation provisions and the differential taxation of dividends and retained earnings had substantial and significant effects on investment. The data imply that the responses to the other components of the user cost of capital (the tax rate and the net cost of funds) are weaker and may not have existed at all. The evidence that tax inducements to increase retained earnings raised investment is consistent with the finding for Britain (Chapter 7) that higher retained earnings raised total national savings. In short, both types of policies appeared to be successful in raising capital formation before the differential taxation of dividends and retained earnings was abandoned in 1958 and the value of accelerated depreciation was eroded by inflation in the late 1960s and 1970s.

A defect of the Feldstein-Flemming study, as well as of the work of Jorgenson and his collaborators, is the assumption that replacement investment is a fixed fraction of the capital stock. In Chapter 16, "Toward an Economic Theory of Replacement Investment," Michael Rothschild and I show that replacement investment is likely to be quite sensitive to changes in tax laws in both the short run and the long run. Since replacement investment is approximately of the same magnitude as net expansion investment, this influence of tax rules is potentially quite important.

A tax change that alters the optimal ratio of capital services to labor is also likely to alter the optimal planned durability of capital and therefore the initial amount of capital stock per unit of capital service. If a particular depreciation change both raises the optimal capital-labor ratio and favors more durable investment, it will raise investment outlays for both reasons. Econometric models that ignore changes in durability will attribute all of the increased investment to the higher capital-labor ratio and will therefore overestimate both the sensitivity of the optimal capital stock to the user cost of capital and the long-run effect of the tax change on investment.

In addition, a tax change may induce firms to accelerate or delay the scrapping and replacement of existing equipment by changing the optimal age of replacement. Chapter 16 shows that under certain conditions, the introduction of accelerated depreciation increases the optimal replacement age. In principle, all replacement investment would then be postponed until the oldest equipment reached the new optimal age. Investment would eventually rise because of the increase in the optimal capital-labor ratio but would fall temporarily because of postponed replacement. An econometric analysis that ignores the delay in replacement would therefore underestimate the response of the optimal capital intensity to the tax change.

These examples illustrate that the simplified specification of replacement investment that still characterizes econometric studies of investment may be an important source of bias in estimating the way in which tax rules affect investment. More generally, the analysis of Chapter 16 implies that the impact of tax rules on replacement investment may be very significant and deserves more careful econometric analysis than it has received.

As I noted in discussing the effective tax rate calculations of Chapter 2, the increasing rate of inflation that began in the mid-1960s has had a major effect on the taxation of capital. This occurs because the taxable income of businesses and individuals is calculated by conventional accounting methods that evaluate nominal rather than real capital income. The use of historic cost depreciation and first-in/first-out inventory accounting causes an understatement of the costs of production and therefore an overstatement of taxable income. The use of nominal interest rather than real interest causes an overstatement of the borrowers' costs and an overstatement of the lenders' income. And the taxation of nominal capital gains causes a rise with inflation in the effective tax rate on individual equity investors. The net result of all three forms of capital income mismeasurement is to raise the effective tax rate on the income from business investment as inflation rises.

This interaction between inflation and tax rules implies a substantial nonneutrality of inflation and shows the importance of an economy's fiscal structure as a determinant of its macroeconomic equilibrium. Chapter 17, "Inflation, Tax Rules, and Investment: Some Econometric Evidence," focuses on the primary effect of the tax-inflation interaction: its impact on nonresidential fixed business investment.

There are a number of complex channels by which the inflation-tax interaction affects business investment. The higher effective tax rate on capital income changes the incentive to save and directs more of aggregate saving into owner-occupied housing. The incentive for business investment is depressed by the lower real net-of-tax return that can be earned on any given investment but is encouraged to the extent that firms use debt finance and face a lower real net-of-tax cost of debt.

Chapter 17 begins by acknowledging that the effect of the tax-inflation interaction on investment is too complex to be described accurately by any single econometric model. Although models like that of Chapter 15 can be useful, they represent a substantial simplification in their specification of technology, of the market environment of firms, of financial behavior, and so on. Because any econometric specification is therefore a "false model," it is useful to estimate alternative specifications in which the potential biases are likely to be different. Because all inference is necessarily based on false models, the robustness of results is the best indication of economic reality.

Three quite different models are presented in Chapter 17. The most explicit specification is an extension of the generalized CES capital stock adjustment specification of Chapter 15 in which substantial care is given to the measurement of the effects of inflation. An alternative model of investment behavior that avoids some of the restrictions of the capital stock adjustment process relates investment to the difference between the net return on investment and the net cost of funds. Finally, there is a model that is more of a reduced form, relating nonresidential investment to the real net return that is earned by those who provide the capital.

All three models indicate that net nonresidential fixed investment is quite sensitive to tax rules and that the interaction of inflation and the U.S. tax rules that prevailed in the 1960s and 1970s can account for much of the nearly 40 percent decline in the net investment share in GNP that occurred between the second half of the 1960s and the 1970s. Although the chapter does not deal explicitly with the 1981 tax legislation that significantly shortened the depreciation lives of plant and equipment, the analysis implies that this change should raise investment substantially and should reduce the sensitivity of effective tax rates and of investment to changes in inflation.

Tax Incidence in a Growing Economy

The five final chapters in this volume look at capital taxation in a general equilibrium framework. The analyses are theoretical and examine economies in steady-state equilibrium growth. A principal focus of each chapter is the impact of some tax on the returns to capital and labor, but the analyses go beyond the issue of tax incidence to examine the more general effects of the tax on the behavior of economic agents.

The first of these studies, "Tax Incidence in a Growing Economy with Variable Factor Supply" (Chapter 18), shows that the long-run incidence of a tax depends only on its effect on the share of national income that is saved. The effect of the tax on the supply of labor is irrelevant in the long run because changes in the supply of labor induce corresponding changes in the supply of capital that make the capital-labor ratio (and therefore the factor returns) independent of the labor supply. The irrelevance of the labor supply response very clearly distinguishes the implications of long-run growth incidence from the implications of static analyses of tax incidence.

The specific analysis of Chapter 18 deals with the effect of a general "payroll tax" on labor income. If the tax does not alter the fraction of national income that is saved, the entire burden of the tax is borne by labor and the return to capital remains unchanged. If, however, some fraction of the taxed income would have been saved while the government saves none of the tax revenue, the effect of the tax is to lower the national saving rate and therefore to reduce the economy's equilibrium capital-labor ratio. This in turn raises the rate of return to capital and lowers the pretax return to labor. In this case, labor bears more than 100 percent of the payroll tax. More generally, the effect of the tax depends on the redistribution of income among groups with different saving rates and the sensitivity of saving to the rate of return.

Chapter 19, "Incidence of a Capital Income Tax in a Growing Economy with Variable Savings Rates," extends the analysis of tax incidence in a growing economy to the case of a tax on capital income. The results of this analysis are again very different from the implications of a static general equilibrium model. In a static general equilibrium model with a fixed capital stock, owners of capital would bear the entire burden of a general tax on capital income. When the capital stock is instead made endogenous, a substantial fraction of the burden of a general tax on capital income may be borne by labor. The precise incidence depends on the elasticity of the saving rates of different types of taxpayers with respect to the net rate of return.

The contrast between the irrelevance of the labor supply elasticity and the sensitivity of the results to the savings elasticities is striking. This difference reflects the fact that capital is a derived factor of production and is thus a function of the labor supply and labor income, while the opposite is not true. It implies that the providers of capital may ultimately avoid some of the burden of any tax in a way that is not available to the providers of labor services.

Although the analysis of Chapter 19 refers to a general tax on capital income rather than a partial tax like the corporate income tax, it suggests that the implications of the traditional static analysis of the corporate income tax would not remain valid if the very long run incidence were examined explicitly.

In an economy with more than one type of capital asset, changes in the taxation of a particular type of capital income cause an immediate change in the price of the corresponding asset and may cause changes in other asset prices as well. These asset price changes capitalize the changes in future net incomes. Such capitalization effects are an important aspect of the distributional effect of a tax change and can also play a key role in the reallocation of assets.

Chapter 20 extends the traditional theory of capitalization and of tax incidence by using a model of a growing economy with overlapping generations. The analysis is applied to a tax on pure land rent, the classic case of a tax that has been assumed to be unshiftable and therefore to be fully capitalized in the price of land. This study, "The Surprising Incidence of a Tax on Pure Rent: A New Answer to an Old Question," shows that even a tax on pure rent can be shifted to other forms of capital.

This surprising conclusion comes from recognizing that land is a store of value as well as a factor of production. When a tax on rent destroys some of the market value of land, savers must hold more reproducible capital as part of their life-cycle saving. The tax on rent thus increases the stock of reproducible capital, thereby raising the capital-land ratio and the capital-labor ratio. The result of this is a higher pretax rent and higher wages. Chapter 20 presents an explicit model of this process and shows how the value of land might even be raised by a tax on rental income.

Although this analysis is limited to the case of pure land rents, it has obvious implications for the corporate income tax, for taxes on natural resources, and for all other partial taxes on particular types of capital income. It shows the importance of describing explicitly the way in which any tax change alters existing capital values and the accumulation of capital.

In Chapter 21, "Corporate Financial Policy and Taxation in a Growing

Economy," Jerry Green, Eytan Sheshinski, and I use the framework of an economy in equilibrium growth to examine how a system of profits taxation affects corporate financial decisions and the net returns to individual investors in debt and equity. The framework of equilibrium growth is important in this context because it constrains the debt-equity ratio and the dividend payment rate to combinations that are consistent with the exogenously given growth of each firm's capital stock. The corporate-type tax system that we study favors both borrowing and retained earnings, but a firm cannot maintain both a high debt-equity ratio and a low dividend payment rate without generating an excessive growth rate for its capital stock.

The effect of the corporate-type tax system on the debt-equity ratio depends on the portfolio balance behavior of individual investors. If an increase in the net yield on debt relative to equity causes a rise in the desired debt-equity ratio, the corporate tax system raises the equilibrium debt-equity ratio.

Changes in the ratio of debt to equity complicate the analysis of the effect of tax rules on asset yields because part of any change in asset yields is their compensation for the change in risk. To clarify the analysis, we assume that the individual portfolio equilibrium requires a constant debt-equity ratio. In this context, we obtain the rather surprising result that an increase in the corporate tax rate reduces the net yield to debt even though interest payments are deductible by the corporation. Similarly, a higher tax rate lowers the net yield on equity and reduces the dividend payment rate.

The analysis shows that the current structure of corporate and personal taxes is significantly nonneutral and can significantly distort the financial behavior of firms and the returns to the provider of capital. Extending our analysis to a two-sector model with an endogenous stock of capital would indicate further aspects of nonneutrality.

The final chapter, "Inflation, Income Taxes, and the Rate of Interest: A Theoretical Analysis," returns to the interaction of inflation and tax rules that provided the basis for the econometric study in Chapter 17. In an economy without income taxes and in which money demand is not a function of the interest rate, a change in the equilibrium rate of inflation has no effect on the real economy. This is the "superneutrality" implied by Irving Fisher's original analysis of inflation. More recently, James Tobin (1965b) has emphasized that the observed inverse relation between inflation and money demand implies that an increase in the rate of inflation causes a portfolio substitution that raises the equilibrium capital intensity of the economy.

In reality, this portfolio substitution effect must be very small. Even a relatively broad definition of the relevant monetary balances implies that the maximum effect is less than 2 percent of total wealth. An economy's tax rules are therefore likely to have a much more substantial effect by influencing the total supply of saving and its allocation among alternative uses.

The analysis of Chapter 22 considers a particularly simple tax structure that illustrates how fully anticipated inflation can change the real return to savers and therefore the rate of saving. The model focuses exclusively on the difference between the tax rate of corporate borrowers and the tax rate of the individual savers who lend to the corporation. The effects of inflation on depreciation, on inventory profits, and on capital gains are all ignored, and all investment is assumed to be financed by debt. In this context, an increase in the rate of inflation raises the net return to savers if the corporate tax rate at which interest payments are deducted exceeds the personal tax rate that is paid on interest receipts. Moreover, since savers in high tax brackets will generally see their rate of return depressed by inflation (because their personal tax rates exceed the corporate rate) while savers in low brackets receive higher rates of return, the net effect on aggregate saving will depend on the relative sensitivity of saving in the different groups.

The studies included in this volume have dealt with only some aspects of the broad subject of capital taxation. These analyses are sufficient, however, to show that the tax system does have substantial and varied effects on the process of capital accumulation. They also indicate the need for continuing research, both theoretical and empirical, on the ever-changing system of actual tax rules and on the possibilities for better alternatives.

PART ONE

The Effects of Taxation on Household and Corporate Saving

1 The Rate of Return, Taxation, and Personal Savings

It is widely believed that the taxation of capital income reduces the rate of saving by more than an equal yield tax on consumption or labor income.[1] While this conclusion may be empirically correct, it is not a necessary implication of economic theory. The substitution of a consumption tax or labor income tax for the current tax on capital income might actually reduce saving. Even when attention is limited to a compensated tax change in a simplified life-cycle model, theory alone cannot tell whether individuals will increase or decrease their saving. The purpose of this chapter is to explain this ambiguity.

The Theoretical Ambiguity

It is important to understand first that the theoretically correct statement that "a compensated price increase unambiguously reduces the demand for a good or increases the supply" does not imply that savings are increased by a compensated rise in the net rate of return. Saving is formally equivalent to the current *expenditure* to purchase future consumption. The "price" of that future consumption (measured in terms of foregone current consumption) varies inversely with net rate of interest. The negative compensated price elasticity of demand for future consumption implies that a compensated increase in the net rate of return will increase the *quantity* of future consumption that is demanded. But since the price of that consumption has also fallen, this extra quantity of future consumption can be achieved with a less than proportionate increase in

Reprinted from the *Economic Journal* 88 (September 1978), pp. 482–487, by permission of Cambridge University Press. An earlier version of this chapter was part of a larger study presented at the 1976 NBER Conference on Research in Taxation.
    1. For assertions of this common proposition, see Bailey (1957), Boskin (1977), Diamond (1970), Feldstein (1977), Harberger (1964), Kaldor (1955, chap. 2), Musgrave and Musgrave (1973, chap. 21), and U.S. Congress (1977).

expenditure on that consumption, that is, in saving. If the compensated demand elasticity is less than one, future consumption will increase but current saving will actually decrease.

This simultaneous increase of future consumption and decrease of current saving appears paradoxical at first. The paradox is resolved when we recognize that a compensated change from a general income tax to a consumption tax will also change the timing of each individual's tax payments. Under a consumption tax, more taxes may be paid when the individual is young and working and less when he is retired. The reduction of the taxes due in retirement permits the individual to save less in early years and still consume more in retirement. This reduction in saving is then used to pay the higher taxes during the working years. Thus private saving can fall while subsequent consumption increases.

To examine this more explicitly, consider a two-period life-cycle model in which a fixed labor income is earned in the first period and none is earned in the second period. By saving S pounds in the first period, the individual "buys" retirement consumption of R pounds. The current price p of retirement consumption satisfies

$$p = e^{-rT}, \tag{1}$$

where r is the net rate of return obtained by the individual and T is the length of the interval between saving and dissaving. The amount of saving, that is, the first-period expenditure on second-period consumption, is

$$S = pR. \tag{2}$$

An increase in the net rate of interest lowers p and alters the demand for retirement consumption. The usual Slutsky decomposition of the demand function implies

$$\frac{\partial R}{\partial p} = \left.\frac{\partial R}{\partial p}\right|_{U} - R\frac{\partial R}{\partial a}, \tag{3}$$

where a is autonomous income. Multiplying by p/R and writing $\sigma = \partial S/\partial a = \partial(pR)/\partial a$ for the marginal propensity to save, yields

$$\frac{p}{R}\frac{\partial R}{\partial p} = \left.\frac{p}{R}\frac{\partial R}{\partial p}\right|_{U} - \sigma, \tag{4}$$

or
$$\eta_{Rp} = \varepsilon_{Rp} - \sigma, \tag{5}$$

where η_{Rp} is the uncompensated elasticity of demand for retirement consumption with respect to its price and ε_{Rp} is the corresponding compensated price elasticity. Since $\varepsilon_{Rp} < 0$ and $\sigma \geq 0$, $\eta_{Rp} < 0$; that is, the uncompensated as well as the compensated demand for retirement consumption will be positively related to the net rate of return. Indeed, the uncompensated effect is even stronger than the compensated effect because of the positive marginal propensity to "spend" on retirement consumption.

Consider now the way in which a compensated increase in the net rate of return would affect *saving*. Equation (2) implies

$$\frac{\partial S}{\partial p} = R + p \frac{\partial R}{\partial p} \tag{6}$$

and the corresponding compensated effect

$$\frac{\partial S}{\partial p}\bigg|_U = R + p \frac{\partial R}{\partial p}\bigg|_U. \tag{7}$$

Multiplying both equations by $p/S = R^{-1}$ yields

$$\eta_{Sp} = 1 + \eta_{Rp} \tag{8}$$

and
$$\varepsilon_{Sp} = 1 + \varepsilon_{Rp}. \tag{9}$$

The compensated elasticity of savings with respect to price is negative (and therefore the compensated effect on saving of an increase in the net interest rate is positive) if and only if $\varepsilon_{Rp} < -1$, that is, if and only if the compensated price elasticity of demand for retirement consumption is algebraically less than -1.

Although this shows that a compensated decrease in the rate of tax on capital income may decrease household saving, this form of analysis obscures the importance of the *type* of compensating tax change. Like all such analyses of the effect of a compensated price change, the current derivation implicitly assumes that the compensation is made by a lump-sum change in the numeraire commodity. In the context of the current problem, this is equivalent to financing the reduced tax on capital income by a higher rate of tax on labor income during the individual's preretirement years. The alternative form of compensation is a higher rate of consumption tax, that is, a higher rate of tax on consumption in both periods. Although both forms of compensation yield the same pattern of household consumption, they differ in the time pattern of disposable income and therefore of household saving. Moreover, both forms of compensation shift at least part of the government's tax receipts from the retirement period (that is, when the household receives its interest income) to the first period (when labor income is earned and some consumption occurs). The government must therefore increase public saving if the time pattern of government purchases of goods and services is to remain unchanged. Total national savings, including both private and public saving, will necessarily increase when a labor income tax or consumption tax is substituted for a tax on capital income even though private saving decreases *if* the government increases its surplus to maintain the original time pattern of public spending.[2]

An Example with Cobb-Douglas Utility

These ideas will be clarified by studying a specific example. Consider an individual with fixed first-period labor income Y who maximizes a symmetric Cobb-Douglas utility function $U = C_1 C_2$. In the absence of any tax, his budget constraint is $C_1 + pC_2 = Y$. Maximizing $U = C_1 C_2$ subject to this constraint implies that optimal first-period consumption is $C_1 = 0.5Y$ and thus saving is $S = 0.5Y$. A capital income tax raises the price of second-period consumption to $(1 + \tau)p$ and thus changes the budget constraint to $C_1' + (1 + \tau)pC_2' = Y$. Because of the special character of the Cobb-Douglas utility function, $C_1' = 0.5Y$ remains unchanged. Moreover, since none of the tax is collected in the first period, $S' = 0.5Y$ also remains unchanged. The capital income tax collects $\tau C_2'$ in the second period; the present value of the tax is thus $p\tau C_2'$.

An equal-yield consumption tax raises the price of consumption in the first period to $(1 + t)$ and the price of retirement consumption to $(1 + t)p$, where t is chosen to produce the same revenue as the capital income tax, that is, so that $tC_1'' + ptC_2'' = p\tau C_2'$. Maximizing utility subject to the budget constraint $(1 + t) C_1'' + (1 + t) pC_2'' = Y$ yields $(1 + t) C_1'' = 0.5Y$. Net consumption expenditure (C_1'') is now less than it was with the capital income tax. However, gross consumption expenditure $[(1 + t) C_1'']$ is the same as before so that the individual's saving remains unchanged at $S'' = S' = 0.5Y$. The individual's tax payments increase by tC_1'' in the first

2. Diamond (1970) concludes that a compensated capital income tax unambiguously reduces savings because he assumes that the tax proceeds are given as a lump sum during the retirement years.

period and fall by a corresponding amount in the second period. The government can therefore increase its net surplus by tC_1'' and maintain the original public consumption path. The entire increase in national saving that results from this change in tax structure is therefore due in the current case to the government surplus since private saving remains unchanged.[3]

The effect of an equal yield tax on labor income is only slightly different. With labor income fixed in the current case, this is equivalent to a lump-sum tax that changes the individual's budget constraint to $C_1 + pC_2 = Y - T$. First-period consumption falls to $C_1^* = 0.5(Y - T)$ but first-period saving also falls to $S^* = Y - T - C_1^* = 0.5(Y - T)$. Since all taxes are now paid in the first period, the government can run an even larger surplus than with an equal-yield consumption tax. Part of this surplus must offset the decrease in private saving.

Because the government surplus is the only possible source of increased national saving in the current context, it is important to examine in more detail how the change in taxes affects the government's multiperiod budget constraint. Such an examination will show that the possibility of increased national saving depends crucially on the nature of the *transition* from the capital income tax to the alternative. If this is not done in the appropriate way, the substitution of a consumption tax or labor income tax is more likely to cause a government deficit than a surplus. The nature of this problem can be illustrated by considering the substitution of a consumption tax in a stationary economy with overlapping generations of identical individuals.[4]

With a pure tax on capital income, the time stream of tax payments by the "young" (that is, individuals in the first period of their life) and by the "old" retirees is

	"Year"			
	1	2	3	. . .
Young	0	0	0	. . .
Old	$\tau C_2'$	$\tau C_2'$	$\tau C_2'$	. . .
Total	$\tau C_2'$	$\tau C_2'$	$\tau C_2'$	. . .

3. This is a direct reflection of the Cobb-Douglas utility function. With a more general utility function, current private saving may decrease or increase. When private saving decreases, national saving can still increase because of the government surplus.

4. This could be extended as Samuelson (1958) did to a growing economy without altering the conclusions of the current analysis as long as the gross rate of return exceeds the rate of population growth.

If a consumption tax is substituted in year 1, the new stream of tax payments becomes

	"Year"			
	1	2	3	. . .
Young	tC_1''	tC_1''	tC_1''	. . .
Old	tC_2''	tC_2''	tC_2''	. . .
Total	$tC_1'' + tC_2''$	$tC_1'' + tC_2''$	$tC_1'' + tC_2''$	. . .

Recall that the consumption tax rate is set to satisfy $tC_1'' + ptC_2'' = p\tau C_2'$, that is, so that the present value of each individual's tax remains unchanged. This implies that each "year's" total tax receipts under the capital income tax exceeds the potential receipts under the consumption tax; that is, $tC_1'' + ptC_2'' = p\tau C_2'$ implies $tC_1'' + tC_2'' < \tau C_2$ since $p < 1$. Since each year's tax receipts under the consumption tax are lower than under the capital income tax, it is impossible to maintain the old level of government spending and run the surplus that is required to increase national saving.

This problem arises because the immediate complete substitution of the consumption tax for the capital income tax lowers the tax burden on the first generation of retirees (that is, the group that is old in year 1) from $\tau C_2'$ to tC_2''. Since the present value of the taxes of all other cohorts remains unchanged, the total present value of all tax receipts falls. The possibility of a government surplus is thus eliminated by giving an inappropriate windfall tax reduction to the first generation of retirees. The correct transition requires maintaining the original tax liability of this first generation. The time stream of tax receipts is then

	"Year"			
	1	2	3	. . .
Young	tC_1''	tC_1''	tC_1''	. . .
Old	$\tau C_2'$	tC_2''	tC_2''	. . .
Total	$tC_1'' + \tau C_2'$	$tC_1'' + tC_2''$	$tC_1'' + tC_2''$	. . .

Tax receipts in year 1 exceed the receipts under the capital income tax by tC_1'' and in each subsequent year fall short by $\tau C_2'' - (tC_1'' + tC_2'') = [(1 - p)/p]tC_1''$.[5] The present value of this future tax shortfall is exactly

5. The equal yield requirement, $p\tau C_2' = tC_1'' + ptC_2''$, implies that $\tau C_2' - (tC_1'' + tC_2'')$ $= tC_1''/p + tC_2'' - tC_1'' - tC_2'' = [(1 - p)/p]tC_1''$.

tC_1'', that is, the first-year surplus can be saved and used to finance all future reductions in tax receipts.[6] The appropriate treatment of the "old retirees" during the transition thus permits the original levels of government spending to be maintained and is crucial if the consumption tax is to increase national saving.

Conclusions

This analysis establishes the theoretical indeterminacy of the effect on private saving of switching to a consumption tax or reducing the tax on capital income by any other compensated tax changes.[7] Only empirical studies can assess the magnitudes of the likely change in private saving.[8] Moreover, whatever the effect on private saving, the overall effect on national saving depends on the way that the government responds to the greater revenue that would result from advancing the time when taxes are due.

6. The present value in year 1 of the tax deficit in year n is $p^{n-1}[(1 - p)/p]tC_1''$. The present value of all deficits beginning in year 2 is thus $(p + p^2 + . . .)[(1 - p)/p]tC_1'' = tC_1''$.

7. Note that the tax rate of the consumption tax or labor income tax could be varied through time to make the revenue in each year equal to what it would have been with the capital income tax. If this is done, the change in private saving is equal to the change in national saving and is therefore positive. Such a policy would no longer be a compensated tax change for each generation.

8. Boskin (1977) presents an econometric analysis of this question with careful attention to measuring the real net rate of return.

2 The Effective Tax Rate and the Pretax Rate of Return

This chapter presents new estimates of the pretax rate of return on nonfinancial corporate capital in the United States and on the effective rate of tax paid on that return. We then use these estimates to examine whether there has been any systematic decline in the rate of return and to study the sources of variation in profitability. Our estimates of the rate of profit during the past quarter century use the most recent national income account revisions and the latest estimates by the Department of Commerce and the Federal Reserve Board of the stocks of reproducible capital and land. In addition, we have developed our own estimates of the property tax paid by nonfinancial corporations (NFCs) to state and local governments, a significant component both of taxes and of pretax profits that was omitted in all previous studies.

These estimates of property taxes and their implications for the pretax rate of return are discussed in the first two sections of the chapter. The effective tax rate reflects the taxes paid by corporations, their shareholders, and their creditors to governments at all levels. The third section of the chapter discusses the estimation of these taxes and the implied behavior of the effective tax rate. The fourth section then examines whether there has been a trend in profitability in the postwar period or a tendency for profits to decline in the 1970s. Several factors that are potential determinants of corporate profitability, including productivity and the ratio of final product prices to intermediate input prices and unit labor costs, are examined in the fifth section. There is no evidence that the broad fluctuations in the effective tax rate over the past twenty-five years induced off-

This chapter was written with James Poterba and Louis Dicks-Mireaux. Reprinted from the *Journal of Public Economics* (Fall 1982) by permission of North-Holland Publishing Company. This study is part of the NBER Study of Capital Formation. An earlier version of the first three sections appeared in NBER Working Paper 508R by Feldstein and Poterba. These sections were revised to reflect new national income and capital account data. Dicks-Mireaux participated in this revision and in the fourth and fifth sections.

setting changes in the pretax rate of return. Changes in the effective tax rate were therefore associated with correspondingly large changes in the net rate of return.

State and Local Taxes Paid by Nonfinancial Corporations

In measuring corporate profits, the national income and product accounts treat state and local property taxes very differently from the profits taxes levied by all levels of government.[1] Pretax profits are defined as profits before corporate income taxes but after all of the state and local property taxes paid by corporations. We believe that this method is conceptually incorrect and that it significantly distorts the measurement of the national rate of return on additions to the stock of corporate capital.[2]

Although all of the taxes paid by corporations are costs from the private viewpoint of the shareholders, these taxes do not represent social costs. Similarly, the taxes paid by business to state and local governments do not represent charges for benefits received. From the national viewpoint, the marginal product of capital is therefore the total addition to national output and not that addition net of the taxes levied on capital or capital income. A correct measure of capital productivity therefore requires adding the state and local property taxes to the national income measure of pretax income.[3] This section presents alternative estimates of the state and local property taxes paid by nonfinancial corporations.

In 1979 state and local governments collected more than $32 billion in taxes on the capital or capital income of nonfinancial corporations. This includes the state personal income taxes on the dividends of shareholders as well as the state and local taxes on corporate property and profits. State and local taxes on the capital income of nonfinancial corporations now exceed 17 percent of real pretax capital income and 70 percent of that income net of all federal, state, and local taxes. It is clear from these fig-

1. The term "property tax" refers to taxes levied on the value of physical assets, while "profits taxes" are levied on the income generated from these assets.

2. The national income accounting convention of treating property taxes as a cost of production rather than as a tax on capital appears to be based on accepting the business accounting convention that the property tax is a "cost" because it is subtracted in calculating business profits; see Ruggles and Ruggles (1956). A further reason offered in defense of the conventional national income accounting method is that the property tax is an "indirect tax" and therefore presumably has a very different incidence than the direct capital income taxes; see Ruggles and Ruggles (1970). We believe that the property tax and the tax on profits cannot usefully be distinguished in either of these ways.

3. This expanded definition of pretax profits differs from the social product of capital if there are externalities, economic rents, nonconstant returns to scale, or monopoly power. This distinction will be ignored in this chapter.

ures alone that recognizing state and local taxes is important for calculating the total effective tax rate on capital income as well as for assessing the pretax rate of return on corporate capital.

Nonfinancial corporations pay two types of state and local taxes that are based on capital or capital income: corporate profits taxes and property taxes. Since there are no official estimates of either type of tax paid by nonfinancial corporations, we now describe our own method of estimation.

The total corporate profits tax accruals of state and local governments for all types of corporations are calculated by the Department of Commerce and published in the *National Income and Product Accounts*.[4] The value for 1979 was $13.0 billion. We divide this amount between nonfinancial and financial corporations in the same ratio as the *federal* corporate income tax accruals are divided between these two types of corporations. In 1979, for example, nonfinancial corporations accounted for 80 percent of total federal corporate tax liabilities.[5] On the basis of this information, we estimate that the state and local corporate tax liability for nonfinancial corporations was $10.4 billion. Similar values for other years since 1948 are shown in column 1 of Table 2.1. Note that the tax rose from only $1.1 billion in 1960 to $2.8 billion in 1970 and $10.4 billion in 1979.

The total value of state and local property tax collections appears in the national income and product accounts (see Table 2.3), but no distinction is made between the taxes levied on the property of nonfinancial corporations and the taxes levied on the property of households, unincorporated businesses, and financial corporations. The total state and local property tax receipts for 1979 were $64.4 billion. Because calculating the share of property taxes levied on nonfinancial corporations is difficult, we present three different estimates based on three different assumptions. All three estimates are based on the Department of Commerce series of the replacement value of stocks of reproducible physical assets and the Federal Reserve estimates of the current market value of landholding.[6]

4. Table 3.4 of the NIPA contains a detailed breakdown of state and local government receipts.

5. The total corporate profits tax liability is reported in table B-19 of the 1981 *Economic Report*, while the corresponding figure for nonfinancial corporations is reported in table B-11. The Department of Commerce follows the same procedure, based on the NFC's share of federal profits, for allocating state and local profits taxes. Therefore, the profits tax liabilities data reported, which include federal, state, and local taxes, reflect the share of NFC federal profit taxes in total profit taxes.

6. These estimates are presented in *Balance Sheets for the U.S. Economy,* a periodical document of the Division of Research and Statistics of the Board of Governors of the Federal Reserve System. The figures used in the calculation presented in this chapter are from the version dated April 1981.

Table 2.1. State and local property tax base and tax payments by nonfinancial corporations (billions of dollars)

Year	State and local corporate profits tax (1)	Property subject to state and local property tax		State and local property tax collections			
		Total (2)	Nonfinancial corporations (3)	Total (4)	Nonfinancial corporations		
					Equal rate (5)	3 to 1 rate (6)	1 to 3 rate (7)
1948	0.6	498.9	157.5	5.9	1.874	3.447	0.791
1949	0.6	531.6	170.5	6.6	2.130	3.893	0.903
1950	0.7	574.4	182.6	7.1	2.271	4.165	0.961
1951	0.8	638.8	200.5	7.7	2.415	4.452	1.018
1952	0.8	686.7	216.7	8.4	2.645	4.866	1.117
1953	0.7	719.3	228.8	9.1	2.893	5.305	1.224
1954	0.7	752.0	239.3	9.7	3.079	5.644	1.303
1955	0.9	802.9	254.7	10.4	3.314	6.083	1.401
1956	1.0	873.2	280.7	11.5	3.682	6.723	1.562
1957	0.9	934.0	306.5	12.6	4.138	7.494	1.765
1958	0.9	981.0	323.1	13.8	4.533	8.198	1.936
1959	1.0	1,033.8	336.8	14.8	4.825	8.765	2.055
1960	1.1	1,081.5	349.4	16.2	5.245	9.560	2.228
1961	1.1	1,121.6	360.0	17.6	5.643	10.310	2.393
1962	1.3	1,168.6	373.3	19.0	6.056	11.086	2.565
1963	1.4	1,214.7	386.3	20.2	6.439	11.806	2.724
1964	1.6	1,272.3	401.0	21.7	6.835	12.577	2.884
1965	1.7	1,353.1	426.1	23.2	7.302	13.440	3.081
1966	2.0	1,452.3	462.2	24.5	7.809	14.314	3.304
1967	2.1	1,556.3	502.3	27.0	8.702	15.866	3.696
1968	2.6	1,677.0	541.5	29.9	9.654	17.597	4.101
1969	2.9	1,824.5	590.5	32.8	10.604	19.312	4.507
1970	2.8	1,970.4	649.1	36.7	12.081	21.848	5.160
1971	3.2	2,117.7	700.2	40.4	13.373	24.149	5.718
1972	4.0	2,318.1	751.9	43.2	14.021	25.513	5.963
1973	4.7	2,638.9	832.8	46.4	14.628	26.905	6.175
1974	5.3	3.079.2	984.8	49.0	15.665	28.661	6.637
1975	5.8	3,469.9	1,134.8	53.4	17.458	31.664	7.442
1976	7.6	3,814.9	1,229.8	58.2	18.776	34.248	7.972
1977	9.0	4,273.5	1,348.2	63.4	20.003	36.794	8.443
1978	9.5	4,908.5	1,510.7	63.9	19.681	36.547	8.254
1979	10.4	5,626.3	1,710.6	64.4	19.581	36.529	8.186

Sources: Column 1, NIPA table 3.3. Remaining columns based on authors' calculations using data from *Economic Report of the President* (tables B-11, B-19) and *Balance Sheets of the U.S. Economy,* tangible asset allocation table.

More specifically, the total value of property that is subject to state and local property tax is calculated as the sum of plant and equipment, land, and residential structures minus the amounts of those types of assets owned by nonprofit institutions.[7] The total value of taxable property estimated for 1979 was $5,626 billion. Within this total, nonfinancial corporate business accounted for $1,711 billion or 30 percent of the total taxable capital stock.[8] Columns 2 and 3 of Table 2.1 present the two series of taxable capital stocks.

If all jurisdictions valued property for tax purposes at the replacement values and taxed all property at the same rate, it would be appropriate to assign state and local property taxes in the same ratio as the value of the property itself. In fact, however, effective tax rates differ substantially among jurisdictions and among property classes within jurisdictions. Within jurisdictions, business property tends to be taxed more heavily than residential property or agricultural land;[9] this implies that nonfinancial corporations bear more than a proportionate share of the total property tax. The variation in effective tax rates among jurisdictions could either strengthen this tendency or reverse it. Because of this uncertainty, we present three separate calculations. The first assigns property taxes in the same ratio as the value of the property; if the variation in tax rates among jurisdictions is uncorrelated with the mix of property types, this "equal tax" assignment is a conservative understatement of the property tax paid by nonfinancial corporations. The second method assumes that the effective tax rate on nonfinancial corporate property is three times the effective tax rate on other property.[10] The third method assumes the op-

7. Data on land and reproducible fixed assets are presented in the table "Tangible Asset Allocations" of the document cited in note 6. For 1979, the total value (including that held by tax-exempt nonprofit institutions) was $5,843 billion. State and local jurisdictions differ in their treatment of inventories; to be conservative, we exclude inventories from the tax base and thereby reduce the fraction of property taxes assigned to nonfinancial corporations.

8. Including inventories would raise the total taxable capital stock by $655 billion to $6,281 billion; for nonfinancial corporations, the increase would be $539 billion to $2,250 billion. This expanded definition would raise the share of nonfinancial corporate property from 0.30 to 0.36. This may seem a surprisingly small share of capital owned by nonfinancial corporations; most of the remaining property is housing (41 percent) and agricultural land (8 percent).

9. The effective tax rate has two components: the assessment-price ratio and the tax rate on assessed value. The 1977 Census of Governments *Taxable Property Values and Assessment-Sales Price Ratios* reports the assessment-price ratio on commercial and industrial property to be higher than that on any other class of property. Netzer's comments (1973) indicate that the equal effective tax rate assumption probably understates the taxation of business property.

10. This implies that for 1979, nonfinancial corporations paid 56.7 percent of the property tax even though they only had 30.4 percent of taxable property.

posite imbalance: the effective tax rate on other property is three times the rate on the property of nonfinancial corporations. (The second and third calculations are almost certain to bound the true value.) For 1979, these two assumptions imply that nonfinancial corporations may pay as much as 56.7 percent of the total state and local property tax or as little as 12.7 percent.

Column 4 of Table 2.1 reports the total state and local property tax collections, while columns 5, 6, and 7 report the property taxes assigned to nonfinancial corporations by the three assumptions. Note that the basic assumption of method 1 (that is, the assumption that nonfinancial corporations pay the same effective tax rate as other property owners) implies that NFCs paid $19.6 billion in property taxes during 1979.

Expanded Profits and the Rate of Return on Capital

Several recent studies have estimated the total pretax return to capital with appropriate adjustment for the effects of inflation on the traditional accounting measures of corporate income.[11] The common procedure in all of these studies is to define total capital income as the sum of (1) corporate interest payments and (2) corporate profits with a capital consumption adjustment and inventory valuation adjustment.[12] The rate of profit is then calculated as the ratio of this measure of total capital income to the replacement value of the corporate capital stock defined to include fixed capital, inventories, and land.[13] This rate of profit is the marginal product of capital if there are constant returns to scale and no economic rents or monopoly profits.

These estimates rely on the work by the Department of Commerce during the past decade that led to their publication of estimates of economic depreciation and of the replacement cost of fixed business capital.[14] The Federal Reserve Board's "Balance Sheets for the U.S. Economy" incorporate these Commerce Department estimates and also provide unpublished Commerce Department estimates of the market value of inven-

11. See Feldstein and Summers (1977), Holland and Myers (1979), and Nordhaus (1974).

12. There is no need to adjust for changes in the real value of corporate debt (due to inflation or interest rate changes) since any gain by the equity owners represents an equal loss to the creditors and leaves total capital income unchanged.

13. Land is, of course, included at an estimated market value. Lovell (1978) presents estimated profit rates that include only plant and equipment in the capital stock; since inventories and land represent about 35 percent of the total NFC capital stock, this measure is seriously incorrect.

14. These data are more fully described in the April 1976 issue of the *Survey of Current Business*.

tories and their own estimates of the market value of land. The capital stock is defined on a "net" basis,[15] and capital income is defined in the corresponding way.

Columns 1 and 2 of Table 2.2 present this conventional measure of total corporate income and the implied net rate of return.[16] Column 3 expands the measure of total corporate income by including the estimate of the state and local property taxes paid by nonfinancial corporations on the assumption of equal effective rates of property tax on all types of property; that is, column 3 is the sum of column 1 of Table 2.2 plus column 5 of Table 2.1. The corresponding rate of return, calculated by dividing column 3 by the same capital stock series that is used to go from column 1 to column 2, is presented in column 4.

For the 32-year period from 1948 through 1979 the total pretax rate of return (column 4) averages 11.5 percent. By contrast, the conventional return based on capital income after state and local property tax payments is only 10.3 percent. The failure to add state and local property taxes back into the total return to capital caused previous estimates to understate the rate of return by about 1.2 percentage points or nearly 11 percent. The estimates for overlapping decades (also shown in Table 2.2) indicate that this difference has remained fairly constant over the postwar period, with some tendency for a larger gap in the second half of the period than in the first half.

Columns 5 and 6 of Table 2.2 present alternative estimates of the net rates of return based on the two extreme assumptions about the property tax rate on nonfinancial corporations and other types of property. The assumption that the nonfinancial corporations pay a property tax rate equal to three times the rate paid on other property yields the series shown in column 5 and implies that the conventional estimate of the rate of return understates the true value by about 2.2 percentage points. Conversely, the extreme assumption of "undertaxation" of nonfinancial corporate property implies that the conventional estimate understates the true rate of return by about 0.5 percentage points (column 6). It seems safe to conclude that the truth lies somewhere between these extremes and that the conventional estimate of the rate of return has been too low by between

15. The capital stock is measured net of depreciation in contrast to a gross capital stock from which scrapping is deducted. All the estimates in this chapter are therefore comparable to the "net" profitability series in Feldstein and Summers (1977) and not to the "gross" profitability series.

16. These figures differ from the r_N series in Feldstein and Summers (1977) because of data revisions. Data revisions affect the earlier years in the series because of the new estimates of the values of land and inventories.

Table 2.2. Corporate income and rates of return on nonfinancial corporate capital

Year	NIPA corporate income[a] (1)	NIPA rate of return (2)	Total corporate income (3)	Total rate of return Equal rate (4)	3 to 1 rate (5)	1 to 3 rate (6)
1948	26.5	12.8	28.4	13.7	14.4	13.2
1949	24.0	10.8	26.1	11.8	12.6	11.3
1950	30.5	12.9	32.7	13.9	14.7	13.3
1951	34.5	13.1	36.9	14.0	14.8	13.5
1952	31.5	11.0	34.2	12.0	12.8	11.4
1953	31.3	10.5	34.2	11.4	12.2	10.9
1954	30.1	9.7	33.2	10.7	11.5	10.1
1955	40.0	12.2	43.4	13.2	14.1	12.6
1956	37.5	10.4	41.2	11.4	12.2	10.8
1957	37.0	9.4	41.2	10.5	11.3	9.9
1958	32.8	8.0	37.4	9.1	10.0	8.5
1959	43.3	10.2	48.1	11.3	12.2	10.7
1960	40.8	9.2	46.1	10.4	11.4	9.7
1961	42.2	9.3	47.8	10.5	11.5	9.8
1962	50.1	10.6	56.2	11.9	12.9	11.1
1963	56.0	11.4	62.5	12.7	13.8	12.0
1964	63.0	12.3	69.8	13.6	14.7	12.9
1965	73.8	13.5	81.1	14.8	16.0	14.1
1966	79.5	13.4	87.3	14.7	15.8	13.9
1967	77.6	11.9	86.3	13.3	14.4	12.5
1968	83.3	11.9	93.0	13.3	14.4	12.5
1969	80.6	10.5	91.2	11.9	13.1	11.1
1970	69.7	8.3	81.7	9.8	10.9	8.9
1971	80.2	8.9	93.5	10.4	11.6	9.6
1972	91.8	9.5	105.8	11.0	12.2	10.1
1973	101.7	9.5	116.3	10.8	12.0	10.0
1974	93.2	7.2	108.9	8.4	9.5	7.7
1975	116.9	7.9	134.3	9.1	10.0	8.4
1976	136.8	8.6	155.6	9.7	10.7	9.1
1977	159.6	9.1	179.6	10.2	11.2	9.6
1978	174.5	8.9	194.1	9.9	10.7	9.3
1979	181.9	8.1	201.4	9.0	9.7	8.4
1950–59	—	10.7	—	11.7	12.6	11.2
1955–64	—	10.3	—	11.5	12.4	10.8
1960–69	—	11.4	—	12.7	13.8	12.0
1965–74	—	10.5	—	11.8	13.0	11.1
1970–79	—	8.6	—	9.8	10.8	9.1
1948–79	—	10.3	—	11.5	12.5	10.8

Sources: Calculations based on data from NIPA table 1.13, Federal Reserve Board *Balance Sheets,* and Table 2.1 of the present work.
   a. The amounts in columns 1 and 3 are in billions of current dollars.

one and two percentage points, implying that the true value exceeds the conventional estimate by between 10 and 20 percent.

Effective Tax Rates

The effective tax rate on the capital income of nonfinancial corporations depends on the federal, state, and local taxes that are paid by the corporation itself and by the corporation's shareholders and creditors. These include the corporate income taxes, the property tax, the personal tax on dividends and capital gains, and the personal and corporate taxes on the interest income received by the creditors of the nonfinancial corporations.

In an earlier paper Summers and I calculated the effective tax rate on the capital income of nonfinancial corporations (Feldstein and Summers 1979). In contrast to previous studies that were limited to the corporate rate, that analysis also included the federal taxes on dividends, capital gains, and interest. The effective tax rate was defined as the ratio of the combined tax liability to the real pretax capital income. The present study redefines this tax rate in two fundamental ways: the total tax burden is expanded to include the state and local taxes discussed in the previous section as well as the state and local taxes paid by shareholders and creditors; and the real capital income of the nonfinancial corporations is also expanded by including the state and local property taxes. Since the effective tax ratio is less than one, adding equal amounts to the numerator and denominator (that is, the state and local taxes paid by the corporations) would raise the ratio. In fact, the numerator is increased by more than the denominator (because of the taxes paid by individuals), so the effective tax ratio rises even more. In addition to this fundamental change in the definition of the effective tax rate, the present study also makes several smaller improvements in the previous Feldstein-Summers procedure.[17] A description of the tax rate data calculations is provided in the Appendix at the end of this chapter.

Table 2.3 presents each of the components of the total effective tax rate. The effective tax rate is expressed as a percentage of what we shall call the "adjusted real capital income" of the nonfinancial corporations.

17. The calculation by Feldstein and Summers was concerned in part with evaluating the effect of an increase in the rate of inflation. The marginal tax rate on nominal profits created this way can differ in minor ways from the tax rate on nominal profits that results from an expansion of the capital stock—for example, because of the special rules affecting life insurance companies. In this chapter we are not concerned with these special effects of changes in the inflation rate. See also note 34.

This adjusted income is the total pretax capital income of the nonfinancial corporations adjusted for the corporation's losses on non-interest-bearing financial assets (cash, demand deposits, and net trade credit). These losses are calculated as the product of the percentage change in the personal consumption deflator and the total value of these non-interest-bearing assets.[18] We adjust these for inflation because they represent a real loss to the corporation without being a real gain to any explicit provider of corporate capital; that is, the loss on net trade credit is similar to a price reduction, the loss on cash is a gain to the government, and the loss on demand deposits is a gain to commercial banks.

The adjusted real capital income series presented in the first column of Table 2.3 is based on the assumption of equal effective property tax rates. This series therefore differs from the figures in column 3 of Table 2.2 only because of the inflation adjustment. A comparison of these two series shows that the adjustment reduces the measure of real corporate income by about 7 percent.

Column 2 of Table 2.3 presents the NFC federal corporate income tax payments as a percentage of this adjusted real capital income. The corresponding state and local corporate tax payments are shown in column 3. It is noteworthy that the state and local payments were only about 5.5 percent of the federal payment in the 1950s but have recently risen to 15 percent of the federal tax. Column 4 presents the state and local property tax payments (based on the equal effective rate assumption). The series shows a general upward trend but appears to have peaked in the early seventies and to be in decline since then. These three taxes have been grouped together because they are all collected directly from the corporation. The combined tax rate for these three types of taxes has dropped from 58.6 percent of adjusted real capital income in the first five years of this sample (1953 through 1957)[19] to 47.2 percent in the five years ending in 1979.

The effective tax rate on dividends depends on the distribution of dividends among different classes of investors (households, pension funds, life insurance companies, and so on) and the average effective tax rate for each class of investor. The present study uses the Flow of Funds data on equity ownership to distribute dividends among classes of investors for

---

18. Annual series for these assets, calculated from the Federal Reserve "Balance Sheets," are presented in columns 1 and 2 of Appendix Table 2.A1. The inflation rate for each year is computed as the first quarter to first quarter change in the personal consumption expenditure deflator.

19. Data limitations on the marginal tax rate series used later in the calculation precluded extension of the effective tax rate series to the years before 1953.

Table 2.3. Components of the total effective tax rate on nonfinancial corporate capital income

Year	Adjusted real capital income (1)	Federal corporate tax (2)	State and local corporate tax (3)	State and local property tax (4)	Tax on dividends (5)	Tax on real capital gains (6)	Tax on nominal capital gains (7)	Tax on interest (8)	Total effective tax rate (9)
					Contributions to total effective tax rate				
1953	33.5	53.0	2.2	8.6	8.5	0.7	0.7	1.0	74.7
1954	32.9	45.4	2.1	9.4	8.7	0.8	0.6	1.2	68.1
1955	42.9	45.0	2.1	7.7	7.7	1.2	0.8	1.0	65.4
1956	40.4	47.4	2.4	9.1	8.7	1.1	1.3	1.1	71.1
1957	39.8	45.7	2.3	10.4	9.0	1.1	1.6	1.5	71.6
1958	36.5	42.1	2.3	12.4	9.7	0.8	0.9	2.0	70.3
1959	47.2	41.7	2.2	10.2	8.0	1.2	1.0	1.8	66.0
1960	45.2	40.1	2.3	11.6	8.6	1.0	0.7	2.1	66.5
1961	47.3	38.9	2.3	11.9	8.3	0.9	0.4	2.3	65.0
1962	55.4	34.9	2.3	10.9	7.5	1.4	0.7	2.2	59.9

1963	61.6	34.7	2.3	10.4	7.5	1.4	0.5	2.0	58.9
1964	69.1	32.4	2.3	9.9	6.6	1.5	0.5	2.0	55.2
1965	80.0	31.8	2.2	9.1	6.2	1.7	0.7	1.9	53.5
1966	85.6	32.2	2.3	9.1	6.4	1.8	1.0	2.3	54.9
1967	84.9	30.2	2.5	10.3	6.8	1.6	1.0	2.7	55.0
1968	90.5	34.0	2.9	10.7	7.2	1.6	1.5	3.2	61.1
1969	88.2	34.3	3.2	12.0	7.2	2.2	2.8	4.3	66.1
1970	78.5	30.8	3.6	15.4	7.7	1.8	3.5	6.6	69.5
1971	90.5	29.4	3.6	14.8	6.7	2.0	3.1	5.9	65.4
1972	103.1	28.7	3.9	13.6	6.2	2.0	2.3	5.4	62.1
1973	111.8	31.5	4.2	13.1	5.8	2.9	3.2	6.1	66.8
1974	99.0	37.1	5.3	15.8	6.8	4.0	6.4	9.3	84.7
1975	125.2	28.3	4.6	13.9	6.4	2.6	6.6	7.8	70.3
1976	149.0	30.2	5.1	12.6	6.5	2.2	3.3	6.3	66.2
1977	171.4	29.4	5.3	11.7	6.2	2.6	3.5	5.9	64.6
1978	184.0	31.4	5.2	10.7	6.6	3.0	4.6	6.6	68.1
1979	187.2	31.7	5.5	10.5	6.9	2.6	4.2	8.0	69.4

Note: Column 1 is in billions of current dollars. All other columns are percentage rates. See the Appendix to this chapter for data sources.

each year since 1953.[20] Brinner and Brooks (1979) have calculated the tax rate on dividends received by individuals, including the state and local taxes; this rate averaged 43.2 percent for the years 1953 through 1979 and was 49 percent for 1979.[21] Individuals account for approximately 93 percent of the equity that the Flow of Funds sector statements of assets and liabilities classify as belonging to "households"; the remaining "household" equity is owned by nonprofit organizations (foundations, universities, and so on) and trusts.[22] We make the conservative assumption that the dividends received by these "other household institutions" are untaxed. For the remaining dividend recipients we follow the procedure of the Feldstein-Summers study (1979) and assume that insurance companies and banks pay a tax rate equal to 15 percent of the corporate tax rate,[23] (that is, 0.069 for 1979) and that pension funds, foreign equity owners, and other miscellaneous investors pay no tax. The relevant weighted average of these tax rates implies an overall tax rate on dividend income in 1979 of 34.9 percent.[24] Since the ratio of dividends to "adjusted real capital income" was 25.2 percent in 1979, the taxes on dividends added 6.9 percentage points ($0.349 \times 0.252 = 0.069$) to the total tax as a percentage of adjusted real capital income. The series for all years is presented in column 5 of Table 2.3. The relative stability of this tax component reflects the underlying stability of the dividend-income ratio and the effective tax rate on dividends.[25]

The appropriate effective rate of capital gains tax reflects the distribution of equity ownership among different classes of investors and the fact that the capital gains tax is payable only when the asset is sold. The distri-

20. This assignment assumes that equity in nonfinancial corporations is distributed in the same way as total equity and that dividends are distributed in proportion to total equity. This represents an improvement over Feldstein and Summers (1979) where the 1976 pattern of ownership was used to assign dividends in all years of the period.

21. To compute the federal tax on dividends, Brinner and Brooks constructed a weighted average of individual tax rates, using the fraction of dividends received by each taxable income class each year and the corresponding statutory marginal rates. State dividend taxes are estimated by assuming that the marginal rate on dividends is 1.5 times the average state personal tax rate, which can be computed from NIPA aggregates. Columns 3 and 4 of Appendix Table 2.A1 provide the separate series for the federal and state taxes, which were kindly provided by Brinner and Brooks.

22. The 93 percent refers to 1975 and is based on a calculation described in Feldstein and Summers (1979); see Securities and Exchange Commission (1977), p. 11. Our calculation assumes 93 percent for all years.

23. In calculating their taxable income, corporations are allowed to exclude 85 percent of the dividends received from other corporations.

24. The complete series of dividend tax rates is presented in column 5 of Appendix Table 2.A1.

25. There is, of course, some decrease in the series after the tax cuts of 1963 and 1964, but the difference is quite small.

bution of equity ownership has already been described in the previous paragraph. For the sample years before 1969, individual capital gains were taxed at half the individual's statutory rate on dividends, but subject to an "alternative" maximum rate of 25 percent. However, gains are taxed only if realized and the effective tax rate is reduced by the postponement of realization.[26] For the period between 1969 and 1978, the effective tax rate on capital gains was raised in a number of ways: the use of the alternative tax was limited, the value of the loss offset was reduced, the "untaxed" portion of capital gains was subject to a minimum tax, and the amount of income qualifying for the maximum tax on personal services income was reduced. There is no way to provide an accurate evaluation of the weighted average capital gains tax rate for each year in our series. Instead, we shall make what we regard as the quite conservative assumption that households paid an effective rate of tax of only 5 percent on accruing capital gains except during the years 1969 through 1978 when the rate was 7.5 percent. Insurance companies and banks are taxed at a 30 percent statutory rate on capital gains realizations. We assume an effective rate of 15 percent on accruing gains because of the effect of deferral. Finally, we assume that pensions, foreign shareholders, and other "miscellaneous" investors pay no tax on capital gains. The overall effective tax rate on capital gains implied by these values was 0.044 in 1979 and 0.062 in 1978 (before the tax change).[27]

The capital gains tax rate must be applied to two kinds of capital gains: the rise in the real value that results from retained earnings, and the rise in the nominal value that results from the general increase in the price level. The national income account estimate of retained earnings is deficient because it ignores the real gain that the equity owners make at the expense of the creditors. For example, at the beginning of 1979 the net debt of nonfinancial corporations was $738.2 billion.[28] The 9.9 percent rise in the personal consumption expenditure deflator implied a gain to the equity owners of $73.1 billion and an equal loss to the creditors.[29] The gain on

26. A gain can permanently escape being "realized" for tax purposes if the asset is bequeathed, since the new owner is permitted to "step up" his basis for future tax liabilities to the market value at the time that the asset is received.

27. A complete series of capital gains tax rates is shown in column 6 of Appendix Table 2.A1. Note that while interest and dividends tax calculations are based on taxes that were actually paid, the capital gains tax rate is an estimate of the present value of the future tax liability that will be due when the gains are realized.

28. Computed from the Flow of Funds tables published by the Federal Reserve Board.

29. Of course, the equity owners "paid for" some of this gain in the form of higher interest rates, and, to that extent, national income account profits are lower. The issue here is clarifying the real allocation of the income between debt and equity and identifying the way in which this extra component of real income is taxed.

outstanding debt must be added to real retained earnings[30] for each year to calculate the real increase in equity value.[31] Multiplying this real increase in equity values by the capital gains tax rate and dividing the product by adjusted real capital income gives the additional tax component shown in column 6 of Table 2.3. This source of tax is responsible for only between one and four percentage points of the total effective tax rate.

An additional capital gains tax liability results from the nominal increase in the value of corporate assets that accompanies a general rise in the price level. We abstract from the year-to-year stock market fluctuations and calculate the nominal rise in the value of the capital stock as the product of the capital stock at the beginning of the year and the rise in the GNP deflator during the year.[32] Multiplying this nominal increase in equity values by the capital gains tax rate and dividing the product by the adjusted real capital income gives the additional tax component shown in column 7 of Table 2.3. This source of tax was responsible for less than 1.5 percentage points of effective tax rate until the late 1960s, but the rise in inflation since then has made this a more significant factor. In the five years ending in 1979, the accrued capital gains tax on this nominal increase was equivalent to an average tax on total income of 4.4 percent.

The final component of the total effective tax rate is the tax borne by the creditors of the nonfinancial corporations. Although there are federal, state, and in some cases, local taxes on interest income, we follow the very conservative procedure of including only the federal tax.[33] The Feldstein-Summers study (1979) used the Flow of Funds accounts for 1976 to estimate the distribution of the net liabilities of nonfinancial cor-

30. The real retained earnings are, of course, after the inventory valuation and capital consumption allowance adjustments.

31. This real increase in equity value is presented in column 7 of Appendix Table 2.A1. We assume that an extra dollar of real retained earnings raises the market value of equities by one dollar. This abstracts from year-to-year fluctuations in stock market valuation. It also ignores the arguments of Auerbach (1979b), Bradford (1979), and King (1977) that the capitalization of future tax liabilities may cause a dollar of retained earnings to raise share prices by less than one dollar.

32. The GNP deflator is too broad an index, while the fixed nonresidential investment deflator is too narrow (because it excludes inventories and land); however, both indices rose almost exactly the same amount over the 17-year period and behaved quite similarly from year to year. Note that the equity owners receive the nominal gain on the entire capital stock and not just on the equity fraction. The value of the beginning-of-year capital stock for each year, found in the "Balance Sheets" document, is presented in column 8 of Appendix Table 2.A1. The calculation abstracts from the depressing effect on share prices of unanticipated changes in inflation; see Feldstein (1980b) and the other research cited therein.

33. We do this because of the difficulty of calculating the state and local taxes on interest income, especially the taxes paid by financial corporations.

porations among households, pensions, commercial banks, savings banks, life insurance companies, government accounts, and a number of smaller categories. We use the relative weights implied by this analysis and also follow Feldstein-Summers in setting the household tax rate on this interest income at 35 percent, the mutual savings bank rate at 24 percent, and the rate for private pensions, government accounts, and "miscellaneous" creditors at zero. Life insurance companies are taxed under a special set of tax rules that make their effective rate depend essentially on the yield on their portfolio as well as the statutory corporate tax rate. We apply these rules to calculate a different tax rate for every year based on the prevailing Baa bond rate.[34] For commercial banks, nonlife insurance companies, and finance companies, we make the conservative assumption that one-third of their interest income is completely sheltered from all corporate taxes.[35] The combined tax rate on interest income[36] multiplied by the annual interest payments of nonfinancial corporations and the product divided by their adjusted real capital income gives the interest component of the total effective tax rate that is presented in column 8 of Table 2.3. This component contributed less than 2.5 percentage points to the total effective tax rate until 1966, but the rising interest rates since then raised this component to more than seven percentage points in 1979.

   The combined total effective tax rate on the capital income of the nonfinancial corporate sector—that is, the sum of federal, state, and local taxes on capital and capital income divided by the adjusted real capital income—is shown in column 9. This tax rate reached 69.4 percent in 1979; taxes took more than two-thirds of the total pretax income. Since 1973, the rate has exceeded 64 percent every year. By comparison, the rate was as low as 54 percent in the mid-1960s. The effective tax rates in the period from 1975 to 1979 were back to the same high level that prevailed in the early 1950s before accelerated depreciation, the investment tax credit, rate reductions, and so on. This increase in effective tax rates occurred because of the interaction of inflation with existing tax rules and

34. These rules (known as the Menge formula) imply that there is one marginal tax rate on the increase in income that occurs when interest rates rise and a different and lower marginal tax rate on the increase in income from an increase in the size of the portfolio. Because of their focus on the effect of inflation, Feldstein and Summers calculated the former; we calculate the latter.

35. This is equivalent to assuming that a larger portion is converted to capital gains or just postponed. The untaxed income is, of course, subject to further tax as the dividends and retained earnings of these financial corporations. We assume the same dividend-payout ratio, 0.461, as Feldstein and Summers.

36. This rate is presented in column 9 of Appendix Table 2.A1.

Table 2.4. Alternative effective tax rates and the real net rate of return

Year	Total effective tax rate (1)	Real net after-tax rate of return (2)	3 to 1 property tax rate assumption (3)	1 to 3 property tax rate assumption (4)	Federal effective tax rate (5)
1953	74.7	2.9	76.4	73.4	72.8
1954	68.1	3.4	70.4	66.3	65.1
1955	65.4	4.6	67.5	63.8	62.8
1956	71.1	3.3	73.1	69.5	68.5
1957	71.6	3.0	73.8	69.8	68.8
1958	70.3	2.7	73.0	68.0	66.5
1959	66.0	3.8	68.6	63.9	62.4
1960	66.5	3.5	69.4	64.1	62.3
1961	65.0	3.7	68.2	62.4	60.5
1962	59.9	4.8	63.2	57.2	54.9
1963	58.9	5.2	62.2	56.3	54.1
1964	55.2	6.1	58.6	52.5	50.0
1965	53.5	6.9	56.8	50.9	48.6
1966	54.9	6.6	58.1	52.4	50.1
1967	55.0	6.0	58.5	52.2	49.6
1968	61.1	5.2	64.2	58.5	56.2
1969	66.1	4.0	69.1	63.5	61.3
1970	69.5	3.0	65.9	66.5	63.9
1971	65.4	3.6	69.1	62.2	59.1
1972	62.1	4.2	65.9	58.9	55.5
1973	66.8	3.6	70.1	64.1	61.5
1974	84.7	1.3	86.5	83.2	82.8
1975	70.3	2.7	73.3	67.7	65.6
1976	66.2	3.3	69.4	63.6	61.0
1977	64.6	3.6	67.8	62.0	59.3
1978	68.1	3.1	70.8	66.0	64.3
1979	69.4	2.7	71.9	67.4	66.1

Note: See the Appendix to this chapter for data definitions.

despite several statutory changes that, in themselves, would reduce the effective tax rate.[37]

Table 2.4 compares alternative effective tax rates and the implied net rate of return. Column 1 represents the combined effective tax rate from column 9 of Table 2.3. The real net rate of return on nonfinancial corporate capital is equal to the product of the pretax rate of return on capital

37. The nature of the interaction between inflation and effective tax rates is discussed in Feldstein (1979) and Feldstein and Summers (1979).

(presented in column 4 of Table 2.2) and one minus the effective tax rate.[38] This return is shown in column 2 of Table 2.4. The real net rate of return for 1979 was only 2.7 percent. For the most recent five years, it averaged only 3.1 percent. The contrast with the mid-1960s is striking; in the five years from 1963 through 1967, the real net return averaged 6.2 percent. Columns 3 and 4 show the effective tax rates corresponding to the two alternative assumptions about state and local property taxes.[39] If the property of nonfinancial corporations is taxed more heavily than other property (column 3), the estimated effective tax rate rises by about three percentage points. Conversely, if nonfinancial corporations are taxed more lightly than other property (column 4), the effective tax rate falls by about two and one-half percentage points.[40]

The last column of Table 2.4 ignores state and local taxes completely and reports the effective federal tax rate defined as the ratio of the total federal tax to the real capital income net of the state and local taxes paid by the corporations.[41] This effective federal rate shows the same general movement over time as the effective total rate. In the five years ending in 1979, the rate averaged 63 percent—twelve percentage points higher than in the years 1963 through 1967.

Is the Rate of Profit Falling?

The average value of the pretax rate of return was 9.8 percent in the 1970s and thus was substantially lower than the corresponding averages of 12.7 for the 1960s and 11.1 for the period from 1953 to 1959. Does the lower rate of return in recent years reflect a fundamental fall in the rate of profit, or has it just been a cyclical or temporary change?

In a previous paper Summers and I attempted to answer that question

38. This is equal to the marginal real net return to providers of capital if the pretax return to capital is the marginal return to capital and if the effective tax rate is an effective marginal rate. As we have already noted, the pretax return to capital may differ from the marginal return if there are nonconstant returns to scale, economic rents, or monopoly profits. The effective tax rate may differ from the marginal effective tax rate if the marginal allocation of saving is different from the average saving pattern. In particular, the marginal tax rate will exceed the average rate if individuals are limited in the amount of low-tax-rate saving that they can do by such things as the limits on pensions and Keogh contributions.

39. These alternative assumptions require changes in both the numerator, for taxes paid, and the denominator, for pretax income, of the effective tax rate ratios.

40. Note that the real net rate of return of column 2 is independent of the assumption about the effective property tax rate.

41. This is an updated version of the effective tax rate series reported in Feldstein and Summers (1979), table 5. The series reported there included state and local profit taxes as well as federal taxes.

with data for a period ending in 1976 (Feldstein and Summers 1977). That study concluded that there was no statistical support for the view that there had been a gradual decline in the rate of return over the postwar period but found that the average return between 1970 and 1976 was some 1 to 2 percent lower than would have been predicted on the basis of fluctuations in capacity utilization alone. The authors also cautioned that factors that contributed to the lower rate of return in the 1970s were likely to be transitory so that the fall in the return might also be only temporary.

In this section we return to that earlier question with a procedure that has been improved in several ways. First, the real rate of return variable (*R*) is based on the recently revised national income account figures and reflects also our new estimates of the taxes paid to state and local governments. Second, we have extended the sample from 1976 to 1979. Third, as we explain below, we have developed a richer set of variables to measure the cyclical condition of the economy. Finally, we consider several other factors that were associated with the fluctuation in the rate of return during the past quarter century.

Equation (1) repeats the basic specification of the earlier Feldstein-Summers paper with the new sample and data. The variable *R* is the real, pretax rate of return shown in column 4 of Table 2.2. The *TIME* variable is an annual trend beginning in 1953, and *DUM70* is a binary variable equal to one in the ten years beginning in 1970 and equal to zero in all previous years. The capacity utilization variable, *UCAP*, is the Federal Reserve Board's index of capacity utilization. The equation is estimated with a first-order autoregressive transformation, and the autoregressive parameter is shown as a coefficient of μ_{-1}. Standard errors are shown in parentheses.

$$R = -1.19 + 0.030 \ TIME - 2.035 \ DUM70 + 0.150 \ UCAP + 0.53\hat{\mu}_{-1}.$$

$$\begin{array}{cccc} (0.070) & (1.035) & (0.058) & (0.027) \end{array} \tag{1}$$

$$\bar{R}^2 = 0.706$$
$$DWS = 1.773$$
$$SSR = 19.45$$
$$1953-1979$$

The results are very similar to the previous estimate. There is no evidence of a general time trend, but an indication that the rate of return was some two percentage points lower in the 1970s than in the previous two decades. A higher rate of capacity utilization tends on average to raise the rate of return, each additional percentage point raising the rate of return

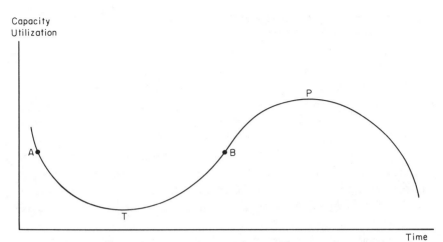

Figure 2.1. Capacity utilization business cycle

by about one-sixth of a percentage point. Replacing the capacity utilization variable with the GNP gap yields very similar results.

Although capacity utilization (or the GNP gap) is intended as an indication of the economy's cyclical condition, it actually describes only one aspect of that cyclical condition. Figure 2.1 presents a business cycle diagram with the amplitude measured in terms of capacity utilization. The use in Eq. (1) of capacity utilization as a measure of the economy's cyclical condition is equivalent to treating points *A* and *B* as equivalent even though *A* occurs during a business cycle contraction (that is, between a peak and the subsequent trough) while *B* occurs during a business cycle expansion (that is, between a trough and the subsequent peak). Early research by Wesley Mitchell (1927, 1951) and others at the National Bureau of Economic Research suggested that profits decline during a business cycle contraction and then increase during a recovery. Although these studies did not use regression methods to distinguish the effect of the level of activity from the cyclical position, we can do so in the current study by including an additional variable that indicates the phase of the cycle. More specifically, we have created a series of quarterly variables defined to equal one in the quarter in which the business cycle trough occurs[42] and in the three subsequent quarters, and to equal zero in all other periods. An

42. The peaks and troughs used for this calculation are the standard NBER turning points: 1954: 2(T), 1957: 3(P), 1958: 2(T), 1960: 2(P), 1961: 1(T), 1969: 4(P), 1970: 4(T), 1973: 4(P), 1975: 1(T), 1980: 1(P).

annual series derived by averaging the quarterly values in each calendar year is denoted *RECOVERY*.

Although this early expansion phase of the business cycle is likely to be a time of above-average profits, further expansion may cause profits to decline. As the economy gets closer to the cyclical peak, there are problems with bottlenecks, older machinery, less experienced employees, and so on. To investigate whether the end of expansion has an effect on profitability that goes beyond the effect of a high level of capacity utilization, we have created a variable that measures how close the economy is to reaching a cyclical peak. We create a quarterly series equal to zero during contractions and otherwise equal to the number of quarters until the peak is reached. The annual average of these quarterly values gives the annual variable *QTILPK*.

Several other cyclical variables were also examined, including the proportion of the year spent in recession, the number of quarters until a cyclical trough, and an indicator of whether a trough occurred in the year. None of these variables had a stable and statistically significant effect on the rate of return.

Equation (2) shows the effect of adding the two additional business cycle variables to the previous specification:

$$R = -16.06 + 0.016\ TIME - 1.415\ DUM70 + 0.315\ UCAP$$
$$(0.048)(0.742)(0.056)$$
$$+\ 1.839\ RECOVERY + 0.093\ QTILPK + 0.50\hat{\mu}_{-1}.$$
$$(0.718)(0.022)(0.25)\qquad\qquad(2)$$

$$\bar{R}^2 = 0.850$$
$$DWS = 1.50$$
$$SSR = 9.05$$
$$1953-1979$$

The coefficient of the *RECOVERY* variable shows that the rate of return tends to be about two percentage points higher during the first year of the recovery than it would otherwise be with the same level of capacity utilization. The coefficient of the *QTILPK* variable shows that the rate of return is higher during expansion than during contractions (when *QTILPK* = 0) but that this excess fades as the economy gets closer to the peak; each quarter further away from the peak adds about one-tenth of a percentage point. Capacity utilization continues to be an important variable; indeed, its coefficient is twice as large in Eq. (2) as it was in Eq. (1)

when the other cycle variables were not taken into account. The coefficients of the time trend variable and the dummy variable for the 1970s are also similar to those of Eq. (1), indicating no time trend but a reduction of about 1.5 percentage points in the 1970s.

The coefficients of Eq. (2) show that the explicit business cycle variables provide information about the fluctuations in profitability that are not captured in simpler measures of aggregate demand like capacity utilization and the GNP gap. As a further test of the usefulness of measuring activity relative to the business cycle peaks and troughs, we added a four-year distributed lag in the capacity utilization variable. The explicit business cycle variables are still very significant; the coefficients are more than three times their standard errors. Of the lagged capacity utilization variables, only the first is statistically significant; its coefficient is negative, small, and a bit less than twice its standard error. For the analysis of profitability, the explicit business cycle variables are clearly better.

The specification of the time trend and level shift in Eqs. (2) and (3) was used to permit comparison with the earlier results in Feldstein and Summers (1977). We have also examined a wide variety of alternative specifications of the relation between time and profitability. Each of these specifications included three variables: (1) a time trend; (2) a level shift variable, that is, a dummy variable equal to zero before a given year and equal to one in that year and beyond; and (3) a trend shift variable, that is, an interaction between the time trend and a dummy variable equal to zero before a given year and equal to one in that year and beyond. The time of the level shift was not constrained to be the same as the time of the trend shift; all years from the mid-1960s to the mid-1970s were considered for both shift variables.

The specification with the lowest sum of squared residuals has a level shift in 1970, just as in Eqs. (1) and (2), and an additional trend shift in 1973:

$$R = -16.74 + 0.082 \ TIME - 1.266 \ DUM70 - 0.053 \ TIME \times DUM73$$
$$\quad\quad\quad\quad (0.035) \quad\quad\quad (0.588) \quad\quad\quad\quad (0.016)$$
$$\quad + 0.313 \ UCAP + 1.875 \ RECOVERY + 0.083 \ QTILPK + 0.15\hat{\mu}_{-1}.$$

$$\quad (0.043) \quad\quad\quad\quad (0.686) \quad\quad\quad\quad\quad\quad (0.017) \quad\quad\quad\quad (0.34)$$

(3)

$$\bar{R}^2 = 0.892$$
$$DWS = 1.630$$
$$SSR = 6.17$$
$$1953\text{–}1979$$

This specification implies a much faster rate of growth of profitability both before 1972 (0.082 percentage points per year) and even after 1973 (0.029 points per year) than the insignificant time trend of Eq. (2). Like the earlier specification, this also implies a drop in profitability of about 1.3 percent in addition to the change in the profitability trend.

It should be emphasized that these three time variables should not be extrapolated outside the sample period. They are really a way of describing the complex time pattern of profitability during the 27-year sample and should not be given a more structural interpretation. A useful way of summarizing the implication of the three time variables is to evaluate the sum of the three effects for each year. The variable constructed in this way shows the pure time-related changes in profitability after excluding the cyclical and random variations in profitability. Column 2 of Table 2.5 presents this composite trend variable. For comparison, column 1 shows the real net return variable. Column 3 presents the cyclically adjusted rate of return, that is, the rate of return with the three cyclical variables evaluated at their sample means.

The mean values of the composite trend variable provide a useful way of assessing the extent to which profitability declined in the 1970s relative to earlier years after taking account of cyclical and random fluctuations. For the period 1953 to 1969, the average value of the composite trend variable was 1.23; by contrast, it was −0.06 for 1970 to 1979. This trend profitability was 1.31 percentage points lower in the 1970s than in the previous seventeen years. A similar comparison between the 1960s and the 1970s shows that trend profitability was 1.59 percentage points lower in the 1970s. Since total profitability fell 2.9 percentage points (from 12.7 percent in the 1960s to 9.8 percent in the 1970s), cyclical and random fluctuations account for 45 percent of the fall (that is, 2.9 minus 1.59 divided by 2.9) and the composite trend accounted for the remainder.

Two specifications in addition to the combination of a 1970 level shift and 1973 trend shift provided nearly as good an explanation of the profitability series; all the other specifications covered in our search were considerably worse. The first of these other two specifications includes a positive level shift in 1969 and a negative trend shift in that same year. The second specification has a negative level shift in 1973 and a negative trend shift in 1970. Although the three specifications imply minor differences in the timing of the change in profitability, they have very similar implications about the change in profitability between the 1970s and the earlier years of the sample. In comparison to the 1.31 percentage point difference implied by Eq. (3), placing both shift dummies in 1969 implies a difference of 1.25 percentage points while placing the shift dummies in 1970 and 1973

Table 2.5. Variations in profitability

Year	Pretax real net rate of return (1)	Composite trend (2)	Cyclically adjusted profitability (3)
1953	11.436	0.572	10.540
1954	10.704	0.654	10.877
1955	13.208	0.736	11.886
1956	11.373	0.817	11.117
1957	10.480	0.899	11.355
1958	9.129	0.981	11.100
1959	11.316	1.063	12.085
1960	10.426	1.144	12.453
1961	10.501	1.226	11.361
1962	11.885	1.308	11.037
1963	12.720	1.390	11.562
1964	13.628	1.471	12.120
1965	14.848	1.553	12.448
1966	14.668	1.635	12.107
1967	13.277	1.717	12.371
1968	13.257	1.798	12.644
1969	11.919	1.880	11.888
1970	9.764	0.695	10.873
1971	10.415	0.777	11.244
1972	10.986	0.859	11.493
1973	10.819	−0.502	10.365
1974	8.450	−0.473	9.387
1975	9.073	−0.445	10.362
1976	9.743	−0.417	10.751
1977	10.226	−0.388	10.789
1978	9.852	−0.360	9.986
1979	8.955	−0.332	9.022
1953–59	11.1	0.82	11.3
1955–64	11.5	1.10	11.6
1960–69	12.7	1.51	12.0
1965–74	11.8	0.99	11.5
1970–79	9.8	−0.06	10.4
1953–69	12.0	1.23	11.7

Note: See the Appendix to this chapter for data definitions.

implies a difference of 1.23 percentage points. Similarly, comparing the 1960s and the 1970s shows differences of 1.59 in the specification of Eq. (2) and 1.58 and 1.61 in the other two specifications. The cyclically adjusted profitability figures shown in column 3 of Table 2.5 show a similar pattern. For the 1970s as a whole, the cyclically adjusted profitability was 1.6 percentage points below the corresponding figures for the 1960s.

It is interesting to note that all three measures of profitability have changed in the same direction and that the effective tax rate moved in the opposite direction. The total effective tax rate averaged 69.6 percent in the 1950s, 59.6 percent in the 1960s, and 68.7 percent in the 1970s. There was obviously no tendency for the pretax return to rise and fall in parallel to the effective tax rate in order to dampen the effect on the net-of-tax rate of return. Instead, the two moved in opposite directions and thereby caused proportionately greater movements in the real net-of-tax rate of return.

It is appropriate to conclude this discussion with a word of caution. Without understanding why profitability was lower in the 1970s than in the earlier period, it is not possible to say whether there has been a permanent or a temporary decline. Only the experience of the future will provide a definite answer. Some additional insight can, however, be obtained by examining some of the factors that may have contributed to the variation in profitability.

Sources of Profitability Variation

To go beyond the trend and cycle analysis of the previous section, we have considered several aspects of the economic environment that have fluctuated significantly over the past two and a half decades and that are potential determinants of the level of profitability. This section describes each variable and its effect both on profitability and on the otherwise unexplained fall in profitability between the 1960s and the 1970s.

The rate of growth of productivity per man-hour rose rapidly in the 1960s and then dropped to successively lower values in the 1970s. Since the reasons for the productivity decline are still poorly understood, "explaining" profitability in terms of productivity growth is of limited value. Nevertheless, any neutral technological shift that reduces productivity is likely to be reflected in profitability. The same is true of lower effective labor inputs per man-hour (because of changes in the composition of the labor force or of individual effort) but would not be true of lower productivity caused by a reduced input of capital.

Equation (4) shows that productivity growth does have a significant effect on profitability and that including it leaves the other coefficients qualitatively unchanged.

$$R = -15.48 + 0.100 \; TIME - 0.041 \; TIME \times DUM73 - 1.667 \; DUM70$$
$$ (0.026) (0.012) (0.437)$$

$$+ \; 0.293 \; UCAP \; + \; 1.632 \; RECOVERY \; + \; 0.046 \; QTILPK$$
$$(0.031) \qquad\qquad (0.454) \qquad\qquad\qquad (0.015)$$

$$+ \; 0.290 \; PRODGRO \; + \; 0.15 \; \hat{\mu}_{-1}.$$

$$(0.073) \qquad\qquad\qquad (0.29) \qquad\qquad\qquad\qquad\qquad (4)$$

$$\bar{R}^2 = 0.940$$
$$DWS = 1.57$$
$$SSR = 3.26$$
$$1953-1979$$

The coefficient of the productivity growth variable (*PRODGRO*) implies that each additional percentage point of productivity growth has associated with it a 0.3 percentage point increase in profitability.

The lower rate of productivity growth in the 1970s contributed significantly to the decline in profitability but was not responsible for the change in the composite trend variable. The coefficients of Eq. (4) imply composite trend values of 0.52 for the 1970s, 1.85 for the 1960s, and 1.50 for the entire sample period before 1970. The gap between the profitability of the 1960s and the 1970s is narrowed to 1.32 percentage points, while the difference between the 1970s and all the preceding years is 0.98 percentage points. The fall in productivity growth from an average of 2.5 in the 1960s to 1.4 in the 1970s decreased profitability by 0.32 percentage points or about 24 percent of the overall profitability decline.

A higher inflation rate can reduce pretax profitability in a variety of ways. For example, firms may seek greater after-tax profits by investing in inventories and other assets with more favorable tax treatment. Alternatively, firms may be misled into making low-profit investments or inappropriate pricing decisions by accounting calculations that do not correctly adjust for inflation. When the annual rate of increase of the GNP deflator is added to the basic specification of Eq. (2), its coefficient is significantly negative and implies that each percentage point of inflation reduces profitability by 0.20 percentage points. The rise in inflation from an average of 2.5 percent a year in the 1960s to 6.5 percent in the 1970s implies a profitability decline of 0.80 percentage points. The inclusion of the inflation variable does not, however, have a substantial effect on the change in the composite trend variable. Its value is calculated to be 2.22 for the 1960s and 1.32 for the 1970s, a decline of 0.90 percentage points. Moreover, when the productivity growth variable is added to the equation, the coefficient of the inflation variable becomes much smaller and statistically insignificant. Therefore, the inflation variable is of interest only if one believes that productivity growth is not a legitimate explanatory variable either because it is an alternative measure of a common phenomenon or because it is itself the result of lower profitability.

One reason why inflation may reduce profitability is that conventional historic cost accounting methods cause an overstatement of profits when there is inflation. Depreciation is understated and artificial inventory profits are recorded (see, for example, Feldstein and Summers 1979). If firms do not see this, they may believe that their costs are lower than they actually are and, as a result, may fail to make as much in real profits as they should. Although this effect is caused by inflation, it is not proportional to current inflation since the depreciation effect depends on the history of inflation and investment as well as on the current inflation value. The national income and product accounts provide annual data on nominal book profits for nonfinancial corporations. When the ratio of these nominal profits to the real profits that we have calculated (and reported in the section on state and local taxes) is added to the basic specification, its coefficient is large and statistically significant (-3.98 with a standard error of 1.21). For the 1970s as a whole, the average value of this nominal to real profits ratio was 0.99, while for the 1960s it was 1.25. The increase in the ratio thus implies a fall in pretax profitability.

Including this accounting ratio variable reduces the size and statistical significance of the time variables. In this specification, the composite trend variable is 0.03 for the 1970s and 0.77 for the 1960s, implying a fall of only 0.74 percentage points. Similarly, between the 1970s and the entire pre-1970 sample period, the difference is only 0.59 percentage points. If this is a correct estimate of the effect of the accounting error, it can be assumed to be only a temporary influence until firms see through the accounting convention and assess costs and profits more accurately.

Adding the productivity growth variable reduces the coefficient of the accounting ratio to -2.13 and raises its standard error to 1.60. In this more general specification, the accounting ratio can at most be considered marginally significant. Moreover, the composite time trend implies a more substantial decline of 1.10 percentage points between the 1960s and 1970s. The inference that a substantial part of the profitability decline is transitory because it reflects an accounting error is therefore conditional on regarding the productivity decline as an inappropriate explanatory variable.

The jump in the price of oil in 1973 and again in 1979 clearly disrupted normal economic behavior. It has been cited as a possible source of the decline in productivity growth (Bruno 1981; Bruno and Sachs 1980; Vinals 1981) and may have contributed directly to the profitability decline as well. This would be true in the short run to the extent that selling prices had already been fixed and even in the longer run to the extent that the higher energy price implies a smaller use of energy inputs that are complementary to capital in production. The coefficient of a dummy variable equal to one in the years 1973, 1974, and 1979 had the expected negative sign: −0.971 with a standard error of 0.438. However, including this variable did not explain any of the composite trend which showed an even larger decline of 1.8 percentage points between the 1960s and 1970s. Adding the productivity variable, however, reduced the coefficient of this dummy variable to the size of its standard error and returned the changes in the composite trend variable to their usual values.

A more general way to incorporate the change in the relative price of oil and of other input prices as well is to use the ratio of an index of final sales prices of nonfinancial corporations to the index of intermediate input prices. The coefficient of this variable was, however, very small and statistically insignificant.

An alternative relative price variable, the ratio of final sales prices to unit labor costs, raised profitability; the coefficient of this price ratio was 20.2 with a standard error of 8.24. The relative price index rose from an average of 0.77 in the 1960s to 0.84 in the 1970s, implying a fall of 1.41 points in profitability. Including this variable did not, however, explain any of the fall in the composite trend variable. The new trend variable declined by 3.3 percentage points between the 1960s and 1970s. Moreover, much of the movement in the relative unit labor cost merely reflects the shift in productivity growth. When both variables are included, only the productivity growth variable is statistically significant, and the composite trend change has the usual value.

In summary, then, we have identified several variables that have influenced profitability during the past decades. Of these variables, only the rate of productivity growth, the rate of general inflation, and the ratio of accounting profits to real profits helped to explain some of the trend decline in pretax profitability. Adding the productivity growth variable to any specification leaves the other new variable statistically insignificant. The implication of this work, therefore, is that although several factors contributing to the profitability decline have been identified, a decline in cyclically adjusted profitability of between 1 and 1.5 percentage points from the 1960s to the 1970s remains to be explained.

It should again be noted in conclusion that the fall in cyclically adjusted pretax profitability between the 1960s and 1970s occurred at the same time as a rise in the effective tax rate. Similarly, the rise in cyclically adjusted pretax profitability between the post–Korean War years of the 1950s and the decade of the 1960s occurred at the same time as a fall in the effective tax rate. There was no tendency for pretax profits to move in a way that offset changes in the effective tax rate.

Conclusion

This chapter has presented new estimates of the taxes paid on nonfinancial corporate capital, of the pretax rate of return to capital, and of the effective tax rate. The basic time series show that both the pretax rate of return and the effective tax rate have varied substantially in the past quarter century.

An explicit analysis indicates that, after adjusting for different aspects of the business cycle, pretax profitability was between 1 and 1.5 percentage points lower in the 1970s than in the 1960s. The rate of profitability in the 1960s was also about one-half of a percentage point greater than the profitability in the seven years of the 1950s after the Korean War.

Changes in productivity growth, in inflation, in relative unit labor costs, and in other variables are all associated with changes in profitability. None of these variables, however, can explain the differences in profitability between the 1950s, 1960s, and 1970s.

Looking at broad decade averages, the effective tax rate and the pretax rate of return move in opposite directions, higher pretax profits occurring when the tax rate is high. Thus there appears to have been no tendency for pretax profits to vary in a way that offsets differences in effective tax rates.

Appendix: Data Description

1. Table 2.3:
   Column 1: (Column 3, Table 2.2) − (Q1 to Q1 change in Personal Consumption Deflator (NIPA, 7.1) × (Mid-year value for holdings of Cash, Demand Deposits, and Net Trade Credit, NFCs [FRBBS])

   The effective tax rates given in columns 2 through 8 are the numbers described below divided by column 1.

   Column 2: Federal Corporate Tax Receipts, NFCs, (ERP, B-11)
   Column 3: Column 1, Table 2.1
   Column 4: Column 5, Table 2.1
   Column 5: (Table 2.A1, column 5) × NFC Dividend Payments (NIPA, 1.13)
   Column 6: (Table 2.A1, column 6) × (Table 2.A1, column 7)
   Column 7: (Table 2.A1, column 6) × (Table 2.A1, column 8)

Column 8: (Table 2.A1, column 9) × (Net Interest Payments of NFCs, NIPA 1.13)

Column 9: Sum of columns 2 through 8 (*ETRATE*)

2. Table 2.4:

Column 1: *ETRATE*

Column 2: (1 − *ETRATE*) × (Column 4, Table 2.2)

Columns 3–4: As in 2, using columns 5 and 6 of Table 2.2

Column 5: See final note in Table 2.A1

3. Table 2.5:

Column 1: Column 4, Table 2.2

Column 2: 0.082 × *TIME* − 1.266 × *DUM70* − 0.053 × *DUM73* × *TIME*, where *TIME* and *DUM70, DUM73* are as defined in text

Column 3: Net Pretax Rate of Return (Table 2.2, column 4) − 0.313 × avg (*UCAP*) − 1.875 × avg (*RECOVERY*) − 0.083 × avg (*QTILPK*), where the averages are the sample means of the exogenous variables for the sample period, 1953–1979

4. Table 2.A1:

Columns 1–2: Data from FRBBS

Column 3: (*TDIVTAX* − *SLTAXRATE*)/(1 − *SLTAXRATE*)

TDIVTAX = unpublished series for the total effective dividend tax rate, all levels of government, provided by Roger Brinner of Data Resources, Inc.

SLTAXRATE = State and Local Personal Tax and Nontax Receipts (NIPA 3.4)/(Rental, Proprietors, Wage and Salary, and Interest Income of Persons, NIPA 1.11)

Column 4: *SLTAXRATE*

Column 5: 0.93 × Household and Nonprofit Equity Ownership (FF) × *TDIVTAX* + 0.15 × *ETRCORP* × (Equity owned by Life and Other Insurance Companies, Savings and Commercial Banks [FF]) all divided by *TOTALEQUITY*. *TOTALEQUITY* is the sum of equity owned by households, pension funds, state and local government retirement plans, commercial banks, savings and loans, and life and other insurance companies

Column 6: 0.93 × Household and Nonprofit Equity Ownership (FF) × *HHCAPRAT* + 0.15 × (Equity Owned by Life and Other Insurance Companies, Savings and Commercial Banks

Table 2.A1. Components of effective tax rate calculations

| Year | Nonfinancial corporate assets | | Individual dividend tax rates | | | Capital gains tax rate (6) | Real increase in equity value (7) | Value of capital stock in current dollars (8) | Tax rate on interest income (9) |
	Cash and demand deposits (1)	Net trade credit (2)	Federal (3)	State/local (4)	Total dividend tax rate (5)				
1953	26.6	9.6	43.7	1.8	38.8	4.8	5.0	292.6	25.6
1954	27.4	9.8	43.6	1.9	38.9	4.8	5.8	305.8	25.3
1955	28.8	10.7	44.4	2.0	39.5	4.8	10.9	314.1	25.4
1956	29.1	11.8	44.1	2.2	39.2	4.8	9.4	342.5	25.8
1957	29.0	12.5	43.1	2.3	38.2	4.8	9.3	381.7	26.8
1958	29.6	13.9	42.8	2.4	38.0	4.7	6.5	403.8	26.8
1959	29.6	15.3	42.5	2.6	37.7	4.7	12.1	414.6	27.2
1960	28.7	16.3	41.5	2.7	36.7	4.7	9.7	435.1	27.2
1961	30.0	18.3	42.4	2.9	37.4	4.7	9.2	448.7	27.1
1962	33.1	19.9	41.5	3.0	36.5	4.7	16.2	462.0	27.0

1963	34.0	19.8	41.7	3.1	36.5	4.7	18.4	482.9	26.7
1964	33.1	19.7	38.0	3.3	33.4	4.6	21.8	499.2	25.7
1965	32.9	24.8	36.4	3.3	31.9	4.6	28.8	525.3	25.0
1966	32.7	26.1	36.9	3.6	32.4	4.6	32.9	566.4	26.1
1967	33.6	23.3	37.8	3.8	32.9	4.5	29.8	624.3	26.8
1968	36.2	24.3	39.2	4.2	34.0	4.5	32.3	675.4	29.4
1969	40.3	25.7	38.5	4.6	33.3	6.5	30.1	727.0	29.1
1970	43.6	27.0	38.3	4.8	32.8	6.4	22.1	803.0	30.6
1971	43.3	28.0	38.6	5.2	32.6	6.4	28.0	871.2	29.9
1972	43.8	31.0	37.8	6.0	31.5	6.3	32.9	924.8	29.3
1973	45.6	32.6	37.9	5.8	30.9	6.3	51.7	1,001.3	29.3
1974	47.0	50.6	39.3	5.8	31.5	6.3	62.7	1,148.3	30.9
1975	50.8	69.5	39.4	6.1	31.4	6.2	52.3	1,429.1	31.8
1976	54.7	72.5	40.7	6.4	32.3	6.2	52.4	1,532.1	31.0
1977	55.9	80.2	42.3	6.6	33.6	6.2	72.1	1,662.0	30.2
1978	59.0	89.0	43.1	6.6	33.9	6.2	90.0	1,850.2	30.9
1979	64.6	95.5	45.5	6.4	34.9	4.4	111.5	2,091.0	31.7

Note: See the section on effective tax rates for data definitions and sources.

[FF]) divided by *TOTALEQUITY,* where *HHCAPRATE* = 0.05 for 1953–1968, 1979 and 0.075 for 1969–1978

Column 7: Undistributed profits of NFCs with IVA and CCA (NIPA, 1.11) and author's calculations of net corporate debt (FF) times the Q1 to Q1 percentage change in consumption deflator (NIPA)

Column 8: Beginning of year replacement value of plant, land, equipment, inventories, and residential structures (FRBBS) × Q1 to Q1 percentage change in the GNP deflator (NIPA, 7.1)

Column 9: This variable uses the net ownership of corporate debt information reported in Feldstein and Summers (1979, table 3). *INTTAXRATE* = 0.35 × (45.5) + 237.7 × *MTR-FINCOS* + 0.24 × 30.7 + 141.7 × *MTRLIFEINS,* all divided by 556.2

Where *ETRCORP* = *FEDCORPRATE* + (Column 1, Table 2.1)/NFC Profits (NIPA 1.13)

MTRFINCOS = 0.66 × *FEDCORPRATE* + (1 − 0.66 × *FED-CORPRATE*) × (0.461 × [Col. 5] + 0.539 × [Col. 6])

FEDCORPRATE = statutory corporate tax rate (DRI)

MTRLIFEINS + *FEDCORPRATE* × (average BAA rate for year [DRI] − 3)/10

To compute the federal component of the tax rates, Column 5 is recomputed using *FEDDIVRATE* (column 3) in place of *TDIVTAX* and *FEDCORPRATE* in place of *ETRCORP.* This new column 5 is then used in computing column 9, and these two tax rates are used in calculating column 5, Table 2.4, that is, a total effective tax rate, as in column 1, Table 2.4, excluding all state and local components

Data sources:

NIPA: National Income and Product Accounts, published in various issues of the *Survey of Current Business.*

ERP: *Economic Report of the President* (Washington, D.C.: Government Printing Office, 1980).

FRBBS: *Balance Sheets for the U.S. Economy,* provided by the Division of Research and Statistics of the Board of Governors of the Federal Reserve System. Dated April 1981.

FF: *Flow of Funds Accounts,* usually sector balances.

DRI: Data series provided courtesy of Data Resources, Inc.

3 Why Do Companies Pay Dividends?

The nearly universal policy of paying substantial dividends is the primary puzzle in the economics of corporate finance. Until 1982 dividends were taxed at rates varying up to 70 percent and averaging nearly 40 percent for individual shareholders. In contrast, retained earnings imply no concurrent tax liability; the rise in the share value that results from retained earnings is taxed only when the stock is sold, and then at least 60 percent of the gain is untaxed.[1] In spite of this significant tax penalty, U.S. corporations continue to distribute a major fraction of their earnings as dividends; during the past fifteen years, dividends have averaged 45 percent of real after-tax profits. In effect, corporations voluntarily impose a tax liability on their shareholders that is currently more than $10 billion a year.[2]

Why do corporations not eliminate (or sharply reduce) their dividends

This chapter was written with Jerry Green. Reprinted from the *American Economic Review* (March 1983) by permission of the American Economic Association. This chapter is part of the NBER Study of Capital Formation and its research program on Business Taxation and Finance. We have benefited from discussion of this work with Alan Auerbach, David Bradford, John Flemming, Mervyn King, Lawrence Summers, and other participants in the NBER's 1979 summer institute.

1. Current law allows 60 percent of the gain to be excluded. This has the effect of taxing realized capital gains at only 40 percent of the regular income tax rate. When shares that are obtained as a bequest are sold, the resulting taxable income is limited to 40 percent of the rise in the value of the shares since the death of the previous owner.

2. There would, of course, be no problem in explaining the existence of dividends if there were no taxes. The analysis of Modigliani and Miller (1958) shows that without taxes dividend policy is essentially irrelevant since shareholders can in principle offset any change in dividend policy by buying or selling shares. Even in the Modigliani-Miller world, the stability of dividend rates would require explanation.

and increase their retained earnings?[3] It is, of course, arguable that if all firms were to adopt such a policy it would raise the aggregate level of investment and therefore depress the rate of return on capital.[4] But any individual firm could now increase its retained earnings without having to take less than the average market return on its capital if it used the additional funds to diversify into new activities or even to acquire new firms.

Several different possible resolutions of the dividend puzzle have been suggested. In reality there is probably some truth to all of these ideas, but we believe that, even collectively, they have failed to provide a satisfactory explanation of the prevailing ratio of dividends to retained earnings. It is useful to distinguish five kinds of explanations.

First, there is the desire on the part of small investors, fiduciaries, and nonprofit organizations for a steady stream of dividends with which to finance consumption. Although the same consumption stream might be financed on a more favorably taxed basis by periodically selling shares, it is argued that small investors might have substantial transaction costs and that some fiduciaries and nonprofit organizations are required to spend only "income" and not "principal." However, transaction costs could be reduced significantly if investors sold shares less frequently. Fiduciaries and nonprofit organizations can often eliminate any required distinction between income and principal.

Miller and Scholes (1978) have offered the ingenious explanation that the current limit on interest deductions implies that there is no marginal tax on dividends. Under current tax law, an individual's deduction for investment interest (that is, interest other than mortgage and business interest) is limited to investment income plus $10,000. An extra dollar of dividend income raises the allowable interest deduction by one dollar. For a taxpayer for whom this constraint is binding, the extra dollar of dividends is just offset by the extra dollar of interest deduction, leaving taxable in-

---

3. There is also in principle the possibility of repurchasing shares instead of paying dividends. The proceeds received by shareholders would be taxed at no more than the capital gains rate and therefore at no more than 40 percent of the rate that would be paid if the same funds were distributed as dividends. There are, however, significant legal impediments to a systematic repurchase policy. Regular periodic repurchases of shares would be construed as equivalent to dividends for tax purposes. Sporadic repurchases would presumably avoid this problem but would subject managers and directors to the risk of shareholder suits on the grounds that they benefited from insider knowledge in deciding when the company should repurchase shares and whether they as individuals should sell at that time. British law forbids the repurchase of shares. This chapter assumes that frequent repurchases would be regarded as income and therefore focuses on the choice between dividends and retained earnings. The possibility of postponed and infrequent share repurchases is expressly considered.

4. The greater retained earnings could also partly or wholly replace debt finance.

come unchanged. Although Miller and Scholes discuss how the use of tax-exempt annuities "should" make this constraint binding for all individual investors, in reality fewer than one-tenth of one percent of taxpayers with dividends actually had large enough interest deductions to make this constraint binding.[5] Moreover, since the limit on interest deductions was only introduced in 1969, the Miller and Scholes thesis is irrelevant for earlier years.

A more plausible explanation is that dividends are required because of the separation of ownership and management. According to one form of this argument, dividends are a signal of the sustainable income of the corporation: management selects a dividend policy to communicate the level and growth of real income because conventional accounting reports are inadequate guides to current income and future prospects.[6] Although this theory remains to be fully elaborated, it does suggest that the steadiness (or safety) of the dividend, as well as its average level, might be used in a dynamic setting. The dividend tax of more than $10 billion does seem to be an inordinately high price to pay for communicating this information; a lower payment ratio might convey nearly the same information without such a tax penalty. Closely related to the signaling idea is the notion that shareholders distrust management and fear that retained earnings will be wasted in poor investments, higher management compensation, and so on. According to this argument, in the absence of taxation shareholders would clearly prefer a "bird in hand," and this preference is strong enough to pressure management to make dividend payments even when this involves a tax penalty. If investors would prefer dividends to retained earnings because of this distrust, it is hard to understand why there is not pressure for a 100 percent dividend payout.[7]

Auerbach (1979a), Bradford (1979), and King (1977) have developed a theory in which positive dividend payments are consistent with shareholder equilibrium because the market value per dollar of retained earnings is less than one dollar. More specifically, if θ is the tax rate on dividends and c is the equivalent accrual tax rate on capital gains,[8] the net

5. Feenberg (1981) uses a large sample of actual tax returns to estimate the number of dividend recipients affected by the interest income deduction limitation. He found that in 1977 only 2.5 percent of dividend income went to constrained taxpayers.

6. For a development of this view, see Bhattacharya (1979), Gordon and Malkiel (1979), and Ross (1977).

7. The argument that dividends reflect the separation of ownership and management appears to be supported by the fact that closely held companies pay few or no dividends. However, such companies can usually achieve a distribution of funds as management salary, which is deductible.

8. The equivalent accrual tax rate on capital gains is the present value of the tax liability that will eventually be paid, per dollar of dividend income.

value of one dollar of dividends is $1 - \theta$ while the net value of one dollar of retained earnings is $(1 - c)p$, where p is the rise in the market value of the firm's shares when an extra dollar of earnings is retained, that is, p is the share price per dollar of equity capital. Auerbach, Bradford, and King point out that shareholders will be indifferent between dividends and retained earnings if the share price per dollar of equity capital is $p = (1 - \theta)/(1 - c) < 1$. At any other value of p, shareholders would prefer either no dividends or no retained earnings, but at $p = (1 - \theta)/(1 - c)$ any value of the dividend payout rate would be equally acceptable. Moreover, in the context of their model, the share price will satisfy this value of p when shares sell at the present value of after-tax dividends. In short, they argue that the existence of dividends is appropriate if the value of retained earnings capitalizes the tax penalty on any eventual distribution.

This line of reasoning is clearly important but raises several problems. First, it has been argued[9] that an equilibrium in which p is less than one is incompatible with new equity finance by the firm. While it is clearly inconsistent for firms to pay dividends and sell shares at the same time (except if dividends are paid for some of the other reasons noted above), the theory is not incompatible with firms having some periods when $p \geq 1$ and new equity is sold and other periods when $p < 1$ and dividends are paid but shares are not sold. In any case, new equity issues by established companies (outside the regulated industries where special considerations are applicable) are relatively rare.

A more important problem with the Auerbach-Bradford-King theory is that it is based on the premise that funds can never be distributed to shareholders in any form other than dividends. This implicitly precludes the possibility of allowing the company to be acquired by another firm or using accumulated retained earnings to repurchase shares. Either of these options permits the earnings to be taxed as capital gains after a delay.[10] The theory that we develop in this chapter explicitly recognizes this possibility.

A further difficulty with the theory is that any payout rate is consistent with equilibrium, and therefore it gives no reason for the observed stability of the payout rate over time for individual companies and for the aggregate. Although such stability could be explained by combining the Auerbach-King-Bradford model with some type of signaling explanation,

9. See, for example, Gordon and Malkiel (1979).

10. Such infrequent share repurchases are very different from a systematic program of substituting regular repurchases for dividends. They do not risk the adverse tax consequence referred to above and, unlike continuous repurchases in lieu of dividends, involve a different growth of equity.

our own analysis based purely on considerations of risk indicates that the payout rate is determinate and that it is likely to be relatively insensitive to fluctuations in annual earnings. (A more explicit dynamic analysis would be necessary to confirm this conclusion.)

The most serious problem with the Auerbach-Bradford-King hypothesis is the implicit assumption that all shareholders have the same tax rates (θ and c). In reality, there is very substantial variation in tax rates and therefore in the value of $p = (1 - \theta)/(1 - c)$ that is compatible with a partial dividend payout. For individuals in the highest tax bracket, $\theta = 0.7$ and the dividend-compatible q is approximately $0.33;$[11] for tax-exempt institutions, the corresponding value is one. The Auerbach-Bradford-King concept of shareholder equilibrium implies that, at any market value of p, almost all shareholders will prefer either no dividends or no retained earnings, depending on whether the market value of p was greater than or less than their own values of the ratio $(1 - \theta)/(1 - c)$. This condition would cause market segmentation and specialization; some firms would pay no dividend while others would have no retained earnings, and each investor would own shares in only one type of firm. Such specialization and market segmentation are clearly counterfactual. Our own current analysis emphasizes the diversity of shareholder tax rates and shows that this is a key to understanding the observed policy of substantial and stable dividends.

An earlier paper (reprinted as Chapter 21 of this volume) studied the long-run growth equilibrium of an economy with corporate and personal taxes. In this context, dividends appear as the difference between after-tax profits and the retained earnings that are consistent with steady-state growth and with the optimal debt-equity ratio. This limits aggregate retained earnings and implies positive aggregate dividends but does not explain why *each firm* will choose to pay positive dividends rather than to grow faster than the economy's natural rate. We suggested that each firm is constrained by the fact that more rapid growth would increase its relative size, thereby making it riskier and reducing the market price of its securities. An explicit model of this relation between size and the "risk-discount" was not presented in the earlier paper but is one of the basic ideas of the general equilibrium analysis that we present here. Unlike the previous paper, the current analysis will not look at properties of the long-run steady state but will examine microeconomic choice in a one-period model.

---

11. This is based on tax rates for 1981 and assumes that postponement and the stepped-up basis at death reduce the accrual equivalent capital gains tax to 10 percent.

The idea of shareholder risk aversion as a limit to a firm's growth and the existence of shareholders in diverse tax situations are the two central components of the analysis developed in this chapter. We consider an economy with two kinds of investors: taxable individuals and untaxed institutions (like pension funds and nonprofit organizations).[12] Firms can distribute profits currently as dividends or they can retain them, grow larger, and ultimately distribute these funds to shareholders as capital gains.[13] In the absence of uncertainty, these assumptions would lead to segmentation and specialization. The taxable individuals would invest only in firms that pay no dividends even though, ceteris paribus, they prefer present dollars to future dollars, while untaxed institutions would invest only in firms that retain no profits. In this equilibrium the share price per dollar of retained earnings would in general be less than one. This type of equilibrium with segmentation and specialization is not observed because of uncertainty. Because investors regard each firm's return as both unique and uncertain, they wish to diversify their investment. We show in this chapter that each firm can in general maximize its share price by attracting both types of investors and that this requires a dividend policy of distributing some fraction of earnings as dividends. Only in the special case of little or no uncertainty or of a limited ability to diversify risks can the equilibrium be of the segmented-market form.

The first section of the chapter presents the basic model of dividend behavior in a two-firm economy with two classes of investors. Some comparative statistics of the resulting equilibrium are developed in the second section. The third section examines the special case in which the two firms have equal expected yields and equal variances. Despite the diversity of taxpayers, both firms choose the same dividend rate. In the fourth section, the symmetry of this equilibrium is contrasted with the segmentation and specialization that can arise with riskless investments, or with risk-neutral individuals. The concluding section suggests directions for further work.

Dividend Behavior in a Two-Company Economy

Our analysis of corporate dividend behavior uses a simple one-period model. At the beginning of the period, each firm has one dollar of net prof-

---

12. The same reasoning would apply if we consider "low-tax-rate" and "high-tax-rate" individuals. See Chapter 14 for the application of such a classification to analyzing the effect of the corporate tax system.

13. This future capital gain distribution could be the result of the firm's shares being acquired by another firm or of a share repurchase by the firm itself.

its that must be divided between dividends and earnings. The firms announce their dividend policies and trading then takes place in the shares. The firms use the amounts that they have retained to make investments in plant and equipment. At the end of the period, the uncertain returns on these investments are realized and the companies are liquidated. All of the end-of-period payments are regarded as capital gains rather than dividends and will be assumed to be untaxed.

There are two kinds of investors in the economy. Households (denoted by a subscript H) are taxed at rate θ on dividend income but pay no tax on capital gains. Institutions (denoted by a subscript I) pay no taxes on either dividends or capital gains. At the beginning of the period, the two types of investors own the following numbers of shares in both companies: $\bar{s}_{H1}$, $\bar{s}_{H2}$, $\bar{s}_{I1}$, and $\bar{s}_{I2}$, where the subscripts 1 and 2 indicate the companies. For notational simplicity, we normalize the number of shares in each company at 1. After the companies announce their dividend policies, the investors can sell their shares (at prices determined in the market that depend on the firms' dividend policies) and can buy other shares. Investors can also place some of the proceeds of their share sales in a riskless asset or can spend those funds on consumption; each dollar invested in this riskless asset has an end-of-period value of R. We assume, however, that investors may not sell shares short. Both types of investors prefer present dollars to future dollars; one present dollar (obtained either as after-tax dividends or from the sale of shares) is worth R dollars. Although R might be expected to differ between households and institutions, we shall assume the same R for both groups.

Each firm has an initial amount of one dollar available for distribution and retention. Company i pays dividend d_i at the beginning of the period and therefore invests amount $1 - d_i$. The end-of-period value of company $i(i = 1,2)$ is r_i per dollar of funds that are retained and invested; the rate of return on the firm's capital is thus $r_i - 1$.[14] The expected value of this uncertain return is r_i^e, and its variance is σ_{ii}. The covariance of the returns of the two firms is σ_{12}. In the analysis that follows, we consider the general case in which the yields and variances are unequal. We then examine in detail the character of the equilibrium in the case in which the mean yields and variances of the two firms are identical. We show that in this situation the degree of uncertainty (as measured by the common variance) and the opportunity for effective diversification (as measured by the correlation between the returns) determine whether both companies pay dividends

---

14. We assume that firms do not borrow and that the stochastic return per dollar of investment does not depend on the amount that is invested.

and are owned by both types of investors or whether there is market segmentation in which one company pays no dividends and is owned by the household investors.

Our strategy of analysis is as follows. We first derive the share demand equations for the two types of investors. These demands depend on the prices of the shares and on their stated dividend policies. We then use the fact that the available number of shares of each type of stock is fixed to calculate the price functions. The price of each type of share depends in general on the dividend policy of that firm and of the other type of firm. We assume that firms select the dividend policy that maximizes the firm's value, that is, that maximizes the price per share.[15] This maximization yields the optimal dividend for each firm. When these dividend values have been obtained, we shall examine the characteristics of the equilibrium and the comparative static response to changes in the tax rate.

Investors' Demands for Shares

We derive each investor's demand functions for shares by maximizing the investor's expected utility subject to the wealth constraint implied by the investor's initial shareholdings and the equilibrium share prices. We assume that the investors' utility functions are quadratic and focus our attention on the role of taxes by assuming that all investors have exactly the same utility function. The nature of the utility function implies that the demand for each type of share is independent of the individual's wealth; we can therefore derive aggregate demand functions for each type of shareholder by treating all of the investors of each type as if they were a single investor.

Consider first the investment problem of the households. If the market equilibrium share prices for the two companies are p_1 and p_2, the value of their initial portfolio is $p_1 \bar{s}_{H1} + p_2 \bar{s}_{H2}$. The initial wealth is exchanged for s_{H1} shares of company 1, s_{H2} shares of company 2, and z dollars of the monetary asset. The new portfolio must satisfy the wealth constraint:

$$p_1 \bar{s}_{H1} + p_2 \bar{s}_{H2} = p_1 s_{H1} + p_2 s_{H2} + z_H. \tag{1}$$

With dividend payouts of d_1 and d_2, the households' total after-tax funds at the beginning of the period are $(1 - \theta)d_1 s_{H1} + (1 - \theta)d_2 s_{H2} + z_H$.

---

15. Maximizing the share price is Pareto-efficient but not uniquely optimal. There are other plausible criteria by which management might in general decide its dividend policy even in a one-period model such as the current one, for example, majority voting of the shareholders.

The additional funds received at the end of the period are the uncertain amount $(1 - d_1)s_{H1}r_1 + (1 - d_2)s_{H2}r_2$. Combining these two with each dollar of beginning-of-period funds equivalent to R dollars of the end-of-period funds yields the argument of the household's utility function:

$$W_H = R(1 - \theta)[s_{H1}d_1 + s_{H2}d_2] + Rz_H + s_{H1}(1 - d_1)r_1 + s_{H2}(1 - d_2)r_2. \tag{2}$$

The quadratic character of the utility function implies that expected utility can be written as a linear combination of the mean and variance of W_H:

$$E[U(W_H)] = E(W_H) - 0.5\gamma \cdot \text{var}(W_H), \tag{3}$$

where $\gamma > 0$ is a measure of risk aversion (and the 0.5 is introduced to simplify subsequent calculations). Equation (2) implies that

$$E(W_H) = R(1 - \theta)(s_{H1}d_1 + s_{H2}d_2) + Rz_H + s_{H1}(1 - d_1)r_1^e + s_{H2}(1 - d_2)r_2^e, \tag{4}$$

and

$$\text{var}(W_H) = s_{H1}^2(1 - d_1)^2\sigma_{11} + s_{H2}^2(1 - d_2)^2\sigma_{22} + 2s_{H1}s_{H2}(1 - d_1)(1 - d_2)\sigma_{12}. \tag{5}$$

The households' optimum portfolio is found by maximizing Eq. (3) subject to the constraint of Eq. (1).[16] The first-order conditions for maximizing expected utility are

$$0 = R(1 - \theta)d_1 + (1 - d_1)r_1^e - Rp_1 - \gamma[s_{H1}(1 - d_1)^2\sigma_{11} + s_{H2}(1 - d_1)(1 - d_2)\sigma_{12}] \tag{6}$$

and

$$0 = R(1 - \theta)d_2 + (1 - d_2)r_2^e - Rp_2 - \gamma[s_{H2}(1 - d_2)^2\sigma_{22} + s_{H1}(1 - d_1)(1 - d_2)\sigma_{12}]. \tag{7}$$

16. We indicate below the important circumstances under which the demands implied by this maximization would violate the "no short sale" constraints. This "limited risk avoidance" case will be considered explicitly in the fourth section.

Collecting terms, we may write the households' pair of demand equations as:

$$\gamma \begin{bmatrix} (1 - d_1)^2 \sigma_{11} & (1 - d_1)(1 - d_2)\sigma_{12} \\ (1 - d_1)(1 - d_2)\sigma_{12} & (1 - d_2)^2 \sigma_{22} \end{bmatrix} \begin{bmatrix} s_{H1} \\ s_{H2} \end{bmatrix}$$
$$= \begin{bmatrix} R(1 - \theta)d_1 + (1 - d_1)r_1^e - Rp_1 \\ R(1 - \theta)d_2 + (1 - d_2)r_2^e - Rp_2 \end{bmatrix}, \tag{8}$$

or, in matrix notation,

$$\gamma \mathbf{A} s_H = a_H - Rp, \tag{9}$$

where the elements of $\mathbf{A}$ and a_H are clear from (8). If the matrix $\mathbf{A}$ is not singular, (8) can be solved for the share demands s_H. It is important to note that $\mathbf{A}$ is singular either when stock is riskless or when the correlation between the two yields is one; in either case, holding a mixed portfolio does not achieve any reduction in risk. The optimal portfolio in this case is an investment in only one type of stock. More generally, when the variances are small or the correlation high, the solution of Eq. (9) may imply demands for shares that violate the constraint on short-selling. The feasible optimum again requires a specialized portfolio and induces extreme dividend behavior in which one company pays no dividend and the other keeps no retained earnings. We shall examine below the characteristics of this "low risk avoidance" equilibrium. Now, however, we shall focus on the case in which $\mathbf{A}$ is nonsingular and the solution of Eq. (9) does not violate the other constraints on portfolio behavior.[17]

Solving Eq. (9) yields the households' share demand equation under the assumption that $s_H \geq 0$ (that is, that short-selling would not be optimal):

$$s_H = \gamma^{-1} \mathbf{A}^{-1}[a_H - Rp]. \tag{10}$$

Analogous share demand equations hold for the institutional investors:

$$s_I = \gamma^{-1} \mathbf{A}^{-1}[a_I - Rp]. \tag{11}$$

The share demands differ only because a_H contains the tax variable ($\theta > 0$), while in a_I the tax variable is implicitly zero.[18]

---

17. We later show that such equilibria can exist for plausible parameter values.

18. If any of the nonnegativity constraints on s_H or s_I are binding, the optimum is no longer given by Eqs. (10) and (11).

Price Functions and Optimal Dividends

By equating the share demands of Eqs. (10) and (11) to the fixed share supplies, we can solve for the market clearing share prices that would correspond to any combination of dividend policies. Since the number of shares of each company was normalized to one, we have

$$s_H + s_I = \begin{bmatrix} 1 \\ 1 \end{bmatrix} \tag{12}$$

or

$$\begin{bmatrix} 1 \\ 1 \end{bmatrix} = \gamma^{-1}\mathbf{A}^{-1}[a_H + a_I - 2Rp]. \tag{13}$$

Solving Eq. (13) for this price vector yields

$$p = \frac{1}{2R} \begin{bmatrix} R(2 - \theta)d_1 + 2(1 - d_1)r_1^e \\ R(2 - \theta)d_2 + 2(1 - d_2)r_2^e \end{bmatrix} \\ - \frac{\gamma}{2R} \begin{bmatrix} (1 - d_1)^2\sigma_{11} + (1 - d_1)(1 - d_2)\sigma_{12} \\ (1 - d_2)^2\sigma_{22} + (1 - d_1)(1 - d_2)\sigma_{12} \end{bmatrix}. \tag{14}$$

The price of each type of share is positively related to its own expected yield and negatively related to the variance of that yield and its covariance with the yield of the other type of stock.

We assume that each firm selects its dividend payout rate to maximize its share price and takes the dividend of the other firm as given.[19] The first order condition for firm 1 is

$$\frac{\partial p_1}{\partial d_1} = 0$$

$$= \frac{1}{2R} \{R(2 - \theta) - 2r_1^e + \gamma[2(1 - d_1)\sigma_{11} \\ + (1 - d_2)\sigma_{12}]\} \tag{15}$$

and implies that the firm's optimal dividend rate (d_1^*) satisfies

$$1 - d_1^* = \frac{2(r_1^e - R) + \theta R}{2\gamma\sigma_{11}} - \frac{\sigma_{12}(1 - d_2)}{2\sigma_{11}}. \tag{16}$$

19. It is easy to show that the process is stable.

Equation (16) describes the first firm's optimal reaction to the dividend policy of the second firm. Symmetrically we obtain the dividend policy reaction function of the second firm:

$$1 - d_2^* = \frac{2(r_2^e - R) + \theta R}{2\gamma\sigma_{22}} - \frac{\sigma_{12}(1 - d_1)}{2\sigma_{22}}. \tag{17}$$

If the returns to the investments by the two firms are not independent ($\sigma_{12} \neq 0$), the optimal dividend policy of each firm depends on the dividend policy of the other firm. The two dividend policy functions can be solved simultaneously to obtain the equilibrium dividend policy of each firm:

$$\begin{bmatrix} 1 - d_1^* \\ 1 - d_2^* \end{bmatrix} =$$

$$\frac{1}{1 - \frac{1}{4}\left(\frac{\sigma_{12}^2}{\sigma_{11}\sigma_{22}}\right)} \begin{bmatrix} \dfrac{2(r_1^e - R) + \theta R}{2\gamma\sigma_{11}} - \dfrac{1}{2}\left(\dfrac{\sigma_{12}}{\sigma_{11}}\right)\dfrac{2(r_2^e - R) + \theta R}{2\gamma\sigma_{22}} \\ \dfrac{2(r_2^e - R) + \theta R}{2\gamma\sigma_{22}} - \dfrac{1}{2}\left(\dfrac{\sigma_{12}}{\sigma_{22}}\right)\dfrac{2(r_1^e - R) + \theta R}{2\gamma\sigma_{11}} \end{bmatrix} \tag{18}$$

Some Comparative Statics

It is immediately clear from Eq. (18) that each firm's optimal retained earnings depend positively on its own expected return and negatively on its own variance.[20] A higher expected yield makes it optimal to retain and invest more in the company, while an increase in the uncertainty of that return makes the immediate payment of dividends more appealing.

If the returns of the two firms are positively correlated ($\sigma_{12} > 0$), each firm's optimal retained earnings vary inversely with the attractiveness of investment in the other firm (that is, with the other firm's expected yield and the inverse of its variance). Intuitively, when retained earnings in one firm are more attractive and therefore increase, the riskiness of retaining earnings in the other firm increases if the yields of the two firms are positively correlated.

The effect of an increase in the rate of tax on dividends is particularly interesting. For firm 1,

---

20. Since $\sigma_{12}^2/\sigma_{11}\sigma_{22}$ is the square of the correlation coefficient between the two yields and is therefore necessarily less than unity, the common multiplier of both terms is positive.

$$\frac{\partial d_1^*}{\partial \theta} = -\frac{1}{1 - \frac{1}{4}\left(\frac{\sigma_{12}^2}{\sigma_{11}\sigma_{22}}\right)} \cdot \frac{R}{2\gamma\sigma_{11}} \cdot \left[1 - \frac{1}{2}\left(\frac{\sigma_{12}}{\sigma_{22}}\right)\right]. \tag{19}$$

The first two terms on the right-hand side are unambiguously positive. If the yields of the two firms are uncorrelated ($\sigma_{12} = 0$), an increase in the tax rate on dividends necessarily reduces the firm's payout. However, when the yields are correlated the effect of the tax rate is ambiguous; that is, the sign of the final term in Eq. (19) can be either positive or negative. Since σ_{12}/σ_{22} is the regression coefficient of the return for the first firm's investment on the return for the second firm's investment,[21] it could exceed 2 and make the final expression negative.

It is easy to understand why a strong covariance between the yields could produce the apparently counterintuitive result that an increase in the tax rate on dividends can actually raise a firm's optimal payout. Note first that an equation similar to (19) holds for firm 2:

$$\frac{\partial d_2^*}{\partial \theta} = -\frac{1}{1 - \frac{1}{4}\left(\frac{\sigma_{12}^2}{\sigma_{11}\sigma_{22}}\right)} \cdot \frac{R}{2\gamma\sigma_{22}} \cdot \left[1 - \frac{1}{2}\left(\frac{\sigma_{12}}{\sigma_{11}}\right)\right]. \tag{20}$$

Adding these two expressions gives the effect of an increase in θ on the total dividends of the two firms combined:

$$\frac{\partial(d_1^* + d_2^*)}{\partial \theta} = -\frac{1}{1 - \frac{1}{4}\left(\frac{\sigma_{12}^2}{\sigma_{11}\sigma_{22}}\right)}$$
$$\cdot \frac{R}{2\gamma\sigma_{11}\sigma_{22}}[\sigma_{22} + \sigma_{11} - \sigma_{12}]. \tag{21}$$

It is easy to show that this is unambiguously negative. This is clearly so if $\sigma_{12} < 0$. To see that this is also true when $\sigma_{12} > 0$, note that the variance of the difference $r_1 - r_2$ is $\sigma_{22} + \sigma_{11} - 2\sigma_{12}$; since this is a variance it is necessarily positive, implying $\sigma_{22} + \sigma_{11} > 2\sigma_{12}$ and therefore that $\sigma_{22} + \sigma_{11} - \sigma_{12} > \sigma_{12} > 0$. Thus an increase in the tax rate on dividends unambiguously reduces total dividends. The dividends of one of the firms may increase, but not the dividends of both of them. The dividends of one firm will increase when the decrease in the dividends of the other is so large

---

21. This regression coefficient is closely related to the beta of capital market theory but refers here to the yields expressed as a return on physical capital rather than share value.

that, given the positive covariance between the returns, the greater risk associated with retained earnings in the first firm outweighs the direct effect of the tax.

It is interesting to consider the magnitude of this sensitivity of the payout policy with respect to the tax parameter. Equation (18) can be used to calculate the elasticity of the aggregate retained earnings with respect to θ. Although it is easy to obtain a general expression, the interpretation of the elasticity is clearer if we assume that the "excess yield" $(r^e - R)$ is the same for both assets.[22] With this assumption, Eq. (18) implies the elasticity

$$\frac{\theta}{2 - d_1^* - d_2^*} \frac{\partial (2 - d_1^* - d_2^*)}{\partial \theta} = \frac{\theta R}{2(r^e - R) + \theta R}. \tag{22}$$

In the special case in which the expected yield is equal to the yield on the riskless asset (that is, $r^e = R$), there are retained earnings only because of the tax effect, and the elasticity of the retained earnings with respect to the dividend tax rate is unity. When there is a positive expected excess return on retained earnings, the tax effect is less important and the elasticity is less than one.[23]

Characteristics of the Symmetric Equilibrium

The special case in which the two firms have equal expected yields and equal variances is particularly interesting to analyze. Together with the assumptions that we have made about the similarity of the two types of investors, this assumption about the firm implies that the only essential source of difference in the model is in the different tax treatments of households and institutions. We commented in the introduction, and will show formally in the next section, that when the advantage of diversification is small (that is, low risk or high correlation), this difference in taxation leads to specialization of ownership and corner solutions for the firms' dividend policies; that is, the firm that remains in business pays no

22. When the excess returns differ for the two firms, $r^e - R$ is replaced by a weighted average including the variances and covariances of the yields.

23. In an early empirical study of the effect of taxes on the dividend policy of British firms (reprinted as Chapters 4 and 5 of this book), I estimated that the elasticity of the *dividend* rate with respect to the inverse of θ was 0.9. Since dividends were about two-thirds of retained earnings in that sample period, the estimated elasticity of 0.9 corresponds to an elasticity of retained earnings with respect to θ of approximately 0.6, and is therefore quite compatible with Eq. (22).

dividend. We now examine the characteristics of the equilibrium in the case in which there is sufficient risk and opportunity for diversification and show that in this case both firms do pay dividends. *The opportunity for advantageous diversification by investors induces positive dividends by firms.*

With $r_1^e = r_2^e$ and $\sigma_{11} = \sigma_{22}$, Eq. (18) shows immediately that $d_1^* = d_2^*$, that is, both firms have the same optimal dividend. In contrast to the "no diversification" case in which the dividend policies are at opposite extremes, advantageous diversification produces identical dividend policies. This common dividend policy satisfies

$$1 - d^* = \frac{2(r^e - R) + \theta R}{\gamma\sigma(2 + \rho)}, \tag{23}$$

where r^e is the common expected yield, σ is the common variance, and ρ is the correlation between the yields.[24]

Note first that $\theta = 0$ and $r^e = R$ together imply $d^* = 1$; when there is no tax on dividends and no "excess return" on funds retained in the firm, all profits will be paid out. The economic reason for this is clear: with no tax or yield incentive for retention, full payout avoids the risk of retained earnings without any loss in after-tax yield.

A small tax on dividends clearly makes $1 - d^* > 0$ and therefore $d^* < 1$, that is, both firms pay out some but not all of their profits as dividends. A positive but partial dividend payout is clearly optimal despite a tax that discriminates against dividends. Of course, a large enough value of θ can make $1 - d^* \geq 1$ and therefore imply $d^* = 0$; when the tax discrimination against dividends is strong enough, no dividends will be paid. Note that the excess return on retained earnings affects the optimal dividends in the same way as the dividend tax. Starting at $\theta = 0$ and $r^e = R$, a small increase in r^e will cause positive but partial dividend payout, while a large enough excess return on retained earnings will cause all dividends to stop.[25]

Consider next the price per share that prevails in this case when both firms adopt the optimal dividend policy. This share price is the value that

24. With $\sigma_{11} = \sigma_{22}$, $\rho = \sigma_{12}/\sigma_{22} = \sigma_{12}/\sigma_{11}$. Equation (23) follows directly from (18) when it is noted that the common multiplier in (18) is the inverse of $1 - (\rho/2)^2$ and that $1 - \frac{1}{2}(\sigma_{12}/\sigma_{11}) = 1 - (\rho/2)$; the ratio of these two is the inverse of $1 + (\rho/2)$.

25. It is tempting to ask what happens as ρ tends to unity. When $\rho = 1$, there is no opportunity for diversification. The economics implies that in this case there will be specialization of ownership and therefore of dividend policy. This *cannot* be seen by setting $\rho = 1$ in Eq. (23) because Eq. (23) does not hold when $\rho = 1$. When $\rho = 1$, the matrix $\mathbf{A}$ of Eq. (9) is singular and the share demand equations (10) and (11) from which (23) is derived do not hold.

investors place on the initial dollar of available profits inside the firm.[26] Since dollars retained in the firms have equal expected yields and equal variances, their share prices must also be equal. Equation (14) confirms this and shows that the common price is

$$p = R^{-1}[(1 - \theta/2)dR + (1 - d)r^e - \tfrac{1}{2}\gamma(1 - d)^2\sigma(1 + \rho)]. \qquad (24)$$

The three terms on the right-hand side of (24) show that the price depends on the net-of-tax value of the current dividend $[(1 - \theta/2)d]$, the expected present value of the retained earnings $[(1 - d)r^e R^{-1}]$, and the offset for the risk associated with the retained earnings $[\gamma(1 - d)^2\sigma(1 + \rho)]R^{-1}$. Substituting the optimal value of the dividend payout rate from Eq. (23) and rearranging terms yields

$$p = 1 - \frac{\theta}{2} + \frac{\gamma\sigma}{2R}(1 - d^*)^2 \qquad (25)$$

or

$$p = 1 - \frac{\theta}{2} + \frac{[r^e - R + R\theta/2]^2}{2R\gamma\sigma(1 + \rho/2)^2}. \qquad (26)$$

Since half of the shareholders pay tax at rate θ while half pay no tax, the average tax rate is $\theta/2$, and $1 - \theta/2$ is the net-of-tax income per dollar of dividends. Equation (25) shows that when it is optimal to pay out all profits as dividends ($d^* = 1$), the share price equals the net-of-tax value of the dividend.[27] More generally, when the firms retain some of their earnings,

---

26. There is an extensive literature on this value, which is sometimes referred to as "Tobin's q." It has been common to assume that the equilibrium value of q is one, an assumption that we accepted in the earlier paper (Chapter 21). Auerbach (1979a), Bradford (1979), and King (1977) analyze a model without uncertainty and with only taxable shareholders; they conclude that if firms are paying positive but partial dividends, the share price must equal $1 - \theta$, that is, a dollar of profits inside the firm must be valued at the amount that can be paid *net of tax* to the shareholder. (Their analysis also allows for a tax on capital gains, which also influences the share price; in the absence of this tax their share price formula reduces to $1 - \theta$.) Studies using the capital asset pricing model to measure the value of a *marginal* dollar inside the firm produce estimates that vary substantially over time, with an average that is in the range of unity or somewhat less; see Gordon and Bradford (1979) and the studies that they cite. Green (1980) shows that changes in share prices on their ex dividend days cannot be used to estimate the value of a marginal dollar of funds inside the firm.

27. This special case thus corresponds to the Auerbach-Bradford-King share price equation extended to the case of heterogeneous taxpayers. It holds, however, only when all profits are paid as dividends by both firms.

the price per share exceeds the net-of-tax amount that could be distributed. This is shown clearly in Eq. (25). The equivalent expression in Eq. (26) indicates why this is so. Since it is optimal for a firm to retain some of its earnings when the returns inside the firm exceed their opportunity cost or when there is a tax penalty on dividends, either of these reasons to limit dividends causes an increase in the share price vis-à-vis the price that would prevail if $d^* = 1$. This is seen explicitly in Eq. (26). To the extent that there is an excess return on retained earnings ($r^e > R$) or that the average tax rate on dividends is positive ($\theta/2 > 0$), the price exceeds the net amount that could be distributed. An increase in risk aversion (γ) or in the riskiness of retained earnings ($\sigma[1 + \rho/2]$) decreases the magnitude of this premium.

It is certainly interesting to note that the price per dollar of earnings inside the firm may be less than, equal to, or greater than unity. When $d^* = 1$, the price is clearly less than one. A high value of excess return can of course produce a share value greater than one. But even if $r^e = R$, the price lies between $1 - \theta/2$ and 1.[28]

The discussion in this section has implicitly assumed that both types of investors hold both assets in an optimal portfolio. It can be demonstrated that this is in fact true unless the product of the risk aversion parameter (γ), the common variance ($\sigma_{11} = \sigma_{22}$), and the tax rate ($\theta$) are relatively high. For a high enough value of $\theta\gamma\sigma_{11}$, the taxable individuals will wish to hold only the riskless asset with yield R. In this case the shares are held only by the tax-free institutions. But if risk aversion and risk are not too high, individuals as well as institutions will want to hold positive amounts of the shares of both firms.

A Numerical Example

To conclude this analysis of the case in which the opportunity for advantageous diversification causes nonspecialization and positive but partial dividend payout, it is useful to present a numerical example in which these properties hold. Consider the case in which the expected return on investment in both firms is $r^e = 1.3$ and the correlation between the returns is $\rho = 0.5$. Let the tax rate be $\theta = 0.5$ and the riskless yield on the alternative asset be $R = 1.1$. The common variance of the returns does not matter as such, only the product of the variance and the risk aversion

---

28. Clearly when $r^e = R$ and $d^* = 0$, the value of the firm is the discounted expected value of the subsequent payout ($r^e/R = 1$) minus any adjustment for risk. When $r^e = R$ but $d^* > 0$, p lies between this upper bound and $1 - \theta/2$.

coefficient $(\gamma\sigma)$. The dividend payout rate (d) and the combined risk parameter $(\gamma\sigma)$ must satisfy the dividend payout condition (Eq. [23]) and the condition that the demand for shares by households and institutions (given by Eqs. [10] and [11]) together equal unity for each firm and separately do not violate the condition that investors may not sell short. The symmetry of the current problem implies that each type of investor will hold equal amounts of both types of shares. These conditions are satisfied if the dividend payout rate is $d = 0.8$ and the risk parameter is $\gamma\sigma = 1.87$. Equation (25) implies that the corresponding price per share is $p = 0.78$.

The Segmented Market Equilibrium

We have been analyzing the case in which firms are identical but in which there is enough opportunity for advantageous diversification to cause investors to hold mixed portfolios. Firms pay out positive dividends in a value-maximizing equilibrium. Qualitatively, these results are not surprising. It is, however, somewhat odd that the equilibrium of our model in the symmetric case is itself symmetric: both firms choose the same dividend payout rate and each investor holds an equal share in the two firms. The conflict between diversification and tax avoidance is completely resolved in favor of the former. One might have thought that the firms would "locate" at different points in the dividend spectrum attracting a different clientele, one more heavily taxed on average than the other, and that investors would accept this incomplete diversification in equilibrium in order to reap the tax advantages.

At present we do not know whether this striking symmetry property is the result of the mean-variance utility, the "two-class" model of investors, or whether it is a phenomenon of more fundamental generality.

In this section we will show that this symmetric equilibrium, which is unique whenever investors are holding shares of both firms, coexists with asymmetric "locational" equilibria when the nonnegativity conditions for portfolios are binding. Such a situation arises when there is little variance in yields or a high correlation between the two firms so that diversification is of only limited benefit.

The phenomenon of asymmetric, segmented market equilibrium is seen most clearly in the extreme case of certainty: $\sigma_{11} = \sigma_{22} = 0$. This lack of risk implies that each investor values shares at the present value of their payouts, net of taxes. For either firm, one dollar paid as dividends is worth $(1 - \theta)R$ to households and R to institutions, while one dollar of retained earnings is worth r to both types of investors.

Consider the case in which $R > r^e > R(1 - \theta)$, that is, in which funds inside the firm have a lower yield than outside the firm ($R > r^e$) but are worth more than funds outside the firm if a dividend tax has to be paid ($r^e > (1 - \theta)R$.[29] In this case, the untaxed institutional investor prefers immediate payout ($d = 1$) because the value of the dividend (R) exceeds the expected value of the funds left in the company (r^e). In contrast, the taxed household investor prefers no dividend payout ($d = 0$) because the value of the net-of-tax dividend ($[1 - \theta]R$) is less than the expected value of the funds left in the company (r^e). The market will accommodate this conflict of preferences by specialization of ownership and dividend policies.

Let us examine the equilibrium prices that would lead to $d_1 = 0$, $d_2 = 1$, with portfolios $s_{H1} = 1$, $s_{H2} = 0$, $s_{I1} = 0$, $s_{I2} = 1$. First, it is clear that unless the initial ownership of shares gives the two classes equal portfolio wealth, the equilibrium prices of the two firms may not be equal. This is not incompatible with the value-maximizing assumption because the firm cannot achieve the other's value by mimicking its dividend policy. Both values will change in this process.

We will show that the equilibrium prices are given by

$$p_1 = R^{-1}r^e \quad \text{and} \quad p_2 \epsilon [(1 - \theta), 1], \tag{27}$$

where the precise value of p_2 in this interval is determined in such a way that the portfolios described above are compatible with the budget equation (1). For households to hold shares of firm 1 in positive quantity we need $p_1 \leqq R^{-1}r^e$, and if they do not hold firm 2, then $p_2 \geqq 1 - \theta$. Similarly, the implications that can be derived from institutions' portfolios are $p_2 \leqq 1$, $p_1 \geqq R^{-1}r^e$. Combining these, we see that (27) is required.

To verify that these prices are indeed equilibria, it is necessary to see what changes would be induced by different dividend policies. This problem is a little curious in that even if dividends were to vary, the same prices and the same portfolios could still persist. Thus the equilibrium sustained by extreme dividend policies is compatible with value maximization only in the sense that firms are indifferent to these choices.

It is of interest to note that the symmetric equilibrium $d_1 = d_2 = 0$ and $p_1 = p_2 = R^{-1}r^e$ is also an equilibrium here.[30] The paradox of symmetric versus segmented equilibria is resolved by noting that the latter are produced when the nonnegativity constraints for portfolios are binding.

---

29. In the alternative case of $r^e > R$, both investors will prefer to have no dividends and both firms will therefore choose $d = 0$. The firms behave identically and there is no market segmentation.

30. Any share ownership will sustain this, and individuals will be indifferent.

Moreover, one can observe that since no taxes are actually collected in either of these cases, the consumption patterns, and hence welfare considerations, are identical.

The results of the riskless case can be extended to the case of small variance or high correlation without changing the essential conclusion. In such cases, the share demands implied by Eqs. (10) and (11) would violate the no-short-selling constraint. The constrained optimum would involve a corner solution in which ownership is specialized. The dividend policy of each company would then be adjusted to the tax situation of its homogeneous group of shareholders. The lack of such homogeneity and the presence of dividends for the majority of major publicly owned companies suggest that the opportunities for advantageous diversification are sufficient to prevent shareholder specialization.[31]

Conclusion

This chapter has provided a simple model of market equilibrium to explain why firms that maximize the value of their shares pay dividends even though the funds could instead be retained and subsequently distributed to shareholders in a way that would allow them to be taxed more favorably as capital gains. Our explanation does not rely on any assymmetry of information or divergence of interests between management and shareholders. The heterogeneity of tax rates and the existence of uncertainty and of risk aversion are explicitly recognized. Indeed, it is the combination of the conflicting preferences of shareholders in different tax brackets and their desire for portfolio diversification in the face of uncertainty that together cause all firms to pay dividends in our model.

The model that we have used should be extended in several directions in order to provide a more realistic framework for analysis. The most important extension would be to an economy with many firms. It can be shown that such an extension preserves the main results of the two-firm model, including all of the characteristics of the symmetric equilibria, if the variance of each firm's return grows with the number of firms in the economy.[32] In contrast, if the variance of each firm remains constant, an increased number of firms will cause a segmented equilibrium in which taxable shareholders invest in one diversified portfolio of firms and non-

31. Other possibilities include a nonhomogeneity of beliefs that are not perfectly correlated with tax status, locked-in investors due to the taxation of capital gains on realization, or intertemporal considerations that are of practical importance but are difficult to model.

32. This case is developed in sections 5 and 6 of the earlier NBER version of the current chapter, NBER Working Paper no. 413, "Why Do Companies Pay Dividends?"

taxable shareholders invest in a different portfolio. This occurs because each investor's portfolio becomes progressively less risky as the number of firms increases, inducing the investor to concentrate on the tax advantages of a specialized portfolio even though that requires some loss of diversification.

We believe that an alternative and more natural generalization that preserves the nonsegmented market equilibrium is to recognize that within each tax class, investors have heterogeneous expectations about individual firms. This implies that each firm is subjectively unique and that both high-tax and low-tax investors will want to invest in all firms.

Another worthwhile extension of the present model would be to recognize that both corporations and portfolio investors can also borrow and that corporations as well as investors can earn the risk-free return. Such a model would have to introduce a layer of corporate taxation if misleading results are to be avoided. Expanding the firm's financial behavior in this way would weaken the link between dividends and real corporate investment that is in the present model. We believe, however, that such a link between dividend policy and real corporate investment would persist, contrary to the Modigliani-Miller theorem or the complete separation of investment and financial decisions.

An explicit multiperiod analysis with growing capital stocks should also be developed. The relationship between each firm's rate of investment and its equilibrium rate of return can be analyzed within this extended framework.

This chapter indicates that the existing tax treatment of dividends distorts corporate financial decisions and may cause a misallocation of total investment. It will be important to see whether these adverse effects remain in the more general analytic framework.

4 Corporate Taxation and Dividend Behavior

There is now a substantial body of theory and evidence to suggest that corporate investment is responsive to changes in retained earnings. If this inference is correct, tax policies that are able to influence the level and timing of corporate saving may have important effects on economic growth and stability. Until 1958, the structure of British profits taxation provided strong incentives for corporate saving by taxing dividends at a substantially higher rate than retained earnings. The purpose of this chapter is to estimate the magnitude and time profile of the impact of changes in the tax incentive.

More specifically, until 1958 all corporate profits were subject to two taxes: an income tax (at a rate which varied after 1950 between 42.5 and 47.5 percent) and a profits tax, assessed at one rate on retained earnings (varying between 2.5 and 10 percent) and a higher rate on dividends (varying between 22.5 and 50 percent). A useful measure of the retention incentive provided by the differential between the profits tax rates is the implied opportunity cost of retained earnings in terms of foregone net dividends. For example, in the year before the abolition of the differential, a company could choose between retaining £1 or paying £0.68 of net dividends.[1] In the next year, a pound of retained earnings had an opportunity cost of one pound of dividends, nearly 50 percent higher.

In spite of this apparently very strong incentive, there has been substantial disagreement about the effectiveness of the tax differential. The

Reprinted from *Review of Economic Studies* 37 (January 1970), pp. 57–72, by permission of the Society of Economic Analysis Ltd. I am grateful for research assistance by Janet Hornby and for comments on earlier versions presented at seminars at Oxford, Cambridge, and Harvard Universities and the London School of Economics.

1. This opportunity cost is calculated on the assumption that the shareholder pays income tax at the "standard rate." For surtax payers, the opportunity cost is less, while for those who pay less than standard rate, the opportunity cost is more.

debate was launched by the Royal Commission on the Taxation of Profits and Income (1955). The majority of the Commission concluded that the differential tax had not been very effective (par. 537), while the dissenting opinion sought to prove the opposite (pars. 101–102). Several years after the tax differential had ended, Rubner (1964) examined three-year moving averages of dividend-profit ratios for the period 1949 to 1961 in an attempt to show that abolishing the differential had had no effect. But his use of moving averages provided only one observation (for 1959–1961) that was entirely in the postabolition period. When we recognize the possibility of a lag in the dividend response, it is not surprising that Rubner's evidence is inconclusive.[2] More recently, Paish (1965) has argued that the incentive had little effect, while Williams (1966) has reached the opposite conclusion.

One reason for so much disagreement is that none of the previous attempts to assess the tax impact used estimated models of dividend or corporate savings behavior. It was therefore difficult to distinguish tax-induced changes in the dividend-profit ratio from the natural cyclical changes that result from the lag between dividends and income. The current chapter investigates the tax effect in the framework of a dynamic model of dividend behavior. The first section discusses the specification of the model. Estimation problems are considered in the second section. The results with aggregate data for all industries are analyzed in the third and fourth sections. Separate results for several individual industries are presented in the fifth section. The concluding section considers some of the broader policy implications of this work.

A Model of Dividend Behavior

The dividend equations estimated in this chapter are generalizations of the model originally suggested by Lintner (1956). The basic components of such a model are (1) an equation defining the firm's "optimum" amount of dividends in the current period (D_t^*) and (2) a dynamic adjustment equation describing how dividends change when the current optimum dividend level is not equal to the actual dividends in the preceding period. The specification of these two equations will now be discussed.

Denoting a particular level of dividends as the "optimum" is not meant to imply any particular objective function for corporate management. Although the optimum dividend equation is consistent with the assump-

2. For a fuller discussion of Rubner's work and some preliminary estimates of a simple dynamic dividend model, see Feldstein (1967b).

tion that management decisions reflect the interests of the typical share-holder, it is not so precisely defined that it precludes more general behavioral assumptions. More specifically, we shall assume that D_t^* reflects the firm's "permanent" or "trend" level of income (Y_{pt}), the tax-determined opportunity cost of one pound of retained earnings in terms of the foregone net dividends (θ_t),[3] and a stochastic disturbance U_t.

The form of the optimum dividend equation,

$$D_t^* = A Y_{pt}^\alpha \theta_t^\beta U_t,\tag{1}$$

implies a constant elasticity (α) of D_t^* with respect to income and a different constant elasticity (β) with respect to the opportunity cost of retained earnings. A change in θ thus changes the optimum ratio of dividends to income at any level of income but does not change the elasticity of dividends with respect to income. Moreover, if $\alpha = 1$, the ratio of optimum dividends to income (D_t^*/Y_{pt}) is independent of the level of income.[4]

Two problems arise in measuring a firm's "permanent income." First, how should income be defined? Second, how should *permanent* income be approximated? Three alternative income definitions are investigated in this chapter: (1) net profits after tax and depreciation (that is, net earnings available for common stockholders); (2) gross profits before tax and depreciation; and (3) maximum possible net profits.[5] To approximate permanent income, the chapter supplements the current income level with information on the current rate of growth.

The opportunity cost of retained earnings in terms of dividends differed among shareholders, being lower for shareholders with high marginal rates of income tax than for those in low income tax brackets. But although the British income tax is highly progressive in its overall structure, there is a very wide range over which the marginal tax rate is constant at what is known as the "standard rate." Although some dividend recipients are surtax payers, others pay no income tax at all (for example,

3. The variable θ is defined by $\theta = (1 - t_y)(1 + t_d - t_y - t_u)^{-1}$ where: t_u = tax rate on undistributed profits; t_d = tax rate on distributed profits; t_y = "standard rate" of income tax. The use of the standard rate is explained below. The values of the three tax rates are those applicable to profits and dividends earned and paid in the observation period and not necessarily the rates actually prevailing during the quarter. Note that θ also measures the ratio of maximum net dividends to maximum net retentions.

4. This interpretation also implies that gross company income is not a function of the tax rates. If tax shifting is important, the coefficient θ measures only the partial effect due to tax-induced changes in the relative cost of retained earnings.

5. Maximum net profits are equal to maximum possible retained earnings, since the firm minimizes its tax by distributing nothing.

nonprofit institutions); as a compromise, the standard rate of income tax is used in this study. A further justification for this simplification is that the firms distributed dividends net of income tax at the standard rate and were therefore likely to think of this as the amount foregone by shareholders if retained earnings were increased.

Equation (1) implies that only the current tax rates influence D_t^*. However, an anticipated increase in θ during the next year would be expected to raise D_t^*. Some of the estimated models include the variable θ_{t+1}^e/θ_t in the optimum dividend equation, where θ_{t+1}^e is the value of θ that could be expected to prevail in year $t + 1$ based on information available in year t. The variable θ_t/θ_{t-1} was also included in some models to investigate whether the optimum dividend level responded immediately to a change in the tax variable.

Although including dynamic variables in an equation that defines an optimum is unusual, it is not inconsistent with the definition of an optimum level. In defining D_t^* no reference is made to a long-run value toward which dividends would eventually converge. Rather, D_t^* is defined as the dividend level toward which firms would adjust in period t.

The dynamic adjustment equation specifies how firms respond (in the aggregate) to a difference between D_t^* and D_{t-1} by changing the dividend level toward D_t^*. For several reasons, the entire difference is not eliminated immediately. First, individual firms are uncertain about the optimum level of dividends and may therefore not change dividends unless the difference between D_t^* and D_{t-1} is substantial or sustained. Second, a rise in dividends could reduce the internal availability of funds required for investment that is already committed. Similarly, a sharp fall in dividends would produce internal funds for which there might be no immediate use. Finally, because firms are notoriously reluctant to lower dividends, if $D_t^* < D_{t-1}$ they may wait until rising income increases D_t^*, while if $D_t^* > D_{t-1}$ they may hesitate to raise dividends because they fear that the rise in optimum dividends is only temporary. This delayed response will be approximated by the partial adjustment model:

$$\frac{D_t}{D_{t-1}} = \left[\frac{D_t^*}{D_{t-1}}\right]^\lambda V_t, \tag{2}$$

where λ is the response elasticity and V_t is a stochastic disturbance. Substituting Eq. (1) into Eq. (2) and taking logarithms yields (writing lowercase letters for logarithms of the corresponding uppercase variables):

$$d_t - d_{t-1} = \lambda a + \lambda \alpha y_{pt} + \lambda \beta \theta_t - \lambda d_{t-1} + w_t, \tag{3}$$

where $w_t = \lambda u_t + v_t$. More generally, the dividend equation is given by:

$$d_t - d_{t-1} = \lambda a + \lambda \alpha_0 y_t + \lambda \alpha_1 (y_t - y_{t-1}) + \lambda \beta_0 \theta_t$$
$$+ \lambda \beta_1 (\theta^e_{t+1} - \theta_t) + \lambda \beta_2 (\theta_t - \theta_{t-1}) - \lambda d_{t-1} + w_t. \quad (4)$$

Estimation Methods

Because the explanatory variables of the dividend behavior equations include a lagged dependent variable,[6] ordinary least squares parameter estimates will be both biased and inconsistent if the disturbance term is autocorrelated (Griliches 1961; Koyck 1954; Orcutt and Cochrane 1949). Moreover, the Durbin-Watson statistic does not provide an adequate test of the serial correlation of the disturbances, being asymptotically biased toward 2, the value which indicates no serial correlation (Griliches 1961; Malinvaud 1961; Nerlove and Wallis 1966).

Three different consistent methods are used in this chapter to estimate the dividend behavior equations. The first of these is an instrumental variable procedure. The other two, quasi-generalized least squares and augmented least squares, are more novel and will be described below.[7]

The analysis of this section and the results presented in the following sections are based on the assumption that the income variables (as well as the tax variables) are exogenous. The exogeneity of income rests on two underlying assumptions: that current dividends do not directly influence current profits, and that the disturbances in the dividend and profit equations are uncorrelated. Although these are reasonable assumptions for gross profits,[8] they are less acceptable for the most economically relevant definition: profits net of depreciation, tax, and preferred dividends, that

6. It is obvious that Eq. (3) can be rewritten with d_t as the dependent variable and $(1 - \lambda)$ as the coefficient of d_{t-1}, without changing any of the parameter estimates.

7. If the disturbances are normally distributed, maximum likelihood estimates can be obtained either by a Newton-Raphson iterative procedure (Sargan 1964) or, more easily, by a one-dimensional search over sufficiently finely spaced values of the autocorrelation coefficient between -1 and $+1$. Although it is in principle desirable to obtain maximum likelihood estimates, the procedure requires substantially more computational work than the sequential procedures that have been used in this study. In particular, investigating the possibility of a higher than first-degree autocorrelation requires a vast increase in the number of grid points to be investigated or a substantial increase in the size of the Newton-Raphson problem. The advantage of maximum likelihood estimation, which in this case is primarily the full asymptotic efficiency property, was considered insufficient to outweigh these computational disadvantages.

8. Strictly speaking, because of autocorrelated disturbances the exogeneity of current profits requires that the disturbance in the profits equation be independent of all lagged disturbances in the dividend equation.

is, net profit available for common stockholders.[9] Fortunately, the evidence discussed below for all three income measures is mutually reinforcing.

Instrumental Variables

Liviatan (1963) has noted that a consistent estimate of a lagged dependent variable equation with autocorrelated disturbances can be obtained by using an instrumental variable method. If the equation to be estimated is of the form

$$y_t = \beta_0 + \beta_1 x_t + \beta_2 y_{t-1} + u_t, \tag{5}$$

Liviatan proposes the use of x_{t-1} as an instrumental variable for y_{t-1}. If the instrumental variable calculation is described as a two-stage least squares procedure, the first stage of Liviatan's method is to estimate (by ordinary least squares) the coefficients of

$$y_{t-1} = \alpha_0 + \alpha_1 x_t + \alpha_2 x_{t-1} + \xi_t, \tag{6}$$

and to calculate the values of $\hat{y}_{t-1} = \hat{\alpha}_0 + \hat{\alpha}_1 x_t + \hat{\alpha}_2 x_{t-1}$. In the second stage the coefficients of

$$y_t = \beta_0 + \beta_1 x_1 + \beta_2 \hat{y}_{t-1} + \varepsilon_t \tag{7}$$

are estimated by ordinary least squares. As instrumental variable estimators, these are consistent estimates of β_0, β_1, and β_2 (Sargan 1958).

Moreover, although Liviatan did not deal with the properties of the calculated residuals ($\hat{\varepsilon}_t = y_t - \hat{\beta}_0 - \hat{\beta}_1 x_t - \hat{\beta}_2 \hat{y}_{t-1}$), it is clear that any rational function of the $\hat{\varepsilon}_t$'s is a consistent estimate of the corresponding function of the ε_t's. More specifically, the large sample autocorrelation coefficients of the $\hat{\varepsilon}_t$'s are consistent estimators of the autocorrelation of the ε_t's.[10] In particular, if d^* is the Durbin-Watson statistic calculated from these residuals, then $1 - d^*/2$ is a consistent estimate of the first-order autocorrelation of the ε_t's. Although the Durbin-Watson test is not strictly applicable to the residuals of an equation estimated by instrumental variables, for large samples $1 - d^*/2$ may be treated as an ordi-

---

9. The central role of this measure of income as the basis on which to determine dividends is indicated by its name in British financial circles, "net earned for ordinary" (that is, for ordinary shareholders rather than preferred).

10. We assume here, as throughout, that the disturbances are of constant variance.

nary correlation coefficient (Hannan 1960, p. 85). This is in direct contrast with the situation when the Durbin-Watson statistic is obtained for the residuals from an ordinary least squares estimate of a lagged dependent variable equation. Of course, if the ε_t's are serially dependent, as would be expected if the u_t's are autocorrelated, the standard errors and variance components of Eq. (7) are asymptotically biased. Evidence that the ε_t's are autocorrelated should serve as a warning against the use of confidence intervals or significance tests defined in the usual way.

A second serious drawback is that the instrumental variable method will generally lead to a loss of efficiency. First, serial correlation of the ε_t's reduces the efficiency of the parameter estimates for any given choice of instrument. Second, when the u_t's are serially independent, the use of the instrumental variable method reduces efficiency in comparison to ordinary least squares. The efficiency of instrumental variables in the absence of autocorrelated disturbances will depend on the partial correlation between $\hat{y}_{t-1}$ and y_{t-1} given x_t. Malinvaud (1964, p. 477) reported that the Liviatan procedure increased standard errors by an average of 50 percent in sampling experiments with twenty observations; unfortunately, no information was given about the partial correlation of the instrument. Two methods of increasing the large-sample efficiency of consistent parameter estimates will now be presented.

Quasi-Generalized Least Squares

If $\hat{u}_t$ is defined by $\hat{u}_t = y_t - \hat{\beta}_0 - \hat{\beta}_1 x_t - \hat{\beta}_2 y_{t-1}$, that is, as the residuals calculated for Eq. (5) using the consistent parameter estimates of Eq. (7), sample autocorrelation coefficients of the $\hat{u}_t$'s are consistent estimates of the population autocorrelation coefficients of the u_t's. These can be used to transform the original variables in a manner analogous to generalized least squares estimation. To consider a specific example, if the $\hat{u}_t$'s indicate only a first-order autocorrelation ($u_t = \rho u_{t-1} + \omega_t$), ordinary least squares could be applied to the transformed equation:

$$y_t - \hat{\rho} y_{t-1} = \beta_0 + \beta_1(x_t - \hat{\rho} x_{t-1}) + \beta_2(y_{t-1} - \hat{\rho} y_{t-2}) + \omega_t. \qquad (8)$$

The estimates of β_1 and β_2 would be consistent and, in large samples, could be expected to have greater efficiency than instrumental variable estimates. Because the regressors include a lagged endogenous variable, these estimates will not have full asymptotic efficiency (Amemiya and Fuller 1965). However, Monte Carlo experiments with samples of size 50 support the assumption that this method yields more efficient parameter estimates than the instrumental variable method and reduces the bias in the standard errors (Wallis 1966).

In applying this method in the current study, the order of serial correlation in the disturbances was determined by comparing equations of the forms

$$\text{(i)} \quad u_t = \rho_1 u_{t-1} + \rho_4 u_{t-4} + \omega_t,$$

$$\text{(ii)} \quad u_t = \sum_{j=1}^{N} \rho_j u_{t-j} + \omega_t, \quad \text{and}$$

$$\text{(iii)} \quad u_t = \rho_N u_{t-N} + \omega_t,$$

with N taking the values one through four, and selecting the form with the highest multiple correlation coefficient ($\bar{R}$).

Augmented Least Squares

Because the generalized least squares method is not fully efficient even in large samples, an alternative and computationally easier procedure was also studied. If Eq. (5) is rewritten in a way that explicitly recognizes the Nth order autocorrelation structure of the disturbance,

$$y_t = \beta_0 + \beta_1 x_t + \beta_2 y_{t-1} + \sum_{j=1}^{N} \rho_j u_{t-j} + v_t, \tag{9}$$

it is immediately clear that the asymptotic bias that occurs when ordinary least squares is applied to Eq. (5) is due to the misspecification of omitting variables (u_{t-j}'s) that are correlated with an explanatory variable (Griliches 1961). This suggests that consistent parameter estimates can be obtained by augmenting the original data matrix with columns containing estimates of the lagged disturbances. More specifically, augmented least squares (ALS) estimates are defined as the ordinary least squares estimates of

$$y_t = \beta_0 + \beta_1 x_t + \beta_2 y_{t-1} + \sum_{j=1}^{N} \rho_j \hat{u}_{t-j} + \eta_t, \tag{10}$$

where $\hat{u}_t$ is defined in the beginning of the section on quasi-generalized least squares.

Although ALS can be shown to be consistent, no specific analytic result about the efficiency of ALS is available. It should be more efficient than the instrumental variable estimation procedure for three reasons. First, Eq. (10) is estimated by ordinary least squares rather than instrumental variables. Second, the estimation equations contain more information (the $\hat{u}_{t-j}$'s). Third, the η_t's should have little or no serial correlation.

In practice, the number of lagged disturbances in Eq. (10) (N) was determined by comparing equations with values of N between 0 and 4, selecting the one with the highest adjusted multiple correlation coefficient ($\bar{R}$).[11]

Some Basic Results

The dividend equations described in the first section of this chapter were estimated with quarterly data for the period from January 1953 through December 1964. The data, derived from the summary of company accounts published monthly in the *Financial Times,* relates to all industrial companies whose financial year ended in that quarter. Lagged values such as D_{t-1} and Y_{t-1} therefore refer to the dividends and income reported one *year* before by those companies.[12]

Table 4.1 presents coefficients of the basic dividend model (Eq. [3]) estimated by ordinary least squares (OLS), instrumental variables (IV), quasi-generalized least squares (GLS), and augmented least squares (ALS). The equilibrium elasticities of dividends (that is, the elasticities of the optimum dividend level, D_t^*) with respect to income and to the opportunity cost of retained earnings, and the time profiles of these elasticities, are also presented. The income variable is here defined as net profits after tax, depreciation, and preferred dividends (that is, net profits available for common stockholders).

Casual inspection of Table 4.1 indicates that the estimates are approximately the same with all four estimation methods. Detailed discussion of the parameter values will therefore be limited to the simplest of the consistent estimators (instrumental variables). A brief comparison with the other methods will then follow.

The impact elasticity of dividends with respect to income is 0.412 ($\lambda\alpha$). A consistent estimate of the corresponding equilibrium elasticity with

11. Two alternative forms were also considered. The first included $\hat{u}_{t-1}$ and $\hat{u}_{t-4}$; the second included only $\hat{u}_{t-4}$.

12. The forty-four quarterly observations are therefore actually four temporally interrelated samples of eleven observations each. Using seasonal dummy variables had little effect on the coefficients. Similarly, preliminary estimates with four separate series also supported the assumption that pooling all forty-four observations would not distort the results.

Table 4.1. The basic dividend model: alternative estimation methods

Estimation method	OLS	IV	GLS	ALS
Coefficients				
(Impact elasticities)				
$\lambda\alpha(y)$	0.387	0.412	0.336	0.381
	(0.042)	(0.044)	(0.045)	(0.040)
$\lambda\beta(\theta)$	0.369	0.389	0.340	0.350
	(0.051)	(0.052)	(0.057)	(0.050)
$\lambda(-d_{-1})$	0.407	0.433	0.363	0.388
	(0.042)	(0.044)	(0.046)	(0.041)
Equilibrium elasticities				
$\alpha(y)$	0.951	0.951	0.926	0.982
$\beta(\theta)$	0.907	0.898	0.937	0.902
Time profile elasticities				
Income				
1 year	0.38 (40)	0.40 (42)	0.33 (35)	0.37 (38)
4 years	0.83 (87)	0.85 (89)	0.76 (83)	0.84 (85)
Tax				
1 year	0.36 (40)	0.38 (42)	0.33 (35)	0.34 (38)
4 years	0.79 (87)	0.80 (89)	0.78 (83)	0.77 (85)
$\bar{R}^2$	0.688	0.694	0.601	0.717
DWS	1.35	1.31	1.69	1.94

Income variable: net profits after tax, depreciation, and preferred dividends. Estimation method: OLS = ordinary least squares; IV = instrumental variables; GLS = quasi-generalized least squares; ALS = augmented least squares.

respect to income is obtained by dividing the impact elasticity by the estimated response elasticity (λ). Although the resulting point estimate of α, 0.951, indicates that the optimum ratio of dividends to income declines slightly as income increases, the standard errors of $\lambda\alpha$ and λ imply that the coefficients are quite compatible with a constant optimum ratio ($\alpha = 1$).

The impact elasticity of dividends with respect to a tax-induced change in the opportunity cost of retained earnings is 0.389. The relatively small standard error (0.052), although possibly biased downward because of the serial correlation of the disturbances, leaves little doubt about the statistical significance of the tax effect. The estimated equilibrium elasticity is 0.898. These elasticities imply that the differential rates of profit tax had a substantial impact on dividend behavior. The abolition of the differential in 1958 increased the value of θ from 0.68 to 1.00. This increase in θ of nearly 50 percent implied that the optimum ratio of dividends to income rose by more than 40 percent. In the first year, dividends would be expected to rise by more than 15 percent.

The speed of adjustment parameter ($\lambda = 0.433$) indicates that, for small relative differences between D_t^* and D_{t-1}, approximately 43 percent of the difference is removed in the first year. Because the dynamic adjustment model (Eq. [2]) assumes a constant *elasticity* response mechanism, the more usual "proportional correction" measure of the speed of adjustment depends on the relative size of the initial change in the income or tax variable. The "time profile elasticities" presented in Table 4.1 relate to 10 percent changes in Y and θ and show the corresponding proportional changes after one and four years; the numbers in parentheses express the proportional changes as percentages of the change in the "optimum" dividend level (that is, the "equilibrium" change). Thus, a 10 percent increase in the value of θ yields a 3.8 percent dividend increase after one year and an 8.0 percent increase by the end of four years; these are 42 and 89 percent of the ultimate dividend increase of 9.0 percent.

Each of the ordinary least squares coefficients is lower than the corresponding instrumental variables estimate. The implied downward bias in the estimate of λ corresponds with a priori expectations; if the disturbance in Eq. (4) is positively autocorrelated, the coefficient of d_{t-1} (that is, $-\lambda$) will be biased upward and therefore the value of λ biased downward. The value of the Durbin-Watson statistic (DWS = 1.35) indicates that the disturbances are positively autocorrelated, since correcting for the bias would lower the Durbin-Watson statistic even further. Because the estimates of $\lambda\alpha$ and $\lambda\beta$ were lower than the corresponding instrumental variable estimates in approximately the same proportion as λ, the estimated equilibrium elasticities were almost the same for both methods.

The quasi-generalized least squares and augmented least squares estimates also support the conclusion that the differential profits tax had a substantial impact on the dividend level. The point elasticities of optimum dividends with respect to θ exceed 0.9; at least 35 percent of this reaction occurs in the first year and 85 percent within four years. The Durbin-Watson statistics indicate that the GLS transformation and the use of ALS both reduce positive serial correlation of the disturbances. Because the ALS method incorporates additional information, it has the highest adjusted multiple correlation coefficient and smallest standard errors.

The estimates shown in Table 4.1 all refer to the simplest specification of the optimum dividend equation. Table 4.2 compares four alternative dynamic specifications. Both augmented least squares and instrumental variable estimates are shown;[13] income is again defined as net profits. Before considering the differences between the eight estimates, we may note that in each case the effect of the tax variable is large, both economically and in relation to its standard error. The estimated impact elasticities range between 0.271 and 0.389; the equilibrium elasticities range between 0.894 and 0.937. It is clear that allowing for more complex dynamic dividend behavior does not weaken the conclusion that the differential profits tax had a substantial influence on dividend behavior.

Specifications 2 through 4 introduce the variable $\dot{y} = \log (Y_t/Y_{t-1})$. Each of the estimated coefficients of this variable is positive and larger than its standard error, implying that the firms' "permanent income" is calculated by projecting the recent rate of growth. More specifically, α_0 is the elasticity of optimum dividends with respect to the permanent level of income, and α_1/α_0 is the implied elasticity of "permanent income" with respect to the ratio of current to previous income. For example, using the ALS estimate of specification 2, if $Y_t/Y_{t-1} = 1.1$, the firm determines its optimum dividend level with reference to a "permanent income" of $Y_t(1.1)^{0.099/0.312} = 1.03 \ Y_t$.[14] All six estimates of α_1/α_0 indicate that Y_t/Y_{t-1} has only a small effect on implied permanent income; $0.32 \leq \alpha_1/\alpha_0 \leq 0.55$. All of the equations also imply that the elasticity of optimum dividends with respect to income is approximately unity.

The estimates of specifications 3 and 4 indicate that neither an expected future change in the tax $[\dot{\theta}_+ = \log (\theta^e_{t+1}/\theta_t)]$ nor a previous change $[\dot{\theta}_- = \log (\theta_t/\theta_{t-1})]$ had a substantial effect on dividend behavior. The coefficients are less than their standard errors and the adjusted multiple correlation coefficients are less than those of specification 2. The point estimates of $\lambda\beta_1$ are all of the correct sign (negative), indicating that an expected increase in the opportunity cost of retained earnings causes retained earnings to rise in the current period. Although the estimates of $\lambda\beta_2$ are of the wrong sign, the very low t values (11/259 and 118/298) indicate that this variable ($\dot{\theta}$) has no real effect.

Because of the more complex dynamic structures, the adjustment elasticity parameter (λ) is no longer an adequate measure of the speed of adjustment. The time profile elasticities for specifications 2 through 4 all in-

13. For each specification, the ALS estimate has a higher $\bar{R}^2$ than the corresponding IV estimate and a DWS of almost exactly two.

14. The positive elasticity of dividends with respect to (Y_t/Y_{t-1}) is in contrast to the common assumption that firms determine "permanent income" as a weighted average of current and past income.

Table 4.2. Alternative dynamic specifications

Specification	1	2	3	4	1	2	3	4
Estimation method	ALS	ALS	ALS	ALS	IV	IV	IV	IV
Coefficients (Impact elasticities)								
$\lambda\alpha_0(y)$	0.381 (0.040)	0.312 (0.059)	0.300 (0.060)	0.300 (0.063)	0.412 (0.044)	0.294 (0.077)	0.284 (0.079)	0.295 (0.085)
$\lambda\alpha_1(\dot{y})$	—	0.099 (0.073)	0.102 (0.074)	0.100 (0.075)	—	0.151 (0.088)	0.154 (0.089)	0.145 (0.092)
$\lambda\beta_0(\theta)$	0.350 (0.050)	0.298 (0.059)	0.278 (0.063)	0.277 (0.069)	0.389 (0.052)	0.288 (0.074)	0.271 (0.078)	0.285 (0.086)
$\lambda\beta_1(\dot{\theta}_+)$	—	—	−0.070 (0.070)	−0.068 (0.086)	—	—	−0.064 (0.081)	−0.042 (0.098)
$\lambda\beta_2(\dot{\theta}_-)$	—	—	—	−0.011 (0.259)	—	—	—	−0.118 (0.298)
$\lambda(-d_{-1})$	0.388 (0.041)	0.318 (0.060)	0.305 (0.062)	0.305 (0.066)	0.433 (0.044)	0.315 (0.080)	0.303 (0.082)	0.316 (0.089)

Equilibrium elasticities							
$\alpha_0(y)$	0.982	0.981	0.984	0.984	0.951	0.933	0.937	0.934
$\beta_0(\theta)$	0.902	0.937	0.911	0.908	0.898	0.914	0.894	0.902
Time profile elasticities								
Income								
1 year	0.37 (38)	0.40 (41)	0.39 (40)	0.39 (40)	0.40 (42)	0.43 (47)	0.43 (46)	0.43 (46)
4 years	0.84 (85)	0.79 (81)	0.78 (79)	0.78 (79)	0.85 (89)	0.77 (83)	0.76 (81)	0.79 (84)
Tax								
1 year	0.34 (38)	0.29 (31)	0.27 (30)	0.26 (28)	0.38 (42)	0.28 (31)	0.26 (29)	0.17 (18)
4 years	0.77 (85)	0.73 (78)	0.69 (76)	0.68 (75)	0.80 (89)	0.70 (77)	0.67 (76)	0.67 (74)
$\bar{R}^2$	0.717	0.725	0.717	0.717	0.694	0.639	0.636	0.627
DWS	1.94	2.00	2.00	2.05	1.31	1.34	1.33	1.34

Income variable: net profits after tax, depreciation, and preferred dividends. Estimation method: ALS = augmented least squares; IV = instrumental variables.

dicate that dividends respond more rapidly to income changes than to changes in the tax. The ALS estimates show that 40 percent of the equilibrium response to a 10 percent income change occurs in the first year, while only 30 percent of the equilibrium response to a 10 percent change in θ occurs in one year. By the end of four years, however, the proportions of the equilibrium responses are nearly equal. Similar but slightly stronger differences are obtained by IV estimation.

The coefficients presented in Tables 4.1 and 4.2 were all estimated with income defined as profits net of tax, depreciation, and preferred dividends. Although this is probably the most appropriate income variable to consider as a determinant of dividends,[15] it has two disadvantages. First, because the amount of tax subtracted in calculating net profits reflected the amount of dividends (until the abolition of the differential profits tax), this income variable is clearly endogenous and the estimated coefficients are therefore biased and inconsistent. Second and more important, the use of the net profits definition blurs the fact that changes in the income and profits tax rates affect dividends through changes in net profits as well as through changes in the opportunity cost of retained earnings.

Table 4.3 compares estimates for three different income definitions: net profits, gross profits before tax and depreciation, and maximum net profits (that is, maximum retained earnings). For simplicity, only specification 1 is presented; both ALS and IV estimates are given. The results support the previous conclusions that the elasticity of dividends with respect to θ is substantial and significant, and that the elasticity of optimum dividends with respect to income is approximately one. Although the impact elasticity with respect to the tax variable is substantially higher when income is measured gross than when it is measured net, the equilibrium elasticities are approximately equal.

However, when the maximum possible profit measure of income is used, a striking and suggestive result appears. Although the estimated response elasticity (λ) and income impact elasticity ($\lambda\alpha$) are almost identical with those of the net profit equation, the impact and equilibrium tax elasticities are nearly 40 percent higher. This difference implies that, during the period under study, tax changes that increased the opportunity cost of retained earnings simultaneously decreased the maximum net profits associated with any given gross profits. The observed changes in dividends therefore reflected a balancing of these two countervailing forces. The implications of this are developed in the next section.

15. See note 10.

Table 4.3. Alternative income definitions

Income definition	Net profits	Gross profits	Maximum profits	Net profits	Gross profits	Maximum profits
Estimation method	ALS	ALS	ALS	IV	IV	IV
Coefficients (Impact elasticities)						
$\lambda\alpha_0(y)$	0.381	0.645	0.381	0.412	0.552	0.405
	(0.040)	(0.044)	(0.040)	(0.044)	(0.058)	(0.046)
$\lambda\beta(\theta)$	0.350	0.538	0.514	0.389	0.525	0.550
	(0.050)	(0.041)	(0.059)	(0.052)	(0.060)	(0.066)
$\lambda(-d_{-1})$	0.388	0.631	0.387	0.433	0.571	0.424
	(0.041)	(0.044)	(0.041)	(0.044)	(0.057)	(0.045)
Equilibrium elasticities						
$\alpha(y)$	0.982	1.022	0.984	0.951	0.967	0.955
$\beta(\theta)$	0.902	0.853	1.328	0.898	0.919	1.297
Time profile elasticities						
Income						
1 year	0.37 (38)	0.63 (62)	0.37 (38)	0.40 (42)	0.54 (56)	0.39 (41)
4 years	0.84 (85)	1.00 (98)	0.84 (85)	0.85 (89)	0.93 (97)	0.86 (88)
Tax						
1 year	0.34	0.53	0.50	0.38	0.51	0.54
4 years	0.77	0.83	1.15	0.80	0.88	1.16
$\bar{R}^2$	0.717	0.880	0.735	0.694	0.706	0.673
DWS	1.94	2.29	1.98	1.31	0.91	1.25

Estimation method: ALS = augmented least squares; IV = instrumental variables.

The Dual Tax Impact

The dual tax impact is best represented by the use of two tax variables in the optimum dividend equation. In addition to the opportunity cost of retained earnings in terms of net dividends foregone (θ), we use the ratio of maximum net profits to gross profits (II). Equation (1) is therefore replaced by

$$D_t^* = A Y_{pt}^\alpha \theta_t^\beta \Pi_t^\gamma U_t, \tag{11}$$

where Y_{pt} refers to gross profits before tax and depreciation. The values of β and γ measure the dual impact of tax changes on the optimum dividend level.

Table 4.4 presents the estimates obtained by substituting Eq. (11) into the dynamic adjustment model specified in Eq. (2). The impact and equilibrium elasticities with respect to income and to the opportunity cost aspect of tax changes are similar to the estimates for gross profits presented in Table 4.3. The implied effect of changes in II is small; the point estimates of the elasticity of D_t^* with respect to Π_t range between 0.111 and 0.313. The estimated standard errors are large relative to the point estimates of $\lambda\gamma$; moreover, because the disturbances of the IV equations are positively autocorrelated, these estimated standard errors are biased downward. But although the high standard errors should serve as a warning that the point estimates of $\lambda\gamma$ and λ may be substantially different from their true values, they should not be interpreted as implying that II has no effect on D^*. The large standard errors are partly a reflection of the small variation in II during the period of observation; the minimum and maximum values were 0.4625 and 0.5500. The safest conclusion from the evidence of Tables 4.3 and 4.4 is that a partial effect of the tax changes which increased the ratio of maximum net profit to gross profit was to increase dividends by an indeterminate amount.

An interesting alternative interpretation of the coefficients in Eq. (11) is also possible. Because θ_t measures the constant rate at which retained earnings may be transformed into dividends, the product $\theta_t \Pi_t$ is the ratio of maximum possible dividends to gross profits. Since $Y_{pt}\theta_t\Pi_t$ is therefore the maximum dividend level, rewriting Eq. (11) as

$$D_t^* = A (Y_{pt}\theta_t\Pi_t)\alpha\theta_t^{\beta-\alpha}\Pi_t^{\gamma-\alpha}U_t \tag{12}$$

shows that α may be interpreted as the elasticity of optimum dividends with respect to maximum dividends, while $\beta - \alpha$ and $\gamma - \alpha$ measure the dual tax impact when the maximum dividend level is held constant. Be-

Table 4.4. The dual tax impact

Specification	1	2	1	2
Estimation method	ALS	ALS	IV	IV
Coefficients (Impact elasticities)				
$\lambda\alpha_0(y)$	0.627	0.581	0.594	0.504
	(0.063)	(0.074)	(0.092)	(0.108)
$\lambda\alpha_1(\dot{y})$	—	0.135	—	0.088
	—	(0.121)	—	(0.159)
$\lambda\beta(\theta)$	0.551	0.504	0.601	0.542
	(0.046)	(0.063)	(0.090)	(0.110)
$\lambda\gamma(\pi)$	0.079	0.066	0.140	0.169
	(0.090)	(0.098)	(0.102)	(0.104)
$\lambda(-d_{-1})$	0.612	0.571	0.616	0.520
	(0.063)	(0.074)	(0.092)	(0.109)
Equilibrium elasticities				
$\alpha_0(y)$	1.026	1.020	0.962	0.967
$\beta(\theta)$	0.895	0.878	0.975	1.044
$\lambda(\pi)$	0.124	0.111	0.219	0.313
Time profile elasticities				
Income				
1 year	0.616 (60)	0.707 (69)	0.582 (60)	0.580 (60)
4 years	1.001 (98)	0.995 (98)	0.940 (98)	0.923 (96)
Tax (θ)				
1 year	0.539 (60)	0.492 (56)	0.589 (60)	0.530 (51)
4 years	0.874 (98)	0.847 (96)	0.952 (98)	0.986 (94)
Tax (II)				
1 year	0.076 (60)	0.063 (57)	0.133 (60)	0.162 (51)
4 years	0.122 (98)	0.108 (96)	0.214 (98)	0.297 (94)
$\bar{R}^2$	0.843	0.817	0.543	0.570
DWS	2.243	2.293	1.180	1.358

Income: gross profits before tax and depreciation. Estimation method: ALS = augmented least squares; IV = instrumental variables.

cause $\beta - \alpha$ appears to be zero or slightly negative, a tax-induced rise in θ may be thought of as increasing D^* by increasing the maximum possible dividend level rather than by changing the opportunity cost of retained earnings. Although we cannot determine whether one of these two explanations is a better behavioral description than the other, the conclusion that the differential profits tax had a substantial effect on dividends and the estimates of that effect both remain unaltered.

There is an important policy implication of the introduction of the variable Π. As already noted, during the period 1953–1964 the values of θ and Π tended to change in opposite directions. However, because Π depends only on the rates of tax on income and undistributed profits, while θ also reflects the tax rate on distributed profits, the two variables can be moved independently while keeping the rate of personal income tax unchanged. This offers substantially greater flexibility than a corporate income tax system under which a given change in θ implies a specific change in Π (unless the rate of personal income tax is altered). This flexibility can be used either to change the retention incentive while keeping the total tax receipts from the corporate sector approximately constant (as in Britain) or to alter the total gross tax "burden" on the corporate sector without changing the retention incentive.

It is therefore somewhat surprising that in 1965 Britain gave up the differential profits tax system for the less flexible corporation tax. The most obvious explanation is that government officials did not recognize that the change would reduce the number of fiscal policy instruments. Because the corporation tax would appear to *firms* to have the same characteristics as the old differential rates of profits tax, the important difference between these tax systems as instruments of public policy was ignored.

Individual Industry Comparisons

The estimates discussed in the two previous sections relate to the behavior of all public industrial corporations. Table 4.5 presents disaggregated results for the manufacturing sector as a whole, for five individual manufacturing industries, and for the industrial classification "finance, land, and property." For some sets of data, information was only available for an eight-year period; the number of observations (32 or 44) is shown at the top of each column. All equations were estimated by augmented least squares.

Although there is substantial variation in the individual parameter estimates, the results as a whole support the conclusions reached above. The dividend model defined by Eqs. (11) and (2) provides a good explanation of annual dividend changes. With the exception of cotton textiles, the individual coefficients are quite plausible; the dividend model is probably inappropriate for cotton textiles because the industry was in a secular decline.

For all other industries except shipbuilding,[16] θ has a substantial posi-

---

16. Shipbuilding was in a period of stagnation and secular decline. This may explain why neither tax variable had any effect.

tive effect. The equilibrium elasticities for these growing industries range between 0.889 and 2.482, implying a tax effect substantially greater than our previous estimate for industrial corporations as a whole. The effect of Π is also generally positive and significant. However, in addition to a near-zero value for shipbuilding, the coefficients are negative for finance, land, and property (but less than the standard error) and for motors and aircraft.

The response elasticities (λ) are generally in the interval 0.3 to 0.5; the only exceptions are a slow response for chemical and allied ($\lambda = 0.145$) and an implausible value for cotton textiles ($\hat{\lambda} = 1.274$). Examination of the time profile elasticities indicates that the response to income change is generally more rapid than the response to tax changes, although by the end of four years the gap is nearly closed. The two industries in which the response to income changes is slower ($\alpha_1 < 0$) are ones with highly cyclical profits; for firms in these industries, Y_{pt} is more reasonably approximated by this average of current and past income than by projecting the current growth rate. For each industry, the equilibrium response to income is approximately one; $\hat{\alpha}$ ranges between 0.859 for finance, land, and property and 1.039 for engineering.

Conclusions

The evidence examined in this chapter shows that the policy of differential profits taxation had a substantial effect on corporate saving.[17] Tax rate changes influenced both the opportunity cost of retained earnings in terms of foregone dividends and the ratio of maximum net profits to gross profits. Dividends responded to these changes with a distributed lag; approximately 40 to 60 percent of the ultimate effect occurred in the first year. The elasticity with respect to tax-induced changes in the opportunity cost of retained earnings appears to be substantially higher than the elasticity with respect to the ratio of maximum possible net profits to gross profits.

Although these results support the original suggestion that tax policies designed to influence the level and timing of corporate saving may have important effects on economic stability and growth, the link between corporate saving and these policy aims must still be investigated. Changes in

17. The strength of this evidence depends on the appropriateness of the dividend model that has been used. It would be useful to investigate whether the conclusions of this chapter would be affected by allowing dividend behavior to be influenced by the factors that determine the firms' total demand for funds: investment opportunities, the rate of interest, depreciation provisions of the tax system, corporate liquidity, and so on. A multiple equation model, such as that used by Dhrymes and Kurz (1967), would be required for this.

Table 4.5. Tax effects in individual industries

Industry	All industries (44)	All manufacturing (32)	Chemical and allied (44)	Engineering (44)	Motors and aircraft (32)	Shipbuilding (44)	Cotton textiles (44)	Finance, land, and property (32)
Coefficients (Impact elasticities)								
$\lambda\alpha_0(y)$	0.581	0.447	0.148	0.446	0.510	0.272	1.194	0.361
	(0.074)	(0.079)	(0.045)	(0.087)	(0.083)	(0.070)	(0.081)	(0.074)
$\lambda\alpha_1(\dot{y})$	0.135	0.165	0.467	−0.035	−0.076	0.295	0.217	0.079
	(0.121)	(0.120)	(0.090)	(0.121)	(0.116)	(0.104)	(0.194)	(0.119)
$\lambda\beta(\theta)$	0.504	0.473	0.339	0.579	0.478	−0.006	6.832	0.909
	(0.063)	(0.080)	(0.087)	(0.092)	(0.100)	(0.113)	(0.765)	(0.110)
$\lambda(\pi)$	0.066	0.178	0.361	0.469	−0.196	−0.030	2.232	−0.093
	(0.098)	(0.113)	(0.081)	(0.244)	(0.181)	(0.010)	(0.225)	(0.115)
$\lambda(-d_{-1})$	0.571	0.433	0.145	0.412	0.535	0.296	1.274	0.417
	(0.074)	(0.083)	(0.048)	(0.101)	(0.078)	(0.076)	(0.133)	(0.077)

Equilibrium elasticities								
α_0	1.020	1.035	1.019	1.039	0.952	0.916	—	0.859
β	0.878	1.099	2.482	1.432	0.889	−0.021	—	2.306
γ	0.111	0.399	2.662	1.146	−0.343	−0.095	—	−0.211
Time profile elasticities								
Income								
1 year	0.707 (69)	0.601 (58)	0.604 (59)	0.433 (40)	0.422 (44)	0.556 (61)	—	0.428 (50)
4 years	0.995 (98)	0.954 (92)	0.758 (74)	0.913 (87)	0.898 (94)	0.789 (86)	—	0.772 (90)
Taxes (θ)								
1 year	0.492 (56)	0.462 (42)	0.328 (13)	0.567 (42)	0.466 (52)	−0.006 (30)	—	0.905 (39)
4 years	0.847 (96)	0.980 (89)	1.092 (44)	1.251 (88)	0.846 (95)	−0.016 (76)	—	2.015 (87)
Taxes (II)								
1 year	0.063	0.171	0.350	0.457	−0.185	−0.028	—	−0.089
4 years	0.108	0.357	1.167	1.003	−0.327	−0.072	—	−0.187
$\bar{R}^2$	0.817	0.911	0.683	0.753	0.783	0.659	0.898	0.847
DWS	2.293	2.499	1.960	1.940	1.638	2.053	1.964	1.712

Income: gross profits before tax and depreciation. Estimation: augmented least squares.

corporate saving may be stabilizing in two ways. First, tax-induced changes in saving could (in principle) lead to higher investment during periods of low aggregate demand and lower investment during periods of high aggregate demand. But the well-established evidence that investment occurs only after a substantial lag (Almon 1965; Eisner 1967; Eisner and Strotz 1963) reduces the potential importance of such countercyclical policy, even if it is accepted that investment would be cyclically sensitive to tax-induced changes in retained earnings. Second, if corporate saving does not affect short-run corporate investment but dividends do influence consumption, tax policies to decrease dividends during periods of high aggregate demand would be stabilizing. Although this may be a potentially useful way of reducing aggregate demand by "forced saving" in high-income groups instead of by lower investment or decreased general consumption, the estimated lag structure indicates that such a policy could only be effective if the government's recognition and implementation lags were sufficiently short.

When we turn to the influence of tax policies on growth, the effectiveness of the differential profits tax in influencing corporate saving raises two further questions. First, does an increase in the internal availability of corporate funds lead to increased corporate investment? Second, does an increase in corporate saving induce a corresponding decrease in personal saving? If the answer to the first question is yes and the answer to the second is no, tax policies to encourage corporate saving will increase aggregate investment. If the answer to both questions is yes, such tax policies will only shift investment from the noncorporate to the corporate sector. Finally, there is no effect on investment if the answer to the first question is no and the answer to the second question is yes.

Previous attempts to estimate the effect of retained earnings on corporate investment have been handicapped by the high degree of multicollinearity between retained earnings, profits, and sales. The tax-induced changes in the "equilibrium" ratios of retained earnings to profits and sales that have occurred in Britain since 1950 may provide a useful set of data with which to estimate the effects of retained earnings. This is currently being explored.

Although the relation between corporate and personal saving has been the subject of theoretical speculation, it has never been empirically estimated. Because both forms of saving are cyclically volatile, multicollinearity problems again arise. The rise in dividends after 1958 and the relative fall that can be expected to follow the 1965 corporation tax may provide a sufficient departure from the secular and cyclical patterns to permit studying the effect of corporate retentions on personal saving.

A preliminary examination of the data for the period after 1958 shows a sharp rise in personal saving and a change in corporate financing from internal to external sources. But only a careful study will reveal whether the tax change had any qualitative effect on the total supply of saving and the level and pattern of investment.

5 Corporate Taxation and Dividend Behavior: A Reply and Extension

In Chapter 4 I showed that the equilibrium dividend payout ratio falls during periods in which retained earnings are taxed at a lower rate than dividends. Although this is contrary to much popular and political opinion, it is implied by qualitative economic analysis. A lower tax rate on retained earnings makes it advantageous for shareholders to save through retained earnings instead of by reinvesting a portion of their dividends. Even if future dividends are taxed at the same higher rate, capital retained within the firm has a relatively higher long-run net yield because these earnings are taxed at a lower rate until they are paid out. This effect on retained earnings is analogous to the effect on personal saving of substituting a consumption tax for an income tax.

Mervyn King's two papers (1971 and 1972) strengthen the conclusion that tax differentials influence dividend policy. Using a longer period of annual observations, a somewhat different data source, and a modified functional form, he also finds that dividends respond to changes in the differential taxation of dividends and retained earnings. The issue is now not *whether* tax policy influences dividend behavior but by *how much*. King's estimate of the elasticity of dividends with respect to the tax variable (θ—the opportunity cost of retained earnings in terms of foregone dividends) is about 0.4 in contrast to my estimate of approximately 1.0. Although I have no a priori reason to believe that the elasticity is of any particular size, I suspect that King's estimate is biased downward.

The first section of this chapter shows that my original elasticity estimate is essentially unaffected by adopting the nonlinear form suggested by King. I then discuss why his lower parameter value is most likely due to differences in data that cause an underestimate of the relevant elasticity. The second section considers the evidence about takeover activity and

Reprinted from *Review of Economic Studies* 39 (April 1972), pp. 235–240, by permission of the Society of Economic Analysis Ltd.

the hypothesis of a "managerial" theory of dividend behavior. I have also taken this occasion to extend the previous analysis by considering the effect on dividend behavior of another important aspect of company tax policy: investment allowances. The results of this extension are presented in the third section.

Nonlinearity, Estimation Method, and Data

In Chapter 4 I specified the optimal dividends equation as

$$D_t^* = A Y_t^\alpha \theta_t^\beta \pi_t^\gamma, \tag{1}$$

where D_t^* is optimal dividends, Y_t is gross profits before tax and depreciation, θ_t is the differential tax variable (the opportunity cost of retained earnings in terms of net foregone dividends), and π_t is the ratio of maximum net profits to gross profits. King correctly pointed out that, to be faithful to my analysis of the dual tax impact, the log-linear approximation of Eq. (1) should be replaced by an implicit function of D_t^*:

$$D_t^* = A \left[Y_t \pi_t - \frac{1 - \theta_t}{\theta_t} D_t^* \right]^\alpha \theta_t^\beta. \tag{2}$$

Using the proportional adjustment model,

$$\frac{D_t}{D_{t-1}} = \left(\frac{D_t^*}{D_{t-1}} \right)^\lambda, \tag{3}$$

yields the dividend equation

$$\frac{D_t}{D_{t-1}} = \left[\frac{A(Y_t \pi_t)^\alpha \left[1 - \frac{1 - \theta_t}{\theta_t} \frac{D_t^*}{Y_t \pi_t} \right]^\alpha \theta_t^\beta}{D_{t-1}} \right]^\lambda, \tag{4}$$

or, in logs,

$$\log D_t = (1 - \lambda) \log D_{t-1} + \lambda \log A + \lambda \alpha \log (Y_t \pi_t)$$
$$+ \lambda \beta \log \theta_t + \alpha \lambda \log \left[1 - \frac{1 - \theta_t}{\theta_t} \frac{D_t^*}{Y_t \pi_t} \right]. \tag{5}$$

Equation (5) cannot be estimated because the last term contains the unobservable D_t^*. In his first paper, King proceeded by dropping this last term and using the remaining variables to estimate the parameters. He then used these parameter estimates to approximate D_t^*, reestimated the full equation (5), and continued iteratively until convergence was achieved. The result was a lower estimate of the differential tax effect ($\hat{\beta} = 0.55$) and an implausibly high income elasticity ($\hat{\alpha} = 1.47$).

I originally suspected that the unorthodox estimation method might be responsible for the low tax elasticity and unacceptable income elasticity. Even if the stochastic disturbance in Eq. (5) (not shown explicitly) were normal, homoskedastic, and serially independent,[1] King's method would not generally yield maximum likelihood estimates. The additional requirement for the method to be a maximum likelihood estimator is quite strong: the equation relating optimal dividends to income and tax variables, Eq. (2), must hold exactly, without any random disturbance. If this is not true, the final term of Eq. (5) will be correlated with the disturbance and the parameter estimates will be inconsistent.[2]

A simple nonlinear maximum likelihood procedure is possible if we adopt the reasonable assumption that the income elasticity, α, is equal to one.[3] Equation (2) can then be solved for D^* to yield:

$$D_t^* = \frac{A Y_t \pi_t \theta_t^\beta}{1 + A(1 - \theta_t)\theta_t^{\beta-1}}. \tag{6}$$

Substituting into the adjustment model, Eq. (3), and adding a disturbance term yields the estimation equation

$$\frac{D_t}{D_{t-1}} = \left[\frac{A Y_t \pi_t \theta_t^\beta}{D_{t-1} + A(1 - \theta_t)\theta_t^{\beta-1}D_{t-1}} \right]^\lambda + u_t. \tag{7}$$

If the u_t's are normal, homoskedastic, and serially independent, the least squares estimates of Eq. (7) are maximum likelihood.[4]

1. The assumption of serial independence is important because of the lagged dependent variable (D_{t-1}). The usual methods of dealing with this problem, discussed at length in Chapter 4, cannot be used in this nonlinear equation. The evidence in Table 4.1 indicates, however, that the problem is not serious; ordinary least squares gave essentially the same long-run parameter estimates as the consistent instrumental variable procedure.

2. His argument that the procedure is nevertheless legitimate because the omitted variable "is small in relation to the dependent variable" (King 1971, p. 379) is incorrect; the biases depend not on the size of the omitted variable but on its partial regression coefficients on the included variables (Thiel 1961).

3. That this would quite obviously be expected on a priori grounds was noted in Chapter 4 and adopted by King as a criterion for judging his own equations. My previous estimates, using the specification of Eq. (1), gave α values between 0.96 and 1.03.

4. See note 1 above. In keeping with the criticism noted in the paragraph above, it might be better to formulate Eq. (7) with a multiplicative error and apply maximum likelihood estimation to its logarithm.

The parameter estimates obtained by this direct nonlinear procedure are very similar to my earlier results. In particular, the differential tax elasticity is not significantly different from one: $\hat{\beta} = 0.900$ with a standard error of 0.085. The other parameters are: $\hat{A} = 0.423$ (S.E. $= 0.014$) and $\lambda = 0.474$ (S.E. $= 0.045$). $\bar{R}^2 = 0.719$ and the Durbin-Watson statistic is 1.894.

The difference between my estimates and King's are therefore not due to the difference between my original log-linear function and King's more complex specification. Moreover, although King is correct that my original log-linear equation with net income implies that the "dual tax effect" equation should be like Eq. (2) and not Eq. (1), it should be remembered that the original log-linear net income equation is itself only an approximation. There is therefore no reason to constrain the "dual tax effect" equation to assume the complex nonlinear form implied by it. One might just as well begin by using Eq. (1). Fortunately the estimates indicate that the choice of approximation does not affect the parameter estimates.

King has now (1972) accepted the suggestion to use a direct maximum likelihood estimator. His new estimates show that the coefficient values are quite insensitive to the choice of estimation method.[5] We must look elsewhere for an explanation of the difference in coefficient values.

There are two features of King's data that are likely to cause a downward bias in his estimate of the tax elasticity. First, he used annual data for the period since 1949, while I used quarterly observations from 1953. In the period before 1953, the activities of the Capital Issues Committee depressed the level of dividends. Including this period in the analysis probably introduces a spurious upward bias in the income elasticity. Since the tax law changes implied that the payout ratio would rise in the second half of King's sample period, the upward bias in the income elasticity causes a downward bias in the tax elasticity.

Second, the use of annual data of the type employed by King may blur the impact of tax changes. Each of my quarterly observations relates to the last twelve months' dividends and income of companies whose financial years end in that quarter and to the tax variables relevant to such companies. King's observations combine data for all of the financial years ending within a calendar year. The tax variable is therefore an average of the different relevant tax variables for each quarter. The tax variable therefore differs from the theoretically relevant magnitude by a random error that is likely to cause a downward bias in the estimated tax effect.

I conclude from these considerations that the true elasticity of divi-

---

5. His 1972 paper shows this for the more general equation with the takeover variable, but King informs me that this is also true for the simpler equation.

dends with respect to the tax variable, θ, is likely to be closer to my original estimate of approximately one than to King's lower values.

The Takeover Threat and "Managerial" Capitalism

King found (1971) that he could obtain a more reasonable value of the income elasticity ($\hat{\alpha} = 0.92$) by introducing a variable that he described as a measure of the threat of takeovers. King interpreted the significance of this variable as evidence for the Marris theory of "managerial" capitalism (1964) and against the "classical" theory of the firm.

In his first paper King's measure of the takeover threat was the *aggregate* expenditure of firms on the acquisition of subsidiaries. Even if there were no change in the number of takeovers, this variable would increase through time merely because of the rising price level and the expanding economy. To avoid this problem, it is better to deflate the expenditure on takeovers by a measure of aggregate corporate size or activity. I have used the "disposable income" of corporations for this purpose.[6] The resulting ratio. which I shall denote T, rises from 0.115 in 1954 to 0.381 in 1964, indicating a substantial increase in the rate of takeover activity.

There is a small problem in converting the annual T values to a quarterly series for use in the regression equation. Each quarterly observation on Y_t and D_t relates to the income and dividends during the previous twelve months of the companies whose accounting year *ended* in that quarter. The annual T values are effectively averages of the relative takeover expenditures during the accounting periods *ending* during that government fiscal year. Thus if $T_{54:q}$ is the relative takeover expenditure of companies whose accounting year ended in quarter q of fiscal 1954, the observable value of T_{54} is a weighted average of four $T_{54:q}$'s. The relative number of companies whose accounting period ends in each quarter provides an adequate basis for these weights. In 1961, 30 percent were in the first quarter, 40 percent in the fourth quarter, and 15 percent in each of the remaining quarters; these fractions are unlikely to vary appreciably with time. The problem therefore is to estimate quarterly values of T whose weighted average is equal to the observed annual average, for example $0.30\,T_{54:1} + 0.15\,T_{54:2} + 0.15\,T_{54:3} + 0.40\,T_{54:4} = T_{54} = 0.115$. The principle used to estimate these quarterly values is based on the assumption that the quarterly T values do not behave erratically but change smoothly.

---

6. The "expenditure on acquisition of subsidiaries" and "disposable income" are taken from the Annual Abstracts of Statistics data on quoted companies.

More specifically, the forty-four quarterly T_t values were estimated by minimizing $\sum_{t=2}^{44} (T_t - T_{t-1})^2$ subject to the eleven annual "weighted average" constraints of the type described above.

Following King, we may redefine the optimal dividend as

$$D_t^* = A \left[Y_t \pi_t - \frac{1 - \theta_t}{\theta_t} D_t^* \right] \theta_t^\beta T_t^\gamma \tag{8}$$

and proceed as before to obtain maximum likelihood estimates. The estimated takeover effect is small and insignificant ($\hat{\gamma} = -0.115$ with a standard error of 0.114). The differential tax parameter is essentially unchanged ($\hat{\beta} = 1.190$, standard error 0.301). If we use the log-linear approximation based on a generalization of Eq. (1), and use instrumental variables for the lagged dependent variable, we obtain

$$\log\left(\frac{D_t}{D_{t-1}}\right) = -0.552 + 0.588 \log Y_t + 0.170 \log \pi_t + 0.539 \log \theta_t$$
$$\phantom{\log\left(\frac{D_t}{D_{t-1}}\right) =} (0.127) \qquad\qquad (0.286) \qquad\qquad (0.143)$$
$$+ 0.028 \log T_t - 0.612 \log D_{t-1}.$$
$$ (0.063) \qquad\quad (0.131) \tag{9}$$

$$\bar{R}^2 = 0.680$$
$$DWS = 2.203$$

The coefficient of the takeover variable is not significantly different from zero, while the differential tax elasticity and income elasticity are not significantly different from one ($\hat{\beta} = 0.881$, $\hat{\alpha} = 0.961$).

The small size and insignificance of the takeover coefficient imply that the data provide no support for the "managerial" hypothesis. This may, of course, be because T is not a good measure of *potential* takeover threats. Indeed there is nothing in Marris's theory to suggest that this potential should be changing. The insignificance of this variable should not therefore be construed as strong evidence against the managerial hypothesis. I was in fact quite careful in Chapter 4 to note that my dividends model was consistent with both classical and more general behavioral assumptions.

In his second paper, King accepts my objection to his use of *aggregate* takeover expenditure and replaces this variable by the ratio of aggregate expenditure to total net assets. He finds that the new variable has approximately the same coefficient as his original aggregate variable. The reason for our difference in this respect is unclear. It may reflect differences in the deflator variables. "Total net assets" is a trend-like variable; King's use of it implies that the relevant measure of activity is the proportion of assets being acquired. "Company disposable income" has a cyclical as well as a general trend behavior; its use measures the fraction of companies' new resources being used for acquisitions. There seems to be no a priori way to choose between them. Alternatively, if King's sample period and use of annual observations do bias the estimated income and tax elasticities (for the reasons noted in the previous section), this would bias the coefficient of the takeover variable. More specifically, since takeover activity was higher in the second half of the sample period, it is positively correlated with both the tax and income variables. The coefficient of the takeover variable would therefore be biased upward, that is, to indicate a positive effect even if there were none.[7]

The most important point about the level of takeover activity is that it is not exogenous. There are two different aspects of the problem. First, within the individual firm expenditure on acquisitions may be determined simultaneously with dividends and with investment in plant and equipment. If so, it is illegitimate to say that any one of the variables influences the level of the other. Second, even if attention is limited to those firms which have no expenditure on acquisitions and which may respond to the level of takeover activity among other firms, it is necessary to bear in mind that the level of takeover activity may in part reflect changes in tax policy. Unfortunately, we currently lack an adequate theory of takeover investment. An examination of the basic data shows that expenditure on acquisitions in Britain had two substantial relative increases in the postwar period, one after the tax change of 1958 and the other after the introduction of the corporation tax. One possible explanation of this is that the increased takeover activity represents the acquisition of those firms that had not adjusted their dividend policies to the new tax incentives. Whatever the mechanism, the association between tax changes and takeover

---

7. To see this more explicitly, consider a model in which there are only two explanatory variables, x and z, with x measured with a random error, ε. If the true equation is $q = \alpha + \beta x + \gamma z + u$ and the measurement error in x is independent of x, z, and u, the probability limit of the OLS estimator of γ is

$$\hat{\gamma} = \gamma + \frac{\beta(z'x)(\varepsilon'\varepsilon)}{(x'x)(z'z) - (x'z)^2 + (z'z)(\varepsilon'\varepsilon)},$$

where terms of the form $(z'x)$ represent the covariance of z and x. In the context of our problem, z is the takeover variable, T, and x the tax variable, θ. Since T and θ are positively correlated and β is positive, the value of γ will be biased upward. Including the income variable would not alter the analysis.

activity should caution against including takeover activity in the equation and then treating the coefficient of the tax variable as a measure of its *total* effect.

Investment Allowances and Dividend Behavior

During the period since 1954 changes in the structure of initial and investment allowances have been an important stimulus to corporate investment (see Chapter 15). Several readers of my dividend study (Chapter 4) suggested that changes in investment allowances that make investment more attractive are also likely to reduce dividends. To test this, the basic dividend equation has been respecified to include a measure of the value of investment allowances:

$$D_t^* = A Y_t \pi_t \left[1 - \frac{\theta_t}{1 - \theta_t} D_t^* \right] \theta_t^\beta I_t^\delta, \tag{10}$$

where I_t is the discounted value of the tax savings due to the depreciation, investment allowances, and initial allowances resulting from one pound of investment.[8]

The nonlinear maximum likelihood estimates of the corresponding dividend equation show the coefficients of the investment allowance variable to be insignificant ($\hat{\delta} = -0.105$, S.E. $= 0.371$) while the remaining coefficients remain unchanged (in particular, $\hat{\beta} = 0.979$ with S.E. $= 0.293$). If the takeover activity variable (T_t) is added to the equation, its coefficient is insignificant ($\hat{\gamma} = -0.114$, S.E. $= 0.117$) and the others are essentially unaffected. Using the log-linear approximation with instrumental variables for the lagged dependent variable yields has similar implications:

$$\log \left(\frac{D_t}{D_{t-1}} \right) = -1.386 + 0.638 \log Y_t + 0.211 \log \pi_t + 0.508 \log \theta_t$$
$$\phantom{\log \left(\frac{D_t}{D_{t-1}} \right) = -1.386 +} (0.097) (0.242) (0.111)$$
$$+ 0.214 \log I_t - 0.665 \log D_{t-1}.$$
$$ (0.182) (0.100) \tag{11}$$

$$\bar{R}^2 = 0.664$$
$$DWS = 2.390$$

In short, although changes in the investment allowance variable had

---

8. See Chapter 15 for further description. It actually refers to the "revised allowance" variable used in that chapter.

substantial effects on investment behavior, dividends remained unaffected. Although this may in part be due to changes in the use of external funds, it is also because the investment and initial allowances themselves provided additional cash flow to firms.

Summary

King's two papers support my original conclusion that differential taxation influences the dividend payout ratio. His analysis indicates a somewhat smaller elasticity of dividends with respect to the tax variable but, as this chapter has shown, his estimate is likely to be biased downward. It is clear that the estimated elasticity is not influenced by the use of a log-linear approximation instead of a more general functional form.

The effect of takeover activity on dividend behavior is unclear. An alternative to King's measure of takeover activity was found to be insignificant, and it was shown that King's estimate might be biased to show a positive coefficient even if there were no real effect. In any case, the takeover activity is endogenous and may be influenced by changes in tax policy. Only further research on this interesting issue will resolve the question.

Finally, changes in the initial and investment allowances that substantially influenced capital formation in this period did not affect dividend behavior.

6 Tax Incentives, Corporate Saving, and Capital Accumulation in the United States

The American system of taxing corporate income provides a strong incentive for companies to save a substantial fraction of their income. While all corporate income is subject to the corporate profits tax, only the portion paid as dividends is taxed as personal income. The capital gains that result from retained earnings are taxed at half of the personal income tax rate and only when realization occurs. There is no constructive realization on assets held until death. The effective tax rate on retained earnings is therefore very much less than the rate on dividend income.

Brittain (1966) has shown that the growing tax incentive associated with rising marginal personal income tax rates has induced companies to increase the fraction of total earnings that is saved.[1] During the 1960s corporate retained earnings were more than 50 percent of net income; gross corporate savings exceeded 75 percent of corporate cash flow after tax. This corporate saving accounts for a large share of total capital formation. From 1962 through 1971, corporate saving was 52 percent of gross private saving and 40 percent of net private saving.

This higher level of corporate saving does not, of course, imply an equal net increase in aggregate capital formation. To the extent that shareholders take corporate saving into account in making their individual saving decisions, the higher level of corporate saving induced by the tax structure will be offset by a lower level of personal saving. The purpose of

Reprinted from the *Journal of Public Economics* 2 (April 1973), pp. 159–171, by permission of North-Holland Publishing Company. This chapter is part of a larger study of the effects of taxation on capital formation and income distribution. I am grateful to the National Science Foundation for financial support and to V. Ambrosini and A. Munnell for assistance with the calculations.

1. Feldstein (Chapters 4 and 5) and King (1972) found that British firms also varied their savings rate in response to tax-induced changes in the opportunity cost of retentions in terms of foregone net dividends.

this chapter is to estimate the net effect of higher company saving on aggregate capital accumulation.[2]

The first section contrasts the relations between corporate savings and personal consumption that are implied by the Keynesian and Fisherian theories of consumption. An alternative model that is more appropriate for an economy with substantial corporate savings is developed. The second section discusses the data sources and specific definitions. The parameter estimates are presented and analyzed in the third section. The fourth section comments on the implications for tax policy and future research.

Corporate Saving and Personal Consumption

There has been almost no empirical analysis of the relation between corporate dividend policy and personal savings. Nearly all econometric consumption functions assume without explicit testing that retained earnings do not have an independent effect on concurrent consumer expenditure. This is surprising, not only because of the importance of the issue but also because the early theoretical literature on the consumption function pointed in a different direction. In the *General Theory,* Keynes (1936) related consumption to a broad definition of income including capital gains and not excluding retained earnings. Harrod's theory of saving (1948) placed great emphasis on retained earnings and assumed that such retentions would generally induce an offsetting decrease in personal saving. Harrod suggested, however, that for some individuals, the retained earnings might exceed total desired saving. He assumed in this case that there could not be a completely offsetting change in personal saving and referred to the increment to total saving as "surplus corporate saving."[3]

Most subsequent developments of consumption theory have ignored the issue.[4] Econometric consumption functions in the "Keynesian" tradition have ignored Keynes's formulation and related consumption to disposable income, including dividends but excluding retained earnings. Since the ratio of retained earnings to disposable income is not constant through time or across income classes, the exclusion of retained earnings

2. A parallel analysis of British postwar experience is presented in Chapter 7.
3. Harrod thus ignores the possibility that the individual's personal savings might be negative, either by borrowing or by the sale of assets.
4. Friedman (1957) was one of the few who specifically noted that retained earnings are not included in his definition of income. He acknowledged that "it is by no means clear that this concept [of income] is best for our purposes."

is a substantial omission. An alternative specification of the consumption function, inspired by Irving Fisher's theory of intertemporal allocation (1890, 1930) and by the life-cycle elaboration of that model developed by Harrod (1948), Modigliani and Brumberg (1954), and Ando and Modigliani (1963), relates consumption to disposable *labor* income and to wealth. In this formulation, neither dividends nor retained earnings as such affect consumption, that is, the earnings of capital have the same effect on consumption whether they are retained or distributed.[5]

The Keynesian and Fisherian specifications of consumer behavior have very different implications about the effect that tax-induced changes in dividend policy will have on aggregate capital formation. The Keynesian theory implies that tax incentives that reduce dividends will also lower concurrent consumer spending and will therefore increase the rate of capital accumulation. In contrast, the Fisherian hypothesis implies that households will lower their personal savings when firms save more; the tax therefore has no effect on aggregate saving.

Although there has been no direct test of whether U.S. savings have been affected by tax-induced changes in corporate dividend policy, Denison (1958) supported the Fisherian hypothesis by showing that the ratio of total private saving to GNP was more stable than the ratio of personal saving to personal income during the ten high-employment peacetime years (1929 and 1948–1956) for which data was available at the time of his study.[6] Modigliani's recent study (1970) of international differences in savings rates is also consistent with the Fisherian view. Modigliani found that, ceteris paribus, the ratio of private saving to income is not significantly related to the ratio of corporate saving to income. However, the Modigliani results are ambiguous and may be interpreted as indicating that, contrary to both the Fisherian and Keynesian views, higher retained earnings increase consumption. The coefficient of the corporate saving variable in each alternative equation was positive and had a large standard error; the coefficients ranged from 0.20 (S.E. 0.32) to 0.48 (S.E. 0.35). Modigliani summarized his results on this issue by noting that "no clear-cut conclusion can be reached from our data" (p. 221).

A different test is suggested by the observation that, if retained earnings do increase concurrent consumption, they do so because they raise the

5. The Cambridge theories of consumption are in a sense more Fisherian than Keynesian since they specify separate consumption propensities for capital and labor income.

6. After this paper was submitted for publication, I received Paul David and J. L. Scadding's "What You Always Wanted to Know about 'Denison's Law' but Were Afraid to Ask." They show that Denison's results are generally supported by data for the much longer period 1897–1968.

level of accrued capital gains. Arena's evidence (1964) that current accrued capital gains do not have an independent effect on consumption
(when disposable income and wealth are taken into account) therefore appears to support the Keynesian position.[7] In a 1972 study (reprinted as
Chapter 7 of this book) Fane and I showed that such an interpretation is
not correct. An insignificant effect of capital gains in general is not incompatible with a substantial concurrent effect of retained earnings. This is
implied by the "components of capital gains" model of consumer behavior that was used in the 1972 study and that will also provide the framework for the empirical analysis in this chapter.

It will be useful to develop the rationale for that specification by starting
with the following simple model:

$$C_t = \beta_0 + \beta_1 Y_t + \beta_2 W_{t-1} + \beta_3 G_t, \tag{1}$$

$$W_t = W_{t-1} + G_t + Y_t - C_t, \tag{2}$$

where C_t is consumer expenditure, Y_t is disposable income, G_t is accrued
capital gains, and W_t is the stock of wealth at the end of period t. A consumption function of the type specified in Eq. (1), with a lagged wealth
variable, implies that a one-dollar increase in income at time T causes a
concurrent increase in consumption of β_1 dollars, followed by an increase
of $\beta_2(1 - \beta_1)$ dollars at $T + 1$, an increase of $\beta_2(1 - \beta_2) \times (1 - \beta_1)$ at
$T + 2$, $\beta_2(1 - \beta_2)^2(1 - \beta_1)$ at $T + 3$, and so on. A unit change in income
at time T thus has an exponentially declining impact beginning at time $T +$
1. The sum of this exponential stream of consumption is clearly $1 - \beta_1$.
Since the consumption in the first year is β_1, the total eventual effect of a
one-dollar increase in Y_t is an increase in consumption of exactly one
dollar. In this special sense, a consumption function with a lagged wealth
variable implies a total long-run marginal propensity to consume of one.[8]
This is of course true not only for disposable income but also for capital
gains. *The coefficients of the consumption function therefore only measure the relative speeds of response of consumption to each of its determinants.*[9]

---

7. Similar estimates are also reported by Bhatia (1971). He obtains a significant coefficient
for accrued gains only when that variable is constrained to have the same coefficient as the
stock of wealth.

8. A life-cycle model with no bequests would have the same implication in finite time for
each individual.

9. This is also true if Eq. (1) is replaced by a more general specification in which a dif-

This interpretation of the parameters of the consumption function implies that a low coefficient of the capital gains variable means only that the response of consumption to a change in the level of capital gains is very slow. There is no reason, however, to assume that households respond to all forms of capital gains at the same rate. The speed of response to a particular type of capital gain is likely to depend on how "permanent" households regard that gain to be, that is, the extent to which it implies that a similar gain will accrue in future years. In 1972 Fane and I suggested (Chapter 7) that households are likely to consider increases in share prices due to retained earnings as more "permanent" than the share price changes due to market revaluations of previously existing assets. If so, the capital gains due to retained earnings would evoke a more rapid response and would therefore have a larger coefficient in the consumption function.

This specification has been described as the components of capital gains model of the capital income hypothesis (see Chapter 7). The capital income hypothesis provides that all forms of capital *income,* whether distributed or not, have a substantial effect on concurrent consumption. It is thus in contrast with the "Keynesian" specification which excludes undistributed income and the Fisherian view which excludes all capital income. More specifically, the components of capital gains model posits that consumption does not respond in the same way to all components of capital gains. As a basis for the empirical analysis of this model, we may write the real accrued capital gains in each year (G_t) as the sum of the capital gains due to retained earnings (λRE_t) and the change in the real market value of existing assets (X_t):[10]

$$G_t = \lambda RE_t + X_t. \tag{3}$$

Since λ is unobservable, the value of X_t cannot be calculated. The compo-

---

ferent distributed lag response is allowed for disposable income and capital gains. In that specification, one can distinguish the short-run marginal propensity to consume, the usual long-run *direct* marginal propensity to consume (that is, ignoring the induced wealth effect), and the long-run *total* marginal propensity to consume of one.

10. One dollar of retained earnings produces $\lambda < 1$ dollars of capital gains because of the future taxes that must be paid. There is no need in this chapter to estimate the value of λ. For evidence that retained earnings do significantly increase share values, see, for example, Nerlove (1968). Note that although Eq. (3) implies that the resulting capital gains are immediate, the actual annual correlation of G_t and RE_t may be low because of substantial variations in X_t. The random walk hypothesis implies that current retained earnings as such cannot lead shareholders to anticipate future capital gains in excess of the normal rate of return.

nents of gains model of the consumption function can, however, be specified without explicit reference to the unobservable variable X_t as

$$C_t = \beta_0 + \beta_1 Y_t + \beta_2 W_{t-1} + \beta_3 G_t + \beta_4 RE_t. \tag{4}$$

With this form, the coefficient of retained earnings represents the *excess* effect of retained earnings over capital gains in general.

Equation (4) provides the basic framework for estimating the effects of retained earnings on household consumption and therefore on aggregate capital accumulation. If the *sum* of β_3 and β_4 is substantially greater than zero, it may be inferred that retained earnings do induce offsetting changes in personal saving behavior. More specifically, the net effect of the tax incentives on capital accumulation is the difference between the marginal propensity to consume out of dividends and the sum of β_3 and β_4.

Several modifications in the specification of Eq. (4) will be examined. Separate distributed lag responses will be estimated for each of the determinants of consumption. The impact of dividends on consumption will be evaluated explicitly. Because unemployment can have a variety of important effects on consumption, the unemployment rate will also be included in some specifications. The estimated effect of retained earnings is very insensitive to these modifications. All of the evidence supports the conclusions that retained earnings do have a substantial effect on consumption and therefore that tax incentives that alter corporate dividend policy have at most a quite limited effect on aggregate capital accumulation.

The Data

The estimates presented below are based on aggregate U.S. data for the period 1929 through 1965, excluding the years 1941 through 1946. It is noteworthy that company savings rose from 32 percent of gross profits in 1929 to 58 percent in 1966. The analysis ends with 1965 because of the lack of comparable data on household assets after that year.

Consumer expenditure (C), disposable personal income (YD), and dividends (DIV) are the usual national income account values, deflated to constant 1958 dollars and divided by population. The measurement of retained earnings raises a problem because of the inadequate data on true economic depreciation. Undistributed profits as reported in the national income accounts is equal to gross profits minus an estimate of corporate capital consumption. Because of the accounting conventions used to calculate capital consumption, this measure of net retained earnings is likely to be an underestimate of true net corporate saving. Gross retained earnings, however, is obviously an overestimate. Separate equations have been estimated with each specification. The similar implications of the results with both measures indicate that further work to improve the measurement of retained earnings would not alter any conclusions.

The wealth variable is the per capita net worth of consumers at market value expressed in 1958 dollars. The series was estimated by Ando and Modigliani (1963) based on Goldsmith's earlier study (1956) and updated by Branson and Klevorick (1969).[11] The variable W_t refers to the wealth at the end of year t.[12] The value of accrued capital gains is defined as the increase in household wealth minus personal savings.

Estimates and Tests of the Components of Capital Gains Model

All of the estimates presented below support the conclusion that retained earnings have a substantial effect on consumer expenditure. The implied marginal propensity to consume retained earnings is approximately one-half and is quite insensitive to the particular specification of the equation. The data clearly support the components of capital gains model: the speed of response to changes in retained earnings is much greater than the response to other components of capital gains. All of the estimates are therefore very similar to the findings for British postwar experience reported in Chapter 7.

Because dividends respond slowly to cyclical changes in corporate profits, retained earnings tend to vary with the cycle. Consumption also tends to vary cyclically, being above normal in years when the unemployment rate is high. There is a danger, therefore, that the estimate of the effect of retained earnings will be biased by a spurious correlation with cyclical conditions. To guard against this, the unemployment rate (RU) has been included explicitly in the equations. The estimated relation between consumption and retained earnings should therefore reflect the secular rise in retained earnings and its response to tax incentives.

Equation (5) of Table 6.1 presents an estimate of the basic specification of the components of capital gains model using a measure of retained earnings that is net of depreciation (RN_t).[13] The estimated direct long-run

11. I am grateful to these authors for making available their unpublished data.

12. Ando and Modigliani actually report the value at the beginning of each year. This is referred to here as the value at the end of the preceding year in order to make the current notation consistent with that in Chapter 7.

13. Since R^2 values are extremely high for all the equations ($R^2 > 0.99$), only the sum of squared residuals and Durbin-Watson statistics are presented.

Table 6.1. The components of capital gains model[a]

Variable	Eq. (5)	Eq. (6)	Eq. (7)	Eq. (8)	Eq. (9)	Eq. (10)
YD_t	0.57	0.57	0.57	0.57	0.59	
	(0.06)	(0.07)	(0.06)	(0.06)	(0.06)	
YD_{t-1}	0.18	0.19	0.19	0.19	0.18	
	(0.04)	(0.05)	(0.03)	(0.04)	(0.04)	
YP_t						0.78
						(0.05)
W_{t-1}	0.024	0.010	0.024	0.023	0.019	0.021
	(0.008)	(0.007)	(0.008)	(0.008)	(0.009)	(0.007)
G_t	−0.12	0.78	0.024	0.023	0.019	0.021
	(2.21)	(2.27)	(0.008)	(0.008)	(0.009)	(0.007)
RN_t	0.49		0.49	0.49	0.47	0.45
	(0.10)		(0.09)	(0.10)	(0.10)	(0.08)
RG_t		0.50				
		(0.12)				
RU_t	2.99	2.14	3.00	2.99	2.79	3.08
	(0.89)	(0.98)	(0.86)	(0.88)	(0.88)	(0.08)
DIV_t				0.034		
				(0.243)		
$DIV25_t$					−0.167	
					(0.277)	
Constant	41	93	41	40	68	31
SSR	2209	2432	2209	2207	1525	2143
DWS	2.03	1.82	2.03	2.05	2.36	—

a. The dependent variable in each equation is real per capita consumption. See the text for definitions and data sources. The period of estimation is 1929–1965 excluding 1941–1946, except for Eq. (9) in which the sample ends in 1960.

propensity to consume disposable income is 0.75.[14] The coefficients of *RN* and *G* indicate that the effect of retained earnings on consumption is very different from the effect of other components of capital gains. Although the negative coefficient of G_t is inadmissible, the very large standard error implies that this parameter is not significantly different

14. Although additional lagged values of income are not statistically significant, this may only reflect collinearity among the variables. A general exponential lag distribution for the coefficients of the income variable is estimated in Eq. (10).

from zero or from the coefficient of W_{t-1}.[15] If X_t, the component of capital gains that is not due to retained earnings, is a purely random variable as suggested by the random walk model of asset prices, households should treat these gains as additions to the stock of wealth. The implication of this, that the coefficient of G_t should be the same as the coefficient of W_{t-1}, is borne out quite precisely by the estimates in Chapter 7 and is not contradicted by Eq. (5).[16]

The coefficients of Eq. (5) indicate that the propensity to consume retained earnings is about one-half. This is approximately two-thirds of the direct long-run propensity to consume disposable income. This estimate contradicts both the Keynesian view that households respond to dividend income but not to retained earnings and the Fisherian position that consumption depends on the stock of wealth but not the flow of capital income.[17] It implies that households "see through the corporate veil." The specific point estimates indicate that the adjustment of personal saving to changes in retained earnings is incomplete. Before considering the implications in more detail, it is useful to examine the sensitivity of the parameter estimates to alternative specifications of the basic framework.

Equation (6) shows that none of the conclusions are affected by the use of retained earnings gross of depreciation (RG) instead of net retained earnings. The coefficients of retained earnings and disposable income are essentially unchanged. The redefinition of retained earnings does, however, lower the coefficient of W_{t-1}. Although the coefficient of G_t is now large and positive, the standard error is so big that the previous conclusion is not altered. A comparison of the sum of squared residuals shows that RN provides a slightly better explanation of variation in consumption.

The very large standard error of the coefficient of G_t supports the theoretical presumption that the accrued capital gains that are due to market revaluation of previously existing assets are treated as part of the shareholders' stock of wealth and do not induce a substantial concurrent increase in consumption. Constraining the coefficients of G_t and W_{t-1} to be

15. An explicit test of this is presented below.

16. Arena's estimated consumption function contained G_t but not retained earnings. He also concluded that the coefficient of G_t was not different from that of W_{t-1}. His low value of the G_t coefficient even when retained earnings are not included in the equation may reflect the fact that for Arena's period of estimation (1946–1958) most of the variation in G_t was not associated with a change in dividend behavior.

17. The estimates might, however, be reinterpreted as consistent with the Fisherian position. Since the rate of interest is not explicitly included in Eq. (5), changes in the flow of capital income with a given capital stock may be interpreted as an indicator of changes in the rate of return.

equal has no effect on any of the other coefficients and does not significantly increase the sum of squared residuals; this is shown in Eq. (7).

The coefficient of the combined variable $(W_{t-1} + G_t)$ is approximately the same as the previous coefficient of wealth. Similar results are obtained with gross retained earnings.

The specification of these equations implies that the aggregate propensity to consume dividend income is the same as the propensity to consume other forms of disposable income. Since these propensities are essentially a measure of the speed of response and since dividends are a very stable form of income, this is quite plausible. Equation (8) adds real per capita dividends (DIV) to the previous explanatory variables: its coefficient measures the *differential* impact of dividends since YD also includes dividends.[18] The coefficient of DIV is very much less than its standard error, and the other coefficients are essentially unchanged.

The dividend variable in Eq. (8) is measured gross of the personal income tax. There is, unfortunately, no complete time series on the average marginal tax rate of shareholders that might be used to approximate net dividends. Brittain (1966) has, however, developed estimates of the marginal tax rates at selected fractiles of the distribution of dividends for each year through 1960. Equation (8) has been reestimated for this shorter period with alternative measures of real net dividends per capita based on the tax rate at the median and 25th percentile. In both cases the dividend variable was insignificant and the other coefficients were very similar to their previous values. Equation (9) shows the results with $DIV25$, the net dividends based on the marginal rate at the 25th percentile; the equation with the median tax rate had a higher sum of squared residuals. The coefficient of the net dividend variable is negative but small and much less than its standard error.

Alternative dynamic specifications also leave these conclusions unchanged. Equation (10) replaces the two-year distributed lag on disposable income by an exponentially declining lag. More specifically, a permanent disposable income variable is defined by the recursive relation $YP_t = (1 - \lambda)YD_t + \lambda YP_{t-1}$. A maximum likelihood estimator is obtained by doing ordinary least squares conditional on values of λ between zero and one and selecting that value of λ that minimizes the sum of squared residuals.[19] The maximum likelihood estimator of $\lambda = 0.24$ implies a rapid

18. These results are unchanged if W_{t-1} and G_t are included separately. Similarly, a lagged value of the dividend variable is insignificant and leaves the other coefficients essentially unchanged.

19. See Maddala and Rao (1971). I am grateful to William Raduchel for the golden section search routine used in this calculation.

response. All of the other parameters, including the long-run direct propensity to consume disposable income, are almost unchanged from the two-year distributed lag specification of Eq. (7).

Additional equations that are not reported show that lagged values of RN_t and G_t are not significant and do not alter the other coefficients. It would of course be wrong to interpret this as implying that the full impact of the retained earnings components of capital gains is immediate. Because the specification contains lagged wealth, a more appropriate interpretation is that after a relatively large initial impact, the effect decays exponentially.

The six estimated equations that are reported here are representative of a very much larger set that have been estimated and examined.[20] All of the equations imply the same basic consumption propensities. The direct marginal propensity to consume disposable income is approximately 0.75, and the marginal propensity to consume retained earnings is approximately 0.50. The difference between the propensities is just about statistically significant at the 5 percent level. In Eq. (7), for example, the exact difference is 0.26 with a standard error of 0.136.

Implications for the Effects of Taxation on Capital Formation

The parameters of the consumption function imply that households see through the corporate veil and adjust their personal savings to changes in corporate savings. The current system of corporate income taxation, which induces corporations to retain a high fraction of earnings, therefore appears to have little if any effect on the aggregate volume of capital formation.

This suggests that the integration of the corporation tax and the personal income tax[21] would not significantly reduce the total rate of capital accumulation. Such integration would, however, eliminate several of the inefficiencies and inequities of our current system. The present incentives distort the distribution of capital accumulation between the corporate sector and the rest of the economy. Within the corporate sector, the reduction in dividends and the increased reliance on retained earnings favor

---

20. I have not, however, examined specifications with different propensities to consume out of the several components of disposable income (for example, entrepreneurial income, taxes, and so on). Klein and Goldberger (1955) and Taylor (1971) provide evidence that such consumption propensities may differ significantly. It would be useful to extend the current analysis in this way.

21. See, for example, Goode (1951) for a discussion of some of the alternative ways in which this might be done.

investment by established firms with substantial cash flow in comparison with new and rapidly growing firms. The lower rate of tax on retained earnings discriminates against some individuals with labor income and certain other types of capital income. At the same time, individuals with low incomes pay a higher tax on their share of corporate earnings than on other forms of income.

The basic empirical findings of this chapter imply that U.S. experience has been similar to the behavior of the British economy reported in Chapter 7 and to the pattern of international savings described by Modigliani. All of these studies have used only aggregate data. Further analysis of this important question at a microeconomic level would obviously be worthwhile.

7 Taxes, Corporate Dividend Policy, and Personal Savings: The British Postwar Experience

Tax policies in Britain and the United States significantly affect corporate dividend behavior. The lower rates of tax on retained earnings than on dividends induce companies to retain a substantial fraction of their cash flow. Since these retained earnings are a large share of gross private saving, the tax incentives could have a major influence on the rate of capital accumulation. The purpose of this chapter is to examine the extent to which tax-induced changes in retained earnings do in fact also influence personal saving and therefore total private capital formation. The results are important not only for the appraisal of tax policy but also for understanding household saving behavior.

Since the current study uses data for the British postwar period, it is useful to begin by describing the nature and effect of the relevant policies that Britain has pursued during those years. Until the introduction of the corporation tax in the mid-1960s, all company profits were subject to the income tax at the "standard rate" and also to separate profits taxes on dividends and retained earnings. In most years, the profits tax rate on dividends was higher than on retained earnings; high-income individuals also paid surtax (in addition to the standard rate of income tax collected from the companies) on dividends but not on retained earnings. The tax differential in favor of retained earnings was quite substantial at times; when the differential was at its maximum, a company could retain 1 pound or pay a net dividend of only 0.6 pound to a shareholder subject to taxation at the standard rate. In a previous study I showed that changes in this tax differential induced substantial shifts in the fraction of profits paid out as dividends (Feldstein 1970a).[1] Under the corporation tax, profits are not subject to *personal* income tax until they are paid to shareholders as divi-

This chapter was written with George Fane. Reprinted from the *Review of Economics and Statistics* 55 (November 1973), pp. 399–411, by permission of North-Holland Publishing Company. We are grateful to John Flemming for discussions.

1. These results are supported by more recent analysis (see Chapter 5). For additional confirmation of the qualitative conclusions, see Brittain (1966) and King (1972).

dends. Capital gains are taxed at lower rates than income and there is no constructive realization at death; the corporation tax combined with this advantageous treatment of capital gains thus provides an important inducement to high retained earnings.

Although the general effect of these tax incentives on company dividend policy is quite clear, their impact on total capital accumulation is ambiguous. There are two separate questions. First, is the rise in company savings offset by a decreased use of external finance, resulting in no change in company investment? Flemming and I studied this issue (see Chapter 15) and found that the tax incentives for retained earnings appear to increase company investment by a significant amount; the estimates imply that an additional 100 pounds of retained earnings increases investment by about 30 pounds. Second, does the rise in company savings reduce personal saving and, if so, by how much? This is the subject of the current study.

An estimate of the effect of changes in retained earnings on private saving is important for an appraisal of the desirability of the tax incentives. Although increased private saving may be a goal of public policy,[2] the tax incentives have offsetting disadvantages. These provisions clearly affect the *form* of capital accumulation, that is, its distribution between the corporate sector and the rest of the economy. Within the corporate sector, the subsidy of internally financed investment may interfere with the efficient allocation of funds among firms. Moreover, the lower rate of tax on retained earnings reduces the overall progressivity of the tax structure and, at each income level, discriminates against individuals with labor income or certain types of capital income. Although any attempt to balance these inefficiencies and inequities against the gains from increased capital formation is beyond the scope of this chapter, measurement of the effects of the tax on gross saving is an important first step.

The tentative conclusions of the current study can be summarized briefly. The evidence is most consistent with a position somewhere between the Keynesian and Fisherian theories. In contrast to the Fisherian model, capital income and not merely the stock of wealth is a determinant of consumer spending but, contrary to the Keynesian position, the division of capital income between dividends and retained earnings has little effect. In particular, the retained earnings of companies have a substantial short-run effect on consumer spending. This influence is sepa-

---

2. Inducements to increase private saving may be sought in order to offset the deterrent effect of the income tax (Kaldor 1955) or because, as Pigou (1920), Sen (1961), and others have argued, undistorted individual preferences would yield an aggregate saving rate that by some political or ethical criterion is deemed to be too low.

rate from and stronger than the impact of total accrued capital gains. In contrast, the marginal propensities to consume out of accrued capital gains and the stock of wealth are small and not significantly different from each other. We shall refer to the resulting specification as the *capital income model* of consumption because it includes *total* capital income in addition to the usual labor income and wealth variables. The implication of this specification is that the tax incentives that increase retained earnings have much less effect on total private saving. An additional pound of retained earnings probably increases total savings by less than 0.50 pound and may increase total savings by as little as 0.12 pound.

The next section discusses the relation between consumption, capital income, and wealth more fully. The third section deals with problems of dynamic specification and estimation. The remaining sections present and discuss the empirical results.

Alternative Models of Consumption Behavior

Although most previous studies of consumption behavior have not dealt with either retained earnings or capital gains, the particular specifications used in these studies do have strong and conflicting implications about their effects on consumer spending. Consider first the Keynesian theories. As in so many other areas of economic theory, the consumption function ideas developed by Keynesian economists depart substantially from Keynes's own propositions. In the *General Theory,* Keynes related consumption to a broad definition of income including unanticipated capital gains and not excluding retained earnings. Moreover, he suggested that the propensity to consume out of unanticipated capital gains is likely to be lower than out of other forms of income. Nearly all of the subsequent empirical developments of Keynesian consumption theory have instead focused on disposable personal income. Although discussions about the role of the real balance effect introduced wealth as a variable in the consumption function, the definition of income used by those who considered themselves verifying or extending the Keynesian approach remained unchanged.[3] Today most econometric models also use disposable personal income as the income measure in their consumption functions.

3. Friedman (1957) notes specifically that he has omitted retained earnings in his definition of income and that "it is by no means clear that this concept of income is best for our purposes" (p. 116). He later explains (p. 123) that he omitted retained earnings "because it was a roughly constant fraction of savings over the period covered" (1897–1949). Since the ratio of retained earnings to dividends did change during the period, we see no reason for Friedman's decision.

This use of disposable income and the omission of both retained earnings and accrued capital gains have important implications about savings behavior in general and about the effects of tax incentives in particular. They imply that a tax-induced switch in dividend policy is an effective way of increasing total private saving. This is illustrated by the simple Keynesian model:

$$C_t = m_0 + m_1[(1 - t_L) YL_t + (1 - t_D) D_t] + m_2 W_{t-1}, \qquad (1)$$

$$W_t = W_{t-1} + [(1 - t_L) YL_t + (1 - t_D) D_t - C_t] + \mu RE_t, \qquad (2)$$

where C_t is consumption, YL_t is labor income, D_t is dividends, W_t is household wealth at the end of period t, and RE_t is retained earnings. The tax parameters t_L and t_D are the constant income tax rates on labor income and dividends. Dividends are assumed to be the only nonlabor income. Equation (2) states that the annual increment in wealth is the sum of personal savings $[(1 - t_1)YL_t + (1 - t_D)D_t - C_t]$ and the increased value of equities due to retained earnings. The coefficient μ, which measures the increment to the market value of equities per pound of retained earnings, is less than one because of future taxes. A 1-pound reduction in dividends reduces consumption (C_t) by $m_1(1 - t_D)$ and reduces personal saving by $(1 - m_1)(1 - t_D)$. The corresponding 1-pound increase in retained earnings in period t has no immediate effect but does raise W_t by μ and therefore C_{t+1} by μm_2. This rise in W_t is partly offset by the fall in personal saving by $(1 - m_1)(1 - t_D)$ due to the reduction in D_t. The net increase in C_{t+1} is therefore $m_2[\mu - (1 - m_1)(1 - t_D)]$. For the two years together, personal consumption falls by $m_1(1 - t_D) - m_2[\mu - (1 - m_1)(1 - t_D)]$. Personal saving therefore falls by only $(1 - m_1)(1 - t_D) + m_2[\mu - (1 - m_1)(1 - t_D)]$. If the marginal propensity to consume disposable income (m_1) is 0.8 and the tax rate on dividends is 40 percent, $(1 - m_1)(1 - t_D) = 0.12$. Estimates of the marginal effect of wealth on consumption always indicate that m_2 is substantially less than 0.1 and generally that $m_2 < 0.05$. Since μ is less than one and $(1 - m_1)(1 - t_D) > 0$, we may conclude that the fall in personal saving is probably less than 0.2 for 1 pound of dividends switched to retained earnings. Total private saving therefore probably rises by more than 0.8 pound per pound increase in retained earnings. This is the type of reasoning that motivated the use of tax incentives to reduce dividends. The key conclusion depends, of course, on the special Keynesian treatment of capital income that is implied by Eqs. (1) and (2).

In contrast, the approach that is derived from the work of Irving Fisher treats capital income very differently and implies that the allocation of profits between retained earnings and dividends has no effect on aggregate savings. In its purest form, the Fisherian approach describes the consumption decision as the allocation of an individual's wealth over his lifetime. This wealth includes not only his marketable physical and intangible assets but also the present value of his future labor income (that is, his human wealth). Current income flows as such, including all forms of capital income, affect current consumption only by increasing wealth.[4] In practice, the uncertainty and illiquidity of human capital pose special problems. For this reason, Ando and Modigliani (1963) in their empirical development of the Fisherian approach used current labor income as a proxy measure of human capital.[5] Their consumption function,

$$C_t = m_3 + m_4(1 - t_L)YL_t + m_5W_{t-1}, \tag{3}$$

specifically excludes any impact of short-run variations in capital income whether it is paid out in dividends or retained. Changes in capital income influence consumption only by altering household wealth; since m_5 is very much less than m_4, changes in wealth have a very small but sustained effect on consumption.[6] This specification clearly implies that any switch in the allocation of profits between dividends and retained earnings would have no effect on consumption or private savings.

The extreme and diametrically opposed conclusions of the Keynesian and Fisherian approaches reflect their strong and arbitrary assumptions about the impact of capital income. First, the Keynesian approach distinguishes sharply between dividends and retained earnings while the Fisherian approach treats all capital income in the same way. Second, both specifications exclude the possibility of any substantial short-run effect on consumption of the retained earnings or capital gain components of capital income. Neither of these implications is really essential to the two underlying theories of consumer behavior. We believe that they represent unintended consequences of specifying consumer behavior without considering the implications of the corporate form of business.[7] Moreover,

---

4. See Harrod (1948, chap. 2), Modigliani (1954), and Tobin (1967) for more complete development of this theory.

5. Ando and Modigliani introduced an adjustment for unemployment which we ignore in the current description.

6. The coefficient m_5 is greater than m_2 of Eq. (1) because, in more Keynesian terms, m_5 represents not only a pure wealth or real balance effect but also the consumption of capital income.

7. The unintended nature of these implications is well illustrated by the recent work of Modigliani and Ando. Because of the difficulties of measuring disposable labor income, Modigliani and Ando have abandoned their original specification (Eq. [3] above) and used total disposable income (as in Eq. [1] above). They apparently consider this fully in accord with their original theory and do not indicate anything about the changed implications for the propensity to consume.

the ratio of company savings to total capital income is now much higher than at the time of Fisher or Keynes. The empirical analysis in this chapter relaxes these restrictive assumptions and studies the possibility that retained earnings have a short-run effect on consumption in addition to its long-run wealth effect. We shall refer to this as the capital income hypothesis to emphasize the importance of short-run flows of capital income.

More specifically, we shall examine two forms of the capital income hypothesis. The pure capital gains model posits that retained earnings increase share prices and that consumers respond to this as they do to other capital gains. The alternative form, the capital gains component model, states that shareholders distinguish between the capital gains due to retained earnings and other capital gains and have a higher marginal propensity to consume out of the former. The remainder of this section will describe these two models more fully.

It is useful to begin by examining the way that the presence of a lagged wealth variable affects the interpretation of the coefficients of the income variables. In order to emphasize the implications for the dynamics of consumption behavior, we shall relate consumption to lagged as well as concurrent income. If Y_t is the appropriate measure of income[8] and W_t is the end-of-period value of wealth, we may write the consumption function and wealth equation as

$$C_t = m_0 + m_1'Y_t + m_1''Y_{t-1} + m_2W_{t-1}, \tag{4}$$

and

$$W_t = W_{t-1} + Y_t - C_t. \tag{5}$$

It is clear that m_1' is the usual short-run marginal propensity to consume. What is the long-run marginal propensity to consume? The traditional measure is $m_1' + m_1''$. This actually measures the total increase in consumption resulting from a one-period increase in income *if the effects of wealth are ignored.* If the wealth effect is taken into account, the total increase in consumption is actually larger. More specifically, it is easy to show[9] that Eqs. (4) and (5) imply that a 1-pound increase in income during

8. We shall for the moment assume that Y_t includes capital income and shall ignore the possibility of different propensities to consume.

9. Consider the time path of consumption associated with a 1-pound increase in income during period $t = T$. During period T consumption rises by m_1'. During period $T + 1$, con-

a single period raises total future consumption by exactly 1 pound.[10]

While it is important to bear in mind that this *total* long-run marginal propensity to consume is always one, this in itself only emphasizes the need to know the effect on consumption over a shorter period. In the current study we found that the *direct* effect of changes in income and in the components of capital gains occurs quite quickly. We therefore describe the effect of income on consumption by reporting the traditional long-run marginal propensity to consume; we shall also do this for each of the components of capital gains. To emphasize that the traditional long-run marginal propensity to consume describes only part of the total response because it ignores the wealth effect, we shall refer to it as the long-run *direct* marginal propensity to consume.

In the pure capital gains model, consumption is related to the past stock of wealth and to distributed lags on disposable income and accrued capital gains. In the components of gains model, a distributed lag on retained earnings is also included. The sum of the coefficients of each distributed lag is the long-run *direct* marginal propensity to consume that type of income. *Note that differences in the long-run* direct *marginal propensities to consume do not imply differences in corresponding* total *marginal propensities.* All of the *total* propensities to consume are one. Differences in the long-run *direct* propensities to consume imply differences in the *timing* of the response of consumption to that component of total income. A higher direct propensity to consume implies a larger increase in con-

---

sumption rises by m_1'' plus $m_2(1 - m_1')$. Since income in $T + 1$ is at the original baseline level, this lowers the stock of wealth by $m_1'' + m_2(1 - m_1')$. (To simplify the calculations we ignore the fact that increases in wealth cause increases in income. If the system is stable this poses no problems.) At the end of period $T + 1$ the stock of wealth has therefore been increased by $1 - m_1' - m_1'' - m_2(1 - m_1') = (1 - m_2)(1 - m_1') - m_1''$. Consumption in $T + 2$ is therefore raised by $m_2[(1 - m_2)(1 - m_1') - m_1'']$ and the stock of wealth at the end of $T + 2$ is $(1 - m_2)^2(1 - m_1') - (1 - m_2)m_1''$ greater than it would otherwise have been. In general, the excess wealth at the end of period $T + s$, for $s \geq 1$, is $(1 - m_2)^{s-1}[(1 - m_2)(1 - m_1') - m_1'']$. Thus, after the initial years in which income has a *direct* effect on consumption, wealth continues to increase consumption by an amount that decreases exponentially by a factor of $(1 - m_2)$. The total of all the consumption resulting from a 1-pound increase in income at time T is thus 1 pound; that is,

$$\sum_{t=T}^{\infty} \Delta C_t = \Delta C_T + \Delta C_{T+1} + \sum_{s=1}^{\infty} \Delta C_{T+s+1} = m_1' + [m_1'' + m_2(1 - m_1')]$$
$$+ m_2[(1 - m_2)(1 - m_1') - m_1''] \sum_{s=1}^{\infty} (1 - m_2)^{s-1}$$

$$= m_1' + [m_1'' + m_2(1 - m_1)] + [(1 - m_2)(1 - m_1') - m_1''] = 1.$$

10. This would also be true for each individual in a model of life-cycle savings and no bequests.

sumption in the earlier years.[11] A higher direct propensity to consume thus means a smaller contribution to capital accumulation.[12]

Why should the direct propensities to consume differ? The higher propensity to consume out of disposable labor income than out of nondisposable capital income is implied by both Keynesian and Fisherian theories. The reasons for this difference are familiar and need not be discussed further here.[13] We must, however, consider the reasons for differences in direct propensities to consume out of the different components of capital gains. We may write the real accrued capital gains in each year (G_t) as the sum of two components: the capital gains due to retained earnings[14] (μRE_t) and the change in the real market value of existing assets (X_t); that is, $G_t = \mu RE_t + X_t$. The pure capital gains model imposes the restriction that consumption responds in the same way to both components of G_t. There are, however, two reasons for believing that there are different propensities to consume different components of capital gains and, in particular, for examining a capital gains components model that has a separate propensity to consume for the portion of capital gains that results from retained earnings.

First, investors may view retained earnings as a more dependable and permanent increase in wealth than the capital gains that result from market revaluation of existing assets. Moreover, an increase in retained earnings, especially if induced by a tax change, may be regarded as a good predictor of future changes in retained earnings. If the market revaluation component of capital gains is viewed as more volatile and uncertain than the retained earnings component, it is likely to induce a smaller *direct* response and to be treated more as a component of the stock of wealth. Stated slightly differently, the proportion of the variance of retained earnings that investors deem to be "permanent" is likely to be much greater than the corresponding proportion of the market revaluations. Since the response of consumption to a "permanent" component is faster, the direct propensity to consume will be higher for the retained earnings portion of capital gains.

11. Although the relative weights within each distributed lag provide more precise information, in the current study this is relatively unimportant.

12. Differences among the direct long-run propensities are therefore good measures of the effects on aggregate saving of tax-induced changes in dividend policy.

13. Most of the reasons suggest why propensities to consume may differ for some years but not why there is a permanent difference. Our distinction between direct and total long-run propensities shows that there is nothing inconsistent about unequal "long-run" propensities as conventionally defined.

14. This chapter will not explicitly investigate the link between retained earnings and capital gains; see Nerlove (1968) for strong evidence that retained earnings do significantly increase future share values.

The second reason for expecting different propensities to consume for different components of capital gains is the special nature of the capital gains that result from changes in interest rates. Although a fall in the rate of interest raises the current value of capital assets, it may have an additional effect on the desired allocation of consumption over the life cycle. If the substitution effects dominate income effects, there would be an increase in short-run consumption. In contrast, if the income effect dominates, consumption would fall in the short run. The rate of return effect is therefore ambiguous; it may either increase or depress the coefficient of retained earnings relative to the coefficient of general capital gains.[15]

The net result of these two influences is obviously uncertain. To test the components of gains model we shall include both retained earnings and total accrued capital gains in the consumption function. Note that we need not subtract an estimate of the retained earnings component from other capital gains in order to test our hypothesis. The coefficient of retained earnings represents the *excess* effect of retained earnings; if it significantly exceeds zero, we shall conclude that retained earnings have a larger effect on consumption than other components of capital gains.

There is little previous empirical study of the effects of capital gains or retained earnings on consumption. The only previous attempts to assess the marginal propensity to consume capital gains are the studies of Arena (1964) and Bhatia (1971). Arena added accrued capital gains (G_t) to our Eq. (1) and estimated the coefficients with annual data for the United States for 1946 through 1968. His basic estimates were:

$$C_t = 114 + 0.52 \ YD_t + 0.052 \ W_{t-1} + 0.015 \ G_t,$$
$$(76) \quad (0.13) \quad\quad (0.018) \quad\quad\quad (0.015) \quad\quad\quad\quad (6)$$

$$R^2 = 0.995$$

where YD_t is disposable personal income; standard errors are shown in parentheses. Arena notes that the coefficient of G_t is not significantly different from zero or from the coefficient of W_{t-1}. Despite these inconclusive results, it is clear that capital gains did not have a large impact on the

15. It would in principle be possible to take this into account explicitly by including the rate of return among the explanatory variables. We have been deterred from trying this by the difficulty of measuring the relevant variable: a return for the relevant holding period and the approximate mix of assets, net of tax and adjusted for expected inflation. Previous attempts to include some rate of return in the consumption function have generally been unsuccessful. Depending on particular variables and functional form, the coefficient is insignificant (for example, Suits 1969), significantly positive (for example, Weber 1970) or significantly negative (for example, Wright 1969). None of these estimates used a real rate of return; see Feldstein (1970).

order of magnitude of the effect of disposable income. Bhatia (1971) improved Arena's specification by allowing YD and G to influence consumption in a distributed lag model through "expected disposable income" and "expected capital gains" series that were constructed using different geometric lag parameters. The estimated coefficient of the capital gains variable was extremely small, negative, and with a t-statistic less than one.[16]

Taken at face value, these results are consistent with the Keynesian view that there is a high marginal propensity to consume disposable capital income but that the accrued capital gains that result from retained earnings only affect consumption through the small propensity to consume previous accumulated wealth. These results must, however, be treated with caution. Arena's specification implies that the direct effects of YD and G are immediate, contrary to the now well established view that consumption responds to income variations with a lag. Bhatia's exclusion of wealth is a source of indeterminate bias in the coefficients of capital gains and income. Both samples are relatively short and, because they are limited to postwar United States experience, do not reflect the results of substantial variations in the equilibrium ratio of dividends to profits.

There is even less previous evidence of the effect of retained earnings on consumption behavior. Denison (1958) provided some support for the capital income hypothesis by noting that in the United States in ten high-employment years (1929 and 1948–1956) there was little variation in the ratio of total private savings to GNP despite changes in company saving behavior, and less than in the ratio of personal savings to personal income. Although this does suggest that individuals consider personal and corporate savings as substitutes, the small size of the sample, lack of formal structure of the analysis, and absence of significant structural change in company dividend policy all imply, as Denison himself insisted, that this inference must be treated with substantial caution. Modigliani (1970) has recently examined international differences in savings rates and noted that, ceteris paribus, the ratio of private savings to income is not significantly related to the ratio of corporate savings to income. Nevertheless, the coefficient of the corporate savings variable was always

16. Unfortunately, Bhatia did not include a wealth variable in this specification. Although the effect on the coefficient of the capital gains variable is indeterminate, it would most likely be positive. In an alternative specification, Bhatia related consumption to labor income and to a single composite wealth variable that included both wealth and a distributed lag on capital gains. Although he concluded from the significant positive coefficient of this variable that accrued capital gains do influence consumption, this analysis provides no estimate of an effect of capital gains other than as a component of wealth.

positive with values between 0.20 (S.E. 0.32) and 0.48 (S.E. 0.35). Modigliani stressed the lack of statistical significance and therefore noted that the data are not in conflict with the life-cycle hypothesis but concluded more agnostically that "no clear-cut conclusion can be reached from our data" (p.221).

Fortunately the evidence that we have analyzed provides a richer source of data for studying this problem. By using the British postwar experience, we can examine a period in which the relative sizes of retained earnings and dividends were varying in response to tax incentives. We thus have substantial variation in the explanatory variables without the special problems that accompany international comparisons.

Dynamic Specification and Estimation

There is nevertheless a limit to the amount that can be learned from our relatively small sample of annual observations. We cannot hope to obtain precise estimates of the several propensities to consume and the time profile of each response. Although we have tried not to be too restrictive in considering different dynamic specifications, it is necessary to restrict the lag patterns in order to limit the number of parameters to be estimated. This section discusses the dynamic specifications that we have used and describes our method of constrained instrumental variable estimation.

One of the best established facts about consumption behavior is that consumer expenditure responds to changes in disposable income with a lag. All of our specifications use the Pascal lag distribution (Solow 1960) to represent this response. The Pascal distributions imply a rich variety of lag forms including, of course, the exponential model implied by the adaptive expectations assumption used by Friedman (1957) and others. Using a Pascal distribution permits a computationally convenient way to represent relatively long mean lags without sacrificing a substantial number of observations; we return to this below.

It is not clear what dynamic forms of response of consumption to the components of capital gains might be expected. The traditional theories that exclude current capital gains and do not distinguish past capital gains from the total stock of wealth imply that capital gains have no immediate effect but then influence consumption over a long period with an impact that decreases exponentially with time.[17] We retain the lagged wealth variable in all of our specifications and therefore imply this long exponential lag in addition to any explicit lag on the capital gains variables

---

17. See the previous section.

themselves. If we include only the current value of capital gains and no lagged values, we implicitly assume that there is a concurrent effect followed by a long exponential lag. For the components of capital gains model this specification is (where L is the lag operator, $L \, x_t = x_{t-1}$):[18]

$$C_t = \beta_0 + \beta_1 \frac{(1 - \lambda)^r}{(1 - \lambda L)^r} \, YD_t + \beta_2 W_{t-1} + \beta_3 G_t + \beta_4 RE_t. \tag{7}$$

We shall also relax this restriction on the lags of the capital gains variables. Although in principle the lag responses to YD, G, and RE could involve three different lag coefficients (λ's) and three different orders (r's), we are forced by the size of our sample to consider more limited generalizations of Eq. (7). First, we shall always assume that all the Pascal lags are of the same order (or that a variable responds with no lag). Second, for $r > 1$ we constrain all the λ's to be equal.[19] For the exponential lag case ($r = 1$), however, we do not impose this restriction.

Because of our relatively small sample, we use the autoregressive form of the Pascal distribution for estimation.[20] We multiply the basic specifications by the appropriate lag operator variables to obtain an autoregressive form with lagged dependent and explanatory variables but no Pascal variables. For example, with a second-order Pascal lag, Eq. (7) becomes

$$C_t = \beta_0(1 - \lambda)^2 + \beta_1(1 - \lambda)^2 \, YD_t + \beta_2 W_{t-1} - 2\lambda\beta_2 W_{t-2} + \lambda^2\beta_2 W_{t-3}$$
$$+ \beta_3 G_t - 2\lambda\beta_3 G_{t-1} + \lambda^2\beta_3 G_{t-2} + \beta_4 RE_t + \lambda^2\beta_4 RE_{t-1}$$
$$- 2\lambda\beta_4 RE_{t-2} + 2\lambda C_{t-1} - \lambda^2 C_{t-2}. \tag{8}$$

Estimating the parameters of an equation like (8) raises two problems. First, the basic parameters are overidentified; there are thirteen coefficients but only six basic parameters (λ and five β's). By imposing the identifying restrictions instead of estimating thirteen unconstrained coef-

18. Although this implies an infinite lag for the direct effect of YD, the actual mean lag is so short that the interpretation suggested in the previous section remains valid.

19. In practice, the residual sum of squares implies that $r = 1$ is preferable to $r = 2$, and we therefore do not consider values higher than $r = 2$.

20. With a large sample, the most desirable way to estimate the parameters of an equation with Pascal lag variables is to construct the Pascal variables explicitly for alternative values of the λ's, calculate the least squares estimates of the corresponding regression coefficients, and select the set of λ's that minimizes the sum of squared residuals. These λ's and the associated regression coefficients are consistent and, if the disturbances are normally distributed and serially independent, are maximum likelihood estimators. Unfortunately, this method requires the loss of a substantial number of observations at the beginning of the sample period.

ficients, we obtain more efficient estimates of the basic parameters. This gain in efficiency is particularly important because of the small size of our sample. The parameter estimates are obtained by minimizing the residual sum of squares with respect to the values of λ and the β's.[21] If the disturbances were serially independent, this would provide consistent estimates of all the parameters.

The second problem in estimating the autoregressive form of the Pascal distribution is that the presence of the lagged dependent variable implies that least squares estimates are biased and inconsistent if the disturbances are serially correlated. If we ignore the identifying restrictions, consistent estimates of all the parameters can be obtained even in the presence of serially correlated disturbances by using instrumental variables instead of ordinary least squares and excluding the lagged dependent variables from the set of instruments. This is equivalent to replacing C_{t-1} and C_{t-2} in Eq. (8) by their fitted values in the regression of these variables on the other variables of Eq. (8) plus additional instrumental variables.[22] We follow Liviatan's suggestion (1963) and use lagged values of the other explanatory variables as instruments.[23] Applying the method of constrained least squares described in the previous paragraph does not affect the consistency of the instrumental variable procedure. Our estimates are therefore consistent and obtain increased efficiency by employing the identifying restrictions of the Pascal distribution.

The estimates are based on annual data for the period 1948 through 1969. All of the variables are per capita values, deflated by the consumer price index to obtain 1963 pounds. The dependent variable is consumers' expenditure as reported in the national income accounts. The retained earnings variable is based on the gross company savings reported in the

21. When there is only one lag parameter (λ) and a fixed order of the lag distribution (r), the minimization is achieved by combining ordinary least squares with a golden section search on λ. We are grateful to William Raduchel for this regression program. Since r takes only integer values, the estimation is repeated for different r's to select the one that minimizes the SSR. When there is more than one different λ, we combine the above procedure with an explicit search with respect to the second λ at intervals of 0.05.

22. The standard errors obtained in this way are slightly different from the values that would be obtained by using the parameter estimates with C_{t-1} and C_{t-2} to obtain the residual sum of squares. The difference is so very small that we have not recomputed the standard errors.

23. The fitted values of C_{t-1} and C_{t-2} are linear combinations of the variables in Eq. (8) plus YD_{t-1} and YD_{t-2}. This ignores the potential simultaneous equations bias that results from the endogeneity of the other explanatory variables, particularly YD. We have examined some estimates in which income and its lagged values are excluded from the instrument set which is expanded to include government expenditure, exports, a time trend, and lagged values of these variables. The estimates were essentially unchanged.

national income accounts; several relatively minor adjustments, reflecting the treatment of investment grants and company reserves, have been made in order to obtain a more appropriate series.[24] Household wealth is defined as the current market value of the fixed and financial assets of the personal sector. The series was constructed by using Revell's (1967) estimated net worth of the personal sector in 1958 as a benchmark, adding the year-to-year changes in net wealth for the entire period, and deflating by the consumer price index.[25] Constant dollar capital gains are defined as the annual increment to wealth minus personal savings. Dividends refer to total dividends of companies but exclude dividends of public corporations.

The Pure Capital Gains Model

All of our estimates of the pure capital gains model imply that current accrued gains do have a significant effect on consumption but that that effect is approximately the same as the subsequent wealth effect. There is no evidence of an additional distributed lag on capital gains other than that implied by the wealth variable itself. In short, accrued capital gains matter, but only as a component of wealth. These estimates would suggest that a tax-induced reduction in dividends leads to a relatively large increase in total private saving. Nevertheless, any such conclusion must await analysis of the separate components of capital gains in the next section.

Equation (9) presents the basic estimates for the pure capital gains model using the exponential form of the first dynamic specification. The coefficient of the income variable is written as the product of the long-run direct marginal propensity to consume and the estimated lag operator. Es-

24. It would be useful to examine the effect of subtracting a measure of depreciation to obtain a net savings variable. Our choice of the gross definition is partly a reflection of the inadequacies of the available depreciation series. We are also influenced by Brittain's finding (1966) that United States companies appear to base dividends on gross cash flow and not on cash flow net of capital consumption allowances. My estimates for the United Kingdom (Chapter 4) seem to support this, but the difference is not substantial.

25. The annual increment to personal sector wealth is the sum of (1) savings net of depreciation and of the excess of capital taxes minus capital transfers; (2) appreciation of fixed assets owned by the personal sector; (3) the net change in the market value of equities due to changes in the price of equities, that is, excluding net new issues; and (4) the net change in the market value of government bonds due to changes in the price of bonds, that is, excluding net new issues. The estimated series for 1947 through 1969 in millions of current pounds is: 57,834; 55,923; 54,878; 55,081; 52,964; 53,504; 57,102; 59,944; 59,020; 59,333; 59,398; 63,883; 71,823; 76,677; 76,713; 79,913; 85,443; 86,008; 86,138; 90,485; 104,748; 118,513; 115,685.

timated approximate standard errors are shown in parentheses. Since all of the equations in this chapter have very high multiple correlation coefficients ($R^2 > 0.99$), only the sum of squared residuals is presented for comparing equations.

$$C_t = 24.5 + 0.781 \cdot \frac{0.64}{1 - 0.36\,L}\, YD_t + 0.019\,G_t + 0.016\,W_{t-1}.$$
$$\quad (6.5)\quad (0.017) \qquad\qquad\qquad (0.008)\quad\;\; (0.008) \qquad (9)$$

$$SSR = 81.24$$

The coefficients of disposable income and wealth are consistent with previous estimates. Although the constant term is statistically significant, it is less than 8 percent of mean per capita consumption. The estimated lag parameter ($\lambda = 0.36$) is relatively short, but this reflects the presence of the wealth variable. The most important feature of the equation is that the coefficient of accrued gains is significantly positive but very close to, and not significantly different from, the coefficient of the wealth variable. This supports Arena's conclusion (1964) and thus the original Ando-Modigliani specification. The current results are actually stronger than Arena's since the similarity of the two coefficients is established not merely by a large standard error on the coefficient of G_t; the coefficient of G_t as well as of W_{t-1} is significantly different from zero.

More general dynamic specifications do not alter these conclusions. If a second-order Pascal distribution is used for the income variable, the consumption propensities and standard errors remain essentially unchanged (none varies more than 0.01) and the lag parameter ($\hat{\lambda} = 0.20$) implies approximately the same mean lag. The sum of squared residuals ($SSR = 81.85$) is higher than for Eq. (9); the simple exponential lag is therefore preferable to higher-order lag distributions.

As an alternative more general lag structure, separate first-order lag distributions for disposable income and capital gains were estimated.[26] The propensities to consume are nearly unchanged from Eq. (9); if anything the results suggest a slightly higher long-run direct propensity to consume out of G_t (0.024) but still approximately the same as the coefficient of wealth (0.017). The lag coefficient for income is almost identical to the estimate of Eq. (9). The lag coefficient of G_t is very small; the implied mean lag is only 0.2 years. These estimates therefore suggest that the more general specification is not preferable to the simpler specification of (9). This

26. The value of the lag parameter for income is determined to the nearest 0.05. See note 21.

is supported by an approximate likelihood ratio test. In large samples, a likelihood ratio test of the restriction that there is no distributed lag for G_t (that is, $\lambda_2 = 0$) can be based on the fact that, on the null hypothesis, minus twice the log of the likelihood ratio is distributed as χ^2 with one degree of freedom. The test statistic is therefore:

$$-2 \ln[SSR \, (\lambda_2 = \hat{\lambda}_2)/SSR \, (\lambda_2 = 0)]^{N/2} = 1.7.$$

Since the critical value of $\chi^2(1)$ for $p = 0.10$ is 2.7, the test supports the conclusion that the distributed lag on G_t can be ignored.

The specification of the distributed lag for G_t is not crucial to the inference about the long-run direct consumption propensities. If the exponential lag coefficient is constrained to be the same for YD_t and G_t, the resulting estimate leaves the previous conclusions unaltered. Using the same second-order Pascal distribution for both YD_t and G_t also has no effect on the coefficient estimates but has a slightly higher sum of squared residuals.

Separating dividend income from total disposable income does not change these conclusions about accrued gains. To avoid the intractable problem of defining disposable dividends, we leave disposable income unchanged and add gross dividends (D_t) to the equation.

$$C_t = 0.86 \frac{0.65}{1 - 0.35L} YD_t + 0.021 \frac{0.87}{1 - 0.13L} G_t$$
$$(0.11) \qquad\qquad\qquad (0.009)$$
$$+ 0.020 \, W_{t-1} - 0.42 \, D_t + 10.45.$$
$$(0.009) \qquad (0.53) \tag{10}$$

$$SSR = 71.72$$

The coefficient of dividends is smaller than its standard error, and its introduction has no effect on the coefficient of G_t.

The estimates in this section are unambiguous: total accrued capital gains have a significant but small effect on concurrent consumption. This suggests that a tax-induced increase in company savings would have no offsetting effect on personal savings. To assess this more carefully we now turn to the more general specification in which the effect of the retained earnings component is distinguished from the effect of total accrued gains.

The Components of Capital Gains Model

All of the estimates in the current section indicate that the retained earnings component of capital gains has a much larger effect on consumption than the other components of capital gains. The estimated direct marginal propensity to consume retained earnings is approximately 0.25. Because of the difference in tax treatments of retained earnings and dividends, the difference between 0.25 and the marginal propensity to consume disposable income (approximately 0.77) substantially overstates the effect on consumption of substituting retained earnings for dividends. A tax-induced reduction in dividends and increase in company savings therefore raises total private saving much less than is suggested by either the traditional Keynesian model or the estimates of the previous section. The current section concentrates on reporting the parameter values for different dynamic specifications. The next section develops a more specific estimate of the effect of the tax policy and the implications for the capital income hypothesis.

Equation (11) extends the basic consumption function to include retained earnings.

$$C_t = 17.8 + 0.77 \frac{0.55}{1 - 0.45L} YD_t + 0.019\, G_t + 0.254\, RE_t$$
$$\quad (5.6) \quad (0.02) \qquad\qquad\qquad (0.007) \qquad (0.127)$$
$$+ 0.017\, W_{t-1}.$$
$$(0.008) \tag{11}$$

$$SSR = 65.66$$

The addition of the new variables leaves the coefficients of all the original variables unchanged. The constant term is smaller and the lag coefficient implies a slower adjustment. The estimated total direct effect of retained earnings on concurrent consumption, that is, the sum of the retained earnings coefficient and some fraction of the capital gains coefficient (the fraction being the concurrent effect of retained earnings on capital gains), exceeds 0.25. The estimates thus indicate strong support for the hypothesis that capital income, whether distributed or not, has a substantial effect on concurrent consumption.

Alternative dynamic specifications do not change these basic results. A higher-order Pascal distribution for the income variable is a slightly inferior specification ($SSR = 68.75$) but yields approximately the same coefficients for retained earnings (0.23), accrued gains (0.016), and the other variables.

All of our attempts to estimate separate lag distributions for the capital gains components indicate that there is no distributed lag in the effect of the gains components other than the exponential lag implied by the wealth variable. For example, when the specification provides for the same lag for RE_t as for G_t and a different lag for YD_t we obtain:

$$C_t = 17.7 + 0.77 \frac{0.55}{1 - 0.45L} YD_t + 0.017 \frac{0.984}{1 - 0.016L} G_t$$
$$\quad (5.6) \quad (0.02) \qquad\qquad\qquad (0.008)$$

$$+ 0.247 \frac{0.984}{1 - 0.016L} RE_t + 0.020\ W_{t-1}.$$
$$\quad (0.130) \qquad\qquad\qquad (0.007) \qquad\qquad\qquad\qquad (12)$$

$$SSR = 65.78$$

The lag coefficient ($\hat{\lambda}_2 = 0.016$) is the smallest positive value considered in the search procedure; the fact that the sum of squared residuals slightly exceeds that for Eq. (11) implies that $\hat{\lambda}_2 = 0$ would be a preferable specification. Similar results are obtained when the lag coefficient of either G_t or RE_t is constrained to zero and separate lag coefficients are estimated for the other variable and for disposable income.

The long-run direct consumption propensities are not very sensitive to the choice of dynamic specification. If, for example, all three income variables (YS_t, G_t, and RE_t) are required to have the same distributed lag coefficient, the estimates are

$$C_t = 23.2 + 0.76 \frac{0.57}{1 - 0.43L} YD_t + 0.037 \frac{0.57}{1 - 0.43L} G_t$$
$$\quad (5.9) \quad (0.02) \qquad\qquad\qquad (0.012)$$

$$+ 0.25 \frac{0.57}{1 - 0.43L} RE_t + 0.014\ W_{t-1}.$$
$$\quad (0.20) \qquad\qquad\qquad (0.007) \qquad\qquad\qquad\qquad (13)$$

$$SSR = 67.47$$

When gross dividend income is added as an additional variable (with net dividends still included in disposable income), its coefficient is not significantly different from zero and the other coefficients are essentially unchanged:

$$C_t = 1.05 + 0.89\frac{0.53}{1 - 0.47L}\ YD_t + 0.0165\ G_t + 0.278\ RE_t$$
$$(14.78)\ \ (0.10) \hspace{3.5cm} (0.0076) \hspace{0.7cm} (0.127)$$
$$-\ 0.607\ D_t + 0.021\ W_{t-1}.$$
$$(0.525) \hspace{0.8cm} (0.009) \hspace{5cm} (14)$$

$$SSR\ =\ 59.70$$

The negative sign of the dividend coefficient implies that the propensity to consume dividends is lower than for other income. The specific point estimate of -0.6 suggests a marginal propensity to consume dividends of approximately zero,[27] the value implied by the pure Fisherian or life-cycle theory. The very large standard error is a warning against imposing such an interpretation. The implied marginal propensity to consume dividends is not significantly different from both the marginal propensity to consume retained earnings and the marginal propensity to consume other disposable income.

A variety of other specifications that will not be reported here, including a redefinition of income to exclude dividends, continue to support the basic estimates of Eq. (11): while capital gains in general have a significant but small effect on concurrent consumption, the marginal propensity to consume the retained earnings component of capital gains is very much larger. The components of capital gains model is the better specification of the capital income hypothesis and suggests quite different effects of tax policy than the pure capital gains model.[28] These implications are the subject of the next section.

Implications and Conclusions

The results of this study suggest a significant respecification of consumer behavior and an important reevaluation of the use of tax incentives to increase company saving. Our evidence supports the capital income hypothesis: capital income, including retained earnings as well as dividends, has a substantial effect on concurrent consumption. More specifically, the estimates favor the components of capital gains model.

27. Since a 1-pound increase in gross dividends provides approximately 0.6 pound of disposable income, the total effect on consumption implied by Eq. (4) is 0.89 (0.6 pound) − 0.607(1 pound) = −0.073 pound.

28. After this chapter was written, an analogous study using U.S. data for 1929–1966 was completed. The results, reported in Chapter 6, are very similar to those reported here for Britain.

Although accrued capital gains in general increase concurrent consumption, their effect is small and approximately the same as the effect of the stock of wealth. In contrast, the retained earnings component has a much larger short-run effect than do the capital gains that result solely from changes in the market value of existing assets. Because retained earnings depress personal savings in this way, tax policies that reduce dividends have a relatively small effect on total private savings.

To evaluate the effect of tax policies that induce firms to substitute retained earnings for dividends, consider the direct impact of a change in tax structure that leaves total tax receipts unchanged. A 1-pound increase in retained earnings is therefore accompanied by a 1-pound decrease in net (disposable) dividends. The additional capital accumulation is the net excess of the increased retained earnings (1 pound) minus the decreased personal saving. An equivalent and more direct measure of additional capital accumulation is the decrease in personal consumption expenditures.[29]

Equation (11) provides a specific basis for estimating the effect on consumption of such a change in company dividends and retained earnings. The effect of the increased retained earnings is to increase consumption by 0.254 plus the product of 0.019 and the impact of retained earnings on accrued capital gains. A pound of retained earnings can be expected to increase accrued gains by some amount less than 1 pound, the exact difference reflecting expected future returns and taxes on the retained earnings. Since the coefficient of accrued gains is itself quite small (0.019), our ability to assess the effect of retained earnings on accrued gains is not a source of serious error. We can conclude that the effect of an addition of 1 pound of retained earnings raises consumption by approximately 0.27 pound.

The estimated long-run direct marginal propensity to consume disposable income, 0.77, is a weighted average of the propensities of different individuals and for different components of disposable income. Several previous studies with U.S. data have estimated that the propensity to consume dividend income is less than the overall propensity to consume (for example, Klein and Goldberger 1955; Holbrook and Stafford 1971). Equation (14) also suggests a lower consumption propensity for dividends (although the difference is not statistically significant). We shall therefore consider the implications of marginal propensities to consume dividends

---

29. There are, of course, also further effects in future years. The increased retained earnings raises wealth and therefore depresses future savings. It also raises future capital income from which additional savings flow.

between a high value of 0.77 and a low value of half that, 0.39.[30] The high marginal propensity implies that the tax change reduces consumption by 0.50 pound (that is, 0.77 pound − 0.27 pound) while the low marginal propensity to consume implies that the tax change reduces consumption by only 0.12 pound (that is, 0.39 pound − 0.27 pound).

Tax policies that raise retained earnings therefore increase total private savings by a substantially smaller amount. Fifty percent should be regarded as a high estimate of the increased total saving relative to increased retained earnings. An effect as small as 10 or 15 percent is also quite plausible.[31]

Differential taxation that favors retained earnings is also a potential source of significant inefficiencies and inequities that must be balanced against the relatively small gain in total savings. A study of the magnitudes of these distortions and of the net effect of differential taxation on aggregate income and its distribution would be of great value.

30. We shall ignore the fact that even the full long-run direct response only occurs with a lag.

31. Retained earnings were defined as gross of depreciation and therefore represent an inaccurate measure of true retained earnings. The coefficient (0.27) is thus likely to be biased downward. A correction for this would further lower the estimated effect of the tax on capital accumulation.

8 Corporate Tax Integration: The Estimated Effects on Capital Accumulation and Tax Distribution of Two Integration Proposals

This chapter examines the effects of complete integration of the corporate and personal income taxes and of a modified partial integration proposal that involves no loss of revenue. More specifically, the "no revenue loss" proposal combines a sharp reduction in the corporate tax rate with integration of the remainder in a way that keeps the total tax on corporate source income unchanged. New microeconomic simulations and previously reported econometric parameter estimates are used to calculate how each proposal would change the aggregate accumulation of capital and the distribution of tax burdens among income levels.[1]

The first section emphasizes that either type of reform would be likely to improve the efficiency of our capital markets, thereby increasing national income and economic well-being. There are four separate ways in which complete integration would increase economic efficiency. Only two of these are relevant if integration is constrained to keep the same total tax burden on the corporate sector.

The second section examines the effect of corporate tax integration on private saving and thus aggregate capital accumulation. Although corporate tax integration has been widely advocated as a means of increasing capital accumulation, there is little or no evidence to support this claim. The analysis presented in the second section shows that integration may be as likely to reduce saving as to increase saving.

Either reform would have the effect of increasing the overall progressi-

This chapter was written with Daniel Frisch. Reprinted with permission from the *National Tax Journal* 30 (March 1977), pp. 37–52. The chapter reports the basic results of a study of corporate tax integration sponsored by the Tax Foundation.

1. For previous discussions of corporate tax integration, see Break (1969), Break and Pechman (1975), and McLure (1976).

vity of the tax system. The third and fourth sections show that the relative tax reductions for low- and middle-income taxpayers would be quite substantial and that high-income taxpayers would pay a greater tax.

Before turning to these sections, it is important to describe the two specific reform proposals that will be discussed. Complete integration is equivalent to treating corporations like partnerships. Corporate profits are included in the individual's taxable income, regardless of whether they are paid out as dividends or retained by the corporation. The corporate income tax as such is completely eliminated. Tax credits are also passed through to individuals.

Corporations might be required to withhold personal income tax at a common rate for all shareholders and remit this tax to the Treasury on behalf of the shareholder. For example, corporations could continue to remit to the Treasury the same payments that they currently do under the corporate income tax, but the individual shareholders would be credited with their proportionate shares of the corporations' tax payments and credits. Individuals with high marginal personal income tax rates would have further payments to make on their corporate income while those with low tax rates could either use the excess withholding to offset other tax liabilities or claim a refund. In this way, integration could easily be limited to individual taxpayers only (that is, excluding pension funds and other fiduciaries, charitable organizations, foreign nationals, and other shareholders not subject to the ordinary U.S. personal income tax provisions) by continuing to withhold the current corporate income tax and allowing a credit only to individual taxpayers. In general, our analysis will assume that integration is limited to individuals in this way, although the discussion in the first section will deal with both possibilities.

A great many different types of *partial* integration methods are possible. The partial integration method analyzed in this chapter has three important features: (1) there is no net revenue cost to the change, (2) the tax burden on corporate source income remains unchanged, and (3) the new rule applies only to individual taxpayers and not to fiduciaries, charities, and so on. These features are achieved by reducing the corporate income tax rate to 15 percent from its current 48 percent and treating all of the after-corporate-tax income on a partnership basis. More specifically, corporations continue to pay tax just as they do now. For nonindividual shareholders, there are no further changes. For individuals, tax payments equivalent to 15 percent of profits are regarded as a corporate profits tax; the remaining tax payments are credited to these shareholders in proportion to their share ownership. The individual shareholders also include in their taxable income their share of the corporate profits in excess of the 15 percent tax. Individuals thus pay more tax on this corporate source income if they have a high tax rate and receive a rebate or a credit to offset other liabilities if they have a low tax rate. The corporate tax rate of 15 percent has been selected because, together with the other rules, it keeps the total tax revenue and the total tax burden on corporate source income approximately unchanged.[2] For reasons that will be clear in the next section, this method of partial integration can be regarded as a move in the direction of complete integration that preserves much of the status quo and thereby has more limited advantages than full integration.

Integration and Capital Market Efficiency

Complete integration of the corporate and personal income taxes would reduce or eliminate four distortions that currently reduce the efficiency of our capital markets and our economy. These inefficiencies represent the major misallocations of productive resources that are caused by our current corporate tax system. Eliminating these distortions would produce a permanent gain in the real value of national income and in the level of economic well-being. In this section we review these distortions and indicate how they would be reduced or eliminated by integration.

The Distortion between Corporate and Noncorporate Activities

Investors divide the available capital stock between corporate and noncorporate activities until the *net-of-tax* rates of return are equalized. A higher rate of tax on corporate source income therefore distorts the allocation of resources toward the noncorporate sector.[3] At the margin, an extra dollar of capital in the corporate sector has a higher before-tax rate of return than an extra dollar of capital in the noncorporate sector. Transferring capital from the noncorporate sector to the corporate sector would therefore raise total real national income. The current tax-induced distortion in favor of noncorporate activities thus represents a pure waste of potential national income.

Stated somewhat differently, the corporation income tax reduces real incomes by more than the amount of revenue that it transfers to the gov-

2. For 1973, the total tax burden on corporate income is reduced by $1.0 billion, less than 2 percent of the combined corporate and personal taxes on corporate income.

3. The relative tax rates on corporate and noncorporate income reflect not only the corporation income tax but also the method of taxing capital gains and the magnitude of real property taxes. See Harberger (1966).

ernment. Arnold Harberger has estimated that the tax-induced misallocation of the capital stock creates a waste equal to 0.5 percent of national income, or currently about $8 billion. This pure waste is equivalent to
throwing away more than 10 percent of total corporate tax revenue.[4]

It is important to realize that this waste or "excess burden" of the corporate income tax does not depend on *who* ultimately bears the burden of
the tax.[5] It is now well understood that the net-of-tax rate of return to capital in all uses will be equalized. It is generally also understood that the
real incomes of labor as well as of capital owners may fall because of the
corporate income tax. This redistribution or shifting of the burden of the
tax does not alter the fundamental fact that the *before-tax* rates of return
in corporate activities will remain higher than the *before-tax* rate of return
in unincorporated activities. The source of the waste or excess burden is
therefore independent of how *net-after-tax* incomes are altered.

Complete integration of the corporation tax would eliminate this source
of excess burden only if all other special ways of taxing capital income
(for example, property taxes on structures but not equipment) were also
eliminated. An exact assessment of the gain from complete integration
without any other changes is therefore not possible. Moreover, integration would require increasing some alternative tax, which would be a new
source of waste. However, even with variable supplies of labor and capital this excess burden is likely to be much less than the excess burden that
would be eliminated by integration. It seems reasonable to conclude that
the reallocation of capital that would be induced by complete integration
would eliminate an excess burden of between $4 billion and $6 billion at
1976 levels of income and capital.[6]

Partial integration of the type that keeps the total tax burden on corporate income constant will not have any appreciable effect on this source

4. This calculation refers only to the misallocation between corporate and noncorporate
activities. The extra waste due to the distortion between present and future consumption
and to misallocation within the corporate sector is discussed below. Shoven (1976) has recently pointed out some arithmetical and conceptual errors in the Harberger analysis but
noted that these errors approximately cancel each other, leaving Harberger's estimate essentially unchanged. Shoven also shows that with a more disaggregated analysis, the estimated loss is even greater.

5. Economists have long used the term "excess burden" to refer to the pure waste, the
excess of total loss of real income over the revenue received by the government. The use of
the term "excess burden" by Break and Pechman (1975) is unconventional and should not
be confused with the current concept.

6. Since capital can only be redeployed slowly, it would take some years before the full
efficiency gain is realized. Of course, the potential gain would grow with the economy and
the size of the capital stock.

of inefficiency. The distortion is reduced for taxpayers with low marginal tax rates but increased for those with high marginal rates.[7]

Note finally that complete integration eliminates the distortion between corporate and noncorporate investment only if the integration is extended to pensions, charities, and other shareholders that are not subject to the income tax. If it is felt that this constitutes too much of a tax reduction for "nontaxable" shareholders, their *total* capital income should be made subject to a new tax. The important point is that the tax should be on their capital income from *all* sources, not just from corporations. The current method of taxing only part of the income of "tax-exempt" institutions is an unnecessary source of inefficiency.

The Distortion between Future Consumption and Present Consumption

Because the extra taxation on corporate income is ultimately borne by all capital, its effect is to lower the net return to all savings.[8] This raises the cost of retirement consumption and distorts households' choices in favor of current consumption. The efficiency loss of excess burden associated with this distortion is likely to be of the same order of magnitude as the waste due to the misallocation of capital between the two sectors.[9]

To avoid confusion, it is important to emphasize that this loss of efficiency does not depend on an assumption that a higher net rate of return would increase savings. If the saving rate is completely insensitive to the net rate of return, the reduced tax on capital income implied by complete integration would eliminate a welfare loss of approximately $7 billion at 1976 levels of income and savings.[10]

Any form of partial integration that lowers the total rate of tax on capital income will reduce the distortion in favor of current consumption. The particular partial integration method described above maintains the same

---

7. There are, of course, other forms of partial integration that lower the effective rate of tax on corporate income and therefore reduce the inefficiency from this source. Feldstein (1975) discusses the advantage in this regard of the 1975 Treasury integration proposal.

8. It is possible but very unlikely that the corporation tax is shifted by more than 100 percent, that is, that the rate of return on all capital is actually raised by the corporation tax; see Harberger (1962) and Chapter 19 of the present work. This possibility is ignored in the current discussion.

9. See Feldstein (1978b) for a discussion of the measurement of this loss and an estimate indicating that the loss is of the same order of magnitude.

10. See Feldstein (1978b). The potential welfare gain is larger if integration would increase savings. This calculation also assumes that the entire reduction in the tax on corporate source income is financed by raising taxes on noncapital income.

tax burden on capital income and therefore has no ability to limit this source of inefficiency.

The Distortion between Dividends and Retained Earnings

Because the current tax system induces corporations to reduce dividends and increase retained earnings, investment is encouraged in established companies with internally generated savings and is discouraged in new companies that must go to the capital market for funds. Moreover, an investment that is worthwhile when it can be financed by retained earnings (thus avoiding the personal income tax) might not be worthwhile if it had to be financed with after-tax dollars. This introduces a further source of misallocation of capital within the corporate sector. Although it is difficult to quantify the magnitude of the loss that results from this distortion against external finance, it could be as large or larger than the losses resulting from the distortions described in the two previous sections.

Under the current tax system, the opportunity cost of one dollar of retained earnings is 68 cents of net after-tax dividends available for spending by shareholders.[11] In contrast, with either complete integration or the partial integration described above, the amount of tax is unaffected by the division between dividends and retained earnings. The opportunity cost of one dollar of retained earnings is one dollar of net spendable dividends. Thus, partial as well as total integration can eliminate the current distortion in corporate dividend policy.[12]

The Distortion between Equity Finance and Debt Finance

In the decade from 1964 to 1974, corporate debt rose 206 percent while corporate profits rose only 11 percent. The concurrent rise in interest rates implies that the ratio of interest payments to total corporate income has risen very sharply—from about 10 percent in the early 1960s to more than 25 percent now.

It is clear that the tax rule permitting the deduction of interest payments

---

11. This is based on the 40 percent marginal personal tax rate for the 81 percent of dividends paid to taxable shareholders. These figures are discussed in the third section.

12. Note that other partial integration methods may not eliminate this distortion. The 1975 Treasury proposal would actually raise the opportunity cost of retained earnings to about $1.20 of net dividends, thereby encouraging too high a dividend rate and, as a result, an inefficiently excessive reliance on external finance. See Feldstein (1975), p. 186.

but not of dividends provides a substantial incentive for debt finance.[13] The disadvantage of such a high ratio of debt to equity is the increased risk of bankruptcy. This general risk, as well as the actual bankruptcies that do occur, affects not only the individual firm that issues a large quantity of debt but also other firms as well. Since there is no offsetting reason for public policy to favor such debt finance, the corporation tax should be altered to eliminate the distinction between debt and equity finance.

Complete tax integration would achieve the desired goal since there would be no separate corporation tax base from which interest payments are deductible. The partial integration method described above would eliminate most of the incentive that now exists by lowering the rate against which interest payments are deducted from 48 percent to 15 percent.[14]

In short, complete corporate tax integration would increase the efficiency of the capital markets and raise real national income in four different ways. (1) Capital would move from less productive uses in the unincorporated sector to more productive uses in the corporate sector. (2) The higher net rate of return to all capital would reduce the current tax bias against future consumption. (3) An increase in the dividend payout rate would encourage investment by new companies and improve the allocation of capital within the corporate sector. (4) Removing the bias in favor of debt finance would reduce the capital market risks caused by high ratios of debt to equity. Each of these is an important reason for substituting an integrated tax system for our current method of taxing corporate source income.[15]

---

13. The incentive to substitute debt for equity has been present as long as the corporate income tax existed. Why has the debt grown so rapidly in recent years? Some economists argue that firms have simply been slow to take advantage of the tax incentive. An alternative explanation is that the reduction in high personal income tax rates in 1964 and 1965 provided an extra inducement to substitute debt for equity. It might also be noted that high rates of inflation have recently made bond finance particularly attractive; corporate borrowers pay high nominal yields but low or negative real yields and use "call" provisions to protect themselves against a future fall in inflation and interest rates. Finally, since new equity issues are always uncommon, the growth of debt may reflect only the failure of gross retained earnings to keep pace with desired investment financing. Feldstein, Green, and Sheshinski (1978) show that inflation increases the bias in favor of debt finance.

14. Although neutrality between debt and equity finance could also be achieved by eliminating the deduction for interest payments under the current corporation tax, this would exacerbate the first two distortions discussed above. This extra distortion could in turn be eliminated by reducing the corporate tax rate to maintain unchanged corporate tax collections. Alternatively, neutrality could be achieved by allowing dividends paid to be deducted from the corporate tax base; this would probably induce corporations to pay out all profits, thus attaining the same tax effect as complete integration.

15. In two recent papers, Stiglitz (1973, 1977) has discussed an alternative theory of the cor-

The partial integration method that reduces the corporation tax rate to 15 percent and attributes all remaining profits to the personal income of the shareholders would achieve the third and fourth goals but not the first two. It would, however, involve no loss of tax revenue and no change in the overall tax burden on corporate source income. Other partial methods of integration could attain greater success in dealing with all four goals but with different consequences for aggregate tax revenue and its distribution.

Integration and Capital Accumulation

Corporate tax integration has frequently been presented as a method of increasing the nation's rate of capital accumulation.[16] This has been an unfortunate source of confusion. There is in fact no way to know at this time whether integration is more likely to increase or to decrease aggregate capital accumulation. Moreover, for the reasons discussed in the previous section, corporate tax integration is desirable even if it does not increase the rate of saving.

Integration would affect savings in three quite different ways: by changing corporate savings (that is, retained earnings), by altering the net rate of return to savings, and by redistributing the tax burden among individuals with different propensities to save. Each of these will now be examined.

The Change in Corporate Savings

Corporate savings are likely to fall as a result of integration. Under current law, a corporation chooses between keeping an extra dollar of retained earnings and increasing the shareholder's *after-tax* income by substantially less, that is, by one dollar minus the shareholder's marginal tax rate. With either complete integration or the partial integration described above, an extra dollar of retained earnings would involve foregone divi-

---

porate income tax which implies that, under certain conditions, a tax of the current type would involve no adverse distortions. However, the critical assumption of Stiglitz's analysis include: (1) there is no risk in the economy (or all investors are risk-neutral); (2) corporations pay no dividends but retain all after-tax profits; and (3) corporations finance all marginal investments by debt. Feldstein, Green, and Sheshinski (Chapter 21) develop an alternative theoretical analysis that explicitly recognizes uncertainty and the effect of taxes on dividends and on the marginal debt-equity ratio.

16. This was the thrust of the testimony of Treasury Secretary William Simon on July 31, 1975, when he introduced the Treasury's proposal for corporate tax integration.

dends of exactly one dollar. The cost of retained earnings would be substantially increased.[17]

Common sense suggests that such a sharp increase in the cost of retained earnings would cause a reduction in retained earnings and an increase in dividends. This is supported by an examination of changing dividend behavior in the United States. In 1929, when the personal income tax rates were negligible, corporate dividends were more than twice the level of retained earnings. In contrast, during the most recent decade (1966–1975), dividends averaged only 95 percent of retained earnings. This reduction of dividends relative to retained earnings is part of a secular development that John Brittain (1966) has estimated is due to the growing differential between the rates of tax on retained and distributed profits.

In a detailed study of the way that British corporations changed their dividend payout rates in response to changes in the tax law, I found that the payout ratio was quite sensitive to tax-induced changes in the relative cost of dividends and retained earnings (Feldstein 1970).[18] More specifically, each 10 percent increase in the tax-determined opportunity cost of retained earnings in terms of foregone net dividends led to a 9 percent increase in the amount of dividends paid. Although firms adjusted to this new payout policy with some delay, the entire adjustment was essentially completed in about four years.

Consider the implication of this estimate for corporate tax integration. Under current law, a general increase in all dividends would be subject to personal income tax at an effective rate of about 32 percent.[19] The opportunity cost of a dollar of retained earnings is thus currently 68 cents of net dividends. Both forms of integration would raise this opportunity cost to one dollar, an increase of about 47 percent. The estimates in the British study suggest that this 47 percent increase would raise dividends by some

17. The 1975 Treasury proposal for what is effectively a dividend deduction would involve an even greater increase in the cost of retained earnings. For example, for a taxpayer whose marginal rate is less than the corporate tax rate, each dollar of retained earnings would cost more than one dollar of dividends. The "cost" of retained earnings would in fact be nearly doubled at every income level. In this respect, the Treasury's 1975 proposal is significantly less favorable to saving than either complete integration or the partial method discussed in this chapter.

18. See also Chapter 5 and King (1971, 1972).

19. This estimate is based on the 1973 Treasury Tax File and the TAXSIM program described in the next section. Increasing each taxpayer's dividends by 1 percent raised total dividends by $187.3 million and total taxes by $74.1 million. Since 19 percent of dividends (paid to noncorporate shareholders) are not subject to the personal income tax (that is, are paid to pension funds, charitable organizations, and so on), the $187.3 million of dividends corresponds to $230.8 million of total dividends. The effective tax rate is thus $74.1 divided by $230.8 or 32 percent.

42 percent. With 1975 dividends of $33 billion, this represents a dividend increase of $14 billion.

The net impact on company saving would depend on whether integration is accompanied by withholding at the corporate level and how corporations and shareholders responded to this arrangement. Consider the case in which the current level of corporate tax payments is continued under complete integration but treated as a withholding of personal income tax. If dividends rise by $14 billion, corporate retained earnings would fall by an equal amount. Fortunately, such a reduction in corporate saving would be substantially offset by an increase in personal saving. If households adjust their consumption to their *total* after-tax income, whether received in cash or retained by the corporation of which they are shareholders, a reduction in retained earnings and an equal increase in dividends would not change consumption. All of this additional net dividend income would therefore be saved. The increase in personal saving would just offset the reduction in company saving.

Although this is an idealized description of household saving behavior,[20] there is statistical evidence that indicates that households do largely if not fully offset changes in corporate dividend policy. In an econometric study of U.S. saving behavior during the period from 1929 through 1966 (excluding 1942–1947), I found that one dollar of retained earnings adds approximately 25 cents more to total private savings than one dollar of net dividends (see Chapter 6). This is consistent with a study of British postwar experience (Chapter 7) in which Fane and I found that reducing retained earnings by one pound and increasing net dividends by a pound would reduce total private saving by between 0.15 pounds and 0.50 pounds. Using the estimate of a 25 percent reduction in total private savings for every dollar transferred from retained earnings to net dividends implies that the fall in corporate saving of $14 billion would reduce total private saving by about $3.5 billion.

This calculation ignores the effect of any net corporate tax reduction and may therefore be regarded as a more appropriate estimate for the partial integration method than for total integration. It is more difficult to estimate how the increased after-tax income due to complete integration would be divided between dividends and retained earnings.[21] Moreover,

---

20. This idealization ignores the fact that the retained earnings are not directly available for consumption. However, retained earnings can accumulate without paying personal income tax. With the current taxation of capital gains, most of this accumulation avoids all personal taxation.

21. One reasonable assumption would be that these incremental funds would, in equilibrium, be divided in the same proportions as the intramarginal funds.

the total impact on saving would depend on how other taxes are changed to recover the lost revenue.

The Change in the Net Return to Saving

A reduced tax burden on corporate source income would in itself increase the after-tax return that savers receive on all forms of capital income.[22] The net change in savers' after-tax rates of return would of course depend on the way in which the reduction of taxes on corporate source income is financed. As long as some of the substitute tax revenue comes from taxing wage and salary income,[23] the overall effect of integration would be to increase the net after-tax return on all forms of capital income.

But an increase in the net rate of return does not imply that there would be an increase in the rate of savings. Economic theory suggests that a higher net rate of return can either increase or decrease savings.[24] Since so many policy discussions assert that a higher net yield would induce more private saving, it is worthwhile to examine why this may not be true. Consider, for example, a man at age 40 who wishes to save for his retirement at age 65.[25] He now believes that he will obtain an average real after-tax return of 4 percent. For every $100 per year that he saves during the next twenty-five years, he will be able to dissave $357 per year from the time he is 65 until he is 80. In light of this opportunity, he decides to save $1,400 per year and thus have $5,000 of dissaving each year when he is retired.[26]

Now consider what happens if his net rate of return rises from 4 percent to 5 percent. This implies that every $100 per year that is saved from age

22. The analysis of this subsection is limited to the complete tax integration since the partial method described above does not reduce the tax burden on corporate source income.

23. The important distinction here is the type of *income* and not the type of *taxpayer*. For example, if effective tax rates were raised in each income class to keep the tax burden the same for that class, there would be a net substitution of tax on salary and other labor income for some of the reduced tax on capital income.

24. Feldstein and Tsiang (1968) argue that an increase in savings may be more likely, but the analysis is basically inconclusive except for those who are currently nonsavers. For them, an increase in the net return can increase savings or leave savings unchanged but will never decrease saving (or increase borrowing).

25. Although this example will be developed in terms of retirement saving, the same type of ambiguity applies to the other motives for saving, including such things as saving to pay for children's education, the future purchase of a home or of consumer durables, or to have funds available for emergencies.

26. This description of individual choice is of course a stylized representation of the actual process of saving. Some kind of calculation of this sort must implicitly be made if a change in the rate of return is to have any effect.

40 through 64 will "buy" substantially more retirement consumption; more specifically, with a 5 percent return the individual could dissave $440 per year instead of the $357 obtained at 4 percent. Faced with this lower "price" of retirement consumption, the individual is very likely to increase the level of planned retirement consumption. *But if the new level of retirement consumption does not increase sufficiently, current saving will actually fall.* For example, if the individual decides to increase his annual retirement dissaving from $5,000 to $5,500, he can actually lower his current saving from $1,400 to $1,303. Only if annual retirement dissaving increased to at least $5,900 would current saving increase. Since we do not know how the demand for retirement consumption responds to its net cost, it is not possible to say whether saving would increase or decrease in response to a higher net rate of return.

Note that this ambiguity involves two separate issues.[27] First, a reduction in the price of retirement consumption (that is, an increase in the net rate of return) will increase the level of retirement consumption if the *un*compensated demand for retirement consumption is a decreasing function of its price. Theory requires only that the compensated demand be a decreasing function of its price. Nevertheless, a nonnegative marginal propensity to save implies that the uncompensated demand will also be a decreasing function of price.

Second, a reduction in the price of retirement consumption will increase the rate of saving only if the demand for retirement income has a price elasticity which is absolutely greater than one. By definition, saving is equal to the product of retirement consumption and its price. The elasticity of saving with respect to that price is thus equal to one plus the elasticity of retirement consumption with respect to its price. If this negative elasticity has an absolute value less than one, it follows that the elasticity of savings with respect to this price is positive. And since this price varies inversely with the net rate of return, in this case the elasticity of savings with respect to the net rate of return is negative.

Unfortunately, the statistical analyses that have been published until now have been inconclusive about this important question. The econometric literature provides estimates that indicate both positive and negative responses of saving to the rate of interest. However, these studies have generally used inadequate measures of the real net rate of return, failing to adjust for either taxes, inflation, or both.[28] Boskin has recently presented

27. These issues are developed more fully in Feldstein (1978b).
28. See, for example, Suits (1963), Weber (1970), and Wright (1969). For a discussion of the likely effects of these misspecifications, see Feldstein (1970).

careful time-series estimates in which the real net rate of return is estimated by using an appropriate series for the average marginal tax rate on interest income and an adaptive expectations model of anticipated inflation.[29] His estimate of the elasticity of saving with respect to the real net rate of return is approximately 0.3, an estimate that he describes as "substantially larger than virtually all previous estimates."[30] Although this estimate is based on the real net return on corporate debt, it is interesting to see the implication of applying a "large" elasticity to the effect of corporate tax integration. The estimates in the next section imply that complete integration for individual taxpayers would reduce the tax on capital income by $7.5 billion in 1973. Since total after-tax capital income in that year was approximately $150 billion, this tax cut would represent an increase in the net return of approximately 5 percent. The elasticity of 0.3 implies a 1.5 percent increase in total savings, an increase of approximately $2 billion.

The Change in the Distribution of Income

The final way in which corporate tax integration—both complete and partial—would affect saving is by redistributing the tax burden among individuals with different propensities to save.

The analysis of the next section shows that the break-even form of partial tax integration redistributes after-tax income from high-income individuals to others with low or middle incomes. The economics profession has long debated whether there are any significant differences between the representative marginal propensities to save at different income levels. The evidence indicates that this redistribution may reduce saving slightly or leave it essentially unchanged.

The distributional effect on saving of complete integration would depend on the tax increase that was chosen to replace the lost revenue. Since this tax increase would probably leave the distribution of the tax burden among income classes approximately the same as it is now, the net effect of any such redistribution would be very small.

A reduction in the tax on corporate source income and an increase in the tax on salaries and other types of labor income in the same income class *may* be a redistribution of the tax burden from capital owners with high propensities to save to those with less capital and lower propensities

29. See Boskin (1977).
30. This estimate refers to the partial effect of the interest rate with fixed income and wealth.

to save. But that is only conjecture. Those who currently receive substantial capital income may actually have lower *marginal* propensities to save than those high-income earners with few capital assets.

The three ways in which integration would affect saving can be summarized briefly: (1) Retained earnings are likely to fall, resulting in a slight reduction in total private saving. (2) The net rate of return to all saving would rise, but this may either increase or decrease saving. (3) The redistribution of the tax burden is likely to have only a negligible effect, although here again our knowledge is weak.

The Distributional Effects of Partial Integration

Complete corporate tax integration is neither progressive nor regressive as such but depends on the method by which the lost revenue is replaced. It is best therefore to begin with the partial integration method, which involves no change in total revenue. The analysis presented here shows that partial integration would involve very substantial reductions in effective tax rates for low- and middle-income taxpayers and significant increases for high-income taxpayers. Because partial integration involves no change in the total tax burden on corporate source income, this analysis will disregard the possibility that the pretax rate of return would be altered by a change in the incidence of the tax.[31]

The current analysis is based on microsimulations using the Treasury Tax File for 1973. The Treasury Tax File is a stratified random sample of 112,441 individual tax returns. We have used a random 25 percent subsample of 28,109 returns. Because the sampling weights are known, the individual records can be used to make estimates for the population of taxpayers.

The analysis uses a computerized model that can apply the 1973 tax laws and any alternative tax rules to individual records like the Treasury Tax File. TAXSIM also includes estimates of each individual's corporate source income and current corporate tax payments. Although TAXSIM can in principle take into account the changes in asset ownership that would result from a change in the corporate income tax, the current simulations *assume no behavioral response*.[32]

31. The incidence of the tax might in fact change if the reallocation of funds by investors at different income levels did not cancel each other. The current assumption is equivalent to assuming that the incidence of a change in the total tax on corporate income is independent of the distribution of the tax by income level.

32. Such behavioral responses can be important. Higher-income individuals could avoid some of the tax increase by switching to other assets, while lower-income individuals would

Each individual's corporate source income and current corporate tax payments are estimated on the basis of his dividends.[33] In 1973, total dividends paid out of the U.S. corporate sector were $24.4 billion. During the same year, profits subject to the corporate tax were $114.3 billion, gross tax liability was $51.8 billion, and credits used against the corporate tax were $13.3 billion.[34] Therefore, each dollar of dividends corresponded to $4.68 of corporate income, $2.12 of gross tax, and $0.54 of credits. Corporate income, tax, and credits for each individual were computed by multiplying these numbers by his dividends. Since individual taxpayers received a total of $19.8 billion in dividends, corporate income, tax, and credits allocated to all individuals were $91.1, $41.3, and $10.6 billion respectively.

Table 8.1 shows the distribution of corporate income and taxes in 1973. The 80.7 million taxpayers are classified by adjusted gross income as defined by the 1973 income tax law. The average dividend per return is shown in column 3. The personal tax on corporate income (column 4) is the amount by which the individual's personal tax would be reduced if he received no dividends instead of the amount shown in column 3; this calculation reflects not only the progressive tax structure but such features as income averaging, the maximum rate on earned income, the proportional standard deduction, and so on. As the previous paragraph explained, each dollar of dividends is associated with $4.68 of pretax corporate income and with $1.58 of net corporate tax liability. Column 5 combines the individual income tax from column 4 with the corporation tax implied by the dividends in column 3. The total tax paid by an individual, column 6, is the sum of his total personal income tax for 1973 and the imputed corporate tax liability. The final three columns relate the total tax on corporate income (column 5) to dividends, corporate income, and full income (defined as the sum of adjusted gross income and corporate source income).[35]

---

purchase more common stock as it became more favorably taxed for individuals at their income level. A more complete analysis with a full behavioral response deserves high priority as the next step in the analysis of the distributional effect of corporate tax integration. The sensitivity of portfolio investors to after-tax rates of return is discussed in Chapter 10.

33. The "individual" is really the taxpaying unit, that is, an individual or couple.

34. Internal Revenue Service (1976). Dividends are defined as distributions to stockholders minus dividends received by U.S. corporations minus capital gains distributions of investment companies. The last three numbers are from the U.S. Department of Commerce (1976). A correction was made for dividends received by individuals from abroad; this number was estimated at $0.5 billion.

35. Note that we adjust the dividends of each taxpayer by the average fraction of dividends received from abroad. This reduces imputed corporate tax payments by approximately 2.5 percent.

Table 8.1. Distribution of corporate income and taxes, 1973

Income class AGI (in thousands) (1)	Number of returns (in thousands) (2)	Dividends (in dollars) (3)	Average amounts per return			Tax on corporate income as percentage of:		
			Personal tax on corporate income (in dollars) (4)	Total tax on corporate income (in dollars) (5)	Tax on all income (in dollars) (6)	Dividends (%)[a] (7)	Corporate income (%)[a] (8)	Full income (%)[a] (9)
0–5	26,691.1	38.9	1.4	61.6	150.9	158.27	34.55	2.37
5–10	20,573.3	104.2	12.1	173.2	851.9	166.31	36.31	2.23
10–15	15,867.5	90.8	14.6	155.1	1,523.0	170.78	37.28	1.22
15–20	8,824.6	187.7	34.8	325.2	2,497.3	173.20	37.81	1.82
20–30	5,805.7	435.1	94.6	767.6	4,296.5	176.40	38.51	3.04
30–50	1,805.8	1,817.8	481.9	3,293.5	9,959.7	181.18	39.56	7.55
50–100	585.0	5,261.5	2,070.0	10,207.2	25,791.8	194.00	42.36	12.03
100–500	130.2	26,941.4	12,090.3	53,728.6	97,984.9	199.43	43.56	21.37
500–1000	2.6	196,101.5	88,017.8	391,318.3	603,470.5	199.55	43.56	28.51
1000+	0.9	596,812.7	248,818.9	1,171,887.0	1,955,847.1	196.36	42.87	27.39
All[b]	80,748.2	246.3	67.9	448.8	1,760.5	182.24	39.79	4.02

a. Figures in these columns relate only to taxpayers with dividend income.
b. Includes AGI less than zero not shown separately.

Columns 7 and 8 show that the present tax on corporate income and dividends is nearly proportional. Since dividends rise sharply with income, this nearly proportional tax on corporate source income significantly reduces the overall progressivity of the tax structure.

The partial integration method analyzed in Table 8.2 reduces the current 48 percent rate of corporate income tax to 15 percent and then treats all income after this corporation tax as personal income. Stated differently, the corporate income in excess of the 15 percent tax is treated as equivalent to dividends whether or not it is paid out. Current corporate tax credits continue to offset corporate tax liabilities. The aggregate effect of this partial integration is a tax loss of only $1.0 billion, or less than 2 percent of total taxes on corporate income.

Column 3 of Table 8.2 shows the change in the average tax liability in each income class. This reflects the reduction in the individual's pro rata corporate tax liability and the corresponding increase in the personal tax liability. Note that these averages refer to *all* individuals in each income class, not just to those with dividend income. The figures indicate a modest average tax cut for those with adjusted gross incomes below $30,000 and substantial tax increases above $50,000.

Column 4 shows that partial integration would reduce current tax liabilities by 25 percent in the lowest income class. Taxes would fall between 8 and 2 percent in income groups up to $30,000, but taxes would rise more than 18 percent at the highest income levels. These results can be seen somewhat differently by looking at the change in effective tax rates (column 5). The average effective tax rates fall by between 0.4 percent and 1.4 percent for incomes below $30,000 but rise by as much as 8 percentage points for high-income groups. These results relate to all taxpayers including those with no dividend income.

The results in columns 6 through 8 relate only to those with dividend income. Column 6 expresses the tax changes as a percentage of corporate income; this is equivalent to the change in the effective tax rate on corporate income. Effective rates fall by more than 20 percentage points at the lowest income and rise by some 13 percentage points at the highest. Column 7 shows the same results in terms of the effective rates on dividends received. Since corporate plus personal tax payments currently exceed dividends received (that is, the effective tax rates on dividends exceed 100 percent), the changes in effective rates appear more dramatic. Effective rates relative to dividends fall by more than 50 percentage points for incomes up to $15,000 and rise more than 50 percentage points at high incomes.

Column 8 shows that partial integration would reduce the total tax paid

Table 8.2. Effects of replacing the current taxation of corporate income by partial integration[a]

Income class AGI (in thousands) (1)	Number of returns (in thousands) (2)	Average change in tax (in dollars) (3)	Change in tax as percentage of:				
			Current total tax (%) (4)	Full income (%) (5)	Corporate income (%)[b] (6)	Dividends (%)[b] (7)	Current tax on corporate income (%)[b] (8)
0–5	26,691.1	−37.2	−24.63	−1.44	−20.85	−95.53	−60.36
5–10	20,573.3	−69.9	−8.20	−0.90	−14.65	−67.11	−40.35
10–15	15,867.5	−50.5	−3.32	−0.40	−12.15	−55.64	−32.58
15–20	8,824.6	−68.0	−2.72	−0.38	−7.91	−36.23	−20.92
20–30	5,805.7	−95.6	−2.23	−0.38	−4.80	−21.97	−12.46
30–50	1,805.8	66.5	0.67	0.15	0.80	3.66	2.02
50–100	585.0	1,052.6	5.83	1.77	6.24	28.56	14.72
100–500	130.2	14,255.2	14.55	5.67	11.56	52.91	26.53
500–1000	2.6	118,612.8	19.66	8.64	13.20	60.49	30.31
1000+	0.9	364,176.8	18.62	8.51	13.32	61.02	31.08
All[c]	80,748.2	−12.4	−0.70	−0.11	−1.10	−5.03	−2.76

a. "Partial integration" taxes corporate income at 15 percent and includes the remainder in personal income. Current corporate tax credits are retained. The simulations assume no behavioral response to the tax change.
b. Figures in these columns relate only to taxpayers with dividend income.
c. Includes AGI less than zero not shown separately.

on corporate income by 60 percent in the lowest income group and by more than 30 percent for incomes up to $15,000. For those with incomes over $100,000, tax on corporate income would rise by 25 to 30 percent.

The Distributional Effects of Complete Integration

This section begins with an analysis that is parallel to the simulations of the previous section; the effect of complete integration is thus analyzed on the assumption that there is no change in each individual's pretax corporate income. However, since complete integration involves a reduction in the tax burden on corporate income of $7.5 billion, this section also discusses the distributional consequences that occur through short-run capitalization and through long-run changes in pretax incomes.

Simulation of Tax Changes by Income Class

The method of complete integration analyzed here treats all corporate income as the personal income of the individual shareholder. Each individual's adjusted gross income is therefore increased by an amount equal to $3.68 per dollar of 1973 dividend income.[36] Corporate tax credits equal to 54 cents per dollar of dividend income are available for each individual to offset against his own final personal tax liability, subject to the limit that the final liability is not negative.

The simulations in Table 8.3 correspond exactly to the partial integration results of Table 8.2. The tax change (in column 3) again shows a moderate cut for low-income taxpayers and a large increase for the richest. Taxpayers in the $30,000 to $100,000 adjusted gross income (AGI) range also experience a drop in taxes. As the relative change in overall tax shows, complete integration is more important than partial in the bottom and middle brackets and less important in the top. The columns that focus on corporate income emphasize this shift. The effective tax rate on corporate income falls a full 31.5 points in the bottom class. Since Table 8.1 shows an original effective rate of 34.6 percent, this fall is essentially to zero. At the top, the effective tax rate on corporate income rises by 9 points. Again a more progressive set of taxes on corporate income is the result.

A useful way to assess the difference between partial integration and

36. Recall that before-tax corporate income in 1973 was 4.68 times the dividends paid. Dividend income was already included in AGI, except for the dividend exclusion, which is eliminated.

Table 8.3. Effects of replacing the current taxation of corporate income by complete integration[a]

Income class AGI (in thousands) (1)	Number of returns (in thousands) (2)	Average change in tax (in dollars) (3)	Change in tax as percentage of:				
			Current total tax (%) (4)	Full income (%) (5)	Corporate income (%)[b] (6)	Dividends (%)[b] (7)	Current tax on corporate income (%)[b] (8)
0–5	26,691.1	−56.1	−37.17	−2.18	−31.48	−144.19	−91.10
5–10	20,573.3	−118.6	−13.93	−1.52	−24.87	−113.91	−68.49
10–15	15,867.5	−91.0	−5.98	−0.71	−21.87	−100.18	−58.66
15–20	8,824.6	−142.3	−5.70	−0.80	−16.55	−75.81	−43.77
20–30	5,805.7	−254.8	−5.93	−1.01	−12.79	−58.57	−33.20
30–50	1,805.8	−489.3	−4.91	−1.12	−5.88	−26.92	−14.86
50–100	585.0	−132.5	0.51	0.16	0.55	2.52	1.30
100–500	130.2	8,415.8	8.59	3.35	6.82	31.24	15.66
500–1000	2.6	78,125.3	12.95	5.69	8.70	39.84	19.96
1000+	0.9	241,184.5	12.33	5.64	8.82	40.41	20.58
All[c]	80,748.2	−93.5	−5.31	−0.84	−8.29	−37.96	−20.83

a. "Complete integration" includes all corporate income and personal income for tax purposes. Current corporate tax credits are retained. The simulations assume no behavioral response to the tax change.

b. Figures in these columns relate only to taxpayers with dividend income.

c. Includes AGI less than zero not shown separately.

complete integration is to see the tax changes that occur if we start with the partial integration rules and change to complete integration. Table 8.4 presents the simulations for this change.[37] Since the partial integration involves a tax revenue loss of $1.0 billion while the revenue loss of complete integration is $7.5 billion, the net revenue loss associated with this change is $6.5 billion. The columns of Table 8.4 correspond exactly to those of Tables 8.2 and 8.3. All taxpayers experience a cut in total taxes, with the largest absolute cuts going to the highest brackets. The percentage fall in total taxes (column 4) is greatest for those with AGI below $10,000. The percentage reduction is approximately 3 percent between $10,000 and $30,000 and approximately 6 percent above $30,000. The percentage fall in taxes on corporate income (column 8) falls sharply as income increases. Since corporate income rises so sharply with AGI, the slightly smaller drop in tax per corporate dollar for the rich can result in a larger drop in overall taxes. Changes in effective tax rates on full income reflect this as well. The overall tax rate falls more on top (column 5), but the effective tax rate on corporate income falls more in lower brackets (column 6). In any case, these changes are roughly equal across AGI classes, so we may conclude that moving from partial to complete integration does not affect progressivity in any degree.

The Short-Run Capitalization of the Corporate Tax Reduction

In the short run, the volume of capital and its distribution among activities are fixed. The pretax earnings of corporations are as a result also fixed for the moment. A reduced tax on corporate source income would therefore be reflected by an increase in the value of common stock. The benefit of this capital gain would accrue to those who own common stock at the time that corporate tax integration is enacted.

How does this capitalization occur? Recall that now the real before-tax return on marginal corporate investment exceeds the corresponding return in the unincorporated sector. The difference between these before-tax returns is large enough to make the after-tax returns equal. A reduction in the effective rate of tax on corporate income eventually induces a reallocation of capital to lower the real before-tax return to corporate investment. But in the short run, the fixity of capital and labor implies that before-tax returns remain unchanged. The reduced tax on corporate income therefore implies that the after-tax income of corporate equity rises.

37. Tables 8.2 and 8.4 can thus be regarded as a decomposition of the complete integration of Table 8.3 into two steps.

Table 8.4. Effects of replacing a partial integration scheme by complete integration[a]

Income class AGI (in thousands) (1)	Number of returns (in thousands) (2)	Average change in tax (in dollars) (3)	Change in tax as percentage of:				
			Current total tax (%) (4)	Full income (%) (5)	Corporate income (%)[b] (6)	Dividends (%)[b] (7)	Current tax on corporate income (%)[b] (8)
0–5	26,691.1	−18.9	−12.54	−0.73	−10.62	−48.66	−77.55
5–10	20,573.3	−48.7	−5.72	−0.63	−10.22	−46.79	−47.17
10–15	15,867.5	−40.5	−2.66	−0.32	−9.72	−44.53	−38.68
15–20	8,824.6	−74.3	−2.98	−0.42	−8.64	−39.58	−28.90
20–30	5,805.7	−159.2	−3.71	−0.63	−7.99	−36.59	−23.69
30–50	1,805.8	−555.8	−5.58	−1.27	−6.68	−30.58	−16.54
50–100	585.0	−1,370.2	−5.31	−1.61	−5.69	−26.04	−11.70
100–500	130.2	−5,834.6	−5.95	−2.32	−4.73	−21.66	−8.58
500–1000	2.6	−40,489.8	−6.71	−2.95	−4.51	−20.65	−7.94
1000+	0.9	−122,993.3	−6.29	−2.87	−4.50	−20.61	−8.01
All	80,748.2	−81.1	−4.61	−0.73	−7.19	−32.93	−18.59

a. "Partial integration" taxes corporate income at 15 percent and includes the remainder in personal income. "Complete integration" includes all corporate and personal income for tax purposes. Current corporate tax credits are retained. The simulations assume no behavioral response to the tax change.

b. Figures in these columns relate only to taxpayers with dividend income.

c. Includes AGI less than zero not shown separately.

If share prices were to remain constant, the net rate of return to owners of equities would be higher than the net rate of return to owners of other assets. Such unequal returns on portfolio assets cannot continue for even a very short period of time. The price of equities must rise until the rates of return to portfolio investors are equal in all assets.

While it is difficult to estimate the magnitude of the change in share values, it is possible to indicate the likely upper limit to that change. If there were no reallocation of capital from the noncorporate sector to the corporate sector, the net corporate income on the original equity capital would remain permanently higher by the value of the tax cut. Moreover, this increase in net income would increase through time as the corporate sector grows with the economy. The proportionate increase in share values would therefore approximate the proportionate increase in 1973 net equity income. Corporate profits net of both corporate and personal taxes were approximately $45 billion. The $7.5 billion tax reduction thus represents an increase in net income of slightly more than 15 percent. In practice, of course, the increase in net income would be attenuated over time as capital moved from the unincorporated sector to the corporate sector until the rates of return were equal.[38] In the same way, the response of savers to higher net rates of return may alter the total capital stock. The likely magnitude of the change in equity values depends on the speed with which the capital stock adjusts; reducing the change from 15 percent to 5 percent might be a reasonable guess. A gradual or delayed introduction of integration would further reduce this windfall gain.

The Long-Run Changes in Real Incomes

Economists generally agree that the rates of return to all forms of capital tend in the long run to become equal.[39] It is appropriate, therefore, to ask how corporate tax integration would affect the return to all capital rather than the return to equity capital or any other single type of capital. Moreover, in the long run, the common rate of return must also equal the real after-tax marginal product of capital.

There is much less professional agreement about the way in which a reduction in the tax on corporate source income would affect the yield to capital and the general level of real wages. Harberger (1962) has argued

38. Since this entails lowering the before-tax return to corporate investment and raising the corresponding return in the noncorporate sector, the value of equities would rise by less than the proportionate increase in short-run net corporate income.

39. Here, as elsewhere in this chapter, rates of return should be understood as "after adjusting for risk."

that, with a fixed capital stock, any change in the effective rate of tax on corporate income is likely to accrue primarily if not wholly to owners of capital. It is quite possible, however, and consistent with Harberger's formal analysis, that some of the benefit of the tax integration would be shifted to labor.[40] The exact incidence depends on the nature of technology in the two sectors and of the demand for corporate and noncorporate goods. Moreover, if the capital stock increases in response to a lower tax on capital income, more of the benefit of the tax is likely to be shifted to labor.[41]

Conclusion

This chapter has explored some of the economic effects of two alternative proposals for corporate tax integration: complete integration and a partial integration method that keeps the tax burden on corporate income unchanged. We have argued that either proposal would be desirable because of the favorable effects on the efficiency of the capital markets. Complete integration would have greater benefits than partial integration, particularly with respect to the allocation of consumption over time and of capital between corporate and noncorporate activities. Microeconomic simulations using the TAXSIM model and the 1973 Treasury Tax File show that either form of integration would reduce taxes relatively more for low-income individuals and would actually raise taxes for high-income individuals.

40. It is sometimes asserted that "consumers" may also enjoy part of the benefit of such a tax reduction, that is, that the reduction is "shifted forward" in the form of "price reductions." In general, this is not a helpful notion. If all consumers are also suppliers of labor or capital services, the idea of a separate incidence on consumers (in addition to the impact on capital and labor income receipts) is without meaning. If there is a separate class of individuals with fixed money incomes (for example, private pensions), this group will be affected by a change in the price level. However, a change in the corporate income tax should not as such affect the price level (as opposed to the *relative* prices of different goods). Any shifting of a corporate tax change to consumers is therefore really the result of the accompanying monetary and fiscal policies.

41. See Chapter 19. This conclusion is independent of the response of labor supply to the changes in net wage rates; see Chapter 18.

PART TWO

The Effects of Taxation on Portfolio Behavior

9 The Effects of Taxation on Risk Taking

The proposition that a proportional tax with full loss offset increases personal risk taking is now widely accepted by professional economists. This conclusion, originally suggested by Domar and Musgrave (1944), has more recently been reached by several economists working in the context of von Neumann–Morgenstern expected-utility maximization (Hall 1960; Penner 1964; Richter 1960; Tobin 1958). A heuristic argument to reconcile this rather surprising result with intuition would be something like this. Because the imposition of a tax decreases both the yield and the "risk" of all assets, it increases the investor's demand for higher yield (raises "the marginal utility of income") and reduces his resistance to assuming more risk (lowers the "marginal disutility of risk"). If the tax lowers the yield and risk of every security in the same proportion (as occurs with the yield and risk measures considered by previous writers), the market risk-yield rate of transformation is unchanged. The result is an increased demand by investors for higher-yielding and more risky assets.

The purpose of this chapter is to demonstrate that the assertion that proportional taxation causes individuals who maximize expected utility[1] to increase risk taking is not generally true. The first section shows that previous attempts to prove that taxation increases risk taking have relied on a variety of restrictive and implausible assumptions. The second section then argues that the concept of risk taking (and therefore of the tax base) should be extended beyond portfolio choice and, in this framework, offers a counterexample to the general proposition that taxation increases risk taking.

Previous Studies in the Expected Utility Framework

In a pioneering article Tobin (1958) applied the von Neumann–Morgenstern theory of expected-utility maximization to portfolio choice

Reprinted from the *Journal of Political Economy* 77 (September–October 1969), pp. 755–764, by permission of the University of Chicago Press. Copyright © 1969 by the University of Chicago.

1. This chapter does not consider earlier demonstrations that do not assume expected-utility maximization (for example, Domar and Musgrave 1944).

and showed that under certain conditions an investor's preferences could be represented by an indifference map in terms of the mathematical expectation of the investment "outcome" (μ) and its standard deviation (σ). The properties of these indifference curves were then derived for two different cases: (1) no restriction placed on the investor's utility function, but the subjective probability distribution of the investment outcome has a two-parameter probability density function; (2) no restriction placed on the probability distribution, but the investor's utility function is quadratic. Analysis of the second and more restrictive case will be given in the second part of this section.

The Analysis of Tobin and Hall

Tobin first shows that a risk averter (an investor with a concave utility function)[2] will be indifferent between two portfolios with unequal outcome variance only if the higher-variance portfolio also has higher expected outcome (that is, $d\mu/d\sigma > 0$ along each indifference curve). He then tries to show that a risk averter with a two-parameter (μ, σ) subjective probability distribution necessarily has convex indifference curves, that is, $d^2\mu/d\sigma^2 > 0$ along each curve. Because Tobin's proof is correct only if the distribution is restricted to a limited subclass of two-parameter distributions (including the normal but not the lognormal),[3] the generality of his result is substantially reduced. Within the restricted framework of convex indifference curves, Tobin's analysis does demonstrate that if an investor divides his portfolio between a riskless asset with no yield ("money") and a risky asset ("bonds"), the effect of a proportional tax with full loss offset would be to increase the proportion held in bonds (if not 100 percent before the imposition of the tax). I show below that this result depends critically on the assumption that one of the assets is riskless. But a theory that rests on the existence of a riskless asset is of little value in a world of uncertain price levels.[4] Moreover, a useful theory

2. A utility function $u(x)$ is concave if $u'(x) > 0$ and $u''(x) < 0$. More generally, a function $f(x)$ is concave if a chord connecting two points on the function lies below the function: $af(x_1) + (1 - a)f(x_2) < f[ax_1 + (1 - a)x_2]$ for all $0 < a < 1$. If the second derivative exists for all x, this definition implies that a concave function has $u''(x) < 0$. The function is convex (sometimes called convex downward) if the chord lies above the function.

3. A counterexample is $u = \log x$ lognormally distributed. For a proof that this is a counterexample, explanation of the limitation of Tobin's proof, and a discussion of the importance of this for Tobin's theory of liquidity preference, see Feldstein (1969).

4. Tobin has recognized this in his later writing on the theory of portfolio selection; see Tobin (1965).

of individual risk taking cannot be limited to the problem of asset choice.[5] If the analysis is extended to occupational and other economic choices involving uncertainty, it is clear that even if money were riskless, the individual would not have the option of a life without risk. To see the crucial role of the riskless asset in Tobin's proof, we turn to Hall's attempt (1960) to extend Tobin's analysis to the general case in which the unacceptable assumption of a riskless asset is dropped.

An investor who divides his portfolio between two risky assets[6] faces a nonlinear μ,σ-opportunity locus. The general shape of this curve is easily derived. Let the two assets have expected yields $\mu_1 > \mu_2$ and variances σ_1^2, σ_2^2. A portfolio with proportion P invested in the first asset has mean $\mu_0 = P\mu_1 + (1 - P)\mu_2$ and variance $\sigma_0^2 = P^2\sigma_1^2 + (1 - P)^2\sigma_2^2 + 2P(1 - P)\rho\sigma_1\sigma_2$, where ρ is the correlation between the yields of the two assets. Therefore μ_0 increases with P at a constant rate $(d\mu_0/dP = \mu_1 - \mu_2)$, while σ_0 decreases with P until $P^* = (\sigma_2^2 - \rho\sigma_1\sigma_2)/(\sigma_1^2 + \sigma_2^2 - 2\rho\sigma_1\sigma_2)$ and then increases with P at an increasing rate. Since portfolios with $P < P^*$ are inefficient (that is, have lower mean and higher variance than at P^*), σ_0 is an increasing function of P throughout the relevant range. One such opportunity locus is drawn in Figure 9.1 as curve AB; point A corresponds to complete specialization of the portfolio in the low-yield asset, while point B corresponds to complete specialization in the high-yield asset.

The investor is in equilibrium when the opportunity locus is tangent to an indifference curve such as I_1 in Figure 9.1. This indifference curve is drawn convex, following Tobin and Hall. At point E the investor's marginal rate of substitution between μ and σ is equal to the marginal rate of transformation.

A proportional tax (with full loss offset) at rate $(1 - \theta)$ decreases the mean and standard deviation of each asset in the same proportion. Therefore the mean and standard deviation corresponding to any portfolio is also decreased in that proportion. Graphically, a new net-of-tax opportunity locus is defined by shifting each point on the gross-of-tax opportunity locus toward the origin along a ray. The distance from the origin to the new point divided by the distance from the origin to the old point equals θ. Figure 9.2 shows the relation between a gross-of-tax opportunity locus AB and the net-of-tax locus $A'B'$.

Hall tries to prove that a proportional tax increases the proportion of

5. Only Hirshleifer (1965) appears to have explicitly recognized this. This idea is developed more fully in the next section.
6. The adjective "risky" is used to denote any asset whose outcome has nonzero variance.

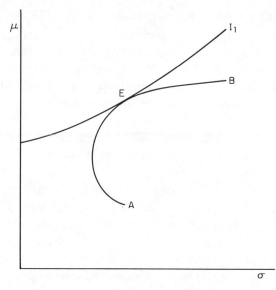

Figure 9.1. Equilibrium portfolio allocation

the riskier asset in the optimum portfolio by showing that the new equilibrium point (F' in Fig. 9.2) corresponds to a point on curve AB between E and B. If this were so, it would imply that the investor's optimum gross-of-tax variance is increased by the tax and that the new portfolio therefore contains more of the riskier asset.

A crucial, but incorrect, step in Hall's argument may be summarized as follows: If the investor does not change the composition of his portfolio, the imposition of the tax will shift his position in the μ,σ-space to the point E' *where the slope of the indifference curve is less than the slope of the opportunity locus.* If the statement in italics were true, the investor would alter the composition of his portfolio by increasing μ and σ and therefore, given the shape of the opportunity locus, moving through points of lower slope on the opportunity locus until he reaches a point such as F' where the opportunity locus is tangent to the indifference curve. But the italicized statement is not true in general. At the point E' the slope of the opportunity locus is obviously the same as at the point E; but the slope of the indifference curve at E' is not necessarily less than at E and may be greater. Figure 9.3 shows that a set of convex indifference curves is not incompatible with the proportional tax causing a decrease in risk taking.

Hall's argument founders on the implicit assumption that, for given σ,

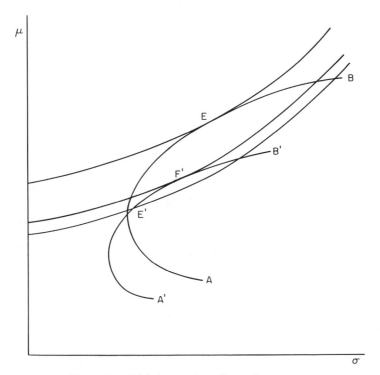

Figure 9.2. Risk-increasing effect of taxation

the value of $d\mu/d\sigma$ along successive indifference curves increases, remains constant, or decreases only slowly as μ increases. If, as in Figure 9.3, $d\mu/d\sigma$ decreases as μ increases for given σ, a proportional tax may decrease demand for riskier assets. The assumption that $d\mu/d\sigma$ decreases as μ increases should not be viewed as an unusual special case. In economic terms, it implies the quite acceptable proposition that an investor with higher income will be less risk-averse, that is, will require less compensation for incurring additional risk.[7]

It is clear that in the general case in which the investor divides his portfolio between two risky assets, or even between a riskless asset and a risky asset with positive yield, it is impossible to predict the effects of proportional taxation without further knowledge of the properties of the indifference curves. But if one of the assets has no yield and no risk, as originally assumed by Tobin, the opportunity locus is a ray from the ori-

7. We return to this in the second part of this section, where this measure of decreasing risk aversion is related to that described by Pratt (1964).

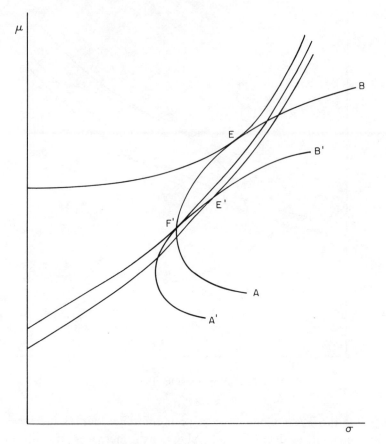

Figure 9.3. Risk-decreasing effect of taxation

gin.[8] If the indifference curves are convex, there can exist no more than one point at which the opportunity locus is tangent to an indifference curve. To return to that point after the imposition of a tax, the investor must increase his holding of the risky asset.[9] This shows both the correctness of Tobin's argument and its critical dependence on the fact that the opportunity locus is a ray from the origin in a world with a riskless, yieldless option. The limited relevance of such a world has already been noted. It must therefore be concluded that the assumption of convex μ,σ indifference curves (or, more fundamentally, of a concave utility function

8. A portfolio consisting of a risky asset with mean μ_1 and variance σ_1^2 and a riskless asset with mean μ_2 has portfolio mean $\mu_0 = P\mu_1 + (1 - P)\mu_2$ and portfolio standard deviation $\sigma_0 = P\sigma_1$. Therefore $d\mu_0/d\sigma_0 = (\mu_1 - \mu_2)/\sigma_1$. If the riskless asset has mean $\mu_2 = 0$, the opportunity locus is the ray with slope μ_1/σ_1.

9. For diagrammatic presentation of the riskless asset case, see Tobin (1958, p. 78).

and a subjective probability distribution in a limited two-parameter class) is insufficient to yield any clear results about the effect of proportional taxation on risk taking.[10]

Quadratic Utility Function Approach

If the investor's utility function is severely restricted by the assumption that it is quadratic over the relevant range, a proportional tax can be shown to increase risk taking regardless of the subjective probability distribution. After proving this,[11] I critically examine the quadratic utility assumption.

If the investor's utility function is quadratic, it can, without loss of generality, be written as

$$u(x) = x + \alpha x^2, \tag{1}$$

with $\alpha < 0$ and $0 \leqslant x \leqslant \dfrac{1}{2|\alpha|}$. The investor therefore maximizes

$$E[u(x)] = Ex + \alpha Ex^2 = \mu + \alpha\sigma^2 + \alpha\mu^2, \tag{2}$$

using $\sigma^2 = Ex^2 - \mu^2$. Constant expected utility curves are therefore concentric circles with one diameter lying along the vertical μ axis and the center at $\sigma = 0, \mu = \dfrac{1}{2|\alpha|}$. The arcs of these circles in the region $\sigma \geqslant 0$ and $0 \leqslant \mu \leqslant \dfrac{1}{2|\alpha|}$ are the relevant indifference curves. It is clear from the geometry of concentric circles that the slope of successive indifference curves increases as μ increases for given σ. The first part of this section showed that this is a sufficient condition to make Hall's proof correct, that is, to make the imposition of a proportional tax cause increased risk taking.

But the assumption of a quadratic utility function is subject to two serious objections. First, a quadratic utility function implies the unlikely characteristic that "risk aversion" increases with income. This is a "local

10. An interesting paper by Mossin (1968), which appeared after this paper was submitted for publication, proves that a proportional tax increases risk taking without any restrictions on the subjective probability distribution. This demonstration does, however, depend on the existence of a riskless asset.

11. The first proof of this was given by Richter (1960). His results were extended to other types of taxation, for example, taxation of one asset only, by Penner (1964).

objection,'' an unacceptable property which holds in the neighborhood of every point in the μ,σ-space or, equivalently, of every point on the utility function. The discussion of indifference curves as arcs of concentric circles showed that this is true if risk aversion is defined as that compensation, in terms of additional expected yield, that must be paid to induce the investor to accept a portfolio of higher risk (σ). A more fundamental definition of risk aversion in terms of the properties of the utility function was suggested independently by Arrow and Schlaifer and developed by Pratt (1964). For utility function $u(x)$, the risk aversion at point x is defined as $r(x) = -u''(x)/u'(x)$, the absolute value of the ratio of the rate of decline of marginal utility to its current value. This corresponds to a measure of the compensation that an individual would require for making a small fair bet when his original position is point x.[12] For the quadratic utility function, $r(x) = -2\alpha(1 + 2\alpha x)^{-1}$; since $\alpha < 0$ and the function is only defined for $1 + 2\alpha x > 0$, risk aversion is an increasing function of x. As the discussion of Figure 9.3 has made clear, this unacceptable property is very important in previous proofs that taxation increases risk taking.

The second objection to the quadratic function refers to its overall shape rather than to a property that holds at each point. In order that the marginal utility of income be everywhere positive, the value of α must be such that $|\alpha| \leq \frac{1}{2}x$ for all relevant x. Because the range of possible outcomes may be very large if the investor's time horizon is long, the required value of α may imply very little curvature of the utility function; that is, both the measure of risk aversion and the absolute elasticity of the marginal utility function may be unreasonably low.

In short, the quadratic utility function is inappropriate as the basis for a general analysis of the effects of taxation on risk taking.

An Alternative Approach

Previous analyses have always posited that the argument of the utility function is the outcome of portfolio investment, and they have restricted attention to the effects of taxation on portfolio composition. However, the optimal portfolio behavior for an individual is not independent of the uncertainty of his other income sources. Moreover, the effects of taxation on other aspects of individual risk taking may be at least as important as the effect on portfolio choice. This section considers the effects of taxation on total risk taking by individuals with constant elasticity utility func-

---

12. For further discussion of the interpretation of $r(x)$, see Pratt (1964).

tions. In this context it is shown that a proportional tax has no effect on risk taking regardless of the investor's subjective probability distribution, while the effect of a progressive tax is indeterminate unless restrictions are placed on the probability distribution.

The utility function of this analysis is defined in terms of "total consumption" (c). The expected level and uncertainty of the individual's lifetime consumption stream depend not only on his portfolio allocation decisions but also on his business or occupation, his choice of location, his savings decisions, and so on. If taxation affects risk taking, it will influence each of these choices and not just portfolio composition. In order to study this problem while avoiding the complications of a dynamic analysis, we consider a two-period "way of life" model in which income in the second period (x) depends on this whole range of economic choices. The term "income" thus refers to all funds (including the value of portfolio assets) which in the absence of taxation would be consumed in the second period of a two-period model.

This income variable will be taken as the tax base for studying the effects of proportional and progressive taxation. If an individual has no income from employment, this is equivalent to a tax on the final value of a portfolio including interest and dividend income. Because we are generally interested in the effects of taxing income and capital gains rather than wealth or consumption, the use of x as a tax base requires some justification. For almost all individuals, taxable employment income, portfolio income, and capital gains are much more important sources of consumption expenditure than the untaxed dissaving of inherited wealth. Moreover, even if income from employment is ignored, in a two-period analysis with the length of the period equal to a large fraction of the investor's adult life, the ratio of final portfolio value to original (and therefore tax exempt) equity would be large. Treating a tax on x as if it were a tax on income plus capital gains therefore introduces only a moderate degree of approximation.

The basic desirable properties of a utility function $u(c)$ are: (1) positive marginal utility, $u'(c) > 0$ for all $c \geq 0$, and (2) diminishing marginal utility, $u''(c) < 0$ for all $c \geq 0$. In addition, it would seem reasonable to require (3) decreasing risk aversion, $r'(c) < 0$ for all $c \geq 0$ where $r(c) = -u''(c)/u'(c)$. A simple class of utility functions which satisfies (1) and (2) is defined by having constant elasticity of the marginal utility function, $c[u''(c)/u'(c)] = \beta < 0$. This class of function also implies the third desired property. Solving this second-order differential equation, we obtain $u(c) = Bc^{\alpha} + u_0$ with $\alpha = \beta + 1$ and arbitrary constants B, u_0 subject to

$\alpha B > 0$. Since the constant term (u_0) can be set equal to zero without loss of generality, it is reasonable to say that the utility function has constant elasticity α.[13]

With this set of specifications it is easy to show that a proportional tax with full loss offset will have no effect on risk taking. In the absence of taxation, consumption (c) equals income (x). The subjective probability distribution associated with the ith "way of life," f_i, is preferred to distribution f_j if and only if

$$\int u(x)f_i(x)dx \equiv E_i[u(x)] > E_j[u(x)] \equiv \int u(x)f_j(x)dx, \qquad (3)$$

or, equivalently,

$$BE_i[x^\alpha] > BE_j[x^\alpha]. \qquad (4)$$

When a proportional tax at rate $1 - \theta$ is introduced, $c = \theta x$. Distribution i is then preferred to distribution j if

$$BE_i[\theta^\alpha x_i^\alpha] > BE_j[\theta^\alpha x_j^\alpha]. \qquad (5)$$

But since $\theta^\alpha > 0$ and is nonrandom, (4) and (5) are equivalent. The preference ordering of distributions is unchanged by the introduction of a proportional tax.

A progressive tax, however, will generally affect the choice of distribution by an individual with a constant elasticity utility function. The tax system which relates disposable income (consumption) to gross income by

$$c = \theta x^\rho, \qquad 0 < \rho < 1, \qquad 0 < \theta \leq 1 \qquad (6)$$

is progressive, with lower values of ρ implying greater progressiveness. If an investor is indifferent between distributions i and j before the introduction of a tax, he will remain indifferent only if $E_i(x^{\alpha\rho}) = E_j(x^{\alpha\rho})$. Because this is not generally true for all $0 < \rho < 1$,[14] introduction of this progres-

---

13. More formally, the defining property can be stated as the constant elasticity of the *marginal* utility function. Functions of this form are also said to exhibit constant relative risk aversion; see Pratt (1964).

14. It is true if the utility function is of the Bernoulli semilogarithmic form, $u(x) = \log x$. The marginal utility function has constant elasticity -1 so that this corresponds to the limiting case of $\alpha = 0$. The introduction of a progressive tax makes the individual maximize $u(x) = \log \theta + \rho \log x$. It is clear that $E_i[u(x)] = E_j[u(x)]$ is independent of ρ.

sive tax will affect the choice of distributions. Without restricting the value of α and the class of subjective probability distributions, it is not possible to say whether this tax will increase or decrease risk taking.

Concluding Remarks

The widely accepted proposition that proportional taxation with full loss offset causes increased risk taking has been shown to rest on weak theoretical foundations. The counterexample of the previous section proves that no completely general theoretical assertion is possible. Further analysis of this problem must therefore rely on the exploration of a variety of restricted but plausible models. In doing so it must be remembered that the results obtained are sensitive to the specification of the model. Policy advice would be more firmly based if the alternative contending theories of economic behavior under uncertainty were taken as working hypotheses for empirical investigation.

10 Personal Taxation and Portfolio Composition: An Econometric Analysis

The theory of portfolio choice has been extensively developed in recent years. This work has substantially improved our understanding of the ways in which the personal income tax may affect household investment behavior. Unfortunately, the theoretical results are generally ambiguous; taxes have a predictable effect on portfolio composition only when strong simplifying assumptions are made. Further improvements in our understanding now require extensive empirical analysis. The purpose of this chapter is to begin the econometric study of this important question.

The first section presents a critical review of previous research on the theory of portfolio choice. The related empirical studies are discussed in the second section. The third section describes the survey data used in the current research and presents estimates of the basic asset composition equations. The fourth section uses these estimates to analyze the relation between relative net yields and portfolio composition. The effects of taxes on mean social rates of return and on risk are described in the fifth section. A brief concluding section summarizes the results and draws some more general conclusions about tax structure.

The Theory of Taxation and Portfolio Composition

Economists' interest in the effect of taxes on portfolio composition began with the sharp rise in U.S. personal income tax rates in the 1940s. There was general concern that the new high rates of tax would reduce the demand for high-yield common stocks and other risky business investments. This in turn would increase the cost of business capital and distort the pattern of investment in the economy. In the first theoretical study of this question, Domar and Musgrave (1944) showed that such a reduction in the demand for the high-yield risky assets was not inevitable. More specifically, they presented a model of investment behavior in which the introduction of a proportional tax with full loss offset necessarily increases

Reprinted from *Econometrica* 44 (July 1976), pp. 631–650, by permission of the Econometric Society. I am grateful to Harvey Rosen for assistance with this research.

the gross (that is, pretax) yield and risk of the investor's portfolio. The reason for this conclusion is not difficult to find. Risk is measured in such a way that the introduction of a proportional tax causes equiproportional reductions in yield and risk while leaving the market rate of transformation between yield and risk unchanged; with the "normal" indifference curves assumed by Domar and Musgrave, the individual therefore responds to the tax by increasing the risk and yield of his portfolio.

Further analysis of this subject began after von Neumann and Morgenstern provided the foundations for the expected-utility maximization theory of choice under uncertainty, and Markowitz (1959) showed how this theory could be applied to problems of portfolio selection. Early results by Hall (1960), Richter (1960), and Tobin (1958) based on expected-utility maximization supported the original conclusion of Domar and Musgrave that taxation increases the demand for the risky asset. However, the generality of this result was later challenged by Mossin (1968), Stiglitz (1969), and myself (Chapter 9), who showed that the conclusion depends on important restrictive assumptions.

To review the development of this theory, it is useful to consider first the case in which the investor divides his wealth between one risky asset and one riskless asset. Tobin (1958) showed that the introduction of a proportional tax with full loss offset would induce a risk-averse investor to increase his demand for the risky asset if the riskless asset has no yield and either the return on the risky asset is distributed normally or the investor's utility function is quadratic. Later Mossin (1968), building on work by Arrow (1965), showed that Tobin's conclusion could be extended to any concave utility function and any distribution of yields on the risky asset.

Unfortunately, dropping the assumption that the riskless asset has zero yield is sufficient to make the effect of the tax ambiguous. If risk aversion decreases sufficiently rapidly as wealth increases, a proportional tax with full loss offset can reduce the demand for the risky asset and increase the demand for a riskless asset with positive yield. Mossin (1968) showed that the original risk-increasing effect of the tax would still prevail even when absolute risk aversion decreases with wealth if relative risk aversion does not decrease too rapidly.[1] Since Arrow (1965) had earlier presented evidence that relative risk aversion actually increases with wealth, Mossin concluded that a proportional tax would increase risk taking.

---

1. See also Stiglitz (1969) for a similar analysis of this case and for a discussion of a wealth tax and of changes in the loss-offset provisions. Arrow (1965) and Pratt (1964) define the concepts of absolute and relative risk aversion.

However, Arrow's interpretation of the evidence on risk aversion deserves further examination. Arrow showed that in a two-asset model in which money has neither risk nor yield, the share of money in total wealth would be an increasing function of wealth if and only if relative risk aversion is also an increasing function of wealth. Arrow then noted that there is time series evidence that the income elasticity of demand for cash balances exceeds one (for example, Friedman 1959) and concluded that this implies increasing relative risk aversion. There are several problems with this inference. The model's assumption that money has neither risk nor yield is not true in a world of uncertain and changing price level. The restriction to two assets is also important; if the existence of equities, bonds, and money is recognized, the behavior of relative risk aversion can no longer be inferred from the wealth elasticity of the demand for money. Moreover, Arrow's model ignores taxes; since tax rates have generally been increasing through time and this lowers the yield on other assets relative to the yield (including the implicit convenience yield) on money, the fraction of wealth held in cash balances might increase even if relative risk aversion is decreasing. Similarly, in Arrow's model the total portfolio size is fixed; Sandmo (1969) later showed that in a two-period model in which investors decide their saving and portfolio composition simultaneously, Arrow's result on the demand for money as a fraction of wealth may no longer hold. In short, it cannot be inferred from the evidence on the demand for money that relative risk aversion is increasing. It then follows from Mossin's analysis that the effect of a proportional tax becomes ambiguous as soon as the riskless asset is permitted to have a nonzero yield.[2]

The ability of Arrow, Mossin, and Stiglitz to analyze asset demand without restricting the distribution of the returns or the form of the utility function depended critically on the assumption that the portfolio contains only one risky asset. Recognizing that money is not a riskless asset or that the relevant choice is between equities and other risky assets substantially complicates the analysis. Richter (1960) showed that with two risky assets and a quadratic utility function, the introduction of a proportional tax with full loss offset would increase pretax portfolio variance. The special and unappealing properties of the quadratic utility function (including

2. Stiglitz (1969) cites Lampman's data (1962) that cash and bonds are a decreasing function of wealth as estate size grows as evidence that relative risk aversion may be a decreasing function of wealth. The interpretation here is subject to the same problem as Arrow's. Moreover, data on cash in estates are notoriously unreliable. Again, tax considerations are likely to be of substantial importance in determining the relative shares of different assets in these portfolios.

increasing absolute risk aversion and a finite level of wealth at which the marginal utility of wealth becomes negative) limit the interest of this result. Although Hall (1960) attempted to extend this result to any case in which the investor's preferences could be described in terms of the mean and variance of the portfolio yield,[3] I showed that this analysis was in error and based on the implicit assumption of properties similar to the quadratic utility function (see Chapter 9).

With more than two assets, the results are even more complex. In the sample case of riskless and yieldless money, and a multivariate normal distribution for the yields of all other assets, Tobin's famous separation theorem implies that a proportional tax decreases the demand for money and increases the demand for all risky assets. Under more general conditions, the result is indeterminate. I provided a counterexample (see Chapter 9) in which an investor would not alter his portfolio in response to the introduction of a proportional tax. Stiglitz (1969, 1972) and Cass and Stiglitz (1970, 1972) subsequently developed a quite complete theory of portfolio allocation with many risky assets. Stiglitz recently summarized the rather negative and unpromising results of this research: "The attempt to derive from portfolio analysis general theorems about the demands for particular assets without imposing severe restrictions on either the asset structures and/or the utility functions seems to have come to a dead end: nor is it surprising that general theorems are not to be had" (1972, pp. 93–94).

Several recent studies have extended the theory of portfolio choice to dynamic multiperiod models with additively separable utility functions. Leland (1968) showed that, by suitable restrictions on the utility function, it can be proved that the introduction of a tax would increase the share of a two-asset portfolio that is held in the risky asset. These restrictions and the assumption that the asset yield in each period follows a normal distribution make this model a dynamic generalization of Tobin's original specification. Merton (1969) extended the dynamic model of Leland and Samuelson (1969) to a continuous time process with continuous portfolio optimization. This has the important implication that the relevant rates of return necessarily follow a multivariate normal distribution. Although Merton did not consider the effects of taxation, Flemming (1971) has shown that Tobin's original conclusions can be obtained in the framework of Merton's continuous time model without imposing any restrictions on

---

3. Although Hall followed Tobin (1958) in claiming that this would allow all two-parameter distributions, I showed that, with more than one risky asset, the mean-variance representation of preferences is limited to the normal distribution (see Chapter 4).

either the utility function or the distributions of returns. The result is of considerable theoretical interest, but its applicability is obviously severely limited by the crucial assumption of continuous portfolio reallocation on which the multivariate normality property depends.[4]

The theory of portfolio choice has thus clarified the basic issues and corrected earlier intuitive speculations about the effect of taxation on portfolio composition. Nevertheless, we are without any clear theoretical presumption about the effect of taxes on asset choice in general and on the demand for equity investments in particular. Moreover, any attempt to evaluate the likely effects of our actual tax system must deal with a variety of special features of the personal income tax. While most of the theoretical analyses have assumed a proportional tax with full loss offset, the actual income tax is of course progressive and the possibility to offset losses is limited.[5] The most important feature of the tax is the existence of different relative tax rates for different types of investments. First, capital gains are taxed at a lower rate than dividends, interest, and rents. Moreover, capital gains are not taxed as they accrue but only when the asset is sold; there is no constructive realization when assets are given away or bequeathed, and the recipient of a bequest takes the current value of the asset as the basis for evaluating future taxable gains. This favorable treatment of capital gains implies a lower effective rate of tax on the yield from investments in equities and real estate.[6] Second, the interest on bonds issued by state and local governments is completely exempt from the income tax. Third, the imputed income on personal residences is not taxed, while mortgage interest and local property taxes are deductible expenses. The gain realized on the sale of a personal residence also enjoys particularly favorable treatment.[7] In addition to these complex features of the tax

4. The implausibility of continuous portfolio reallocation suggests other issues about the possible relevance of the dynamic model. Even if expected utility maximization is accepted as an adequate descriptive model in simple static situations, how plausible is the corresponding dynamic programming problem as a description of investment behavior through time? In the absence of competitive behavior that threatens the survival of households, why should we assume that individuals successfully optimize? Moreover, the exclusive focus on portfolio choice fails to recognize that the individual must simultaneously choose an uncertain stream of labor income and a portfolio.

5. I showed that the progressivity of the tax can change the qualitative results of the analysis (see Chapter 4); in an example in which a proportional case is neutral, a progressive tax does affect portfolio choice. Stiglitz (1969) examined the implication of limited loss offset.

6. Penner (1964) specifically examined the effect of different tax rates for different types of assets. He showed that with a quadratic utility function, the introduction of a tax on one asset only could actually increase the demand for the other asset.

7. Other differential tax rates arise from the special tax treatment of individual investment in oil and gas and from the provisions for accelerated depreciation of certain residential housing, pollution control facilities, and so on. Asset choices may also be influenced by the estate tax and by the tax treatment of charitable contributions of appreciated assets.

law, a variety of restrictions in the asset markets also affect actual portfolio choice. These include limits on the minimum investment in certain assets, transaction cost, margin requirements, and special rules about negative ("short") positions.

It is clear from this brief summary of the theoretical studies and the institutional complexities that direct empirical research now offers the greatest promise for improving our understanding of the effects of taxation on the demand for portfolio assets.

Empirical Studies of Portfolio Choice

Although there has been no econometric study of the effects of taxation on portfolio choice, several previous empirical studies are relevant to the current research. These include surveys of investors' attitudes and perceptions, indirect evidence on the effects of taxes on individual investment behavior, and general econometric studies of portfolio choice and asset demand.

The most frequently cited evidence is a 1949 survey in which Butters, Thompson, and Ballinger (1953) asked a nonrandom sample of 746 "active investors" how they had responded to the rise in tax rates in the 1940s. Approximately 69 percent indicated that the higher tax rates had no influence on their investment behavior. Of those who said they were influenced, the great majority (71 percent) indicated that the higher tax rates induced them to hold a more conservative portfolio. Even among the 193 investors with 1949 incomes over $25,000, approximately 43 percent claimed that the taxes did not affect their investment behavior. A more recent study by the University of Michigan Survey Research Center (1966) also concluded that a large fraction of investors are not influenced by tax considerations: "The awareness of preferential tax treatment and the inclination to take advantage of it appeared to be confined to a small minority of high-income people, with the notable exception of the tax advantages of capital gain" (p. 171). Even for capital gains, only about one-fifth of those with appreciated assets said that they were deterred from selling them because of tax considerations.

This reported lack of sensitivity to taxes is contrary to other evidence on household investment behavior. Bailey (1969) estimated that at least 70 percent of common stocks with accrued capital gains are never sold, presumably because individuals are induced to avoid the capital gains tax by holding the assets until death or by giving them to others. Laidler (1969) presented evidence that the demand for owner-occupied housing is quite sensitive to the price differences that result from not taxing the imputed income while allowing the deduction of mortgage interest. The substantial effect of taxes on corporate dividend behavior found by Brittain (1966) and in my own research (Chapters 4 and 5) provides indirect evidence that individuals are sensitive to tax changes.

None of the direct econometric studies of portfolio choice have dealt explicitly with the effects of taxes. Time series studies of the demand for money and other portfolio assets have used gross interest rates and have ignored the effects of the income tax, for example, DeLeeuw (1965) and Friedman (1959). Even in the postwar period, changes in tax rates and in the distribution of taxable income have altered the relative net-of-tax yields on different assets and, of course, the yields relative to cash. For studies that use much longer time series, the consequences of ignoring tax changes are obviously more significant.

Studies using cross-section data have also generally ignored the potential effect of taxes (Atkinson 1956; Claycamp 1963; Crockett and Friend 1967; Lydall 1955; Uhler and Cragg 1971; Watts and Tobin 1967). Since *gross* assets yields are the same for all individuals,[8] the relative *net* yields on different assets vary among individuals only because of taxes. Because these studies have ignored taxes, they have not tried to relate portfolio choice to the relative yields on different assets. The result is to impute an effect to income (or wealth if income is not included in the equation) that is at least partly a price effect due to the tax structure. The bias is most obvious in analyzing the demand for money, since the yield on money (either zero or the imputed value of convenience or liquidity) is untaxed while the net yields on all other assets (except nontaxable state and local bonds) fall as income and the marginal tax rate rise. The result is an overestimate of the pure income elasticity of demand for money. Since the tax rate also varies among assets for each individual (for example, the lower tax rate on capital gains), the tax rates are also relevant to more general studies of portfolio composition.

Portfolio Composition Equations

This study uses household survey data to study the effects of taxes on portfolio composition. The first stage of the analysis relates the proportions of wealth held in each type of asset to the individual's tax bracket, wealth, and other relevant variables. The coefficients of these equations are then used to assess the impact of tax rates on asset demand. The next section shows how the effect of taxes on net yields can explain both the

8. More precisely, although individuals have different ex ante gross yields, the researcher can only observe average ex post gross variables.

income class distribution of owners of each type of asset and the composition of assets held by each income class.

In 1962 the Board of Governors of the Federal Reserve System conducted a national survey of the income and assets of 2,557 households (Projector and Weiss 1966). With the assistance of the Internal Revenue Service, the survey was able to greatly oversample high-income individuals.[9] The survey includes detailed information on the composition of assets and the sources of income. Although the survey was done in 1962, these data no doubt remain the best source of information for the current analysis.

The theoretical models of the first section provide the basic framework for this study. The proportional composition of each household's portfolio is assumed to depend on its wealth and on its perception of the probability distribution of net asset yields. The age and sex of the head of the household and the ratio of human capital to total wealth are also permitted to influence portfolio composition. Additional differences in risk aversion among individuals become part of the unexplained residual variation in asset choice. No attempt is made to separate the effect of wealth on risk aversion from its effect through economies of scale in asset management.

Differences among individuals in the perceived distribution of net yields reflect two things: (1) differences in the individuals' subjective probability distributions of gross yields, and (2) objective differences in the individuals' tax situations. Since no information is available on the individuals' subjective perceptions, the study assumes that these perceptions are independent of wealth and of the tax situation and can therefore be excluded from the equation without biasing the coefficients of the remaining variables. Each individual's tax situation can be described completely by the set of tax rates applicable to each type of asset. However, such detail is obviously unnecessary. Once an individual's taxable income is specified, all of the tax rates are uniquely defined. Because of the large number of observations, it is possible to classify individuals by income and to use a set of binary variables to represent the tax situations. This permits assessing the effect of the tax without imposing parametric restrictions. The reinterpretation of these tax situation variables in terms of individual tax rates is developed below.

9. For example, 18 percent of the sample but less than 1 percent of the population had 1962 incomes over $25,000. Nearly 10 percent of the sample had wealth of more than $500,000, while only 0.2 percent of the population had that much wealth. See Projector and Weiss (1966) for a description of the survey methods and for counts of the number of respondents by income, wealth, and so on. Ferber (1969) discusses the problems of reporting errors in this data.

For the purpose of this study, financial assets have been grouped into seven types: (1) common stock, including mutual funds;[10] (2) preferred stock; (3) taxable fixed income securities, including corporate and government bonds, loans, and mortgages; (4) state and local tax-exempt bonds; (5) U.S. savings bonds; (6) bank accounts, including checking accounts and savings accounts at all types of financial institutions; and (7) interest in trusts, wills in probate, and so on. The dependent variable in each of the portfolio composition equations is the ratio of the investor's holding of the corresponding asset to the total value of the financial portfolio. There is no attempt to explain the holding of such nonfinancial assets as real estate or unincorporated business nor the extent and type of the individual's indebtedness.

The portfolio composition equation takes the form

$$p_{ji} = \sum_k \beta_{jk} TAX_{ki} + \sum_l \gamma_{jl} W_{li} + \sum_m \delta_{jm} AGE_{mi} + \alpha_{j1} SEX_i$$

$$+ \alpha_{j2} RATIO_i + \alpha_{j0} + \varepsilon_{ji}, \tag{1}$$

where p_{ji} is the proportion of total financial assets held in the type j by individual i; TAX_{ki} is a binary variable equal to one if the individual is in income class k and otherwise equal to zero; W_{li} is a binary variable for net worth class; AGE_{mi} is a binary variable for age class; SEX_i is equal to one if the head of the household is female; $RATIO_i$ is the ratio of human capital to nonhuman net worth; and ε_{ji} is a random error. Singularity of the covariance matrix is avoided by omitting one group from each of the TAX, W, and AGE sets of binary variables.

The individual's *actual* income cannot be used to define the tax situation variable. If actual income were used, the tax situation variable would depend on the mix of assets that the individual chooses. This simultaneity would clearly bias the resulting parameter estimates. It is therefore more appropriate to replace the individual's actual asset income and realized gains by an average amount that would be earned on a portfolio of his size with a "standard" mix of assets. For this purpose, the standard yield on portfolio wealth (excluding unrealized capital gains) was assumed to be 5 percent.[11] Because there is insufficient information to estimate the indi-

10. All mutual funds are included with common stock even though about 15 percent of the assets of these funds were invested in bonds or cash. This 15 percent is very small in relation to the total value of all common stock and mutual funds.

11. Labor income was defined to include wages, salaries, and earnings from partnerships, proprietorships, and farming. A substantially higher "standard yield" of 15 percent reduced the explanatory power of Eq. (1) but did not substantially alter the results of the analysis.

vidual's personal deductions, the tax situation variable is defined in terms of this measure of adjusted income. More specifically, the tax situation variables (*TAX*) are defined by nine separate brackets of adjusted income: less than $3,000; $3,000—; $5,000—; $7,000—; $10,000—; $15,000—; $25,000—; $50,000—; and over $100,000.

The net worth variable is based on a complete list of the individual's assets and liabilities, not merely portfolio assets.[12] Nine net worth classes are used to define the W_{li} variables: less than $1,000; $1,000—; $5,000—; $10,000—; $25,000—; $50,000—; $100,000—; $200,000—; and over $500,000. The *AGE* classes are: less than 35, 35–54, 55–64, and over 65.

The value of human capital is measured by the discounted future earnings with an allowance for the probability of death before retirement. More specifically, the combined effects of growing earnings, the discounting of future receipts, and the increasing probability of death are approximated by discounting a constant stream until age 65 of the individual's current labor income at the rate of 5 percent. In households with two earners, the sum of the two human capital variables is used. The variable *RATIO* is the ratio of household human capital to nonhuman net worth. Although this measure of human capital could obviously be made much more precise, further refinements do not seem useful in the current context; the coefficients of the tax variable are quite insensitive to the exclusion of the *RATIO* variable.

Table 10.1 presents the coefficients of the *TAX* variables for the six basic portfolio composition equations.[13] Since income below $3,000 is the omitted category, the coefficients show the effect of being in each tax situation relative to the portfolio composition when income is less than $3,000. For example, the first coefficient in the common stock equation (5.588) implies that the percentage of common stock in the portfolio is increased by 5.6 percentage points when the individual's tax situation changes from an adjusted income less than $3,000 to an adjusted income of $3,000 to $5,000. This difference represents the effect of the *TAX* variable only since the equation adjusts for the effects of net worth, age, sex, and the ratio of human capital to net worth.

Before the results are examined, three points of caution should be

12. See Projector and Weiss (1966) for a description of this variable. No attempt is made to allow for the value of the individual's future benefits from social security or private pensions; see Feldstein (1974).

13. The sample of 1,799 households excludes the observation in the original survey that did not have positive portfolio assets. A table showing the coefficients for all of the variables is available on request. The other coefficients are economically sensible, and there is no evidence that collinearity is a severe problem.

Table 10.1. Portfolio composition equations[a]

Tax situation variable (T_{ki})	Common stock	Preferred stock	Bonds (excluding municipal and savings)	Municipal bonds	Savings bonds	Bank accounts
3,000–	5.588	0.203	−0.265	0.088	−1.345	−2.886
	(2.715)	(0.378)	(0.955)	(0.480)	(2.172)	(3.281)
5,000–	5.664	0.615	−0.483	0.118	2.304	−6.175
	(2.614)	(0.364)	(0.919)	(0.463)	(2.091)	(3.159)
7,500–	6.632	0.376	−0.601	0.267	3.202	−8.276
	(2.674)	(0.372)	(0.940)	(0.473)	(2.138)	(3.231)
10,000–	11.177	0.281	−0.809	0.101	3.436	−12.683
	(2.773)	(0.380)	(0.961)	(0.484)	(2.186)	(3.303)
15,000–	16.152	0.171	−0.517	0.610	0.045	−14.309
	(3.092)	(0.430)	(1.087)	(0.547)	(2.473)	(3.737)
25,000–	19.496	−0.243	−0.253	0.276	−0.568	−13.733
	(3.781)	(0.526)	(1.329)	(0.669)	(3.024)	(4.569)
50,000–	23.143	0.566	−0.147	1.840	−0.443	−22.231
	(4.311)	(0.600)	(1.516)	(0.763)	(3.448)	(5.210)
100,000–	30.587	−0.761	−3.790	4.782	−2.302	−27.725
	(5.128)	(0.713)	(1.803)	(0.907)	(4.101)	(6.197)
$\bar{R}^2$	0.37	0.02	0.19	0.15	0.03	0.33

a. These coefficients refer only to the tax situation variables of Eq. (1); the other coefficients were estimated but are not shown. All coefficients have been multiplied by 100, rescaling the dependent variable to percentage composition. Standard errors are shown in parentheses.

noted. First, the linear specification of Eq. (1) implies no interaction among the *TAX*, *W*, *AGE*, *SEX*, and *RATIO* variables and makes no specific allowance for the limited range of the dependent variable. Second, the use of current income ignores the possibility of transitory income effects; the individual may choose a portfolio in response to his average or long-run tax rate rather than that prevailing in the survey year. Third, no allowance is made for the "locked-in" effect of taxing only *realized* capital gains; the individual's current portfolio may be dependent on previous decisions.

Casual inspection of the table indicates that the tax effects are quite important. The coefficients in each equation differ substantially and, in general, vary monotonically with the *TAX* variable. The increased holding of common stock is striking; the proportion of common stock increases by 31 percentage points from the lowest tax bracket to the highest. This is offset in the highest tax group by lower holdings of bonds (except municipal bonds) and of bank deposits. The holding of nontaxable municipal bonds also increases rapidly with the individuals' tax brackets. By contrast, bank accounts (which enjoy no tax advantage) drop sharply as a percentage of portfolio assets.

The coefficients of Table 10.1 can be used to provide a direct measure of the effect of tax rates on portfolio composition. Consider the equation

$$\hat{\beta}_{jk} = a_j + b_j M_k + u_{jk},\qquad(2)$$

where $\hat{\beta}_{jk}$ is an estimate of the coefficient for asset j and TAX class k (see Eq. [1]) and M_k is the marginal tax rate corresponding to TAX class k. The coefficient b_j indicates the change in the fraction of the portfolio held in asset j when the marginal tax rate rises 1 percent. It should be stressed that by using the $\hat{\beta}_{jk}$'s instead of the original p_{jk}'s, Eq. (2) focuses on the effect of the TAX variable after adjusting for the effect of W, age, sex, and the amount of human capital. The statutory marginal rates (M_k's) for 1962 were evaluated at the mean *taxable* income in each TAX class. For this purpose, the mean adjusted income in each class was regarded as a measure of adjusted gross income (AGI), and the mean taxable income at the level of AGI was derived from the official analyses of 1962 tax returns. The marginal tax rates varied from 0.20 in the lowest class to 0.43 for incomes between \$15,000 and \$25,000 and to 0.89 in the highest class.[14] Table 10.2 presents the values of a_j, b_j, and the corresponding $\bar{R}^2$ and significance level for each of the six assets.

These estimates show that *with the special features of the American tax system*, higher marginal rates increase the demand for common stock and municipal bonds and decrease the demand for other types of financial assets. The $\bar{R}^2$ values and associated significance levels (based on 7 degrees of freedom) indicate that the tax effect has a statistically significant effect for all assets with the possible exception of preferred stock. Moreover, using a linear specification for Eq. (2) understates the effect of the tax and gives only the *average* effect of the tax over its entire range.[15]

14. An alternative measure of the marginal tax rate was obtained by comparing the difference in taxes paid between successive tax brackets with the corresponding difference in income; these calculations were also based on the official Internal Revenue Service data. When this measure of the tax rate was used in Eq. (2), the results were generally similar but had lower explanatory power. This may reflect the fact that the "effective" marginal rate computed from tax return data is not the "price" faced by households but the result of the statutory rates and the individuals' adaptation of their portfolio.

15. The coefficients of Table 10.1 suggest some nonlinearity, but there are too few observations to examine this issue. An alternative test of whether taxes matter could be done with the F-statistic for the hypothesis that all of the β_{jk}'s in Eq. (1) are zero. However, the power of this test would be low because it would not use the information that the M_k's differ little among several classes and therefore that the corresponding β_{jk}'s would not be expected to differ substantially.

Table 10.2. Marginal tax rates and portfolio composition[a]

Asset	Constant term (a_j)	Tax rate (b_j)	$\bar{R}^2$	Significance level
Common stock	−2.683	36.855 (3.403)	0.94	>0.99
Preferred stock	0.521	−0.900 (0.517)	0.20	>0.87
Bonds, excluding municipal and savings	0.394	−2.691 (1.340)	0.28	>0.90
Municipal bonds	−1.258	5.014 (1.233)	0.66	>0.99
Savings bonds	2.428	−4.530 (2.379)	0.25	>0.90
Bank accounts	1.739	−31.935 (4.501)	0.86	>0.99

a. The dependent variables are the portfolio composition coefficients of Table 10.1. Standard errors are shown in parentheses. Significance levels are based on 7 degrees of freedom for each equation.

Nevertheless, it is clear that tax rates do have substantial effects, especially on the holdings of common stock, bank deposits, and municipal bonds.

These results stand in sharp contrast to some previous assertions that tax rates have only a small effect. The substantial increase in common stock holding at high tax rates is also contrary to the report by Butters, Thompson, and Ballinger (1953) that investors reported that high tax rates generally induced those who altered their investments to hold a more conservative portfolio.

It should be emphasized that the coefficients of the tax situation variables in Table 10.1 and the corresponding parameter estimates of Table 10.2 are the *partial* effect of the tax situation variable in an equation that adjusts for the effects of wealth (as well as age, sex, and the ratio of non-human to human capital). These tax situation variables therefore are not a reflection of risk aversion or economies of scale in the holding of particular types of assets, both of which are associated with wealth and not income or tax situation.

Although the effect of higher tax rates on the demand for common stock was the original impetus for the theoretical work discussed in the first section, the current results are not directly relevant to the theoretical propositions. In particular, the increase in the demand for common stock at high tax rates is undoubtedly a reflection of the favorable tax treatment of capital gains.[16] Thus, while it is clear from Tables 10.1 and 10.2 that our current tax structure actually encourages individuals with high tax rates to hold common stock, this does not imply that high tax rates per se increase the demand for common stock or other risky assets. For a better understanding of the way in which the tax structure affects asset demand, it is necessary to go beyond the simple form of Eq. (1) and to develop a model that relates asset demand to relative net yields. This is the purpose of the next section.

Relative Net Yields and Asset Choice

The basic portfolio composition equations of the previous section show how the individual's portfolio responds to his tax situation after adjusting for the effects of net worth, age, sex, and the ratio of human capital to nonhuman capital. These estimated effects of the tax situation will now be used to assess the relation between portfolio composition and the relative *net-of-tax* yields of different assets.

The analysis of this section begins by looking separately at *each type of asset* and asking the following question: Why do different income classes hold different fractions of their portfolios in this asset? More specifically, after adjusting for the effects of net worth and of demographic factors, how much of the variation among taxable income classes in the fraction of portfolio wealth held in this asset can be explained by the differences among them in the relative mean net yield of this asset?

After dealing with this question, the analysis looks separately at *each income class* and asks the following question: When adjustment is made for the effects of net worth and of demographic factors, how much of the variation in the fraction of wealth held in each type of asset by this income class can be explained by differences among the assets in relative mean net yield?

Composition of Owners by Asset Type

Because of the personal income tax, the net yield of each type of asset depends on the owner's marginal tax rate. Moreover, the special treatment of capital gains and the exemption of interest on state and local bonds imply that the net yields on all assets are not lowered in the same

---

16. Recall that in 1962 capital gains were taxed at half of regular rates with a maximum of 25 percent. Moreover, there is no tax on accrued gains and no constructive realization at death.

proportions, that is, the tax alters the *relative* net yields on different assets received by *each* person. For example, the yield on time deposits falls by the individual's marginal tax rate while the yield on tax-exempt bonds remains unchanged and the yield on capital gains falls by about half of the marginal rate.

This section examines the effects of these differences in relative mean yields on the ownership of each type of asset. The coefficients of the income variables in the basic portfolio composition equation for asset j(that is, the β_{jk}'s of Eq. [1]) measure the differences among income classes in the mean fraction of portfolio wealth held in that asset after adjusting for the effects of differences among income classes in the distribution of net worth, age, sex, and the ratio of human capital to nonhuman capital. The evidence presented below indicates that, for each asset, a substantial fraction of the variance of the β_{jk}'s among the nine income classes can be explained by the differences among them in the relative mean net yield of asset j, that is, by differences in the mean net yield on asset j relative to the mean net yield on a "standard portfolio."

More explicitly, the *relative* net yield of asset j to an individual in income class k is defined by

$$\frac{r_{jk}^N}{r_{\cdot k}^N} = \frac{r_{jk}^N}{\sum\limits_{q=1}^{6} r_{qk}^N P_{q\cdot}}, \tag{3}$$

where r_{qk}^N is the after-tax yield on asset q to an individual in income class k and $P_{q\cdot}$ is the mean proportion of portfolio wealth held in assets of type q by all investors. To make the estimated relations between the β_{jk}'s and corresponding relative net returns comparable for different types of assets, the dependent variable is measured by the adjusted income class differential (β_{jk}) relative to the mean holding of the asset $(P_{j\cdot})$ and rescaled to make the mean of the dependent variable zero. The equation estimated for each type of asset is thus

$$\frac{\beta_{jk} - \beta_{j\cdot}}{P_{j\cdot}} = \pi_{0j} + \pi_{1j}\frac{r_{jk}^N}{r_{\cdot k}^N} + v_{jk}. \tag{4}$$

The net rate of return on each asset in each income class was calculated by applying the appropriate statutory marginal rate at the mean level of taxable income in that class to the gross yield on that type of asset at the time of the survey (1962–1963). Municipal bonds were assumed untaxed. Stock dividends were taxed at the regular rate while capital gains were

Table 10.3. Relative net yields and asset ownership[a]

Asset	Constant (π_{0j})	Relative yield (π_{1j})	$\bar{R}^2$	Significance level
Common stock	−1.963	1.220 (0.234)	0.77	>0.99
Preferred stock	−5.007	4.890 (2.018)	0.38	>0.95
Bonds, excluding municipal and savings	−4.038	4.082 (1.035)	0.65	>0.99
Municipal bonds	−2.068	1.590 (0.135)	0.95	>0.99
Savings bonds	−1.002	1.149 (0.556)	0.29	>0.90
Bank accounts	−0.957	1.148 (0.235)	0.74	>0.99

a. Estimates refer to Eq. (4). Standard errors are shown in parentheses.

taxed at half of that rate.[17] The gross yields are estimates of the return for one-year investments. Thus the gross yield on bank deposits is a weighted average of currently prevailing rates. Similarly, the estimated gross yields on municipal bonds, taxable bonds, and preferred stock assume no expected change in market rates and therefore use the yield to maturity on those assets to measure the yield for one year. Because of retained earnings, the yield on equities includes both dividends and expected appreciation. There are two methods of assessing the expected appreciation: (1) the ratio of retained earnings per share to the price of the corresponding share, and (2) the actual rate of increase in share prices in the recent past. Using the Standard and Poor's index of 500 common stocks yields very similar results by both methods: 2.4 percent based on retained earnings and 2.6 percent based on appreciation during the past year. The value based on actual appreciation was used in the current estimates.

Table 10.3 presents the estimates of Eq. (4). Recall that in the absence of taxes the yield on each type of asset would be the same for all investors and the independent variable $r_{jk}^N/r_{\cdot k}^N$ would be a constant in each equation. The variation in $r_{jk}^N/r_{\cdot k}^N$ in each equation reflects only the differences in tax

17. This calculation ignores state income taxes, but these were still quite small in 1962–1963. It also ignores certain other features of the federal income tax, including the small dividend exclusions and the alternative tax on capital gains. More importantly, it assumes that equities are sold after one year. These simplifications all cause an underestimate of the net yield on equities and an underestimate of the relative advantage of equities to high-income individuals.

rates and special tax provisions. If tax considerations did not affect who held each type of asset, the equation would have no explanatory power. Table 10.3 shows that the equations do have substantial explanatory power and the effect of taxes on the ownership of assets is very important. For five of the asset types, the relation is significant at the 95 percent level or higher; for the remaining asset (savings bonds), the relation is significant at the 90 percent level. The explanatory power of the equations is surprisingly high in view of the simplicity of the model: the demand for each asset depends on all net yields but only through a single ratio; only mean yields are considered and all considerations of risk are ignored; the class of assets and yields is restricted to portfolio investments; and several special features such as the potential capital gains of convertible preferred stock and the postponement of tax liabilities with common stock and savings bonds are ignored.

To interpret the regression coefficients, recall that the dependent and explanatory variables are both unit-free numbers: the dependent variable is the proportional deviation of each income class from the mean holdings of the asset and the explanatory variable is the relative net yield on the asset for the corresponding income class. The regression coefficients are therefore similar to elasticities; for example, the coefficient of 1.220 for common stock implies that an increase of 1 percent in the *relative* net yield on equities (not the net yield itself) would increase the *relative* holding of the asset by 1.22 percent. The coefficients are quite similar for all of the asset types except preferred stock and taxable marketable bonds, where they are substantially larger. Since the relative net yields of common stock and municipal bonds increase with taxable income, these equations indicate that the current tax system substantially increases the demand for these assets by those individuals who generally have the largest total portfolio.

Composition of Portfolio by Income Class

The composition of the average portfolio in each income class is substantially affected by the relative net yields on each asset among income classes. More specifically, for each income class I have estimated the relation between the holding of each type of asset relative to the average holding by all households of that asset and the net yield of that asset in that income class relative to the average net yield on that asset:

$$\frac{\beta_{jk} - \beta_{j\cdot}}{P_{j\cdot}} = \mu_{0k} + \mu_{1k}\frac{r_{jk}^N}{r_{j\cdot}^N} + \omega_{jk}, \tag{5}$$

Table 10.4. Composition of portfolios by income class[a]

Income class ($)	Constant (μ_{0k})	Relative net yield (μ_{1k})	$\bar{R}^2$	Significance level
<3,000	−2.46 (1.44)	1.803 (1.138)	0.23	0.81
3,000−	−2.03 (0.72)	1.526 (0.568)	0.55	0.95
5,000−	−3.14 (1.71)	2.616 (1.390)	0.34	0.87
7,500−	−2.34 (0.96)	2.005 (0.814)	0.50	0.93
10,000−	−3.60 (1.20)	3.159 (1.061)	0.61	0.96
15,000−	−3.32 (2.59)	3.468 (2.709)	0.12	0.73
25,000−	−0.30 (1.20)	0.198 (1.663)	−0.25	0.09
50,000−	−0.76 (0.43)	2.233 (0.736)	0.63	0.96
100,000−	−2.45 (0.54)	7.263 (1.157)	0.88	0.99

a. Estimates refer to Eq. (5). Standard errors are shown in parentheses.

where r_j^N is a weighted average of r_{jk}^N over all individuals. Note that the dependent variable measures the effect of being in income class k on the holding of asset j relative to the average holding of that asset after adjusting for the effects of wealth, age, sex, and the ratio of human capital to nonhuman capital. The results are shown in Table 10.4.

The coefficients generally indicate a substantial and statistically significant response. In general, if the net yield on asset j is 10 percent higher than average in income class k, the proportion of asset j in the portfolio of income class k will be about 20 percent higher than average. In the highest income class the coefficient is much greater (7.263), indicating that a 10 percent difference in net yield would be associated with a 70 percent difference in portfolio composition.

It is important to note that these effects are solely a reflection of the tax differences. In the absence of the tax, r_{jk}^N would be the same for all income classes; each r_j^N would equal the common value of r_{jk}^N, making the explanatory variable a constant. The explanatory power of these equations and the typical sizes of the coefficients indicate the important effects of tax-induced differences in net rates of return or the demands for portfolio assets.

Effects of Taxes on Social Return and Portfolio Risk

Until now, the analysis in this chapter has focused on explaining the *behavior* of the portfolio investor. I now return to the basic question that motivated economists' interest in the effect of taxation on portfolio choice: does the progressive tax system deter high-income individuals from holding portfolios with high social (that is, pretax) rates of return? Although the effect of the tax on pretax portfolio risk is only of interest because of the assumed association between high risk and high yield, the focus in the theoretical research on the effect of taxes on risk taking as such makes it interesting to ask whether our tax system discourages individuals with high taxable income from holding portfolios with greater pretax risk.

To answer these questions, I return to the individual survey observations used in the third section of this chapter to estimate the basic portfolio composition equations. The pretax social rate of return on each individual's portfolio is generally evaluated as the average of the gross yields on each type of asset, weighted by the fraction of that asset in the individual's portfolio.[18] The appropriate definition of the social rates of return on common stock and preferred stock raises a special problem. Because of the corporation tax, the owners of common and preferred stock receive only about half of pretax corporate profits in the forms of pretax dividends and retained earnings. The estimates of this section therefore also use an alternative measure of the social rate of return on each individual's portfolio in which the social return on common stock and preferred stock is twice the gross yield to the shareholder.[19]

Although the social rate of return on each investor's portfolio is an objective value that can in principle be measured accurately, the pretax risk on that portfolio is a subjective attribute that defies precise measurement. The procedure used here is to measure risk by a variance estimated with historical data for the fifteen-year period before the survey. Because the analysis is concerned with yields and risk for a one-year holding period, the returns on bank accounts and savings deposits were assumed to be known with certainty. For the other four types of assets, a covariance matrix was calculated using one-year rates of return as the basic observations. For common stock, these one-year rates of return were measured

18. The measurement of these gross yields was discussed in the first part of the fourth section.

19. This may overstate the social return on private equity capital because the method of accelerated depreciation causes the effective rate of tax on the social return to be less than 50 percent.

as the sum of the dividend yield and the capital gain or loss on the sale of a Standard and Poor's "portfolio" of 500 common stocks purchased one year earlier; a similar measure was used for preferred stocks. For marketable bonds, the one-year capital gain or loss was calculated from the observed change in the market interest rate as the change in the present value of a bond with fifteen years to maturity and a coupon interest rate equal at the beginning of the year to the original yield to maturity. From the covariance matrix estimated with these annual values, the pretax variance of each investor's portfolio was calculated using the fractions of each type of asset as the appropriate weights in the quadratic form.[20]

This method of estimating portfolio variance ignores the problem of inflation. When the future price level is uncertain, the *real* one-year yields on bank accounts and savings bonds can no longer be regarded as known with certainty. The variances and covariances of the other types of assets are also changed. The covariance matrix for the set of six real yields was calculated by first subtracting each year's rate of consumer price inflation from the nominal yields of the four types of marketable securities, and then regarding the nominal yields on bank accounts and savings bonds as nonstochastic so that their variances and covariances reflected only the changes in the annual rate of consumer price inflation. With this enlarged covariance matrix of real yields, the variance of each individual's portfolio was again calculated using the fractions of each type of asset as the weights in the relevant quadratic form.

A social rate of return equation was estimated using the sample of 1,799 households described in the third section. The independent variables were again classificatory binary variables for adjusted income, net worth, age, and sex, and a continuous variable measuring the ratio of human capital to nonhuman capital. The specification is thus identical to Eq. (1) except that the dependent variable is now the social rate of return on the portfolio. The equation was also estimated with the two estimates of the pretax risk of the portfolio as the dependent variable.

The results for the income class variables are presented in Table 10.5. Column 1 presents the results with the social returns on equity investments measured by the gross yield to shareholders, that is, after the corporation tax; in column 2, twice this gross yield is used, that is, before the corporation tax. Both sets of coefficients rise with income, with the more rapid rise when the social return on equity is valued before the corpora-

---

20. No attempt was made to allow for the greater risk that individuals bear by holding a small number of securities of each type or for differences in the riskiness of specific stocks or bonds.

Table 10.5. Effects of taxation on social return and pretax risk[a]

Tax situation variable (T_{ki})	Social rate of return		Portfolio risk before tax	
	After corporation tax (1)	Before corporation tax (2)	Nominal yields (3)	Real yields (4)
3,000–	0.067	0.268	0.647	0.048
	(0.065)	(0.234)	(0.264)	(0.084)
5,000–	0.120	0.454	0.874	0.080
	(0.064)	(0.231)	(0.254)	(0.083)
7,500–	0.108	0.422	1.000	0.060
	(0.065)	(0.234)	(0.261)	(0.084)
10,000–	0.205	0.763	1.652	0.104
	(0.066)	(0.239)	(0.267)	(0.085)
15,000–	0.303	1.129	2.256	0.046
	(0.075)	(0.271)	(0.301)	(0.097)
25,000–	0.425	1.558	2.672	0.173
	(0.088)	(0.318)	(0.365)	(0.114)
50,000–	0.422	1.581	2.960	0.123
	(0.093)	(0.336)	(0.413)	(0.120)
100,000–	0.383	1.397	2.969	0.146
	(0.074)	(0.268)	(0.493)	(0.096)
$\bar{R}^2$	0.40	0.41	0.22	0.23
Mean	4.24	5.63	2.85	6.20

a. These coefficients refer only to the tax situation variables. The coefficients for net worth, age, sex, and human capital were estimated but are not shown. The values of $\bar{R}^2$ refer to the complete equations. Standard errors are shown in parentheses.

tion tax. Only in the very highest bracket (over $100,000 of adjusted income) is there any suggestion that a higher tax rate induces investment in a portfolio with a lower social yield; here the fall is quite small and is presumably due primarily to the greater fraction of municipal bonds in these portfolios.

The coefficients presented in column 3 show that nominal risk taking as measured by the pretax portfolio variance of nominal yields rises substantially and monotonically with income. The current system of taxation with its special provisions for the favorable tax treatment of equities induces individuals in high-income brackets to hold portfolios with greater nominal pretax risk. However, when the risks of inflation are recognized, the results are substantially changed. Column 4 shows that the portfolio variance of *real* pretax one-year rate of return is affected very little by the individual's tax situation.

In considering these results it should be remarked that the equations from which the coefficients of Table 10.5 are taken also contain variables for net worth, age, sex, and the human capital ratio. These coefficients therefore measure the effect of the individual's tax situation after adjusting for the effects of wealth and demographic influences.

Conclusion

The basic results of this study can be summarized briefly:

1. The personal income tax has a very powerful effect on individuals' demands for portfolio assets, after adjusting for the effects of net worth, age, sex, and the ratio of human to nonhuman capital.

2. Differences among *income classes* in the relative net yields for *each type of asset* explain the pattern of ownership of that type of asset.

3. Differences among *assets* in the relative net yields explain the mix of assets held by *each income class*.

4. Higher-income individuals are encouraged by the current tax system to hold a larger share of their portfolios in common stock. The primary stimulus for this demand for equities is the special treatment of capital gains.

5. The means of the pretax yield on individuals' portfolios are an increasing function of the individuals' tax rates. The current system of taxation appears to encourage a socially more productive allocation of portfolio wealth than would otherwise have prevailed.

6. The pretax portfolio variance of nominal yields rises substantially with income, but the pretax portfolio variance of real yields is largely unaffected.

It should also be noted that this chapter deals only with financial portfolio investments. The household's total investment may also include real estate, unincorporated business, and such tax-favored assets as partnership interests in oil drilling ventures. It would obviously be of interest to extend the current analysis to a broader class of investments if a method of estimating yields for such assets could be found.

The analysis of the composition of portfolios and the distribution of asset ownership in the fourth section focused on the impact of the tax system through its effects on relative yields with no explicit attention to the effects on risk. Although the results of Tables 10.3 and 10.4 show that this approach can provide substantial explanation of the pattern of asset ownership, it is clear that a more general analysis would be desirable.

11 The Effects of the Capital Gains Tax on the Selling and Switching of Common Stock

The present method of taxing capital gains is one of the most widely criticized features of the U.S. tax system. Under current law, capital gains are taxed only when an asset is sold and are generally subject to a special tax rate that is less than or equal to half of the tax rate that would apply to ordinary income; the tax applies to the nominal increase in value with no adjustment for inflation. Reformers in the Haig-Simons tradition advocate taxing all realized capital gains at ordinary tax rates and regard the current system as a $5 billion tax subsidy to wealthy investors. Other suggestions for reform include taxing capital gains on an accrual basis (usually by adjusting the tax liability at a time when gains are realized for the implicit postponement of taxes), adjusting the amount of the capital gain for the effects of inflation, eliminating the "alternative tax" procedure that limits the tax rate to 25 percent, reducing the tax rate as a function of the holding period, taxing all capital gains at the death of the owner, or abandoning the taxation of capital gains completely in favor of a tax on consumption or wealth.[1]

The choice between the present tax law and any of the proposed reforms should reflect the way in which the behavior of investors is affected by taxation. For example, the criticism that the current rules keep investors "locked into" previously purchased securities (because taxes are postponed until the asset is sold) would apply with even greater force to

This chapter was written with Shlomo Yitzhaki. Reprinted from the *Journal of Public Economics* 9 (February 1978), pp. 17–36, by permission of North-Holland Publishing Company. We are grateful to two referees of the *Journal* for their careful comments and suggestions, to David Bradford, Harvey Galper, Nelson McClung, and George Tolley for helpful discussions, and to the Office of Tax Analysis of the U.S. Treasury for financing this research.

1. Alternative proposals to reform the taxation of capital gains are discussed in (among others): Andrews (1974), Break and Pechman (1975), Brinner (1973), David (1968), Diamond (1975), Feldstein (1976), Flemming and Little (1974), and Surrey, McDaniel, and Pechman (1976). The estimated tax subsidy is presented in U.S. Senate (1976).

the proposal to tax realized gains at ordinary tax rates but would be avoided by appropriate systems of accrual taxation or by the substitution of a consumption tax. The importance of this issue depends on the extent to which tax considerations do influence investors' decisions to sell assets.

This chapter presents what we believe to be the first econometric estimates of the effect of taxation on the selling of common stock.[2] Our analysis indicates that investors are quite sensitive to tax considerations in their decisions to sell common stock. An important feature of our data is that they permit separating "switches" of common stock (that is, sales followed by purchases of different stock or other financial assets) from "net sales" in which the proceeds are not reinvested; the evidence indicates that the portfolio reallocation decisions ("switches") are particularly sensitive to tax considerations.[3]

The first section of the chapter discusses the way in which taxes and other variables might be expected to affect the common stock sales of individual investors. The second section describes the household survey data that are used in the chapter. The estimated parameters are discussed in the third and fourth sections, and simulations of three alternative tax policies are presented in the fifth section. There is a brief concluding section in which we indicate possible directions for future work.

Taxation and Common Stock Sales

In considering how taxes are likely to affect the sales of common stock, it is useful to begin with the prior question of why individuals sell the stock that they own. Two quite different types of selling can be distinguished. First, individuals sell stock to finance consumption during retirement or to pay for the college education of children, the purchase of an automobile, or other large expenses. We shall refer to such transactions as "net sales" because the proceeds are not reinvested. Second, individuals sell stock to reallocate their portfolios into different stocks and other financial assets. The data analyzed below indicate that most of the pro-

---

2. There have, of course, been previous studies of the likely effect of taxation on the sale of stocks and other assets, but none of these presented specific econometric evidence. See in particular the valuable studies by Bailey (1969), Barlow, Brazer, and Morgan (1966), David (1968), Holt and Shelton (1962), and McClung (1966).

3. There is the further issue of how the tax treatment of capital gains affects the way that investors allocate their wealth between common stock and other assets. In Chapter 10 I present evidence that the current rules substantially increase investment in common stock by individuals with high marginal tax rates.

ceeds of stock sales are in fact reinvested in other stock; we shall refer to such sales as "stock switches." More generally, "financial switches" (that is, sales of common stock with the proceeds reinvested within one year in stocks or other financial assets) account for about two-thirds of the value of common stock sales.

Although the theory of efficient markets might at first seem to imply that individuals can do as well by holding their initial portfolios as they can by switching securities,[4] there are two distinct reasons why a rational investor who believes in the efficiency of the stock market would sell one stock and buy another. The general theory of optimal portfolio selection implies that even with unchanged expectations and tastes, individuals should continually rediversify their portfolios by selling some of the stocks that have appreciated in value and buying more of the stocks that have declined in value.[5] In addition, the optimal portfolio of an individual will change if there is a change in his risk aversion, induced for example by a change in his wealth.[6] In practice, of course, individual investors frequently believe that stocks do have different ex ante expected yields even with the same risk characteristics; that is, investors implicitly reject the idea that the stock market is fully efficient and believe that their insights, judgments, and tips are sufficient to "beat the market." Each of these reasons implies that, in the absence of transaction costs and tax considerations, investors would engage in frequent and substantial asset switches.

The current tax law should reduce "switch sales" and may also reduce "net sales." Switch sales are deterred because the seller cannot reinvest all of the proceeds but must pay some of his receipts as a capital gains tax. This tax is an increasing function of both the individual's marginal tax rate and of the fraction of the sale proceeds that represents capital gain. More specifically, the rate of tax on capital gains is one-half of the individual's tax rate for ordinary income, up to a maximum capital gains tax rate of 25 percent; no capital gains tax is due when an investor dies, and all assets are then revalued to the current market price, thereby permanently eliminating any tax liability for previous gains.[7] An example will illustrate the

4. For a brief summary of the theory of efficient markets and extensive references, see Jensen (1972).

5. See, for example, the analyses of Merton (1969) and Samuelson (1969).

6. If money is not regarded as a riskless asset (because of uncertain inflation), a change in risk aversion would in principle require a general reallocation of portfolio wealth and not just changing the shares of money and non-money assets.

7. This was the rule prevailing in the year for which our data were collected (1963). The maximum tax rate for ordinary income was then 92 percent. Assets held less than six months were subject to tax at the ordinary income rate; we ignore the special six-month rule in our current analysis.

potential importance of these rules. An individual with a 50 percent marginal tax rate who sells $100 worth of stock that has doubled in price since he bought it[8] pays a capital gains tax of $12.50. This tax could be postponed and therefore reduced in present value if the stock were instead sold at a later date; the tax would be avoided completely if the individual died before the stock was sold. The higher an individual's marginal tax rate on capital gains, the greater is the deterrent to switch selling.

The effect of the tax on *net* sales is ambiguous because of two countervailing effects that are similar to substitution and income effects. The "substitution" effect of the higher tax rate induces the investor to postpone consumption, to reduce the size of major purchases, and to plan larger bequests. The offsetting "income" effect occurs because a higher rate means that a larger gross sale must be made to obtain any given amount of after-tax revenue. If the expenditures to be financed by selling assets cannot easily be postponed or reduced in size, the effect of the tax will be to increase net selling. Since an increase in the individual's marginal tax rate on capital gains strengthens both the income and substitution effects, the relation between net selling and the individual's marginal tax rate is ambiguous.

The special provision for revaluing assets when the investor dies (known as "stepping up" the basis of the asset to market value) implies that the tax deterrent to selling should increase with the investor's age. For any given positive marginal tax rate, an older investor has a higher expected tax saving by postponing a sale for a year. This is reinforced by the tendency for the assets of older investors to have a higher ratio of accrued gain to market value. Both of these reasons should make selling and especially switching a decreasing function of age. We shall refer to this as the pure age effect.

The effects of the individual's age and marginal tax rate also interact to reinforce each other. The greater deterrent to selling that is associated with a higher marginal tax rate is an increasing function of age. Similarly, the greater deterrent to selling that is associated with older age is an increasing function of the individual's marginal tax rate. This suggests that we consider the possibility of a positive age-tax interaction effect.

Age also has an effect on net selling that has nothing to do with taxes. Older individuals are more likely to be net sellers in order to finance retirement consumption. This makes the effect of age ambiguous for net selling but does not alter the implications for switch selling.

---

8. On average, stock bought in 1954 had more than doubled in price by 1963 (the year of the survey).

Two other variables are likely to affect the individual's decision to sell common stock and the fraction of all such stock that he sells: the value of the stock in the individual's portfolio and the level of the individual's income. To understand the likely effect of the size of the portfolio or the probability and value of different types of asset sales, it is useful to think of the portfolio as a collection of different individual stocks. A larger portfolio is likely to have a greater number of different stocks so that the probability of selling at least one stock should be an increasing function of portfolio size. Individuals with larger portfolios may also be more likely to switch securities because they can justify a greater investment of time and resources in acquiring relevant information. Although the probability of selling is therefore likely to be an increasing function of portfolio size, the ratio of sales to portfolio value is likely for two reasons to vary inversely with the size of the portfolio. First, switching two or three securities in a small portfolio could involve switching 50 percent of the portfolio's market value. In addition, any net sale of stock to finance a major consumption expenditure could more easily represent a large fraction of a small portfolio.

The probability of switching at least some stock and the ratio of such switch sales to the total value of stock should both, ceteris paribus, increase with the investor's income. Higher-income individuals can afford the risks of speculation, generally have greater confidence in their own ability to make good investment decisions, and are more likely to have access to relevant investment information. Again, net sales are not likely to follow the same pattern as switches; individuals with lower money incomes are more likely to be retired or otherwise below their permanent income and therefore more likely to want the proceeds of the net sales of common stock.

Data and Definitions

In 1963 and 1964, the Board of Governors of the Federal Reserve System conducted a national survey of 2,557 households.[9] With the assistance of the Internal Revenue Service, the survey was able to oversample greatly the high-income population; for example, 18 percent of the sample but less than 1 percent of the population had incomes over $25,000. Although the survey was done almost twenty years ago, these data remain

9. See Projector and Weiss (1966) for a description of the survey methods and for counts of the number of respondents by income, wealth, and so on. Ferber (1969) discusses the problems of reporting errors in these data. I used these data to analyze the effects of taxation on portfolio composition (see Chapter 10).

the best source of information for the current analysis because they permit separate measurement of "switch" selling and "net" selling.

The survey includes detailed information on the composition of assets, the sources of income, and the sales and purchases of assets during 1963.[10] Of the 2,557 households, 646 usable observations had common stock at the end of 1962;[11] these 646 observations, representing a population of 7.7 million common stock owners,[12] are the basic data used in our study.

Based on our sample, 27 percent of stock owners in the population sold common stock in 1963.[13] The value of the shares sold by this group was 12 percent of the total value of the common stock that they owned. A majority (56 percent) of those who sold stock during the year also purchased other stock, that is, were "switch sellers." An additional 11 percent of stock sellers purchased financial assets other than stock;[14] that is, financial switch sellers constituted 67 percent of all stock sellers. Hlaf of this group (33 percent of all stock sellers) reinvested all of the proceeds of their stock sales (net of tax) in stock or other financial assets.

Stock switches accounted for 58 percent of the *value* of common stock sales, that is, 58 percent of the value of common stock sale proceeds were reinvested in common stock by the end of 1963.[15] Using the broader concept of "financial switches," that is, reinvestment in stock or other financial assets, raises the value of switches to 65 percent of stock sales. The stock sellers who reinvested *all* of their proceeds in stocks or other financial assets accounted for 28 percent of stock sales.

The marginal tax rate that is relevant for decisions about the sale of common stock is equal to the lesser of (1) one-half of the individual's marginal tax rate and (2) 0.25. To prevent simultaneity between common stock sales and the marginal tax rate, we use the marginal tax rate applicable to the first dollar of capital gains. The survey did not specifically ask for the individual's taxable income or marginal tax rate. To estimate the

10. There is no reliable information on the amount of gain realized on these common stock sales.

11. There were 751 observations with common stock, but 105 of these lacked other information required for our study.

12. This estimate is based on the sampling weights in the survey. Note that it treats a household as a single owner.

13. This percentage and the other figures in this and the next paragraph are estimates of population values based on the sampling probabilities associated with our 646 observations.

14. That is, made *net* investments in other financial assets. We exclude cash and demand deposits in defining financial assets.

15. More formally, the value of "switch sales" is the minimum of the values of sales and stock purchases, both in 1963. Since stock sold in 1963 and reinvested in stock in 1964 is not counted, the 58 percent is likely to be an underestimate.

relevant marginal tax rate, we first calculate total income from all taxable sources excluding capital gains. We then subtract the value of personal exemptions and an estimate of total deductions based on the value of the individual's residence, his outstanding debt, and the mean of the other itemized deductions in his income class. With this as an estimate of taxable income before capital gains, we use the relevant tax schedule to find the individual's marginal tax rate.[16]

The survey contains information about the age of the household head, the value of common stock owned at the end of 1962, and the total income (including tax-free income but excluding capital gains) for 1962 and 1963. We average the incomes of 1962 and 1963 to achieve a better measure of permanent income. Finally, in our estimates we use classificatory dummy variables for age, wealth, and income to avoid imposing any unnecessary constraints on the form of the functional relations.

Common Stock Sales: Basic Estimates

Although we have emphasized the likely behavioral differences between switch sales and net sales, we begin our econometric analysis by studying all sales combined. This yields a measure of the overall tax impact and provides estimates that can be compared with future results in other bodies of data that lack information on reinvestment.[17]

The estimates presented in Table 11.1 imply that higher tax rates are a substantial deterrent to the sale of common stock. To appreciate the magnitude of this effect, it is useful to discuss the tax rate coefficient in Eq. (1)

16. The use of mean deductions by income class implies that the estimated marginal tax rate for each individual will not be an exact measure but (to a linear approximation) the mean value for such individuals. This type of measurement error introduces no bias in the estimated regression coefficients because the error is uncorrelated with the observed value. A different problem results from our inability to observe accounting losses (for example, oil depletion allowances, accelerated depreciation, and so on) that reduce the adjusted gross income of high-income individuals. To the extent that such losses still leave the individual's marginal tax rate above 50 percent (that is, a taxable income of $36,000 for a married couple in 1963), they have no effect on the estimated marginal tax rate for capital gains; this is the likely effect since investments with substantial accounting losses are generally unprofitable at lower tax rates. Insofar as the actual capital gains tax rates of high-income individuals are lower on average than the values we have used, our estimated coefficient will understate the responsiveness of sales to the tax rate.

17. All of the equations in this study have been estimated by ordinary least squares. The equations might have been estimated by a logit regression, but with nearly half of the sample selling stock, there is likely to be little difference between logit and linear ordinary least squares regression. A Tobit procedure would be inappropriate for the equations dealing with the ratio of sales to value since the total value of the individual's common stock has opposite effects on the probability of selling and the conditional value of the sales.

Table 11.1. The effects of taxation on common stock sales[a]

Explanatory variables	Ratio of sales to value			Decision to sell			Ratio of sales to value among sellers	
	(1)	(2)	(3)	(4)	(5)	(6)	(7)	(8)
Tax rate on capital gains	−3.20	−3.16	−2.15	−0.65	−0.84	+0.21	−4.93	−4.70
	(1.04)	(1.10)	(1.36)	(0.58)	(0.62)	(0.76)	(1.95)	(2.04)
Age								
<35	0.15	—	1.10	0.16	—	0.42	0.01	—
	(0.14)	—	(0.34)	(0.08)	—	(0.19)	(0.31)	—
36–45	0.04	—	0.18	0.14	—	0.33	−0.06	—
	(0.12)	—	(0.29)	(0.06)	—	(0.16)	(0.24)	—
46–55	0.01	—	0.31	0.08	—	0.28	−0.03	—
	(0.11)	—	(0.28)	(0.06)	—	(0.16)	(0.22)	—
56–65	0.02	—	0.11	0.03	—	0.28	0.07	—
	(0.10)	—	(0.28)	(0.06)	—	(0.16)	(0.21)	—
Tax rate–Age interaction								
<35	—	−0.16	−6.66	—	0.61	−1.58	—	−1.45
	—	(0.84)	(2.13)	—	(0.47)	(1.19)	—	(1.68)
36–45	—	0.02	−0.78	—	0.49	−1.09	—	−0.18
	—	(0.62)	(1.56)	—	(0.34)	(0.88)	—	(1.13)
46–55	—	−0.23	−1.68	—	0.22	−0.22	—	−0.30
	—	(0.55)	(1.45)	—	(0.30)	(0.81)	—	(1.00)
56–65	—	−0.03	−0.54	—	−0.06	−1.37	—	0.30
	—	(0.51)	(1.42)	—	(0.29)	(0.80)	—	(0.95)
Value of common stock								
Less than $4,000	0.32	0.36	0.34	−0.46	−0.45	−0.46	1.71	1.75
	(0.13)	(0.13)	(0.13)	(0.07)	(0.07)	(0.07)	(0.29)	(0.28)
$4,000–$10,000	0.42	0.44	0.45	−0.23	−0.22	−0.22	1.05	1.08
	(0.14)	(0.15)	(0.14)	(0.08)	(0.08)	(0.08)	(0.28)	(0.28)
$10,000–$50,000	0.16	0.17	0.19	−0.30	−0.30	−0.29	0.44	0.44
	(0.12)	(0.12)	(0.12)	(0.07)	(0.07)	(0.07)	(0.22)	(0.23)
$50,000–$200,000	0.25	0.26	0.28	−0.18	−0.17	−0.17	0.49	0.51
	(0.12)	(0.12)	(0.12)	(0.06)	(0.07)	(0.07)	(0.21)	(0.21)
Income								
Less than $10,000	−0.73	−0.73	−0.76	−0.25	−0.26	−0.27	−1.11	−1.10
	(0.19)	(0.19)	(0.19)	(0.11)	(0.10)	(0.11)	(0.40)	(0.39)
$10,000–$25,000	−0.52	−0.53	−0.55	−0.15	−0.15	−0.17	−0.87	−0.88
	(0.15)	(0.15)	(0.15)	(0.08)	(0.08)	(0.08)	(0.29)	(0.29)
$25,000–$60,000	−0.13	−0.13	−0.14	0.01	0.01	0.01	−0.14	−0.15
	(0.10)	(0.10)	(0.10)	(0.06)	(0.06)	(0.06)	(0.18)	(0.18)
Constant	0.91	0.93	0.72	0.82	0.89	0.67	1.37	1.36
	(0.27)	(0.27)	(0.32)	(0.15)	(0.15)	(0.18)	(0.51)	(0.49)

Table 11.1 (*cont.*)

Explanatory variables	Ratio of sales to value			Decision to sell			Ratio of sales to value among sellers	
	(1)	(2)	(3)	(4)	(5)	(6)	(7)	(8)
R^2	0.04	0.04	0.06	0.17	0.17	0.18	0.19	0.19
Sample size	646	646	646	646	646	646	263	263
Mean	0.24	0.24	0.24	0.41	0.41	0.41	0.59	0.59
S.D.	0.82	0.82	0.82	0.49	0.49	0.49	1.20	1.20
Population mean	0.12	0.12	0.12	0.27	0.27	0.27	0.22	0.22

a. Coefficients of the omitted groups for Age, Tax-Age interaction, Value of common stock, and Income are all zero by construction. Standard errors are shown in parentheses. Population means in columns 1, 2, 3, 7, and 8 are weighted by value of common stock. See text for definitions.

(column 1 in Table 11.1) in some detail before turning to the other equations. The dependent variable of this equation is the ratio of the value of common stock sales to the value of the initial holding of common stock.[18] The capital gains tax rate variable has a coefficient of -3.2 with a standard error of 1.0. This point estimate indicates that the capital gains tax has a very powerful effect. It implies, for example, that a capital gains marginal tax rate of 0.15 (based on an ordinary marginal tax rate of 0.30) reduces the ratio of sales to value by 0.48.[19] This is twice the sample mean of the sales-value ratio (0.24),, implying that in the absence of the capital gains tax the value of common stock sales for individuals with this marginal rate would have been about three times as large as it was in 1963.

Although this may seem a very large response to a seemingly small tax change, two things should be borne in mind. First, many investors already sell very much more than the average. Since the standard deviation of the sales-value ratio in the sample is 0.82, the calculated change of 0.48 represents an increase of about one-half a standard deviation. Second, the tax rate may not be small in relation to the gains that would otherwise motivate individuals to sell assets. An individual might well sell one stock and buy another for an expected gain of 5 percent if there were no tax but would be dissuaded from making the switch if a tax of as little as, say, 6

18. Note that a high sales-value ratio can indicate that a large fraction of shares are sold or that a small fraction is subject to very frequent turnover or any combination of these two.

19. A marginal tax rate of 0.30 was approximately the weighted average of the marginal tax rates for common stock owners as of 1973, weighting by the amounts of dividends that they receive.

percent (that is, a 15 percent tax on a gain equal to 40 percent of the value of the stock to be sold) had to be paid.

Equations (4) and (7) show that taxes affect both the decision to sell (that is, the probability that a stock owner will sell any positive amount) and the conditional ratio of sales to value among those who do sell. The estimated effect on the conditional sales-value ratio is both larger and statistically more significant than the effect on the probability of selling. The difference between the two coefficients and the fact that less than half of the stock owners sold anything suggest that there may be three different types of investors: those who prefer to sell nothing under the current tax rules and are not affected by variations of tax rates within the observed sample; those whose decision of whether or not to sell at all is sensitive to differences in the tax rate; and those who sell a positive amount that varies with the tax rate. Only a different kind of longitudinal data would permit a further analysis of this idea. In any case, the very powerful response of the conditional ratio of sales to value indicates either that the effect of taxes on switch-selling dominates a countervailing effect on net-selling or that both effects operate in the same direction.

The coefficients of the age variables generally support the importance of the tax effect. The ratio of sales to value decreases monotonically with age in Eq. (1).[20] This implies that the tax incentive not to sell that results from the stepped-up basis at death and the likely increase in the gain-value ratio with age outweigh (or at least offset) the greater volume of net sales that would be expected in older age to finance retirement consumption. Comparing Eqs. (4) and (7) shows that age affects the decision to sell rather than the ratio of sales to value among sellers. The probability of selling in the youngest age group exceeds the probability of those over age 65 by 0.16 (S.E. = 0.08), and the differential declines monotonically with age.

The same picture emerges when the age and tax variables are allowed to interact. In Eq. (5) the age dummy variables are each multiplied by the individual's capital gains tax rate. This implies that the coefficient of the tax rate varies from -0.23 $(= -0.84 + 0.61)$ for those under age 35 to -0.90 $(= -0.84 - 0.06)$ for those aged 55 to 64 and -0.84 for those over age 65. The tax effect on the decision to sell thus changes from a rather mild deterrent in the youngest age group to a quite powerful effect for those for whom the gain-value ratio is higher and the stepped-up basis at

20. Note that the coefficient of the omitted age group variable (age 65 and older) is zero by construction. One such dummy variable must be omitted from each of the classificatory variable groups to prevent complete collinearity.

death appears as a more significant consideration; with a capital gains marginal tax rate of 0.15, the coefficient of -0.23 implies a reduction in the probability of selling of 0.034 (about 13 percent of the population's average probability of selling), while a coefficient of -0.90 implies a reduction in the probability of 0.135 (about 50 percent of the population's probability of selling). Equation (6) shows that the data are not rich enough to yield useful separate estimates of a pure age effect and an age-tax interaction effect. Equation (8) shows no age-tax interaction effects, just as Eq. (7) had shown no pure age effect. An equation with both a pure age effect and an age-tax interaction (not shown) provided no further indication of any age effect.

We indicated in the first section why the probability of at least one sale is likely to increase with the size of the common stock portfolio while the conditional ratio of sales to value is likely to decrease. Equations (4) through (6) show that the probability of a sale does increase substantially with portfolio size. The probability differs between the smallest and largest portfolio classes by 0.46, nearly twice the mean probability for the population as a whole. Equations (7) and (8) also conform to our expectations, registering a sharp drop in the conditional ratio of sales to value with increasing portfolio size. The net effect, shown in Eqs. (1) through (3), is a relatively weak pattern in which the sales-value ratio does not differ significantly among small- and moderate-size portfolios but is significantly lower among the largest portfolios.

All of the equations show that the probability of selling and the conditional value of sales increase with income. This seems to confirm that those with higher income act as if they have more information, more confidence in their ability to make choices, and a greater ability to bear risk. These effects appear to dominate retirement and other departures from permanent income as influences that would tend to increase selling at lower income levels.[21]

Switching versus Net Selling

The estimates to which we now turn indicate that there is a substantial difference between switching and net selling. As we should expect for the reasons discussed in the first section, the tax has a much more powerful effect on switching than on net selling.

21. It is of course possible that the income and tax variables are not measured well enough so that some of the observed pattern of the coefficients reflects interdependent measurement error. Differences in incomes and tax rates are so great that we doubt this, but further analysis must await a better set of data.

For the equations in Table 11.2, switching is defined as selling common stock and buying other common stock. All sellers who are not switchers are classified as net sellers; that is, a stock owner is classified as a net seller if he sold common stock in 1963 but did not buy any. The value of switches for each individual is the minimum of his sales and his purchases of common stock. Net sales are defined as the value of sales, since by definition net sellers buy no stock.

Equation (1) of Table 11.2 shows that the *ratio of switches to value* is significantly and substantially reduced by higher tax rates on capital gains.[22] The coefficient of -2.78 (S.E. $= 0.94$) implies that a capital gains tax rate of 0.15 reduces the ratio of switches to total value by 0.42. For comparison, the mean switch-value ratio in the sample is 0.16 and in the population it is 0.07.[23] The coefficients of the age variables are not significantly different from zero but have such large standard errors that they are also consistent with a variety of other possible patterns.

While the *probability that an individual will switch* some stock (Eqs. [3] and [4]) does not appear to be influenced by differences in tax rates, the coefficients of the age variables do suggest that individuals are sensitive to the stepped-up basis at death or the greater gain-value ratios that are associated with older age. There is a slight fall in the probability of selling as age rises to about 50 years, followed by quite substantial and statistically significant reductions for investors over age 55.

Table 11.2 does not present estimated equations for the *conditional value* of switches (analogous to Eqs. [7] and [8] of Table 11.1). It is, however, clear from a comparison of Eqs. (1) and (3) that the powerful effect of taxes on the ratio of switches to value is due to the effect that taxes have on the conditional value of switches among those who do switch.

Equations (5) and (6) show that on balance taxes have no effect on the ratio of *net sales to value*. Equations (7) and (8) show a small tax effect on the *probability of a net sale*, but the effect is statistically weak. Of course, this absence of any overall effect is not evidence that investors ignore tax considerations when deciding whether and by how much to reduce the value of their common stock holdings. As we explained in the first section, taxes have offsetting income and substitution type effects which

22. Note that Eq. (1) of Table 11.2 has exactly the same right-hand-side explanatory variables as Eq. (1) of Table 11.1. To simplify presentation, the coefficients of the income and wealth variables and the constant term are not shown. These coefficients are also omitted in all of the remaining equations of Tables 11.2 and 11.3.

23. The population mean of 0.07 weights observations by the value of common stock; this is equivalent to defining the population mean as the ratio of aggregate sales to aggregate value.

Table 11.2. Effects of taxation on common stock switching and net selling[a]

Explanatory variables[b] (partial list)	Switching to common stock				Net selling			
	Ratio of switches to value		Decision to switch		Ratio of net sales to value		Decision to sell net	
	(1)	(2)	(3)	(4)	(5)	(6)	(7)	(8)
Tax rate on capital gains	−2.78 (0.94)	−2.63 (1.00)	−0.04 (0.53)	−0.42 (0.56)	0.02 (0.32)	0.01 (0.34)	−0.60 (0.42)	−0.42 (0.44)
Age								
<35	0.08 (0.12)	— —	0.16 (0.07)	— —	0.03 (0.04)	— —	0.00 (0.05)	— —
36–45	−0.00 (0.10)	— —	0.14 (0.06)	— —	−0.00 (0.04)	— —	−0.01 (0.05)	— —
46–55	−0.04 (0.10)	— —	0.12 (0.05)	— —	0.02 (0.03)	— —	−0.03 (0.04)	— —
56–65	−0.01 (0.09)	— —	0.05 (0.05)	— —	0.01 (0.03)	— —	−0.02 (0.04)	— —
Tax rate–Age interaction								
<35	— —	−0.59 (0.76)	— —	0.49 (0.43)	— —	0.31 (0.26)	— —	0.11 (0.34)
36–45	— —	−0.16 (0.56)	— —	0.63 (0.32)	— —	−0.06 (0.19)	— —	−0.14 (0.25)
46–55	— —	−0.39 (0.49)	— —	0.52 (0.28)	— —	0.05 (0.16)	— —	−0.30 (0.22)
56–65	— —	−0.12 (0.46)	— —	0.22 (0.26)	—	0.03 (0.16)	— —	−0.28 (0.21)
R^2	0.03	0.03	0.18	0.18	0.12	0.02	0.02	0.02
Sample size	646	646	646	646	646	646	646	646
Mean	0.16	0.16	0.29	0.29	0.06	0.06	0.12	0.12
S.D.	0.74	0.74	0.45	0.45	0.25	0.25	0.33	0.33
Population mean	0.07	0.07	0.15	0.15	0.02	0.02	0.12	0.12

a. A "switcher" is anyone who sells common stock and also buys common stock. The value of "switches" is the lesser of the values of the sales and the purchases. "Net sellers" are all others who sell common stock.

b. The variables for the Value of common stock and Income and the constant term are not presented but were included in the regression. The coefficients for the omitted groups for Age and Tax–Age interaction variables are zero by construction. Standard errors are shown in parentheses. Population means in columns 1, 2, 5, and 6 are weighted by value of common stock. See text for more detailed definitions.

make the overall impact indeterminate even if each effect is substantial separately. Similarly, while the substitution effect of the tax should be a more powerful deterrent to net sales among older persons, sales of stock to finance retirement consumption offset this pure tax effect; this could in principle account for the essentially monotonic decrease in the probability of net selling until age 65 followed by a substantial increase.

Recall that "financial switches"—that is, sales of common stock in which the proceeds are reinvested in stock or other financial assets (excluding cash and demand deposits)—account for about two-thirds of the value of all common stock sales. The estimates of Table 11.2 (as well as other equations not presented here in which net selling is defined with respect to financial assets and not just stock) also indicate that such financial switches are also the primary if not the sole way in which the capital gains tax affects the actual value of assets sold. In the remainder of this section we shall therefore examine the effect of taxes on financial switches in more detail.

Table 11.3 distinguishes "partial" switching to financial assets from "total" switching. A "partial switcher" is anyone who sells common stock but does not dissave the entire amount of the sale, that is, who reinvests some of the proceeds in stock or in the net accumulation of other financial assets. The value of the partial switch is the lesser of the value of the stock sold and the sum of the purchases of common stock plus other additions to net financial assets. A "total switcher" is anyone who sells common stock and switches *all* of the proceeds (net of tax) into either new common stock or other financial assets.[24] It is clear from these definitions that all "total switchers" are also partial switchers. The importance of "total switchers" is that they represent the pure case in which stock is sold to change the mix of portfolio assets and not to finance any consumption or nonportfolio investment. Unfortunately, such "total switching" is relatively uncommon and therefore difficult to study; only 20 percent of sample stock owners were total switchers, in comparison to the 41 percent who sold any stock. In the population, total switching accounted for only one-fourth of the value of stock sales. Moreover, the line between total switching and partial switching places too much emphasis on the discrete distinction of *total* reinvestment; this is bound to be a source of random variation that weakens the estimated effect.

The first four columns of Table 11.3 describe the effects of taxes and

---

24. The tax is calculated on the assumption that 40 percent of the value of the sale is taxable gain.

Table 11.3. Effects of taxation on switching to all financial assets[a]

Explanatory variables[b] (partial list)	Partial switching to financial assets				Total switching to financial assets			
	Ratio of switches to value		Decision to switch		Ratio of sales to value		Decision to switch	
	(1)	(2)	(3)	(4)	(5)	(6)	(7)	(8)
Tax rate on capital gains	−2.26 (0.85)	−2.29 (0.90)	−0.05 (0.55)	−0.27 (0.59)	−1.07 (0.67)	−0.90 (0.71)	0.27 (0.49)	0.26 (0.52)
Age								
<35	0.15 (0.11)	—	0.14 (0.07)	—	0.12 (0.09)	—	0.05 (0.06)	—
36–45	0.10 (0.09)	—	0.10 (0.06)	—	−0.02 (0.07)	—	0.03 (0.05)	—
46–55	0.04 (0.09)	—	0.09 (0.06)	—	−0.00 (0.07)	—	0.02 (0.05)	—
56–65	0.01 (0.08)	—	0.03 (0.05)	—	0.00 (0.07)	—	0.02 (0.05)	—
Tax rate–Age interaction								
<35	—	−0.25 (0.68)	—	0.59 (0.45)	—	−0.30 (0.54)	—	−0.01 (0.40)
36–45	—	0.27 (0.50)	—	0.37 (0.33)	—	−0.36 (0.39)	—	−0.02 (0.29)
46–55	—	−0.05 (0.44)	—	0.33 (0.29)	—	−0.20 (0.35)	—	−0.04 (0.25)
56–65	—	−0.19 (0.42)	—	0.03 (0.27)	—	−0.18 (0.33)	—	−0.01 (0.24)
R^2	0.03	0.02	0.15	0.15	0.02	0.02	0.09	0.09
Sample size	646	646	646	646	646	646	646	646
Mean	0.15	0.15	0.31	0.31	0.10	0.10	0.20	0.20
S.D.	0.66	0.66	0.46	0.46	0.52	0.52	0.40	0.40
Population mean	0.08	0.08	0.18	0.18	0.03	0.03	0.09	0.09

a. A "partial switcher to financial assets" is anyone who sells common stock but does not dissave the entire amount of the sale. The value of the switch is the lesser of the value of the stock sold and the sum of the purchases of common stock plus other additions to net financial assets. A "total switcher" is anyone who sells common stock but switches all of the proceeds net of tax into either new common stock or other financial assets.

b. The variables for the Value of common stock and Income and the constant term are not presented but were included in the regression. The coefficients for the omitted groups for Age and Tax–Age interaction variables are zero by construction. Standard errors are shown in parentheses. Population means in columns 1, 2, 5, and 6 are weighted by value of common stock. See text for more detailed definitions.

age on partial financial switching.[25] These dependent variables are quite similar to the common stock switching analyzed in Table 11.2. The results are also quite similar and need not be reviewed in detail. One difference might be noted: with the broader definition of switching used in Table 11.3, the pure age effect shows a clearer pattern of sales that decrease monotonically with age.

The results for total switching are generally consistent with the corresponding partial switching coefficients. The arbitrariness of the total switching classification and the decrease in the number of nonzero observations make the coefficients rather unreliable. But, taken at face value, the point estimate of the tax variable in Eq. (5) (-1.07, S.E. $= 0.67$) implies a quite powerful effect relative to the mean value of this ratio of total switch sales to market value; a 15 percent capital gains tax rate reduces the ratio of sales to value by 0.16, more than 150 percent of the current mean sample value of that ratio. In relation to the population mean switch to value ratio of 0.03, the effect of the capital gains tax is relatively much larger.

Simulations of Alternative Capital Gains Tax Policies

The parameter estimates described above can be used to simulate the possible aggregate effects of alternative tax treatments of capital gains. In considering the simulations that will be presented in this section, readers should bear in mind the relatively small simulation sample to which we are restricted. For policies that will reduce the selling of stock, the simulation can only make use of the 263 households with sales in 1963. Moreover, the value of sales is highly concentrated; for example, 50 percent of the value of common stock sales was from portfolios with common stock of more than $200,000, a group represented by only 90 sellers in the sample. In short, although the data can be used to estimate reliable regression coefficients, the simulation results must be regarded as illustrative and indicative rather than precise.

Three alternative policies have been simulated. The smallest change ("option 1") is to remove the 25 percent ceiling on the capital gains tax rate[26] and tax capital gains at one-half of the taxpayer's marginal tax rate. Since tax rates in 1963 rose to 92 percent, this change could increase some

25. As in Table 11.2, the income and portfolio size variables were included in the regressions, but the coefficients are not presented here in order to save space.

26. This 25 percent ceiling is known as the "alternative tax" method of calculating the tax on capital gains. Since 1963, the tax law has been modified to restrict this 25 percent ceiling to the first $50,000 of gains that a taxpayer realizes each year.

investors' capital gains tax rate from 25 percent to 46 percent. Our "option 2" change is the full Haig-Simons treatment of capital gains; that is, capital gains are taxed fully at the taxpayer's ordinary income tax rate.[27] Finally, our "option 3" is to eliminate all taxation of capital gains. While option 3 is no doubt politically as unviable as option 2, this simulation can indicate the effect that the actual law had in 1963.

Our simulations use the effect of the tax rate estimated in Eq. (1) of Table 11.1. The change in each individual's common stock sales is calculated as -3.2 times the change in his marginal tax rate.[28] To derive the individual's "new" level of sales, this change is added to the observed actual 1963 sales.[29] If the calculated decrease in sales is so large that the implied "new" level is negative, the new sales are set equal to zero. For option 3 we make the very conservative assumption that all of the increased sales are made by individuals who were already selling under the 1963 law. The stock sales of all the individuals in the sample are aggregated to national totals by using the appropriate sampling weights as adjusted for nonresponse and missing data. Since we are interested in the total effect of each proposed tax change, we make no distinction in the simulations between switches and net sales.[30]

The results of the simulations are presented in Table 11.4. Although separate analyses are presented by income and by common stock value, these figures must be regarded with great caution since each group contains only about 60 sample observations. Note that the sample implies that there were 7.7 million households with common stock worth $191 billion at the end of 1962.[31] Of these, 2.1 million households sold stock in 1963 worth $23 billion.

Removing the 25 percent ceiling on the capital gains tax rate (option 1) is calculated to reduce the number of sellers by only 4 percent (column 6) but to cut the value of sales by 23 percent (column 8). Almost all of the reduction occurs among high-income individuals since they are the only

27. We do not, however, introduce constructive realization at death or when gifts are made.

28. The simulations thus take the initial value of the individual's common stock as given, even though over time investors would adjust their holding of common stock in response to the change in the effective tax rate on the gains from common stock.

29. Note that this is equivalent to using Eq. (1) of Table 11.1 to predict each individual's level of sales for the specific tax option with the individual's constant term modified by adding his residual from the initial regression equation.

30. Readers should note the simplification involved in applying a fixed tax coefficient to large changes in the tax rate. Moreover, the capital gains tax rates involved in options 1 and 2 lie outside the range of experience.

31. This figure is lower than other estimates of the value of stock owned by individuals (see, for example, Internal Revenue Service [1967]), perhaps reflecting response bias in the survey.

Table 11.4. Simulations of alternative tax policies[a]

Taxpayer group	No. of common stock owners, 1962 (000) (1)	No. of common stock sellers, 1962 (000) (2)	Value of common stock, 1962 ($ million) (3)	Value of common stock of sellers, 1962 ($ million) (4)	Value of common stock sales, 1963 ($ million) (5)	Ratio of predicted no. of sellers to actual, 1963		Ratio of predicted sales value to actual, 1963		
						Option 1 (6)	Option 2 (7)	Option 1 (8)	Option 2 (9)	Option 3 (10)
Income										
Less than $10,000	5,036	1,063	$62,429	$21,186	$6,976	1.00	0.65	1.00	0.17	2.07
$10,000–$25,000	2,193	780	28,144	13,051	7,143	1.00	0.41	1.00	0.74	1.97
$25,000–$60,000	403	185	35,539	22,761	3,428	0.87	0.13	0.74	0.15	6.15
$60,000+	102	70	64,629	52,178	6,104	0.23	0.06	0.26	0.00	7.82
Value of common stock										
Less than $4,000	4,488	913	4,714	894	715	1.00	0.85	1.00	0.59	1.55
$4,000–$10,000	1,087	433	6,480	2,720	2,142	1.00	0.36	1.00	0.69	1.54
$10,000–$50,000	1,533	408	30,325	7,615	2,323	0.99	0.22	0.98	0.25	2.80
$50,000–$200,000	373	170	30,029	13,898	6,215	0.94	0.09	0.95	0.64	2.31
$200,000+	251	173	119,194	84,049	12,256	0.65	0.02	0.59	0.04	5.88
All common stock owners	7,732	2,097	190,736	109,173	23,651	0.96	0.49	0.77	0.30	4.12

a. These simulations use the estimated tax parameter of Eq. (1) of Table 11.1. Individual observations are weighted to represent the entire 1963 population of common stock owners. Because these simulations are based on a total of only 646 observations with 264 sellers in 1963, the simulated predictions must be regarded as subject to substantial sampling variation. The alternative policies are option 1: remove 25 percent ceiling; option 2: tax capital gains at 1963 ordinary income rates; option 3: no tax on capital gains. Columns may not add exactly to total because of rounding difference.

ones for whom the 25 percent ceiling is a binding constraint. Although the effect appears large—for example, individuals with incomes over $60,000 cut sales by 74 percent—it must be remembered that in 1963 a married couple reached the 50 percent tax rate with $36,000 of taxable income and a 75 percent rate with $100,000 of income.

Taxing all capital gains at ordinary rates (option 2) would entail a dramatic rise in tax rates and result in a sharp fall in selling. The simulation (column 7) indicates that half of those who sold in 1963 would not sell anything if their capital gains tax rate were increased by 100 percent or more as it would be under option 2. Since the relative tax rate increase is greater for higher-income individuals (who would lose the 25 percent ceiling as well), the predicted *value* of sales falls by an even greater percentage. With this treatment of realized gains, the value of sales is predicted to fall to 30 percent of its 1963 level. The fall is particularly dramatic for investors with high incomes.[32]

Finally, the elimination of the capital gains tax is predicted to increase sales to more than four times their 1963 level. Note that applying the factor of 4.12 to the 1963 sales of $23.7 billion implies sales of $97.6 billion, somewhat less than the value of the common stock of those who sold in 1963 ($109.2 billion).

In concluding this section, we should reiterate that the simulations are based on only 263 observations and must therefore be regarded as subject to substantial sampling variation. The details are particularly unreliable. But the simulations as a whole are indicative of the powerful effect that the current tax law and alternative changes in the treatment of capital gains can have.

Conclusion

In this chapter we have presented a first set of econometric estimates of the effect of the capital gains tax on the selling of common stock. The evidence indicates that there is a very substantial effect, especially on the "switching" that constitutes about two-thirds of all common stock sales.

There are several directions in which this empirical work might be extended as appropriate data become available. A possible first step would be to analyze how the distribution of holding periods varies among individuals with different tax situations. A more complete analysis would include information on the extent of capital gains and losses as well as on the volume of sales. It would clearly be useful if the effects of the tax

---

32. Such a fall in sales would actually decrease total tax revenue even though the tax rates on capital gains would more than double.

could be analyzed within a model of investor behavior that could be used to infer how such complex changes as varying the tax rate with the holding period would affect selling decisions.

The estimates in this chapter do provide at least a preliminary basis for reexamining the desirability of alternative changes in the taxation of capital gains. The apparent sensitivity of investors to tax rules indicates the importance of considering the incentive and efficiency consequences as well as equity criteria when redesigning this aspect of the current tax law.

Appendix

The two tables presented in this appendix contain the regression coefficients that were omitted in the presentation of Tables 11.2 and 11.3.

Table 11.A1. Supplement to Table 11.2: Effects of taxation on common stock switching and net selling[a]

Explanatory variables (partial list)	Switching to common stock				Net selling			
	Ratio of switches to value		Decision to switch		Ratio of net sales to value		Decision to net	
	(1)	(2)	(3)	(4)	(5)	(6)	(7)	(8)
Value of common stock								
Less than $4,000	0.24	0.27	−0.42	−0.41	0.10	0.10	−0.04	−0.04
	(0.11)	(0.11)	(0.06)	(0.06)	(0.04)	(0.04)	(0.05)	(0.05)
$4,000–$10,000	0.36	0.39	−0.30	−0.30	0.06	0.06	0.07	0.07
	(0.13)	(0.13)	(0.07)	(0.07)	(0.04)	(0.05)	(0.06)	(0.06)
$10,000–$50,000	0.12	0.13	−0.32	−0.33	0.05	0.05	0.02	0.03
	(0.11)	(0.11)	(0.06)	(0.06)	(0.04)	(0.04)	(0.05)	(0.05)
$50,000–$200,000	0.19	0.21	−0.22	−0.21	0.05	0.05	0.04	0.04
	(0.10)	(0.11)	(0.06)	(0.06)	(0.04)	(0.04)	(0.05)	(0.05)
Income								
Less than $10,000	−0.64	−0.64	−0.16	−0.17	−0.01	−0.01	−0.09	−0.09
	(0.17)	(0.17)	(0.10)	(0.10)	(0.06)	(0.06)	(0.08)	(0.08)
$10,000–$25,000	−0.45	−0.46	−0.08	−0.08	−0.04	−0.03	−0.07	−0.07
	(0.14)	(0.14)	(0.08)	(0.08)	(0.05)	(0.05)	(0.06)	(0.06)
$25,000–$60,000	−0.11	−0.12	0.05	0.05	−0.01	−0.01	−0.04	−0.04
	(0.09)	(0.09)	(0.05)	(0.03)	(0.03)	(0.03)	(0.04)	(0.04)
Constant	0.80	0.79	0.53	0.62	−0.00	−0.00	0.29	0.27
	(0.25)	(0.24)	(0.14)	(0.14)	(0.09)	(0.08)	(0.11)	(0.10)

a. These coefficients are from the equations presented in Table 11.2 and omitted there to simplify presentation.

Table 11.A2. Supplement to Table 11.3: Additional coefficients for effects of taxation on switching to all financial assets[a]

Explanatory variables (partial list)	Partial switching to financial assets				Total switching to financial assets			
	Ratio of switches to value		Decision to switch		Ratio of sales to value		Decision to switch	
	(1)	(2)	(3)	(4)	(5)	(6)	(7)	(8)
Value of common stock								
Less than $4,000	0.04	0.08	−0.38	−0.37	0.07	0.10	−0.20	−0.19
	(0.10)	(0.10)	(0.07)	(0.07)	(0.08)	(0.08)	(0.06)	(0.00)
$4,000–$10,000	0.17	0.19	−0.24	−0.23	0.17	0.19	−0.13	−0.13
	(0.12)	(0.12)	(0.08)	(0.08)	(0.09)	(0.09)	(0.07)	(0.07)
$10,000–$50,000	0.02	0.03	−0.24	−0.24	0.04	0.05	−0.14	0.13
	(0.10)	(0.10)	(0.06)	(0.06)	(0.07)	(0.08)	(0.06)	(0.06)
$50,000–$200,000	0.21	0.13	0.18	−0.18	0.02	0.03	−0.14	−0.13
	(0.09)	(0.10)	(0.06)	(0.06)	(0.07)	(0.07)	(0.05)	(0.06)
Income								
Less than $10,000	−0.37	−0.38	−0.19	−0.20	−0.20	−0.20	−0.13	−0.13
	(0.15)	(0.15)	(0.10)	(0.12)	(0.12)	(0.12)	(0.05)	(0.09)
$10,000–$25,000	−0.23	−0.23	−0.10	−0.10	−0.11	−0.12	−0.08	−0.08
	(0.12)	(0.12)	(0.08)	(0.08)	(0.10)	(0.10)	(0.07)	(0.07)
$25,000–$60,000	0.03	0.00	−0.01	−0.01	−0.03	−0.03	0.00	0.00
	(0.08)	(0.08)	(0.05)	(0.05)	(0.07)	(0.07)	(0.05)	(0.05)
Constant	0.61	0.65	0.56	0.62	0.32	0.31	0.31	0.33
	(0.22)	(0.22)	(0.14)	(0.14)	(0.17)	(0.17)	(0.13)	(0.13)

a. These coefficients are from the equations presented in Table 11.3 and omitted there to simplify presentation.

12 The Effects of Taxation on the Selling of Corporate Stock and the Realization of Capital Gains

The effective rates at which capital gains are taxed have increased substantially in recent years. Debate continues on proposals to change the tax law in ways that would further increase these tax rates as well as on proposals to reduce the effective tax on capital gains. This chapter uses a new, rich body of microeconomic data to estimate how taxation affects the selling of corporate stock and the realizing of capital gains. The results indicate that the current high rates of tax on capital gains substantially reduce the selling of corporate stock, particularly sales that would involve recognizing net capital gains.

Until 1969, the tax rate on long-term capital gains[1] was limited by a ceiling of 25 percent. Individuals whose marginal tax rates were below 50 percent could exclude half of their gains, thereby paying a tax rate of less than 25 percent. Higher-income individuals could use the "alternative tax" method that subjected the entire gain to a 25 percent tax. Since then, several statutory changes have combined to raise the tax on capital gains. The alternative tax method is now limited to the first $50,000 of capital gains per taxpayer; since 50 percent of the gains in excess of this amount are excluded from taxable income, the personal tax rate on marginal capital gains can now be as high as 35 percent. A "minimum tax," originally introduced in the Tax Reform Act of 1969, now subjects the excluded half

This chapter was written with Joel Slemrod and Shlomo Yitzhaki. Reprinted from the *Quarterly Journal of Economics* 94 (June 1980), pp. 777–791, by permission of John Wiley and Sons. We are grateful to the Office of Tax Analysis of the U.S. Treasury for financing this work, for making available the special data on which this research is based, and for comments on earlier versions of this chapter that were presented at the Treasury. This chapter was written in 1978, and the "current" tax law referred to in the text is the law as of 1978.

1. At this time, the long-term capital gain rate applied to assets held for at least six months.

of capital gains for some taxpayers to an additional tax of 15 percent. In 1969, the tax on capital gains was effectively raised further for some high-income individuals by a provision that made the tax rate that such individuals must pay on wage and salary income depend on the amount of capital gains that they realize.[2] The combination of these tax changes makes the current marginal capital gains tax rate exceed 40 percent for many individuals, substantially more than the previous 25 percent maximum.[3]

In addition to these statutory tax changes, the effective tax on real capital gains has been raised substantially by inflation. Under current law, the capital gains tax is levied on nominal capital gains with no adjustment for changes in the price level since the stock was acquired. This not only overstates the value of real capital gains, but by converting real losses to nominal gains, also reduces investors' opportunities to offset capital losses against capital gains. An earlier study (Feldstein and Slemrod 1978) analyzed the corporate stock sold by individuals in 1973. It found that adjusting the costs of these stocks for the increase in consumer prices since they were acquired would change the $4.6 billion gain on which taxes were paid to a loss of nearly $1 billion and would cut the corresponding tax liability in half.

A wide range of proposals to change the taxation of capital gains is being actively discussed.[4] The Treasury has proposed eliminating the alternative tax completely. Other proposals to increase the tax on capital gains include raising the minimum tax or even eliminating the 50 percent exclusion. The effective tax rate would be lowered by proposals to tax only real gains or to decrease the tax rate with the length of the holding period, or to repeal the minimum and maximum tax rules related to capital gains. More radical proposals include extending the "rollover" provision (in which capital gains are not taxed if the proceeds are reinvested) to cor-

2. Under the "maximum tax" provisions, the marginal tax rate on wages, salaries, and other personal services income is limited to 50 percent. The 1969 change provides that, for each two dollars of capital gain, the individual must reduce the income that he subjects to the 50 percent "maximum tax" by one dollar and subject that dollar to his ordinary tax. This reclassified dollar may then be taxed at a personal rate of up to 70 percent. For an individual with a 70 percent marginal tax rate, this reclassification adds 20 cents per two dollars of capital gain.

3. Several other statutory changes have also raised the tax on capital gains: the holding period required to qualify as long-term capital gains has increased; the basis of capital assets transferred at death is no longer increased to market value; the ability to donate capital gain property to charities has been limited, and so on. In addition, state income tax on capital gains has become increasingly important.

4. See, among others, Break and Pechman (1975), Brinner (1973), and David (1968).

porate stock or a more general substitution of an expenditure tax for the current income tax.

A prerequisite for sound policy decisions is an understanding of how alternative tax rules would affect investor behavior. It is particularly important to know whether high tax rates "lock investors in" existing stocks, thereby reducing the efficiency of the capital market. Similarly, it is important to know whether increasing the tax rate on capital gains would actually increase revenue, or by substantially reducing the realization of gains, would decrease revenue.

This study provides the first econometric analysis of the effect of taxation on the realization of capital gains. The analysis thus extends and complements the earlier Feldstein-Yitzhaki study of the effect of taxation on the selling of corporate stock (Chapter 11). The present analysis, using a large, new body of data obtained from individual tax returns, supports the earlier finding that corporate stock sales are quite sensitive to tax rates and then shows that the effect on the realization of capital gains is even stronger.

The first section of this chapter discusses the data used in this analysis. The second section presents estimates of the effect of the tax on common stock sales and compares these results with those of Chapter 11. The third section discusses the corresponding estimates of the response of realized capital gains. Simulations of the effects of several alternative policies are presented in the fourth section. There is a brief concluding section.

Data and Definitions

Each year, the Internal Revenue Service and the Treasury select a stratified random sample of approximately 100,000 individual tax returns with which to study income sources, deductions, and tax liabilities. The information for each taxpayer consists of the major items on the individual's tax return (form 1040). The sample is drawn so that the sampling fraction increases to 100 percent for taxpayers with adjusted gross incomes over $200,000. As a result, the sample can be used to make accurate estimates even for the high-income groups that consist of relatively small numbers of people. Moreover, because the sampling probabilities are known, unbiased estimates for all taxpayers or for any subgroup can be constructed.

In 1973, the Treasury collected more detailed information on the capital gains and losses reported on these tax returns. In addition to the usual information on each tax return, this special study recorded the nature of the asset (stock, real estate, and so on) the purchase price, date acquired, sale price, and date sold for each sale of a capital asset (as reported on schedule D of form 1040). Our analysis focuses exclusively on the sale of corporate stock.

In order to study the effect of tax rates on the selling of corporate stock, we require a probability sample of all the taxpayers who own stock and not just of those who sold stock in 1973. Although the tax returns provide no direct information about the ownership of corporate stock, we can use the receipt of dividends to identify stockholders. Our sample consists of 53,523 taxpayers who received dividends in 1973; the sample weights imply that this group represents a population of 11.5 million taxpaying units that owned stock in 1973. All taxpayers without dividend income are eliminated from the sample.

The analysis that we present in the following sections of this chapter relates the value of the stock sold and of the net capital gain realized by each stockowner in the sample to his "capital gains tax rate" and to other determinants of sales and gains. To calculate each individual's capital gains tax rate, we use a sophisticated computer program (TAXSIM) that embodies the basic features of the tax law as of 1973. This program calculates the effect on the individual's total tax liability of another dollar of capital gains, including such calculations as the use of the alternative tax, the extra "minimum tax," and the change in the standard deduction for those who do not itemize their deductions. The capital gains tax rate is a marginal tax rate defined as the extra tax liability due on an additional dollar of capital gain.

Since the capital gains tax rate of an individual can vary with the amount of capital gain that he realizes, there are several possible ways of calculating our capital gains tax rate variable.[5] The simplest procedure is to use the capital gains tax rate that would apply to the first dollar of corporate stock capital gain that the individual realizes, that is, the extra tax liability that would be due on a dollar of capital gain if the individual had no other sales of corporate stock. This "first dollar capital gains tax rate" has the statistical advantage of being exogenous in the sense that it is independent of the individual's decision about how much gain to realize.[6]

---

5. In effect, the individual faces a schedule of capital gains tax rates rather than a single rate.

6. There is, of course, the possibility that the individual adjusts his other taxable income (by, for example, taking other losses) during the year to the amount of gain that he realizes, thus making even this "first dollar" tax rate endogenous. To reflect this would require a much more elaborate behavioral model than we have. This is an issue we hope to investigate in future research.

However, for very wealthy individuals who typically realize large gains, these "first dollar" rates could differ substantially from the tax rates at which marginal decisions were actually made in 1973. The most appropriate rate to use for each individual is the "last dollar capital gains rate," that is, the additional tax liability that would be incurred if the individual increased his capital gain in 1973 by one dollar. Because this tax rate is endogenous to the individual's decision, an equation using this rate cannot be estimated by ordinary least squares. We therefore use a consistent instrumental variable estimation procedure.[7] Fortunately, both definitions of the tax rate yield quite similar results.

The specification of the equations that we have estimated and the precise definitions of the other variables will be discussed in the following section, where the estimates of selling behavior are presented. Before turning to this, it is useful to comment briefly on the difference between the data used in the current study and the data used in the earlier Feldstein-Yitzhaki analysis (Chapter 11). That study was based on the 1963–1964 Federal Reserve Board survey of 646 households that owned common stock at the end of 1962. The information collected for each household included the value of common stock owned at the end of 1962 and the amounts sold and purchased during 1963. This permitted studying "stock switching" and "net selling" separately. There was no reliable information on the amount of gain realized, and tax rates had to be estimated on the basis of income data reported in the survey. Despite these problems and the relatively small sample, the Feldstein-Yitzhaki analysis found clear evidence that the sale of corporate stock is very sensitive to individual differences in capital gain tax rates.

The Selling of Corporate Stock

Our analysis of the selling of corporate stock focuses on the value of corporate stock sales per dollar of dividends received during 1973. We use dividends in this way to represent the value of the stock in each individual's portfolio, since the tax returns contain no direct measure of the portfolio value. There is some evidence that the ratio of dividends to portfolio value varies inversely with the adjusted gross income (Blume, Crockett, and Friend 1974). This suggests that the tax rate appears to have a smaller

---

7. The instrumental variables are the exogenous "first dollar capital gains tax rate" and a "predicted last dollar capital gains tax rate" based on the average capital gains of individuals with that income and dividends.

effect on the sales-dividend ratio than it actually does on the sales-value ratio, and that our parameter estimates understate the effect of the tax on the selling of corporate stock.

In 1973 the average dividend yield on corporate stock was approximately 3 percent.[8] By restricting our sample to taxpayers with at least $3,000 of dividends, we limit our attention to individuals with portfolios of approximately $100,000 or more. Such taxpayers accounted for 79 percent of all dividends reported by individuals for 1973. Restricting the sample in this way eliminates the implausibly high ratios of sales to dividends that occur in smaller portfolios because of chance fluctuations and measurement errors. Taxpayers with larger portfolios are also less likely to distort the estimates by altering the timing of capital gains and losses to take advantage of the very small opportunities to offset long-term losses against short-term gains, and so on.

The age of the taxpayer affects the selling decisions in a number of ways. The tax rules that prevailed in 1973 provided that the basis (or "cost") of assets transferred at death would be revalued to the current market value. This implies that the tax deterrent to selling should increase with the taxpayer's age and should be particularly strong for older taxpayers. Older taxpayers are also likely to have held their stock for a longer time, thus increasing the ratio of gain to total share value and increasing the incentive not to sell. These considerations apply to selling in order to reinvest the proceeds in other assets. In Chapter 11 this "switch selling" was contrasted with the "net selling" used to finance consumption. Older individuals are more likely to be net sellers in order to finance consumption. Although the tax return data do not include an exact age, we can distinguish taxpayers who are age 65 or older; we include a dummy variable wherever at least one individual in the taxpaying unit is at least age 65. Since our data do not allow us to distinguish switch selling from net selling, the overall effect of age is ambiguous.

Two other variables are likely to affect the individual's decision to sell common stock: the value of the stock in his portfolio and the level of the individual's income. Although the probability of selling at least some stock is likely to increase with portfolio size, the ratio of sales to dividends is likely to vary inversely with the size of the portfolio for two reasons. First, any net sale of stock to finance a major consumption expenditure or nonportfolio investment could more easily represent a large fraction of a small portfolio. In addition, switching two or three se-

8. The yield on the Standard and Poor's 500 stocks was 0.0306.

curities in a small portfolio could involve selling a very large fraction of the total value of the portfolio. Although we do not have a direct measure of the value of stock to include in the equation, we can again use the value of dividends to represent the value of the stock. We include the logarithm of dividends so that the variable will not be dominated by the largest portfolios.

Individuals with lower money incomes are more likely to be retired (or below their permanent income for other reasons) and are therefore more likely to want the proceeds of the net sales of common stock. Again, switch sales are not likely to follow the same pattern as net sales. Higher-income individuals are more likely to switch stocks because they can better afford the risks of speculation and are more likely to have access to relevant investment information. We include the logarithm of adjusted gross income in our equation without any prior theory about its sign.[9]

Equation (1) of Table 12.1 presents the estimated coefficients for this equation. The coefficient of the tax variable (-62.4 with a standard error of 5.98) indicates that the taxation of capital gains has a very powerful effect on the selling of corporate stock. For example, a 10 percentage point increase in the tax rate on capital gains reduces the ratio of long-term sales to dividends by 6.2.

The negative coefficient on the age variable indicates that older taxpayers are less likely to sell than younger taxpayers. The tax incentives to postpone switch selling thus dominate the need to finance retirement consumption. The sales-to-dividend ratio also varies inversely with portfolio size and income.

Several variants of Eq. (1) that have been estimated (but are not presented) deserve comment. Using the "first dollar" marginal tax rate, that is, the marginal tax rate on long-term capital gains that the individual would face before he realized any capital gains, reduces the coefficient of the tax variable only slightly (from -62.4 to -45.4), and leaves the other coefficients essentially unchanged.[10] Extending the sample to all shareholders (and not just to those with more than $3,000 of dividends) eliminates the estimated effect of the tax; the coefficient of the tax variable is

---

9. To eliminate the simultaneity of adjusted gross income and sales, we exclude the actual capital gains included in AGI from AGI but add back in a predicted value of "included" capital gains based on a tabulation by income and dividends.

10. Using a marginal tax rate based on "predicted capital gains" introduces substantial random error and results in a substantially reduced tax coefficient.

Table 12.1. The effects of taxation on the selling of corporate stock and the realization of capital gains[a]

Equation	Dependent variable	Population		Estimated coefficients					Sample size
			Tax	Age 65	Logarithm of dividends	Logarithm of adjusted net AGI	Constant	
(1)	Long-term sales Dividends	All	−62.4 (5.98)	−1.13 (0.557)	−2.80 (0.188)	−0.483 (0.184)	38.8 (2.11)	27,832
(2)	Probability of selling	All	−0.650 (0.069)	−0.0295 (0.00639)	0.022 (0.00216)	0.00420 (0.00212)	0.519 (0.0242)	27,832
(3)	Long-term sales Dividends	Aged only	−59.6 (7.00)	—	−2.48 (0.203)	0.450 (0.265)	42.5 (2.46)	9,348
(4)	Probability of selling	Aged only	−0.729 (0.131)	—	0.0198 (0.00379)	0.00605 (0.00494)	0.516 (0.0458)	9,348
(5)	Long-term gains Dividends	All	−49.7 (3.79)	0.176 (0.353)	−1.23 (0.119)	−0.504 (0.117)	35.0 (1.33)	27,832
(6)	Long-term gains Dividends	Aged only	−51.8 (5.74)	—	−1.19 (0.167)	0.204 (0.217)	26.9 (2.01)	9,348

Sample statistics

	Sales dividends	Gains dividends	Probability of selling	Tax (actual last dollar)	Age 65	Logarithm of dividends	Logarithm of adjusted net AGI
Mean	7.75	3.50	0.614	0.264	0.336	10.22	11.61
Standard deviation	42.61	26.63	0.487	0.090	0.472	1.45	2.08

a. In all cases the sample is limited to returns with at least $3,000 in dividends. Figures in parentheses are the adjusted standard error of estimate.

very small and less than its standard error. As we noted above, we believe that this reflects the problems of measuring behavior of investors with small portfolios, but it may also indicate that such investors are less sensitive to tax considerations.

In 1973, 50 percent of shareholders with more than $3,000 in dividends sold some corporate stock. Equation (2) of Table 12.1 shows that the decision to sell anything, as well as the amount of selling, is sensitive to the individual's tax rate. The tax coefficient of -0.650 (with a standard error of 0.069) implies that a 10 percentage point increase in the marginal tax rate reduces the probability of selling something by 6.5 percentage points. The other estimated coefficients show that older people are less likely to sell, that investors with larger portfolios are more likely to sell something, and that higher-income individuals are also more likely to sell.

Equations (3) and (4) describe the selling behavior of taxpayers age 65 and over.[11] The tax coefficient in Eq. (3) is lower than in Eq. (1) but is still substantial. The probability of selling (Eq. [4]) shows an even greater sensitivity for older taxpayers than for the population as a whole.

The evidence in this section confirms the earlier findings of the Feldstein-Yitzhaki study (Chapter 11) that current tax laws have a very substantial effect on the selling of corporate stock. Indeed, the basic tax coefficient estimate of -62.4 in our *sales-to-dividend* equation is roughly similar to the earlier estimate that the *sales-to-market value* responds to the marginal tax rate with a coefficient of -3.20 (standard error = 1.04). Since the dividend-to-market value ratio is approximately 0.03, the current estimate of -62.4 is equivalent to -1.87 in the units of the earlier study.

Two problems should be borne in mind in interpreting the current estimates and the results presented in the next section. First, we have information on the individual's tax rate only for 1973. An individual whose tax rate varies substantially from year to year will tend to sell more when his rate is low. To the extent that low rates in 1973 are only temporarily low, our estimates will overstate the sensitivity of selling to the tax rate. We have no way of knowing how important this is. Second, our analysis is based on the 1973 experience and therefore on the bequest rules that applied then. In 1973, the tax rules provided for a full revaluation of assets transferred at death. Current law provides only for a carry-forward of the basis of assets that are bequeathed. Since this change reduces the advantage of not selling, investor behavior may be somewhat less sensitive to tax rates now than in 1973.

---

11. More precisely, at least one ''age exemption'' was claimed by these taxpaying units.

The Realizing of Capital Gains

A unique advantage of our current set of data is that it contains accurate information on capital gains and losses. We are therefore able to make the first estimates of the effects of the tax law on the realizing of net capital gains. This section follows the structure of the previous one and focuses on the net capital gains (positive or negative) realized in 1973 per dollar of dividends. Again, we examine the effect of the marginal tax rate and the taxpayer's age, portfolio size, and income.

Equation (5) of Table 12.1 shows that the realizing of capital gains is very sensitive to the marginal tax rate. The coefficient of −49.7 (with a standard error of 3.79) implies that a 10 percentage point change in the marginal tax rate changes the gain-to-dividend ratio by 4.97. An important implication of this high coefficient is that a reduction in the tax rate on capital gains would actually increase the total revenue collected.[12]

The realization of capital gains varies with portfolio size and income in the same way that selling does. The effect of age is more difficult to interpret. Equation (5) indicates that age does not have a statistically significant effect when the tax rate, income, and portfolio size are taken into account. Comparing Eqs. (1) and (5) thus suggests that the ratio of capital gains to sales rises with age, a quite plausible implication since older taxpayers are likely to have held their assets longer. Limiting the sample to older taxpayers (Eq. [6]) indicates that as a group they are equally responsive to the tax rate.

Simulating Alternative Tax Rules

The estimated coefficients imply that corporate stock sales and the recognition of capital gains are both very sensitive to marginal tax rates. In this section we use the estimated parameter values to calculate the impact of alternative tax rules on the aggregate volume of selling and the aggregate value of capital gains. For this purpose, we contrast the observed behavior under the 1973 law with two alternatives: option 1 limits the rate of tax on long-term capital gains to 0.25 (and eliminates the minimum tax), while option 2 taxes all capital gains as short-term gains, thus eliminating both the alternative tax and the exclusion.[13]

12. When this equation is reestimated for the "first dollar" marginal tax rate, the coefficient estimates are very similar: the tax coefficient is = 37.1 (S.E. 1.96). When the sample is extended to all dividend recipients, the standard errors are large, and the parameter estimates are unstable.

13. For both options, net capital losses are constrained to be less than $3,000, the value anticipated in the 1978 tax rules. For the sake of comparison, this constraint has been im-

It is important to emphasize that these simulations are not "forecasts" but measures of what, ceteris paribus, sales and realized gains would have been in steady state in 1973 under different tax rules. Any *change* in tax rules would involve transitional adjustments that are difficult to predict and that could last for several years.

Our simulation of the effect of tax changes on selling uses the tax coefficient in Eq. (1) of Table 12.1, -62.4. For each individual, we calculate the tax rate change implied by going from the 1973 law to the option being studied.[14] We then multiply this difference between marginal tax rates by -62.4. This yields the predicted change in the individual's ratio of long-term sales to dividends. This is added to his actual 1973 long-term-sales-to-dividend ratio to get a new predicted value. This new predicted value is multiplied by the individual's actual 1973 dividends to get a predicted long-term sales for the individual. This predicted value (or zero if the predicted value is negative) is aggregated over all individuals using the appropriate sampling weights. This gives the total predicted sales for the particular option. A similar calculation is done for capital gains using the coefficient of -49.7 from Eq. (4). In both cases, the calculation is limited to individuals with dividends of at least $3,000; this causes our calculations to understate the effect of tax changes, but the understatement is small, since these individuals represent 79 percent of the dividends and, having generally higher incomes, are more sensitive to changes in the tax rules.[15]

The results of our simulation are presented in Table 12.2 for seven adjusted gross income classes as well as for all taxpayers together.

Consider first the impact of the tax options on the value of corporate stock sales. Limiting the long-term capital gains tax rate to 0.25 (option 1) increases corporate stock sales to $44.6 billion from the $29.2 billion under the 1973 law. In contrast, treating all capital gains like short-term gains (option 2) reduces selling to $18.5 billion, nearly one-half its 1973

---

posed on the 1973 "current law" simulations as well. Note that option 1 does not coincide with any actual proposal for cutting capital gains tax rates, since it simply reduces the tax rate on all individuals currently facing a rate higher than 0.25, and leaves all other rates unchanged.

14. More specifically, we use the marginal tax rate on the last dollar of actual capital gain under the two alternatives.

15. Note that we do not use all of the estimated coefficients of Eqs. (1) and (5) to predict selling and gains under alternative tax rules. The very low explanatory power of the equations would make such predictions very inaccurate. Instead we use the precisely estimated tax coefficient to calculate *changes* in selling and gains. An alternative way of describing our procedure is to say that we add the calculated residual for each individual to the predicted value based on all the coefficients.

Table 12.2. Simulations of alternative tax policies[a]

	Adjusted gross income class							
	Less than $10,000	$10,000 to $20,000	$20,000 to $50,000	$50,000 to $100,000	$100,000 to $200,000	$200,000 to $500,000	More than $500,000	Total
1973 Law								
Sales	1,652	2,149	7,337	6,667	4,654	3,730	3,050	29,249
Net gains	145	271	1,046	776	883	1,000	1,139	5,262
Tax liability	6	29	142	170	239	321	401	1,308
Option 1								
Sales	1,652	2,226	7,683	8,472	8,187	8,923	7,482	44,624
Net gains	145	334	1,320	2,152	3,625	5,072	4,630	17,279
Tax liability	6	44	210	509	889	1,258	1,149	4,066
Option 2								
Sales	1,481	1,297	3,832	4,141	2,841	2,583	2,346	18,521
Net gains	184	124	117	306	442	616	791	2,580
Tax liability	−5	7	4	69	132	234	346	786

a. Option 1 limits the rate of tax on long-term corporate stock capital gains to 0.25. Option 2 taxes all corporate stock capital gains as short-term gains. All figures refer to population with dividends greater than $3,000. For both options, net gains are constrained to be greater than $3,000 for each return. For the sake of comparison, this constraint has been imposed on the 1973 law estimates as well. Figures are in millions of dollars.

level. Not surprisingly, the relative changes are greatest for the higher-income taxpayers.

The changes in realized gains are even more dramatic than the changes in sales. Limiting the tax rate to 25 percent causes a more than threefold increase in realized gains, from $5.3 billion to $17.2 billion. The higher tax rates under option 2 would substantially contract the value of realized gains.

It is interesting to note the revenue effects of the tax changes. A decrease in the tax rate causes a substantial increase in tax revenue, while a rise in the tax rate causes tax revenue to fall sharply.[16] Since the analysis pertains specifically to 1973, these estimates are directly applicable to current tax law changes only with the qualifications that changing conditions may suggest.[17] For example, since 1973 there have been alterations in a number of important aspects of the taxation of capital gains, which doubtless interact with the effects of simple changes in the rate of tax.[18]

16. Note that this calculation, like all the analysis in this chapter, refers only to corporate stock. The total revenue effect for all capital gains cannot be determined without further analysis of other asset types.

The revenue estimates that are presented in Table 12.2 are approximations to the actual tax revenue from capital gains. For the ''1973 law'' calculations, the actual last-dollar marginal rate of tax applicable to short-term gains is applied to the total short-term gains, and the actual last-dollar marginal rate of tax on long-term gains is applied to long-term gains. For option 1, the long-term tax rate is limited to 0.25 and is applied to the estimated long-term gains. Short-term realized gains are assumed to be unchanged. For option 2, the short-term tax rate is applied to both actual short-term gains and estimated long-term gains.

17. It has been suggested to us that one important qualification concerns the limitation that the stock of accrued gain has on the realizations which can be made from that stock. This raises two points. The first is whether, in our regression analysis, a measure of the amount of accrued gain available for realization by the individual should be included as an explanatory variable. We think so, but unfortunately no such measure was available. Second, it suggests that our aggregate estimate of realizations should be bounded in some way by the total accrued gain that exists. This seems a reasonable concern. We can, however, easily show that on a *continuing* basis the gains that accrue on average each year significantly exceed the realization rate predicted in the simulation of option 1.

In 1973, total dividends of nonfinancial corporations were $23.9 billion. The average ratio of dividends to share prices was 3.06 percent in that year for the 500 companies in the Standard and Poor's index. These figures imply a total market value of corporate stock of $780 billion. Realized capital gains of $17 billion would thus represent approximately 2.1 percent of the market value of the stock. While accrued gains in any year will depend on the chance fluctuations of the stock market, over the long run gains can be expected to accrue on the basis of retained earnings and the general rise in the price level. According to Standard and Poor's, retained earnings averaged 4.06 percent of market value. Even if inflation could be ignored, our calculated value of realized capital gains would be only half of accrued gain. Even a 4 percent rate of inflation would make the accrued gain equal to 8 percent of market value and would make our calculated realized gain equal to only one-fourth of the accrued gain.

18. Some of these statutory changes are listed in note 2.

Conclusion

The estimates presented in this chapter confirm the earlier finding of the Feldstein-Yitzhaki study (Chapter 11) that the selling of corporate stock is sensitive to the tax rates, and show that the realizing of capital gains is even more responsive. More generally, this chapter provides further evidence of the powerful effects that our tax system has on the process of capital formation.

The results indicate that reducing the tax on capital gains would not only encourage a more active market in corporate stock but would also increase tax revenue. There are a number of other proposals to alter the taxation of capital gains that would also increase selling: adjusting the cost of assets for the general rise in the consumer price level; constructive realization of gains at death; taxing accrued gains directly or retroactively with interest; or allowing tax-free rollovers. Analyzing the effects of such proposals requires a more complete model of the decision to sell corporate stock. The development of such a model would be an important extension of the current analysis.

13 The Lock-in Effect of the Capital Gains Tax: Some Time-Series Evidence

One issue in the current debate about lowering capital gains tax rates is the revenue cost of such a reduction. Much of the controversy has centered around the increased tax revenue that would result if the tax reduction stimulated the economy to a higher level of national income. Another, more direct possibility is that the tax revenue loss would be mitigated by an increased volume of capital gains realizations coming at any given level of national income. Investors holding appreciated assets would be less "locked in" to their current portfolio when faced with a lower tax penalty on selling assets.

Some work we have done recently at the National Bureau of Economic Research suggests that the positive response of corporate stock capital gains realizations to reduction in the capital gains tax rate is quite substantial. In fact, it may be so large that a cut in the capital gains tax would actually increase revenue from this type of capital gain. These studies (reprinted as Chapters 11 and 12 of this book) used two different cross-sectional data sets to investigate the response of individual transactions behavior to the taxation of gains.

New Evidence on Lock-in Effects

Our purpose in this chapter is to present some new evidence that a lock-in of capital gains can also be detected by looking at the aggregate data on all capital gains before and after the changes in the taxation of capital gains. *The lock-in effect is evident once we divide individuals into categories on the basis of how much the tax changes have affected them.*

We divide individuals into three categories: (1) those with adjusted gross income (AGI) less than $100,000; (2) those with AGI between $100,000 and $500,000; and (3) those with more than $500,000 in AGI. Our reasoning is that the limitation on the alternative tax, the introduction of

This chapter was written with Joel Slemrod. Reprinted with permission from *Tax Notes* (August 7, 1978), pp. 134–135.

the tax on preference income, and the "poisoning" of earned income would primarily affect only those in the latter two categories, and would affect the highest-income group more intensively than the middle group. This is illustrated by the following evidence.

In 1974 (the latest year for which such information is available), 57 percent of the income in the highest class came from returns subject to the minimum tax. The cutoff of the alternative tax similarly affected largely the upper two groups, where the greatest concentration of returns with long-term capital gains exceeding $50,000 occurs.

In 1974, 98 percent of all the net capital gains of the highest group were made by returns with at least $25,000 net gain (note that $50,000 of long-term capital gain is equal to $25,000 of net gain as defined by the IRS). Eighty percent of the net capital gain of the middle group was so concentrated, while only 22 percent of net capital gain of the lowest income group had at least $25,000 net gain per return. Clearly the limitation of the alternative tax affects the highest-income asset sellers much more often than the lowest.

Table 13.1 presents the recent history of the net gain from the sale of capital assets by income class. The first thing one notices is that the total net gain bounces around substantially from year to year, even when the tax law is unchanged. Obviously there are factors other than taxes that influence realization of gains.

The most important legal changes increasing the capital gains tax were contained in the Tax Reform Act of 1969, the relevant provisions of which took effect in the succeeding three years. In order to discern a lock-in effect, we ought to compare 1969 and before with 1970 and after. In addition, we might expect increased gains realized in 1969 in anticipation of higher taxes starting in 1970.

Table 13.1. Net gain from sales of capital assets, 1967–1976 (billions of dollars)

Adjusted gross income	1967	1968	1969	1970	1971	1972	1973	1974	1975	1976
Less than $100,000	10.3	12.7	10.3	7.7	10.4	12.9	13.5	11.8	11.9	15.2
$100,000 to $500,000	2.6	3.6	3.1	1.9	2.6	3.4	3.2	2.4	2.4	3.2
More than $500,000	1.7	2.6	2.7	1.1	1.6	2.1	1.5	1.2	1.2	1.5
Total	14.6	18.9	16.1	10.7	14.6	18.4	18.2	15.4	15.5	19.9

Source: U.S. Internal Revenue Service, *Statistics of Income: Individual Tax Returns, 1972 to 1976* (Washington, D.C.: Government Printing Office). 1975 and 1976 data are preliminary. Figures for 1971 and before are taken from the historical summary presented in the 1972 volume.

The Simplest Comparison

The simplest comparison, between 1969 and 1970, provides the most striking evidence of a lock-in effect. While net gains of the presumably unaffected under-$100,000 class were 34 percent higher in 1969 than in 1970, they were 63 percent higher for the $100,000 to $500,000 class, and the over-$500,000 class had 145 percent more gains in 1969. If we adjust the trend in gains by the change in the lowest-income class, the gains of the highest-income class were 111 percent higher in 1969 than in 1970.

Comparing these two years may be unfair, however, if 1969 included anticipatory selling by the higher-income classes, and there is some evidence that it did: while net gains of the lowest income class fell 19 percent from 1968 to 1969, net gains of the highest income class actually increased 4 percent.

A More Relevant Comparison

A fairer and more relevant comparison would be an average of 1967 and 1968 net gains on the one hand, and, on the other, an average of 1975 and 1976, the two most recent years for which data is available. Table 13.2 makes this comparison. Note first that in 1975–1976 the net gains of the lowest income class were somewhat higher than in 1967–1968, so if anything the trend since then has been upward. Nevertheless, we see that the net gains of the middle group were about 12 percent lower in 1975–1976 than they were in 1967–1968, and that the net gains of the highest income class were 35 percent lower in 1975–1976 than in 1967–1968. This is an indication that the highest-income individuals were much less likely to realize gains after the Tax Reform Act of 1969 than before.

The evidence does not depend on the assumption that the relative respective income classes have remained constant over the past decade. If we normalize the net gains in each class by some measure of total income in the group, a similar (and more powerful) relationship holds. Table

Table 13.2. Comparison of net capital gains for 1967–1968 and 1975–1976 (billions of dollars)

Adjusted gross income	1967–1968	1975–1976	Percent change
Less than $100,000	11.47	13.52	+17.9
$100,000–$500,000	3.14	2.76	−12.1
More than $500,000	2.12	1.38	−34.9

Table 13.3. Net capital gains as a percentage of adjusted gross income net of gains 1967–1968 and 1975–1976

Adjusted gross income	1967–1968	1975–1976	Percent change
Less than $100,000	2.36	1.42	−39.8
$100,000–$500,000	37.40	9.72	−74.0
More than $500,000	154.70	36.30	−76.5

13.3 specifically shows net capital gains as a percentage of adjusted gross income (not including the net capital gains) for our three groups.

While there has been a large decrease in the gain percentage for all groups, the decline for the upper two groups was far more extreme than that for the lowest income group.

Summary

In sum, we can detect evidence of a lock-in effect in the aggregate data on net gains from capital assets. This, in addition to evidence from cross-sectional research, indicates that estimates of the revenue effect of a change in capital gains taxation—if they are based on the assumption of unchanged net realized gains—may be misleading.

14 Personal Taxation, Portfolio Choice, and the Effect of the Corporation Income Tax

The current theory of public finance views the corporate income tax as an extra tax on income in the corporate sector.[1] This implies that the corporate income tax penalizes activity in the corporate sector. As a result, the corporate sector uses a smaller fraction of the nation's capital stock than it would use if corporations were taxed like partnerships.

This widely accepted conclusion rests on the simplifying assumption that all investors have the same personal tax rate. In fact, of course, personal tax rates vary greatly. Some investors pay no personal income tax, while others pay tax rates of up to 70 percent. This chapter shows that this variation in the personal tax rate may be very important for understanding the allocative effect of the corporate income tax.

Recognizing differences in personal income tax rates significantly changes the analytic structure of the problem and implies that our corporate income tax system could actually increase the fraction of the nation's capital stock that is employed in the corporate sector. The basic reason is that, under the corporate income tax system, retained earnings are not subject to the personal income tax. While dividends are taxed twice, retained earnings are taxed only at the corporate income tax rate, which is lower than the personal rate for many shareholders. Although personal tax may eventually be paid on the increase in share value that results from the retained earnings, this tax would be at the lower capital gain rate and could be postponed for a long time. For those high-income investors whose marginal rates of personal income tax are significantly

This chapter was written with Joel Slemrod. Reprinted from the *Journal of Political Economy* 88 (October 1980), pp. 854–866, by permission of the University of Chicago Press. Copyright © 1980 by the University of Chicago.

1. Harberger (1962) is the best and most widely known statement of this theory. The more recent analyses by Shoven (1976) and Shoven and Whalley (1972) also start from this premise.

greater than the corporate tax rate, the corporate income tax shelters retained earnings from the higher rate of personal income tax. Thus, although the corporate income tax system represents an increase in the total tax on corporate sector income (that is, on the pretax profits of corporations) for lower-income and middle-income investors, for many investors with high tax rates the corporate tax system actually lowers the effective tax rate on corporate-source income to less than the tax rate on income from noncorporate investments.

If all investors are considered together, the corporate tax system does represent a double taxation of dividends and does on balance raise the effective tax rate on corporate-source income. But it is inappropriate for an analysis of the allocative effects of the tax to combine investors in this way if high- and low-income investors differ in their sensitivity to after-tax yields on corporate and noncorporate investments. If the high-income investors for whom the corporate tax system lowers the effective tax rate on corporate income are more responsive to the after-tax yield differential than the lower-income investors for whom the corporate tax system raises the effective tax rate, the net effect of the corporate income tax may be to increase the amount of capital used in the corporate sector.

This chapter presents a portfolio model of the corporate income tax in an economy in which investors have different personal tax rates. The structure of the model is presented in the first section. Numerical simulations are presented in the second section. The final section comments briefly on the implications of this new model for the incidence and efficiency effects of the corporate income tax and suggests directions for extending the current analysis.

A General Equilibrium Model with Portfolio Behavior

The basic features of our problem can be represented by an economy with two classes of investors, a high-income group (denoted by a subscript H) and a low-income group (denoted by a subscript L). The low-income investors pay a personal tax rate of t_L^u on investment income in unincorporated activities and an effective tax rate on corporate-source investment income (including both the corporate and personal income taxes) of t_L^c. For this group, we make the usual assumption that a corporate tax system implies $t_L^c > t_L^u$. For the high-income group, the corresponding tax rates are t_H^u and t_H^c. We shall draw the line between "high" and "low" so that $t_H^u > t_H^c$, that is, so that the high-income group pays a lower effective tax rate on corporate income than on unincorporated income.[2] In the next section we shall also consider the case in which $t_H^u < t_H^c$ but in which the additional corporate tax burden is relatively more important to the low-income group.

The unequal tax rates create an immediate problem for the traditional model of investor equilibrium. Harberger (1959, 1962, 1966) and others have always assumed that the risk-adjusted after-tax yields on corporate and noncorporate investments were equal in equilibrium. With $t_L^c > t_L^u$ and $t_H^c < t_H^u$, this equality of after-tax yields cannot be true for both classes of investors. To see this explicitly, let F_k^c be the marginal product of capital in the corporate sector and F_k^u be the marginal product of capital in the unincorporated sector. Let the corporate sector good be chosen as numeraire (so that its price is 1) while the price of the unincorporated sector's good is p. The after-tax return on corporate investment to investors in class i is thus $(1 - t_i^c)F_k^c$, while the corresponding after-tax return on unincorporated investment is $(1 - t_i^u)pF_k^u$. Since $[(1 - t_H^c) / (1 - t_H^u)] \neq [(1 - t_L^c)/(1 - t_L^u)]$, it is clear that after-tax yields cannot be equal for both groups in both sectors.

If unequal after-tax yields are incompatible with equilibrium, both classes of investors cannot own both types of assets. To see this, consider what happens if the lower-income group does hold both types of assets, that is, if $(1 - t_L^c)F_k^c = (1 - t_L^u)pF_k^u$. Since $t_L^c > t_L^u$, this implies $F_k^c > pF_k^u$. The high-income investors will then hold only corporate investments because $F_k^c > pF_k^u$ and $t_H^c < t_H^u$ implies $(1 - t_H^c)F_k^c > (1 - t_H^u)pF_k^u$.[3]

Such specialization is not consistent with the observed ownership of corporate and noncorporate investments. High-income investors do make investments in real estate and other unincorporated businesses as well as in corporate equity.[4] To reconcile observed asset ownership with the existence of unequal relative tax rates, it is necessary to replace the equal-net-yield model of equilibrium asset ownership with a more general portfolio balance description of this equilibrium.

2. To see that this is possible with our actual tax rates, consider an individual with a marginal personal tax rate of 70 percent. This is his effective rate of tax on additional income from unincorporated investments. If he invests in a corporation that earns $100 of taxable profit, the corporation pays $48 of corporate income tax. If 40 percent of the remaining $52 is paid as dividends, the individual pays an additional 0.7 ($20) = $14 of personal tax. His total tax is thus $62, substantially lower than the personal tax rate. Even if the $30 of retained earnings is subject to capital gains tax in the future, the present value of that tax is unlikely to be as large as the $8 differential.

3. Note that specialization does not require $t_H^c < t_H^u$ but only that $[(1 - t_H^c) / (1 - t_H^u)] \neq [(1 - t_L^c)/(1 - t_L^u)]$.

4. See, for example, the evidence in Projector and Weiss (1966).

In an economy in which both corporate and noncorporate investments have uncertain yields, individual investors will want to hold both assets in their portfolios.[5] The relative quantities of both assets that an individual demands depend on their expected net-of-tax yields and on the net-of-tax risk structure of the assets. We shall not derive explicit portfolio choice equations from a basic model of utility maximization but will posit a constant-elasticity asset demand equation relating the fraction of his portfolio that an individual holds in each asset to the relative expected yields of the two assets and the relative standard deviations of those yields. We recognize that this equation, like the production functions and commodity demand equations of our model that are introduced below, is only a rough approximation of reality.

In this framework, we shall write F_k^c and F_k^u for the expected marginal products of the corporate and unincorporated sectors, respectively.[6] We also write σ_c and σ_u for the pretax standard deviations of these returns. For the high-income investors, the after-tax expected returns are thus $(1 - t_H^c)F_k^c$ and $(1 - t_H^u)pF_k^u$, and the after-tax standard deviations of these returns are $(1 - t_H^c)\sigma_c$ and $(1 - t_H^u)\sigma_u$. If $\bar{K}_H$ denotes the total amount of capital owned by high-income individuals and K_H^c the amount of that capital invested in the corporate sector, the constant-elasticity portfolio demand equation for high-income investors can be written

$$\frac{K_H^c}{\bar{K}_H} = k_H \left[\frac{(1 - t_H^c)F_k^c}{(1 - t_H^u)pF_k^u} \right]^{\mu_H} \left[\frac{(1 - t_H^c)\sigma_c}{(1 - t_H^u)\sigma_u} \right]^{\eta_H}, \tag{1}$$

where $\mu_H > 0$ and $\eta_H \leq 0$, and k_H is the share of the capital of high-income individuals that would be invested in the corporate sector if the expected net yields and associated net risks were the same in both sectors. Changes in the sectoral allocation of capital and labor will change the expected marginal products of capital according to production-function conditions that we shall specify below. There is no obvious way to specify the determination of the relative pretax risk, σ_c/σ_u. It would not be unreasonable to assume that these standard deviations were independent of the respective means and that σ_c/σ_u is therefore a constant. Alternatively, the relative pretax risks might remain constant, making

5. For a useful statement of basic portfolio theory in a model with two risky assets, see Tobin (1965). For analyses that deal explicitly with tax considerations in such a model, see Richter (1960), Stiglitz (1969), and Chapter 9 of the present work. For a brief summary of this theory and of more general contributions, see Chapter 10.

6. Recall that the corporate good is numeraire in our model so that its price is implicitly one.

σ_c/σ_u proportional to F_k^c/pF_k^u. We specify a more general constant-elasticity relation which includes both possibilities as special cases:

$$\frac{\sigma_c}{\sigma_u} = R\left(\frac{F_k^c}{pF_k^u}\right)^\gamma. \tag{2}$$

Substituting Eq. (2) into Eq. (1) yields

$$\frac{K_H^c}{\bar{K}_H} = \lambda_H \left(\frac{F_k^c}{pF_k^u}\right)^{\mu_H+\gamma\eta_H} \left(\frac{1-t_H^c}{1-t_H^u}\right)^{\mu_H+\eta_H}, \tag{3}$$

where $\lambda_H = R^{\eta_H}k_H$, the share of the capital of high-income individuals that would be invested in the corporate sector if there were no taxes and the expected yields were equal. Note that in the special case of constant relative pretax risk ($\gamma = 1$), Eq. (3) implies that the demand for corporate capital depends only on the relative net-of-tax expected yields.[7] A similar equation describes the portfolio equilibrium of the low-income group.

These two portfolio balance equations can be embodied in a general equilibrium model that is a natural generalization of Harberger's 1962 analysis extended to an economy with two groups of capital owners.[8] We follow Harberger in specifying (1) a production function for each sector, (2) a labor market equilibrium condition that the marginal revenue product of labor must be equal in both sectors, and (3) a simple demand equation in which the relative demand for corporate and noncorporate goods depends on the relative price and not on the distribution of income. For each class of investors, there is a constraint that the total available capital must be divided exhaustively between the two sectors. For each sector, there is a constraint that the total capital used in production is the sum of the capital received from the two classes of investors. Finally, a constraint that the total labor ($\bar{L}$) is divided between the corporate (L^c) and noncorporate (L^u) uses completes the model. These eleven equations determine the eleven endogenous variables: the outputs of the two sectors, the relative price of the two goods, and the allocation of labor and capital (L^c, L^u, K^c, K^u, K_H^c, K_H^u, K_L^c, K_L^u). The exogenous variables of the model are the total labor supply ($\bar{L}$), the capital stocks of the two income classes ($\bar{K}_H$ and $\bar{K}_L$), and the four tax rates.

---

7. For evidence of the ability of this simple model to explain individual portfolio composition, see Chapter 10. We assume that $\mu_i + \eta_i > 0$, that is, that the expected net yield dominates the net risk as a determinant of portfolio allocation.

8. The full model is stated explicitly in NBER Working Paper no. 241-R, an earlier but more complete version of this chapter.

In this more general model, substituting a corporate income tax system for the partnership method of taxing corporate-sector income can actually increase the share of total capital that is used in the corporate sector even though the average tax rate on corporate income is then higher than it would be if the same pattern of ownership were taxed by the partnership method. More formally, K^c/K^u can rise when we replace a tax system in which $t_L^c = t_L^u$ and $t_H^c = t_H^u$ by one in which $t_L^c > t_L^u$ and $t_H^c < t_H^u$, even though $t_L^c K_L^c + t_H^c K_H^c > t_L^u K_L^c + t_H^u K_H^c$.

This "counterintuitive" result can occur if the capital that is withdrawn from the corporate sector by low-income investors (because $t_L^c > t_L^u$) is less than the capital that is added by the high-income investors (because $t_H^c < t_H^u$). The likelihood of this occurring depends on the relative amounts of capital owned by each group ($\bar{K}_L$ and $\bar{K}_H$), the differentials in the tax rates under the corporate tax system, and the relative asset demand elasticities of both groups (the μ_i's and η_i's). Consider an obvious extreme case: If $\gamma = 1$ and $\mu_L + \eta_L = 0$ while $\mu_H + \eta_H > 0$, the corporate capital stock would be increased by a corporate tax system since high-income investors would switch assets to the corporate sector while low-income investors would leave their portfolios unchanged. Such an extreme assumption is not necessary. The next section presents an explicit numerical calculation to show that this surprising effect of the corporate tax system is possible with more plausible parameter values. More generally, the analysis of the next section shows that, with more realistic parameter values, recognition of portfolio behavior does not reverse the usual direction of the capital flow but does substantially reduce its magnitude.

Numerical Solutions of the Model for Alternative Tax Rules

We have used a specific numerical version of the model presented in the previous section to calculate how the allocation of the nation's capital stock between the corporate and noncorporate sectors could change if the current corporate tax system were eliminated and the profits arising in corporate activities were instead taxed like ordinary income. The initial values of the model with the corporate income tax in place are a stylized characterization of the U.S. economy in 1973.

To create two classes of investors, we have drawn a dividing line at $50,000 of adjusted gross income. With the help of a microeconomic simulation model which incorporates some 28,000 individual tax returns for 1973, we are able to calculate the average tax rates on additional corporate and noncorporate income for the high- and low-income investors defined in this way.[9]

On the basis of Kendrick's recent estimates of national wealth (1976), we take total privately owned capital in 1973 to be about $3.6 trillion. Twenty-five percent, or $0.9 trillion, we assign to the corporate sector.[10] To divide the ownership of this capital between high- and low-income investors, we have used the Federal Reserve Board *Survey of Financial Characteristics of Consumers* (Projector and Weiss 1966); although this survey is becoming dated, it remains the only source of such information. The survey showed that households with 1962 incomes over $25,000 owned approximately 25 percent of total wealth and 45 percent of publicly traded corporate stock. Since per capita personal income in 1973 was 2.1 times the 1962 level, we use these proportions to describe the wealth holdings corresponding to the $50,000 income level in 1973. These approximations imply that the $3.6 trillion capital stock is divided as follows: High-income investors own $405 billion of corporate equity and $495 billion of other assets, while low-income investors own $495 billion of corporate equity and $2,205 billion of other assets.[11]

The production functions for the two sectors are specified to be Cobb-Douglas. The parameter values, based on the two-sector version of the recent analysis by Shoven (1976),[12] have a capital coefficient of 0.207 in the corporate sector and 0.320 in the noncorporate sector. Our labor al-

---

9. For a description of this TAXSIM computer model and its use with corporate source income, see Chapter 8.

10. The Flow-of-Funds accounts list the market value of corporate equities in 1973 to be $911 billion.

11. Our analysis classifies corporate debt with "other assets" because the corporate income tax applies only to the equity component of corporate capital. We regard this as a crude approximation since we believe that debt and equity cannot be regarded as independent in this way. We also regard the Harberger-Shoven-Whalley assumption of a fixed debt-equity ratio as unsatisfactory. The problem of including corporate debt is compounded by the fact that much of the debt is held by financial intermediaries and not by the individuals themselves. This analysis, in common with previous studies of the corporation tax, ignores the role of financial intermediaries. Because of the special tax rules applicable to banks and insurance companies, this indirect form of ownership cannot be treated as if it were the same as direct ownership by individuals. We reiterate that our current analysis is intended to illustrate the effect of the corporate tax system in a stylized economy and cannot accurately portray the U.S. economy.

12. Shoven's table 2 presents his corrected version of Harberger's original data. By reallocating 45 percent of the corporate capital and labor (the approximate percentage not backed by equity) to the noncorporate sector, the new factor shares can be calculated. Our noncorporate sector, a mix of Shoven's corporate sector and highly capital-intensive noncorporate sector, is thus less capital-intensive than Shoven's noncorporate sector.

locations are based in a similar fashion on the wage bills paid in 1973 by the corporate and noncorporate sectors; we have 253 billion units in the corporate sector and 263 billion units in the noncorporate sector.[13] In specifying the demand function, we follow the original assumption of Harberger that the share of national income spent on corporate-sector goods is not affected by the relative price of these goods or by changes in the distribution of income.[14]

With realistic values of the tax rates and dividend payout ratios, the corporate tax system is not a "shelter" for the group that we refer to as high-income investors. Nevertheless, the simulation shows that disaggregating by income class and using a plausible portfolio response elasticity can substantially alter the conclusions of the traditional analysis. For this calculation, we assume an effective corporate tax rate of 0.491; this is the average ratio of corporate tax payments to real corporate profits (after adjusting inventory profits and capital consumption for inflation) for the period 1965–1975.[15] The ratio of dividends to real after-tax profits during the period 1956–1975, 0.659, will be used as the dividend payout rate for the simulations.

The weighted-average marginal personal tax rate for individuals whose adjusted gross incomes exceeded $50,000 in 1973 was 0.568. For individuals with adjusted gross incomes below $50,000, the weighted-average rate was 0.257. We take these to be the two tax rates on distributed dividends and on income from unincorporated investments: $t_L^u = 0.257$ and $t_H^u = 0.568$. Finally, we assume that the effective tax rate on the capital gains resulting from retained earnings is one-fourth of the individual's ordinary marginal tax rate.[16]

With these assumptions, the overall tax rates on corporate-source income are $t_H^c = 0.706$ for the high-income group and $t_L^c = 0.588$ for the

13. The corporate wage bill in 1973 was $460.6 billion, the private noncorporate approximately $55.6 billion. Allocating 45 percent of the corporate wage bill to our noncorporate sector yields these numbers.

14. Our other assumptions determine this share to be about 45 percent.

15. This makes no adjustment for the real gains that corporations accrue as inflation lowers the real value of their debt. Making such an adjustment would strengthen our conclusion by lowering the effective corporate tax rate. This would require an offsetting change in the effective tax rate on the debt income. These compensating changes are difficult to make within the framework of the current analysis. More generally, see Feldstein and Summers (1979).

16. Recall that 50 percent of long-term capital gains is excluded in calculating taxable income and that the tax is collected only when (and if) the stock is sold. This implies that the effective capital gains rate is 0.142 for the high-income group and 0.064 for the low-income group.

low-income group.[17] Note that both of these corporate income rates exceed the corresponding rates on unincorporated income: $t_H^u = 0.568$ and $t_L^u = 0.257$. Since the corporate tax system raises the tax rate on corporate-source income for both groups, there is an unambiguous shift of capital away from the corporate sector. The extent of this shift depends, however, on the nature of portfolio behavior. If we assume that the portfolio balance elasticities are both equal to 0.5,[18] the effect of integration would be to raise the corporate capital stock from $900 billion to $1.045 trillion, an increase of $145 billion or 16 percent. The corporate capital stock of the high-income group increases by 10 percent, while the corporate capital stock of the low-income group rises by more than 20 percent.

These calculations differ significantly from the capital shift implied by the traditional two-sector model that aggregates all individuals and assumes an infinite elasticity of substitution between corporate and noncorporate assets in investors' portfolios. Combining the two classes of investors implies a weighted overall tax rate on unincorporated income of $t^u = 0.397$ and a corresponding rate on corporate income of $t^c = 0.641$.[19] With these tax rates and the requirement that the net-of-tax yields are equal now and would again be equalized after integration, the switch from the current rule to an integrated system would increase the corporate capital stock from $900 billion to $1.291 trillion. This is an increase of 43 percent, nearly three times as great as the shift implied by the disaggregated model.

With parameter values that are somewhat less realistic, our model can imply that integration actually reduces capital in the corporate sector. Consider an effective corporate tax rate of 0.40, a dividend payout rate of 0.30, and no effective tax on capital gains. With personal tax rates of $t_L^u = 0.257$ and $t_H^u = 0.568$, these assumptions imply total taxes on corporate-source income of $t_L^c = 0.446$ and $t_H^c = 0.502$. Since the relative

17. The calculations are $0.491 + 0.509[0.659(0.568) + 0.341(0.142)] = 0.706$ for the high-income group and $0.491 + 0.509[0.659(0.257) + 0.341(0.064)] = 0.588$ for the low-income group.

18. That is, $_H + _H = _L + _L = 0.5$.

19. Recall that the tax rates use a weighted average of personal marginal tax rates using dividends as the weights. Since the low-income group receives 55 percent of the dividends, the disaggregated rates (t_L^u, t_H^u, and so on) are combined in the 11:9 ratio. To ensure that the equilibrium corporate capital stock under the current tax system is 900 billion, the share of national income spent on corporate goods was increased to 0.46. Note that this implies a slightly different equilibrium allocation of labor than the one presented earlier (259 billion units in the corporate sector and 257 billion units in the noncorporate sector).

tax rates on the two kinds of capital income are now reversed, the switch to an integrated tax will have the counterintuitive effect of reducing corporate capital if the portfolio balance response of the high-income group is sufficiently greater than the portfolio balance response of the low-income group (that is, if $\mu_H + \eta_H$ is sufficiently greater than $\mu_L + \eta_L$).

A greater portfolio balance response for the high-income group seems plausible; their greater wealth provides a greater variety of investment opportunities and a greater incentive to be concerned about their investment strategies. With portfolio balance elasticities of $\eta_H + \mu_H = 0.80$ for the high-income group and $\eta_L + \mu_L = 0.29$ for the low-income group, a switch from the corporate tax system to an integrated system with equal tax yield has no effect on the total corporate capital stock. The corporate capital of the low-income investors rises from \$495.0 billion to \$538.5 billion, while the corporate capital of the high-income group falls by an equal amount. With a smaller difference between the portfolio balance elasticities, the switch from the corporate tax system to the integrated system has the traditional effect of increasing the total corporate capital. With a greater difference between the price sensitivities, the switch in tax regimes has the counterintuitive effect of decreasing corporate-sector capital.[20]

It is clear that the traditional view of the allocative effect of the corporate tax system deserves careful reconsideration. A central feature in any such analysis should be a model of portfolio behavior that goes beyond the conventional assumption of equal net yields. The disaggregation of investors by income class emphasizes the importance of such portfolio behavior and opens the possibility of differences in sensitivity among different income groups. Obviously, more empirical information on such portfolio behavior is needed to reach any valid conclusions about the actual effects of the corporate income tax system.

Conclusion

In this chapter we have extended the traditional analysis of the corporate income tax to an economy with a progressive personal income tax. This extension implies a fundamental change in the analysis of the corporation tax itself. Analyzing such an economy requires replacing the traditional equilibrium condition that after-tax yields are equal on corporate and noncorporate investment with a more general portfolio balance re-

20. See table I of our NBER Working Paper no. 241-R for specific numerical results.

quirement.[21] Our analysis of this more realistic model shows that the introduction of a corporate income tax system could actually increase the fraction of the nation's capital stock that is used in the corporate sector even though the overall effective tax rate on corporate investment income is increased. The previous section showed that this surprising result can occur even for quite feasible values of the portfolio balance behavioral elasticities. With parameter values that are a more realistic description of the current U.S. corporate tax system, we showed that the more general disaggregated portfolio balance model implies a very substantial reduction in the extent to which the corporate tax system shifts the capital stock.

Our analysis has dealt with the effect of the corporate tax system on the allocation of the capital stock but not with the incidence of the corporate income tax. With the special assumptions of the previous section that the technology is Cobb-Douglas in both sectors and that the shares of expenditure on the corporate and noncorporate goods are fixed, the form of the tax system does not affect the incidence of the tax: All of the tax is borne by capital. The Cobb-Douglas technologies and competitive markets imply that labor receives fixed shares of the value of each sector's product regardless of the tax system; the fixed shares of expenditure going to each sector then imply that labor receives a fixed fraction of total national income. With labor income fixed, capital must bear the cost of any resources collected by the government. This is exactly the same reasoning that applies to the Cobb-Douglas model in Harberger's 1962 paper; the disaggregation of capital ownership is irrelevant for this even when it affects the sectoral allocation of total capital.[22] But if a more general technology or expenditure behavior is assumed, the distribution of income will generally depend on the form of the tax and the magnitudes of the portfolio balance elasticities.

Although we have not dealt explicitly with the efficiency aspects of the corporate income tax, this chapter implies that evaluating the excess burden of the corporate income tax should involve considerations that have previously been ignored. In the traditional analysis of the efficiency effects of the corporate income tax,[23] the welfare cost reflects the produc-

21. Note that this portfolio balance model is appropriate even if $t_H^c = t_H^u$ as long as the relative net yields cannot be equated, that is, as long as $[(1 - t_H^c)/(1 - t_H^u)]$ $\neq [(1 - t_L^c)/(1 - t_L^u)]$.

22. This defines incidence in the standard way, without any allowance for risk bearing.

23. Harberger is again the pioneer in this analysis; see Harberger (1962). Feldstein (1978b), Shoven (1976), and Shoven and Whalley (1972) present further developments within this framework.

tion inefficiency that results from the misallocation of capital between the corporate and noncorporate sectors. Since we have seen that the introduction of a corporate tax system can leave the allocation of total capital unchanged, it is important to stress that even in this case the corporate tax still does affect economic efficiency. Although there is no change in the production efficiency of the economy, there is a change in the way that risk is borne (that is, in what we may call "portfolio efficiency"). Without an explicit theory of the optimal taxation of risky assets, it is not possible to say whether a move from equal tax rates on corporate and noncorporate investments (that is, equal for any given taxpayer) to a system of unequal tax rates causes a welfare gain or welfare loss. More generally, a full evaluation of the welfare loss (or gain) that results from the introduction of a corporate income tax requires assessing the effects on both production efficiency and portfolio efficiency.[24]

This chapter shows that quantifying the effects of the corporate income tax requires a better understanding of portfolio behavior than we currently have. First, the analysis of portfolio behavior should be extended to include the role and special tax treatment of financial intermediaries as well as of the portfolios held directly by individuals. Second, within this extended model we need reliable estimates of the basic portfolio balance elasticities. When this information is available, it will be possible to assess more accurately the likely effects of changes in corporate tax rules and to evaluate the welfare implications of those changes.

24. The effect on capital accumulation must also be considered when the simplifying assumption of fixed capital stocks by income class is dropped. The earlier analysis of this source of welfare loss by Feldstein (1978b) assumed a single class of investors and therefore that the corporate income tax, by raising the total tax rate on corporate income, distorted individual choice by raising the relative cost of future consumption. The current chapter shows that the corporate tax system may distort the choices of low- and high-income investors in opposite directions. It is again necessary to consider the disaggregated welfare losses since both groups may incur welfare burdens from this source even if the aggregate consumption pattern is unchanged.

PART THREE

The Effects of Taxation on Business Investment

15 Tax Policy, Corporate Saving, and Investment Behavior in Britain

Much of tax policy in Britain during the past two decades has been aimed at increasing investment. Britain pioneered the use of investment allowances several years before they were adopted in the United States. In addition, during much of the period tax incentives were used to reduce dividends and encourage corporate saving in the belief that this would increase investment spending. Despite this continuing interest in the use of tax policy to stimulate capital accumulation, there has been little analysis of the direct effect of investment allowances and no analysis of the indirect effect of changes in retention behavior.

This chapter reports a study of quarterly aggregate investment in equipment and structures for the period 1954:2 to 1967:4. The analysis builds on the powerful neoclassical investment theory developed and applied by Jorgenson and his collaborators (for example, Fromm 1970; Hall and Jorgenson 1967, 1969; Jorgenson 1963, 1965; Jorgenson and Stephenson 1967, 1968) and, in modified form, by Bischoff (1968, 1969), Coen (1969), and Eisner and Nadiri (1968). The formulation used here differs from that of Jorgenson in several ways which will be explained below. Differences of particular importance for studying the effect of tax policy are that (1) the elasticity of the desired capital stock with respect to tax-induced changes in the user cost of capital is not constrained to be one or even to equal the elasticities with respect to other observed changes in the user cost, and (2) the impact of tax-induced changes in retention is explicitly studied.

The first section briefly reviews the previous studies and opinions on the impact of British tax policy on investment. The second section then presents the theory of investment behavior that forms the basis for our es-

This chapter was written with John Flemming. Reprinted from the *Review of Economic Studies* 38 (October 1971), pp. 415–434, by permission of the Society for Economic Analysis Ltd. We are grateful to Ann Black and Gary Chamberlain for research assistance.

timates. The third section considers the estimation problems raised by this formulation. We present and discuss the estimates in the fourth section and then use them, in the fifth section, to calculate both the effects that policy changes had on investment and the effects that alternative policies would have had. The results are summarized in a brief final section. A description of the data is presented in the Appendix.

Previous Studies and Opinion

On the basis of qualitative survey evidence (Corner and Williams 1965; Hart and Prusmann 1963) and an informal analysis of the aggregate national income statistics, several economists (Little 1962; Musgrave and Musgrave 1968; Williams 1966) have concluded that the investment allowances had a stimulating effect on capital accumulation.[1] None of these discussions offered any estimate of the magnitude of the effect on either investment spending or the long-run capital intensity of production.[2] The impact of tax-induced changes in retention behavior has received even less attention. This is particularly surprising since the effect of retained earnings on company investment has long been an unresolved issue because of the usual multicollinearity among output, output change, and retained earnings; the tax change provides a way of separating shifts in the equilibrium retention ratio[3] from transitory cyclical variations in retained earnings.[4]

1. We limit our discussion here to empirical studies, excluding theoretical discussion of the expected impact of policies; see, for example, Black (1959).

2. Agarwala and Goodson (1969) recently estimated an annual investment equation (for the short period 1958 through 1966) and calculated the effect of investment incentives. Their specification—that gross investment is a linear function of the expected rate of return and the cash flow—makes it difficult to give any economic interpretation to their result. For example, a change in rate of return would have the same absolute effect on investment regardless of the scale of output. As a result of this specification, the cash flow variable is the only one that reflects the scale of the economy; it would therefore have a positive coefficient even if internal availability of funds as such had no economic effect. Although Balapoulos (1967) included an investment allowance variable in an equation that was part of a macroeconomic model of the British economy, the specification of the equation and the definition of the allowance variable cast doubt on any interpretation of his result.

3. In Chapter 4 I showed that British tax policy was successful in influencing corporate saving but did not investigate the implications for investment.

4. Despite the absence of research on this subject, there has been no dearth of opinions. The Royal Commission on Taxation (1955) argued against the then prevailing tax incentive for retention on the grounds that it "does not encourage companies to plough back profits so much as to retain them" (par. 536). Balogh (1958) and Streeten (1960) concurred in this view, while Musgrave and Musgrave (1968) and Williams (1966) suggested that greater internal availability of funds could stimulate investment.

The Model of Investment Behavior

The formulation and implications of neoclassical investment theory are now very well known (see, for example, Jorgenson 1963, 1965). If product and factor markets (including the market for old capital goods) are perfectly competitive, if the production function has constant returns to scale and a constant elasticity of substitution between capital and labor, and if capital is completely malleable, then the optimum capital stock at time t is

$$K_t^* = \mu^\sigma \left(\frac{p_t}{c_t}\right)^\sigma Q_t, \tag{1}$$

where Q_t is output, p_t is the product price, c_t is the user cost of capital, σ is the elasticity of substitution, and μ is the coefficient of capital in the production function. In the special Cobb-Douglas case adopted by Jorgenson, σ is of course one and μ is the production function elasticity of output with respect to capital. The user cost of capital, which is equivalent to the price at which a unit of the capital good would rent in a competitive market, is equal to

$$c = \frac{q(r + \delta)(1 - A)}{(1 - u)}, \tag{2}$$

where q is the purchase price of a unit of the capital good, r is the after-tax rate of return, δ is the constant proportional rate of actual depreciation, u is the rate of tax on company profits,[5] and A is the discounted value of the tax savings due to the depreciation allowances, investment credits, and so on, which follow one "dollar" of investment. By assuming that the current tax rates and depreciation provisions will remain unchanged and that the interest rate is either a short rate or will remain unchanged, the current values of the right-hand-side variables can be used to define c_t.

The dynamic response of net investment to changes in K^* and the capital replacement based on proportional depreciation together determine the path of gross investment. More specifically, Jorgenson has used a variety of dynamic adjustment patterns of the general form

$$K_t - K_{t-1} = \sum_{j=0}^{\infty} \gamma_j(K_{t-j}^* - K_{t-j-1}^*) + e_t. \tag{3}$$

5. In studying U.S. investment, researchers have ignored the personal income tax and identified u as the corporation tax rate. As described below, we have used a combination of personal and company tax rates.

Net investment is thus a distributed lag function of past changes in desired capital stocks, with weights reflecting ordering and delivery lags.[6]

The theoretical importance of Jorgenson's approach is that it develops empirical analysis of aggregate investment behavior from an explicit model of optimization by firms. Its great practical strength is that adopting a specific microeconomic model simplifies estimation by limiting the form of the relation and restricting the parameter values. It is important, however, to investigate whether any questionable assumptions of the underlying model are crucial for the policy conclusions implied by the estimates. For example, Eisner (1969) and Eisner and Nadiri (1968) noted that, because a Cobb-Douglas production function entails unitary price elasticity of K^* with respect to c, Hall and Jorgenson (1967, 1969) have imposed rather than estimated the long-run effect of tax policy.[7] Bischoff (1969) and Eisner and Nadiri (1968) also criticized the dynamic specification for restricting the response structure to be the same for changes in all components of K^*.[8] In addition, all of the previous work assumed that each of the components of the user cost of capital was fully allowed for by the firm in the way suggested by Eqs. (1) through (3). For example, none of the studies examined whether the interest rate is given more or less weight relative to the value of the depreciation allowance than the formula for c implies. Similarly, the time structure of the response to all of the cost variables was always assumed to be the same.

In planning this study we wished to avoid constraining the results by the assumptions of Cobb-Douglas technology, capital malleability, and a perfect capital goods market. Without the last two assumptions, the optimal investment decision is no longer myopic: the future values of output, of tax and depreciation rates, of capital and the product prices, and of

---

6. For a full justification of this lag structure, see, for example, Jorgenson (1965). In estimating Eq. (3), Jorgenson and his colleagues used the rational distributed lag model for the weights, that is, the generating function of the γ_j's was a ratio of polynomials. In practice, relatively low order polynomials were statistically acceptable. More recently, Hall and Jorgenson (1970) found that they could not reject further restrictions on the generating function which implied that the estimating equation could be specified without lagged dependent variables and with the coefficients of the $(K^*_{t-j} - K^*_{t-j-1})$ variable constrained by an Almon lag procedure (1965) to satisfy low order polynomials.

7. Agarwala and Goodson (1969) also implicitly constrain the effectiveness of the tax variable by assuming a Cobb-Douglas technology.

8. If the assumption of perfectly malleable capital is replaced by the putty-clay hypothesis (that is, that the capital-output ratio of *old* equipment cannot be changed), the response to changes in output (Q) should be faster than the response to changes in the user cost of capital. This more general dynamic model cannot be tested in a framework of which Eq. (3) is a special case. When slightly different models in the neoclassical spirit were studied, the slower response to changes in the user cost of capital was observed (Bischoff 1969; Eisner and Nadiri 1968).

the interest rate must be taken in account.[9] Because these future values are unknown at the time of the investment decision, a fully developed model of investment behavior would incorporate a theory of choice under uncertainty. Despite the need for a more complex model, and notwithstanding the sometimes acrimonious debate that has developed about the neoclassical investment function, we believe that the primary virtues of Jorgenson's formulation can be retained for empirical analysis. Rather than introduce a series of more specific assumptions to incorporate the desired generalizations,[10] we prefer to use several rather simple extensions of Eqs. (1) and (2) as an approximation to the more general model.

In place of the *current* values of the variables that enter K^* in the myopic formulation, we consider short distributed lags.[11] More specifically, we replace the current output variable (Q_t) of Eq. (1) by an expression of the form

$$Q_t^+ = (1 + g^*)^{\alpha_*}(1 + g_t)^{\alpha_0}(1 + g_{t-1})^{\alpha_1} \cdots (1 + g_{t-m})^{\alpha_m}Q_t, \qquad (4)$$

where g_{t-i} is the growth rate for the year ending in quarter $t - i$, and g^* is the expected long-run growth rate. This implies that the output level for which the firm plans its capital stock reflects recent growth rates as well as the current output level.[12] Similarly, each of the variables affecting the user cost of capital is also allowed to be either a single value or a short distributed lag.[13] More details will be given when the estimates are presented in the fourth section.

A second generalization of the standard neoclassical investment model is a less restricted definition of the relative cost of capital:

$$\left(\frac{c}{p}\right)^+ = \left(\frac{q}{p}\right)^{\beta_1} (r + \delta)^{\beta_2}(1 - u)^{-\beta_3}(1 - A)^{\beta_4}F^\lambda. \qquad (5)$$

Permitting the β's to differ from unity recognizes that, for example, firms

9. Arrow (1964) and Tobin (1967) both noted the necessity of these assumptions for the myopic rules of Jorgenson's formulation.

10. See Bischoff (1969) for an example of how restrictive such assumptions have to be.

11. In addition, as described below, we retain an adjustment model equivalent to Eq. (3).

12. The constant term $(1 + g^*)^{\alpha_*}$ plays no part in the empirical analysis but permits Q_t^+ to be generally equal to or greater than Q_t even if $\Sigma_0^m\alpha_i < 0$.

13. There is evidence of substantial delay in the United States in adopting favorable accelerated depreciation schedules; see Bischoff (1969). In Britain, dividend policy responded to changes in differential profits taxation with a lag (see Chapter 4). Helliwell and Glorieux (1970) emphasize that because of delivery lags the target capital stock of the current period reflects the decisions of previous years.

may not respond to changes in the value of allowances (A) in the same way as they do to other components of user cost; this extra generality is particularly important in view of the tax policies that are the focus of this chapter. The variable F refers to the availability of internally generated funds; if $\lambda < 0$, the firm treats retained earnings as a less expensive source of funds than borrowing or new capital issues.[14] Including F in the user cost of capital implies an effect on the optimal capital-output ratio and not just on the timing of investment. For this reason F should represent long-run changes in the internal availability of funds and not merely cyclical variations. One of the measures of F studied below, the ratio of company saving (retained earnings plus depreciation allowances) to trend output, is likely to be too sensitive to cyclical fluctuations even when averaged over several periods. The value of F may be better represented as a function of the optimal dividend payout rate implied by the current tax structure. This also facilitates estimating the effect of changes in payout policy induced by differential profits taxation. In Chapter 4 I estimated that $(D_t^*/Y_t) = k\theta_t^\eta$, where D_t^* is the optimal dividend level, Y_t is gross profits, θ_t is the differential tax parameter (that is, the opportunity cost of retained earnings in terms of foregone dividends),[15] η is approximately 0.9, and k is a constant. It is most convenient to measure F by $(D_t^*/Y_t)^{-1}$, the inverse of the optimal payout ratio; using the previous approximation, this is computationally equivalent to replacing F by θ and its coefficient by $-\eta\lambda$.[16]

As a further generalization, the technology was not assumed to be Cobb-Douglas. Of course, if none of the β's in Eq. (5) is constrained to unity, separate estimates of σ and the β's cannot be obtained from the data. Even if the β's were all constrained to equal one, the increased complexity from allowing $\sigma \neq 1$ would be a very low price to pay for the benefit of not prejudging the long-run elasticity of K^* with respect to the user cost.[17]

14. Duesenberry (1958) provides the most thorough discussion of why managers may treat retained earnings as a cheaper source of funds. See also Eisner and Strotz (1963), Evans (1969, chap. 5), Meyer and Kuh (1957), and Smith (1961). Note that including F as part of a general model is very different from the naive "liquidity" model examined critically by Jorgenson and Siebert (1968). Although it would be theoretically more satisfactory to allow F to modify r and not $r + \delta$, computational difficulties prevent this.

15. The variable θ is defined by $\theta = (1 - t_y)(1 + t_d - t_y - t_u)^{-1}$ where: t_u = tax rate on undistributed profits; t_d = tax rate on distributed profits; t_y = "standard rate" of income tax.

16. This also introduces an additional constant term, $k^{-\lambda}$, in Eq. (5).

17. Jorgenson and Stephenson (1967b) argue that a large number of cross-section studies of U.S. production data have shown that the elasticity of substitution is not significantly different from one. However, the historical priority of the Cobb-Douglas function seems inade-

Finally, we introduce a multiplicative error term (V_t) in the definition of K_t^* to allow for omitted variables and for the simplicity of our functional form. The result is

$$K_t^* = \mu^\sigma \left[\frac{p^+}{c}\right]^\sigma Q_t^+ V_t. \tag{6}$$

Our adjustment dynamics are represented by writing Eq. (3) as

$$K_t = \sum_{j=0}^{\infty} w_j K_{t-j}^* + u_t, \tag{7}$$

and imposing restrictions of the generating function of the w_j's.[18] Although Jorgenson could use his very restricted definition of K^* to calculate the K^* values explicitly and then estimate quite complex lag structures, we must estimate the parameters of K^* and the lag structure simultaneously. The price of our quite general specification of K^* is the need to impose a more restricted structure of the w_j's than the rational distributed lag model. Nevertheless, we can employ the Pascal distribution, a rich two-parameter class capable of representing a wide variety of lag patterns. The weights are given by $w_j = C_{r+j}^r \pi^j$, where $0 < \pi < 1$ and C_{r+j}^r is the combinatorial factor; the generating function of this lag structure is given by $(1 - \pi L)^{-(r+1)}$ where L is the lag operator.

Equation (7) can therefore be written

$$K_t = (1 - \pi)^{r+1}(1 - \pi L)^{-(r+1)} K_t^* + \zeta_t. \tag{8}$$

Multiplying both sides of the equation by $(1 - \pi L)^{r+1}$ yields

$$(1 - \pi L)^{r+1} K_t = (1 - \pi)^{r+1} K_t^* + (1 - \pi L)^{r+1} \zeta_t. \tag{9}$$

---

quate reason for granting it the status of null hypothesis and therefore accepting $\sigma = 1$ even though there is substantial variation in the point estimates of σ. Moreover, there is very little evidence on the elasticity of substitution for Britain. Cross-section estimates obtained with the reduced form procedure of Arrow et al. (1961) varied between 0.640 and 1.103; direct estimates for the same observations varied between 1.5 and 1.9 (Feldstein (1967a).

18. Rewriting Eq. (3) as Eq. (7) changes the properties of the disturbance. If the e_t's of Eq. (3) are serially independent, the u_t's of Eq. (7) are not, and vice versa. Jorgenson and his collaborators originally assumed the e_t's to be serially independent but tests by Bischoff (1969) showed this to be false. If it is assumed that for $t = 0$, $K_0 = K_0^* = 0$, there is no other difference between the "first difference" form of Eq. (3) and the "level" form of Eq. (7).

The simplest case of the Pascal distribution ($r = 0$) is the familiar geometric distribution; Eq. (9) then becomes

$$K_t - \pi K_{t-1} = (1 - \pi)K_t^* + (\zeta_t - \pi\zeta_{t-1}). \tag{10}$$

Higher values of r introduce more lagged values of K_t, implying that the weights first increase and then fall;[19] in our applications we studied $r = 0, 1$, and 2.[20]

Although the Pascal distribution is less versatile than the rational distributed lag, the combination of the Pascal distribution for the w_j's and individual dynamic structures for the components of K^* provide what is in important ways a more general dynamic model. Our results indicate that this tradeoff was probably worthwhile.

Since the capital stock is generated by the relation $K_t = I_t + (1 - \delta)K_{t-1}$, Eqs. (7) to (9) can be replaced by investment functions of the form:[21]

$$I_t = \sum_{j=0}^{\infty} w_i K_{t-1}^* - (1 - \delta)K_{t-1} + u_t. \tag{11}$$

In the case of the geometric lag this becomes

$$I_t = (1 - \pi)K_t^* - (1 - \delta - \pi)K_{t-1} + v_t, \tag{12}$$

and for the Pascal lag with $r = 1$,

$$I_t = (1 - \pi)^2 K_t^* - (1 - \delta - 2\pi)K_{t-1} - \pi^2 K_{t-2} + v_t. \tag{13}$$

Estimation Problems

Consider for simplicity the geometric distribution ($r = 0$); the estimation problems and methods discussed for this case are generalized in an

19. For a full discussion see Solow (1960) and Malinvaud (1966, pp. 480–481).

20. The results were mutually reinforcing in indicating that higher-order structures were not necessary; the reasons for this will be clear when the estimates are presented in the fourth section.

21. This of course implies that the replacement investment component of gross investment is a constant proportion of the lagged capital stock. A recent study (Feldstein and Foot 1971) indicates that this common assumption may be too simple and a source of error in estimating the determinants of *net* investment behavior.

obvious way to the Pascal distribution with $r > 0$. Combining Eqs. (4),(5),(6), and (12), the equation to be estimated is

$$I_t = Q_t \left\{ B \cdot \left[\left(\frac{q}{p} \right)^{\beta_1} (r + \delta)^{\beta_2} (1 - u)^{-\beta_3} (1 - A)^{\beta_4} \theta^{-\eta\lambda} \right]^{-\sigma} \right.$$

$$\left. \times \left[\prod_j (1 + g_{t-j})^{\alpha_j} \right] \cdot V_t \right\} - (1 - \delta - \pi)K_{t-1} + v_t, \qquad (14)$$

where $B = \mu^\sigma k^{-\sigma\lambda}(1 + g^*)^{\alpha_0}(1 - \pi)$, and the other variables and parameters are defined in the second section. For notational convenience in considering the estimation problems, we rewrite (14) as

$$I_t = Q_t \cdot BZ_t^\alpha V_t - (1 - \delta - \pi)K_{t-1} + v_t. \qquad (15)$$

Transferring the lagged capital stock to the left-hand side and dividing both sides by Q_t yields

$$\frac{I_t + (1 - \delta - \pi)K_{t-1}}{Q_t} = BZ_t^\alpha V_t + \frac{v_t}{Q_t}. \qquad (16)$$

Assume temporarily that $1 - \delta - \pi$ is a known parameter; this permits postponing discussion of the problems introduced by the presence of a lagged dependent variable.[22] The equation to be estimated is nonlinear and can be linearized by a logarithmic transformation only if the additive disturbance is ignored. Ignoring v_t would be equivalent to assuming that the errors in investment behavior can be parametricized instead as multiplicative disturbances (V_t) in the levels of the optimal capital stock. Because there is no operational way of distinguishing a disturbance in K_t^* from an error in the adjustment path to K_t^*, respecifying the model without v_t should not raise serious objections. It is, however, reassuring to know that ignoring v_t/Q_t in the estimation even though it should be in the model can be shown to introduce no large-sample bias to a first-order approximation and is likely to introduce little bias to a second-order approximation.

---

22. The lagged dependent variable problem is seen more clearly if I_t is rewritten as $K_t - (1 - \delta)K_{t-1}$.

Taking logarithms of both sides of Eq. (16) and expanding the right-hand side in a second-order Taylor's series around $BZ_t^\alpha V_t$ yields

$$\log \frac{I_t + (1 - \delta - \pi)K_{t-1}}{Q_t} = \log B + \alpha \log Z_t + \log V_t$$

$$+ \frac{v_t}{Q_t BZ_t^\alpha V_t} - \frac{v_t^2}{2(Q_t BZ_t^\alpha V_t)^2}. \qquad (17)$$

The biases in the estimates of $\log B$ and α that result from ignoring v_t in a least squares regression can be easily calculated following Theil's analysis (1961) of bias due to omitted variables. To a first-order approximation (that is, ignoring the v_t^2 term), it is clear that there is no bias if v_t has mean zero and is independent of Z_t and K_t^*. Moreover, it may be reasonable to assume that the second-order bias is small: if v_t is not homoskedastic but has a standard deviation that is proportional to $K_t^* = Q_t BZ_t^\alpha V_t$, the composite term $v_t^2/(Q_t BZ_t^\alpha V_t)^2$ has constant expected value and only the estimate of the constant term ($\log B$) is biased by omitting the second-order term.

We now drop the assumption that $1 - \delta - \pi$ is known. The nonlinear (logarithmic) transformation of the composite left-hand side variable of Eq. (16) precludes using Liviatan's (1963) instrumental variable method to obtain consistent estimates of all the parameters including the coefficient of the lagged dependent variable. The alternative common procedure of maximum likelihood estimation by a search technique is unsuitable in the current context because of the strong assumptions that must be made about the disturbances. If the disturbances are assumed to be normally distributed and serially independent, the minimum sum of squared residuals in a one-dimensional search over values of $1 - \delta - \pi$ between 0 and 1 corresponds to maximum likelihood estimates of all the parameters. Since the composite disturbances are the result of multiplication by a lag operator and subsequent logarithmic transformation, neither normality nor serial independence is plausible. Even the assumption of first- or second-order autocorrelation, which would require a two- or three-dimensional search, is likely to be unduly restrictive. The usual method of maximum likelihood estimation would therefore not be appropriate.

Fortunately, however, in all of the equations studied we have been able to identify narrow ranges that contain consistent estimates of the basic long-run investment parameters. The basis for this is the fact that if the true value of $1 - \delta - \pi$ is substituted in the left-hand side, the least squares estimates of the other parameters are consistent regardless of the serial correlation or nonnormality of the disturbances. In practice, the estimates of the long-run parameters were affected very little by varying $1 - \delta - \pi$ over a grid between 0 and 1. Since one set of these estimates is consistent and all the estimates are very similar, we can identify narrow ranges within which consistent estimates lie, even though we neither know nor can estimate the value of $1 - \delta - \pi$. In the estimates in the following section, such a range is presented for each parameter.

This solution to the estimation problem implies that we are not able to obtain information about the speed with which investment responds to changes in policy instruments. However, because this study is concerned with policies designed to have a long-run impact on capital formation rather than with stabilization, this is not a serious limitation.[23]

The Parameter Estimates

The results presented in this section indicate that both investment allowances and tax policies that induce higher retention ratios have a significant impact on investment behavior. They also show that the generalized neoclassical model of Eq. (14) is much more satisfactory than the constrained version of Eqs. (2) and (3). The estimated elasticities of K^* with respect to the several components of the user cost of capital differ substantially. Constraining them to be equal yields seriously misleading policy implications.

More specifically, the elasticity of K^* with respect to the allowance variable[24] is approximately one, while the elasticity with respect to the composite user cost of capital is only about 0.3. This does not necessarily imply that the true long-run elasticity of K^* with respect to a "permanent" change in the value of any variable (such as p/q or $1 - u$) is lower than one. A low estimated elasticity may indicate only that the *observed* variations in (p/q), r, and $(1 - u)$ are unrelated to changes in the relevant expected future values, even when polynomial distributed lags are used to extrapolate recent observations. Alternatively, the differences among the elasticities of K^* with respect to the components of the user cost variable may reflect suboptimal behavior by firms.

23. The estimation problems discussed in this section could be substantially simplified if the dynamic adjustment process of Eq. (7) were replaced by an analogous logarithmic equation, $\log K_t = \Sigma \, w_j \log K^*_{t-j} + \zeta_t$. However, as Jorgenson and Stephenson (1967b) have argued, this is economically very different and no longer equivalent to the adjustment process specified in Eq. (3). Some preliminary experiments with this formulation showed the explanatory power to be very much lower and the coefficients less sensible.

24. The allowance variable is $1 - A$, where A is the present value of tax reductions due to depreciation, allowance, and so on which follow a "dollar" of investment.

This helps to reconcile the apparent conflict between Jorgenson and his followers, who cite cross-section evidence that the elasticity of substitution of the production function is approximately one, and Eisner and others, who estimate that the price elasticity of demand for capital with respect to the composite user cost is very much lower. Even if *technology* is Cobb-Douglas, the *behavioral* elasticity of K^* with respect to observed user cost may be substantially less than one. To estimate and predict the effect of changes in the policy variables, it is necessary to estimate each elasticity separately. Neither an imposed technologically determined elasticity nor an estimated elasticity with respect to composite user cost will be correct.

Because the estimates to be presented indicate no reasonable and significant response to observed changes in (p/q), $(1 - u)$, and $(r + \delta)$, we begin by considering equations in which these variables are held constant (that is, ignored). We then study the effect of introducing them alone and in combination. Tables 15.1 and 15.2 relate to the geometric lag distribution; Table 15.3 presents estimates for higher-order Pascal distributions that show that the lag distribution has almost no effect on the estimated parameters of the demand for capital.

Table 15.1 presents parameter estimates for an equation of the form:

$$I_t = B \cdot Q_t^+ \cdot (1 - A)^{-\beta\sigma}\theta^{\eta\lambda\sigma} - (1 - \delta - \pi)K_{t-1}, \qquad (18)$$

or, more explicitly,[25]

$$\log \frac{I_t + (1 - \delta - \pi)K_{t-1}}{Q_t} = \log B + \sum_{j=0}^{7} \alpha_j \log (1 + g_{t-j})$$

$$- \beta\sigma \sum_{j=0}^{7} w_{1j} \log (1 - A_{t-j})$$

$$+ \eta\lambda\sigma \sum_{j=0}^{7} w_{2j} \log \theta_{t-j}. \qquad (19)$$

The lag weights (α_j's, w_{1j}'s, and w_{2j}'s) are constrained to satisfy a

25. Each g_{t-j} is the rate of growth of output for the four quarters ending in period $t - j$. A_{t-j}, defined in the previous footnote, reflects the law prevailing in quarter $t - j$. Similarly, θ_{t-j} is the effective opportunity cost of retained earnings in terms of foregone dividends in quarter $t - j$.

Table 15.1. Parameters of basic investment equations

Equation	Output change $\Sigma\alpha_j$	Tax incentive $\eta\gamma\sigma$	Allowance $-\beta\sigma$	Revised allowance $-\beta\sigma$	Output change α_0	Output change α_3	Tax incentive $\eta\gamma\sigma\cdot w_{22}$	Tax incentive $\eta\gamma\sigma\cdot w_{24}$	Revised allowance $-\beta\sigma\cdot w_{12}$	IGF	SER	$\bar{R}^2$
1.1	−2.84 (0.52) [−2.49, −2.92]	−0.14 (0.061) [−0.12, −0.14]	−1.74 (0.17) [−1.72, −1.74]	—	—	—	—	—	—	—	0.040 [0.039, 0.042]	0.78 [0.77, 0.79]
1.2	−1.95 (0.15) [−1.67, −2.02]	−0.15 (0.015) [−0.15, −0.16]	—	−1.39 (0.032) [−1.38, −1.42]	—	—	—	—	—	—	0.011 [0.011, 0.014]	0.98 [0.97, 0.98]
1.3	−1.71 (0.25) [−1.51, −1.79]	−0.12 (0.030) [−0.12, −0.12]	—	—	—	—	—	—	−1.28 (0.061) [−1.28, −1.31]	—	0.022 [0.022, 0.024]	0.93 [0.93, 0.93]
1.4	−1.49 (0.19) [−1.05, −1.59]	—	—	−1.29 (0.041) [−1.28, −1.29]	—	—	−0.056 (0.025) [−0.026, −0.062]	−0.046 (0.026) [−0.045, −0.052]	—	—	0.015 [0.015, 0.021]	0.97 [0.95, 0.97]
1.5	—	−0.14 (0.017) [−0.14, −0.15]	—	−1.34 (0.035) [−1.33, −1.39]	−0.95 (0.096) [−0.93, −1.05]	−0.63 (0.093) [−0.56, −0.64]	—	—	—	—	0.012 [0.012, 0.014]	0.98 [0.98, 0.98]
1.6	−2.06 (0.33) [−1.38, −2.21]	—	—	−1.17 (0.043) [−1.17, −1.18]	—	—	—	—	—	0.0038 (0.051) [−0.011, −0.0073]	0.020 [0.019, 0.022]	0.95 [0.93, 0.95]

second-order polynomial with the final weight (an 8 quarter lag) equal to zero; the w_{1j}'s and w_{2j}'s are assumed to sum to one.[26]

To save space, only the sums of the individual estimates are presented; that is, $\Sigma\alpha_j, \beta\sigma$, and $\eta\lambda\sigma$. The top line for each equation gives estimates corresponding to $\delta + \pi = 0.75$. The standard errors are given in parentheses immediately below the estimates. The square brackets indicate the minimum and maximum values of the coefficients obtained as $\delta + \pi$ was varied over six values from 0.05 to 0.95. The column headed SER gives the standard error of the regression for $\delta + \pi = 0.75$ and, in brackets, the range of SER's as $\delta + \pi$ varies over the six values. The final column presents similar information for the corrected coefficient of determination ($\bar{R}^2$). For each equation in Table 15.1, varying $\delta + \pi$ had almost no effect on either the long-run parameter estimates or the standard error of the regression.[27]

Equation (1.1) indicates that, for any current level of output, there is a negative elasticity of derived output capacity (Q_t^+) with respect to recent increases in output; that is, the estimates of $\Sigma\alpha_j$ range from -2.49 to -2.92. This implies that firms neither ignore nor extrapolate the very recent growth path but rather assume that deviations from the long-run trend are primarily cyclical. Since the distributed lag refers to eight quarterly observations on annual growth rates or three years of growth, $\Sigma\hat{\alpha}_j = -2.84$ implies that an increased growth during the past three years has approximately no effect on Q^+; for example, a 1 percent increase in the growth rate raises Q_t by 3 percent after three years but Q_t^+ rises by less than 0.5 percent. If the higher growth rate is sustained longer, the effect through Q_t outbalances the cyclical effect through $\Sigma\alpha_j$. Although the relation between historical output levels and desired output capacity is only tangential to the current study and will not be discussed further in this chapter, the observed nonmyopic determination of Q^+ and K^* deserves more careful study by those who develop investment equations for forecasting purposes.

The estimated elasticity with respect to the user cost of capital as affected by the allowance variable is large and highly significant. The esti-

---

26. The equations were estimated using a modification of the Almon polynomial distributed lag procedure (1965) developed by Robert Hall and incorporated into the Harvard version of a program entitled Time Series Processor.

27. The internal structure of the lag distributions did change as $\delta + \pi$ was varied. The changes indicated that the time response can be estimated more accurately than the complete agnosticism with respect to $\delta + \pi$ suggests. Because the remaining uncertainty is still great and the issue of timing tangential to our primary concern, we shall not pursue this further.

mates are very insensitive to $\delta + \pi$; $-\hat{\beta}\hat{\sigma}$ ranges between -1.72 and -1.74; the individual weights (w_{1j}'s) generally decline over the eight lag periods. The value of $\hat{\beta}\hat{\sigma}$ is surprisingly high, possibly unrealistically so if β is assumed to be approximately one. We believe that the high value in this equation is spurious and will return to discuss this in considering Eq. (1.2) below.

The negative estimated elasticity with respect to the tax variable θ indicates that tax inducements for higher retention are successful in increasing capital accumulation. There are two aspects to assessing the actual magnitude of this effect: the change in investment and the change in the desired capital-output ratio. Because the elasticity of dividends with respect to θ is approximately 0.9 (see Chapter 4) and the retained earnings plus capital consumption allowances were approximately twice dividends,[28] the long-run effect of a 10 percent decrease in θ would be a 9 percent decrease in dividends and a 4.5 percent rise in internally available funds. The estimated coefficient indicates that a 10 percent fall in θ would raise the equilibrium capital-output ratio, and therefore the equilibrium rate of gross investment, by only 1.4 percent. Since gross fixed investment is approximately equal to internally available funds, the comparison of 1.4 percent and 4.5 percent implies that about two-thirds of the effect of tax changes on retained earnings is offset by a change in the use of external funds. Despite this dilution of the effect of taxes, the historical variation in θ has implied economically important changes in capital formation.[29] When the tax differential was ended in 1958, raising θ from 0.66 to 1.00, the desired capital-output ratio (K^*/Q^+) fell by more than 6 percent. This would have both a substantial impact on investment during the adjustment period and an important long-run effect on output per man.[30]

Examining the observed and fitted values of investment corresponding to this equation indicated an important misspecification. For the period from the first observation in the period of fit (1954: 2) through 1955: 4, observed investment was always substantially higher than the fitted values; after that date there ceased to be any systematic difference. This pattern suggested a misspecification of the allowance variable. In 1954 the "initial

28. Higher during the period of differential taxation.

29. It should be noted that, unlike changes in depreciation allowances, θ can be used to increase investment without any reduction in tax collections.

30. The large size of this tax effect can also be seen by calculating the change in the interest rate that would alter $K^*/Q +$ by 6 percent. If technology is Cobb-Douglas, $K^*/Q +$ rises by 6 percent when $(r + \delta)$ falls by 6 percent. If $r + \delta \geqq 0.16$ percent, the net rate of interest (r) must fall by more than 1 percent. The effect of the differential tax system was therefore roughly equivalent to a 1 percent fall in the net rate of interest or somewhat more than a 2 percent fall in the gross rate of interest.

allowances" were generally replaced by "investment allowances" that in effect permitted more than 100 percent depreciation. These remained in effect until 1956:1 when the original initial allowances were reinstated. The pattern of residuals indicates that some firms failed to recognize that the investment allowance was more valuable or were very slow to respond to the change. To reflect this we replaced the actual allowance values through 1956:1 with a linear interpolation between the 1952:1 value (0.27) and the 1956:1 value (0.30). The result was to end the systematic divergence between actual and fitted values of the dependent variable during the early observations and to lower substantially the standard error of the regression in each equation.

The revised allowance variable is therefore used in Eq. (1.2) and all subsequent equations. The output change coefficient ($\Sigma\alpha_j$) is somewhat lower but still indicates a substantial correction for cyclical variation in output. The tax coefficient ($\eta\lambda\sigma$) is almost identical but has a very much smaller standard error. The revised allowance elasticity ($-\beta\sigma$) ranges between -1.38 and -1.42, showing a substantial impact of allowances on investment behavior. Although these coefficients are significantly greater than one, they do not necessarily conflict with the assumption of Cobb-Douglas technology ($\sigma = 1$) since β may exceed one. There are two reasons for this. First, higher allowances increased the flow of internally available funds, which may have had an independent positive effect on investment. Second, the frequent changes of the allowance rate may have induced firms to try to concentrate investment expenditures on periods in which rates were high by accelerating investment when allowance rates were raised and postponing when they were expected to rise in the future. The estimates of approximately -1.4 may therefore reflect the timing of government policy; more frequent changes, and particularly more decreases, might have resulted in an even greater responsiveness.[31]

Equations (1.3) through (1.5) show that none of the conclusions based on Eq. (1.2) are altered if the distributed lags are replaced by simpler dynamic structures. In (1.3) the revised allowance variable is represented by a single observation lagged two periods; in terms of Eq. (1.5), $w_{12} = 1$ and

---

31. Note that this is exactly opposite to the view stated by the Royal Commission (1955) and endorsed by Williams (1966) that varying the allowance rates would reduce the effectiveness of this instrument.

In general, the coefficients estimate the way firms responded to the actual variation in the explanatory variables and not the way they might respond to a very different time pattern of exogenous variable changes. This is of course a quite general problem; the coefficients of a simple accelerator model would become inappropriate if the sales of a firm ceased to be highly autocorrelated and became a purely random series.

$w_{1j} = 0$ for $j \neq 2$. The resulting estimates (-1.28 to -1.31) are very close to the previous range, reflecting the substantial autocorrelation in the allowance series. Equation (1.4) measures the tax impact by two lagged values, θ_{t-2} and θ_{t-4}. The sum of their coefficients is somewhat less than when a full distributed lag is used, but the basic quantitative implications are unchanged. Similarly, in (1.5) the output change is measured by two observations, g_t and g_{t-3}, and the sum of their coefficients is slightly less than with the distributed lag. In each of these three equations, replacing one of the distributed lags leaves the other coefficient sums essentially unchanged.

Equation (1.6) replaces the tax variable by a direct measure of internally available funds: IGF is a four-quarter average of internally generated funds divided by the trend level of output. The extremely low and completely insignificant estimated elasticities may reflect this method of measuring available funds, the inadequacies of the basic data,[32] the use of output as a deflator, or the possibility of simultaneous equations bias. In any case, the estimate is in striking contrast to the significant elasticity with respect to the tax variable. If the estimate is accepted as correct, this contrast suggests that K^* is unaffected by the substantial transitory cyclical variation of IGF and responds only to long-run shifts in the retention ratio such as that caused by changes in the tax variable.[33]

The equations in Table 15.2 show that introducing the other components of user cost (r, q, and u) and the price of output produces unsatisfactory results, especially when all the coefficients are constrained by the user cost of capital formation to imply a single price elasticity of demand for K^*. Equation (2.1) corresponds to the "pure" neoclassical formulation

$$\log \left[\frac{I_t + (1 - \delta - \pi)K_{t-1}}{Q_t} \right] = \log B + \Sigma \alpha_j \log (1 + g_{t-j})$$

$$- \sigma \Sigma w_{1j} \cdot \log \left(\frac{c}{p} \right)_{t-j}, \qquad (20)$$

in which all the variables affecting the cost of capital services are constrained to operate through a single user cost variable, $c_t = q_t(r_t + \delta)$

32. The *quarterly* series of company savings involves a somewhat arbitrary allocation of dividends and earnings over the year.

33. It should be noted that the current formulation does not test whether cyclical variation in the availability of funds affects the timing of investment.

Table 15.2. Parameters of investment equations with decomposed user cost

Equation	Output change[a]	Tax incentive (θ)	Revised allowance ($1 - A$)	Deflated user cost (c/p)	Price ratio (q/p)	User cost per £ of capital goods $[(r + \delta)(1 - A)(1 - u)]$	Gross required return $[(r + \delta)/(1 - u)]$	Net required return ($r + \delta$)	Tax rate ($1 - u$)	SER	$\bar{R}^2$
2.1	−2.26	—	—	−0.40	—	—	—	—	—	0.071	0.31
	(0.75)			(0.10)							
	[−2.23, −2.36]			[−0.38, −0.49]						[0.070, 0.071]	[0.29, 0.40]
2.2	−2.02	0.28	—	−0.23	—	—	—	—	—	0.050	0.66
	(0.53)	(0.12)		(0.16)							
	[−1.98, −2.17]	[0.19, 0.30]		[−0.19, −0.41]						[0.050, 0.054]	[0.66, 0.67]
2.3	−0.72	0.24	—	—	−3.27	0.33	—	—	—	0.028	0.90
	(0.32)	(0.070)			(0.34)	(0.11)					
	[−0.69, −0.82]	[0.14, 0.26]			[−3.19, −3.61]	[0.17, 0.37]				[0.028, 0.033]	[0.88, 0.90]
2.4	−1.66	−0.16	−1.60	—	0.77	—	—	—	—	0.011	0.98
	(0.13)	(0.021)	(0.094)		(0.26)						
	[−1.51, −1.82]	[−0.16, −0.16]	[−1.60, −1.61]		[0.46, 0.84]					[0.011, 0.016]	[0.97, 0.98]
2.5	−1.75	−0.082	−1.25	—	—	—	0.10	—	—	0.015	0.97
	(0.18)	(0.042)	(0.08)				(0.06)				
	[−1.69, −1.98]	[−0.052, −0.210]	[−1.18, −1.58]				[−0.075, −0.140]			[0.014, 0.017]	[0.97, 0.97]
2.6	−1.34	−0.23	−1.44	—	—	—	—	0.13	0.24	0.012	0.98
	(0.21)	(0.05)	(0.11)					(0.10)	(0.10)		
	[−1.33, −1.41]	[−0.20, −0.38]	[−1.38, −1.75]					[0.014, 0.160]	[0.17, 0.51]	[0.011, 0.014]	[0.98, 0.98]

a. Output change is measured by two values (g_t and g_{t-3}), as in Eq. 1.5, instead of the 8 quarter distributed lag.

$(1 - A_t)/(1 - u_t)$. The equation is a generalization of the original Jorgenson formulation; the price elasticity (σ) is not constrained to one, and recent growth of output is taken into account. The estimates of σ, ranging between $+0.38$ and $+0.49$, are reminiscent of the values obtained for U.S. data with similarly formulated equations (Eisner and Nadiri 1968; Coen 1969). However, because this equation hides the high elasticity with respect to the allowance variable, it explains investment very much less well than the equations of Table 15.1; the standard error of the estimate is more than six times larger than for Eq. (1.2).

Equation (2.2) indicates that constraining the allowance variable to be part of the user cost of capital causes the tax variable to enter with the wrong sign. Equation (2.3) shows that splitting $\log (c/p)$ into $\log (q/p)$ and $\log [(r + \delta)(1 - A)/(1 - u)]$ has implausible results: an unreasonably high negative elasticity with respect to q/p and a positive elasticity with respect to the other components of cost.

Equation (2.4) shows that the previous coefficient of (q/p) reflected the use of a composite cost of capital variable and the exclusion of the allowance variable as such. When r and u are held constant, as in (2.4), the allowance, tax, and output change variables appear as they did in the equations of Table 15.1. The elasticity with respect to the relative price variable is positive and therefore still implausible. It seems most sensible to conclude that the observed variation of the price ratio is not closely enough related to expectations about future movements on which firms act to have any explanatory value. In the presence of substantial uncertainty, short-run relative price variations contribute too little information to have an economic impact. This variable will therefore be ignored in subsequent equations.

The required gross rate of return $[(r + \delta)/(1 - u)]$ is introduced in Eq. (2.5), where it is completely insignificant. When the required net rate of return $(r + \delta)$ and the tax variable $(1 - u)$ are separated in Eq. (2.6), the rate of return variable has the wrong sign (positive).[34]

Table 15.3 presents estimates for the more general second- and third-degree Pascal distributed lags.[35] Again the value of $\delta + \pi$ is varied over six values in the interval from 0.05 to 0.95. To conserve space, not all esti-

34. This coefficient may be biased because r is measured as a nominal rate rather than a real rate; for estimates of the magnitude of this bias and evidence that it could account for the incorrect sign, see Feldstein (1970). Unfortunately, the possible importance of this bias was recognized only after the estimation for this chapter was completed.

35. That is, for $r + 1$ equal to 2 and to 3 in the lag operator generating function $(1 - \pi L)^{-(r+1)}$; the geometric lags considered in Tables 15.1 and 15.2 correspond to $r + 1 = 1$.

Table 15.3. Nonlinear investment equations

Equation	$r+1$	$\pi+\delta$	Output change	Revised allowance $(1-A)$	Tax incentive (θ)	Deflated user cost (c/p)	SER	$\bar{R}^2$
3.1	2	0.25 to 0.95	−1.62 (0.21) −1.74 (0.14)	−1.28 (0.038) −1.31 (0.057)	−0.10 (0.027) −0.12 (0.018)	—	[0.012, 0.018]	[0.96, 0.98]
		0.05	1.91 (2.05)	−1.24 (0.54)	−0.16 (0.25)		0.17	0.21
	3	0.35 to 0.95	−1.71 (0.18) −1.77 (0.15)	−1.28 (0.038) −1.30 (0.047)	−0.11 (0.022) −0.12 (0.018)	—	[0.012, 0.015]	[0.97, 0.98]
		0.25	−1.22 (0.98)	−1.32 (0.26)	−0.10 (0.12)		0.082	0.53
3.2	2	0.25 to 0.95	−1.29 (0.76) −1.58 (0.75)	—	—	−0.21 (0.086) −0.28 (0.080)	[0.078, 0.080]	[0.13, 0.13]
		0.05	2.02 (1.69)			−0.29 (0.19)	0.18	0.10
	3	0.35 to 0.95	−1.45 (0.76) −1.58 (0.75)	—	—	−0.21 (0.086) −0.22 (0.087)	[0.078, 0.080]	[0.13, 0.13]
		0.25	−1.02 (1.06)			−0.27 (0.12)	0.11	0.087
		0.05	2.69 (5.99)			0.014 (0.69)	0.63	0.02
3.3	2	0.25 to 0.95	−2.54 (0.60) −2.62 (0.61)	—	0.16 (0.13) 0.24 (0.12)	−0.28 (0.17) −0.43 (0.17)	[0.049, 0.051]	[0.67, 0.68]
		0.05	−0.48 (2.09)		−0.54 (0.42)	−1.34 (0.58)	0.17	0.23
	3	0.35 to 0.95	−2.54 (0.60) −2.61 (0.61)	—	—	−0.28 (0.17) −0.36 (0.17)	[0.049, 0.050]	[0.68, 0.68]
		0.25	−2.49 (1.14)		−0.080 (0.23)	−0.57 (0.32)	0.093	0.39
		0.05	10.53 (7.73)		1.04 (1.55)	2.52 (2.15)	0.63	0.075

mates are presented. For each value of $r + 1$, the table indicates the *range* of estimates of each of the parameters. Because the estimates corresponding to low values of $\pi + \delta$ (that is, $\pi + \delta = 0.05$ and, for $r + 1 = 3$, also $\pi + \delta = 0.25$) generally differed substantially from the others, these estimates are shown separately. Wherever there is a substantial difference in the estimates, the equations corresponding to low $\pi + \delta$ values are markedly inferior in terms of explanatory power.

The basic implication of Table 15.3 is that using more general distributed lags does not alter the conclusions based on the geometric lags of Tables 15.1 and 15.2. Equation (3.1) corresponds to the most satisfactory of the previous specifications, Eq. (1.2). The new estimates are very close to those obtained with the geometric lag, although generally slightly lower in absolute value.[36] The elasticity with respect to the allowance variable is approximately -1.3, and with respect to the tax incentive variable it is -0.11. The ratio of desired capacity output to current output is negatively related to the recent growth rates. Equation (3.2) is the "pure" neoclassical investment function slightly generalized by including recent output growth rates. The results are similar to Eq. (2.1), but the estimated price elasticity of demand for capital is even lower (approximately 0.22 in comparison to 0.40) and the explanatory power of the equation even worse. The specification of Eq. (3.3) is analogous to (2.2) and confirms that when the measure of the tax incentive to retain is introduced into the "pure" neoclassical equation (3.2), it has the wrong sign and leaves the equation substantially worse than the more general specification (3.1).

In summary, our results show that both the investment allowances and the tax incentive for increased retention had substantial impact on investment. The generalized neoclassical investment function is substantially better than the "pure" neoclassical function in which all variables affecting the cost of capital services are constrained to operate through a composite user cost variable. Such constraints are misleading; the resulting estimates understate the effect of investment allowances, ignore the effect of retained earnings, and overstate the effect of the other components of user cost.

Simulations of Alternative Policies

This section assesses the effects on capital formation of the changing allowance (A) and tax (θ) policies since 1952. The potential impact of

---

36. No estimate is presented for $r + 1 = 3$ and $\pi + \delta = 0.05$ because the equation had no explanatory ability.

alternative policies is also evaluated. These simulations measure only the direct effects of the policy variables; the indirect effects through changes in aggregate output and in the market rates of interest are ignored. All of the simulations use the parameter estimates of Eq. (1.2). Detailed results are presented for the response corresponding to $\pi = \delta = 0.95$; this implies that the capital stock responds to a change in desired capital stock with a mean lag of approximately seventeen quarters. This speed is similar to the estimates by Hall and Jorgenson (1967) for the United States; they found mean lags of five to eight quarters for equipment and fifteen to thirty quarters for structures. Less detailed results are also presented for the more rapid response corresponding to $\pi + \delta = 0.75$. It should be remembered that, in both cases, there is an additional distributed lag of up to seven quarters in the response of the desired capital stock to changes in the underlying variables.

Three different allowance policies were considered. Policy A1 corresponds to the actual time path of all the explanatory variables: the adjusted allowance variable rises slowly in the early years, has large increases in 1959 and 1962, and decreases slightly in 1966. Policy A2 keeps the allowance variable at the 1952 value of 0.27 for the entire interval, while policy A3 uses the highest value (0.41, actually reached in 1962) for the entire interval. For each simulation, the actual values of θ as well as of the nonpolicy variables are used while the lagged values of the capital stock are generated endogenously.

The results are presented in Table 15.4; to conserve space, only the value for the final quarter of each year is given. The A1 policy shows substantial rises in investment after the allowance variable increases of 1959 and 1962. The A2 simulation shows that the rate of investment would have been very much lower throughout the period without the changes in investment allowances. If the most generous depreciation policy ($A = 0.41$) had been adopted in 1953 (as in simulation A3), the rate of capital formation would have been substantially greater during the 1950s than that which actually prevailed, somewhat lower during the first half of the 1960s, and approximately equal thereafter.

The simplest measure of the effect of the different allowance policies is a comparison of the capital stock growth over the entire period from 1954:4 to 1967:4. In 1958 prices, the relevant capital stock was £20,600 million in 1954:4. By 1967:4, the actual constant price capital stock was £37,880 million; this is matched almost exactly by the A1 simulation, £38,007 million. In comparison, the A2 policy simulation indicates a capital stock in 1967:4 of only £29,506 million, while the expansionary A3 policy indicates a capital stock of £40,387 million. With no change in depreciation policy

Table 15.4. Investment predicted by alternative allowance policies

| Period | (£ million at constant prices, quarterly rate) | | |
	Policy A1	Policy A2	Policy A3
1954: 4	321	297	746
1955: 4	358	313	704
1956: 4	383	323	668
1957: 4	373	311	611
1958: 4	376	299	561
1959: 4	429	264	485
1960: 4	488	240	430
1961: 4	513	284	473
1962: 4	472	275	446
1963: 4	559	250	398
1964: 4	548	244	381
1965: 4	643	342	508
1966: 4	561	354	519
1967: 4	599	425	612

after 1953 (that is, A2), the capital stock would have grown 49 percent less than with the actual depreciation policy, while the immediate change of policy (A3) would have increased the capital stock growth by 14 percent.

Very similar overall results are obtained when a more rapid rate of adjustment ($\pi + \delta = 0.75$) is assumed. The final capital stocks are now £37,965 million (A1), £28,899 million (A2), and £39,297 million (A3). The paths of investment differ substantially between the $\pi + \delta = 0.95$ and the $\pi + \delta = 0.75$ simulations. In particular, the more rapid response ($\pi + \delta = 0.75$) implies implausibly high rates of investment in the early 1950s and extremely volatile gross investment series corresponding to policies A2 and A3. Although the simulation corresponding to the actual policy (A1) did not imply any implausible behavior, the correlation between the predicted and actual gross investment series ($r = 0.70$) was lower than for the corresponding simulation for the slower response speed ($r = 0.95$).[37]

Four different tax policies affecting the retention of profits were examined. Policy T1 corresponds to the actual time path of all the explanatory variables: the θ variable varies between 0.741 and 0.680 until the end of differential profits taxation in 1958, then rises to 1.00 where it remains until the corporation tax introduced a differential that lowered θ to 0.59 in

---

37. This suggests an approach to choosing among the different response speeds, but we shall not pursue this further here.

Table 15.5. Investment predicted by alternative differential taxation policies

	(£ million at constant prices, quarterly rate)			
Period	Policy T1	Policy T2	Policy T3	Policy T4
1954: 4	321	321	321	259
1955: 4	358	358	357	301
1956: 4	383	383	384	334
1957: 4	373	373	373	329
1958: 4	376	376	361	322
1959: 4	429	424	407	369
1960: 4	488	549	533	492
1961: 4	513	619	604	561
1962: 4	472	563	550	512
1963: 4	559	645	631	591
1964: 4	548	624	612	574
1965: 4	643	719	707	664
1966: 4	561	652	641	603
1967: 4	599	559	549	517

1966. The T1 simulation is of course exactly the same as the A1 simulation. Policy T2 is the same as T1 until 1958 but then, instead of discontinuing the differential, it maintains $\theta = 0.680$ for the remaining years. The result, shown in Table 15.5, is a substantially higher level of investment during the 1960s (until 1967 when the effect of the actual 1966 tax change has made its impact). Policy T3 keeps the original 1953 tax differential ($\theta = 0.733$) for the entire period. The corresponding investment falls slightly below the actual level in the late 1950s in response to the actual fall in θ but is then higher during the 1960s. Capital formation is of course not as great as with policy T2. Finally, policy T4 has no differential taxation, that is, $\theta = 1$ for the entire period. The implied investment is substantially lower than the T1 policy for the 1950s; during the 1960s (when the values of θ are the same) the investment is lower with T1 reflecting the greater previous accumulation of capital.

A comparison of the final period capital stocks is again informative. In comparison to the T1 stock of £38,007 million, not ending the differential in 1957 (T2) implies a capital stock of £40,103 million. The constant differential at $\theta = 0.733$ (T3) produces a capital stock of £39,628 million, while the constant no differential policy (T4) indicates a capital stock of £37,601 million.[38] The effect on capital formation of differential taxation

38. The capital stock accumulations with the more rapid response ($\pi + \delta = 0.75$) were quite similar: £37,965 million (T1), £39,616 million (T2), £39,062 million (T3), and £36,850 million (T4).

can therefore be considerable: with no differential, the capital stock increased 82.5 percent in thirteen years, while with the expansionary T2 policy the increase is 94.7 percent. It should be remembered that, unlike the allowance policies, differential taxation changes reflected in θ need not reduce tax revenues.

Summary

This chapter has used a generalized neoclassical investment function to assess the effects of tax policy on investment in Britain during the period from 1954 through 1967. The estimates show that both the accelerated depreciation allowances and the use of differential taxation to induce the retention of corporate profits had substantial and significant impacts on investment behavior.

The generalized neoclassical investment function relaxes the assumption that the price elasticities of the desired capital stock with respect to the components of the user cost of capital are all equal. The time patterns of each price response and of the response to increased output are also not constrained to be the same. Both generalizations are shown to be important. The constrained "pure" neoclassical investment function yields misleading results; the estimates understate the effect of investment allowances, ignore the effect of retained earnings, and overstate the effect of the other components of user cost.

Simulations with the investment equation showed that the increases in depreciation allowances accounted for approximately 45 percent of net capital accumulation in the period after 1954. Until differential profits taxation ended in 1958, it raised annual investment by some £240 million or about 15 percent of gross investment. If differential profits taxation had not been abandoned in 1958, the capital stock would have been greater when the corporation tax reintroduced a retention incentive in 1966. In short, both types of tax policy had important effects on capital accumulation.

Appendix

Data Definitions and Sources

Investment (I_t) is gross fixed capital formation in manufacturing, construction, distribution, and other services. *Economic Trends* (1969) presents this data seasonally adjusted in constant 1958 dollars for the period after 1956:1. For earlier quarters, the series was calculated from unadjusted data at current prices as published in *Economic Trends* (1958).

Capital stock (K_t) is calculated from the capital stock identity, $K_t = (1 - \delta)K_{t-1} + I_t$. The value of δ was estimated by requiring that the capital stocks for 1954 and 1967 in 1958 prices, as reported in the 1967 *National Income and Expenditure*, be consistent with the investment series and the capital stock identity.

Output (Q_t) is constructed from the indices of industrial production for manufacturing, construction, distribution, and other services as reported in *Economic Trends* (1968) for the period 1958:4 to 1967:4. For the earlier years, it was necessary to use an annual index of real GDP derived from the *National Income and Expenditure* Blue Book and interpolate to obtain quarterly figures; output in manufacturing, construction, distribution, and other services accounts for about 80 percent of GDP.

The rate of return (r_t) is a weighted combination of equity and debenture yields quoted in the *Monthly Digest of Statistics*. For debentures, the "flat yield" on irredeemable industrial debentures was used for 1952:1 through 1962:4. From 1965:1, redemption yields on 20-year industrial debentures are used with a correction of 0.4 percentage points based on a comparison of long-term and irredeemable government bonds. For the interval from 1963:1 to 1964:4, the redemption yield on long-term government bonds, with an adjustment of 1.1 percentage points inferred from relative levels in 1961–1962, was used.

The relative price variable (p_t/q_t) is the ratio of the price index for total output to the price index for fixed assets. Annual data in the *National Income and Expenditure* Blue Book was interpolated to a quarterly basis.

The tax rate (u_t) is the rate of tax on the income of a company with the average payout ratio. This reflects the income, profits, and corporation tax rates. The tax differential (θ_t) is the opportunity cost of retained earnings in terms of foregone dividends; see Chapter 4 for a more specific definition. The tax rates are presented in the annual *Report of the Commission of Inland Revenue*.

The allowance variable (A_t) is the discounted value of the tax savings due to depreciation, investment allowances, and initial allowances. Depreciation is based on the allowable diminishing balance rate of depreciation, and the discount rate is a constant 10 percent. The allowance variable is a weighted average of the appropriate value for each asset class weighted by its average share in the relevant gross investment over the period.

16 Toward an Economic Theory of Replacement Investment

Large variations in capital spending continue to motivate econometric studies of investment behavior. The past decade has seen the development of attempts to model *net* investment as the adjustment of the capital stock to a desirable level. Building on earlier work by Haavelmo (1960), Lutz (1951), and others, Jorgenson and his collaborators (for example, Hall and Jorgenson 1967; Jorgenson 1970; Jorgenson and Stephenson 1967) have provided an operational model of net capital accumulation that relates desired capital to the cost of capital services. Although serious objections have been raised about the specification of the optimal capital stock (including Bischoff 1971; Eisner 1969; Feldstein 1971; and Fisher 1971) and about the arbitrary nature of the adjustment dynamics (Nerlove 1972), it is likely that some form of this general model will continue to provide a framework for future investment studies.

In contrast to these developments of a theory of capital expansion, replacement investment continues to be analyzed in terms of a noneconomic model of technical necessity. Jorgenson and others have adopted the simplifying assumption that replacement investment is a constant proportion of the capital stock.[1] This assumption has been challenged and contrary evidence has been offered by Eisner (1972) and Feldstein and Foot (1971). The purpose of this chapter is to examine several aspects of a theory of replacement investment. We hope not only to show that a model with a constant replacement rate is implausible and unsatisfactory but also to provide a basis for better empirical work in the future. The magnitude of replacement investment (the annual rate of replacement investment generally exceeds expansion investment) makes this issue a matter of substantial importance.

This chapter was written with Michael Rothschild. Reprinted from *Econometrica* 42 (May 1974), pp. 393–423, by permission of the Econometric Society. We are indebted to Paul David, Zvi Griliches, and Bert Hickman for helpful discussions.

1. Jorgenson has provided a formal statement of and an attempted justification for this assumption in several places (including Jorgenson 1965, 1970). See Jorgenson (1973) for his most complete statement of the basis for assuming proportional replacement.

Introduction

Much of the confusion in the current analysis of replacement investment results from a failure to distinguish several related but quite different
concepts which, partly following common usage, we shall label deterioration, output decay, input decay, depreciation, scrapping, and replacement investment.[2]

The *deterioration* of a piece of equipment is the increase in real
resource cost per unit of output as the machine ages. Deterioration assumes two quite different forms. First, as a machine ages it may yield less
output. We shall refer to this output decrease as *output decay*. Second, an
older machine may absorb more inputs of materials, labor, maintenance,
and so on while maintaining or nearly maintaining the original level of output; we shall refer to this as *input decay*. The relative importance of these
two forms of deterioration for any particular machine is generally a matter
for economic decision by the firm. The technical possibilities, relative
costs, and short-run position of the firm influence the extent to which additional expenditures on inputs and on maintenance are used to prevent
output from declining.

Depreciation is the fall in the price of a machine as it ages. If there are
no installation costs and no uncertainty, the rate of depreciation reflects
the overall rate of deterioration and the rate of technological obsolescence
(Hall 1968).[3] Even when the rate of obsolescence can be separately accounted for, the rate of depreciation cannot be used to measure the rate of
output decay but only the combined effects of output decay and input
decay. We return to this in the third section of this chapter.

Scrapping is the complete withdrawal of a piece of equipment from a
firm's capital stock. A machine is scrapped when, no matter how it is
used, it cannot earn a positive quasi-rent. Scrapping thus reflects obsolescence, deterioration, and a limited ability to reduce the labor input on old
equipment (Solow et al. 1966).

Replacement investment is the actual purchase of equipment to maintain the output capacity that is lost through output decay and scrapping.
Note that replacement investment is not equivalent to deterioration, depreciation, or scrapping. Since both output decay and scrapping represent
economic choices by the firm, the amount of replacement investment in
any year is also an economic choice and not a technological necessity.

2. See Griliches (1962) for an early attempt to distinguish among some similar pheno-
mena.
3. Technological obsolescence is the fall in the real resource cost per unit of output on
new *vintages* of equipment.

By examining alternative technological assumptions and models of investment behavior, we shall show how inappropriate it is to assume that the replacement ratio—the ratio of replacement investment to the capital stock—is constant. We also hope to identify and elucidate the features that should be incorporated in a complete theory of replacement investment.

We begin in the next section by adopting Jorgenson's extremely restrictive assumption that all deterioration is output decay and that obsolescence can be ignored. All replacement investment is, therefore, technically necessary rather than the result of specific economic choice. Moreover, we also adopt the assumption that this technical decay function remains unchanged through time. Contrary to Jorgenson's assertions, even these restrictions are not sufficient to imply that the replacement ratio is, or tends to, a constant. We show in the next section that, except for numerical accidents of no economic interest, even a tendency toward a constant replacement ratio will emerge only if either (1) each piece of equipment is subject to output decay at the same constant exponential rate, or (2) the entire capital stock, and therefore both net and gross investment, grows at a constant exponential rate.[4] Neither of these assumptions is acceptable; the extent to which the actual economy departs from these assumptions is sufficient to cause economically important variations in the replacement ratio.

The third section shows the inadequacy of the evidence that has been used to support the assertion that output decay occurs at a constant geometric rate. Appeal to depreciation estimates is, of course, not conclusive because exponential depreciation of a machine does not imply exponential output decay. Moreover, exponential output decay for individual machines does not imply a constant aggregate decay rate unless all equipment decays at the same rate or the composition of the capital stock does not change. Since all the depreciation evidence comes from studies of the second-hand markets for motor vehicles (and even that indicates variability in "the" rate of decay by model year and type of vehicle), there is little reason to believe that the economy's capital stock decays at a constant exponential rate.

A constant growth rate of the capital stock is not only contrary to fact but also makes a theory of investment unnecessary. We shall show in the fourth section that the normal historical mix of deviations from constant

4. Jorgenson's attempted generalization of the standard renewal theorem (1973) will be shown to be invalid except in the extreme and uninteresting case of an economy with constant exponential growth of capital.

exponential growth is sufficient to imply significant fluctuations in replacement rates in even the very long run.

Even if output growth were exponential, the replacement rate would alter because of changes in the tax laws, the interest rate, and the nature of technical progress. The same economic forces that alter the desired capital intensity of production, and therefore influence expansion investment, will alter the planned life of equipment and the decision to replace existing equipment. Any theory of investment should reflect these economic forces in explaining replacement as well as expansion investment. We begin a study of these influences in the fifth section by considering the relatively simple case in which a machine's physical durability is determined in advance. We show how changes in interest rates and tax laws alter the optimal durability of equipment and how this in turn influences the replacement rate in the long run and the short run. We then consider (in the sixth section) a model of embodied technical change and putty-clay capital goods in which the durability of a machine is an ex post economic decision. We show how changes in factor prices and the tax law alter the rate of replacement. The analysis of both sections shows that interest rate and tax changes are likely to have as large an effect on the amount of replacement investment as on the amount of expansion investment.

A theory of replacement investment that is adequate for econometric work must also reflect the lags and other aspects of timing that affect replacement investment. The seventh section discusses the problems of short-run timing of replacement investment and comments on the implications of our analysis for previous econometric studies of investment behavior.[5]

Conditions for a Constant Replacement Ratio

The presumed theoretical basis for assuming a constant replacement ratio is well summarized by Jorgenson's statement: "It is a fundamental result of renewal theory that the distribution of replacements . . . approaches a constant fraction of the capital stock for (almost) any distribution of replacements over time and for any initial distribution of capital stock. This result holds for a constant stock and for a growing stock as well" (1965, p. 51). This passage seems to imply that in most investment processes, if they proceed for a long enough time, the replacement ratio approaches a constant. In this section we examine this claim through the analysis of a simple discrete time model of capital accumula-

---

5. To avoid more complex notation, we shall use some letters as symbols for very different things in the separate sections.

tion and deterioration. Our analysis leads to a rejection of this attempt to extend the results of renewal theory. Specifically, we show that, barring numerical accidents of no economic significance, the replacement ratio will not approach a constant unless either the entire capital stock happens to deteriorate at a constant exponential rate or the capital stock is growing at a constant exponential rate. Of course, if the capital stock is growing at a constant rate then both net and gross investment grow at a constant rate. But an econometric specification that states that there is a varying rate of net investment which is determined by economic forces while replacement is a constant fraction of the capital stock cannot be justified by appeal to renewal theory. Such a procedure is justified if, and only if, deterioration occurs at a constant exponential rate. We shall now establish this necessary and sufficient condition. The next section then examines the evidence for the assertion of constant exponential deterioration.

Our model is the simplest possible one. Capital lasts V years,[6] and deterioration consists solely of output decay. A machine in the vth year of its life yields s_{v-1} as much service as it did in year $v - 1$.[7] We adopt the convenient normalization rule that in the first period of its life a machine delivers a single unit of service. More generally, we shall measure capital in efficiency units; the number of units of capital of each age is measured by the number of units of service they provide per period. The capital stock at time t may be described by a vector, $M(t)$, whose components represent the amount of capital of each age at time t, that is,

$$M(t) = \begin{bmatrix} M_1(t) \\ M_2(t) \\ \cdot \\ \cdot \\ \cdot \\ M_v(t) \\ \cdot \\ \cdot \\ \cdot \end{bmatrix} \tag{1}$$

The total amount of the capital services rendered at time t is, given our conventions, simply the sum of the components of $M(t)$. Thus

$$K(t) = \sum_v M_v(t). \tag{2}$$

---

6. At this stage, V may be finite or infinite; in the latter part of this section we shall, for expositional simplicity, assume that V is finite.

7. Thus, if V is finite, $s_V = 0$.

If there are no additions, the capital stock that produced $K(t)$ units of service in period t will produce only $K(t + 1) = \sum_{v=1}^{V} M_v(t)s_v$ units of service in period $t + 1$. An investment of

$$R(t) = \sum_{v=1}^{V} M_v(t)(1 - s_v) \tag{3}$$

is required to keep the capital service constant. Thus $\Sigma\, M_v(t)(1 - s_v)$ is the standard definition of the replacement requirement. We define the replacement ratio at time t, $r(t)$, as the replacement requirement divided by the capital stock:

$$r(t) = \frac{\sum_{v=1}^{V} M_v(t)(1 - s_v)}{K(t)}. \tag{4}$$

Observe that the replacement ratio does not depend on the absolute size of the capital stock but only the proportionate contributions of capital goods of each age to the total capital services. Thus, if we define the vector

$$a(t) = \frac{1}{K(t)} M(t) \tag{5}$$

as the age structure of the capital stock, we see that $r(t)$ depends only on $a(t)$ and not on $K(t)$:

$$r(t) = \sum_{v} a_v(t)(1 - s_v). \tag{6}$$

We shall take advantage of this fact to abuse our notation on occasion by writing $r(a)$ to denote the replacement ratio associated with a particular age structure.

We are interested in the circumstances under which $r(t)$ will be a constant. It is clear that this will happen only if either the replacement ratio is independent of the age structure or if the age structure only assumes certain limited values. We now examine these restrictions.

The implications of independence between the replacement ratio and the age structure are both strong and familiar. A sufficient condition for

$$r(a) = \sum_{v=1}^{V} a_v(1 - s_v) = r \quad \text{for all } a_v \geq 0 \text{ such that } \sum_{v=1}^{V} a_v = 1 \tag{7}$$

is that all capital deteriorates at the same constant exponential rate. This is also a necessary condition except in the economically uninteresting special case of $V = 1$ (which we ignore from now on). To see this, observe that (7) holds if and only if

$$s_v = s \qquad (v = 1, \ldots, V). \tag{8}$$

Since $s_V = 0$, (8) can only hold if $V = 1$ or $V = \infty$; if $V = \infty$, (8) implies constant exponential decay.

If the pattern of decay is not exponential, the movements of the age structure must be restricted. More specifically, barring numerical accident,[8] the age structure must remain unchanged. We therefore consider under what circumstances the age structure of the capital stock will actually remain constant. We shall show that this will happen only if net, gross, and replacement investment all eventually grow at the same constant rate. The proof we give is confined to finite-lived capital goods ($V < \infty$). We assume that goods last exactly V years so that $s_v > 0$ for $v = 1, \ldots, V - 1$.

To examine how the age structure of the capital stock changes, it is necessary to examine how the capital stock changes. We may describe gross investment in each period as the sum of replacement investment, $R(t)$, and net investment, $N(t)$. Also as a matter of notation, we state that investment in period t is installed in period $t + 1$. Thus

$$M_1(t + 1) = R(t) + N(t). \tag{9}$$

The other components of the capital stock are determined by the aging of the previous period's capital stock so that

$$M_v(t + 1) = s_{v-1} M_{v-1}(t) \qquad (v = 2, \ldots, V). \tag{10}$$

It is convenient to define the nonnegative variable $q(t)$ as the solution of the equation

$$M_1(t + 1) = q(t) \cdot \sum_{v-1}^{V} M_v(t). \tag{11}$$

Note that $q(t)$ is the ratio of gross investment to the capital stock; we shall

---

8. The possibility of satisfying Eq. (7) by numerical accident represents the fact that the set of vectors $a(t)$ satisfying Eq. (6) is a hyperplane. We are unable to give any economic meaning to the condition that the sequence of age structures belongs to this particular hyperplane and therefore ignore this as a numerical accident of no economic interest.

refer to it as the expansion coefficient. With this definition, we can describe the sequence of capital stock vectors by the equation

$$M(t + 1) = B[q(t)] \cdot M(t), \tag{12}$$

where the $V \times V$ matrix B is given by

$$B(q) = \begin{bmatrix} q & q & q & \cdots & q \\ s_1 & 0 & 0 & \cdots & 0 \\ 0 & s_2 & 0 & \cdots & 0 \\ & \cdot & & & \\ & \cdot & & & \\ & \cdot & & & \\ 0 & \cdots & \cdots & s_V & 0 \end{bmatrix} \tag{13}$$

It is quite straightforward to show that if the expansion coefficients q are constant, then the capital stock grows at a constant rate and the age structure approaches a constant. More formally, this is stated by the following theorem, which is proved in the Appendix.

THEOREM 1: *If $q(t) = q$ for all $t > 0$, then there exists a nonnegative vector $E(q)$ such that $\|E(q) - a(t)\| \to$ (where $\|x_v\| = \Sigma|x_v|$).*

This is the correct generalization of the basic result of renewal theory; it is also a well-known result of stable population theory. It implies that even if the capital stock does not decay exponentially, the replacement ratio would eventually be constant in the very special case in which gross investment is a constant fraction of the capital stock and therefore in which the capital stock eventually grows at a constant exponential rate.

This in itself is not very interesting because the required condition does not hold. Theorem 2, which is roughly the converse of theorem 1, is much more important. It states that if the age structure is to approach a constant, then the expansion coefficient must also.

THEOREM 2: *If (1) $M_1(t) > 0$ for all t, (2) $0 < q \leq q(t) \leq \bar{q}$ for all t, and (3) $\lim_{t \to \infty} a(t) = a$, then the sequence $q(t)$ converges.*

This theorem is proved in the Appendix; here we comment on its content and economic meaning. Assumption (1) states that gross investment is positive in every year; assumption (2) states that the expansion coefficient has finite lower and upper bounds.[9] Given these very weak assumptions, the theorem asserts that the age structure is or tends to a constant only if the sequence of expansion coefficients also converges to a constant. This implies that if the capital stock does not decay exponentially, the replacement ratio would (even eventually) be constant *only* in the very special case in which gross investment is a constant fraction of the capital stock and therefore in which the capital stock eventually grows at a constant exponential rate.

The analysis of this section has shown that renewal theory does not justify treating the replacement ratio as a constant. Theorem 2 shows, roughly speaking, that the renewal theory type result can be obtained only for an economy in which investment grows at a constant exponential rate. Gross investment has not grown at a constant exponential rate in any economy. We therefore conclude that the only possible justification for treating the replacement ratio as a constant would be that output decay occurs at a constant exponential rate.[10] In the next section we consider the evidence for this proposition.

The Pattern of Output Decay

Has output decay occurred at a constant exponential rate? In the last section we showed that the legitimacy of assuming a constant replacement ratio hinged on an affirmative answer to this question. In this section we examine the case for the proposition that output decay follows a constant exponential pattern. Our conclusion is that it has not. Because direct evidence about output decay simply does not exist, our analysis is based on the interpretation of data on scrapping and depreciation. The argument of this section in brief is as follows: We first establish that different kinds of capital goods have different patterns of deterioration. We then show that a capital stock composed of machines with different deterioration patterns will exhibit exponential output decay only if (1) output decay of each machine occurs at some constant exponential rate, *and* (2) the composition of the capital stock by deterioration type remains constant. Our analysis of the available evidence shows that neither the first nor the second condition is an adequate description of the U.S. capital stock since

9. The theorem also holds if we impose the weaker condition $0 \leq q(t) \leq \bar{q}$; the argument is both obvious and cumbersome and we omit it.

10. It might also be argued that treating the replacement ratio as constant is justified in empirical work because departures from constancy are not economically important. We show below that this is not true and, in particular, that historical variations in the rate of growth can account for substantial variation in the replacement ratio.

1929. Although the data are neither so abundant nor so good that we can claim to have definitely refuted the notion of exponential output decay, it is clear that the evidence does not imply such a pattern of deterioration.

It seems hardly necessary to argue that there are differences in the deterioration patterns of capital goods. Everyone knows that computers become obsolete more quickly than typewriters, that Volkswagens depreciate less quickly than Corvairs, that light fixtures outlast the light bulbs in them. These casual observations are confirmed by more systematic evidence. The United States Treasury Department's Bulletin F indicates a wide variety of average lives for different forms of plant and equipment.[11] An even more useful source of data is Winfrey's report (1935) of the mortality curves compiled by workers at the Engineering Experiment Station of Iowa State College during the 1920s and 1930s. Winfrey used eighteen different mortality curves to summarize the data on the 176 different groups of property that he analyzed.[12]

Studies of depreciation also indicate considerable variability in deterioration patterns even within the very narrow class of goods (that is, motor vehicles) for which depreciation studies are available. The estimated rate of depreciation varies from year to year and among types of vehicles. Griliches (1970) reports that for tractors the rate of depreciation was somewhat higher in the 1930s than in the 1950s. Cagan (1971) devotes an appendix to the problem of "depreciation drift," which he defines as "the tendency for the average rate of depreciation of successive model years to change slightly." Wycoff (1970) reports rates of depreciation that vary from 0.30 to 0.43 in the first year and from 0.17 to 0.27 for subsequent years in the vehicle's life. The results of a study by Ramm (1971) show that age-specific depreciation rates on automobiles vary from year to year. The only study that does not report significant differences in depreciation patterns by type of vehicles (including model year) is that of Hall

11. Although the basis for the 1942 Bulletin F lives has never been published, Grant and Norton (1955) note that the 1931 Internal Revenue Service estimated lives were apparently obtained through conferences with industry and that a number of statistical studies were made between 1931 and 1942. Additional statistical analyses were used to revise the Bulletin F lives in 1957.

12. Winfrey's *Statistical Analysis of Industrial Property Retirements*, published in 1935, has never been superseded or updated. The Office of Business Economics still uses a modification of Winfrey's S-3 curve (a Pearson type II curve with parameters due to Winfrey) to calculate the distribution of lives of all capital goods in the Office of Business Economics' capital stock project; see U.S. Department of Commerce (1971). The S-3 curve is in effect a weighted average of the eighteen individual curves that Winfrey developed to describe different mortality distributions. See also Marston and Agg (1936) and Terborgh (1954).

(1971), whose study is limited to half-ton Ford and Chevrolet pickup trucks.

The implications of heterogeneity are both immediate and strong. Suppose that the capital stock at time t is composed of H kinds of machines. It follows from the argument of the previous section that, barring numerical accidents, the replacement ratio of each component will be a constant independent of the age structure only if each type of machine deteriorates at a constant geometric rate. However, even this is not sufficient to ensure that the aggregate capital stock will experience output decay at a constant geometric rate. If machines of type h deteriorate at the geometric rate d_h and if $M_h(t)$ is the number of units of capital of type h at time t, the replacement requirements at time t are given by $R(t) = \sum_h M_h(t)d_h$ and the replacement ratio is $r(t) = R(t)/\sum_h M_h(t)$. If we define

$$m_h(t) = \frac{M_h(t)}{\sum_h M_h(t)},$$

then we may write the replacement ratio as a function of the $m_h(t)$, the shares of capital goods of different types in the total capital stock. That is,

$$r(t) = \sum_h m_h(t)\, d_h.$$

Clearly, $r(t)$ will be a constant only if (1) $d_h = d$ for all h, or (2) if the $m_h(t)$ remain constant, or (3) if the $M_h(t)$ change over time but in such a way that they remain on the hyperplane defined by

$$\sum_h m_h(t)\, d_h = \bar{r}.$$

We may dismiss (1) as being inconsistent with the observed heterogeneity of the capital stock discussed above, while (3) is a numerical accident of no economic interest. We are left with the proposition that the capital stock will decay exponentially only if each component decays exponentially *and* in addition the composition of the capital stock, by durability, remains constant. We now present evidence that neither of these statements is true.

We first consider whether the composition of the capital stock by durability has remained constant. Since no classifications of capital goods by the relevant durability type exist,[13] it is difficult to establish whether the composition of the capital stock, in the desired sense, has changed. However, there is evidence that the composition of the capital stock by deterioration pattern has changed. Since Bulletin F lists the average life of each type of capital good, a detailed breakdown of investment by type of capital good could be used to calculate the average life expectancy of new investment for different years. A change in this figure would suggest that the composition of the capital stock by deterioration type had changed. Unfortunately, published data do not permit this calculation to be made at any but the most gross level of aggregation. However, a very crude breakdown shows a significant change in the average expected age of new non-farm investment: it declined from 19.8 years in 1929 to 15.3 years in 1963.[14]

Other indications of the changing age composition of the capital stock may be gleaned from the tables of the Office of Business Economics' capital stock study (1971). The age distribution of the gross capital stock has changed markedly. For example, in 1925 34.4 percent of the gross capital stock was less than nine years old; the comparable figure was 23.1 percent in 1938, 52.5 percent in 1958, 50.7 percent in 1963, and 54.4 percent in 1968 (U.S. Department of Commerce 1971, p. 109). Some of the change in the age distribution of the capital stock is due to changes in the rate of capital formation; the rest is due to changes in the average life expectancy of new investment. Disentangling these two effects on the basis of published data is very difficult, but it seems most unreasonable to attribute the entire shift to changes in the growth rate.

We turn now to the question of whether or not all capital goods experience output decay at a constant proportional rate. On its face this proposition seems so unlikely that it is hard to understand why anyone would believe it in the absence of strong evidence in its favor. Yet the actual evidence on deterioration patterns is so scanty and fragmentary that it is hard to refute definitely any proposition about output decay, even this one. We present two bits of evidence that strongly suggest to us that output decay is not exponential.

Consider first the evidence based on studies of depreciation of motor

13. That is, by the exponential rate of output decay. One reason that no such classification exists in the published literature is that, as we argue below, it is most unlikely that all capital goods exhibit exponential output decay.

14. Calculated by applying 85 percent of the average Bulletin F lives for structures and equipment for both manufacturing and nonmanufacturing to the gross investment data reported in the Office of Business Economics capital stock study (1971). The 85 percent factor was also based on the OBE study.

vehicles.[15] In his useful survey, Jorgenson (1973) cites four: Griliches' (1970) study of tractors, Cagan's (1971) and Wykoff's (1970) studies of passenger cars, and Hall's (1971) study of pickup trucks. These investigators found the data on prices of used cars consistent with constant rates of depreciation, but only for vehicles that were more than one year old. Since the greatest percentage amount of depreciation takes place in the first year of a vehicle's life, this omission is significant—just how significant can be seen in Wykoff's conclusion.[16] As Jorgenson noted, Wykoff wrote that "after the first year cars do appear to decay exponentially." However, Wykoff also observed that "first-year depreciation is almost twice the rate in succeeding years" and concluded flatly that "depreciation rates for automobiles are not exponential" (1970, pp. 171–172). These studies of motor vehicles therefore do not support the conclusion that output decay for even this segment of the capital stock has been exponential.[17]

Even if it were conceded that depreciation occurs at a constant exponential rate, it would not follow that output decay also occurs at a constant exponential rate. Data on depreciation cannot be transformed into evidence about output decay without assumptions about input decay.[18] Consider a machine that becomes more inefficient as it ages. It does the same amount of work each period but requires more inputs to produce these services.[19] Even if the machine never becomes so inefficient that it is scrapped, its value will decline from period to period. Such depreciation will never generate any replacement investment. If we pursue these considerations a bit further, we see immediately that output decay is not simply a technological phenomenon. The amount of output a machine will

15. These studies are based on recorded prices of used goods. Studies of deterioration based on secondhand prices probably show too much depreciation. It is most likely that the vehicles that appear on such markets are less good than average vehicles. Whether or not this is an accurate statement, people believe it and prices reflect it. What effect this bias, which Akerloff (1970) calls the "lemon effect," will have on determining whether the rate of depreciation is independent of age is not clear. We are inclined to guess that it is of greater absolute importance for young equipment than for old but have no idea at what ages the *relative* bias (which is at issue here) is greatest.

16. All of the studies cited but Wykoff's are limited to the depreciation of vehicles after their first year.

17. Although Ramm's (1971) study of depreciation rates of passenger cars indicates the annual percentage rate of depreciation declines with an automobile's age, Ramm observes that the exponential function fits "quite well" (p. 79).

18. As Hall (1968) emphasized, depreciation will also reflect technical progress. Even in the absence of input decay, separate rates of output decay and technical progress can only be identified under special conditions.

19. There is some evidence that this pattern of deterioration occurs on equipment used to generate electrical power; see Balinfante (1972).

generate in any year is a function of the inputs used with it as well as its age. How much input will be used with a machine depends on economic considerations. For example, automobiles last much longer, and travel many more miles, in Israel (where labor is relatively cheap and new cars are taxed heavily) than in the United States. Depreciation patterns, output decay patterns, and, more importantly, the relation between the two, depend on relative prices. In short, exponential depreciation need not imply exponential output decay.

Consider now the class of capital goods in which all output decay occurs at one time, that is, "one-horse-shay" deterioration. Light bulbs deliver the same amount of illumination from their day of installation until their filament burns out. Railroad ties and telephone poles generate no replacement until they are torn up and replaced. We shall refer to goods that deliver a constant amount of output over their useful lives as *failing goods*. The mere fact that a kind of capital good produces a constant amount of output until it is replaced might seem to preclude an exponential replacement pattern. This is not so because service lives of such capital goods are stochastic. Some light bulbs last longer than others. One may calculate, from a sample of light bulb lives, the probability that a light bulb will fail after a given length of service. The resulting mortality distribution is, for the analysis of replacement investment, equivalent to the pattern of output decay for a good with nonstochastic service life. A failing good with a 10 percent probability of failure in its fifth year of life will, on average, generate in that year the same replacements as a nonstochastic good whose output decays 10 percent in its fifth year.

If the mortality distribution of a capital good is exponential, a capital stock composed of a large number of such goods will have a constant replacement ratio independent of its age distribution. A capital stock of failing goods with any other mortality distribution will not generate a constant replacement ratio. It follows that the mortality distributions of failing goods may be used to determine whether or not output decay occurs at a constant geometric rate. Winfrey's monograph (1935), the most comprehensive study of the distribution of service lives known to us, contains data on many different failing goods, including underground cables, electric lamps, railroad trestles, gas meters, and telephone poles. Only one of Winfrey's 176 empirical frequency curves looks remotely like an exponential distribution.[20] The only conclusion that Winfrey's study permits is that the service lives of failing goods are not distributed exponentially.

---

20. The curve in question (number 105) is for telephone switchboards. No other curve even shows the required monotonically declining probability of replacement. The telephone switchboard curve seems not to have been due to a technical characteristic of telephone

The attention that economists and operations researchers have devoted to the problem of determining the optimal replacement policy for failing goods[21] provides evidence of a different sort that the service lives of these goods are not distributed exponentially. If the mortality distribution were exponential, there would be no point in developing such a policy. An exponential distribution of service lives implies that the expected future life of any functioning piece of equipment is independent of its age. No replacement policy can improve over the practice of replacing equipment only after it fails. This conclusion is independent of objective functions, relative costs of repair and of down time, and the like. If optimal replacement policies are of any practical use, the mortality distributions of failing goods are not exponential.

The analysis of this section can be summarized briefly. We first noted that different kinds of capital goods have different deterioration patterns. We next established that this implies that the capital stock will exhibit exponential output decay only if both (1) the composition of the capital stock by deterioration type remains constant and (2) output decay of each machine occurs at a constant exponential rate. We then showed that neither of these conditions appears to be true.[22] The implication of this section and the previous one is that the replacement ratio neither is nor tends to a constant. The most reasonable interpretation of most of the evidence is that the replacement ratio has fluctuated. The next section assesses the importance of departure from exponential output decay as a source of a fluctuating replacement ratio. Other causes of variation in the replacement ratio are then considered in succeeding sections.

Deviations from Constant Growth

The previous sections indicated that the assumption of constant proportional growth is crucial in the use of the renewal theorem to establish a constant ratio of replacement of the capital stock even under the restricted assumption that all deterioration is output decay. This section illustrates the order of magnitude of the variation in the replacement ratio that results from realistic variations in the rate of growth of the capital stock.

---

switchboards but to the conjunction of rapid growth of demand and sudden obsolescence of this type of switchboard (Winfrey 1935, p. 153).

21. See, for example, Jorgenson, McCall, and Radner (1967).

22. This conclusion is based on a reasonably comprehensive survey of the U.S. evidence. We have not undertaken a systematic survey of the evidence from other countries. The other reports that we have come across (Barna's [1961] questionnaire study of scrapping dates in British industry and Parkinson's [1957] study of the scrapping of ships) tend to support our negative conclusions.

To emphasize the importance of the constant proportional growth assumption, we retain all of the other assumptions that tend to reduce variation in the aggregate replacement rate. In particular we continue (1) to ignore the distinction between replacement and decay, implicitly assuming that all deterioration is output decay; (2) to assume that the capital-output ratio of new investment is constant; and (3) to assume that the replacement pattern of new investment remains unchanged.

Our analysis proceeds with the aid of a simulation model. In place of the assumption that output and the capital stock grow at a constant exponential rate, we start with the assumption that the rate of growth of output satisfies a first-order stochastic difference equation:

$$g_t = \alpha_0 + \alpha_1 g_{t-1} + u_t, \tag{14}$$

where $g_t = \ln (X_t/X_{t-1})$ and X_t is real gross national product. Exponential growth at a constant rate corresponds to the special case of $\alpha_1 = 0$ and $\sigma_{uu} = 0$, where σ_{uu} is the variance of the stochastic disturbance. Equation (14) was estimated for the United States for the period 1932 through 1970; the parameter estimates are:[23]

$$g_t = 0.021 + 0.466g_{t-1}, \qquad \sigma_{uu} = 0.0553. \tag{15}$$

Equation (15) is used to generate a growth rate for each period. The actual level of output is then given by:[24]

$$X_t = X_{t-1} \cdot \exp(g_t). \tag{16}$$

The desired capital stock (K_t^*) is assumed to be a constant multiple of the output level:[25] $K_t^* = kX_t$. A multiple of $k = 2$ is used in the simulations; the value of k has no effect on the long-run results presented below. Net investment (N_t) is then given by the stochastic capital stock adjustment model:

$$N_t = \mu(K_t^* - K_{t-1}) + \varepsilon_t. \tag{17}$$

23. This simple specification was selected after using the method of Box and Jenkins (1970) to examine a more general mixed second-order autoregressive and second-order moving average process. The moving average terms and the second-order term of the autoregressive process were not significant.

24. The initial conditions are $g_0 = 0$ and $X_0 = 1$.

25. This corresponds to the assumption employed by Jorgenson (1963); it is equivalent to the traditional "accelerator" assumption or to the "neoclassical theory" with a constant

The speed of adjustment (μ) is kept constant at one-half and the disturbance is drawn from a normal distribution with mean zero and a very small variance ($\sigma_{\varepsilon\varepsilon} = 0.01$).

Gross investment (I_t) and replacement investment (R_t)[26] are defined in terms of net investment by the equations

$$R_t = \sum_{v=1}^{V} d_v I_{t-v} \tag{18}$$

and

$$I_t = N_t + R_t, \tag{19}$$

where d_v is the fraction of the original gross investment replaced after v years. The pattern of decay (the d_v's) is discussed below.

The model is completed by the identities defining the capital stock,

$$K_t = K_{t-1} + N_t, \tag{20}$$

and the aggregate replacement ratio,

$$r_t = R_t / K_{t-1}. \tag{21}$$

In order to focus on the asymptotic behavior of the replacement ratio and to avoid influencing the results by the choice of initial conditions, the model is simulated for 200 years, and only the behavior during the final 100 years is studied.

The second section showed that, if the replacement distribution (that is, the d_v's of Eq. [18]) represents exponential decay at a constant rate and if the length of the replacement distribution (V of Eq. [18]) is great enough that all replacement has effectively occurred by year V (that is, $\Sigma_{v=1}^{V} d_v \sim 1$), then the aggregate replacement ratio will also be constant regardless of the time path of net investment. If either of these restrictive assumptions is dropped, the aggregate replacement rate will *not* be a constant but will vary in a way that reflects past fluctuations in gross investment. The conclusion of a constant aggregate replacement rate therefore

user cost, constant product price, and constant technology. Relaxing any of these assumptions and allowing variation in capital intensity would introduce another source of variation in the replacement ratio.

26. Recall that we are adopting Jorgenson's assumption of identifying replacement with output decay.

depends crucially on positing either constant exponential growth or constant exponential decay of all investments.

The third section showed that the assumption of exponential decay of all equipment at the same constant rate is untenable. Moreover, even if equipment does decay exponentially during its economic life, it is often scrapped well before its output has decayed to near zero. We shall therefore investigate the implications of alternative departures from the assumption of exponential decay with infinite life. We are not concerned with selecting a decay function that accurately represents the decay of any particular type of machine but only with simple parametric representations of decay that is not both exponential and complete.

Two models of decay will be studied: the Pascal distribution and the truncated exponential distribution. The Pascal distribution is a two-parameter family that includes the exponential as a special case. In simulating with the Pascal distributions, we have assumed that the date of final scrapping is sufficiently distant that almost all of the capital has decayed before that time. The Pascal distribution (truncated in this way) implies that the proportion of the original capital good that decays in period v is given by

$$d_v = (1 - \delta)^{h+1} C_{h+j}^h \varepsilon^v \qquad (v = 1, \ldots, V - 1),$$

$$d_V = 1 - \sum_1^{V-1} d_v, \tag{22}$$

where C_{h+v}^h is the combinational term. For $h = 0$, this is the exponential distribution. For $h \geq 1$, d_v rises and then declines. By choosing $V = 25$ years for all of the Pascal distributions with $h \geq 1$, we limit the final year scrapping to less than 8 percent of the original investment. Our alternative departure from complete exponential decay was the truncated exponential distribution, that is, we let $v = 0$ but set V so that a substantial proportion of the original investment remained to be replaced in the final year.

Table 16.1 shows the effect of substituting alternative decay functions for complete exponential decay; the seven simulations shown were selected from a much larger set with similar implications. The basic result for each alternative specification is shown in column 7, the coefficient of variation of the replacement ratio during the final 100 years of the simulation. Several things should be borne in mind in interpreting each of these values. First, the assumption of constant exponential decay is equivalent to assuming that the coefficient of variation of the replacement ratio is zero. Second, the corresponding coefficient of variation estimated by

Table 16.1. Variation in the replacement ratio

Simulation (1)	Distribution parameters			Final scrapping V (5)	Replacement ratio	
	h (2)	δ (3)	V (4)		Mean (6)	Coefficient of variation (7)
1	0	0.15	25	0.02	0.15	0.005
2	0	0.05	25	0.29	0.06	0.146
3	0	0.10	15	0.23	0.12	0.078
4	0	0.15	10	0.23	0.18	0.054
5	1	0.25	25	0.01	0.14	0.061
6	2	0.25	25	0.00	0.10	0.088
7	3	0.25	25	0.07	0.06	0.123

Feldstein and Foot (1971) from McGraw-Hill survey data is 0.095. Third, a coefficient of variation of 0.10 implies very substantial fluctuations in investment. There is currently about $56 billion of replacement investment, excluding residential construction. A one-standard-deviation range around this value (that is, ±10 percent) therefore corresponds to more than $5 billion per year.[27]

Simulation 1 corresponds to (almost) complete exponential decay. With constant decay of 15 percent of the remaining capital, 98 percent is depreciated by year 25. This is sufficiently close to the hypothetical complete exponential decay to keep the coefficient of variation of the annual replacement ratio to only 0.5 percent. Simulations 2 through 4 correspond to the truncated exponential. With different combinations of δ and V that imply a final year scrapping of approximately one-fourth of the original investment, the coefficient of variation rises to between 5 and 15 percent. In simulations 5 through 7 the decay is almost complete, but the decay proportions follow higher-order Pascal distributions. The coefficients of variation again rise to between 6 and 15 percent.

The results of our simulations may be summarized briefly. Relatively small departures from complete exponential decay imply annual variations in the replacement ratio that are economically important and of the same order of magnitude as the observed variation. These simulations are of course only illustrative and reflect the strong assumptions that replacement is equivalent to output decay and that the pattern of output decay remains unchanged. The next sections consider the economic incentives that also contribute to variation in the replacement ratio.

27. This is based on extrapolating the average recent McGraw-Hill ratio of replacement to total investment (0.52) to all nonresidential fixed investment in 1971.

Changing Durability: Interest Rates, Taxes, and Optimal Planned Durability

The simulations of the previous section showed that fluctuations in the rate of net investment would imply variations in the replacement ratio even if all new investment continued to have the same capital-output ratio and the same durability (output decay function). Changes in the capital-output ratio and in the durability of equipment introduce a further source of variation in the replacement rate. More specifically, an altered capital-output ratio would change the replacement ratio during a long period of transition but would then leave the mean replacement ratio at the original level. In contrast, a change in the average durability of equipment implies a permanent change in the replacement ratio. This section and the next analyze the effect of changes in the tax law and in the rate of interest on the durability of equipment and thus on the replacement ratio. We find that tax and interest rate changes have approximately the same size effects on replacement and net investment in both the short run and the long run.

Economic variables affect the pattern of durability in two distinct ways. First, the physical lives of capital equipment are not immutable. Machines of different durability may be produced at different costs. The lives of machines actually produced thus reflect economic decisions and are affected by changes in economic parameters. Second, the time pattern of output produced by a machine (and thus the replacement requirements it generates) depends on the machine's economic life as well as its physical durability. For example, in the putty-clay model (Johansen 1959; Phelps 1963; Solow 1966), machines are scrapped when their quasi-rents are zero even though they remain physically capable of continuing to produce output.

To simplify the exposition we shall analyze the effects of taxes and the interest rate on physical durability and on economic obsolescence separately. We begin in this section by ignoring economic obsolescence and study the optimal planned durability. The next section assumes that machines have an infinite physical life but that embodied technical progress limits their economic life. In both sections we limit our analysis to the finite life formulation of the problem: "one-horse-shay" decay in this section and a putty-clay technology in the next. Moreover, we make the standard assumptions of static expectations and no adjustment costs; we return to this in the seventh section.

Consider a firm producing output with the production function $Q = F(K, L)$ where L is labor services and K is capital services. A machine of type V (which can be bought at cost $C(V)$) produces one unit of capital services for exactly V years, after which it dies. The firm has two decisions: choosing V and choosing the K/L ratio. The problems are to some extent independent. Whatever the K/L ratio, the firm will choose V so as to minimize the total discounted cost of providing a constant level of capital services until the end of time.[28]

The problem of optimal durability is then equivalent to selecting the machine life that minimizes the discounted cost of providing a unit of capital services forever. Let the cost of producing a machine with life V years be $C(V)$. The net cost of a machine also reflects any initial investment tax credit and the discounted value of the tax savings due to depreciation allowances. If $D_V(s)$ is the tax depreciation allowed at age s of a machine with life V years, k the initial investment credit, α the fraction of the tax credit that is deducted in calculating allowable depreciation, θ the marginal rate of corporate income tax, and ρ the interest rate, then the present value of the tax savings is $\theta[1 - \alpha k] \int_0^V D_V(s) e^{-\rho s} ds$ where $\int D_V(s) ds = 1$. The *net* cost of a machine is thus $h(V) \cdot C(V)$ where

$$h(V) = 1 - k - \theta(1 - \alpha k) \int_0^V D_V(s) e^{-\rho s} ds. \qquad (23)$$

In steady state a machine is bought every V years. The present value of the cost of providing one unit of capital services is thus

$$B(V) = h(V) \cdot C(V)[1 + e^{-\rho V} + e^{-2\rho V} + \ldots] = \frac{h(V)C(V)}{1 - e^{-\rho V}}. \qquad (24)$$

The optimal durability, V^*, is a solution of the equation $B'(V^*) = 0$ so that

$$(1 - e^{-\rho V^*})[h'(V^*) \cdot C(V^*) + h(V^*) \cdot C'(V^*)]$$
$$= h(V^*) \cdot C(V^*)\rho e^{-\rho V^*} \qquad (25)$$

or

$$\frac{h'(V^*)}{h(V^*)} + \frac{C'(V^*)}{C(V)} = \frac{\rho e^{-\rho V^*}}{1 - e^{-\rho V^*}}. \qquad (26)$$

28. Our analysis is thus similar to Wicksell's discussion (1934) of Ackerman's problem. Formulating the analysis this way is legitimate if the demand for capital services is nondecreasing. If, for example, the firm has static expectations, this is the correct model. Swan (1970) has shown that this formulation is correct independent of the competitive or monopolistic structure of the industry that produces or uses investment goods.

We shall derive explicit expressions for $h'(V)/h(V)$ and $C'(V)/C(V)$ and use these to find the optimal V^*. We can then relate changes in V^* to changes in the replacement ratio.

To derive explicit expressions for $h'(V)/h(V)$ under different tax depreciation rules we shall assume that the actual life of the machine is the same as the allowable tax depreciation life. This is more reasonable than is sometimes supposed. In practice, allowable tax depreciation lives have been at least partly dependent on the actual historical replacement policy of the firm. Although the Internal Revenue Service established official guideline lives, many firms used shorter tax depreciation lives because they could show that their actual durability was less. The new asset lives established in 1962 were significantly lower than before but still left 30 percent of the firms in each industry with shorter actual lives. The official adoption of the reserve ratio test in 1962 facilitated firms' establishment of depreciation lives shorter than the guideline when their experience warranted and also prevented firms' use of the guideline lives when their actual lives were longer.[29]

We now derive $h'(V)/h(V)$ and show how it is affected by changes in tax laws. Before 1954 all depreciation was straight line and there was no investment credit. The present value of depreciation was therefore

$$\int_0^V \frac{1}{V} e^{-\rho s}\, ds = \frac{1 - e^{-\rho V}}{\rho V}. \tag{27}$$

Equation (23) then implies

$$h(V) = 1 - \frac{\theta}{\rho V}(1 - e^{-\rho V}). \tag{28}$$

Therefore,

$$h'(V) = \frac{\theta}{\rho V^2}\{1 - e^{-\rho V}(1 + \rho V)\} \tag{29}$$

and

$$\frac{h'(V)}{h(V)} = \frac{\theta[1 - e^{-\rho V}(1 + \rho V)]}{V[\rho V - \theta(1 - e^{-\rho V})]}. \tag{30}$$

29. See Andrews (1969, pp. 339–340) and *Prentice-Hall Federal Handbook* (1972, pp. 286–296) for further details.

In 1954 the law changed to permit sum of the years digits and double declining balance depreciation. Although firms responded slowly and incompletely to these more advantageous options (Ture 1967; Wales 1966), the depreciation of a majority of assets was altered. The sum of the years digits is generally preferable and was more commonly adopted. For the sum of the years digits it can be shown (Hall 1968) that

$$\int_0^V D_V(s)\, e^{-\rho s}\, ds = \frac{2}{\rho V}\left[1 - \frac{1}{\rho V}(1 - e^{-\rho V})\right]. \tag{31}$$

Therefore,

$$h(V) = 1 - \frac{2\theta}{\rho V}\left[1 - \frac{1}{\rho V}(1 - e^{-\rho V})\right] \tag{32}$$

and

$$\frac{h'(V)}{h(V)} = \frac{2\theta\{\rho V(1 + e^{-\rho V}) - 2(1 - e^{-\rho V})\}}{V\{\rho^2 V^2 - 2\theta[\rho V - (1 - e^{-\rho V})]\}}. \tag{33}$$

In 1962 the investment tax credit was introduced ($k = 0.07$) and depreciation was allowed on 93 percent of the investment ($\alpha = 1$). Using Eqs. (23) and (31) yields

$$h(V) = (1 - k) - \theta(1 - k)\left\{\frac{2}{\rho V}\left[1 - \frac{1}{\rho V}(1 - e^{-\rho V})\right]\right\} \tag{34}$$

or

$$h(V) = (1 - k)\left\{1 - \frac{2\theta}{\rho V}\left[1 - \frac{1}{\rho V}(1 - e^{-\rho V})\right]\right\}. \tag{35}$$

It is clear from comparing Eqs. (32) and (35) that the investment tax credit left $h'(V)/h(V)$ unchanged.

The repeal of the Long Amendment in 1964 provided that the tax credit would not alter the full depreciation of the original cost of the investment ($\alpha = 0$). From Eqs. (23) and (30) it then follows that

$$h(V) = 1 - k - \frac{2\theta}{\rho V}\left[1 - \frac{1}{\rho V}(1 - e^{-\rho V})\right]. \tag{36}$$

Here $h'(V)$ is the same as with no investment credit but

$$\frac{h'(V)}{h(V)} = \frac{2\theta\{\rho V[1 + e^{-\rho V}] - 2[1 - e^{-\rho V}]\}}{V\{(1 - k)\rho^2 V^2 - 2\theta[\rho V - (1 - e^{-\rho V})]\}}. \tag{37}$$

Comparing Eqs. (33) and (37) shows that the investment credit lowers the denominator and therefore raises $h'(V)/h(V)$.

In 1964 θ was lowered from 0.52 to 0.50 and then in 1965 to 0.48. It is clear that $\partial[h'(V)/h(V)]/\partial\theta > 0$ so that these decreases in θ lowered $h'(V)/h(V)$.

We now examine the implications of these tax changes for the optimal machine life. The optimality condition of Eq. (25) can be rewritten:

$$\frac{V^*C'(V^*)}{C(V^*)} = \frac{V^*\rho\, e^{-\rho V^*}}{1 - e^{-\rho V^*}} - \frac{V^*h'(V^*)}{h(V^*)}. \tag{38}$$

If the cost function $C(V)$ can be approximated in the relevant range by a constant elasticity relation,

$$C(V) = C_0 V^n, \tag{39}$$

the left-hand side of (38) is just equal to the constant η.[30] Equations (30), (33), and (37) show that for each tax system the value of $Vh'(V)/h(V)$ depends only on the product of ρ and V and not on each separately. As a result, the entire right-hand side of (38) also depends only on the product ρV^*. Table 16.2 presents the optimal values of V for various values of η over the relevant range assuming an interest rate of 10 percent. The reader may use the fact that ρV^* is a constant to calculate the optimal V's for other interest rates; it is clear that all the V^*'s in Table 16.2 would change in the same proportion. Five different tax systems, identified as A, B, C, D, and E, are analyzed. System A is the one prevailing prior to 1954. Only straight line depreciation is allowed, there is no investment tax credit, and the corporate tax rate is 52 percent. System B differs from system A only in that accelerated depreciation (sum of the years digits) is allowed. System C corresponds to the tax system prevailing after the 7 percent investment tax credit was introduced and the depreciation base was reduced by the amount of the credit. As we observed above, the change from tax system B to C entails no change in V^*. In system D the

---

30. It is clear that $0 < \eta < 1$ since $\eta \leq 0$ would imply that increased durability could be obtained at no extra cost while $\eta \geq 1$ would imply that a shorter life was optimal.

Table 16.2. Tax systems and optimal machine lives (V^*)

Cost elasticity	Tax systems[a]				
(η)	A	B	C	D	E
0.10	20.6	20.7	20.7	19.6	20.8
0.20	15.8	16.3	16.3	15.5	16.4
0.30	12.2	12.9	12.9	12.3	13.0
0.40	9.4	10.2	10.2	9.6	10.2
0.50	7.1	7.9	7.9	7.4	7.9
0.60	5.2	5.9	5.9	5.5	5.9
0.70	3.6	4.1	4.1	3.9	4.2

a. Tax systems: A—straight line depreciation, $\theta = 0.52$; B—sum of the years digits, $\theta = 0.52$; C—sum of the years digits, $\theta = 0.52$, investment tax credit with reduced depreciation base; D—sum of the years digits, $\theta = 0.52$, investment tax credit with full depreciation base; E—as D, but $\theta = 0.48$.

full depreciation base is restored, and in system E the marginal tax rate is reduced to 48 percent.

These figures can be put into perspective by comparing the effect of tax changes on replacement investment and on expansion investment. In making such a comparison it is important to bear in mind the two quite distinct sources of the change in replacement investment. First, a change in the equilibrium ratio of capital to output has an equal proportional effect on the ratios of expansion investment to output and replacement investment to output. Since expansion and replacement investment are on average approximately equal in magnitude, the change in the capital-output ratio has approximately equal absolute effects on expansion and replacement investment. Second, the tax laws alter the optimum machine life and therefore the replacement ratio. If the capital intensity and the replacement ratio vary in the same direction, the change in the amount of replacement investment will exceed the change in the amount of expansion investment. In the comparisons presented below we show that the change in the replacement ratio has been about as important as the change in the capital-output ratio. Indeed, even when the two effects were in opposite directions, the change in the replacement ratio was so large that the *net* effect was to alter the level of replacement investment by almost as much as the level of expansion investment.

Jorgenson's model of expansion investment provides a convenient framework for this analysis. Since $B(V^*)$ is the present value of the cost of providing one unit of capital services forever with the optimal machine life, we can measure the user cost of capital services by $b = \rho \cdot B(V^*)$.

Table 16.3. User cost of capital and investment ratios

Tax systems[a]	User cost of capital			Investment ratios		
	(1) $b = \rho B$	(2) HJ1[b]	(3) HJ2[b]	(4) N/Q	(5) R/K	(6) R/Q
A	100.0	100.0	100.0	100.0	100.0	100.0
B	91.0	91.9	91.9	109.9	96.1	105.6
C	84.7	86.4	84.2	118.1	96.1	113.5
D	81.6	—	—	122.6	102.5	125.6
E	85.0	84.6	82.5	117.7	95.3	112.2

a. Tax systems are as in Table 16.2.

b. The Hall and Jorgenson user cost values are calculated from data in Hall and Jorgenson (1970). We have assumed the price of capital goods constant for these calculations. Since our model deals with the case in which actual lives are equal to tax lives, we do not reflect the 1962 change in depreciation life guidelines. HJ1 neglects these and HJ2 takes them into account for C and E. The difference is quite small. Hall and Jorgenson do not present results for system D.

By substituting the optimal V^*'s into Eq. (24) and assuming the constant elasticity cost function of Eq. (39), we can calculate this user cost explicitly. With this user cost and the machine life of Table 16.2, we can find the effect of tax changes on the ratio of net investment to output and the ratios of replacement investment to output and capital for any given growth rate of output and elasticity of substitution. More specifically, if the optimal capital stock (K^*) is determined by marginal productivity conditions with an exogenously given output level (Q) and the production technology is Cobb-Douglas,[31] then $K^* = C_1 Q/b$ where C_1 is an arbitrary constant. With output growing at rate g, the ratio of net investment to output is gC_1/b. If machines last V^* years, the replacement ratio equals $g/[(1 + g)^{V^*} - 1]$.

In Table 16.3 we show the results of this analysis for the five tax systems described above; the calculations correspond to an output growth rate (g) of 3.2 percent and a cost function elasticity (η) of 0.20. Because C_0 in Eq. (39) is an unknown constant, the figures are standardized so that for each variable the value corresponding to the original tax system (A) is 100. The first three columns refer to the user cost of capital. Column 1 gives the theoretical values of $b = \rho B(V^*)$ derived with the current model. For comparison we also report (in columns 2 and 3) Hall and Jorgenson's estimates (1971) of the user cost of capital for these tax

31. These are, of course, the assumptions used by Jorgenson and his collaborators.

systems; although their model differs from the current one, the results are substantially similar. The last three columns present the ratios of expansion investment (N) to output and of replacement investment (R) to the capital stock and to output.

Consider, for example, the effects of introducing accelerated depreciation, that is, the switch from tax system A to B. The user cost of capital falls by 9 percent (to 91.0). With the assumed Cobb-Douglas technology, the equilibrium capital-output ratio, and therefore the ratio of expansion investment to output, rises by 9.9 percent. This is shown in column 4. The accelerated depreciation encourages longer-lived assets and therefore a lower replacement ratio. More specifically, column 5 shows that the optimal replacement ratio falls by 3.9 percent. The net effect of the higher capital-output ratio and the lower replacement-capital ratio is a rise in the ratio of replacement investment to output. For the change from tax system B to C there is no variation in the replacement ratio, and therefore it has equal effects on expansion and replacement investment. For the two subsequent tax changes, the shift in the replacement ratio is in the same direction as the change in the capital-output ratio. In both cases, therefore, replacement investment changes substantially more than expansion investment.

So far we have discussed only the long-run effects of tax changes. The short-run effects are quite different. This is seen most easily if we consider the introduction of the investment tax credit, that is, the change from tax system B to C. Such a change has no long-run effect on the replacement ratio but does have considerable short-run consequences. If the optimal machine life is V^* years, introduction of the investment tax credit can only affect replacement investment after a delay of V^* years. During that period the capital-output ratio is increased and the replacement ratio therefore falls.[32]

If a tax change also alters optimal machine life, the short-run effects are more complex. Consider for simplicity a tax change that does not affect the cost of capital and thus the desired capital stock but does change the optimal life of machines. If the optimal machine life increases, the cost per machine will also increase. Since the number of machines to be replaced in the period immediately after the tax change is unaffected, the total dollar cost of replacement increases. Since the capital stock is unaffected, the replacement ratio rises.

---

32. If a constant replacement ratio is assumed for econometric analysis, the amount of net expansion investment in the period following the tax change will be understated. The consequence is likely to be an underestimate of the price elasticity of demand for capital and/or the speed of adjustment.

When tax changes alter both the optimal capital stock and the optimal machine life, the replacement ratio will reflect both effects. The relative magnitudes of the short-run impact on replacement and expansion investment depend on the ex post malleability of the capital stock. The greater the malleability, the more rapid will be the expansion of the capital stock in response to a fall in the user cost of capital. With complete ex post substitutability of capital and labor, a tax change would have a much larger immediate effect on expansion investment. In the more realistic case of very restricted ex post substitutability,[33] the immediate effect on expansion investment would be much more limited.

The conclusions of this section can be summarized briefly. Optimal planned durability is sensitive to changes in the interest rate and tax laws. Such changes would have as large an effect on the long-run replacement ratio as on the level of net investment. In the shorter run, these changes will also have a significant effect on the replacement ratio. The assumption of a constant replacement ratio is thus unwarranted even if there is no variation in the growth of output.

Optimal Ex Post Replacement

The previous section assumed that operating costs were constant over the machine's technologically determined life. It is illuminating to consider a model with the opposite extreme assumptions: a world with a putty-clay technology in which operating costs rise as machines age so that, even if machines are infinitely durable at no additional cost, they are replaced as they become economically obsolete.

Operating costs of old machines can rise for two reasons: (1) input decay and (2) rising wages due to embodied technical change. Consider first the case of technical change. In an economy with putty-clay technology, machines of each vintage are identified by their labor requirements. To produce a unit of output with labor requirements λ a machine of size $f(\lambda)$ must be built; clearly $f'(\lambda) < 0$ and $f''(\lambda) > 0$. In the conveniently tractable Cobb-Douglas case $f(\lambda) = \lambda^{-\alpha}$, where $\alpha = (1 - \beta)/\beta$ and β is the output elasticity of capital in the putty technology. If labor augmenting embodied technical change is occurring at rate γ the labor requirement of a machine of a given size decreases at that rate. Thus a machine of size $\lambda^{-\alpha}$ installed at time 0 has an annual labor requirement of λ whenever it is operated, while a machine of size $\lambda^{-\alpha}$ installed at time t has a permanent annual labor requirement of $\lambda\, e^{-\gamma t}$. With wages rising at the same rate γ, that is, $w(t) = w\, e^{\gamma t}$, the *initial* labor cost of operating a new

---

33. See Bischoff (1971) and Eisner (1969) for evidence on this.

machine of size $\lambda^{-\alpha}$ at time T is $\lambda\ e^{-\gamma T} \cdot w\ e^{\gamma T} = \lambda w$, independent of T. Exactly the same pattern of costs on installed machines will be observed if there is no technical progress, wages are constant, and input decay occurs at the constant exponential rate γ. The model of this section also applies if embodied technical progress (with rising wages) occurs at rate γ_1 while input decay takes place at rate γ_2 where $\gamma_1 + \gamma_2 = \gamma$.

As in the previous section we wish to analyze this model to determine, under conditions of steady-state growth, the optimal life of a machine, the replacement ratio, the capital-output ratio, and the sensitivity of these parameters to changes in the tax laws.[34] We first consider the problem of producing a constant stream of one unit of output forever at minimum cost. This means choosing a sequence of replacement intervals V_1, V_2, . . . and a sequence of technologies (machine sizes) λ_1, λ_2, . . . so that the total discounted cost of production is minimized. The optimal policy is clearly stationary, that is, it entails replacement of new equipment every V years. The variable cost of producing a unit of output on a best practice machine installed at time T_0 is, at time $T_0 + t$, equal to $w\lambda e^{\gamma t}$ and is independent of T_0. The total variable cost of producing one unit of output for V years, when discounted back to the time of installation of the new machine, is $\lambda W(V)$ where

$$W(V) = \frac{w}{\gamma - \rho}[e^{(\gamma - \rho)V} - 1]. \tag{40}$$

The net cost of a machine of size $\lambda^{-\alpha}$ is $\lambda^{-\alpha}C_0 h(V)$ where C_0 is the cost of a unit of capital (putty)[35] and $h(V)$, as defined in Eq. (23), reflects the present value of tax savings and investment tax credits associated with the purchase of a unit of capital of life V. The total discounted cost of producing one unit of output for V years with technology λ is

$$\lambda^{-\alpha}C_0 h(V) + (1 - \theta)\lambda W(V). \tag{41}$$

The optimal λ, which we denote $\lambda(V)$, is chosen to minimize Eq. (41). Noting that $\beta = (1 + \alpha)^{-1}$, we may express the optimal λ as

$$\lambda(V) = C_1\left[\frac{h(V)}{W(V)}\right]^\beta \tag{42}$$

34. For earlier analyses of the effects of tax laws on optimal machine life, see Kelley (1971) and Smith (1963).

35. The constants C_0, C_1, . . . used in this section do not have the same meanings as they did in the previous section.

and the cost-minimizing capital-output ratio as

$$\lambda(V)^{-\alpha} = C_2 \left[\frac{W(V)}{h(V)}\right]^{1-\beta}, \tag{43}$$

where the C_i are inessential constants.

Substituting into Eq. (41) and rearranging implies that the total discounted cost of producing a unit of output for V years at the cost-minimizing technology is

$$J(V) = C_3 h(V)^\beta W(V)^{1-\beta}, \tag{44}$$

while the total discounted cost of producing a unit of output forever is

$$J(V)[1 + e^{-\rho V} + e^{-2\rho V} + \ldots] = C_3 h(V)^\beta W(V)^{1-\beta}[1 - e^{-\rho V}]^{-1}. \tag{45}$$

Setting the first derivative of the logarithm of this total discounted cost to zero shows that the cost minimizing V^* satisfies

$$\frac{\rho \, e^{-\rho V^*}}{1 - e^{-\rho V^*}} = \beta \frac{h'(V^*)}{h(V^*)} + \frac{(1-\beta)(\gamma-\rho) \, e^{(\gamma-\rho)V^*}}{e^{(\gamma-\rho)V^*} - 1}. \tag{46}$$

Note that this is analogous to Eq. (26) of the previous section. Note also that V^* is independent of the wage rate (w) and the cost of capital goods (C_0).

We shall now examine how changes in the interest rate and the tax law alter the optimal life of machines, the rate of replacement investment, and the capital-output ratio. The values of $h'(V)/h(V)$ derived in the previous section are again applicable.

Table 16.4 presents the values of V^* derived from Eq. (46) for various rates of technical progress plus input decay and for the five tax systems described in the previous section. We use the Cobb-Douglas production function with capital elasticity of 0.33; that is, $\beta = 0.33$ or $\alpha = 2$.

We can put these figures in better perspective by comparing the changes in replacement and expansion investment corresponding to the shifts from one tax system to the next. We use Eq. (43) to derive the optimal capital-output ratios corresponding to the V^* values of Table 16.4. For any given rate of growth of output we can then calculate the steady-state ratios of expansion investment (N) to output (Q), replacement investment (R) to capital (K), and replacement investment to output. The results corresponding to an output growth rate of 3.2 percent, an

Table 16.4. Optimal life of equipment with embodied technical progress (V^*)

Rate of technical progress plus input decay	Interest rate	Tax system[a]				
		A	B	C	D	E
0.01	0.10	21.7	21.4	21.4	20.2	21.5
	0.15	15.9	15.4	15.4	14.6	15.5
0.02	0.10	16.8	17.1	17.1	16.3	17.2
	0.15	13.2	13.2	13.2	12.5	13.3
0.03	0.10	13.6	14.1	14.1	13.5	14.2
	0.15	11.2	11.4	11.4	10.9	11.4

a. Tax systems are as in Table 16.2.

interest rate of 0.10, and $\gamma = 0.03$ are presented in Table 16.5. The values for the initial tax system (A) are standardized at 100.

As before, the long-run effects of tax changes on net investment and on the replacement ratio are of the same order of magnitude. Whenever the capital-output ratio and the replacement ratio vary in the same direction, the tax change has a larger impact on replacement investment (R/Q) than on expansion investment (N/Q). For example, the repeal of the Long Amendment (that is, the switch from C to D) increases the ratio of expansion investment to output by less than 2 percent (from 112.6 to 114.4) but increases the ratio of replacement investment to output by 7 percent (from 107.7 to 115.4).

The short-run effects of tax changes are quite different from the case of fixed durability examined in the last section. With the life of a machine an ex post decision, the immediate impact of a tax change on replacement investment is much larger. The effect of an increase in V^* is an immediate halt to scrapping until the youngest machine reaches the new optimal age.

Table 16.5. Capital-output and investment ratios

Tax systems[a]	Capital-output ratio	Investment ratios		
		(N/Q)	(R/K)	(R/Q)
A	100.0	100.0	100.0	100.0
B	107.3	107.3	95.6	102.6
C	112.6	112.6	95.6	107.7
D	114.4	114.4	100.9	115.4
E	112.6	112.6	94.8	106.7

a. Tax systems are as in Table 16.2.

Similarly, a decrease in V^* would cause a scrapping of all equipment that is older than the new optimal age. For example, with $\gamma = 0.01$ and $\rho = 0.10$, the introduction of the 7 percent investment tax credit lowers the optimal life from 21.4 years to 20.2 years. In principle, firms should adjust by scrapping all equipment older than 20.2 years.

If the capital stock has been growing at an annual rate of 3 percent, this would require a replacement of nearly 4.5 percent of the capital stock. This is approximately half the additional expansion investment required to obtain the desired capital intensity. In practice, there would of course be lags in these adjustments. If ex post malleability is low (as assumed in the current section), the short-run replacement effect would be much larger than the short-run expansion effect.[36]

Finally, as we noted in discussing Eq. (46), the optimal life of a machine does not depend on the net cost of a machine but only on the sensitivity of that cost to machine life. Similarly, the optimal capital intensity of production is unaffected if the cost of machines and final products change in the same proportion. This is not true of the short-run replacement decision. A fall in the price of new machines (or in their net acquisition cost because of the introduction of an investment credit with the credit deducted from depreciable value) would induce firms to scrap old equipment sooner. Conversely, an unanticipated increase in machine prices or the removal of an investment credit would cause a postponement in replacement. Unanticipated inflation, for example, will in this way have a depressing effect on replacement investment.

The Timing of Replacement Investment

The analysis of the last two sections ignored both adjustment costs and financing preferences. We now consider the influence of these factors on the short-run timing of replacement investment.

It has long been recognized that the managerial and installation costs of a given amount of investment depend on the speed with which that investment is done. Following Eisner and Strotz (1963), a number of studies including Gould (1968), Rothschild (1971), and Treadway (1969) have analyzed how firms would optimally adapt their timing of investment to reflect these adjustment costs. Although those studies focused on expansion

---

36. The putty-clay technology implies that capital intensity could only be increased as machines are replaced. This implies a much slower response of expansion investment than of replacement investment. For evidence supporting this (although in models that do not deal fully with the determinants of replacement investment), see Eisner (1969) and Bischoff (1971).

investment, the timing of replacement investment would also be altered because of adjustment costs. This introduces an additional potential source of variation in the replacement ratio.

Moreover, firms may give primacy to increasing output capacity while concentrating their timing adjustments on replacement investment. There is evidence that firms can delay or accelerate scrapping for several years with very little effect on total discounted costs, that is, the actual cost relations corresponding to the $J(V)$ functions of the previous section are quite flat in the neighborhood of V^* (Howard 1960; Smith 1957). In contrast, the postponement of expansion investment may entail more substantial losses of profit, especially when the expansion corresponds to the introduction of new products. Estimates of a short-run replacement function (Feldstein and Foot 1971) support this notion that, ceteris paribus, firms vary the rate of replacement to offset fluctuations in expansion investment.[37]

Financing preferences are also likely to affect the timing of investment. Because dividends are adjusted quite slowly to changes in profits, the amount of retained earnings varies substantially with the cyclical fluctuation in profits. Coen (1971) provides evidence that firms may advance their expansion investment when internal funds are more ample and delay such investment when internal funds are scarce. The effect of internally available funds on replacement investment is likely to be greater. Since costs are generally affected relatively little by small shifts in the timing of replacement, the discretionary part of replacement expenditure can be used as a buffer to absorb fluctuations in available funds. Foot and I found strong evidence of such behavior (Feldstein and Foot 1971); those estimates imply that an additional dollar of retained earnings causes, ceteris paribus, an increase of 30 cents in replacement spending.

Finally, there will be short-run variations in the replacement ratio because of the uncertain delivery lags for capital goods. Jorgenson has argued that delivery lags do not affect the timing of replacement because, unlike expansion investment, firms can anticipate their replacement requirements and place orders sufficiently far in advance so that the replacement machines are delivered when needed. Even in the context of Jorgenson's own model, this is incorrect unless firms know the delivery lags with certainty. Moreover, the economic nature of the replacement

---

37. For further evidence on this, see Foot (1972). Jorgenson's objection (1973), that these estimates are based on an inappropriate measure of the capital stock, is unwarranted. He overlooks the estimates that Feldstein and Foot (1971) present based on a capital stock measure that they derive to be consistent with their replacement series. Moreover, as they show, the estimates are not at all sensitive to the choice of capital stock measure.

decision makes delivery lags even more important. As the fifth and sixth sections showed, changes in tax laws or interest rates cause a sudden change in the desired short-run rate of replacement investment. Because of delivery lags, the change in actual replacement would be spread over several years.

Conclusion

This chapter has investigated several reasons why the assumption of a technologically constant rate of replacement is incorrect. In the introductory section we discussed the difference between replacement and deterioration, stressing the distinction between output decay and input decay. The second section proved that the renewal theorem only implies an asymptotically constant rate of output decay in two very special circumstances: constant exponential decay at the same rate for all equipment and constant exponential growth of the capital stock. The third section showed that the evidence about depreciation does not imply constant exponential decay for each type of equipment. The simulation results of the fourth section demonstrated that the historical variations in the rate of output growth would cause substantial variations in the rate of replacement. All of this is consistent with previous survey evidence that the rate of replacement investment does have appreciable fluctuations.

The remaining sections examined the different aspects of optimal replacement investment that should be taken into account in specifying an econometric model of investment behavior. The fifth section focused on the economic choice of physical durability, while the sixth section dealt with the economic obsolescence implied by embodied technical progress. The long-run and short-run effects of changes in the interest rate and in tax laws were examined. Finally, the seventh section discussed how adjustment costs, financing preferences, and delivery lags alter the timing of replacement spending.

The failure to specify correctly the behavior of replacement investment has serious consequences. As the analyses of the fifth and sixth sections have shown, changes in tax laws and the rate of interest are likely to affect expenditure on replacement investment as much as expenditure on expansion investment. Moreover, the cyclical variation in total investment spending will be incorrectly anticipated if the dynamics of replacement investment are ignored. Finally, if replacement investment is incorrectly specified, the estimated parameters of the capital expansion process will be biased. We hope that the analysis of this chapter will provide a basis for better empirical work in the future.

Appendix

In this appendix we state and prove two results about the system which evolves according to the rule

$$M(t) = \prod_{\tau=1}^{t} B[q(\tau)]M(0), \qquad (A.1)$$

where

$$M(0) \geqslant 0 \qquad (A.2)$$

is a vector belonging to R^V and $B[q(t)]$ is a nonnegative $V \times V$ matrix defined by

$$B[q(t)] = \begin{bmatrix} q(t) & q(t) & \cdots & q(t) \\ s_1 & 0 & \cdots & 0 \\ 0 & s_2 & \cdots & 0 \\ \cdot & & & 0 \\ \cdot & & & \\ \cdot & & & 0 \\ 0 & & s_{V-1} & 0 \end{bmatrix} \qquad (A.3)$$

for

$$q(t) > 0 \qquad (A.4)$$

and

$$s_v > 0, \qquad v = 1, \ldots, V - 1. \qquad (A.5)$$

Let $M_v(t)$ be the vth component of $M(t)$ and define

$$a(t) = \|M(t)\|^{-1} a(t) = \left[\sum_{v=1}^{V} M_v(t) \right]^{-1} M(t).$$

THEOREM 1: *If* $q(t) = q$ *for all* t, *then there exists a nonnegative vector* $E(q)$ *such that*

$$\|E(q) - a(t)\| \to 0.$$

PROOF: This well-known result follows from the fact that $B(q)$, being nonnegative and indecomposable, has a unique real positive eigenvalue $\lambda(q)$ corresponding to a unique real nonnegative eigenvector $E(q)$ of unit length. The details of the argument may be found in Enzer (1966).

THEOREM 2: *If* (1) $M_1(t) > 0$ *for all t,* (2) $0 < \underline{q} \leqslant q(t) < \bar{q}$ *for all t, and* (3) $\lim_{t \to \infty} a(t) = a$, *then the sequence* $q(t)$ *converges to a constant q.*

PROOF: Since the sequence $\{q(t)\}$ is bounded it has limit points. We prove the theorem by showing that if q and $\hat{q}$ are limit points of $\{q(t)\}$, then $q = \hat{q}$. Let $\gamma(t) = \|B[q(t)]a(t-1)\|^{-1}$. Then the sequence $\{\gamma(t)\}$ is bounded and the sequence $\{a(t)\}$ evolves according to

$$a(t) = \gamma(t)B[q(t)]a(t-1). \tag{A.6}$$

If q is a limit point of $\{q(t)\}$, then there is a subsequence $\{t_j\}$ such that $\lim_{j \to \infty} q(t_j) = q$. Clearly, $\lim_{j \to \infty} a(t_j) = q$ and $\lim_{j \to \infty} \gamma(t_j)$ exists and is equal to $\|B(q)a\|^{-1}$. Calling this quantity γ we see that

$$\gamma = q + S_1 q_2 + \dots + S_{V-1} a_V. \tag{A.7}$$

Taking these limits in (A.7) we see that

$$a = \gamma B(q)a. \tag{A.8}$$

Similarly, if $\hat{q}$ is another limit point of $\{q(t)\}$, then

$$a = \hat{\gamma} B(\hat{q})a, \tag{A.9}$$

where

$$\hat{\gamma} = (\hat{q} + s_1 a_2 + \dots + s_{V-1} a_V)^{-1}. \tag{A.10}$$

Writing out (A.8) and (A.9) component by component, we see that $\gamma = \hat{\gamma}$ so that $q = \hat{q}$.

17 Inflation, Tax Rules, and Investment: Some Econometric Evidence

My subject in this chapter is one to which Irving Fisher devoted considerable analytic and econometric effort: the effect of inflation on financial markets and capital formation.[1] Nowadays every student learns of Fisher's conclusion that each percentage point increase in the steady-state inflation rate raises the nominal interest rate by 1 percent, leaving the real rate of interest unchanged. Moreover, since the supply of saving depends on the *real* rate of interest and the demand for investable funds also depends on the *real* rate of interest, a change in the rate of inflation would have essentially no effect on the economy's real equilibrium. I say "essentially" no effect because another great Yale economist, James Tobin, reminded us in the 1964 Fisher Lecture that an increase in the nominal interest rate could cause households to substitute capital for money in their portfolios, thereby reducing the real interest rate.

The Fisher-Tobin analysis, like most theoretical analyses of macroeconomic equilibrium, ignores the role of the taxes levied on capital income. While this may have been a reasonable simplification at some time in the past, it is quite inappropriate today. Taxes on capital income with marginal rates that are often between one-third and two-thirds can have profound effects on the real macroeconomic equilibrium and on the way in which inflation affects that real equilibrium.

A simple example will illustrate the potential for substantial departures from Irving Fisher's famous neutrality result. Consider an economy in which saving and the demand for money are both perfectly inelastic, in which there is no inflation, and in which the marginal product of capital is 10 percent. If we ignore risk and assume that all marginal investments are

Reprinted from *Econometrica* (July 1982) by permission of the Econometric Society. This chapter was presented as the Fisher-Schultz Lecture at the World Congress of the Econometric Society, August 29, 1980. I am grateful to Charles Horioka for assistance with calculations and to Louis Dicks-Mireaux, James Poterba, and Lawrence Summers for earlier collaborative work.

1. See, for example, Fisher (1896, 1930).

debt-financed,[2] the rate of interest in the economy will also be 10 percent. A permanent increase in the expected rate of inflation from zero to 5 percent would raise the nominal internal rate of return on all investments by 5 percent, which would in turn raise the equilibrium rate of interest in the economy from 10 percent to 15 percent. All of this is just as Irving Fisher would have it.

But now consider the introduction of a corporate tax of 100 τ percent on the profits of the business with a deduction allowed for the interest payments. It is easily shown that, if economic depreciation is allowed, the interest rate that firms can afford to pay remains 10 percent in the absence of inflation. But inflation now raises the interest rate not by any increase in the inflation rate but by that increase in inflation divided by $1 - \tau$.[3] If τ is 50 percent, the 5 percent increase in expected inflation raises the interest rate by 10 percent to 20 percent. This is easily understood since the 10 percent increase only costs a firm a net-of-tax 5 percent, just the amount by which inflation has raised the nominal return on capital.

In this example, the effect of a 5 percent inflation rate is to raise the *real* rate of interest received by savers from 10 percent to 15 percent. Their real *net-of-tax* rate of interest will, however, depend on the extent to which the interest income is subject to personal tax. If every lender's tax rate is exactly equal to the corporate rate, the real net rate of interest will be unaffected by the rate of inflation.[4] But more generally, individual tax rates differ substantially,[5] and the real net-of-tax return rises for those individuals with tax rates below the corporate rate and falls for the others. If saving is sensitive to the real net return, these changes will alter the capital intensity of the economy, which in turn will change the marginal product of capital. The effect on the final equilibrium of a change in the expected rate of inflation will depend on the capital-labor substitutability, on the distribution of individual and business tax rates, and on the interest

2. Intramarginal investments may be financed by the equity resulting from the entrepreneurs' original investment and from subsequent retained earnings. See Stiglitz (1973) for such a model.

3. I have examined this simple case as well as the more general situation in which both saving and money demand are sensitive to the rate of return (Feldstein 1976). If f' is the marginal product of capital and π is the rate of inflation, the nominal interest rate satisfies $i = f' + \pi/(1 - \tau)$.

4. If lenders are taxed at 100 θ percent, the net-of-tax nominal interest rate rises by $(1 - \theta)/(1 - \tau)$ times the increase in the rate of inflation. With $\theta = \tau$, this is one and the real net interest rate therefore remains unchanged.

5. Individual tax rates include not only the statutory personal tax rates but the tax rates on savings channeled through pension funds, insurance, and other financial intermediaries.

sensitivity of saving and money demand (as well as on the correlation between these sensitivities and the personal tax rates). In general terms, inflation will raise capital intensity in this model if the rate at which savers are taxed is less than the tax rate on borrowers.

Introducing a more realistic description of depreciation radically alters this conclusion. In calculating taxable profits, firms are generally allowed to deduct the cost of capital investments only over several years. Because these deductions are usually based on the original or "historic" cost of the assets, the real value of these depreciation deductions can be substantially reduced during a period of inflation. This raises the real tax rate on investment income and therefore lowers the real interest rate that firms can afford to offer. The change in the nominal interest rate may be greater or less than the change in inflation and depends on the balance between the positive effect of interest rate deductibility and the adverse effect of original cost depreciation. This conclusion can be extended directly to an economy with equity as well as debt finance (Feldstein, Green, and Sheshinski 1978) and to an economy with government debt (Feldstein 1980a).

In short, the impact of inflation and of monetary policy depends critically on the fiscal setting. It is therefore unfortunate, but all too common, that theoretical analyses of inflation and of monetary policy ignore the tax structure and assume that all taxes are lump-sum levies.

Because capital tax rules differ substantially among countries, inflation can have very different effects in different countries on the rate and composition of capital accumulation. In the past several years, I have tried to explore the theoretical relationship between inflation and tax rules and to measure the impact of inflation in the United States on effective tax rates (Feldstein and Summers 1979) and on the yields on real capital, on debt, and on equity.[6] These studies, together with the results presented in this chapter, have led me to conclude that the interaction of inflation and the existing tax rules has contributed substantially to the decline of business investment in the United States.

The rate of business fixed investment in the United States has fallen quite sharply since the mid-1960s. The share of national income devoted to net nonresidential fixed investment fell by more than one-third between the last half of the 1960s and the decade of the 1970s: the ratio of net fixed nonresidential investment to GNP averaged 0.040 from 1965 through 1969

6. See Chapter 2 of the present work with respect to yields on real capital; Feldstein and Chamberlain (1973), Feldstein and Eckstein (1970), and Feldstein and Summers (1978) with respect to yields on debt; and Feldstein (1980b, 1980c) with respect to equity yields.

but only 0.025 from 1970 through 1979.[7] The corresponding rate of growth of the nonresidential capital stock declined by an even greater percentage: between 1965 and 1969, the annual rate of growth of the fixed nonresidential capital stock averaged 5.5 percent; in the 1970s, this average dropped to 3.2 percent.[8]

This chapter shows how U.S. tax rules and a high rate of inflation interact to discourage investment. The nature of this interaction is complex and operates through several different channels. For example, while nominal interest rates have been unusually high in recent years, the deductibility of nominal interest costs in the calculation of taxable profits implies that the real net-of-tax interest rates that firms pay actually became negative! In itself, this would of course encourage an increased rate of investment. But, since existing tax rules limit the depreciation deduction to amounts based on the original cost of the assets, a higher rate of inflation reduces the maximum real rate of return that firms can afford to pay. The effect of inflation on the incentive to invest depends on balancing the change in the cost of funds (including equity as well as debt), against the change in the maximum potential return that firms can afford to pay. This explanation of investment behavior, which is close to Irving Fisher's own approach, is developed more precisely later in this chapter (in the section on investment and the rate of return over cost) and is then related to the observed variation of investment since 1955.

The interaction of tax rules and inflation can also be seen in a simpler and more direct way. The combined effects of original cost depreciation, the taxation of nominal capital gains, and other tax rules raise the effective tax rate paid on the capital income of the corporate sector by the corporations, their owners, and their creditors. This reduces the real net rate of return that the ultimate suppliers of capital can obtain on nonresidential fixed investment. This in turn reduces the incentive to save and distorts the flow of saving away from fixed nonresidential investment. Even without specifying the mechanism by which the financial markets and managerial decisions achieve this reallocation, the variations in investment during the past three decades can be related to changes in this real net rate of return. This approach is pursued later in the chapter in the section on investment and the real net rate of return.

---

7. Data on net fixed nonresidential investment are presented in table 5.3 of the National Income and Product Accounts. The full time series is presented in Table 17.1 of the present work. The figures used in this chapter do not reflect national income account revisions after July 1980.

8. See Table 17.1 for the annual values. Data on the net stock of fixed nonresidential capital are presented in the *Survey of Current Business*, April 1976 and subsequent issues.

In addition to these two approaches, I have also examined the implications of inflation in a capital stock adjustment model of the type developed by Jorgenson and his collaborators.[9] These results are presented in the section on the flexible capital stock adjustment model.

On Estimating False Models

My focus in this chapter is on assessing the extent to which investment responds to changes in the incentives that are conditioned by tax rules. Separate calculations based on previous research are then used to evaluate the effect on investment of the interaction between inflation and the tax rules.

Despite the extensive amount of research that has been done on investment behavior, there are still many economists who question whether investment does respond significantly to what might generally be called "price incentives" and not just to business cycle conditions.[10] One important reason for these doubts is the failure of previous studies to reflect correctly the impact of inflation. When the price incentive variable is significantly mismeasured, it is not surprising that its impact on investment is understated. A further, and, I believe, more fundamental reason is that the investment process is far too complex for any single econometric model to be convincing. Moreover, making a statistical model more complicated in an attempt to represent some particular key features of "reality" or of rational optimization often requires imposing other explicit and implausible assumptions as maintained hypotheses.

The problem posed for the applied econometrician by the complexity of reality and the incompleteness of available theory is certainly not limited to studies of investment. In my experience, there are relatively few problems in which the standard textbook procedure of specifying "the correct model" and then estimating the unknown parameters can produce convincing estimates. Much more common is the situation in which the specifications suggested by a rich economic theory overexhaust the information in the data. In time series analysis this exhaustion occurs rapidly because of the limited degrees of freedom. But even with very large cross-section samples, collinearity problems reduce the effective degrees of freedom and make it impossible to consider all of the variables or func-

9. See Gordon and Jorgenson (1976), Hall (1977), Hall and Jorgenson (1967), and Jorgenson (1963), among others.

10. See, for example, the article by Clark (1979) and the book by Eisner (1979) for recent examples of studies that conclude that price incentive effects are economically insignificant or, at most, are quite small.

tional forms that a rich theory would suggest. These problems are exacerbated by the inadequate character of the data themselves. Even when information is available and measurement errors are small, the accounting measures used by business firms and national income accounts rarely correspond to the concepts of economic theory.

The result of all this is that in practice all econometric specifications are necessarily "false" models. They are false models not only in the innocuous sense that the residuals reflect omitted variables but also in the more serious sense that the omissions and other misspecifications make it impossible to obtain unbiased or consistent estimates of the parameters even by sophisticated transformations of the data. The applied econometrician, like the theorist, soon discovers from experience that a useful model is not one that is "true" or "realistic" but one that is parsimonious, plausible, and informative.

Unfortunately, econometric research is not often described in such humble terms. The resulting clash between the conventional textbook interpretation of econometric estimates and the obvious limitations of false models has led to an increasing skepticism in the profession about the usefulness of econometric evidence. While some of this skepticism may be a justifiable antidote to naive optimism and exaggerated claims, I believe it is based on a misunderstanding of the potential contribution of empirical research in economics.

I am convinced that econometric analysis helps us to learn about the economy and that better econometric methods help us to make more reliable inferences from the evidence. But I would reject the traditional view of statistical inference that regards the estimation of an econometric equation as analogous to the "critical experiment" of the natural sciences that can, with a single experiment, provide a definitive answer to a central scientific question. I would similarly reject an over-simplified Bayesian view of inference that presumes that the economist can specify an explicit prior distribution over the set of all possible true models or that the likelihood function is so informative that it permits transforming a very diffuse prior over all possible models into a very concentrated posterior distribution.

Although I am very sympathetic to the general Bayesian logic, I think that such well-specified priors and such informative likelihood functions are incompatible with the "false models" and inadequate data with which we are forced to work. I think that the learning process is more complex. Perhaps the phrase "expert inference" best captures what I have in mind. The expert sees not one study but many. He examines not only the regression coefficients but also the data themselves. He understands the limits of the data and the nature of the institutions. He forms his judgments about the importance of omitted variables and about the plausibility of restrictions on the basis of all this knowledge and of his understanding of the theory of economics and statistics. In a general way, he behaves like the Bayesian who combines prior information and sample evidence to form a posterior distribution, but, because of the limitations and diversity of the data and the models that have been estimated, he cannot follow the formal rules of Bayesian inference.[11]

As a practical matter, we often need different studies to learn about different aspects of any problem. The idea of estimating a single complete model that tells about all the parameters of interest and tests all implicit restrictions is generally not feasible with the available data. Instead, judgments must be formed by studying the results of several studies, each of which focuses on part of the problem and makes false assumptions about other parts.

The basic reference on this type of "expert inference" is not Jeffreys, Zellner, or Leamer. It is the children's fable about the five blind men who examined an elephant. The important lesson in that story is not the fact that each blind man came away with a partial and "incorrect" piece of evidence; the lesson is rather that an intelligent maharajah who studied the findings of these five men could probably piece together a good judgmental picture of an elephant, especially if he had previously seen some other four-footed animal.

The danger in this procedure, of course, is that any study based on a false model may yield biased estimates of the effects of interest. Although informed judgment may help the researcher to distinguish innocuous maintained hypotheses from harmful ones, some doubt will always remain. *In general, however, the biases in different studies will not be the same.* If the biases are substantial, different studies will point to significantly different conclusions. In contrast, a finding that the results of several quite different studies all point to the same conclusion suggests that the specification errors in each of the studies are relatively innocuous.

When the data cannot be used to distinguish among alternative plausible models, the overall economic process is underidentified. This may matter for some purposes but not for others. Even if the process as a whole is underidentified, the implications with respect to some particular variable (that is, the conditional predictions of the effect of changing some variable) may be the same for all models and therefore unaffected by the

11. Leamer (1978) presents very insightful comments about the problems of inference and specification search as well as some specific techniques that can be rigorously justified in certain simple contexts.

underidentification. This "partial identification" is achieved because the data contain a clear message that is not sensitive to model specification.

Of course, not all issues can be resolved in this satisfying way. For many problems, different plausible specifications lead to quite different conclusions. When this happens, the aspect that is of interest (that is, the predicted effect of changing a particular variable) is effectively underidentified. No matter how precisely the coefficients of any particular specification may appear to be estimated, the relevant likelihood function is very flat. In these cases, estimating alternative models to study the same question can be a useful reminder of the limits of our knowledge.[12]

Using Alternative Models of Investment Behavior

The potential advantage of using several alternative parsimonious models is well illustrated by the analysis of investment behavior. There are a wide variety of empirical issues that are of substantial importance for both understanding the economy and assessing the importance of different government policies. How sensitive is investment to tax incentives? To interest rates? To share prices? To the expectation of future changes in tax rules or market conditions? And what is the time-pattern of the response to these stimuli? While an estimate of "the correct model" of investment behavior could in principle answer all of these questions at once, it is in practice necessary to pursue different questions with different studies. The purpose of the present study, as I indicated at the beginning of the chapter, is to assess the extent to which changes in tax incentives and disincentives—and particularly those changes that are due to inflation—alter the flow of investment. Focusing on this issue means that some assumptions must explicitly or implicitly be made about the other issues and that the estimated effect of the tax changes is conditional on those assumptions. I find it quite reassuring, therefore, that estimates based on three quite different kinds of models all point to the same conclusion about the likely magnitude of the response to inflation and to effective tax rates.

The current state of investment theory also indicates the need to examine alternative models. While there is probably considerable agreement about the essential features of a very simple theoretical model of invest-

---

12. For a simplified formal analogy, consider the problem of estimating the elasticity of demand for some product with respect to permanent income. Since permanent income is not observed, some proxy must be used. Each potential proxy is, however, likely to introduce a bias of its own. If the estimated elasticity is similar for several quite different proxies, there is a reasonable presumption that each bias is relatively small.

ment behavior, there is much less consensus about the appropriate framework for applied studies of investment behavior. The disagreements about empirical specification can conveniently be grouped in four areas.[13]

Technology

The traditional capital stock adjustment models assume that capital is homogeneous and that the purpose of investment is to increase the size of this homogeneous stock until, roughly speaking, the return on the last unit of capital is reduced to the cost of funds. An alternative and more realistic view sees capital as quite heterogeneous. There are two aspects of such heterogeneity. First, capital consists of a large number of different kinds of equipment and structures. At any point in time there may be too much of one kind of capital and too little of another. A simple aggregate relationship loses this potentially important information. A much more fundamental kind of heterogeneity is associated with the *flow* of new investment opportunities. Each year, new investment possibilities are created by innovations in technology, taste, and market conditions. This exogenous flow of new investment opportunities with high rates of return can induce investment even when the total stock of capital is too large in the sense that the marginal product of an equiproportional increase in all types of capital is less than the cost of funds or the value of Tobin's q-ratio is less than one.[14]

Even within the framework of homogeneous capital models, there has been much debate about the choice between putty-putty models, in which all investment decisions are reversible, and the putty-clay models, in which invested capital has a permanently fixed capital-labor ratio.[15] While the truth no doubt lies somewhere between these extremes (old equipment and processes can be modified but not costlessly "melted down" and reformed), the more complex putty-clay model is undoubtedly a more realistic microeconomic description than the putty-putty model.

Closely related is the issue of replacement investment, a quite significant issue since roughly one-half of gross investment is absorbed in replacement. The simplest model of replacement is that a constant fraction of the homogeneous capital stock wears out each period. A more

13. No attempt is made here to survey the existing empirical research on investment or to examine all of the arguments about specification. For recent surveys, see Nickell (1978) and Rowley and Trivedi (1975).

14. This is quite separate from the reason for investing when q is less than one that is implied by the analysis of Auerbach (1979), Bradford (1979), and King (1977).

15. See Nickell (1978) for an extensive discussion of putty-clay specifications.

realistic description would recognize that output decay is not exponential but varies with the age of the equipment. More generally, the timing of replacement and the level of maintenance expenditure are economic decisions that will respond to actual and anticipated changes in the cost of capital and other inputs.[16]

Market Environment

The conventional Keynesian picture of investment that motivates the accelerator model of investment and most other capital stock adjustment models assumes that each firm's sales are exogenous. The firm is assumed to take the price of its product and the level of its sales as given, and then to select the capacity to produce this level of output. A more general specification would recognize that the firm sets its own level of output, taking as given either the market price of its product or the demand function for its product.

There are analogous issues about the nature of the markets in which the firms buy inputs. The simplest assumption is that these markets are perfect and that the market prices do not depend on the quantities purchased. A more realistic description would recognize that the short-run supply function of labor to the individual firm is likely to be less than infinitely elastic and that, for the economy as a whole, the short-run supply price of capital as well as labor is an increasing function of the quantity purchased.[17]

Closely related is the sensitivity of adjustment costs to the volume of investment. The simplest assumption is that there are no adjustment costs and that the total cost of any total investment is independent of the speed at which it is done. In contrast, the managerial and planning costs may be a significant part of the cost of capital acquisition and may rise exponentially with the rates of net and gross investment. Abel (1978) has shown how a capital stock adjustment model can be extended to include adjustment costs and how doing so can explain why the firm increases its rate of investment only slowly even when the marginal return on installed capital substantially exceeds its cost.

16. See Feldstein and Rothschild (1974) for a critique of the constant proportional replacement hypothesis and an analysis of the potential effects on replacement investment of changes in tax rates and interest rates.

17. Keynes (1936) emphasized that rising cost of inputs is a principal reason for the declining marginal efficiency of investment in the short run. See Brechling (1975) on the empirical importance of this.

Financial Behavior

There remains much controversy about the role of internal and external finance and about the related issue of the factors determining the cost of funds to the firm. The simplest model assumes that the costs of debt and equity funds are independent of both the debt-equity ratio and the volume of the firm's external finance. More general analyses reject the extreme Modigliani-Miller result and recognize that, beyond a certain point, increases in the debt-equity ratio raise the cost of funds. Similarly, it is frequently argued that the availability of retained earnings lowers the cost of funds (at least in the eyes of management) and therefore affects the timing even if not the equilibrium level of investment.[18]

Tax rules significantly affect the costs to the firm of debt and equity finance. The implications of this obvious statement have been the subject of much research and debate in the past few years.[19] At one extreme is the conclusion of Stiglitz (1973) that U.S. firms should finance marginal investments exclusively by debt, retaining earnings to avoid the dividend tax and using the retained earnings to finance intramarginal investments. Auerbach (1978), Bradford (1979), and King (1977) have argued that retaining earnings does not avoid the dividend tax but only postpones it without lowering its present value; this implies that retained earnings are substantially less costly than new equity funds and that the capital stock should be expanded even if the market valuation of additional capital is less than one-for-one.[20] These types of conclusions reflect a world of certainty and one in which all individual investors have the same personal income tax rates. Although complete models with uncertainty and diverse individual tax rates have not yet been fully worked out, it is clear from partial studies (for example, Chapters 3 and 14) that these extensions can significantly alter conventional results.

Expectations and the Decision Process

With a putty-putty technology and reversible investment, expectations are irrelevant. But when an investment commits the firm to a future capital stock with a fixed capital-labor ratio, expectations about the future are

---

18. See, for example, Coen (1968) and Feldstein and Flemming (1971) for evidence on this point.

19. See, among others, Auerbach (1978), Bradford (1979), Feldstein, Green, and Sheshinski (1978), King (1977), Miller (1977), and Stiglitz (1973).

20. For an application of this theory to the empirical study of investment behavior, see Summers (1980).

crucial. Although simple moving averages of past variables are the most common representation of the process by which expectations are formed, this simplification may cause serious misspecification errors in some contexts. Helliwell and Glorieux (1970) and Abel (1978) have developed forward-looking models of expectations. Lucas (1976) has emphasized the potential instability of all such fixed-coefficient average representations, while Sargent (1978) and Summers (1980) have shown both the possibility and the difficulty of developing even quite simple models of factor demand that are consistent with rational expectations.

Even when investment models acknowledge that expectations are uncertain, the assumption of risk neutrality is usually invoked to simplify the analysis. In fact, investment behavior may be substantially influenced by risk aversion, changes in risk perception, and the pursuit of strategies that reduce the risk of major capital commitments.

In each of the cases that I have been describing, the researcher must choose (implicitly or explicitly) between a more tractable but usually less realistic assumption and an assumption that is more realistic but also more difficult to apply statistically. In general, the choice has gone in favor of the more tractable but less realistic specification. Moreover, implementing any one of the more complex assumptions often makes it too difficult to implement some other more realistic assumption, thus inevitably forcing the researcher to choose among false models.

The work of Jorgenson and his collaborators[21] illustrates well this problem of choice. In each case, Jorgenson and his colleagues have selected the more tractable but less realistic assumption. Because they impose the further restriction that the technology of each firm is Cobb-Douglas, the data are required only to determine the time pattern of the response of investment to prior changes in the desired capital stock.[22] There is no separate estimation of the effect of tax rules and no specific tests of the implied effect on investment of changes in tax rules and inflation. Later in this chapter I adopt the general Jorgenson specification but relax the constraint that the technology is Cobb-Douglas and also the constraint that the response of firms to the tax-induced changes in the user cost of capital is the same as their response to other sources of variation in

21. See the references cited in note 9.

22. The Jorgenson procedure also estimates a further parameter that should equal the capital coefficient in the Cobb-Douglas production function, that is, the share of capital income in total output. Estimates of this parameter are almost invariably far too low; although this indicates that the model is "false," it does not necessarily imply that the estimated effects of tax rules and inflation are misleading.

the user cost of capital. The results indicate that a correct measurement of the impact of inflation in the context of this model substantially increases its explanatory power, and that with the correctly measured variables the data are consistent with an elasticity of substitution of one and with the assumption that firms respond in the same way to all changes in the user cost of capital.

Of course, the support for this conclusion is conditional on all of the other false maintained assumptions. I have, however, also examined two other quite different models that do not impose these constraints. The analysis in the next section, which relates investment to the real net-of-tax rate of return received by the suppliers of capital, avoids any reference to financial market variables. While it is therefore obviously completely uninformative about many potentially interesting issues, it avoids conditioning the estimated responsiveness of investment on any theory of corporate finance. The specification in terms of the flow of investment avoids the assumption of homogeneous capital or a putty-putty technology. Again, this makes the model uninformative about important issues but avoids constraining the results by some obviously strong assumptions of a false model. There are of course potential biases in this approach, since it fails to distinguish different reasons for changes in investment and omits variables that may be significant (for example, changes in government debt, international capital flow, or other factors that would in principle be reflected in financial variables).

The third approach, presented in the section on investment and the rate of return over cost, avoids some of these problems, but, of course, at the cost of introducing new ones. This specification relates the flow of investment to the difference between the cost of funds to the firm and the maximum potential rate of return that the firm can afford to pay on a standard investment project. The financial cost of funds is thus explicitly included. Unfortunately, this requires specifying the "true" cost of debt and equity funds and their relative importance. The specification does, however, avoid restrictive assumptions about technology and other aspects of investment behavior. But, like the other two specifications, this return-over-cost specification is a false model whose coefficients might well be biased.

The strength of the empirical evidence therefore rests on the fact that all three quite different specifications support the same conclusion that the heavier tax burden associated with inflation has substantially depressed nonresidential investment in the United States. The magnitude of the effect implied by each of these three models indicates that the adverse changes in the tax variables since 1965 have depressed investment by more than 1 percent of the GNP, a reduction which exceeds 40 percent of the rate of investment in recent years.

Investment and the Real Net Rate of Return

Individuals divide their income between saving and consuming, and, to the extent that they save, those resources are distributed among housing, inventories, plant and equipment, and investments abroad. Individuals make these decisions not only directly, but also through financial intermediaries, and through the corporations of which they are direct and indirect shareholders.

The most fundamental determinant of the extent to which individuals channel resources into nonresidential fixed investment should be the real net-of-tax rate of return on that investment, a variable that I will denote RN.[23] Although the idea of the real net-of-tax return is conceptually simple, its calculation involves a number of practical as well as theoretical difficulties. Because of data limitations, the calculation is restricted to nonfinancial corporations even though total nonresidential fixed investment refers to a somewhat broader set of firms. The real net return is defined as the product of the real pretax return on capital (R) and one minus the effective tax rate $(1 - ETR)$ on that return.

The pretax return is estimated as the ratio of profits plus interest expenses to the value of the capital stock. Profits are based on economic depreciation and a correct measure of inventory costs; capital gains and losses on the corporate debt are irrelevant since the calculation deals with the combined return to debt and equity. The value of the capital stock includes the replacement cost value of fixed capital and inventories and the market value of land. The pretax rate of return is shown in column 3 of Table 17.1.[24]

The effective tax rate on this capital income includes the taxes paid by the corporations, their shareholders, and their creditors to the federal government and to the state and local governments. The shareholders and

23. The rate of return on other types of investments might also matter. Since the interaction of inflation and tax rules raises the potential return on owner-occupied housing (Feldstein 1980d; Poterba 1980), the effect of RN may be overestimated, but this overstatement only reflects another way in which inflational and tax rules interact to reduce nonresidential fixed investment.

24. Feldstein and Summers (1977) discuss the conceptual problems in measuring the capital income and rate of return. Feldstein and Poterba (1980) use the new capital stock data provided by the Commerce Department and Federal Reserve Bank to calculate the pretax rate of return shown in Table 17.1.

Table 17.1. Investment and the real net return to capital

Year	Investment GNP ratio (I^n/Y) (1)	Investment capital ratio (I^n/K^n) (2)	Pretax return (R) (3)	Effective tax rate (ETR) (4)	Net return (RN) (5)	Cyclically adjusted return		
						Pretax (RA) (6)	Effective tax rate $(ETRA)$ (7)	Net return (RNA) (8)
1953	0.027	0.040	0.114	0.745	0.029	0.105	—	—
1954	0.023	0.033	0.107	0.687	0.034	0.117	0.754	0.029
1955	0.028	0.041	0.132	0.665	0.044	0.130	0.712	0.037
1956	0.031	0.044	0.114	0.724	0.032	0.117	0.714	0.034
1957	0.029	0.040	0.105	0.717	0.030	0.114	0.715	0.032
1958	0.017	0.023	0.090	0.707	0.026	0.113	0.713	0.032
1959	0.020	0.028	0.112	0.673	0.036	0.125	0.694	0.038
1960	0.022	0.030	0.104	0.665	0.035	0.122	0.714	0.035
1961	0.019	0.027	0.103	0.664	0.035	0.124	0.689	0.038
1962	0.023	0.033	0.117	0.615	0.045	0.130	0.643	0.046
1963	0.023	0.033	0.124	0.606	0.049	0.136	0.629	0.050
1964	0.029	0.041	0.134	0.562	0.059	0.141	0.591	0.057
1965	0.040	0.057	0.145	0.551	0.065	0.145	0.573	0.062
1966	0.045	0.064	0.145	0.560	0.064	0.137	0.595	0.055
1967	0.038	0.052	0.130	0.564	0.057	0.126	0.603	0.050
1968	0.037	0.051	0.130	0.626	0.049	0.123	0.663	0.041
1969	0.038	0.051	0.117	0.673	0.038	0.113	0.762	0.027
1970	0.031	0.040	0.096	0.705	0.028	0.106	0.792	0.022
1971	0.025	0.032	0.100	0.677	0.032	0.112	0.782	0.025
1972	0.028	0.037	0.108	0.625	0.041	0.113	0.720	0.032
1973	0.034	0.046	0.105	0.701	0.031	0.102	0.795	0.021
1974	0.031	0.040	0.082	0.901	0.008	0.096	1.079	−0.008
1975	0.014	0.017	0.086	0.724	0.024	0.115	0.852	0.017
1976	0.015	0.019	0.095	0.681	0.030	0.114	0.850	0.017
1977	0.020	0.026	0.097	0.683	0.031	0.109	—	—
1978	0.025	0.033	0.097	0.722	0.027	0.104	—	—

creditors consist not only of individuals but also of various financial intermediaries including banks, pension funds, and insurance companies. In an earlier study Lawrence Summers and I did a detailed analysis of the distribution of corporate equity and debt among the different classes of shareholders and creditors and of the relevant marginal federal tax rates for each such investor (Feldstein and Summers 1979). More recently, James Poterba, Louis Dicks-Mireaux, and I refined this analysis (Chapter 2) and extended it to include the taxes paid to state and local governments. The effective rate of tax is shown in column 4 of Table 17.1; the resulting net-of-tax rate of return is shown in the fifth column.

The pretax rate of return varies cyclically as well as from year to year but has experienced no overall trend.[25] The average return from 1953 through 1979 was 11.0 percent. The effective tax rate was quite high in the 1950s and then declined sharply in the 1960s; at the individual level this reflected a significant reduction in personal tax rates, while at the corporate level this reflected changes in depreciation rules and the statutory corporate tax rate. Since the mid-1960s, the effective tax rate has moved sharply and somewhat erratically upward, primarily reflecting the overstatement of capital income that occurs when inflation distorts the measurement of depreciation, inventory profits, interest payments, and capital gains.[26] The growth of state and local taxes and various changes in personal tax rates contributed somewhat to this overall increase. The real net rate of return shows a general pattern that reflects the changing effective tax rate as well as the cyclical and year-to-year fluctuations in the pretax rate of return. This key rate of return varied around 3.3 percent in the 1950s, rose by the mid-1960s to 6.5 percent while averaging 5.0 percent for the 1960s as a whole, and then dropped in the 1970s to an average of only 2.8 percent.

Since the net rate of return varies cyclically, its estimated impact on investment can reflect cyclical as well as more fundamental influences. To separate these effects, the equations in this section relate the investment rate to a cyclical measure of aggregate demand as well as to the real net return. It is also useful to consider two more explicit ways of focusing on the more fundamental changes in the real rate of return. A cyclically adjusted measure of the real net return was calculated as follows. First, the real pretax rate of return (R) is adjusted by regressing it on the difference between GNP and capacity GNP and then calculating the rate of return for each year at a standard GNP gap of 1.7 percent; this variable, denoted RA (for adjusted) and shown in column 6 of Table 17.1, eliminates cyclical but not year-to-year variations in the pretax return. Since there is no trend in the pretax return, eliminating random as well as cyclical variations in the pretax return would leave only a constant.

The cyclical and random fluctuations in the effective tax rate were eliminated in a more fundamental way by using the explicit statutory provisions. Using a method developed in an earlier study (Feldstein and

25. Feldstein and Summers (1977) showed that the apparent downtrend in the first half of the 1970s was not statistically significant. (More recent evidence, presented in Chapter 2 of the current work, indicates that the yield in the 1970s was about 1.5 percentage points lower than in the 1960s.)

26. This impact of inflation is discussed in Feldstein, Green, and Sheshinski (1978) and calculated in detail in Feldstein and Summers (1979).

Summers 1978) and described more fully in the next section of this chapter, I calculated the real net rate of return that a firm could afford to pay on the debt and equity used to finance a new investment that, in the absence of all taxes, would have a real yield of 12 percent. This net rate of return varies from year to year because of changes in the tax rules and in the anticipated rate of inflation. The ratio of the net rate of return on a mix of debt and equity to the assumed 12 percent real pretax return measures the changes in the effective tax rate that are not due to fluctuations in the pretax rate of return, the rate of current investment, or other year-to-year fluctuations. More formally, this ratio equals $1 - ETRA$; the $ETRA$ value is shown in column 7 of Table 17.1.[27]

Combining the adjusted pretax return and the adjusted effective tax rate gives the adjusted net return ($RNA = RA\,[1 - ETRA]$), shown in column 8 of Table 17.1.

Although this variable is purged of cyclical variation, it still reflects year-to-year variation in the pretax return. Eliminating all such variation and treating the pretax return as a constant implies that all of the variation in the net return comes from the effective tax rate variable. This possibility is tested below in the context of a more general specification in which both RNA and $1 - ETRA$ are included separately.

The basic specification relates the ratio of real net investment to real GNP (I^n/Y) to the real net rate of return (RN) and the Federal Reserve Board's measure of capacity utilization ($UCAP$).[28] I use annual data and lag both regressors one year:[29]

$$\frac{I^n_t}{Y_t} = a_0 + a_1 RN_{t-1} + a_2 UCAP_{t-1} + u_t, \tag{1}$$

where u_t is a random disturbance about which more will be said below.

Although quarterly data could have been constructed, much of the

27. This measure of the effective tax rate differs conceptually from the unadjusted measure in a number of ways. It is an *ex ante* concept for new investment rather than an *ex post* measure on existing capital. No account is taken of the important effect of inflation on the taxation of artificial inventory profits or of the changing rates of state and local taxes. The tax rates on shareholders and creditors are also measured much more crudely.

28. This specification in terms of investment flows represents a disequilibrium process rather than an equal stock adjustment. The special problems of capital heterogeneity and putty-clay technology may make this direct disequilibrium specification more appropriate, especially for explaining and predicting changes in investment over a period of ten to twenty years.

29. Note that since the equation refers to net investment, the past capital stock is not included. I return to this issue later in the chapter.

basic information that is used to calculate the net return variable is available only annually; the within-year variations in a quarterly series would therefore be largely interpolations of doubtful economic meaning.[30]

A lag in response has been found in all previous investment studies and reflects the delays in decision making and in the production and delivery of plant and equipment. The lag also avoids the obvious problem of simultaneity between concurrent investment and capacity utilization or other measures of business cycle activity. More general lag structures and other possible explanatory variables have been considered; these results are also described below.

All of the specifications are estimated by least squares with a first-order autocorrelation correction. The autocorrelation correction algorithm estimates the first-order autocorrelation parameter simultaneously with the other coefficients using a procedure that is equivalent to maximum likelihood if the disturbances are normally distributed. This correction adds to the efficiency of the estimates and, more importantly, avoids the potentially serious downward bias in the estimated standard errors about which Granger and Newbold (1974) have so persuasively warned. For many of the basic specifications I have also checked the constraint implied by the first-order transformation and found that it cannot be rejected; I have also estimated the specification in first-difference form and found similar coefficients. The evidence on this is presented below. (I might also add that simple OLS estimates without autocorrelation correction also produce essentially the same results.)

The basic result is shown in Eq. (2):

$$\frac{I_t^n}{Y_t} = -0.014 + \underset{(0.095)}{0.459}\ RN_{t-1} + \underset{(0.025)}{0.028}\ UCAP_{t-1} + \underset{(0.25)}{0.29}\ u_{t-1},$$

$$\bar{R}^2 = 0.754 \qquad (2)$$
$$DWS = 2.04$$
$$SSR = 3.438\ (10^{-4})$$
$$1954-1978$$

with standard errors shown in parentheses and the coefficient of u_{t-1} indicating the first-order autocorrelation correction parameter. Before looking at other specifications, it is useful to consider briefly the magnitude of

---

30. Extending the analysis to quarterly observations might nevertheless provide more information about the time pattern of response and about the effect of changes in capacity utilization. Of course, the combination of measurement problems and the inherent autocorrelation of the data imply that using quarterly observations would not increase the *effective* degrees of information by anything like a factor of four.

the estimated coefficients. Since the net return variable had a standard deviation of 0.013 for the sample period, a move of RN from one standard deviation below the mean to one standard deviation above would increase the investment ratio by about 0.012, approximately 1.5 times its standard deviation and 45 percent of its 25-year average value. Since the capacity utilization variable has a standard deviation of 0.044, a two-standard-deviation increase in this variable would raise the investment ratio by about 0.0025 or only one-fifth of the change induced by a similar change in RN.[31]

Reestimating Eq. (2) in first-difference form (for 1955 through 1978) shows that the estimated coefficient of RN is quite robust: its coefficient is 0.471 with a standard error of 0.113. The capacity utilization coefficient falls to 0.008 with a standard error of 0.021, and the Durbin-Watson statistic indicates negative serial correlation. To test the constraints imposed by the first-order autocorrelation adjustment, I estimated the ordinary least squares regression of the investment ratio on its own lagged value and on one- and two-period lags in RN and $UCAP$. The reduction in the residual sum of squares was only 6 percent, and the corresponding F-statistic of 0.54 was far less than the 5 percent critical value of 3.55.

Using the cyclically adjusted measure of the net return (RNA) gives greater weight to the cyclical capacity utilization variable and slightly lowers the estimated effect of changes in the fundamental determinants of the net return:[32]

$$\frac{I_t^n}{Y_t} = -0.023 + \underset{(0.106)}{0.386} \ RNA_{t-1} + \underset{(0.023)}{0.045} \ UCAP_{t-1} + \underset{(0.20)}{0.63} \ u_{t-1}.$$

$$\bar{R}^2 = 0.746 \qquad (3)$$
$$DWS = 2.076$$
$$SSR = 3.443 \ (10^{-4})$$
$$1955-1977$$

Several different, more general distributed lag specifications were also estimated. There is some weak evidence that the mean lag between RN and the investment ratio is longer than a year and that the cumulative effect of RN on the investment ratio is larger than Eq. (2) implies. For example, when the variable RN_{t-2} is added to the earlier specification, its

---

31. Since the standard error of the capacity utilization coefficient is relatively large, the coefficient of 0.028 should be regarded as subject to considerable error.

32. The sample is two years shorter because the information required to calculate $ETRA$ is not available before 1954 or after 1976.

coefficient is 0.20 with a standard error of 0.14; the sum of the coefficients on RN_{t-1} and RN_{t-2} becomes 0.60. Second-order polynomial distributed lags with a four- or five-year span and a final value constrained to be zero imply that the coefficients of RN_{t-1} and RN_{t-2} are significantly different from zero but that further coefficients are not; the sum of the coefficients varies between 0.45 and 0.55, depending on the exact specification. Further lags on the capacity utilization variables are never both positive and significantly different from zero.

Redefining the investment variable as the ratio of net investment to *capacity* GNP has essentially no effect; the coefficient of *RN* rises to 0.50 (standard error = 0.10) and the capacity utilization coefficient remains essentially unchanged at 0.026 (S.E. = 0.026).

All of the equations are estimated using the *net* rate of investment because I believe that the Commerce Department's very disaggregated procedure for calculating economic depreciation, while far from perfect, is better than the alternative of studying gross investment and assuming that depreciation is a constant fraction of the past year's capital stock. Nevertheless, as a further test of the robustness of the conclusion that *RN* is important, I have estimated such a gross investment equation:

$$\frac{I_t^g}{Y_t} = -0.123 + \underset{(0.082)}{0.314} \ RN_{t-1} + \underset{(0.028)}{0.106} \ UCAP_{t-1}$$

$$+ \underset{(0.030)}{0.163} \ \frac{K_{t-1}^n}{Y_{t-1}} + \underset{(0.295)}{0.050} \ u_{t-1}. \tag{4}$$

$$\bar{R}^2 = 0.715$$
$$DWS = 1.98$$
$$SSR = 2.70 \ (10^{-4})$$
$$1954 - 1978$$

These coefficients confirm the importance of *RN* but suggest that the net investment specification overstates the importance of *RN* relative to *UCAP*. However, the very large coefficient of the lagged capital variable, implying an implausible 16 percent annual depreciation rate for plant and equipment, is a warning against giving too much weight to this specification.[33]

The results are not sensitive to the use of capacity utilization to mea-

---

33. Further evidence in favor of using the net investment series is given in the next section of this chapter.

sure the effect of aggregate demand. Using the unemployment rate for men over 19 years old leaves the coefficient of RN at 0.454 (S.E. = 0.077), while using the proportional gap between GNP and capacity GNP leaves the coefficient of RN at 0.405 (S.E. = 0.070). A one-percentage-point decline in this unemployment rate raises the investment ratio by a relatively small 0.0016; similarly, a one-percentage-point decline in the GNP gap raises the investment ratio by only 0.0010. Additional accelerator variables (that is, a distributed lag of proportional changes in GNP) were insignificant when capacity utilization was included in the equation.

Several additional variables that are sometimes associated with investment were added to Eq. (2). Three of these variables were each insignificant and changed the coefficient of RN by less than 0.02: the ratio of corporate cash flow to GNP lagged one year; the ratio of the federal government deficit to GNP lagged one year;[34] and a time trend. When the one year lagged value of Tobin's q variable is included,[35] its coefficient is 0.011 (with a standard error of 0.074) and the coefficient of RN drops slightly to 0.391 (S.E. = 0.117).

The actual inflation rate (lagged one year), and the predicted long-term inflation rate[36] (also lagged one year) were completely insignificant and had very little effect on the coefficient of RN. Including both the actual and expected inflation rates did not change this conclusion. The full effect of inflation on investment is captured in the current specification by the RN variable itself.

All of the specification experiments described in the past several paragraphs have also been repeated with the cyclically adjusted RNA variable, with very similar results.

The specification in terms of the net return assumes that investment responds equally to changes in the pretax return and in the effective tax rate. Two tests of this assumption indicate that it is consistent with the data. If instead of using RN_{t-1} Eq. (2) is reestimated with R_{t-1} and $1 - ETR_{t-1}$ as separate variables, the sum of squared residuals actually

34. When the concurrent ratio of the federal deficit to GNP is included, its coefficient is -0.26 (with a standard error of 0.06) and the coefficient of RN drops to 0.21 (S.E. = 0.10). This may be evidence of crowding out, or it may merely reflect the tendency of more investment to increase concurrent national income and thereby reduce the government deficit.

35. This variable is the Holland and Meyers (1979) measure, defined as the ratio of the aggregate market value of nonfinancial corporations to the net replacement cost of plant, equipment, and inventories. Essentially the same result is obtained with their broader measure in which all other nonfinancial assets are included.

36. The predicted inflation rate is based on a rolling series of ARIMA regressions; see Feldstein and Summers (1978, pp. 84–87).

rises; that is, the two variables actually explain less than their product does. An explicit statistical test is possible if *RN* in Eq. (2) is replaced by its logarithm; since ln RN = ln R + ln $(1 - ETR)$, the equality of the two coefficients of ln R and ln $(1 - ETR)$ can be tested explicitly.[37] Neither coefficient is estimated very precisely (each has a *t*-statistic of less than 1.5), and the equality of the two coefficients is easily accepted (the *F*-statistic is only 0.51).

Estimating the analogous decomposition for the cyclically adjusted variables, that is, replacing *RNA* by *RA* and $1 - ETRA$, is interesting because it sheds light on the question of whether the year-to-year noncyclical variations in the pretax return matter. Two things should be noted. First, this substitution reduces the explanatory power of the equation as measured by the corrected $\bar{R}^2$; this favors keeping the simple specification in terms of *RNA*. Second, if both variables are included separately, the coefficient of the *RA* variable is much less than its standard error (0.033 with a standard error of 0.172) while the coefficient of the *ETRA* variable is statistically significant and economically important: -0.044 with a standard error of 0.017. This suggests that year-to-year fluctuations in the pretax return have not been important but that the rise in *ETRA* from about 0.57 in the mid-1960s to about 0.85 in the mid-1970s was enough to reduce the investment ratio by more than one percentage point.

An important indication of the plausibility and reliability of any simple model is the stability of the coefficients in different subperiods. Equations (5) and (6) show the result of splitting the sample in half:

$$\frac{I_t^n}{Y_t} = -0.066 + \underset{(0.078)}{0.448} \ RN_{t-1} + \underset{(0.024)}{0.090} \ UCAP_{t-1} + \underset{(0.25)}{0.62} \ u_{t-1},$$

$$\begin{aligned} \bar{R}^2 &= 0.784 \\ DWS &= 2.20 \\ SSR &= 1.291 \ (10^{-4}) \\ &1954-1966 \end{aligned} \quad (5)$$

$$\frac{I_t^n}{Y_t} = -0.222 + \underset{(0.108)}{0.443} \ RN_{t-1} + \underset{(0.025)}{0.041} \ UCAP_{t-1} + \underset{(0.32)}{0.58} \ u_{t-1}.$$

$$\begin{aligned} \bar{R}^2 &= 0.839 \\ DWS &= 1.48 \\ SSR &= 0.930 \ (10^{-4}) \\ &1967-1978 \end{aligned} \quad (6)$$

37. The switch from *RN* to ln *RN* causes a small decrease in the explanatory power of the equation.

Table 17.2. Actual and predicted investment ratios

Year	Ratio			Change in ratio		
	Actual (1)	Predicted (RN) (2)	Predicted (MPNR − COF) (3)	Actual (4)	Predicted (RN) (5)	Predicted (MPNR − COF) (6)
1971	0.025	0.019	0.024	—	—	—
1972	0.028	0.020	0.027	0.003	0.001	0.003
1973	0.034	0.028	0.033	0.006	0.008	0.006
1974	0.031	0.027	0.026	−0.003	−0.001	−0.007
1975	0.014	0.015	0.004	−0.017	−0.012	−0.022
1976	0.015	0.012	0.012	0.001	−0.003	0.008
1977	0.020	0.020	0.016	0.005	0.008	0.004
1978	0.025	0.022	—	0.005	0.002	—

Note: Predictors are based on equations fitted through 1970 only. Columns 2 and 5 are based on the specification of Eq. (1), while columns 3 and 6 are based on the specification of Eq. (12).

The coefficients of *RN* are remarkably similar, and the relevant *F*-statistic indicates that the hypothesis of equal coefficients for the two subperiods cannot be rejected at the 5 percent level.[38]

A further test of the robustness and usefulness of an equation is its performance in out-of-sample forecasts. The basic specification was reestimated for the period from 1954 through 1970, and this equation was then used to predict the investment ratio for each year from 1971 through 1978. These predictions are based on the two lagged variables only (RN_{t-1} and $UCAP_{t-1}$) and do not use the lagged disturbance (u_{t-1}) or any lagged dependent variable. The results, shown in Table 17.2, are remarkably good. The mean absolute prediction error (0.0035) is only two-thirds of the mean year-to-year change (0.0050) in the investment ratio. The year-to-year changes are also predicted quite well, with the correct sign in six of the seven years and a mean error that is only one-third of the average change.

To conclude the discussion of the net return model of investment behavior, it is useful to consider its implication for understanding the decline in the investment ratio since 1966. The first column of Table 17.3 shows that the investment ratio fell from 0.045 in 1966 to less than half that value in the last four years of the sample period. The 1965 value of *RN* was 0.065, the highest of any year in the sample, and the 1965 value of

---

38. Even the two coefficients of the capacity utilization variable do not differ in a statistically significant way; the difference between them of 0.049 has a standard error of 0.035.

Table 17.3. Actual and conditional ratios of net nonresidential investment to GNP

Year	Actual investment ratio (1)	Investment ratio conditional on:[a]				
		$RN =$ 0.065 (2)	$UCAP =$ 0.896 (3)	$INF =$ 0.0 (4)	$MPNR - COF =$ 0.043 (5)	$UCAP =$ 0.896 (6)
1954	0.023	0.040	0.023	—	—	—
1955	0.028	0.043	0.031	0.031	0.039	0.035
1956	0.031	0.041	0.032	0.035	0.041	0.033
1957	0.029	0.045	0.030	0.035	0.036	0.032
1958	0.017	0.033	0.019	0.023	0.024	0.021
1959	0.020	0.038	0.024	0.024	0.024	0.031
1960	0.022	0.035	0.024	0.026	0.026	0.028
1961	0.019	0.033	0.022	0.023	0.023	0.026
1962	0.023	0.037	0.027	0.026	0.024	0.032
1963	0.023	0.033	0.026	0.025	0.025	0.029
1964	0.029	0.036	0.030	0.032	0.030	0.033
1965	0.040	0.043	0.041	0.042	0.040	0.043
1966	0.045	0.045	0.045	0.048	0.045	0.045
1967	0.038	0.038	0.037	0.042	0.041	0.036
1968	0.037	0.041	0.038	0.041	0.038	0.039
1969	0.038	0.046	0.039	0.043	0.042	0.040
1970	0.031	0.043	0.032	0.038	0.038	0.033
1971	0.025	0.042	0.028	0.031	0.033	0.032
1972	0.028	0.044	0.032	0.033	0.034	0.037
1973	0.034	0.046	0.036	0.039	0.038	0.039
1974	0.031	0.047	0.032	0.041	0.041	0.033
1975	0.014	0.040	0.015	0.030	0.038	0.018
1976	0.015	0.034	0.019	0.024	0.028	0.027
1977	0.020	0.036	0.023	0.028	0.033	0.027
1978	0.025	0.041	0.027	0.034	—	—

a. Columns 2, 3, and 4 are based on Eq. (2); columns 5 and 6 are based on Eq. (13).

UCAP was 0.896, the second highest value and only slightly below the 1966 *UCAP* value of 0.911. Column 2 uses the estimated effect of changes in *RN*—that is, 0.459 from Eq. (2)—to calculate the investment ratio for each of the twenty-five sample years conditional on $RN = 0.065$; that is, each figure in column 2 equals the corresponding figure in column 1 plus 0.459 times $(0.065 - RN_{t-1})$. Similarly, column 3 uses the estimated effect of changes in *UCAP* to calculate the investment ratio conditional on $UCAP = 0.896$.[39] It is clear from the figures in column 2 that the fall in

39. Columns 5 and 6 will be considered in the next section.

RN can account for most of the decline in the investment ratio since 1966 and that the post-1966 fluctuations in *UCAP* cannot account for much of the decline. If *RN* had been kept at its 1965 level, net investment from 1970 to 1978 would have taken an average of 4.1 percent of GNP instead of the actual average of only 2.5 percent, an increase of two-thirds. By contrast, maintaining the high 1965 level of capacity utilization would have raised the average investment-GNP ratio by only 0.5 percentage points. It is also worth noting that if the 1965 level of *RN* had been reached a decade earlier, investment during that decade would have averaged an additional 1.2 percent of GNP. Equation (2) can also be used to estimate an approximate but explicit effect of inflation on the invest-ment ratio. In an earlier study Lawrence Summers and I estimated the change in the tax liability on corporate source income that is caused by the interaction of inflation and the tax laws.[40] For example, in 1977 (the last year of our study) inflation raised the tax liability by \$32.3 billion or 1.9 percent of the corresponding capital stock.[41] The estimate of RN_{t-1} in Eq. (2) implies that a 1.9 percentage point increase in *RN* for 1977 would raise the 1978 investment ratio by 0.009 to 0.034; this value is shown in column 4 of Table 17.3. Similarly calculated values for earlier years indi-cate that the interaction between inflation and the tax rules reduced in-vestment in the 1970s by an average of 0.8 percent of GNP or about one-third of the actual level of net investment.

Investment and the Rate of Return over Cost[42]

In the absence of taxes, the simplest specification of a firm's investment behavior is that it invests whenever the rate of return on an available pro-ject exceeds the cost of additional funds. More generally, the costs of changing the rate of investment and the uncertainty associated with in-vestment returns make the firm's decision problem more complex.[43] It is nevertheless useful to describe the firm's rate of investment as responding to the difference between potential rates of return and the cost of funds.

In terms of the traditional marginal efficiency of investment schedule

---

40. See Feldstein and Summers (1979), table 4, column 9 for the series of inflation-induced tax increases.

41. For the capital stock figures, see Chapter 2, Table 2.A1, column 8.

42. I have borrowed Irving Fisher's phrase "the rate of return over cost" but not his exact meaning. The model in this section is nevertheless very close in spirit to Fisher's anal-ysis.

43. See Abel (1978) for an explicit derivation of the optimum rule when there are en-dogenous adjustment costs.

that Keynes borrowed from Irving Fisher, an upward shift of the marginal efficiency schedule or a downward shift in the cost of funds will increase the rate of investment. If we select a particular rate of investment, we can measure the upward shift of the marginal efficiency schedule by what happens to the internal rate of return at that rate of investment.[44] A rise in the difference between the internal rate of return and the cost of funds should induce a higher rate of investment.

This idea can be extended to an economy with a complex tax structure and with inflation. A change in the tax rules or in the expected rate of inflation alters the rate of return on all projects (in a sense that I will make more precise below). These fiscal and inflation changes therefore act in a way that is equivalent to shifting the marginal efficiency of investment schedule in a simpler economy.

When we switch from a taxless economy to one with company taxes and depreciation rules, the concept of the internal rate of return must be extended to what I shall call the maximum potential net return (*MPNR*). For simplicity I shall describe this first for the case in which the firm relies exclusively on debt finance. I shall then note how the analysis is easily extended to include equity finance as well.

In a taxless economy the internal rate of return on a project is the maximum rate of return that a firm can afford to pay on a loan used to finance that project. If L_t is the loan balance at time t and x_t (for $t = 1, 2, \ldots , T$) is the net cash flow of the project in year t (before interest expenses), the internal rate of return is the interest rate r that satisfies the difference equation:

$$L_t - L_{t-1} = rL_{t-1} - x_t, \tag{7}$$

where L_0 is the initial cost of the project and $L_T = 0$. The solution of Eq. (7) is exactly equivalent to the familiar definition of r as the solution to the polynomial equation:

$$L_0 = \sum_{t=1}^{T} \frac{x_t}{(1 + r)^t}. \tag{8}$$

When a tax at rate τ is levied on the net output minus the sum of the interest payment and the allowable depreciation (d_t), the maximum potential interest rate (*MPIR*) is defined according to

$$L_t - L_{t-1} = rL_{t-1} - x_t + \tau(x_t - d_t - rL_{t-1}), \tag{9}$$

44. Unless the shift is a uniform one, the answer will depend on the initial point that is selected. This is a typical index number type problem.

where $L_T = 0$ and L_0 equals the initial cost of the project minus any investment tax credit.

If x_t is the *real* cash flow of the project, inflation at a constant rate π has the effect of increasing the nominal cash flow to $(1 + \pi)^t x_t$, and the *MPIR* rises to the value of r that solves:

$$L_t - L_{t-1} = rL_{t-1} - (1 + \pi)^t x_t + \tau[(1 + \pi)^t x_t - d_t - rL_{t-1}]. \quad (10)$$

Although in a taxless world the *MPIR* would rise by the rate of inflation, the relative importance of historic cost depreciation and the deductibility of nominal interest payments determines whether r rises by more or less than the increase in π.

The calculation of the *MPIR* is made operational by specifying the real cash flow from a hypothetical project and the associated series of allowable tax depreciation. I adopt here the same specifications that I used in Feldstein and Summers (1979). The hypothetical project is a "sandwich" of which 66.2 percent of the investment in the first year is a structure that lasts thirty years and the remainder is an equipment investment that is replaced at the end of ten years and twenty years.[45] The internal rate of return in the absence of taxes is set at 12 percent for both the equipment and structure components. The net output of the equipment is subject to exponential decay at 13 percent until it is scrapped, while the net output of the structure is subject to 3 percent decay. The depreciation rules, tax rate, and credits are then varied from year to year as the law changes.

The expected rate of inflation in each year is calculated from the consumer expenditure deflator using the optimal ARIMA forecasting procedure of Box and Jenkins (1970).[46] The calculation assumes that forecasts made at each date are based only on the information available at that time and that the ARIMA process estimated at each date is based only on the most recent ten years of quarterly data. The calculation of the *MPIR* is based on the entire sequence of forecasted future inflation rates and not on any single average long-term expected inflation rate.[47]

45. The 66.2 percent ratio is selected to produce a steady-state investment mix corresponding to the average composition over the past twenty years. Note that this specification ignores inventories and therefore the very substantial extra tax burden caused by inflation with FIFO inventory accounting. While this need not affect decisions to substitute capital for labor, it does influence the return on capital expansion to the extent that this involves greater inventories.

46. The calculation of expected inflation series is described in Feldstein and Summers (1978, pp. 84–87).

47. To meet the need for a series of expected long-term inflation rates for other purposes, Feldstein and Summers (1978) calculate a weighted average of these future inflation rates where the weights are equivalent to discounting at a fixed interest rate.

If firms did finance marginal projects exclusively by debt, it would be sufficient to relate the net rate of investment to the difference between the *MPIR* and the long-term nominal interest rate (as well as to capacity utilization or some other measure of cyclical demand). The correct assumption about the marginal debt-equity mix is not clear. In the current analysis I have assumed that firms use debt and equity at the margin in the same ratio that they do on average, that is, that debt accounts for only one-third of total finance. The notion of the *MPIR* must therefore be extended to the maximum potential net return (*MPNR*), defined as the maximum net-of-corporate-tax nominal yield that the firm can pay on its mix of funds.

The method of calculating the *MPIR* in the all-debt case can be applied directly to find the value of the *MPNR*. In the special all-debt case, the $MPNR = (1 - \tau)r$; the solution of a difference equation like (10) is therefore equivalent to finding $MPNR/(1 - \tau)$ in the all-debt case. More generally, however, regardless of the mix of debt and equity finance, the solution of Eq. (10) can be interpreted as equivalent to $MPNR/(1 - \tau)$. Since τ is known, this yields *MPNR* directly. Annual values for *MPNR* are presented in column 1 of Table 17.4.

Note that the *MPNR* is defined in terms of a hypothetical project with a fixed pretax yield of 12 percent. All of the year-to-year variation in the *MPNR* is due to changes in tax rules and expected inflation. An alternative *MPNR* series has also been calculated in which the pretax rate of return is allowed to vary; more specifically, *MPNRVP* (*VP* for varying profitability) replaces the 12 percent assumption with a cyclically adjusted profitability series for each year's new investment that is very similar to the *RA* variable discussed in the previous section.[48] The *MPNRVP* series is presented in column 2 of Table 17.4.

The *MPNR* is the net nominal amount that firms can potentially afford to pay for funds. The actual net nominal cost of funds is

$$COF = \frac{1}{3}(1 - \tau)i + \frac{2}{3}(e + \pi), \tag{11}$$

where i is the long-term bond interest rate and e is the real equity earnings per dollar of share value.[49] The cost of funds series is presented in column 3.

48. See Feldstein and Summers (1978, p. 90) for a description of the cyclically adjusted return series used in the present calculation.
49. Recall that the x_t values of Eq. (10) for each tax regime were calculated on the assumption that the project has a 12 percent pretax rate of return. The procedure that produces *MPNRVP* replaces 12 percent with the cyclically adjusted *RA* series of Table 17.1, column 6.

Table 17.4. Potential and actual net costs of funds

Year	MPNR (1)	MPNRVP (2)	COF (3)	MPNR − COF (4)	MPNRVP− COF (5)
1954	0.087	0.078	0.078	0.009	0.000
1955	0.089	0.084	0.077	0.012	0.007
1956	0.089	0.074	0.067	0.023	0.008
1957	0.091	0.073	0.070	0.020	0.002
1958	0.090	0.075	0.058	0.032	0.017
1959	0.090	0.081	0.060	0.031	0.022
1960	0.090	0.078	0.059	0.031	0.018
1961	0.090	0.081	0.049	0.041	0.032
1962	0.093	0.088	0.056	0.037	0.032
1963	0.094	0.091	0.056	0.038	0.035
1964	0.099	0.098	0.055	0.044	0.043
1965	0.102	0.102	0.058	0.043	0.043
1966	0.101	0.097	0.067	0.034	0.030
1967	0.101	0.092	0.061	0.040	0.031
1968	0.097	0.087	0.066	0.030	0.021
1969	0.093	0.075	0.074	0.020	0.001
1970	0.097	0.073	0.078	0.019	−0.006
1971	0.102	0.081	0.075	0.027	0.006
1972	0.105	0.082	0.071	0.034	0.010
1973	0.106	0.072	0.095	0.011	−0.022
1974	0.111	0.062	0.144	−0.034	−0.082
1975	0.110	0.083	0.108	0.002	−0.025
1976	0.109	0.080	0.107	0.002	−0.027

This section examines a model that makes the rate of net investment a function of (1) the difference between the potential and actual cost of funds and (2) the rate of capacity utilization:

$$\frac{I_t^n}{Y_t} = b_0 + b_1 \, (MPNR - COF)_{t-1} + b_2 \, UCAP_{t-1} + u_t. \qquad (12)$$

Columns 4 and 5 of Table 17.4 present the time series of this yield difference. These figures indicate that the incentive was low in the 1950s, became quite powerful in the mid-1960s, began to fall in the early 1970s, and then dropped very sharply in the mid-1970s.

The pattern of the past decade reflects the fact that, because of historic cost depreciation, inflation raised the *MPNR* rather little while the cost of funds rose substantially.[50] Between 1966 and 1976, the cost of funds rose by four percentage points while the *MPNR* rose by less than one percentage point.[51]

As in the earlier section, the current analysis uses annual data and lags both regressors one year. Equation (12) and a variety of related specifications have been estimated by least squares with a first-order autocorrelation correction. Specific tests for the basic specifications show that the implied constraints are not binding, that is, that the first-order autocorrelation correction is not inferior to a more general first-order ARMA process. Estimates in first-difference form also produce very similar coefficients to those obtained with the autocorrelation transformation.

The basic parameter estimates,

$$\frac{I^n_t}{Y_t} = -0.040 + \underset{(0.066)}{0.316}\ (MPNR - COF)_{t-1}$$

$$+ \underset{(0.020)}{0.073}\ UCAP_{t-1} + \underset{(0.17)}{0.70}\ u_{t-1}, \qquad (13)$$

$$\bar{R}^2 = 0.784$$
$$DWS = 1.79$$
$$SSR = 2.936\ (10^{-4})$$
$$1955-1977$$

indicate that the yield differential has a powerful effect and that the variations in capacity utilization are also important.[52]

Since the return-over-cost variable had a standard deviation of 0.017 over the sample period, a move from one standard deviation below the mean to one standard deviation above would raise the investment ratio by 0.011, approximately 1.3 times its standard deviation and 40 percent of its 25-year average value. A two-standard-deviation move in capacity utilization would raise investment by 0.006, or only about half as much.

---

50. Inflation also raised the cost of funds because the cost of equity funds was raised more than the cost of debt funds fell.

51. This is roughly consistent with a regression equation that indicates that, for the sample as a whole, each one-percentage-point increase in the long-term expected inflation rate reduced the difference *MPNR* − *COF* by about 1.25 percentage points. Between 1966 and 1976, the long-term expected inflation rate (demand from the ARIMA forecasts) rose 3.2 percentage points.

52. Because *MPNR* does not reflect cyclical variations in the rate of return, these parameter values are most appropriately compared to those of Eq. (3) rather than Eq. (1).

Using the varying-profitability measure of the potential net return reduces the corresponding coefficient:

$$\frac{I_t^n}{Y_t} = -0.031 + 0.219 \ (MPNRVP - COF)_{t-1}$$
$$(0.049)$$
$$+ \ 0.069 \ UCAP_{t-1} + 0.71 \ u_{t-1}.$$
$$(0.020) \qquad\qquad (0.17) \qquad\qquad\qquad (14)$$

$$\bar{R}^2 = 0.784$$
$$DWS = 2.02$$
$$SSR = 2.931 \ (10^{-4})$$
$$1955-1977$$

However, since this measure is much more variable (the standard deviation of $MPNRVP - COF$ is 0.028), a two-standard-deviation move implies a slightly bigger change of 0.012 in the investment ratio.

Lagged values of the regressors were insignificant, and polynomial distributed lags of different lengths for the return-over-cost variable did not alter the implications of Eqs. (12) and (13). Redefining the investment variable as a ratio to capacity GNP had no effect on the coefficients. Similarly, substituting for capacity utilization the unemployment rate for men over age 19 or the GNP gap ratio did not significantly alter the coefficient of the return-over-cost variable. Moreover, a distributed lag of proportional changes in past output was insignificant when capacity utilization was included in the equation.

The switch from the net investment equation to a gross investment equation caused some reduction in the coefficient of the return-over-cost variable (to 0.215 with a standard error of 0.072), but the extremely small and totally insignificant coefficient of the lagged capital stock variables (0.002 with a standard error of 0.093) makes this gross investment specification implausible.

A time trend and a lagged ratio of corporate cash flow to GNP were tried as additional variables; neither was significant, and the coefficient of the return-over-cost variable remained unchanged. A lagged ratio of retained earnings to GNP was "mildly significant" (a t-statistic of 1.3) but left the coefficient of the return-over-cost variable unchanged. The lagged ratio of the federal government deficit to GNP had a surprisingly positive coefficient, but its inclusion did not alter the coefficient of the return-over-cost variable. The one-year lagged value of Tobin's q-ratio had a coefficient of 0.012 (with a standard error of 0.009), while the coefficient of the return-over-cost variable remained essentially unchanged at 0.289

(with a standard error of 0.068). Neither the current inflation rate nor the expected inflation rate was statistically significant.

A powerful test of the appropriateness of Eq. (13) is obtained by estimating separate coefficients for the rate of return ($MPNR$) and cost of funds (COF) variables:

$$\frac{I_t^n}{Y_t} = -0.055 + \underset{(0.261)}{0.469}\ MPNR_{t-1} - \underset{(0.068)}{0.319}\ COF_{t-1}$$

$$+ \underset{(0.021)}{0.074}\ UCAP_{t-1} + \underset{(0.20)}{0.66}\ u_{t-1}. \tag{15}$$

$$\bar{R}^2 = 0.775$$
$$DWS = 1.81$$
$$SSR = 2.895\ (10^{-4})$$
$$1955-1977$$

A comparison of the sum of squared residuals of Eqs. (13) and (15) shows that the coefficients of $MPNR$ and COF do not differ significantly. The separate coefficient of COF in Eq. (15) is almost identical to the combined return-over-cost coefficient in Eq. (13); the coefficient of the return variable is larger but so too is its standard error.

The separate estimate of the $MPNR$ coefficient in Eq. (15) is also particularly important because the $MPNR$ variable reflects only the interaction of tax rules and inflation but not the market interest rate or equity yield. The finding that the $MPNR$ coefficient is even larger than the COF coefficient is therefore powerful evidence of the effect of the tax-inflation interaction.[53]

A test of the stability of the basic coefficients over time also provides reassuring support about the plausibility and reliability of the model. Equations (16) and (17) show the result of splitting the sample in half:

$$\frac{I_t^n}{Y_t} = -0.036 + \underset{(0.266)}{0.465}\ (MPNR - COF)_{t-1} + \underset{(0.040)}{0.065}\ UCAP_{t-1}$$

$$+ \underset{(0.21)}{0.81}\ u_{t-1}, \tag{16}$$

$$\bar{R}^2 = 0.599$$
$$DWS = 1.24$$
$$SSR = 2.276\ (10^{-4})$$
$$1955-1966$$

53. A similar analysis with the varying profitability measure of return provides even more striking confirmation: the coefficient of $MPNRVP$ is 0.253 (S.E. = 0.155), while the coefficient of COF is -0.202 (S.E. = 0.084).

$$\frac{I_t^n}{Y_t} = -0.044 + \underset{(0.030)}{0.300} \ (MPNR - COF)_{t-1} + \underset{(0.011)}{0.081} \ UCAP_{t-1}$$

$$- \underset{(0.43)}{0.02} \ u_{t-1}.$$

(17)

$$\bar{R}^2 = 0.963$$
$$DWS = 1.75$$
$$SSR = 0.201 \ (10^{-4})$$
$$1967-1977$$

The coefficients are quite similar, and the F-statistic of 0.695 indicates that the hypothesis of an unchanged structure cannot be rejected at any conventional level of significance. The results for the varying-profitability specification are even more striking: the coefficient of the return-over-cost variable is 0.206 (S.E. = 0.089) in the first half of the period and 0.200 (S.E. = 0.033) in the second half.

Out-of-sample forecasts based on estimating Eq. (12) for 1955 through 1970 are shown in Table 17.2. The agreement between the actual and predicted investment ratios is quite close. The mean absolute prediction error (0.0035) is the same as with the net return equation and only two-thirds of the mean year-to-year change in the investment ratio. The year-to-year changes are predicted even more closely and both turning points are correctly identified.

The parameter estimates of Eq. (13) can be used to analyze the sharp decline in net investment since 1966. Column 5 of Table 17.2 shows the investment ratio which in principle would have been observed if the return-over-cost had remained at its 1965 value of 0.043. Instead of dropping to an average of only 0.025 from 1970 through 1977, it would have averaged 40 percent higher, 0.035. By contrast, even if the capacity utilization rate could have been kept at the overheated level of 0.896, the investment ratio in the 1970–1977 period would have increased only 20 percent to 0.030.

The specific contribution of inflation to the decline in the value of the return-over-cost variable is difficult to determine. One simple way of measuring this effect is by a regression of the return-over-cost variable on the predicted long-term inflation rate. The coefficient in this regression (-1.27 with a standard error of 0.11) and the rise in the long-term inflation variable by 0.034 between 1965 and 1976 together imply that inflation reduced the return-over-cost by 0.0432 during this period. The coefficient of the return-over-cost variable, 0.316 in Eq. (13), implies that inflation reduced the investment ratio by 0.014 over this period. This equals almost all of the 0.015 fall in the investment ratio caused by the decline in the return-over-cost[54] and more than half of the observed decline in the investment ratio between 1966 and 1977.

The Flexible Capital Stock Adjustment Model

The flexible capital stock adjustment model developed by Jorgenson and his collaborators is the direct descendant of that great workhorse of investment equations, the accelerator. Instead of the accelerator's assumption of a fixed capital-output ratio, the more general model allows the capital-output ratio to respond to changes in the cost of capital ownership and therefore to changes in tax rules and inflation. Implicit in the simplest version of this model are a number of very strong assumptions, including homogeneous capital, a putty-putty technology, constant proportional replacement, myopic and risk-neutral decision making, and a known, exogenous financial mix. The present section accepts these assumptions in order to focus on the problem of measuring the effect of inflation in the framework of this popular and influential model. The analysis shows that the traditional implementation of the model has not given adequate attention to inflation and that any attempt to analyze the recent investment experience on the basis of that implementation would be misleading.

The analysis here is limited to investment in equipment. The procedure of estimating separate investment equations for equipment and structures is traditional in this framework because the tax rules differ for the two types of equipment. The implicit assumption of two independent investment demand functions, one for equipment-capital and the other for structure-capital, is clearly a poor description of reality. To the extent that investments in structures and equipment are decided as a package, the model of the previous section is a preferable specification.[55]

The basic model is well known and can be summarized briefly. Each firm has a desired capital stock at each time (K_t^*), and, to the extent that its actual capital falls short of the desired capital, the firm immediately orders capital goods to eliminate the difference. The sum of installed capital and capital-on-order is thus equal to the desired capital stock at the end of each period. This implies that in each period the stock of outstanding orders is increased or decreased by exactly the change in the desired capi-

---

54. This 0.015 is the difference between the actual 1977 investment ratio of 0.020 and the predicted ratio of 0.035 conditional on maintaining the 1965 level of the return-over-cost.

55. This specification also ignores the adverse effect of inflation through the taxation of artificial inventory profits. This will matter to the extent that inventories, equipment, and structures are part of a combined investment-output decision.

tal stock, $K_t^* - K_{t-1}^*$. Since there are delivery delays, the observed net investment can be represented by a distributed lag distribution of these orders:

$$I_t^n = \sum_{j=1}^{T} w_j (K_{t-j}^* - K_{t-j-1}^*).\tag{18}$$

This specification is based on an implicit assumption about replacement investment: The existing stock decays exponentially at a constant rate d, requiring replacement investment of dK_{t-1} to be made in year t to maintain the capital stock. Since firms know the delivery lag distribution exactly, they can anticipate the replacement investment that will be required in each future year (up to the length of the longest delivery lag) and can therefore order replacement investment far enough in advance to make exactly the required replacement. Gross investment is therefore given by:

$$I_t^q = \sum_{j=1}^{T} w_j (K_{t-j}^* - K_{t-j-1}^*) + dK_{t-1}.\tag{19}$$

With a constant elasticity of substitution production function, the first-order conditions of profit maximization imply that the desired capital stock is related to the level of output (Q), the price of output (p), and the annual cost of capital services (c) according to:[56]

$$K_t^* = a^\sigma (p/c)_t^\sigma Q_t,\tag{20}$$

where σ is the elasticity of substitution between capital and labor and a is the capital coefficient in the production function. Substituting (20) into (19) yields:

$$I_t^q = a^\sigma \sum_{j=1}^{T} w_j [(p/c)_{t-j}^\sigma Q_{t-j} - (p/c)_{t-j-1}^\sigma Q_{t-j-1}] + dK_{t-1}.\tag{21}$$

The accelerator model implicitly assumes $\sigma = 0$, while the Cobb-Douglas technology assumed by Jorgenson and his collaborators implies $\sigma = 1$. In this section, I shall show that the flexible model with $\sigma > 0$ is more strongly supported by the data than the simpler accelerator model. The

---

56. Output is measured by the gross domestic product of nonfinancial corporations and p is the implicit price deflator for that output. The value of c is defined below.

maximum likelihood estimate of σ is less than one, but the likelihood function is too flat to reject the Cobb-Douglas assumption.[57]

The annual cost of capital services reflects the price level for investment goods (p_I), the real net cost of funds (R), the exponential rate of depreciation (d), the corporate tax rate (τ), the investment tax credit (X),[58] and the present value of the depreciation allowances per dollar of investment (Z):

$$c = \frac{p_I\,(1 - Z - X)(R + d)}{1 - \tau}. \tag{22}$$

Inflation affects the value of this crucial variable in two important ways, through the cost of funds (R) and through the present value of depreciation (Z). In their original study, Hall and Jorgenson (1967) assumed a fixed nominal interest rate of 20 percent for the cost of funds. In the most recent of the Jorgenson studies, this assumption was replaced by the specification that $R = (1 - \tau)i$, where i is a long-term bond interest rate (Gordon and Jorgenson 1976). This overstates the cost of debt capital (by ignoring inflation) and ignores the role of equity capital. The expected real net cost of debt capital is $(1 - \tau)i - \pi$ (where π is expected inflation), since the debt is repaid in depreciated dollars.[59] Column 1 of Table 17.5 presents this measure of the real net cost of debt. Despite the rapid rise in the Baa rate itself, the real net cost of debt funds actually declined since the mid-1960s.

The cost of equity capital (e) is the ratio of equity earnings per dollar of share price. The conventional earnings-price ratio can be misleading when there is inflation, since it is based on book earnings rather than real economic earnings. Book earnings overstate real earnings by using historic cost depreciation and some FIFO inventory accounting but also understate real earnings by excluding the real reduction in the value of

57. I should again stress that these inferences are all conditional on very strong and obviously "false" assumptions. For example, it seems very likely that the assumption of a "putty-putty" technology causes an understatement of the true long-run elasticity of substitution if the true technology is putty-clay.

58. To simplify notation, I use X to refer to the investment tax credit with the Long-amendment adjustment when appropriate. Data on the investment tax credit refer to actual practice and were supplied by Data Resources, Inc.

59. The putty-putty technology allows all decisions to be myopic and therefore in principle makes the short-term interest rate and short-term inflation rate the relevant variables (Hall 1977). A more realistic description of finance and technology makes a long-term interest rate and inflation the appropriate variables. I have in fact used the Baa corporate bond rate and the long-term inflation expectation derived from the "rolling"-ARIMA estimates presented in Feldstein and Summers (1978).

Table 17.5. Correct and incorrect measures of the cost of capital services

Year	Real net cost of funds			Net nominal cost of funds	Depreciation allowances		Relative cost of capital services			
	Debt (1)	Equity (2)	Combined (3)	(4)	Correct (5)	Incorrect (6)	Correct (7)	Incorrect (8)	No inflation no. 1 (9)	No inflation no. 2 (10)
1954	−0.013	0.067	0.040	0.069	0.644	0.549	0.241	0.221	0.211	0.237
1955	−0.010	0.066	0.041	0.068	0.677	0.582	0.236	0.218	0.207	0.233
1956	−0.008	0.059	0.037	0.063	0.713	0.604	0.230	0.223	0.211	0.233
1957	−0.004	0.065	0.042	0.068	0.703	0.613	0.246	0.234	0.216	0.242
1958	0.000	0.053	0.035	0.057	0.745	0.620	0.227	0.228	0.214	0.235
1959	0.001	0.051	0.034	0.057	0.749	0.625	0.226	0.234	0.215	0.235
1960	0.000	0.055	0.037	0.061	0.739	0.629	0.233	0.233	0.216	0.237
1961	0.005	0.044	0.031	0.050	0.781	0.633	0.215	0.230	0.214	0.231
1962	0.006	0.064	0.044	0.061	0.756	0.652	0.231	0.218	0.205	0.230
1963	0.006	0.062	0.043	0.060	0.776	0.671	0.224	0.214	0.203	0.225
1964	0.006	0.058	0.041	0.058	0.782	0.673	0.206	0.203	0.190	0.210
1965	0.006	0.062	0.043	0.061	0.774	0.674	0.204	0.197	0.204	0.204
1966	0.009	0.076	0.053	0.073	0.740	0.675	0.226	0.206	0.190	0.213
1967	0.012	0.067	0.049	0.068	0.757	0.676	0.217	0.208	0.189	0.210
1968	0.008	0.068	0.048	0.071	0.749	0.676	0.221	0.214	0.185	0.213
1969	0.004	0.075	0.052	0.083	0.718	0.677	0.253	0.239	0.204	0.234
1970	0.011	0.084	0.059	0.092	0.695	0.677	0.263	0.241	0.205	0.234
1971	0.006	0.061	0.042	0.078	0.762	0.714	0.214	0.216	0.190	0.207
1972	0.008	0.062	0.044	0.076	0.767	0.714	0.206	0.206	0.182	0.199
1973	−0.003	0.085	0.056	0.099	0.717	0.714	0.222	0.202	0.176	0.198
1974	−0.034	0.116	0.066	0.146	0.629	0.714	0.244	0.202	0.169	0.195
1975	−0.001	0.100	0.067	0.119	0.678	0.714	0.236	0.203	0.168	0.196
1976	−0.005	0.080	0.052	0.104	0.707	0.714	0.214	0.200	0.169	0.190
1977	−0.012	0.114	0.072	0.127	0.663	0.715	0.245	0.197	0.168	0.198

outstanding debt that occurs because of inflation.[60] The correct earnings-price ratio is presented in column 2 of Table 17.5. The cost of equity funds clearly rose substantially since the mid-1960s, even when the conventional series is appropriately corrected.

Defining the real net cost of funds (R) as a fixed-weight average with one-third debt (the average ratio of debt to capital for the past two decades) implies:[61]

$$R = \frac{1}{3}[(1 - \tau)i - \pi] + \frac{2}{3}e. \tag{23}$$

This series, presented in column 3 of Table 17.5, shows no trend from the mid-1950s through the mid-1960s but then a gradual but substantial rise to the mid-1970s.

The second important way in which inflation affects the cost of capital services is through the value of the depreciation that is allowed in calculating taxable income. Since depreciation allowances are fixed in nominal terms, the real present value of the depreciation allowances (Z) is reduced when the rate of inflation rises. This present value should be calculated using a nominal cost of funds, or, equivalently, the future depreciation allowances should be restated in real terms and then discounted at the real cost of funds. Column 4 of Table 17.5 presents the nominal cost of funds; this is the real cost of funds (shown in column 3) plus the expected rate of inflation.[62] The values of Z presented in column 5 reflect changes in this discount rate as well as changes in the depreciation rules.[63] In the early years Z rises significantly, but since 1964 Z has drifted down because of the rising discount rate, despite the continuing acceleration of depreciation.

The importance of specifying this discount rate correctly can be seen by comparing these Z values with the alternative "$Z10$" values presented in

60. The corrected earnings-price ratio (e) is the ratio of corrected equity earnings per share to the price per share for the Standard and Poor's Index. The usual earnings-price ratio is based on "book earnings" without adjustment for CCA, IVA, or the difference between nominal and real interest rates. I have calculated such a series by using the national income account corrections for debt and inventories and adding the inflation rate times the net debt of the corporation. The consumer expenditure deflator is used to measure inflation. The ratio of corrected equity earnings to book profits multiplied by the conventional earnings-price ratio gives the corrected earnings-price ratio (e).

61. Note that $R + \pi$ equals the *COF* variable of the previous section.

62. In the pure debt case, this would just be the net-of-tax nominal interest rate.

63. The calculation of Z reflects the introduction of accelerated depreciation and the several reductions in the allowable depreciation life.

column 6; the $Z10$ values are calculated with a constant 10 percent discount rate, the procedure used by Jorgenson and his collaborators. With a constant discount rate, the evolution of the $Z10$ variable reflects only the increasingly favorable statutory rules, and therefore it has actually increased during the past decade while the true value has been declining.

The composite relative cost of capital services (that is, the c variable defined in Eq. (22) deflated by the output price) is presented in column 7 of Table 17.5. This measure of the relative cost of capital services falls gradually from the 1950s to a low point in the mid-1960s and then begins rising again. By the end of the sample period (1977), the relative cost of capital is back to its level of the 1950s. This reversal of the incentive to invest is observed if the inflation-induced changes in Z and R are ignored; column 8 presents a false relative cost series that incorporates $Z10$ (that is, a constant 10 percent discount rate to value depreciation) and that measures the cost of funds by the net nominal interest rate.

The Cobb-Douglas technology assumed by Jorgenson and his collaborators is a convenient place to begin testing the significance of the relative cost of capital services. I have estimated Eq. (21) subject to the restriction that the elasticity of substitution is one and compared it to the simpler accelerator model in which the elasticity of substitution is zero. In both specifications, the distributed lag weights were constrained to fit a third-degree polynomial (with four years of lags and a fifth year constrained to zero).

By purely statistical criteria the evidence clearly favors the Cobb-Douglas price sensitivity model over the accelerator model. With the Cobb-Douglas technology, the $\bar{R}^2$ is 0.980 and the sum of squared residuals is 112.3. By contrast, for the accelerator model the $\bar{R}^2$ is only 0.961 and the sum of squared residuals is 215.9. An approximate likelihood ratio test strongly rejects the restriction to a zero substitution elasticity.[64]

Misspecifying the cost of capital series by failing to represent correctly the effect of inflation also reduces the explanatory power of the model. Following the Jorgenson procedure of evaluating depreciation allowances with a fixed 10 percent interest rate and defining the cost of funds in terms of the net nominal rate (that is, using the incorrect c/p series presented in column 8 of Table 17.5) causes the $\bar{R}^2$ to fall to 0.970 (from 0.980) and raises the sum of squared residuals to 167.4 (from 112.3).

---

64. In both the Cobb-Douglas and accelerator specifications, the estimated value of the depreciation rate (that is, the coefficient of the lagged capital stock variable) is approximately 0.18, a reasonable value for equipment capital although higher than the value of 0.138 used in the cost of capital services formula and than the Department of Commerce depreciation rate.

Although relaxing the Cobb-Douglas assumption and estimating the elasticity of substitution could in principle indicate the sensitivity of investment, the data are not informative enough to provide a precise value for this parameter. With the correctly measured value of the user cost of capital, the maximum likelihood estimate of the substitution elasticity is 0.9 but the reduction in the sum of squared residuals to 112.2 is trivial.[65]

Further tests of the cost-sensitivity assumption can in principle be achieved by allowing separate elasticities with respect to the different components of the cost of capital services. In place of Eq. (20), the more general specification is:

$$K_t^* = Q_t \left[\frac{p}{P_I}\right]^{-\sigma_1} \left[\frac{d + R}{1 - \tau}\right]^{-\sigma_2} (1 - Z - X)^{-\sigma_3}. \tag{24}$$

Instead of trying to estimate all these elasticities, three different forms of Eq. (24) were tried. The first constrains $\sigma_1 = 1$. The resulting estimates for σ_2 and σ_3 were 1.8 and 3.2, respectively, but the reduction in the sum of squared residuals to 100.4 from 112.3 in the Cobb-Douglas case is not significant. The second specification, which constrains $\sigma_1 = \sigma_3$, implies estimates of $\sigma_2 = 0.6$ and $\sigma_1 = \sigma_3 = 1$, but the sum of squared residuals (106.6) is again not significantly lower than in the Cobb-Douglas specification. Finally, the constraint that $\sigma_1 = \sigma_2$ implies estimates of $\sigma_1 = \sigma_2 = 0.5$ and $\sigma_3 = 1.0$; the sum of squared residuals of 97.0 is again not sufficiently low to cause a rejection of the Cobb-Douglas assumption.

The Chow test for the stability of the coefficients easily sustains the hypothesis of no change between the first and second halves of the sample, but this is more a reflection of the small sample than of any close agreement in parameter values.

It should be clear from the remarks earlier in this chapter that I believe that the assumptions involved in the present model are far too restrictive and implausible for the model to be regarded as "true" in any sense. It is, however, of some importance that, even within the highly constrained assumptions of the present model, the data provide clear support for a responsiveness of investment to changes in a correctly measured cost of capital services in general and to the changes caused by inflation in particular. Although the data are not rich enough to provide precise estimates of the

---

65. The value of 0.9 is obtained by searching over a grid at intervals of 0.1. It is worth noting that a mismeasurement of the cost of capital series distorts the estimate of the elasticity of substitution. Using the incorrect c/p series of column 8 leads to an estimated elasticity of substitution of 0.6. The reduction in the sum of squared residuals to 157.4 (from 167.4 in the Cobb-Douglas case) is, however, small and not statistically significant.

responsiveness of investment to the individual components of the cost of capital, it is worth noting that the evidence shows that a correct accounting of the impact of inflation substantially improves the ability of the analysis to explain the variation in investment over the past twenty-five years.

On the assumption of a Cobb-Douglas technology, the fall in the relative cost of capital services between the mid-1950s and the mid-1960s was enough to raise the desired ratio of equipment capital to output by nearly 12 percent.[66] Since net equipment investment averaged only about 3 percent of the equipment capital stock at the beginning of the period, the desired increase in capital would require a rise of more than 40 percent in the ratio of equipment investment to capital to achieve the desired capital-output ratio within a decade and a bigger rise to achieve the adjustment sooner. In fact, the investment-capital ratio in 1966–1969 was 0.065, more than double its average in 1956–1965.

The subsequent rise in the value of c/p to an average of 0.235 for the years 1974–1977 reversed the previous change in the desired capital-output ratio. A Cobb-Douglas technology implies a reduction in the desired capital-output ratio of nearly 10 percent between the mid-1960s and the mid-1970s. Achieving this 10 percent change in the capital-output ratio required a much larger proportional fall in investment during the transition period. In fact, the rate of growth of the net equipment capital stock fell sharply, from 0.065 in 1966–1969 to 0.036 in 1976–1979. This in turn implied a one-third fall in the ratio of equipment investment to GNP, from 2.0 in the mid-1960s to 1.3 percent in the mid-1970s.

The specific impact of inflation in this model operates through two channels. First, inflation increases the cost of capital services by reducing the present value of depreciation allowances (Z), a reduction that reflects the increasing *nominal* cost of funds. Second, inflation can increase the cost of capital services directly by raising the real cost of funds (R).[67] The combined effect of both of these changes can be seen by comparing the actual cost of capital services (column 7 of Table 17.5) with the cost of capital services calculated with the real and nominal costs of funds held constant at their 1965 levels (column 9). Instead of rising between the mid-1960s and the mid-1970s, the cost of capital falls sharply, reflecting the favorable changes in statutory tax rules. A similar although less dramatic conclusion appears even if the effect of inflation in raising the real

66. The value of c/p in column 7 of Table 17.5 fell from an average of 0.238 in 1954–1957 to 0.213 in 1964–1967. The Cobb-Douglas technology implies (see Eq. [20]) that the optimal capital-output ratio is increased by a factor of $238/215 = 1.117$.

67. Inflation raises R to the extent that the required equity yield rises by more than the real cost of debt capital falls.

cost of funds is ignored. The figures in column 10 calculate Z by using a nominal cost of funds constructed as the actual real cost of funds plus the 1965 expected inflation rate of 1.8 percent. Although the difference between columns 7 and 10 understates the adverse effect of inflation, even this measure shows that without the increase in inflation the incentive to investment would have become stronger rather than weaker in the decade after the mid-1960s.

Concluding Remarks

I began this chapter by emphasizing that theoretical models of macroeconomic equilibrium should specify explicitly the role of distortionary taxes, especially taxes on capital income. The failure to include such tax rules can have dramatic and misleading effects on the qualitative as well as the quantitative properties of macroeconomic theories. The statistical evidence presented later in the chapter bears out the likely importance of these fiscal effects in studying the nonneutrality of expected inflation.

In discussing the problem of statistical inference, I noted that the complexity of economic problems, the inadequacies of economic data, and the weakness of the restrictions imposed by general economic theory together make it impossible to apply in practice the textbook injunction to estimate a "true" model within which all parameter values can be inferred and all hypotheses tested. Learning in economics is a more complex and imperfectly understood process in which we develop judgments and convictions by combining econometric estimates, theoretical insights, and institutional knowledge. The use of several alternative "false" models can strengthen our understanding and confidence because the *same* biases are not likely to be present in quite different models.

This view of the problem of statistical inference in econometrics leads me to conclude that as practicing econometricians we should be both more humble and more optimistic than is currently fashionable. We should have the humility to recognize that each econometric study is just another piece of information about a complex subject rather than *the* definitive estimate of some true model. But we should also be more optimistic that the accumulating and sifting of this econometric information will permit specialists to make better and more informed judgments.

I illustrated these theoretical and statistical ideas by estimating alternative models of investment behavior with a focus on understanding how the interaction between inflation and existing rules has influenced investment behavior. The results of each of these models show that the rising rate of inflation has, because of the structure of existing U.S. tax rules, substantially discouraged investment in the past fifteen years.

A more general implication of these results is that monetary policy is far from neutral with respect to economic activity, even in the long run when the induced change in inflation is fully anticipated. Because of the nonindexed fiscal structure, even a fully anticipated rate of inflation causes a misallocation of resources in general and a distortion of resources away from investment in plant and equipment in particular.[68] The traditional idea of ''easy money to encourage investment'' that has guided U.S. policy for the past twenty years has backfired and, by raising the rate of inflation, has actually caused a reduction in investment.[69]

It would of course be useful to extend the current analysis in a number of ways. I am currently examining how the interaction of inflation and tax rules affects the demand for consumption in general and for housing capital in particular. Further studies should be done on the effects of inflation and tax rules on the demand for government debt, on financial markets, and on international capital flows.[70] More information about investment behavior could be developed by applying the three models of this chapter on a more disaggregated basis.

I began this chapter by commenting that Irving Fisher's analysis of inflation had ignored the effects of taxation. Even so, Fisher favored the very tax reform that would eliminate the distorting effects of inflation on the taxation of capital income. In a lecture published in the January 1937 issue of *Econometrica* entitled ''Income in Theory and Income Taxation in Practice,'' Fisher advocated a progressive expenditure or consumption tax. Although his reasons for preferring such a tax did not include its inflation neutrality, my remarks here give a further reason for thinking that Fisher was right.

68. This conclusion stands in sharp contrast to the early view of Hayek and others that inflation encourages investment by raising profits or the appearance of profits. That view not only ignored fiscal effects but also was essentially a short-run theory since wages and other costs, as well as expectations, would naturally adjust to inflation.

69. On the role of the fiscal structure in the mismanagement of monetary policy, see Feldstein (1980d).

70. Poterba (1980) and Summers (1980) discuss the theoretical impact of inflation on the demand for housing capital. Hartman (1979) presents an analysis of the effect on international capital flows, and Feldstein (1980a) treats the demand for government debt. Empirical applications are, however, still lacking.

PART FOUR

Tax Incidence in a Growing Economy

18 Tax Incidence in a Growing Economy with Variable Factor Supply

Traditional tax theory implies that the incidence of a tax depends on the elasticities of supply and demand for the taxed good or service.[1] The basic lesson of these partial equilibrium analyses is that the share of the tax burden borne by the suppliers of the taxed good decreases as their supply elasticity increases relative to the elasticity of demand. The purpose of this chapter is to extend these results by developing appropriate models with which to study the effects of supply elasticities on the incidence of *general* taxes on the incomes of labor and capital.

There is substantial scope for the supplies of both labor and capital to vary in response to a change in tax rates. Although empirical analyses of labor supply have concentrated on average working hours and labor force participation rates, these are primarily relevant for married women, youths, and older workers. More important sources of long-run variation in the supply of labor services, especially for prime age males, are differences in formal education and on-the-job training, in the choice of occupation, and in the intensity of effort with which these occupations are pursued. The relative growth of employment in white collar and service occupations and the general rise in the standard of living increase these opportunities for individual discretion, that is, for personal choices between less arduous work and the prospect of higher lifetime income.

The response of capital accumulation to tax changes is more complex. A tax may alter the saving rate by changing the net yield on capital and by redistributing disposable income among groups with different savings propensities. A tax on labor income may also affect the stock of capital indirectly: if a tax on labor income reduces the supply of labor, it may also, by increasing the capital-labor ratio and thus decreasing the yield on capital, cause a reduction in the rate of capital accumulation.

Unfortunately, the partial equilibrium framework that yields the tradi-

Reprinted from the *Quarterly Journal of Economics* 88 (November 1974), pp. 551–573, by permission of John Wiley and Sons. I am grateful to Amy Taylor for assistance with the numerical calculations in this chapter.
1. See, for example, Dalton (1954, chaps. 7 and 8) and Musgrave (1959, chaps. 10–14).

tional conclusion about the effects of supply and demand elasticities is not suitable for analyzing the incidence of a tax on the income of a major factor of production. A partial equilibrium analysis of a tax on labor income, for example, involves an aggregate national demand function for labor that is neither clearly defined nor directly estimable. Moreover, a partial equilibrium analysis of a labor income tax fails to reflect the supply behavior of capital and the long-run interdependence of labor supply and capital accumulation. Nevertheless, more appropriate general equilibrium models of tax incidence in an economy with variable factor supply have not previously been presented. It is the purpose of this chapter to begin closing this gap.

More specifically, this chapter develops two related general equilibrium analyses of tax incidence, a comparative static analysis, and a comparison of long-run steady-state paths of a growing economy. The comparative static formulation provides an explicit statement of the relation of the tax incidence to the supply elasticities of labor and capital and the properties of the aggregate production function. It implies that labor bears the entire burden of a tax on labor income if the supply of labor is fixed but that a substantial portion of that burden can be avoided if the labor supply is an increasing function of the wage rate. These conclusions apply, mutatis mutandis, to a tax on capital income.

The long-run results implied by a comparison of steady-state growth paths are very different from the implications of the comparative static analysis and quite surprising to one whose intuition is based on the traditional partial equilibrium conclusions. *In the long run, labor will bear at least 100 percent of the net burden of a tax on labor income even if there is a substantial positive elasticity of labor supply. The steady-state rate of return is likely to rise in response to the introduction of the tax on labor income; owners of capital actually gain from the imposition of the tax rather than sharing its burden. Moreover, in sharp contrast to the comparative static results, neither these general conclusions nor the specific incidence value is affected by the elasticity of the labor supply function.*

It should be emphasized that these results refer only to the asymptotic long-run growth path. Since there may be a substantial delay before these equilibrium values are closely approximated, it is important to have results that apply over a shorter horizon. If the ex post technology is adequately variable, the comparative static analysis with a fixed capital stock indicates the short-run effects of a tax change. To illustrate the path of transition from this short-run tax impact to the long-run steady-state equilibrium, a specific numerical example will be presented.

The first section of the chapter develops the comparative static general equilibrium analysis. A simple numerical example is used in the second section to illustrate the sensitivity of the incidence and the excess burden to the relative supply elasticities. The third section then analyzes the long-run incidence in the context of a general neoclassical growth model. A numerical illustration of the transition from initial incidence to final growth equilibrium is discussed in the fourth section. There is a brief concluding comment on some of the limits of the current analysis.

A One-Sector General Equilibrium Analysis

The simplest general equilibrium framework within which to analyze the implications of variable factor supply is the static one-product two-factor model of a competitive economy. This captures the basic features of an explicitly specified technology and of supply functions for labor and capital. This variability of factor supply represents a significant extension of previous general equilibrium models of tax incidence.[2] At the same time, however, the specification of only a one-product market precludes the analysis of product substitution and partial-factor taxes that have characterized past general equilibrium analyses. It would obviously be useful to extend the current analyses by considering an economy with more than one sector.

Any comparative static analysis simplifies by treating capital as a primary factor and thus ignores the interdependence of labor income, the savings rate, and the capital stock. These restrictions are relaxed in the third section by extending the model to a growing economy with an endogenous capital stock. Since these results relate only to the long-run steady-state path, it is useful to have estimates that relate to a shorter period. If there is sufficient ex post technological variability, the comparative static analysis with a fixed capital stock shows the short-run response to a tax change. More generally, the comparative static analysis with a variable capital stock can be regarded as an approximate description of the economy's response over a longer horizon.

The following analysis will deal with a proportional tax on labor income. Since capital and labor enter the current model symmetrically, the analysis applies equally well to a tax on capital income.

The basis components of the one-sector static model are a production function, the two-factor price equations, and the two-factor supply functions. The production function,

$$Y = F(K, L), \tag{1}$$

2. These include early general equilibrium studies by Jeade (1955), Johnson (1956), and Shephard (1944), and more recent applications by Harberger (1962), Mieszkowski (1967), and Shoven and Whalley (1972).

which relates output (Y) to the services of capital (K) and labor (L), will be assumed to be homogeneous of degree one. Using subscripts to denote partial derivatives (for example $F_K = \partial Y/\partial K, F_{KL} = \partial^2 Y/\partial K \partial L$, and so on), we may write the usual technological assumptions as $F_i > 0, F_{ii} < 0$, and $F_{ij} > 0$.

The competitiveness of markets implies that both factors are paid their marginal products:

$$F_L = w(1 + \tau),\tag{2}$$

and

$$F_K = r.\tag{3}$$

Here r is the rate of interest and $w (1 + \tau)$ is the gross wage in the presence of a payroll or labor income tax at $100\,\tau$ percent. Since there is only one product, its price is taken as numeraire.

The system is completed by the two-factor supply equations:

$$L = L(w),\tag{4}$$

and

$$K = K(r).\tag{5}$$

For the following analysis it will be assumed that the supply of each factor is either inelastic or an increasing function of its net renumeration.

The effect of a small change in the tax rate can be studied by totally differentiating Eqs. (1) through (5). The proportional change in the wage rate that results from a change in the tax rate is found to be

$$\frac{1}{w}\frac{dw}{d\tau} = -\frac{F_{KK}K_r - 1}{(F_{KK}K_r - 1)(1 + \tau) + F_{LL}L_w}.\tag{6}$$

Equation (6) implies that if both factors are nondecreasing functions of their own net price,

$$0 \le -\frac{1 + \tau}{w}\frac{dw}{d\tau} \le 1,\tag{7}$$

that is, the net wage falls or remains unchanged, but a 1 percent increase in the tax rate does not lower the wage rate by more than 1 percent. To see this, note first that Eq. (6) can be rewritten as

$$\frac{1 + \tau}{w} \frac{dw}{d\tau} = \frac{-1}{1 + \frac{F_{LL}L_w}{(F_{KK}K_r - 1)} \frac{1}{1 + \tau}}. \tag{8}$$

It follows from the properties of the production function that $F_{KK} < 0$ and therefore that $F_{KK}K_r - 1 < 0$ if $K_r \geq 0$. Since $F_{LL} < 0$ and therefore $F_{LL}L_w \leq 0$ for $L_w \geq 0$, the ratio in the denominator is nonnegative. The net wage rate therefore always falls when the tax increases, and, since the denominator is greater than one, the fall is less than proportional.

Note that an increase in L_w reduces the fall in the wage rate. It is tempting to interpret this as implying that a more sensitive labor supply reduces the burden borne by labor. However, L_w is not unit-free and depends on the size of the labor force and the level of wages. It is useful therefore to rewrite Eq. (6) in terms of the supply elasticities of labor and capital. At the same time we can express the relevant local properties of the production function in terms of the implied factor shares and the Hicks-Allen elasticity of substitution.

Labor's contribution to aggregate output will be denoted by $a = (1 + \tau)wL/Y$. This may be constant as with the Cobb-Douglas technology but need not be; a is used only to describe a local property of the production function in the neighborhood where the economy is operating when the tax is introduced. The local elasticity of substitution σ also satisfies the equation:

$$\sigma = -\frac{(1 + \tau)w(1 - a)}{F_{LL}L} = -\frac{ra}{F_{KK}K}. \tag{9}$$

Using $\eta_L = L_w w L^{-1}$ and $\eta_K = K_r r K^{-1}$ to represent the supply elasticities of labor and capital, we may rewrite Eq. (6) as

$$\frac{1 + \tau}{w} \frac{dw}{d\tau} = -\frac{1 + a(\eta_K/\sigma)}{1 + a(\eta_K/\sigma) + (1 - a)(\eta_L/\sigma)}. \tag{10}$$

It is clear from this equation that an increase in the elasticity of labor supply does reduce the effect of the tax on the wage rate. The importance of the elasticity of substitution is also apparent. A higher elasticity of substitution specifically reduces the effect of variable factor supply; the greater the elasticity of substitution, the smaller is the effect that a change in factor supplies has on relative factor prices. Indeed, Eq. (10) indicates that it is only the ratio of each factor supply elasticity to the elasticity of substitution that matters. We may refer to these ratios as the deflated supply elasticities and note that the fall in wages is reduced by a higher deflated labor supply elasticity, but increased by a higher deflated capital supply elasticity.

Equation (10) can now be used to derive an explicit expression for the incidence of the tax. Note first that the change in labor's income that results from a change in the tax rate may be expressed as

$$\frac{d(wL)}{d\tau} = L\frac{dw}{d\tau} + w\frac{dL}{d\tau}. \tag{11}$$

The second term represents the fall in income[3] due to a decrease in labor supply. This fall in the receipt of income does not entail a net loss of satisfaction because it is exactly offset by the value of the increased leisure: since w is the money value of leisure at the margin, $w(dL/d\tau)$ is the money value of the increased leisure. The net loss of labor income, that is, the money loss minus the value of the additional leisure, is thus the first term; I shall write this net loss as $-dW^* = -Ldw$.

The incidence of an incremental tax can be defined as the ratio of labor's *net* income loss to the change in total tax receipts,[4] $dT = wLd\tau + \tau[Ldw + wdL]$, that is,

$$-\frac{dW^*}{dT} = \frac{-Ldw}{wLd\tau + \tau Ldw + \tau wdL}. \tag{12}$$

The incidence can be evaluated by substituting from Eq. (10); for notational simplicity the deflated supply elasticities will be denoted by adding a prime and deleting the σ, that is, $\eta'_L = \eta_L/\sigma$. The incidence can now be written as

$$-\frac{dW^*}{dT} = \frac{1 + a\eta'_K}{(1 + a\eta'_K)(1 - \tau\eta_L) + (1 - a)\eta'_L(1 + \tau)}. \tag{13}$$

---

3. This assumes that the substitution effect dominates the income effect. If $dL/dw < 0$, the second term is an increase in income, and the subsequent statements must be modified in the obvious way.

4. Note that using *net* income makes the definition of incidence essentially a measure of "utility" lost by labor per dollar of taxes raised. With a fixed labor supply there is no difference between this and the loss of money income. Note also that this definition of inci-

Consider first the case of a new tax, that is, $\tau = 0$. If the supply of labor is fixed ($\eta'_L = 0$), labor's loss equals the entire tax revenue. This is independent of the value of η'_K. As the value of η'_L increases, labor's share of the total tax burden decreases.[5] It is interesting to consider the conditions in which labor is able to shift so much of the payroll tax that the actual incidence on capital and labor are in proportion to their original shares in national income, that is, so that the incidence corresponds to what is usually thought of as that of a general income tax. Equation (13) implies that $- dW^*/dT \leqslant a$ if and only if $a(\eta'_L - \eta'_K) \geqslant 1$. For example, if $\eta'_K = 0$ and labor's share of national income (a) is two-thirds, the payroll tax will be paid in proportion to original shares in national income if the deflated labor supply elasticity is equal to 1.5. Even with a substantially lower supply elasticity, the incidence may be closer to the original factor shares usually associated with a general income tax than to the full burden falling on labor that is usually associated with a payroll tax. More specifically, if $- dW^*/dT > a$, a necessary and sufficient condition for $(-dW^*/dT - a) < (1 + dW^*/dT)$ is that $a(\eta'_L - \eta'_K) > 1 - \eta'_L$. Thus, with $\eta'_K = 0$ and $a = \frac{2}{3}$, the incidence of payroll tax more closely resembles that of the traditional income tax incidence whenever $\eta'_L \geqslant 0.6$.

The analysis of an incremental change in a previously existing payroll tax is somewhat more complex. Equation (13) shows that this introduces additional terms in the denominator that are equivalent to $-(\tau\eta'_L)[\sigma - (1 - a) + a\eta_K]$. Since $\sigma > 1 - a$ is implied by all empirical analyses of aggregate production functions, the additional terms reduce the value of the denominator if $\eta'_L > 0$ and $\eta_K \geqslant 0$. Now labor's net loss $(- dW^*)$ can actually exceed the additional revenue raised. This will occur if $(1 + a\eta'_K)\tau\eta_L > (1 - a)\eta'_L(1 + \tau)$, that is, if $\sigma(1 + a\eta'_K)/(1 - a) > (1 + \tau)/\tau$.[6]

---

dence corresponds to a balanced budget concept of incidence rather than a differential tax incidence. The analysis assumes in effect that the government spends the tax receipts to buy the same quantities of factor inputs as the taxpayers would have but that the government purchases do not affect factor supply. See Musgrave (1959, chap. 10).

5. These general equilibrium results can be compared with the partial equilibrium measure: $- dW^*/dT = \eta_D/(\eta_S + \eta_D)$, where η_S and η_D are the supply and demand elasticities for labor. If labor supply is fixed ($\eta_S = 0$), labor's loss equals the entire tax revenue. As the value of η_S increases, labor's share of the total tax burden decreases. The applicability of this partial equilibrium analysis is limited by the ambiguity of the demand function. With a variable supply of capital, the demand for labor at each gross wage cannot be assumed to be independent of the tax rate. Moreover, the use of an aggregate demand function fails to indicate the way in which incidence is affected by the variability of the capital stock and the nature of the technology.

6. The denominator remains positive; it can be shown that $dT/d\tau > 0$ implies that the denominator is positive.

Moreover, the effect of an increase in the elasticity of labor supply is no longer unambiguous. Labor's net loss per dollar of tax revenue $(-dW^*/dT)$ *can be an increasing or decreasing function of labor's supply elasticity.* More specifically,

$$\frac{d[-dW^*/dT]}{d\eta_L} = \frac{dW^*}{dT} \cdot \frac{\frac{1-a}{\sigma}(1+\tau) - \tau(1+a\eta_K')}{(1+a\eta_K')(1-\tau\eta_L) + (1-a)\eta_L'(1+\tau)}. \quad (14)$$

An increase in η_L therefore increases labor's loss per dollar of tax revenue if $\sigma(1 + a\eta_K')/(1 - a) > (1 + \tau)/\tau$; that is, if labor's net loss exceeds the tax revenue, an increase in η_L will increase labor's net loss per dollar of tax revenue. What is the reason for this surprising possibility? A clue is provided by the fact that the higher the original tax rate, the more likely it is that an increase in η_L will increase labor's net loss. One result of the reduction in labor supply is to reduce the tax collected at the old rate. Raising a given incremental tax revenue therefore requires a greater increase in the tax rate if the labor supply is elastic. The higher tax rate increases labor's net loss. The effect of a greater supply elasticity therefore depends on the relative strength of this tax revenue effect and the relative factor supply effect.

Note that the presence of a previously existing tax implies that the incremental tax revenue is less than the sum of the net losses of labor and capital. Denoting the change in net profits by $d\pi^* = Kdr$, it can be shown by calculations analogous to those leading to Eq. (6) that

$$-\frac{d\pi^* + dW^*}{dT} = \frac{(1 + a\eta_K') + (1 - a)\eta_L'}{(1 + a\eta_K')(1 - \eta_L\tau) + (1 - a)\eta_L'(1 + \tau)}. \quad (15)$$

When there is no preexisting tax, the net loss to labor and capital combined is equal to the tax revenue.[7] But when $\tau > 0$, the decrease in labor supply that results from an increase in the tax rate can be expected to decrease labor income and therefore to reduce revenue.[8] Stated somewhat differently, there is a loss in total "net" factor incomes (and therefore in welfare) because the marginal value of leisure is less than the gross wage rate.[9] This also explains why labor's incremental net loss can actually exceed the additional revenue that is raised.

---

7. This is, of course, a first-order approximation, since terms of order $(d\tau)^2$ are ignored.
8. This will occur unless $\sigma - (1 - a) + \sigma a\eta_K' < 0$.
9. Equation (15) shows that there is a welfare loss or excess burden even to a first-order approximation when a preexisting tax is increased. It is well known that there is no welfare

Although a preexisting tax alters labor's net loss per dollar of additional tax revenue, it does not change the relative losses of labor and capital. It follows from Eqs. (13) and (15) that, independent of the value of τ,

$$\frac{dW^*}{dW^* + d\pi^*} = \frac{1 + a\eta_K'}{1 + a\eta_K' + (1 - a)\eta_L'}. \tag{16}$$

This provides an alternative measure of the incidence of a tax: the ratio of the loss of net labor income to the total tax burden, that is, to the total loss of labor and capital income. Labor's share of the total tax burden is an unambiguously decreasing function of its own deflated supply elasticity and an increasing function of capital's deflated supply elasticity. Equation (16) implies that, just as in the absence of a preexisting tax, labor's share of the tax burden will be less than its share of national income if $a(\eta_L - \eta_K) > 1$.

Until now it has been assumed that the factor supplies are nondecreasing functions of their own prices. The equations of course continue to hold even if this is not true. Equation (16), for example, shows that if $\eta_L' < 0$ and $\eta_K' \geq 0$, the introduction of a payroll tax lowers labor's net income by more than the tax and raises the income accruing to capital. Thus, if $\eta_K' = 0$, $\eta_L' = -\frac{1}{2}$, and $a = \frac{2}{3}$, labor will pay 1.2 times the tax revenue and capital will gain one-fifth of the tax revenue from a new tax.

The analysis of this section has indicated the dangers of trying to assess tax incidence without allowing variations in factor supply. The simple general equilibrium model indicates, in a way that the partial equilibrium analysis cannot, how the two supply elasticities and the properties of the production function influence the incidence of the tax. Although the current analysis was developed in terms of a payroll tax, the extension to a general tax on capital income or to a combination of payroll and interest income taxes is obvious. The variability of factor supplies implies that only under very special circumstances will a general income tax be borne in proportion to original factor incomes.

The specific measures of tax incidence reflect the first-order approximation involved in calculating $dw/d\tau$ and in defining dW^*. To show that the error introduced by this approximation is quite small and to indicate the relative order of magnitude of the effect of supply elasticities, the next section presents a brief numerical application. By adopting specific functional forms, one can calculate the tax effects without resorting to linear approximations.

---

loss to a first-order approximation when a new tax is introduced in the absence of any previous distortions.

A Numerical Example

The Cobb-Douglas production function and constant elasticity supply functions provide a tractable and easy-to-interpret example. With this specification Eqs. (1) through (5) become

$$Y = AL^a K^{1-a}, \tag{17}$$

$$w(1 + \tau) = aYL^{-1}, \tag{18}$$

$$r = (1 - a)YK^{-1}, \tag{19}$$

$$L = \lambda_w \eta_L, \tag{20}$$

and

$$K = kr_K^\eta. \tag{21}$$

Equations (17) through (21) are linear in the logarithms of all the variables and can therefore be solved directly for the wage rate and interest rate prevailing after the introduction of a tax at 100τ percent. Subscripts 1 and 2 will be used to distinguish before-tax and after-tax equilibrium values of the variables. Without loss of generality units of measurement may be chosen so that $A = L_1 = K_1 = 1$. With this notation the wage and interest rates are

$$w_2 = a\left(\frac{1}{1 + \tau}\right)^{\frac{1 + \alpha\eta_K}{1 + \alpha\eta_K + \eta_L(1 - \alpha)}} \tag{22}$$

and

$$r_2 = (1 - a)\left(\frac{1}{1 + \tau}\right)^{\frac{\alpha\eta_L}{1 + \alpha\eta_K + \eta_L(1 - \alpha)}}. \tag{23}$$

Note that if $\tau = 0$, $w_1 = a$ and $r_1 = 1 - a$, as clearly implied by Eqs. (18) and (19) with the chosen units of measurement of capital, labor, and output. Note also that, if $\eta_L = 0$, labor bears the entire tax: the gross wage remains unchanged $[w_2(1 + \tau) = a = w_1]$, and the net interest rate is also unaffected by the rate of tax $[r_2 = (1 - a) = r_1]$. If the individual supply elasticities are positive, the net wage rate and the interest rate are both decreasing functions of τ.

These explicit expressions for w and r permit a comparison between exact measures of incidence and the linear first-order approximations of the previous section. This comparison also brings out the pure excess burden associated with introducing a substantial tax when the supply elasticities are nonzero. Since the linear approximation becomes worse as the tax rate and supply elasticities increase, relatively high values of these parameters will be assumed in order to assess the accuracy of the approximation. More specifically, we consider the case of a 20 percent tax rate ($\tau = 0.20$), supply elasticities of 1.0, and a production function coefficient for labor of $a = 0.7$.

The gross wage rate after the introduction of the tax is $w_2 = 0.7(1.2)^{-1.7/2} = 0.600$. Since the wage rate before the introduction of the tax was $w_1 = 0.70$, the fall in the wage rate is 0.100. With a supply elasticity of one the quantity of labor services falls from $L_1 = 1.0$ to $L_2 = 0.856$. The total money income of labor therefore falls from 0.700 to 0.513. The value of the increased leisure lies between $w_2(L_1 - L_2)$ and $w_1(L_1 - L_2)$, that is, between 0.086 and 0.101. Evaluating the leisure at the average of the pretax and after-tax wages, $(w_1 + w_2)/2$ implies that the value of the incremental leisure is 0.093. The value of labor's net income loss is therefore

$$w_1L_1 - w_2L_2 - 0.5(w_1 + w_2)(L_1 - L_2)$$

$$= 0.5(w_1L_1 - w_2L_2 - w_2L_1 + w_1L_2)$$

$$= 0.5(w_1 - w_2)(L_1 + L_2) = 0.093.$$

A similar calculation shows that capital's real income loss is

$$0.5(r_1 - r_2)(K_1 + K_2) = 0.018.$$

Since the total tax receipts are $\tau w_2 L_2 = 0.103$, there is an excess burden of

$$0.5[(w_1 - w_2)(L_1 + L_2) + (r_1 - r_2)(k_1 + k_2)] - \tau w_2 L_2 = 0.0086,$$

or 8.3 percent of the total tax revenue. Labor's real income loss corresponds to 84 percent of the combined loss of labor and capital. Labor can thus avoid a substantial portion of the tax if its supply is variable, even though the supply of capital has the same elasticity.

These calculations can be compared with the first-order approximations

Table 18.1. Comparison of exact and approximate estimates of tax effects

Effect of tax	Exact solution	Approximation $\tau = 0.10$	Approximation $\tau = 0$
$-dw/w$	0.143	0.155	0.170
$-dW^*/dT$	0.909	0.914	0.850
$dW^*/(dW^* + d\pi^*)$	0.839	0.850	0.850

derived in the previous section. Table 18.1 presents the exact values and the corresponding approximations for $\tau = 0$ and $\tau = 0.10$. It is clear that, even with a relatively high tax rate and substantial supply elasticities, the linear approximations are quite accurate, particularly for $\tau = 0.10$.

As noted in the previous section, the special case of $\eta_K = 0$ is of particular interest because it corresponds to the short-run response to a tax if there is sufficient ex post capital malleability. With $\eta_K = 0$ and $\eta_L = 1$, labor bears only 75 percent of the combined burden of labor and capital. There is also an excess burden of 7.5 percent of the tax revenue. Labor's ability to avoid a significant portion of the total burden remains even with a much lower supply elasticity; with $\eta_L = 0.33$, labor bears 90 percent of the total burden.

More generally, the impact of the supply elasticities is illustrated by Table 18.2, which presents the ratio of labor's net loss to the total burden for different combinations of η_L and η_K. All of the values correspond to a tax rate of 20 percent and to $a = 0.7$. A similar comparison of relative excess burdens, that is, the ratio of the excess burden to total tax collections, is presented in Table 18.3.

Table 18.2. Factor supply elasticities and tax incidence[a]

Elasticity of capital supply η_K	Elasticity of labor supply (η_L)				
	0.0	0.33	0.67	1.00	1.33
0.0	1.00	0.90	0.82	0.75	0.70
0.33	1.00	0.92	0.85	0.79	0.74
0.67	1.00	0.93	0.87	0.82	0.77
1.00	1.00	0.94	0.89	0.84	0.80
1.33	1.00	0.95	0.90	0.86	0.82

a. The tax incidence values are the ratio of labor's net loss to the total net loss of labor and capital.

Table 18.3. Factor supply elasticities and percentage excess burden[a]

Elasticity of capital supply (η_K)	Elasticity of labor supply (η_L)				
	0.0	0.33	0.67	1.00	1.33
0.0	0.0	2.81	5.33	7.47	9.35
0.33	0.0	2.86	5.52	7.84	9.94
0.67	0.0	2.90	5.66	8.13	10.41
1.00	0.0	2.92	5.76	8.34	10.76
1.33	0.0	2.94	5.84	8.51	11.05

a. Percentage excess burden is the excess burden as a percentage of total tax collections.

Long-Run Incidence in a Growing Economy

The comparative static general equilibrium analysis that has just been considered shows the effect on tax incidence of differences in the supply responses of capital and labor but does not reflect the relation between labor supply and capital formation that prevails in a dynamic economy. An explicit growth model emphasizes the difference between the supply of labor and of capital, that is, that labor is a primary factor, while the stock of capital depends on savings out of the previous incomes of labor and capital. The current stock of capital is therefore affected by the past supply of labor in two distinct ways: directly through saving out of labor income and indirectly through the effect of labor supply on capital income and therefore on the savings of capital owners. This dependence of the capital growth on past labor supply implies that a payroll tax that reduces labor supply also reduces the steady-state supply of capital.[10]

This section will show that this interdependence has very important implications for long-run tax incidence. Under quite general conditions the long-run incidence of a tax change does not depend on the supply response of labor. The steady-state fall in the net wage rate is the same regardless of whether labor is supplied inelastically or responds to a fall in the wage rate. The incidence does, however, generally depend on the response of the savings rate to the return on capital, on the parameters of the production function, and on the previously prevailing rate of tax.

It must be borne in mind that the results to be derived in this section refer to the long-run steady state. Since the adjustment to a tax change re-

10. For other analyses of tax incidence in a growing economy see Diamond (1970), Feldstein (Chapter 19 of the current work), Hall (1968), Krzyzaniak (1966, 1967, 1970), K. Sato (1967), and R. Sato (1963).

mains substantially incomplete for a long period of time,[11] these steady-state results are inadequate as a guide to the short run and intermediate period. During the adjustment period the incidence does depend on the response of the labor supply. In the very short run, the change in labor supply has no effect on the capital stock, and the results of the comparative static analysis of the previous two sections are relevant.[12] The path of adjustment may be regarded as a transition from the comparative static equilibrium of the previous section to the long-run steady-state equilibrium of a growing economy. To illustrate the adjustment path, the next section will present an explicit numerical example of the path of wage adjustment and the change in incidence through time.

The steady-state growth equilibrium may be characterized by the same constant returns to scale production function and factor price equations as in the static model:

$$Y = F(L, K), \tag{24}$$

$$F_L = w(1 + \tau), \tag{25}$$

and

$$F_K = r. \tag{26}$$

The difference between the stationary and growing economies lies in the factor supply relations. Equation (27) relates the aggregate savings volume to the distribution of income with different savings propensities for labor income (s_L), capital income (s_K), and government tax receipts (s_G):

$$S = s_L w L + s_K r K + s_G \tau w L. \tag{27}$$

The savings propensities out of labor and capital income will each be assumed to be some nondecreasing function of the rate of return:

$$s_L = s_L(r), \qquad s_L' \geq 0; \tag{28}$$

---

11. See R. Sato (1963) for a discussion and some estimates of this. He shows in a particular case that for reasonable parameter values it takes thirty years for 50 percent of the change in equilibrium to occur. In the analysis in the next section of this chapter, half of the change in equilibrium values occurs after twenty years.

12. This is true to the extent that the technology is malleable ex post. The analysis of the incidence path in a putty-clay economy is an important problem, but lies beyond this chapter.

and

$$s_K = S_K(r), \qquad s'_K \geqslant 0. \tag{29}$$

The economy tends toward a balanced growth path along which the pro-portional rate of growth of the capital stock $K^{-1}(dK/dt)$ is equal to the rate of growth of the labor force (n). Since the volume of savings (S) is equal to the increment to the capital stock (dK/dt),[13] the balanced growth equilibrium is characterized by

$$nK = s_L wL + s_K rK + s_G \tau wL. \tag{30}$$

The labor supply function relates the quantity of labor services (L) to the population (N):

$$L = l(w)N. \tag{31}$$

Note that the wage rate is not assumed to affect the rate of growth of the population but only the average quantity of labor services supplied per capita. The long-run rate of growth of labor services is therefore the same as the growth rate of the population.

This completes the specification of the model. The special problem of measuring tax incidence in a growing economy must now be considered. If there is some saving out of labor income, any reduction in current labor income leads to a future reduction in the capital income of workers. Since this reduction merely reflects a postponement of labor's reduced con-sumption, it would be inappropriate to regard this as part of the tax that falls on capital. It is best therefore to assess tax incidence by calculating the relative changes in the wage rate and the rate of interest. The propor-tional fall in the wage rate is equal to the proportional fall in labor income at a constant labor supply, and, therefore, to a first approximation, to the fall in labor income compensated for the increased leisure. The propor-tional change in the interest rate is also equivalent to the proportional fall in the income of "pure capitalists" (that is, those with no labor income) at a fixed supply of their capital and therefore, again to a first approximation, to the fall in capitalist income compensated for their change in consump-tion. The proportional changes in the factor prices are therefore a useful way of describing incidence in an economy in which labor owns a share of the capital stock and in which that share is influenced by the tax rate.

---

13. This follows the usual procedure of ignoring depreciation. Including depreciation af-fects the long-run equilibrium in the same way as a change in the rate of population growth.

From the proportional changes in factor prices, it is also possible to calculate the changes in *net* factor incomes and therefore the measures of incidence used in the first section. Note again that by compensating for the change in leisure and the postponement of consumption, these measures of incidence refer to individual welfare and not just to money incomes.

From Eqs. (24) through (31) it is possible to show by a substantial amount of simple but tedious algebra that the proportional change in the net wage rate induced by a proportional change in the tax price $(1 + \tau)$ is given by

$$-\frac{1+\tau}{w}\frac{dw}{d\tau}$$

$$= \frac{\dfrac{s_L}{1-a}\left(1+\dfrac{a}{\sigma}\epsilon_L\right) + \dfrac{s_K}{\sigma}(1+\epsilon_K)(1+\tau) + s_G\tau\left(\dfrac{1}{1-a} - \dfrac{1}{\sigma}\right) - \dfrac{s_G}{\sigma}}{\dfrac{s_L}{1-a}\left(1+\dfrac{a}{\sigma}\epsilon_L\right) + \dfrac{s_K}{\sigma}(1+\epsilon_K)(1+\tau) + s_G\tau\left(\dfrac{1}{1-a} - \dfrac{1}{\sigma}\right) - \dfrac{s_L}{\sigma}},$$

$$(32)$$

where a is the elasticity of output with respect to the labor input $[a = w(1 + \tau)L/Y]$, σ is the elasticity of substitution of the production function, ϵ_L is the elasticity of the saving rate out of labor income with respect to the rate of interest $[\epsilon_L = (r/s_L)s_L']$, and ϵ_K is the corresponding elasticity for the saving rate out of capital income. All of these parameters refer to the local equilibrium values. Similarly, it can be shown that the change in the rate of return satisfies

$$\frac{1+\tau}{r}\frac{dr}{d\tau}$$

$$= \frac{-(s_G - s_L)\dfrac{1}{\sigma}\dfrac{a}{1-a}}{\dfrac{s_L}{1-a}\left(1+\dfrac{a}{\sigma}\epsilon_L\right) + \dfrac{s_K}{\sigma}(1+\epsilon_K)(1+\tau) + s_G\tau\left(\dfrac{1}{1-a} - \dfrac{1}{\sigma}\right) - \dfrac{s_L}{\sigma}}.$$

$$(33)$$

It is obvious from these equations that labor's supply response $(\partial L/\partial w)$ has no effect on the long-run incidence of the tax change. The changes in the steady-state wage rate and rate of return are the same if the labor services supplied per capita remain constant or change with the wage rate. This result is in sharp contrast with the conclusion of the simpler comparative static analysis of the previous sections. It is perhaps easiest to understand by noting that the wage rate and rate of interest in the long-run equilibrium of a growing economy with a constant return to scale technology do not depend on the absolute size of the labor force but only on its rate of growth. The elasticity of labor supply in effect only alters the size of the labor force and therefore does not affect gross factor prices. The formal derivation of Eqs. (32) and (33) shows that the conclusions of this line of argument are correct, even though, unlike the traditional model of the growing economy, the labor supply is an endogenous variable in the current analysis. It is also clear that the incidence does depend on the response of the aggregate savings rate (that is, on the differences in the savings rates and their elasticities with respect to the rate of return) and the parameters of the production function. These determinants of the incidence will now be considered in greater detail.

If we continue as in the previous sections to define labor's net loss (adjusted for the increase in leisure) by $-L(dw/d\tau)$ and capital's net loss by $-K(dr/d\tau)$, Eqs. (32) and (33) can be used to show that the revenue raised by the introduction of a new tax is (to a first-order approximation) equal to the sum of the net losses of labor and capital. The condition $[(1 + \tau)/w](dw/d\tau) = -1$ therefore implies that labor bears the entire burden of a *new* tax; that is, this condition implies that $-Ldw = Lwd\tau$: labor's net loss $(-Ldw)$ is equal to the tax revenue $(wLd\tau)$. For the same reasons discussed in the first section, an increase in an *existing* tax rate causes the sum of the net factor income losses to exceed the additional tax revenues. Labor's share of the burden of an increase in an existing tax therefore cannot be inferred from the elasticity of w with respect to $(1 + \tau)$.

It is easy, however, to identify the case in which labor bears the entire burden of an increase in an existing tax or of the introduction of a new tax. By definition, labor bears the entire burden when capital bears no burden, that is, when $dr/d\tau = 0$. Equation (33) shows that a necessary and sufficient condition for $dr/d\tau = 0$ is the equality of s_L and s_G. It is also clear from Eq. (32) that $s_L = s_G$ implies $[(1 + \tau)/w](dw/d\tau) = -1$ and therefore that labor's net loss from a new tax is exactly equal to the revenue raised by the tax.

To discuss the incidence when $s_L \neq s_G$, we examine the realistic case in which $s_L > s_G$ and in which the denominator on the right-hand side of Eqs. (32) and (33) is positive.[14] A higher saving propensity out of labor in-

---

14. This denominator will be positive when the elasticity of substitution (σ) exceeds capital's share in national income $(1 - a)$. It will also be positive for $s_L \geq s_G > 0$ and $\sigma/(1 - a) < 1$ if either $s_K > 0$ or $\epsilon_L > 0$.

come than out of tax revenues ($s_L > s_G$) implies that the tax directly lowers the rate of capital formation and therefore further penalizes labor. This is seen most easily in Eq. (32). The numerator and the denominator differ only in the final term. Since the numerator and denominator are both positive, $s_L > s_G$ implies $-[(1 + \tau)/w](dw/d\tau) > 1$, that is, that the tax increase lowers the *gross* wage rate and therefore lowers the net wage rate by more than the tax. Equation (33) shows that the effect of the tax is actually to raise the rate of interest since the equilibrium capital intensity of production is decreased. Although the higher yield on savings out of past labor income partially mitigates the lower wage rate, it is an unqualified gain for the pure capitalists.

As in the first section, it is useful to assess the extent to which the tax lowers the wage rate by comparing labor's net loss ($-Ldw$) to the additional tax yield ($dT = \tau Ldw + \tau wdL + wLd\tau$). A series of simple substitutions yields

$$-\frac{Ldw}{dT} = \frac{-\dfrac{dw}{wd\tau}}{1 + (1 + \eta_L)\dfrac{\tau}{1 + \tau}\left[\dfrac{1 + \tau}{w}\dfrac{dw}{d\tau}\right]}, \qquad (34)$$

where η_L is the elasticity of the labor supply with respect to the net wage. Equation (34) shows that, although η_L does not affect the factor prices, it does influence the additional tax revenues from an incremental tax and therefore the ratio of labor's net loss to the additional tax revenues. Because the effect of $\eta_L \neq 0$ is to change the yield from the previous tax rate, it has no effect when a new tax is being introduced; when $\tau = 0$, the denominator is one, and the ratio of labor's adjusted loss to the tax revenue is equal to the elasticity $-[(1 + \tau)/w](dw/d\tau)$. More generally, for any finite value of η_L, labor's adjusted loss ratio is an increasing function of that elasticity. Except for an implausibly high negative value of η_L, the denominator of Eq. (34) is less than one if $\tau > 0$ so that labor's loss ratio exceeds the absolute wage elasticity.[15]

Equation (32) shows that the absolute wage rate elasticity is equal to or greater than one for $s_L > s_G$. More specifically, the relative labor and capital savings rates, the supply elasticities of those rates, and the properties of the production function influence the wage rate elasticity by affecting the way in which the tax affects capital accumulation and the impact of

---

15. The denominator is <1 if $\eta > -1$. A value of $\eta < -1$ would imply that labor responds to a fall in the wage rate by an absolute increase in earnings.

that change in capital accumulation on factor prices. The general implication of $s_L > s_G$ is that the tax reduces the fraction of national income that is saved. High values of ϵ_K and ϵ_L mean that the capital stock falls less in response to the tax because the rising interest rate induces additional saving. For any given value of s_G, a higher ratio of s_K to s_L implies that savings are affected relatively less by the tax. Since both of these influences reduce the fall in the capital stock, they also limit the reduction in the wage rate. Finally, a high elasticity of substitution σ implies that any given fall in the K/L ratio will have a smaller effect on relative factor prices. All of these effects are shown explicitly by Eq. (32). Since the absolute wage elasticity equals one even if there is no change in the K/L ratio, the effects of the saving and factor substitution parameter cannot reduce the elasticity below one. Labor's net loss must always equal or exceed the additional tax revenue.

The results obtained in this section, and in particular the conclusion that the long-run incidence of a tax on labor income does not depend on the supply response of that factor, cannot be extended by analogy to a tax on profits. In this way the use of the long-run growth equilibrium to analyze incidence differs very significantly from the use of the comparative static framework. The results obtained in the first section could be used to describe a tax on interest income merely by relabeling the capital and labor variables. The growth model emphasizes that the two inputs are very different in kind and that their supplies cannot be regarded as independent variables. This lack of symmetry of capital and labor implies that the incidence of an interest income tax does depend on the way in which the supply of the taxed factor (capital) responds to the tax.[16] More specifically, it can be shown that the incidence of an interest income tax depends on the savings elasticities (ϵ_L and ϵ_K), but not on the elasticity of labor supply. Since a proportional general income tax is a combination of a payroll tax and an interest income tax, it is clear that its incidence also depends on the savings elasticities, but not on the elasticity of labor supply.

It must again be emphasized that the conclusions of this section and the specific incidence expressions refer only to the long-run growth equilibrium. Since the actual factor prices may differ substantially from the equilibrium values for a very long time, the long-run results are not sufficient information for policy analysis. Over a relatively long horizon, the supply elasticity of labor will affect the incidence of the tax. If the tax will reduce wages less, labor will bear a smaller share of the tax burden than would be the case if the labor supply were fixed. In the very short run the stock of

16. For an analysis of this problem see Chapter 19.

capital is fixed, and a reduction in labor supply clearly lowers the rate of return and shifts part of the tax burden. With a sufficiently malleable technology in the short run, the comparative static results of the first section can be applied with $\eta_K = 0$. The actual time path of factor prices then represents a transition from this initial new equilibrium to the steady-state growth path. The next section presents a specific numerical example to illustrate this path of adjustment.

The Path of Adjustment

An economy with Cobb-Douglas technology and constant savings rates ($\epsilon_L = \epsilon_K = 0$) provides a simple model with which to study the path of adjustment to a tax on labor income. With a Cobb-Douglas technology, Eqs. (24) through (27) become

$$Y_t = L_t^a K_t^{1-a}, \tag{35}$$

$$w_t(1 + \tau_t) = aL_t^{a-1}K_t^{1-a}, \tag{36}$$

$$r_t = (1 - a)L_t^a K_t^{1-a}, \tag{37}$$

and

$$S_t = s_L w_t L_t + s_K r_t K_t + s_g \tau_t w_t L_t. \tag{38}$$

K_t is the stock of capital at the *beginning* of period t. A simple model of the evolution of the capital stock is given by

$$K_t = (1 - \delta)K_{t-1} + S_{t-1}, \tag{39}$$

where δ is a constant proportional rate of decay of the capital stock. Introducing a decay rate does not alter any qualitative equilibrium behavior but does permit more realistic parameter values.[17] Finally, the growth of the labor supply is specified by

$$L_t = \lambda w_t^\eta (1 + n)^t. \tag{40}$$

These six equations can be evaluated in each year for the six variables $Y_t, w_t, r_t, S_t, L_t,$ and K_t. The initial conditions are set by assuming that at

17. The assumption of a *constant proportional* rate of decay when the economy is not in steady-state growth is a crude but common approximation. See Chapter 16.

$t = 0$ the economy is on a balanced growth path with no tax and by selecting units of measurement so that the initial stock of labor (L_0) is 1. The balanced growth condition is $S_0 = (n + \delta)K_0$. Evaluating S_0 at $L_0 = 1$ implies that

$$K_0 = \left(\frac{as_L + (1 - a)s_K}{n + \delta}\right)^{1/a}. \tag{41}$$

Substituting in Eqs. (36) and (37) then gives the initial factor prices. The value of λ in Eq. (40) is found by substituting $L_0 = 1$ and w_0.

For a numerical example I have examined first the special case in which all savings rates are equal; more specifically, $s_L = s_K = s_G = 0.2$. The labor coefficient of the production function is $a = 0.7$. The supply of labor is an increasing function of the net wage with supply elasticity $\eta = 1$. The growth and decay rates are $n = 0.03$ and $\delta = 0.04$. In steady-state growth before the imposition of the tax, the capital-output ratio is $s/(n + \delta)$ $= 2.86$. The rate of return on capital is 0.105, and the wage rate is 1.098. A 20 percent tax on net labor income is then introduced; $\tau = 0.20$. Because $s_L = s_G$, all of the tax is borne by labor in the very long run. By contrast, in the very short run the stock of capital is fixed; because the labor supply falls in response to the tax, the short-run burden of the tax is divided between labor and capital.

More specifically, in the first year after the introduction of the tax, the wage rate falls 13 percent to 0.956, and the rate of return on capital falls 9 percent to 0.0947. The less rapid accumulation of capital that follows depresses the capital-labor ratio until, in the new steady-state growth equilibrium, the wage rate falls to 0.915. Columns 1 and 2 of Table 18.4 show the path of the wage rate and rate of return at ten- and twenty-year intervals. It is clear that a period of twenty years is required for the rate of return to recover half of its initial loss. In this same twenty-year period, the wage rate falls half of the distance from its initial posttax equilibrium to the final steady-state loss. An additional twenty-year period is required to halve the remaining gaps.

A very special feature of this example is the equality of all the savings rates. The proportion of national income that is saved is therefore unaffected by the introduction of the tax. Although this specification influences the eventual equilibrium growth path, it does not as such alter the speed of adjustment. This is seen by modifying the previous example by setting $s_G = 0$. The tax therefore decreases the overall saving rate, raises the equilibrium rate of return, and further lowers the equilibrium wage rate. The specific time paths shown in columns 3 and 4 of Table 18.4

Table 18.4. Path of adjustment to tax change

Year	Equal savings rates		$S_L = S_K$ and $S_G = 0$	
	w_t (1)	r_t (2)	w_t (3)	r_t (4)
1	0.956	0.0947	0.954	0.0952
10	0.945	0.0974	0.930	0.1009
20	0.936	0.0997	0.911	0.1059
40	0.925	0.1024	0.889	0.1124
60	0.920	0.1038	0.878	0.1157
80	0.917	0.1044	0.872	0.1173
100	0.916	0.1047	0.870	0.1181
120	0.915	0.1049	0.869	0.1185
140	0.915	0.1049	0.868	0.1187
160	0.915	0.1050	0.868	0.1188
No tax	1.098	0.1050	1.098	0.1050

Note: See text for specific assumptions and parameter values.

again show that a period of twenty years is required for half of the adjustment from the initial posttax values to the final equilibrium values.

The important implication of these two examples is that the rate of adjustment may be very slow. Although the supply elasticity of labor has no effect on the ultimate steady-state growth path, it does continue to influence the incidence of the tax for a very long time. If the supply of labor is reduced when the wage falls, labor will bear a smaller fraction of the total burden, and the rate of return will fall correspondingly.

Conclusion

This chapter has emphasized that the incidence of any tax depends on the net effect of the tax on relative factor supplies. If the supply of the taxed factor is fixed, that factor will bear the entire burden of the tax. If the supply of the taxed factor falls relative to the supply of the untaxed factor, the tax burden will be divided between them.

The specific analyses focused on a general payroll tax on labor income. The first section examined the incidence of the tax in a general equilibrium framework with variable supplies of labor and capital. Any comparative static analysis ignores the interdependence of labor supply and capital accumulation in a growing economy. A simple growth model in which the per capita labor supply depends on the wage rate and the savings propensities out of labor and capital income depend on the rate of return was used to analyze long-run tax incidence in the third section. The conclusions are quite surprising. The incidence of the tax in the new steady-state equilibrium is completely independent of the extent to which the supply of labor responds to the net wage. The distribution of the burden of the tax depends only on the effect of the tax on the economy's overall saving propensity and the technological characteristic of production. Labor bears exactly 100 percent of the entire tax burden if and only if the tax has no effect on the overall saving propensity.

Because the economy adjusts slowly from the immediate posttax equilibrium to the ultimate steady-state growth path, the eventual irrelevance of the elasticity of labor supply should not disguise its potential short-run importance. If technology is sufficiently malleable, the comparative static results provide an appropriate description of the short-run effect of the tax. Some specific numerical examples of the economy's path of adjustment, presented in the fourth section, indicate that some twenty years are required to complete half of the adjustment from the initial posttax values to the final steady-state equilibrium. For a very long time, therefore, it remains true that the incidence of a tax in a growing economy depends on the supply elasticities of labor and capital.

A final caveat is appropriate. All of the conclusions in this chapter have been based on simple one-sector competitive models of the economy. More general models are necessary to examine the implications of relaxing these restrictive assumptions. Only better empirical analysis, however, will permit the assumptions to be more realistic without making the conclusions more ambiguous.

19 Incidence of a Capital Income Tax in a Growing Economy with Variable Savings Rates

The theory of economic growth has emphasized that the capital stock, unlike the labor force, is not an "original" factor of production but represents the accumulation of past incomes.[1] Any analysis of the incidence of a tax on capital income should therefore begin by considering how the tax affects the stock of capital. Although a comparative static analysis with a varying capital stock can be instructive, the process of capital accumulation is represented best by a model of economic growth.

The purpose of this chapter is to examine how savings behavior affects the long-run incidence of a tax on profits[2] in a growing economy. The analysis is in terms of a general tax on all capital income, but the results are obviously relevant to understanding the incidence of the corporate income tax. With a fixed capital stock, owners of capital would bear the entire burden of a general tax on profits[3] and would avoid some of the burden of a partial tax on capital (such as the corporate income tax) to the extent that capital can shift away from the taxed sector to the untaxed sector without significantly reducing the marginal product of capital in the untaxed sector. Harberger's analysis (1962) of such a model has shown that, with reasonable parameter values, the U.S. corporate income tax is borne almost entirely by capital and is therefore quite similar in incidence to a general tax on capital income with a fixed capital stock.

This chapter shows that replacing the usual static model and fixed capi-

Reprinted from the *Review of Economic Studies* 41 (October 1974), pp. 505–513, by permission of the Society of Economic Analysis Ltd.

1. The emphasis on this distinction between capital and labor is much older than modern growth theory and can be traced at least to Shove's important review (1933) of Hicks's *Theory of Wages* (1932).

2. The terms "profits" and "capital income" are used interchangeably. Interest income would therefore be included with profits.

3. Mieszkowski (1969) notes this in his very useful survey of tax incidence and, because he only considers the case of fixed capital and labor, provides no further analysis of the incidence of general factor taxes.

tal stock by a model of a growing economy with variable savings rates substantially alters the conclusions about the incidence of a general tax on profits. For a wide range of plausible parameter values, a substantial fraction of the burden of a general profits tax is borne by labor. The assumption of a fixed capital stock may, therefore, also yield quite misleading conclusions in the analysis of the corporate income tax.

The Effects of a Profits Tax

The current analysis distinguishes separate savings propensities out of capital and labor incomes. This specification is an approximation to the important characteristic of modern economies that a great deal of the capital stock is owned and accumulated by a relatively small group for whom capital income is much greater than labor income.[4] Taxes affect the accumulation of capital through changes in the factor distribution of disposable income and, by altering the net yield on capital, through changes in the savings propensities. The transfer of revenues from the private sector to the government will reduce capital accumulation if the government does not itself save some part of marginal tax receipts. This section assumes no government capital accumulation, while the next section abstracts from this problem by comparing the incidence of equal yield taxes on capital and labor incomes.

The technology of the economy may be summarized by the production function

$$y = f(k), \tag{1}$$

where y is output per man and k is capital per man. No restrictions will be imposed on the form of the production function. The *local* elasticity of substitution, which will be denoted σ, need not be constant.

The population grows at rate n. The labor force participation rate is assumed to be constant; relaxing this assumption would not alter the long-run incidence of the tax.[5] Similarly, ignoring technical progress and depreciation has no effect on the current analysis.

---

4. The current analysis is therefore complementary with Diamond's study (1970) in which all capital accumulation represents life-cycle saving by workers who earn and save in the first period of their life and retire and dissave in the second period.

5. In Chapter 18 I showed that the elasticity of labor supply with respect to the wage rate does not affect the incidence of a tax on labor income. The analysis presented there indicates that the same conclusion is applicable to a tax on capital income.

The equality of marginal products and gross factor prices implies

$$f' = r(1 + t) \tag{2}$$

and

$$y - kf' = w, \tag{3}$$

where r is the net rate of return and w is the wage rate. The tax at rate t is expressed as a fraction of the net rate of return. If the tax were levied at rate θ on the gross rate, Eq. (2) would instead be $(1 - \theta)f' = r$; the two methods of taxation are therefore equivalent for $(1 - \theta)^{-1} = 1 + t$.

Savings per man (s) is

$$s = S_L w + S_K rk, \tag{4}$$

where S_L and S_K are the propensities to save out of net labor and capital incomes. The propensities are related to the net rate of return by

$$S_L = S_L(r) \tag{5}$$

and

$$S_K = S_K(r). \tag{6}$$

The savings rate elasticities will be denoted $E_L = rS_L^{-1}(dS_L/dr)$ and $E_K = rS_K^{-1}(dS_K/dr)$.

The equilibrium condition for steady-state growth is that all saving is invested and therefore that

$$s = nk. \tag{7}$$

These seven equations describe a complete model for the seven variables y, k, r, w, s, S_L, and S_K.[6]

The usual way to measure the incidence of a factor tax is to compare the changes in total net profits and total labor income. Since the current

---

6. Krzyzaniak (1967) and Sato (1967) studied a special case of this model in which the technology is Cobb-Douglas and savings propensities are constant ($E_K = E_L = 0$). Their savings functions are somewhat different from Eq. (4).

analysis recognizes that the tax alters the size of the capital stock, such a measure of incidence is inappropriate. More specifically, a small change in the tax rate alters total net profits per capita by

$$\frac{d(rk)}{dt} = k\frac{dr}{dt} + r\frac{dk}{dt}. \tag{8}$$

While the first term on the right-hand side represents an unambiguous loss to the owners of capital (or gain if $dr/dt > 0$), the second term represents only a change in the timing of consumption. Since the net rate of return measures (to a first-order approximation) the value of the individuals' time preference, this change in the timing of consumption represents no net gain or loss of utility. The appropriate analysis of tax incidence is therefore based on $k(dr/dt)$, the effect of the tax change on the income attributable to the original capital stock.[7]

The incidence of a *new* tax is conveniently measured by the ratio of capital's loss $(-kdr)$ to the tax revenue $(rkdt)$. I shall refer to this measure as capital's *tax share ratio*. The analysis is more complex when a preexisting tax is changed. The additional tax revenue is then not $rkdt$ but $rkdt + rtdk + ktdr$. The incremental tax revenue is less than the combined loss of labor income (dw) and adjusted capital income (kdr); that is, there is a welfare loss (or excess burden) even to a first-order approximation. The capital tax share ratio is therefore an ambiguous measure of incidence since the sum of the capital and labor tax share is less than one. The incidence of an increase in a preexisting tax is therefore better measured by the ratio of capital's loss $[-kdr]$ to the total loss of real income $[-(kdr + dw)]$. I shall refer to this ratio as capital's *income share ratio*. For the introduction of a new tax, the tax share ratio and the income share ratio are obviously equivalent.

---

7. The assertion that the second term (dk/dt) can be ignored because a small change in timing of consumption involves no net change in utility can be illustrated by a simple two-period model of consumption. Let $U(C_1, C_2)$ be the utility of an individual who consumes C_1 in period 1 and C_2 in period 2. Let Y_1 be the initial endowment (including labor income in period 1) and Y_2 be the labor income of period 2. The individual's budget constraint is thus $(Y_1 - C_1)(1 + r) + Y_2 = C_2$. The capital stock of such an individual (that is, the analog of k in Eq. [8]) is equivalent to the assets that remain after consuming C_1, that is, $Y_1 - C_1 = (C_2 - Y_2)/(1 + r)$. A decrease in the capital stock (with fixed values of Y_1, Y_2, and r) is given by $dC_1 = - dC_2/(1 + r)$. The utility change associated with such a redistribution is (with $U_i = \partial U/\partial C_i$): $dU = U_1 dC_1 + U_2 dC_2 = U_1 dC_1 - U_2 dC_1(1 + r)$. Since the first-order condition for maximizing $U(C_1, C_2)$ subject to $(Y_1 - C_1)(1 + r) + Y_2 = C_2$ is $U_1 = (1 + r)U_2$, it follows that $dU = 0$.

It will be convenient for later analysis to derive dr/dt and dw/dt by first obtaining dk/dt, the effect of the tax on capital intensity. Combining Eqs. (2), (3), (4), and (7) yields

$$nk = S_L(y - kf') + S_K kf'(1 + t)^{-1}. \tag{9}$$

Totally differentiating Eq. (9), substituting for dr from the total derivative of Eq. (2) and for n from Eq. (9) itself, yields after some simplification:[8]

$$\frac{dk}{dt} = -\frac{k}{1 + t}\frac{\sigma}{\alpha}\left\{\frac{\alpha E_L S_L + (1 - \alpha)S_K(1 + E_K)(1 + t)^{-1}}{S_L(\alpha + \sigma - 1 + \alpha E_L) + S_K(1 - \alpha)(1 + E_K)(1 + t)^{-1}}\right\}, \tag{10}$$

where α is the share of wages in total income and $1 - \alpha$ is therefore the share of *gross* profits in total income. Since $r = (1 + t)^{-1}f'$, it follows that

$$\frac{dr}{dt} = \frac{f''}{(1 + t)}\frac{dk}{dt} - \frac{f'}{(1 + t)^2}. \tag{11}$$

Similarly, from $w = f - kf'$, we obtain

$$\frac{dw}{dt} = -kf''\frac{dk}{dt}. \tag{12}$$

Consider now an increase in the rate of an existing tax; the corresponding results for the introduction of a new tax can then be seen as a special case. It follows from Eqs. (10), (11), and (12) that the income share ratio is (Appendix A.2):

$$\frac{kdr}{kdr + dw} = \frac{1}{1 + J}, \tag{13}$$

where

$$J = \frac{(1 + t)\alpha E_L + (1 - \alpha)\left(\dfrac{S_K}{S_L}\right)(1 + E_K)}{\alpha + \sigma - 1}. \tag{14}$$

8. A complete derivation is presented in section (A.1) of the Appendix. Other derivations that are omitted in the chapter but presented in the Appendix are indicated in the text by giving the relevant Appendix section number.

For all plausible sets of parameter values, $J > 0$ and the income share ratio is therefore less than one. Labor as well as capital bears part of the burden of the profits tax.

The assumption of a Cobb-Douglas technology ($\sigma = 1$) with savings rates that are fixed ($E_K = E_L = 0$) provides a conservative illustration of the magnitude of tax shifting implied by Eqs. (13) and (14). With these assumptions, the income share ratio is

$$\frac{kdr}{kdr + dw} = \frac{1}{1 + \dfrac{S_K}{S_L}\dfrac{1 - \alpha}{\alpha}}. \tag{15}$$

If labor receives two-thirds of national income ($\alpha = \frac{2}{3}$) and the savings propensities are equal ($S_K = S_L$), the income share ratio is two-thirds; that is, capital shifts away one-third of the tax. If the saving propensity of capital is twice that of labor ($S_K = 2S_L$), Eq. (15) implies that the burden of the profits tax is divided equally between capital and labor.

In the special case in which there is no saving from labor income ($S_L = 0$), Eqs. (13) and (14) imply that capital bears none of the burden of a tax on capital income. This follows directly from Eqs. (4) and (7) of the basic model. With $S_L = 0$, the equilibrium condition for steady-state growth is $S_K rk = nk$. Since S_K depends only on r, this condition implies that there is a unique value of r for each value of n. Since changes in the tax do not alter r, capital bears none of the tax.

More generally, it is clear from Eq. (13) that any increase in J reduces capital's share of the tax burden. Equation (14) shows that J increases with the savings elasticities (E_L and E_K), with the relative savings propensities (S_K/S_L), and with the preexisting tax rate (if $E_L > 0$). The value of J is particularly sensitive to the elasticity of substitution, σ; since $\alpha - 1$ is approximately $-\frac{1}{3}$, reducing σ from 1 to $\frac{2}{3}$ would double J. For the introduction of a new tax, the only difference in this analysis is that $t = 0$ in Eq. (14).

These calculations have shown a very substantial shifting of a general tax on profits. The magnitude of this effect is due in part to the assumption that the government does no investment with its tax revenue. The transfer of funds from the private sector to the government therefore decreases national saving and reduces the capital intensity of production. This lowers the real wage and increases the gross rate of return. This section is therefore relevant for analyzing the distributional effect of government spending financed by a profits tax.[9] An important alternative question is the difference in distributional impact of using a profits tax or a payroll tax to finance a given level of government spending. Such an analysis of the differential incidence of the two taxes abstracts from the effect on capital formation of transferring funds from the private sector to the public sector. The differential incidence depends on how the taxes alter capital accumulation out of a fixed disposable income. I now turn to this question.

A Comparison of Equal Yield Taxes

This section compares the effects on capital income of using either a profits tax or a payroll tax to raise a given amount of revenue. The tax on labor income can be introduced in the model of the previous section by replacing the wage equation (Eq. [3]) by

$$f - kf' = (1 + \tau)w, \tag{16}$$

where τ is the rate of tax on the net wage.

An explicit comparison of equal yield profits and payroll taxes is simplest to obtain and easiest to understand if attention is limited to the introduction of a new tax in the absence of all other taxes. In this case, the loss of real capital income per unit of profits tax revenue is $-kdr/rkdt = -r^{-1}(dr/dt)$. Similarly, the loss of real capital income per unit of payroll tax revenue is $-kdr/wd\tau = -k/w(dr/d\tau)$. To obtain equal revenue from the profits tax and the payroll tax, the required tax rates (dt and $d\tau$) are inversely proportional to the pretax factor shares in national income: $d\tau = [(1 - \alpha)/\alpha]dt$, where α is the pretax share of labor in national income.[10]

The excess loss of capital income if the profits tax is used instead of the payroll tax is therefore

$$D = -\frac{1}{r}\frac{dr}{dt} + \frac{k}{w}\frac{dr}{d\tau}, \tag{17}$$

---

9. This assumes that the government spending does not induce additional private saving. This section is analogous to "balanced budget incidence analysis" in static models of incidence; see Musgrave (1959).

10. Since the yield of the profits tax is $rkdt$ and the yield of the payroll tax is $wd\tau$, the tax rates have equal yields if $d\tau = (rk/w)dt$ or $d\tau = [(1 - \alpha)/\alpha]dt$.

where dt and $d\tau$ represent equal yield taxes. For the profits tax, it can be shown (Appendix A.3) from Eqs. (10) and (11) that

$$-\frac{1}{r}\frac{dr}{dt} = \frac{(\alpha + \sigma - 1)S_L}{S_L(\alpha + \sigma - 1 + \alpha E_L) + S_K(1 + E_K)(1 - \alpha)}. \tag{18}$$

For the payroll tax, Eq. (10) is replaced by

$$\frac{dr}{d\tau} = f''\frac{dk}{d\tau}. \tag{19}$$

The steady-state equilibrium is characterized by

$$nk = S_L(f - kf')(1 + \tau)^{-1} + S_K kf'. \tag{20}$$

Totally differentiating Eq. (20) and using Eq. (19) yields (Appendix A.4):

$$\frac{dk}{d\tau} = -\frac{k}{(1 + \tau)}\frac{\sigma S_L}{S_L(\alpha + \sigma - 1 + \alpha E_L) + S_K(1 - \alpha)(1 + E_K)(1 + \tau)}. \tag{21}$$

Combining Eqs. (19) and (21) and simplifying, we obtain (at $\tau = 0$):

$$\frac{k}{w}\frac{dr}{d\tau} = \frac{(1 - \alpha)S_L}{S_L(\alpha + \sigma - 1 + \alpha E_L) + S_K(1 - \alpha)(1 + E_K)}. \tag{22}$$

Substituting Eqs. (18) and (22) into Eq. (17) gives the fundamental equation for the differential loss of capital income:

$$D = \frac{\sigma}{\alpha + \sigma - 1 + \alpha E_L + \left(\dfrac{S_K}{S_L}\right)(1 + E_K)(1 - \alpha)}. \tag{23}$$

If a profits tax is used, the owners of capital lose D dollars more per dollar of tax revenue than they would if a payroll tax were used. If D is one, capital bears the entire burden of a shift from a payroll tax to a profits tax.[11] If D is less than one, capital is able to shift part of the burden; that is,

11. Recall that for the introduction of a new tax there is no excess burden to a first-order approximation.

switching the nominal tax base from labor to capital does not lower real capital income by the amount of the tax.

In the special case in which the savings propensities out of capital income and labor income are equal ($S_K = S_L$) and are not affected by the rate of interest ($E_K = E_L = 0$), the value of D is one and real capital income falls by the entire amount of the tax that is switched from the profits base to the payroll base. However, more plausible assumptions imply that capital is able to shift a substantial fraction of the tax. It is clear from Eq. (23) that the differential incidence on capital is reduced if $S_K > S_L$, if $E_K > 0$, or if $E_L > 0$.

To appreciate the order of magnitude of these effects, consider first the case in which savings is interest-inelastic ($E_K = E_L = 0$) but the savings propensity out of capital income exceeds the savings propensity out of labor income. With these assumptions, Eq. (23) reduces to

$$D = \frac{1}{1 + \left(\dfrac{S_K}{S_L} - 1\right)\dfrac{1 - \alpha}{\sigma}}. \tag{24}$$

For $\sigma = 1$, $\alpha = \frac{2}{3}$, and $S_K/S_L = 2$, this implies $D = 0.75$. Capital avoids 25 percent of the tax burden.[12] A lower value of σ increases the shifting and a higher value decreases it.

Alternatively, if the savings propensities are equal ($S_K = S_L$) but have equal nonzero elasticities with respect to the net rate of return ($E_K = E_L = E \neq 0$), Eq. (23) becomes

$$D = \frac{1}{1 + E/\sigma}. \tag{25}$$

For values of E between one-quarter and one-half,[13] a Cobb-Douglas technology ($\sigma = 1$) implies values of D between 0.67 and 0.80. The value of D again varies inversely with σ.

12. This compares with a 50 percent shifting when the profits tax was compared to no tax rather than to the payroll tax.

13. The empirical evidence on the relation between savings and the rate of interest is inconclusive. Although most studies of the consumption function have found no significant effect of the interest rate, all of this work has used the nominal interest rate instead of the real interest rate. I showed that this is likely to result in a very substantial bias toward zero (Feldstein 1970).

Combining unequal savings propensities and interest-elastic saving has a more than additive effect on the magnitude of shifting:

$$D = \cfrac{1}{1 + \left(\dfrac{S_K}{S_L} - 1\right)\dfrac{1 - \alpha}{\sigma} + \dfrac{\alpha E}{\sigma} + \left(\dfrac{S_K}{S_L}\right)\dfrac{E(1 - \alpha)}{\sigma}}. \qquad (26)$$

Thus in a Cobb-Douglas economy with $\alpha = \frac{2}{3}$, if $S_K = 2S_L$ and $E = \frac{1}{3}$, $D = \frac{9}{17}$. Even if $S_K = 1.5\ S_L$ and $E = 0.25$, capital shifts more than one-third of the burden to labor; $D = \frac{24}{37}$.

In short, quite plausible assumptions about savings behavior imply that the differential incidence of a profits tax (in place of a payroll tax) is divided between capital and labor with capital bearing the larger share but labor still bearing a significant portion.

Concluding Remarks

The traditional theory of tax incidence emphasized that a general factor tax is borne entirely by the factor on which the tax is levied. In contrast, this chapter shows that in the long run the burden of a general profits tax is more likely to be divided between capital and labor. This shifting of the tax is particularly large for a balanced budget tax change in which an increased profits tax is used to finance additional government spending. But even a differential tax change in which a profits tax is substituted for a payroll tax is likely to be shifted by a substantial amount.

The magnitude of the tax shifting depends on the effect of the tax on the fraction of income that is saved and thus on the capital intensity of production. The effect of the tax on the overall savings rate depends on the difference in savings propensities between capital and labor and on the elasticity of these savings rates to the net rate of interest. The capital intensity of production is quite sensitive to changes in this overall savings rate. The elasticity of the capital intensity with respect to the overall savings rate is equal to the inverse of labor's pretax share of national income (α) and is therefore significantly greater than one.[14]

In his important analysis of the corporation tax, Harberger (1962) incorrectly assumed the opposite, that is, that the percentage excess of the capital stock in the presence of any tax over the capital stock in its absence

---

14. If the overall savings rate is denoted $S(= s/y)$, the condition for equilibrium growth is $Sy = nk$. Totally differentiating yields $ydS + Sf'dk = ndk$. Thus $dk/dS = y(n - Sf')^{-1} = yS^{-1}(k^{-1}y - f')^{-1} = yS^{-1}k(y - kf')^{-1} = S^{-1}k/\alpha$. For the elasticity, $(S/k)(dk/dS) = \alpha^{-1}$.

can "never be greater than the percentage excess of the savings rate that would have existed in the absence of the tax over the savings rate in the presence of the tax " (pp. 235–236). He therefore underestimated the effect of a change in savings on the capital intensity of the economy and concluded inappropriately that "allowing for a rather substantial effect of the corporate income tax on the rate of saving leads to only a minor modification of my overall conclusion that capital bears close to the full burden of the tax" (p. 236). In contrast, the current results suggest that capital may avoid a substantial portion of the burden of the tax if the corporation tax does have a significant effect on the overall savings rate, that is, if $S_K > S_L$ or the savings propensities are interest-sensitive or both. It would be useful to examine this question explicitly by extending the present analysis to look at partial factor taxes in a two-sector model with an endogenous capital stock.[15]

The most basic conclusion of this chapter is the importance of considering capital formation in the analysis of tax incidence. The simple growth model considered here shows the possibility of substantial shifting of general factor taxes. It therefore raises doubts about previous theoretical estimates of the incidence of partial taxes on products and factor incomes. It is clear that much remains to be done to develop both more general theoretical models and a better empirical basis with which to study the relation between capital accumulation and tax incidence.

Appendix

This appendix derives a number of the results used in the text. The appendix is divided into sections to permit easy reference in the chapter. Text equations are referred to by number and appendix equations are identified by section, for example (A.1.1).

Section (A.1)

This section derives Eq. (10) for dk/dt. Equation (9) states (writing f instead of y):

$$nk = S_L f - S_L k f' + S_R k f'(1 + t)^{-1}. \tag{A.1.1}$$

---

15. Feldstein (Chapter 18) and Shoven and Whalley (1972) have analyzed comparative static models with an endogenous capital stock. Because these are not growth models, the response of the capital stock is rather arbitrary and does not reflect the process of capital accumulation.

Totally differentiating gives

$$ndk = fS_L'dr + S_Lf'dk - S_Lf'dk - S_Lkf''dk - kf'S_L'dr + S_Kf'(1 + t)^{-1}dk$$

$$+ S_Kk(1 + t)^{-1}f''dk - S_Kkf'(1 + t)^{-2}dt + kf'(1 + t)^{-1}S_K'dr. \tag{A.1.2}$$

From Eq. (3),

$$dr = f''(1 + t)^{-1}dk - f'(1 + t)^{-2}dt. \tag{A.1.3}$$

Substituting in Eq. (A.1.2) for dr (from [A.1.3]) and for n (from [A.1.1]) yields an equation in terms of dk and dt:

$$[S_Lfk^{-1} - S_Lf' + S_Kf'(1 + t)^{-1} - fS_L'f''(1 + t)^{-1} + S_Lkf''$$

$$+ kf'S_L'f''(1 + t)^{-1} - S_Kf'(1 + t)^{-1} - S_Kkf''(1 + t)^{-1}$$

$$- kf'f''S_K'(1 + t)^{-2}]dk = -[fS_L'f'(1 + t)^{-2} - k(f')^2S_L'(1 + t)^{-2}$$

$$+_{\scriptscriptstyle\uparrow} S_Kkf'(1 + t)^{-2} + k(f')^2S_K'(1 + t)^{-3}]dt. \tag{A.1.4}$$

This can be simplified by using $E_L = S_L'r/S_L = f'S_L'(1 + t)^{-1}S_L^{-1}$ and $E_K = f'S_K'(1 + t)^{-1}S_K^{-1}$. Capital's pretax share of income is kf'/f and is denoted $1 - \alpha$. Labor's share is $(f - kf')/f = \alpha$. Finally, $\sigma = -\alpha f'/kf''$ is the local elasticity of substitution (R.G.D. Allen, *Mathematical Analysis for Economists*, p. 340). These terms can be used to simplify (A.1.4) to Eq. (10) in the text.

Section (A.2)

This section derives capital's income share ratio, Eqs. (13) and (14) in the text. From Eqs. (11) and (12) we obtain

$$\frac{kdr}{kdr + dw} = \frac{kf''(1 + t)^{-1}(dk/dt) - kf'(1 + t)^{-2}}{kf''(1 + t)^{-1}(dk/dt) - kf'(1 + t)^{-2} - kf''\dfrac{dk}{dt}}. \tag{A.2.1}$$

Factoring out $k(1 + t)^{-2}$ and dividing the numerator into the denominator gives

$$\frac{kdr}{kdr + dw} = \frac{1}{1 + J},$$
(A.2.2)

where

$$J = \frac{-(1 + t)^2 f''(dk/dt)}{f''(1 + t)(dk/dt) - f'}.$$
(A.2.3)

Substituting for (dk/dt) from Eq. (10) yields

$$J = \frac{(1 + t)^2 f''[k\sigma/\alpha(1 + t)]\{\alpha E_L S_L + (1 - \alpha)S_K(1 + E_K)(1 + t)^{-1}\}}{-f''(1 + t)[k\sigma/\alpha(1 + t)]\{\alpha E_L S_L + (1 - \alpha)S_K(1 + E_K)(1 + t)^{-1}\}}$$

$$- f'\{S_L(\alpha + \sigma - 1 + \alpha E_L) + S_K(1 - \alpha)(1 + E_K)(1 + t)^{-1}\}.$$
(A.2.4)

Since $\sigma = -\alpha f'/kf''$, Eq. (A.2.4) simplifies immediately to Eq. (14) of the text.

Section (A.3)

To obtain $-r^{-1}(dr/dt)$, we note that $r = (1 + t)^{-1}f'$ and use Eq. (11) to yield

$$-\frac{1}{r}\frac{dr}{dt} = -\frac{f''}{f'}\frac{dk}{dt} + \frac{1}{1 + t}.$$
(A.3.1)

Using Eq. (10) for dk/dt and setting $t = 0$ gives:

$$-\frac{1}{r}\frac{dr}{dt} = \frac{f''}{f'}\frac{k\sigma}{\alpha}\left\{\frac{\alpha E_L S_L + (1 - \alpha)S_K(1 + E_K)}{S_L(\alpha + \sigma - 1 + \alpha E_L) + S_K(1 - \alpha)(1 + E_K)}\right\} + 1.$$
(A.3.2)

Since $\sigma = -\alpha f'/kf''$, we have

$$-\frac{1}{r}\frac{dr}{dt} = 1 - \frac{\alpha E_L S_L + (1 - \alpha)S_K(1 + E_K)}{S_L(\alpha + \sigma - 1 + \alpha E_L) + S_K(1 - \alpha)(1 + E_K)}.$$
(A.3.3)

Equation (18) follows directly.

Section (A.4)

The derivation of $dk/d\tau$ is parallel to section (A.1). Equation (20) is:

$$nk = S_L f(1 + \tau)^{-1} - S_L kf'(1 + \tau)^{-1} + S_K kf'. \qquad \text{(A.4:1)}$$

Since there is no tax on profits ($t = 0$), we have $dr = f''dk$. Totally differentiating (A.4.1) therefore gives

$$ndk = S_L(1 + \tau)^{-1}f'dk + f(1 + \tau)^{-1}S_L'f''dk - S_L f(1 + \tau)^{-2}d\tau$$

$$- S_L kf''(1 + \tau)^{-1}dk - S_L f'(1 + \tau)^{-1}dk - kf'S_L'f''(1 + \tau)^{-1}dk$$

$$+ S_L kf'(1 + \tau)^{-2}d\tau + S_K kf''dk + S_K f'dk + kf'S_K'f''dk. \quad \text{(A.4.2)}$$

Collecting terms and substituting τ, E_K, E_L, and σ yields Eq. (21). From Eqs. (19) and (21) we obtain (at $\tau = 0$):

$$\frac{k}{w}\frac{dr}{d\tau} = -\frac{kf''}{w} \frac{k\sigma S_L}{S_L(\alpha + \sigma - 1 + \alpha E_L) + S_K(1 - \alpha)(1 + E_K)}.$$
$$\text{(A.4.3)}$$

But $-kf''k\sigma/w = -(f'k/w)(f''k\sigma/f') = -(f''k\sigma/f')(1 - \alpha)/\alpha$. Since $\sigma = -\alpha f'/kf''$, we obtain $-kf''k\sigma/w = 1 - \alpha$. Equation (A.4.3) is therefore equivalent to Eq. (22).

20 The Surprising Incidence of a Tax on Pure Rent: A New Answer to an Old Question

The classic example of an unshiftable tax has been the general tax on pure rental income.[1] Ever since Ricardo, economists have believed that the annual net rental income of unimproved land falls by the amount of the annual tax and that the price of the land falls by the capitalized value of this tax. This chapter will show that these conclusions are false, that the tax on pure land rents is at least partly shifted, and that the price of land may actually be increased by the imposition of a tax.

The reasoning that leads to the traditional conclusion can be summarized briefly: consider a one-good economy in which a tax on the pure rents of unimproved land is used to finance some additional government expenditure that does not increase utility vis-à-vis the no-tax situation.[2] In the static, general-equilibrium theory of tax incidence, a tax can be shifted only by reducing the supply of the taxed activity. For if the level of the taxed activity does not change, the original set of gross prices continues to be the solution of the economy's general-equilibrium system. With the original gross prices, the only net price that changes is the price of the taxed factor. Since the prices of all of the other goods and factors remain unchanged, the taxed factor bears the entire burden of the tax. The general tax on the rents of unimproved land is a clear case in which the taxed activity cannot be varied.

Reprinted from the *Journal of Political Economy* 85 (April 1977), pp. 349–360, by permission of the University of Chicago Press. Copyright © 1977 by the University of Chicago. I am grateful to John Flemming, Jerry Green, Thomas Schelling, Eytan Sheshinski, and Richard Zeckhauser for comments on a previous draft.

1. The analysis goes back at least to Ricardo (1951) and has been reasserted by Pigou (1947), Dalton (1954), and later writers.
2. For example, an exogenous change in international conditions that requires a tax to maintain the previous level of national security. The assumption of an economy with a single good avoids any effect of the tax on the composition of a demand. It is important to recognize that this is a crucial assumption. The conclusions of both the traditional analysis and of my own study would be different if the revenue were used to accumulate capital, to finance transfer payments to the aged, and so on.

It is clear that this analysis is false if the tax on pure land rent has income effects that alter the supplies of labor or capital. For example, if the landowners were also the farmers who worked the land, the income effect of a tax on the pure land rent (presumably imputed) might cause the landlord farmers to work harder. This would raise the ratio of labor services to land and would therefore increase the pretax land rent. To preclude this form of shifting, the analysis must specify that the landowners are pure landowners who do not supply labor or capital.[3] Even if this assumption is made, factor prices will change if the proceeds of the tax on pure land rents are distributed as lump-sum payments or as reductions in a pre-existing lump-sum tax. For example, laborers who receive lump-sum transfers are likely to reduce their labor supply, causing a fall in the pretax land rent. This type of differential tax incidence thus suggests that landlords would bear more than 100 percent of the tax. The traditional conclusion that the landlords bear exactly 100 percent of the tax therefore rests on the two assumptions that the government's use of the tax proceeds does not change anyone's well-being and that landlords do not supply any other factors of production.[4] These two assumptions are sufficient to eliminate any shifting through income effects.

But even if income effects are excluded, the traditional analysis is wrong in two important ways. First, it overlooks the fact that, because land is an asset, a tax on rent can change the supply of other factors even if there are no income effects. The first two sections of this chapter will examine the way in which the tax causes an increase in the accumulation of produced capital and will assess the effects of this induced capital accumulation. Second, the traditional theory ignores the effect of the portfolio balance requirements; this is the subject of the third section. A brief concluding section comments on issues of efficiency and directions in which the current analysis can be extended.

A Model of Savings Equilibrium with a Tax on Pure Land Rent

The essential oversight of the classical analysis is to ignore the fact that land and produced capital are alternative components of individual life-cycle wealth. Each generation wishes to accumulate a certain level of wealth with which to finance retirement in old age.[5] If the tax on pure land

3. I believe that this assumption that landlords are a distinct class was at least implicit in the early theory of this subject and was historically justified.

4. As note 2 indicates, it is not necessary to assume that the tax proceeds are wasted.

5. I ignore for the moment the important fact that this desired level of wealth depends on the rate of return. I deal with this below.

rent reduces the value of land, a larger amount of the desired wealth must be accumulated in the form of produced capital. The tax on rental income thus induces an increase in the equilibrium capital stock and therefore in the equilibrium ratio of capital to land. This raises the marginal productivity of land and reduces the rate of interest at which net land rents are capitalized. Part of the tax on pure rent is thus shifted in the form of a lower net yield on capital and a higher wage rate. Moreover, the price of land does not fall by as much as the traditional theory predicts.

This brief statement of the analysis is, of course, only indicative of the line of proof that follows. More specifically, the formal model assumes an economy with a fixed quantity of land, T, and a fixed supply of labor, L, in each generation.[6] A single commodity is produced from land, labor, and produced capital, K, according to the aggregate production function

$$X = F(K, L, T). \tag{1}$$

The usual properties of positive marginal product, constant returns to scale, and concavity are assumed.[7] It is clear that, with fixed L and T, a stable equilibrium with constant factor rewards will exist only if we assume that, corresponding to each rate of property tax, there is a fixed value of K that does not change through time.

Each member of the labor force lives two periods.[8] In the first period of his life, he works and earns a wage income equal to $W = F_L$. He saves a fraction of this and consumes the rest. The savings rate, σ, depends on the rate of interest, F_K:

$$\sigma = S(F_K). \tag{2}$$

The savings are used to purchase assets that, when he reaches the second and final period of his life, will be sold to the then young generation. The wage is paid and the consumption decision is made at the beginning of the first period. The assets are redeemed for consumption goods at the beginning of the second period.

The aggregate savings must equal the sum of the values of the assets purchased with those savings. Since we are dealing with a one-sector model, the price of capital goods is the same as the price of consumption goods. This price is taken to be the numeraire. The price of land will be

6. Not only the number of workers but also the amount of effort per worker is constant. This precludes any income effect on labor supply.

7. More specifically, $F_{ii} < 0$ and $F_{ij} > 0$ for $i \neq j$ are assumed.

8. This is the basic overlapping-generations model first presented by Samuelson (1958).

denoted p; the determinants of this price will be discussed immediately below. Therefore the savings equilibrium condition is

$$\sigma WL = K + pT. \tag{3}$$

If the marginal products of capital and land are known with certainty,[9] both assets will be held by savers only if they have the same after-tax rate of return. Therefore

$$F_K = \frac{(1 - \theta)F_T}{p}, \tag{4}$$

where θ is the rate of tax on the pure land rent F_T.[10] Substituting from Eq. (4) into Eq. (3) yields

$$\sigma WL = K + \frac{(1 - \theta)F_T T}{F_K}. \tag{5}$$

Finally, substituting $W = F_L$ and $\sigma = S(F_K)$, we obtain the basic savings equilibrium as a function of K and θ only:[11]

$$S(F_K) \cdot F_L L - \frac{(1 - \theta)F_T T}{F_K} - K = 0. \tag{6}$$

Note that the demand for produced capital is equal to the savings minus the value of the land. It will be convenient for later reference to label this

$$D = S(F_K) \cdot F_L L - \frac{(1 - \theta)F_T T}{F_K}. \tag{7}$$

Equation (6) states that the excess demand for produced capital must be zero in equilibrium. It is a further stability condition that the derivative of this excess demand with respect to K must be less than zero, that is, that

9. This is implied by the nonstochastic production function of Eq. (1). I return to the case of uncertain yields in the third section.

10. Recall that the tax revenues are assumed to be used to finance some additional government expenditure that does not increase utility vis-à-vis the no-tax situation. The same general results would be true if the revenues were paid as a lump sum to the first generation, since their labor supply is fixed. If all revenues are paid to the older age group, the traditional results are maintained.

11. Recall that L and T are fixed so that F_L, F_K, and F_T are functions of K only.

an increase in K does not induce an equally large increase in the demand for K: $\partial D/\partial K < 1$.

Effects of a Change in the Rate of Tax

An increase in the rate of tax on pure land rent causes an increase in the equilibrium capital stock. Totally differentiating Eq. (6) and making use of Eq. (7) yields

$$\left(\frac{\partial D}{\partial K} - 1\right)dK + \frac{F_T T}{F_K}\,d\theta = 0 \tag{8}$$

or

$$\frac{dK}{d\theta} = \frac{-\,TF_T/F_K}{[(\partial D/\partial K) - 1]}. \tag{9}$$

The stability condition that $\partial D/\partial K < 1$ implies $dK/d\theta > 0$.

The effects of the tax on gross factor rewards follow immediately from the increase in the capital stock and the characteristics of the technology. Since the supplies of labor and land are fixed, the increase in capital raises the wage rate (F_L) and the gross rent (F_T) but lowers the rate of interest (F_K). Part of the tax is thus shifted from land to capital; wage rates increase as a by-product.

The induced change in the capital stock may actually cause a shifting of more than 100 percent of the tax on land rent, that is, the *net* yield on land may actually *rise* when the tax is increased:

$$\frac{d(1 - \theta)F_T}{d\theta} = -F_T + (1 - \theta)F_{TK}\left(\frac{dK}{d\theta}\right), \tag{10}$$

$$= -F_T - \frac{(1 - \theta)F_{TK}TF_T/F_K}{[(\partial D/\partial K) - 1]}. \tag{11}$$

Thus $d(1 - \theta)F_T/d\theta > 0$ if and only if

$$(1 - \theta)\frac{F_{TK}T}{F_K} > 1 - \frac{\partial D}{\partial K}. \tag{12}$$

This condition can be satisfied in practice. The left-hand side is $(1 - \theta)$ times the elasticity of the marginal product of capital with respect to the supply of land. The lower the elasticity of substitution between capital and land, the higher will be this value. The right-hand side is positive but can be arbitrarily small. A specific example with a Cobb-Douglas technology will be presented in the Appendix.

Even if the net rental income falls, the value of the land will rise if the rate of interest (F_K) falls proportionately more. In this case also, the current owners of the land gain from the imposition of the tax, since they are concerned with the value at which it can be sold and transformed into consumption for their retirement period.[12] It follows from Eq. (4) that

$$\frac{dp}{d\theta} = -\frac{F_T}{F_K} + (1 - \theta)\frac{d(F_T/F_K)}{dK} \cdot \frac{dK}{d\theta}. \tag{13}$$

Since T is fixed, $[d(F_T/F_K)]/dK = F_T/(KF_K\varepsilon)$, where ε is the local elasticity of substitution between land and capital. Equation (13) therefore implies $dp/d\theta > 0$ if and only if

$$-\frac{F_T}{F_K}\left[1 + \frac{1}{\varepsilon}\frac{pT}{K}\frac{1}{(\partial D/\partial K) - 1}\right] > 0, \tag{14}$$

or, equivalently,

$$\frac{pT}{K} \cdot \frac{1}{\varepsilon} > 1 - \frac{\partial D}{\partial K}. \tag{15}$$

Since the right-hand side is bounded only by zero, this inequality is easily satisfied. Moreover, Eq. (15) can be true even if Eq. (12) is not satisfied; that is, there exist conditions under which

$$\frac{1}{\varepsilon}\frac{pT}{K} > 1 - \frac{\partial D}{\partial K} > (1 - \theta)\frac{F_{TK}T}{F_K}. \tag{16}$$

An example will be given in the Appendix.

The possibility of an increase in the price of land may rightly puzzle the reader. It would seem at first that an increase in the price of land would

---

12. It is useful to think of the landowners as the older generation at the beginning of the second period of their life. If the tax rate changes just before they sell their land to finance their retirement consumption, the change in the price of land can be thought of as unambiguously borne by this group. The analysis would obviously be more complex in a model in which there are multiple overlapping generations, each living for many periods.

mean, with a given level of savings, that less capital accumulation would occur. With less capital, there is a lower marginal product of land and a higher interest rate. This implies a lower price of land, that is, a contradiction. The puzzle is easily solved. A higher price of land is consistent with more accumulation of produced capital if the rate of saving increases sufficiently when the rate of interest falls. A sufficient increase in savings can absorb both the higher value of land and a larger stock of capital.

Although it is common to regard savings as positively related to the rate of interest, this is only a special case. If the individual chooses his saving rate by maximizing a two-period utility function $u(C_1, C_2)$ subject to the budget constraint $C_2 = (W - C_1)(1 + F_K)$, a decrease in F_K will increase $S = W - C_1$ if the local elasticity of substitution between C_1 and C_2 is less than one.

Risk Aversion, Portfolio Composition, and Short-Run Incidence

Until now, this chapter has examined the incidence of a land tax after there has been sufficient time for the capital stock to change to the new equilibrium value. In the present model, the transition to the new long-run equilibrium takes one generation. In contrast, this section will examine the way in which the pure land tax is shifted in the very short run when no change in the capital stock occurs. Of course the change in the price at which land can be sold to the next generation will affect the present short-run price. To abstract from this effect of future changes in the capital stock, this section will assume that the capital stock is permanently fixed.

Unlike the previous sections, in this section the yields on land and produced capital will no longer be considered as riskless. Because of these risk considerations, land and produced capital are not perfect substitutes in investors' portfolios. The relative shares of capital and land in the investors' desired portfolios will depend on their relative yields and risk characteristics. This section shows that a tax on rental income will generally cause investors to want to alter their portfolio composition. Since the actual quantities of capital and land are fixed, the relative yields must change to make investors content with the available quantities. This change in yields causes a partial offset to the reduction in the price of land.

More specifically, if the traditional capitalization of the tax occurred, the investors' wealth would decline, and the entire reduction in wealth would occur in the value of the land. After this capitalization, the yield on land would return to its original value. The relative riskiness of land (for example, the standard deviation of net income rental relative to the price of land) would also be unchanged. With no change in the relative yields and riskiness of the two assets, investors would not wish to hold the new and much larger portion of their wealth in the form of produced capital.[13] Since the physical quantities of capital and land are fixed, the process of trying to switch assets results only in a bidding up of the price of land, that is, a shifting of the tax.

Consider a more explicit model in which, in the absence of the tax, the relative shares of land and capital in the investors' aggregate portfolio are a constant elasticity function of the relative expected rates of return,[14]

$$\frac{pT}{K} = R \left(\frac{F_T}{pF_K} \right)^\lambda,$$

(17)

where R is the ratio that would prevail with equal expected yields.

Introducing a tax on land has two effects. First, it reduces the net expected return per unit of land to $(1 - \theta)F_T$. Second, it reduces the riskiness per unit of land vis-à-vis produced capital, which in itself increases the desirability of land. The portfolio-balance relation can be approximated by

$$\frac{pT}{K} = R \left(\frac{F_T}{pF_K} \right)^\lambda (1 - \theta)^\mu,$$

(18)

where $\mu < \lambda$ represents the effect of the tax on risk.

Solving Eq. (18) for p yields

$$p = [R(K/T)(F_t/F_K)^\lambda]^{1/(1+\lambda)}(1 - \theta)^{\mu/(1+\lambda)}.$$

(19)

The elasticity of p with respect to $(1 - \theta)$ is

$$\frac{(1 - \theta)}{p} \frac{dp}{d(1 - \theta)} = \frac{\mu}{1 + \lambda}.$$

(20)

13. This is certainly true if there is constant proportional risk aversion. The argument above would be false only if the desired share of wealth decreased extremely rapidly with portfolio size, $\partial pT / \partial (pT + K) = 1$.

14. Here F_T and F_K are expected rates of return. Note that the current model assumes that individuals' consumption is predetermined for the short run, so that K is fixed. The price of capital goods remains at unity because these goods can be sold to the next generation for consumption.

The traditional conclusion that the tax is fully capitalized corresponds to perfect substitutability of the assets in portfolios, that is, to the infinite demand elasticities $\lambda = \mu = \infty$. With smaller values of λ and μ, Eq. (20) implies that the land price falls by less than the capitalized value of the tax. For example, if $\mu = 0.9$ and $\lambda = 1$ implies $d(\ln P)/d\ln(1 - \theta) = 0.45$, introduction of a 10 percent tax reduces the price of land by less than 5 percent.

The current analysis thus implies that, if individual portfolios differ because of differences in risk perception or risk aversion, the owners of the land will be able to shift some of the tax, in the sense that they could sell their land to other members of the same generation at a loss that is less than the capitalized value of the tax.

Of course this portfolio-balance effect will continue in the future. The long-run incidence will therefore reflect both the capital-accumulation effect discussed in the previous sections and the current portfolio-balance effect. A general model, combining both effects in the long run, is a task for the future.

Conclusion

Although this chapter has focused on the incidence of a tax on pure land rent, the analysis has implications for a broader range of problems. The conclusions apply directly to taxes on natural resources and to such provisions as the oil- and gas-depletion allowance. Increasing the effective rate of tax on natural resources creates a capital loss for the current owners and thus induces additional capital accumulation.[15]

Corporate profits are in part economic rents on patents and on unpatented knowledge. Part of the value of equity shares is the capitalized value of these economic rents and of the rents on innovations that are expected to occur in the future. The corporation tax is thus in part a tax on these economic rents, and the analysis in this chapter is again applicable.[16] More generally, it is clear that any general income tax is in part a tax on pure rents. A full analysis of the effect of such a tax should include the induced effects on capital accumulation.

The current analysis also emphasizes the importance of looking at tax incidence in the context of a growing economy and of paying particular

15. The additional accumulation can, as noted above, actually result in a gain to the owners of the natural resource.

16. This view of the corporation tax is developed in Stiglitz (1973). Note that the economic rents earned on innate human skills are quite different; because they cannot be sold to the next generation, the current analysis does not extend to such rents.

attention to its impact within the individual's life cycle. Otherwise identical taxes and transfers will have very different effects if they come at different stages of the life cycle.

One of the reasons that economists have long been interested in the tax on pure rental income is that it is a tax without excess burden. Because the owners of land cannot alter the supply of land, the tax induces no distortions and therefore no welfare loss. Although the current analysis has shown that the tax is actually shifted to some extent, the conclusion of no excess burden is unaltered. The effect of the tax is simply to change initial endowments. The alteration in the capital stock is a response to this different endowment and does not involve any distortion in capital supply per se. There is no wedge between the marginal product of capital and the return to savers. Of course, if there were a preexisting tax on capital income, the tax on pure land rent would in general cause a welfare loss or gain.

A tax on pure land rent can affect the dynamic efficiency of the economy in quite a different way. By increasing the capital intensity of production, an economy in which the marginal product of capital exceeds the rate of growth is moved closer to the golden-rule point. This is of course not an unambiguous welfare gain, since the first generation will typically have a lower level of consumption.

There are a number of directions in which the present research might usefully be pursued. A model of the long-run incidence that combines capital accumulation and portfolio balance should be developed. It would be interesting to extend the analysis to a two-sector economy in which the induced increase in capital would have more complex effects.

Dropping the current conclusion that labor is inelastically supplied should also be explored. A greater capital stock increases the wage rate, which in turn increases labor supply. The elasticity of labor supply will affect the final incidence of the tax on land rent. This result is quite different from the type of results obtained in an economy in which labor and capital are the only factors of production. The elasticity of labor supply is then irrelevant for tax incidence, because any change in labor supply results, in long-run equilibrium, in an equiproportional change in the capital stock (Feldstein 1974). Since a change in labor supply cannot induce a change in the stock of land, the real equilibrium will be altered.

Finally, it would be useful to integrate this analysis into a model with growing population. The equilibrium in such an economy with land might be defined by the constancy of gross factor shares $[(TF_T)/(KF_K)]$ instead of the usual constancy of relative rates of return (F_T/F_K). It seems likely that the current results would continue to prevail in this more general context.

Appendix. An Example with Cobb-Douglas Technology

The magnitudes of the effects of the tax can be illustrated by examining an economy with a Cobb-Douglas technology. This example also shows the possibility of the result that an increase in the tax rate can increase the net rental income on the value of land.

The production function is now

$$X = aK^{\alpha}L^{\beta}T^{\gamma}, \tag{A.1}$$

where a is an arbitrary constant.

With this technology, the price of land is

$$p = \frac{(1 - \theta)F_T}{F_K} = \frac{(1 - \theta)\gamma K}{\alpha T}. \tag{A.2}$$

The basic savings equilibrium of Eq. (6) can be written

$$S(F_K) \cdot X\beta - \frac{(1 - \theta)\gamma K}{\alpha} - K = 0. \tag{A.3}$$

The total derivative of (A.3) with respect to K and θ yields

$$\left\{ \beta[XS'(F_K) \cdot F_{KK} + SF_K] - \frac{(1 - \theta)\gamma}{\alpha} - 1 \right\} dK = - [\gamma K/\alpha]\, d\theta. \tag{A.4}$$

If the elasticity of saving with respect to the interest rate is denoted $\eta_S = F_K \cdot S'(F_K)/S$ and we recognize that $KF_{KK}/F_K = \alpha - 1$, Eq. (A.4) can be rewritten as

$$\frac{1 - \theta}{K} \frac{dK}{d(1 - \theta)} = \frac{(1 - \theta)\gamma/\alpha}{\sigma\beta(X/K)[\eta_S(\alpha - 1) + \alpha] - [(1 - \theta)\gamma/\alpha] - 1}. \tag{A.5}$$

The basic savings equilibrium (Eq. [A.3]) implies

$$\sigma\beta \left(\frac{X}{K} \right) = \frac{(1 - \theta)\gamma}{\alpha} + 1. \tag{A.6}$$

Substituting this into Eq. (A.5) yields[17]

$$\frac{1 - \theta}{K} \frac{dK}{d(1 - \theta)} = \frac{(1 - \theta)\gamma}{[(1 - \theta)\gamma + \alpha](\eta_S + 1)(\alpha - 1)}. \tag{A.7}$$

17. Note that this equation implies that a necessary condition for stability is $\eta_S > -1$.

Some plausible values of the production parameters, the tax rate, and the savings elasticity, will indicate the magnitude of the elasticity of capital with respect to $(1 - \theta)$. Let the labor elasticity be $\beta = 0.7$; the capital elasticity, $\alpha = 0.2$; and the land elasticity, $\gamma = 0.1$. Evaluating the elasticity at $\theta = 0.5$ yields

$$\frac{1 - \theta}{K} \frac{dK}{d(1 - \theta)} = \frac{-0.25}{(1 + \eta_S)}. \tag{A.8}$$

If $-1 < \eta_S \leq 0$, the elasticity of K with respect to $1 - \theta$ is absolutely greater than 0.25.[18] For example, with $\eta_S = -0.5$, a tax increase from $\theta = 0.5$ to $\theta = 0.6$ raises K by approximately 10 percent.

Equation (A.8) can be used to approximate the effect of introducing a substantial tax. With the approximation that the savings function has a constant elasticity with respect to F_K, it is easily shown that the introduction of a tax at $\theta = 0.50$ causes an increase of more than 12.5 percent in the capital intensity if $\eta_S = 0$. With $\eta_S = -0.5$, the increase exceeds 25 percent, while if $\eta = +0.5$, the capital intensity rises by about 8 percent.

Consider the effect of the tax on the *net* return to land. Using Eqs. (11) and (A.7) and the derivatives of the Cobb-Douglas production function, we obtain

$$\frac{1}{F_T} \frac{d(1 - \theta)F_T}{d\theta} = \frac{-(1 - \theta)\alpha\gamma}{[(1 - \theta)\gamma + \alpha](\alpha - 1)(1 + \eta_S)} - 1. \tag{A.9}$$

With the previous values of $\theta = 0.5$, $\alpha = 0.2$, and $\gamma = 0.1$, this equation implies

$$\frac{1}{F_T} \frac{d(1 - \theta)F_T}{d\theta} = \frac{0.05}{1 + \eta_S} - 1. \tag{A.10}$$

Unless the elasticity of η_S is absolutely greater than -0.95, Eq. (A.10) indicates that an increase in θ has the expected effect of decreasing $(1 - \theta)F_T$. But with $\eta_S < -0.95$, an increase in the tax has the surprising effect of raising the net rental income.[19] This occurs because, even with a Cobb-Douglas technology, the increase in the capital stock causes a sufficient increase in the gross yield.[20] A large negative savings elasticity

18. Recall that $\eta_S > -1$ is a condition of stability.
19. For the introduction of a new tax, that is, evaluating (A.9) at $\theta = 0$, the result is similar. Unless $\eta_S > 0.91$, $d[(1 - \theta)F_T]/d\theta < 0$.
20. There is an apparent paradox. An increase in capital lowers the rate of interest. If the net rental rises, how can the land and capital have equal yields, as required for both assets to

permits the savings rate to rise sufficiently to absorb the greater value of land and the larger capital stock.[21]

Finally, the current example can be used to show that the price of land may rise even though the net rental falls. From Eq. (13),

$$\frac{dp}{d\theta} = -\frac{F_T}{F_K}\left[1 - \frac{(1 - \theta)}{K}\frac{dK}{d\theta}\right] \qquad \text{(A.11)}$$

or, using (A.7)

$$\frac{1}{p}\frac{dp}{d\theta} = \frac{-(1 - \theta)\gamma}{[(1 - \theta)\gamma + \alpha](1 + \eta_S)(\alpha - 1)} - 1. \qquad \text{(A.12)}$$

Comparing (A.12) with the condition in (A.9) for $d[(1 - \theta)F_T]/d\theta > 0$ shows that they are identical except that a factor of α is missing in the numerator of (A.12). It is much easier, therefore, to satisfy the condition required by (A.12) to make $(dp)/(d\theta) > 0$. With the previous values of $\theta = 0.5, \gamma = 0.1$, and $\alpha = 0.2$, Eq. (A.12) becomes

$$\frac{1}{p}\frac{dp}{d\theta} = \frac{0.25}{1 + \eta_S} - 1. \qquad \text{(A.13)}$$

Therefore, if $\eta_S < -0.75$, an increase in the tax will raise the value of land. For the introduction of a new tax (that is, evaluating [A.12] at $\theta = 0$), a savings elasticity of -0.59 or less implies that the price of land will rise.

---

be held? They will have equal yields if the price of land rises sufficiently, which it automatically will since $p = (1 - \theta)(F_T/F_K)$.

21. Recall that the negative savings elasticity cannot be regarded as especially unacceptable.

21 Corporate Financial Policy and Taxation in a Growing Economy

This chapter presents a model of corporate financial policy in a growing economy and then uses this model to study the effects of changes in corporate and personal taxes. Our picture of the firm includes a flexible debt-equity ratio and a flexible dividend payout rate. The costs to the firm of both debt and equity capital are increasing functions of the firm's debt-equity ratio. We use a realistic description of the tax system that includes a corporate income tax with deductible interest expenses, a personal income tax, and a favorable tax treatment of retained earnings.

Our work builds on earlier research[1] on both corporate finance and taxation but provides a more general and realistic model. This new model implies a unique optimal debt-equity ratio instead of the indeterminacy associated with the Modigliani-Miller tradition. The model also implies that firms will choose a positive equilibrium payout rate in spite of the favorable taxation of retained earnings. We know of no other model that explains why firms simultaneously borrow and pay dividends in an economy with corporate and personal taxation.

The model is presented and explained in the first section. The second and third sections then examine the effects of changes in the corporate tax rate and in the differential between the taxation of dividends and of retained earnings. The nonneutrality of the corporation tax is discussed more generally in the fourth section.

The framework for our analysis is an economy in steady-state growth with a fixed saving rate. To avoid the usual complexities and ambiguities of corporate tax shifting in a two-sector model, we assume that all busi-

This chapter was written with Jerry Green and Eytan Sheshinski. Reprinted from the *Quarterly Journal of Economics* 93 (August 1979), pp. 411–432, by permission of John Wiley and Sons. The revision of this chapter benefited from comments by participants in the NBER workshop, by a referee of the *Quarterly Journal of Economics,* and by Alan Auerbach, Gregory Ballentine, Joel Slemrod, and Lawrence Summers.

1. See in particular Harberger (1962), Jakobsson (1974), Lintner (1964), Miller (1976), Modigliani and Miller (1958), Solow (1971), and Stiglitz (1973, 1976), as well as our own previous research reported in Feldstein, Green, and Sheshinski (1978).

ness activity takes a corporate form. These simplifying assumptions allow us to focus on the effects of the tax system on financial behavior (the debt-equity ratio and the dividend payout rate) and on the after-tax yields on stocks and bonds. The implications of recognizing a noncorporate business sector and of allowing the saving rate to vary with asset yields are discussed briefly in the fourth section.

A Model of Financial Equilibrium

In order to study these questions, we extend the simple one-sector, nonmonetary growth model to include a specification of the financial behavior of firms and households. By virtue of the assumptions that aggregate savings are insensitive to the rate of return and that population grows exogenously at a fixed rate n, the economy's capital-labor ratio will be constant in the long-run equilibria that we analyze. Under the usual neoclassical conditions, this means that the gross rate of return per unit of capital f' is also a constant.

In the following subsections we discuss the behavior of firms and investors in the context of a simple tax structure that is designed to capture the basic features of the U.S. tax system.

Firms' Decisions and the Posttax and Pretax Returns

The decision variables on which we focus are concerned with the way in which investment is financed. There are two financial instruments, debt and equity; the proportion of capital financed by debt is denoted b. Firms must also choose their payout rate p, which is the fraction of the total return to equity holders (before any personal taxes are paid) that they receive in the form of dividends.

As a first step in the analysis, it is necessary to relate the net-of-tax yields of investors to the corresponding costs of finance to firms. Debt costs the firm i per unit of capital raised, and this return is taxed at the personal interest income rate θ. Thus, the net rate return to bond holders is

$$i_N = i(1 - \theta). \tag{1}$$

The return to equity is e and consists of pe paid in the form of dividends and $(1 - p)e$ retained for capital accumulation by the firm.[2] We assume

2. This assumes that the increase in the market value of the firm resulting from acquiring a dollar's worth of capital goods is one dollar; that is, that Tobin's parameter q equals one (Tobin 1969). This is a crucial difference between our analysis and that of Auerbach (1979a) and Bradford (1978).

that dividends are taxed at the same rate as interest but that retained earnings are in effect taxed at a lower rate ($\mu\theta$), where μ is between zero and one. The reason for the effectively preferential treatment of retained earnings is that no personal taxes are levied on corporate income held within the firm. Taxes are paid upon realization of the resulting gains, but they are below the ordinary income tax rate both because of the differential treatment of capital gains and because of the delay that is typically entailed in taxing only realized capital gains. Overall, the net return to equity is, therefore,

$$e_N = pe(1 - \theta) + (1 - p)e(1 - \mu\theta). \tag{2}$$

It will be convenient to have a special symbol for the effective rate of taxation on equity income, which depends on the firm's control variable p as well as the tax rate; let

$$x = p(1 - \theta) + (1 - p)(1 - \mu\theta) \tag{3}$$

so that

$$e_N = ex. \tag{4}$$

Before the decisions of the firm can be studied, we must describe the economic environment in which it is embedded. Its securities must compete with those of other firms that are substitutes, but not perfect substitutes because their risk characteristics differ. From the household investors' point of view, the relevant variables are assumed to be the expected returns net of tax offered on the two types of securities issued, and the risk characteristics of these assets as determined by the debt-equity ratio the firm has chosen.

We shall use carets to denote the variables relating to all other firms collectively considered; the offered returns are $\hat{e}_N$ and $\hat{i}_N$ for equity and debt, respectively. The debt per unit of capital held by all other firms is $\hat{b}$.

In an equilibrium the firm's sources and uses of funds must be in balance. Its gross income per unit of capital is f'. Interest costs of bi per unit of capital are deductible for tax purposes. The residual is taxed at the rate τ. The return to equity holders per unit of equity before personal taxation is thus defined as

$$(1 - \tau)(f' - bi)/(1 - b) = e. \tag{5}$$

We assume that a firm, in marketing its securities, perceives rising supply prices for both debt and equity capital as its debt-equity ratio rises.[3] This assumption is clearly contradictory to the extreme form of the Modigliani-Miller view that the debt-equity ratio has no effect on the costs of either debt or equity. As we note below, this Modigliani-Miller view is not compatible with an interior solution for corporate debt policy. We also share the view of Myers (1977) and others that a high debt-equity ratio restricts a firm's real investment options, thereby reducing the value of its shares. In addition, we reject the extreme view that "home-made leverage" and corporate leverage are perfect substitutes.

It will be most convenient to express these schedules as giving the net required return to investors. They also depend on the debt-equity ratio of all other firms $\hat{b}$, and their promised returns to the two types of securities, net of personal taxes $\hat{\imath}_N$ and $\hat{e}_N$:

$$i_N = \phi(b,\hat{b},\hat{e}_N,\hat{\imath}_N), \qquad e_N = \psi(b,\hat{b},\hat{e}_N,\hat{\imath}_N). \tag{6}$$

Higher returns available elsewhere, $\hat{e}_N$ and $\hat{\imath}_N$, shift these schedules up. More riskiness in the "market" portfolio $\hat{b}$ will have the opposite effect. We shall assume that the cross-partials of the ϕ and ψ schedules are zero.[4]

We are now ready to discuss the way in which firms operate. Firms choose b and p so as to minimize the net cost of capital N, defined as

$$N = b(1 - \tau)i + (1 - b)e. \tag{7}$$

It is important to remember that i and e in this formula are interpreted as the supply prices to the firm. The economic actions of other firms enter into this decision problem as parameters of the ϕ and ψ functions. Note that minimizing the cost of capital is equivalent to maximizing the present value of the equity in the company with our assumption that a dollar of retained earnings adds one dollar to the market value of the firm.[5]

Although it is clear that the risk considerations that make the firm's costs of debt and equity an increasing function of b cause the firm to find an optimal mixture of debt and equity, it is natural to ask why such a firm

---

3. We assume that both prices rise, although our analysis requires only that at least one rise.

4. Perhaps a more natural assumption would be that the elasticities with respect to b are independent of the levels of the other variables, but this would complicate the comparative statics significantly, without adding much of interest. The results do not depend in any way on the assumed effects of $\hat{e}_N$, $\hat{\imath}_N$, and $\hat{b}$ on the individual firm's cost of funds schedules.

5. This equivalence is discussed by Auerbach (1979a).

would ever pay dividends. By retaining everything possible ($p = 0$), the firm can apparently lower the effective tax rate on equity earnings (x) and thus lower the cost of equity finance associated with any fixed level of the net return to equity holders. Since p is not an argument of ϕ or ψ, the policy $p = 0$ would seem always to be the best.

The answer to this line of argument is that if all earnings were retained, the equity of the firm would grow at a rate equal to the rate of return on equity gross of personal income tax. In order to maintain a constant debt-equity ratio,[6] debt finance must also increase at the same rate. Hence the policy $p = 0$ may force the firm's total capital stock to grow at a rate that exceeds the rate of growth of the economy. In this event the risk class represented by this firm's securities would become very large relative to the market, and it would not be able to raise enough capital in the long run. Since we are restricting firms to choose steady policies only, such a program would be infeasible. The firm could sustain a rate of growth higher than the economy as a whole in the short run only, but the ensuing shifts in the ϕ and ψ schedules would eventually cause the zero profit condition to be violated.

The rate of growth of the effective labor force is denoted by n. The firm operates under the constraint, $n \geq (1 - p)e$. Growing at a faster rate would cause the firm to become too large a risk relative to the remainder of the economy and would thus raise its cost of capital. The firm's problem is therefore

$$\min N = b(1 - \tau)i + (1 - b)e \tag{8}$$

subject to

$$n \geq (1 - p)e. \tag{9}$$

Writing the cost of capital as

$$N = b(1 - \tau)\phi/(1 - \theta) + (1 - b)\psi/x, \tag{10}$$

we see that the Lagrangean for this problem is

$$L = b(1 - \tau)\frac{\phi}{1 - \theta} + (1 - b)\frac{\psi}{x} + \rho\left(n - (1 - p)\frac{\psi}{x}\right), \tag{11}$$

6. We consider only steady policies—that is, choices of p and b that could be pursued indefinitely—throughout this chapter.

where ρ is the Lagrange multiplier of the growth-rate constraint. Differentiating with respect to b, p, and ρ, we obtain the firm's optimality conditions:

$$0 = \frac{1 - \tau}{1 - \theta} (i_N + b\phi') - \frac{e_N}{x} + \frac{(1 - b)}{x} \psi' - \rho \frac{(1 - p)\psi'}{x}, \tag{12}$$

$$0 = (1 - b)e_N(\mu\theta - \theta)/x^2 + \rho e_N(-x + (1 - p)\theta(1 - \mu))/x^2, \tag{13}$$

$$0 = n - (1 - p)e_N/x, \tag{14}$$

where ϕ' and ψ' are the derivatives with respect to b. Solving (13) for ρ, we have

$$\rho = -(1 - b)\theta(1 - \mu)/(1 - \theta). \tag{15}$$

Note that ρ is negative, as might have been anticipated. A higher growth rate would make feasible a financial policy in which retentions increase sheltering equity income to a greater extent, thus lowering the gross return equivalent to the required net return.

Substituting the solution for ρ into (12) and simplifying, we obtain

$$0 = \frac{1 - \tau}{1 - \theta} (i_N + b\phi') - \frac{e_N}{x} + \frac{(1 - b)\psi'}{1 - \theta}. \tag{16}$$

Equations (14) and (16) describe the first-order conditions for the firm's problem of selecting a debt proportion b and a payout ratio p that minimizes the cost of capital subject to the firm's equity growth constraint.[7]

Aggregate Portfolio Balance Conditions

The analysis given above is a complete specification of the suppliers of corporate securities. To close the system, some description of investors'

7. For a given economic environment, as specified by $\hat{b}, \hat{e}N, \hat{i}_N, n$, and the functions ϕ and ψ, the term's choice of b and p that minimizes the cost of capital may not also satisfy the equilibrium cash flow condition (Eq. [5]). If these choices were actually affected, there would be a surplus or deficit in the firm of $z = (f' - bi)(1 - \psi) - e(1 - b)$, which it is natural to assume would accrue to equity as they are the residual claimants. Thus, the true disequilibrium return to equity would be $z/(1 - b) + e$. Investors would be off their ψ schedules, and an adjustment would be necessary. In this chapter we do not give any specification of the process of achieving equilibrium. It would be necessary to do so if one were to use the assumed stability of such a mechanism to derive comparative static results.

risk preferences and their resulting market behavior must be given. The simplest method is to write the market's desired, or acceptable, level of debt per unit of capital as

$$\hat{b} = \eta(\hat{i}_N - \hat{e}_N). \tag{17}$$

The sign of η' can be either positive or negative. We shall deal primarily with the case of $\eta' = 0$ to isolate risk changes from other effects, but we shall also discuss other cases.

Because of the symmetry of firms, in equilibrium the market (careted) variables will equal the corresponding firm-specific variables $\hat{b} = b$, $\hat{i}_N = i_N$, $\hat{e}_N = e_N$. This reduces the system to a determination of b, i_N, e_N, and p. Of course, in this determination each individual firm treats the market variables $(\hat{b}, \hat{i}_N, \hat{e}_N)$ as given parameters of its own problem.

The Complete System

Using Eqs. (3) and (9) to write p in terms of x and the rate of growth, we see that in the long run, the system can be specified by the four relations

$$0 = b - \eta(i_N - e_N), \tag{18}$$

$$0 = f' - \frac{bi_N}{1 - \theta} - \frac{1 - b}{1 - \tau}\frac{e_N}{x}, \tag{19}$$

$$0 = (1 - \mu)\theta x n - (x + \theta - 1)e_N, \tag{20}$$

$$0 = \frac{1 - \tau}{1 - \theta}(i_N + b\phi') - \frac{e_N}{x} + \frac{(1 - b)\psi'}{1 - \theta}, \tag{21}$$

which are, respectively, the portfolio balance condition, the financial balance condition, and the two first-order conditions for the firm's optimization.

Notation

For the reader's convenience, before proceeding, our notation is recapitulated below in tabular form.

Tax Rates

θ = personal income tax rate, applicable to interest and dividend income.

$\mu\theta$ = personal tax rate on retained earnings (through eventual capital gains).

τ = corporate tax rate on profits; interest is deductible.

Financial Variables for the Firm

e = cost of equity finance.

i = cost of debt finance.

b = debt as a proportion of capital.

p = payout rate, the proportion of postcorporate tax earnings paid in the form of dividends.

e_N = the supply price for net rate of return on equity of the firm.

i_N = the supply price for net rate of return on debt of the firm.

Macroeconomic Variables

f' = gross return per unit of capital.

n = rate of growth.

$\hat{b}$ = market debt as a proportion of capital stock.

$\hat{e}_N$ = market rate of return on equity.

$\hat{i}_N$ = market rate of return on debt.

Effects of Changes in the Profit Tax Rate

In this section we examine how an increase in the rate of profits tax affects the decisions of the representative firm and the net returns to debt and equity investors. The differential taxation of dividends and retained earnings (that is, the value of μ) is assumed to remain unchanged.[8]

Our analysis will focus primarily on the case in which $\eta' = 0$; that is, in which the debt-to-capital ratio (b) remains fixed because the market's demand for relative quantities of debt and equity is not sensitive to differences in their yields. We focus on this case because only when b is constant can the predicted changes in e_N and i_N be interpreted unambiguously. With a fixed debt-capital ratio, the values of e_N and i_N are good reflections of the welfare of the owners of debt and equity capital. In contrast, when

---

8. The next section considers changes in μ as well as compensated increases in τ and decreases in μ that keep total tax revenue unchanged. In contrast, the increase in τ in the current section increases tax revenues.

b changes in response to a change in the tax law, parts of the observed changes in e_N and i_N reflect compensation for the new level of risk associated with the new value of b.[9]

Totally differentiating Eqs. (18)–(21) in the general case of $\eta' \neq 0$ with respect to b, e_N, i_N, x, and the predetermined τ yields[10]

$$
\begin{bmatrix}
1 & \eta' & -\eta' & 0 \\
\dfrac{1-\tau}{1-\theta}i_N - \dfrac{e_N}{x} & \dfrac{1-b}{x} & \dfrac{1-\tau}{1-\theta}b & -\dfrac{(1-b)e_N}{x^2} \\
0 & 1-x-\theta & 0 & (1-\mu)\theta n - e_N \\
Z & -\dfrac{1}{x} & \dfrac{1-\tau}{1-\theta} & \dfrac{e_N}{x^2}
\end{bmatrix}
\begin{bmatrix}
db \\
de_N \\
di_N \\
dx
\end{bmatrix}
$$

$$
= \begin{bmatrix}
0 \\
\dfrac{bi_N}{1-\theta} - f' \\
0 \\
\dfrac{i_N + b\phi'}{1-\theta}
\end{bmatrix} d\tau,
\tag{22}
$$

where $Z = \partial^2 N / \partial b^2$. The second-order condition for choosing b to minimize the cost of capital implies that $Z > 0$.

The Debt-Capital Ratio

Although we shall concentrate on the case in which inelastic market demand ($\eta' = 0$) keeps the debt-capital ratio (b) fixed, it is useful to examine first the effect of the corporation tax on the debt ratio in the more general case in which $\eta' \neq 0$. Solving Eq. (22) implies that

$$
\frac{db}{d\tau} = \Delta^{-1}\eta' \left\{ \frac{e_N}{x}\left(\frac{i_N}{1-\theta} - \tau f'\right) - b\phi'\left[\frac{1-\tau}{1-\theta}b((1-\mu)\theta n - e_N)\right.\right.
$$

$$
\left.\left. + \frac{1-b}{x}((1-\mu)\theta n - e_N) + \frac{(1-b)e_N}{x^2}(1-x-\theta)\right]\right\},
\tag{23}
$$

9. A more complete analysis of risk and risk aversion would be required to provide a precise welfare measure.

10. Recall that we have assumed that the cross-derivatives of ϕ and ψ are zero.

where Δ, the determinant of the matrix in (22), is

$$\Delta = \frac{1 - \tau}{1 - \theta} \frac{e_N}{x} + \eta'Z - \eta'\tau \left[\frac{1 - \tau}{1 - \theta} b\phi' + \frac{1 - b}{1 - \theta} \psi' + Zb \right]. \quad (24)$$

Consider first the case in which $\eta' > 0$. Equations (23) and (24) show unambiguously that the introduction of a corporate income tax induces a substitution of debt for equity finance when $\tau = 0$. Equations (23) and (24) then yield

$$\frac{db}{d\tau} = \eta' \left\{ i_N e_N - b\phi' \left[\left(\frac{b}{1 - \theta} + \frac{1 - b}{x} \right) ((1 - \mu)\theta n - e_N) \right. \right.$$

$$\left. \left. + \frac{(1 - b)e_N}{x^2} (1 - x - \theta) \right] \right\} > 0, \quad (25)$$

since $(1 - \mu)\theta n = ((\theta - 1)e_N)/x < 0$ and $(1 - x - \theta) = -(1 - p)$ $(1 - \mu)\theta < 0$. It is easy to understand the reason for this. The corporation tax permits the deduction of interest payments in the calculation of taxable income. It thus raises the cost to the firm of providing a dollar of net equity income relative to the cost of providing net interest income. The firm's cost of capital is therefore minimized by substituting debt for equity. The extent of this substitution is limited by the market's reaction to the increased riskiness implied by an increasing ratio of debt to equity.

If $\eta' < 0$, the numerator is negative, and $db/d\tau > 0$ only if the denominator is also negative. The sign of the denominator can be negative if $\eta' < 0$, but without quantitative information on the magnitudes of η' and Z, it is not possible to be certain of the sign. Stability considerations do not provide a definite answer unless arbitrary restrictions are imposed on the adjustment process.

The Net Rate of Interest

Previous studies of the corporation tax have not provided a satisfactory analysis of the effect of the tax on the net rate of interest received by bondholders. Harberger's discussion (1962) of corporate tax incidence ignored debt completely and assumed that all investment is equity-financed. Stiglitz (1973) considered the opposite extreme case in which all marginal investment is financed by debt and therefore in which a change in the corporate tax rate does not alter the net rate of interest; that is, $di_N/d\tau = 0$.

We now show that when firms combine debt and equity finance, the introduction of a corporation tax (or the increase in a preexisting tax rate) with full interest deductibility reduces the net yield to bondholders. To abstract from changes in i_N that just compensate for the increased debt-equity ratio, we consider the case in which $\eta' = 0$ and therefore b is constant. Equations (22) and (24) then imply that

$$\frac{di_N}{d\tau} = -\frac{1 - \theta}{1 - \tau}\left[f - i - \frac{b(1 - b)\phi'}{1 - \theta}\right]. \tag{26}$$

Combining (19) and (21) implies that

$$f' - i = \frac{(1 - b)b\phi'}{1 - \theta} + \frac{(1 - b)^2}{(1 - \tau)(1 - \theta)}\psi'$$

and therefore that

$$\frac{di_N}{d\tau} = -\frac{(1 - b)^2\psi'}{(1 - \tau)^2} < 0, \tag{27}$$

since ψ' will be positive (even when ϕ' is zero or very small) because equity risk is sensitive to corporate leverage. Thus $di_N/d\tau$ is always negative.

It may at first seem paradoxical that a higher rate of corporation tax changes the yield on debt even though interest payments are fully deductible in calculating the corporation's taxable income. Looked at in this way, it would seem that the interest rate should be unaffected by a corporation tax and that all of the tax should be absorbed by a reduction in equity income.[11] Such an outcome is not compatible with the firms' financing and cost minimization conditions (Eqs. [19], [20], and [21]). If the interest rate remained unchanged, firms would try to reduce their supply of bonds; since $\eta' = 0$ implies that b cannot change, equilibrium must be reestablished by a fall in i_N.

To obtain an indication of the order of magnitude of the effect of changes in the corporate tax rate, we can evaluate Eq. (27) for plausible values of the relevant parameters under the further assumption that

11. Recall that we are dealing with the case of $\eta' = 0$ in which individual investors wish to hold the same portfolio regardless of the relative values of i_N and e_N. With $\eta' > 0$, a fall in e_N would increase the households' demand for bonds, and this in turn would be a further reason for i_N to fall.

$\phi' = 0.$[12] For this calculation it is useful to use Eqs. (4), (5), and (21) to express the unobservable ψ' as $\psi' = (1 - \theta)(f' - i)/(1 - b)$. We shall set the effective rate of corporate tax at $\tau = 0.40$ and the personal rate of tax on bond interest and dividend income at $\theta = 0.30$, values that are roughly appropriate for the United States. The marginal product of capital of U.S. nonfinancial corporations has been about $f' = 0.11$ in the past twenty-five years (Feldstein and Summers 1977). The ratio of corporate debt to the replacement cost of capital for the same period implies that $b = 0.3$ is a reasonable approximation. The real rate of interest on medium-grade corporate bonds has been approximately $i = 0.03.$[13] Substituting these figures into (27) implies that $di_N/d\tau = -0.11$. An increase in the effective corporate tax rate by 0.1 (that is, from 0.40 to 0.50) would lower i_N by 1.1 percentage points. Since $i = 0.03$ and $\theta = 0.3$ imply $i_N = 0.021$, this would cut the net yield in half. Note also that a fall of 1.1 in i_N implies a fall of $1.1/(1 - \theta) = 1.6$ percentage points in the real rate of interest, from 3.0 to 1.4 percent.[14]

The Net Yield on Equity

The fall in the net rate of interest that we have just calculated shows that the burden of the corporation tax is borne by both debt and equity investors. To assess the share borne by each, we must complement the calculation of the previous section by calculating the effect on e_N of an increase in the corporate tax rate.

It follows directly from Eqs. (22) and (24) that, with $\eta' = 0$,

$$\frac{de_N}{d\tau} = \frac{[(1 - \mu)\theta n - e_N](f' + (b^2\phi/1 - \theta))}{e_N/x}. \tag{28}$$

Since Eq. (20) implies that $(1 - \mu)\theta n - e_N = (\theta - 1)e_N/x$, we have that when $\phi' = 0$, Eq. (28) simplifies to

$$\frac{de_N}{d\tau} = -(1 - \theta)f'. \tag{29}$$

12. The magnitude of ϕ cannot be ascertained in general, since it depends on the substitutability among debt issues in investors' portfolios. Close substitutability implies that ϕ is small.

13. During a decade of relative price stability (1954–1964), the yield on Moody's Baa bonds averaged 4.6 percent and the implicit price deflator for gross domestic product rose at 2.0 percent a year.

14. The issue is more complex where there is a positive rate of inflation. See Feldstein, Green, and Sheshinski (1978).

This is a striking result. It implies that the reduction in the equilibrium equity yield in response to an increase in the corporate tax rate is independent of the debt-equity ratio, the dividend payout rate, and the preferential treatment of retained earnings[15] when corporations' borrowing rates are perfectly elastic.

The numerical values suggested above imply that $de_N/d\tau = -0.077$. An increase in the corporate tax rate from 0.40 to 0.50 would thus lower e_N by 0.77 percentage points, less than the reduction in the net interest rate.

Total income of equity investors per dollar of capital is $E_N = (1 - b)e_N$, and the corresponding income of bondholders is $I_N = bi_N$. The relative income change can therefore be written in the case of $\phi' = 0$ directly from Eqs. (27) and (29) as

$$\frac{dE_N/d\tau}{dI_N/d\tau} = \frac{1-b}{b}\frac{de_N/d\tau}{di_N/d\tau} = \frac{1-b}{b} \cdot \frac{(1-\theta)f'}{(1-b)^2(1-\tau)^2\psi'}. \tag{30}$$

Using $\psi' = (1 - \theta)(f' - i)(1 - b)^{-1}$, this simplifies to

$$\frac{dE_N/d\tau}{dI_N/d\tau} = \frac{(1-\tau)^2 f'}{b(f'-i)}. \tag{31}$$

With our values of $\tau = 0.40$, $f' = 0.11$, $b = 0.30$, and $i = 0.03$, $dE_N/d\tau = 1.65\, dI_N/d\tau$. Equity owners bear only about 65 percent of the tax burden even though they account for 92 percent of the pretax corporate income and 89 percent of the after-tax income.[16]

We turn finally to the effect of the corporation tax on the dividend payout ratio p. Recall that the balanced growth of the corporation at the common growth rate of the economy (n) requires that the corporation's

---

15. Note that Eqs. (27) and (29) together imply that introducing a new corporate income tax reduces the earnings on the average portfolio of debt and equity by $d[b i_N + (1 - b)e_N]d\tau = -(1 - \theta)(f' - bi)$. This is of course just the revenue raised by taxing the return to equity, $f' - bi$, when the net income is otherwise subject to personal tax at rate θ.

16. On a pretax basis, bondholders receive only $bi = 0.009$ per dollar of capital, while equity receives (before tax) $(1 - b)e = f' - bi = 0.101$ per dollar of capital. Net of tax, bondholders receive $(1 - \theta)bi = 0.0063$ per dollar of capital. To calculate the net income of equity investors, $(1 - b)e_N = x(1 - b)e$, note that $x = p(1 - \theta) + (1 - p)(1 - \mu\theta)$. Values of $p = 0.5$ for the dividend payout ratio and $\mu = 0.2$ for the relative rate of tax on retained earnings (allowing for the effect of postponement and the lower capital gains tax rate) are reasonable for the United States; these imply that $x = 0.82$. From $(1 - b)e = (1 - \tau)(f' - bi)$, we obtain $(1 - b)e_N = x(1 - \tau)(f' - bi) = 0.497$. Total after-tax income per dollar of capital is therefore 0.0560, of which equity investors receive 89 percent.

equity also grow at this rate. Equation (9) noted that this balanced growth condition could be written as

$$n = (1 - p)e. \tag{32}$$

If we substitute e_N for e, this becomes

$$n = \frac{1 - p}{p(1 - \theta) + (1 - p)(1 - \mu\theta)} e_N. \tag{33}$$

When an increase in the corporate tax rate lowers e_N, the balanced growth condition requires an offsetting increase in the remaining part of the right-hand side of (33). Since this expression varies inversely with p for any feasible values of θ and μ, an increase in the corporate tax rate requires a reduction in the dividend payout rate.[17]

We calculated that, with b constant, increasing from 0.40 to 0.50 would reduce e_N by 0.0077. Since $e_N = 0.071$ at the initial numerical values,[18] this is a reduction of 10.8 percent. To continue to satisfy the balanced growth equation, the dividend payout rate must fall from 0.50 to 0.43.[19]

Effects of Changes in the Taxation of Retained Earnings

A central feature of the corporate-type tax is that retained earnings are taxed at a lower effective rate than dividends. Under current U.S. law, retained earnings are not subject to any personal income tax as such. The resulting capital gains are taxed at a rate less than the rate on dividend income, and the tax is assessed only when the asset is sold. We have parameterized the extent to which retained earnings are sheltered by μ: $\mu = 1$ representing no advantage to retained earnings over dividend income, and $\mu = 0$ representing a zero effective tax on retained earnings. Thus, differentiating with respect to μ corresponds to studying decreased levels of sheltering.

The effects of changing μ run through two channels. Directly, μ alters the effective tax rate on equity income x. Thus, μ influences the cost of capital for fixed values of e_N and i_N. Indirectly, the induced change in e, after firms have adjusted to the new cost of capital, will influence the payout rate p necessary to satisfy the steady-state equation. This feeds back onto the effective tax rate because it alters the part of equity income that is sheltered.

17. More formally, it can be shown that $1/(1 - p)d(1 - p)/d\tau = -f'/e$.
18. Note 16 showed that $(1 - b)e_N = 0.497$. Since $b = 0.3, e_N = 0.071$.
19. More generally, Eq. (22) can be used to calculate $dx/d\tau$ and then $dp/d\tau$ derived by using the definition that $x = (1 - \mu\theta) - (1 - \mu)\theta p$.

Intuitively, we would expect to find that reducing the extent of sheltering lowers the after-tax total return to equity e_N. This is true in this model. Moreover, we shall show that changes in the retained earnings provisions are otherwise neutral (provided that $\eta' = 0$), leaving the gross returns, the net interest rate, and the dividend payout rate unaffected.

Uncompensated Shifts in μ

Recall that our basic equation system, (18)–(21), and its total differentiation (22) are written in terms of the endogenous variables, b, e_N, i_N, and x, with μ as a fixed parameter. This form is inconvenient for the purpose of studying the effects of varying μ because μ enters into the definition of x. By rewriting the system with p, instead of x, as the fourth endogenous variable, we can see the effects of μ more simply. To do so, note that p, μ, and x are related by the definition

$$x \equiv p(1 - \theta) + (1 - p)(1 - \mu\theta). \tag{34}$$

Thus, in differentiating Eqs. (18)–(21) totally with respect to b, e_N, i_N, p, and μ, it is only necessary to use

$$\frac{\partial x}{\partial \mu} = -\theta(1 - p) \quad \text{and} \quad \frac{\partial x}{\partial p} = -\theta(1 - \mu) \tag{35}$$

to convert Eq. (22) into an equivalent system in these variables. This gives

$$
\begin{bmatrix}
1 & \eta' & -\eta' & 0 \\
\dfrac{1-\tau}{1-\theta} i_N & \dfrac{e_N}{x} - \dfrac{1-b}{x}\dfrac{1-\tau}{1-\theta}b & \dfrac{(1-b)e_N\theta(1-\mu)}{x^2} \\
0 & 1 - \theta - x & 0 & -[(1-\mu)\theta n - e_N]\theta(1-\mu) \\
Z & \dfrac{-1}{x} & \dfrac{1-\tau}{1-\theta} & \dfrac{-e_N}{x^2}\theta(1-\mu)
\end{bmatrix}
\begin{bmatrix}
db \\
de_N \\
di_N \\
dp
\end{bmatrix}
$$

$$
=
\begin{bmatrix}
0 \\
-(1-b)\dfrac{e_N\theta(1-p)}{x^2} \\
[(1-\mu)\theta n - e_N]\theta(1-p) + \theta nx \\
\dfrac{e_N\theta(1-p)}{x^2}
\end{bmatrix}
d\mu. \tag{36}
$$

The matrix on the left-hand side of (36) is just the same as that in (22) with the last column multiplied by $dx/dp = -\theta(1 - \mu)$. Thus assuming that $\eta' = 0$,[20] we see that its determinant is

$$-\Delta\theta(1 - \mu) = -\frac{1 - \tau}{1 - \theta} \frac{e_N\theta(1 - \mu)}{x}. \tag{37}$$

We obtain the following comparative static results:

$$\frac{de_N}{d\mu} = -\theta n < 0, \tag{38}$$

$$\frac{di_N}{d\mu} = 0. \tag{39}$$

The particularly simple form of these expressions is worthy of note. The decrease in e_N in response to a higher effective tax on equity is no surprise. Its dependence on n, the growth rate, results from the fact that retentions are constrained in equilibrium by the growth rate. Therefore, in a faster-growing economy with a higher retention rate, the nature of the taxation of retained earnings and capital gains will be more important to equity owners.

The result that i_N is unaffected is somewhat more surprising and is an important conclusion that follows from the behavioral equations of the model. When μ increases, the initial impact is felt on all the equations of the system (except $b = \eta[i_N - e_N]$, which does not matter when $\eta' = 0$). The firm has a cash flow deficit, as can be seen from Eqs. (19) and (35). The retention ratio is no longer compatible with a steady state (from [20]); and bond finance becomes underutilized, since the value of e necessary to provide the original net return e_N is higher. It is important to note that if e_N and p were to change so as to restore cash-flow balance, they would also re-equilibrate the cost of capital at its original level. This can be seen simply by noting that e_N and p enter both of these equations in the form e_N/x only. Since i_N does not enter the steady-state equation at all, it is clear that the new equilibrium is achieved only by changing e_N and x, and leaving i_N at its original level.[21]

---

20. Throughout this section we shall maintain this condition. Little in the way of precise analytic results can be obtained if the aggregate debt-equity ratio is flexible and can respond to shifts in the composition of the cost of capital. Of course, on the firm level in our model, the cost of capital can be affected by financing changes of this type.
    21. This follows formally from the singularity of the matrix in (36), when the coefficients of $d\mu$ are substituted for the third column.

To summarize in economic terms, the constancy of i_N results from the fact that the cost-of-capital equation and the cash flow equation both embody e_N, x, and μ in precisely the same functional form. Viewed in this way, the result is no surprise at all. These equilibrium relations are concerned with firms' behavior and as such depend only on the returns to capital gross of personal taxation; in particular, the tax on retained earnings enters only through e, which is fixed in steady-state equilibrium.

Note that since i_N and θ are unchanged, so is i. Therefore, the cost of capital minimization can be compatible with a fixed b only if e is also unchanged.

From the steady-state condition, $n = (1 - p)e$, it is clear that p must also be constant. An uncompensated-for change in the sheltering provision for retained earnings affects only the net return to equity through a shift in the effective tax on equity income. There are no further repercussions through the general equilibrium of the system. In this sense the differential taxation of retained earnings, unlike the corporate profits tax itself, is neutral.[22]

Compensated Shifts in μ

In concluding this section, it is interesting to ask what happens when μ and τ are changed simultaneously in a way that keeps the net burden of the tax unchanged while increasing the degree of sheltering of retained earnings. In our notation this involves lowering μ and raising τ in a way that keeps $bi_N + (1 - b)e_N$ unchanged.[23] This can also be interpreted as making the tax more like a corporation tax. In the extreme case of complete integration of the personal and corporate taxes, $\mu = 1$ and $\tau = 0$; there is then no difference in the taxation of dividends, retained earnings, and interest; as μ falls and τ rises, we move toward the current type of corporation tax.

Since an increase in τ lowers i_N, while a change in μ does not alter i_N, the combined change in τ and μ also lowers i_N. The requirement that the net portfolio yield $(bi_N + [1 - b]e_N)$ remain unchanged implies that e_N must rise. As the equal yield tax changes in the direction of a corporate-style tax, the net equity yield increases, while the net return on debt falls. Moreover, since $dp/d\tau < 0$ and $dp/d\mu = 0$, the compensated change of increased sheltering has the effect of increasing the fraction of income that is retained.

22. It should be emphasized again that this neutrality holds only in the special case of $\eta' = 0$ that we are examining in this section.

23. Recall that we are assuming that $\eta' = 0$ and therefore that b is fixed. Fixing the net portfolio yield $bi_N + (1 - b)e_N$ is equivalent to fixing the net burden of the tax.

The Nonneutrality of the Corporate Income Tax

Our analysis has shown that the current structure of corporate and personal taxes can substantially distort the financial behavior of firms. This occurs even though we have assumed that the stock of capital at each instant of time is fixed and that all business activity occurs in a corporate form. If we drop either of these assumptions, there is a further source of distortion in either the intertemporal or intersectoral allocation of resources. Before discussing the possibility of such additional distortions, we shall examine the nature of the nonneutrality of the corporation tax in a one-sector economy with a fixed growth rate.

Consider first the nonneutrality of the tax law with respect to the debt-equity ratio. Our analysis showed that the current tax system induces firms to increase their debt-equity ratio. The essential reason for this substitution is that interest payments are deductible in calculating taxable income, while the returns to equity are not. The extent of the substitution is limited because every rise in the firm's debt-equity ratio increases the perceived uncertainty of the firm's interest and equity payments, and this perceived risk raises the cost to the firm of both debt and equity capital. A new equilibrium debt-equity ratio is established at the point where the tax advantage of deductibility just balances the cost induced by the increased riskiness of heavier leverage.

This analysis stands in sharp contrast to two models recently developed by Stiglitz that imply that the corporation tax does not affect the debt-equity ratio. In the first model (1973) Stiglitz postulated that firms retain all of their earnings (that is, pay no dividends) and can borrow at a fixed interest rate to finance investment in excess of these retained earnings. Since all marginal investments are financed wholly by debt in that model, the introduction of a corporate income tax has no effect. The important contribution of that paper is the reminder that previous studies of the corporation tax have been deficient in assuming that all corporate investment is financed wholly by equity. Stiglitz's own assumption that firms can borrow as much as they want at a fixed interest rate is crucial to his conclusion. Stiglitz explicitly recognizes that his assumption would only be tenable in an economy in which there is no uncertainty and would then imply that the marginal product of capital equals the rate of interest ($f' = i$). The inability of this model to explain why any dividends are paid is a further warning against accepting its other conclusions.[24]

24. These remarks should not be regarded as a criticism of Stiglitz's model (which we believe makes an important analytic contribution) but as an explanation of why its implications should not be regarded as directly relevant for any actual economy.

In a subsequent analysis Stiglitz developed a quite different model in which the interest rate paid by the firm is an increasing function of the firm's debt-equity ratio (1976, sec. 5). In the context of this model Stiglitz again concluded that a corporate income tax would not change the firm's optimal debt-equity ratio. More specifically, Stiglitz posited an individual investor who divides his wealth between investment in a corporation (which he controls and which also borrows from others at a rate of interest that is an increasing function of the firm's debt-equity ratio) and investment in an unspecified alternative asset with a fixed return. In Stiglitz's formulation of the problem, the introduction of a corporate income tax does not alter the investor's optimal investment or borrowing decisions. This conclusion rests on the unwarranted assumption that the introduction of a corporation tax at rate τ reduces the net yield on the "alternative asset" by the same factor of $1 - \tau$ that is applied to net corporate income.[25] No reason is offered for this critical assumption. Moreover, the assumption is clearly false if the "alternative asset" is assumed to be the market portfolio of debt and equity or the debt issued by other corporations. The yield on the alternative asset will fall by the corporate tax rate only if this alternative asset consists *exclusively* of equity in other firms. However, this implies that any individual who owns corporate equity invests *only* in corporate equity regardless of the tax, while corporate bonds are held by a wholly separate group. It thus appears that Stiglitz's result that the debt-equity ratio remains unaffected by the tax follows from an implicit assumption that there are two classes of investors, one of which invests only in equity while the other invests only in debt. We therefore reject the "neutrality" conclusion of Stiglitz's second model.

In their justifiably famous article Modigliani and Miller (1958) showed that under certain conditions a firm's debt-equity ratio is indeterminate. One of these crucial conditions is the absence of any taxes. The introduction of the corporation tax in the simplest Modigliani-Miller framework implies that firms will finance their investment by debt only. In his recent presidential address to the American Finance Association, Miller (1976) surveyed the attempts to extend the model to include taxes without reaching this extreme and unrealistic implication. Miller concluded correctly that previous analyses have ignored the tax features that favor equity finance, that is, the absence of any personal tax on retained earnings and the relatively low rate of tax on capital gains. He then argued that this favorable treatment of equity could reestablish the indeter-

25. The crucial character of this assumption is clear, since Stiglitz's argument rests on the tax simply multiplying all terms in the first-order condition by $1 - \tau$.

minacy of the debt-equity ratio and could therefore explain (without introducing considerations of risk related to the debt-equity ratio) why firms have not relied more on debt finance. More specifically, Miller pointed out that the debt-equity ratio is indeterminate if (in our notation) $(1 - \theta) = (1 - \tau) \times [p(1 - \theta) + (1 - p)(1 - \mu\theta)]$; that is, if the after-tax yields on debt and equity are equal. However, since $\theta < \tau$ and $p(1 - \theta) + (1 - p)(1 - \mu\theta) < 1$, this required "indifference condition" is definitely not satisfied in practice. Although Miller is right to stress the full structure of tax incentives, we believe the observed mix of debt and equity can be explained only by incorporating the risk-premium effects of changes in the debt-equity ratio (that is, $\phi' > 0$ and $\psi' > 0$).[26]

In addition to noting the potential effect of the corporation tax on the debt-equity ratio, our own analysis pointed out that the corporate tax lowers the net rate of interest[27] (as well as the yield on equity capital) and reduces the dividend payout rate. Thus, even in the case of an all-corporate economy with a fixed capital stock, the corporate income tax affects every margin of choice.

It is useful to consider the implications of extending our analysis to the type of two-sector economy studied by Harberger (1962, 1966). In this economy, fixed total supplies of capital and labor are divided between corporate and noncorporate production. All capital is equity capital. The introduction of a tax on capital income in the corporate sector involves an excess burden because the allocation of capital and labor between the two sectors is distorted. The introduction of debt finance along the lines developed in our model does not eliminate this excess burden. It is clear from the second section that i_N and e_N are both decreased by the introduction of a corporate income tax; this would induce a shift of capital from the corporate to the noncorporate sector until the net rates of return were again in equilibrium.[28] Note that this change in the allocation of capital and labor might also change the marginal product of labor.

If the savings rate is not fixed, but depends on the net yield to savers, the corporate income tax will also distort the intertemporal allocation of

---

26. Miller appears to accept this at certain places in his address but generally stresses the "indifference condition" and minimizes the importance of uncertainty. Since Miller does not present an explicit complete model, we are uncertain of his final judgment.

27. Stiglitz (1973) concluded that the net rate of interest would be unchanged by the corporation tax, but this rests on the assumption that marginal investments are financed wholly by debt and thus indirectly on the assumption of a riskless economy.

28. The corporation tax reduces the risk as well as the yield of corporate sector investment. The risk effect could in principle outweigh the yield effect and cause capital to flow into the corporate sector (Penner 1964). The implication would still be that the tax is distortionary and creates an excess burden.

resources. In the all-corporate economy, the corporate tax reduces i_N and e_N and therefore the return on the market portfolio. This raises the price of future consumption relative to the price of current consumption and therefore distorts individual consumption and saving decisions. This entails an efficiency loss even if there is no net change in private saving (Feldstein 1977). The distortion is more complex in an economy with noncorporate as well as corporate firms, but the conclusion concerning a potentially large intertemporal misallocation of resources remains unchanged.

Conclusion

In this chapter we have examined the long-run effects of a corporate-type profits tax in a growing economy. Our model explicitly includes optimization by individual firms of their debt-equity ratio and dividend payout rate.

The analysis shows that the corporate-style tax is nonneutral in several important ways even though debt finance is available and the interest payments are deductible in the calculation of taxable income. Even if the economy's saving rate is fixed and all business activity occurs in the corporate form, changes in the tax rate would alter the firms' debt-equity ratio and the dividend payout rate as well as the net-of-tax rates of return earned on both equity and debt investments. With a more general specification of saving behavior and the recognition of an untaxed noncorporate sector, it is clear that this reduction in the net equity and debt yields will alter both saving and the allocation of capital between the corporate and noncorporate sectors.

There are several directions in which the current model should be extended. We have ignored inflation here even though we previously found (with a simpler model) that the interaction of inflation and taxation can be of substantial importance.[29] Although we have discussed the general implications of our research for a two-sector economy, an explicit analysis of the effect of a corporation tax when there is debt and equity finance of the type we analyze and an untaxed noncorporate sector remains to be done. Finally, we have dealt exclusively with the long-run, steady-state characteristics of the economy; it would clearly be useful to analyze the transitional behavior of both corporate borrowing and dividend decisions.

---

29. See Chapter 22 of the present work and Feldstein, Green, and Sheshinski (1978).

22 Inflation, Income Taxes, and the Rate of Interest: A Theoretical Analysis

Income taxes are a central feature of economic life but not of the growth models that we use to study the long-run effects of monetary and fiscal policies. The taxes in current monetary growth models are lump-sum transfers that alter disposable income but do not directly affect factor rewards or the cost of capital. In contrast, the actual personal and corporate income taxes do influence the cost of capital to firms and the net rate of return to savers. The existence of such taxes also in general changes the effect of inflation on the rate of interest and on the process of capital accumulation.[1]

This chapter presents a neoclassical monetary growth model in which the influence of such taxes can be studied. The model is then used in the second and third sections to study the effect of inflation on the rate of interest and on the capital intensity of the economy. James Tobin's early result (1955, 1965) that inflation increases capital intensity appears as a possible special case. More generally, the tax rates and saving behavior determine whether an increase in the rate of inflation will increase or decrease steady-state capital intensity.

The analysis also shows that the net real rate of interest received by savers may be substantially altered by the rate of inflation. The third section discusses the desirability of adjusting the taxation of interest income to eliminate these arbitrary effects of inflation. The fourth section discusses the implications of this for the welfare effects of inflation and the optimal rate of growth of the money supply.

Reprinted from the *American Economic Review* 66 (December 1976), pp. 809–820, by permission of the American Economic Association. I am grateful to the University of California at Berkeley for the opportunity to prepare this paper while I was Ford Research Professor. I am grateful for discussions with Stanley Fischer, Steven Goldman, and David Hartman.

1. Income taxes have been studied in *nonmonetary* growth models by Diamond, K. Sato, and myself (see Chapters 18 and 19). Of course, the effects of inflation cannot be examined in such models.

A Growing Economy with Inflation and Income Taxes

This section presents a one-sector neoclassical model of economic growth with inflation and income taxes. The model differs from that of Tobin (1965) in two fundamental ways: (1) the savings rate depends on the net real rate of return earned by savers; and (2) there are personal and corporate interest income taxes as well as a lump-sum tax.[2] Because the analysis of the model in the next section will focus on comparative steady-state dynamics, only these steady-state properties will be discussed here.

The steady-state economy will be characterized by an inflation rate $\pi = Dp/p$ and a nominal interest rate of i. The real rate of interest is, by definition, $r = i - \pi$. In order to consider the effects of adjusting the tax treatment for the rate of inflation, separate tax rates will be specified for the real and inflation components of the nominal rate of interest. The personal income tax will tax real interest payments at θ_1 and the inflation component at θ_2. The net nominal rate of return is thus $i_N = (1 - \theta_1)r + (1 - \theta_2)\pi$. In our current tax law $\theta_1 = \theta_2$ so that $i_N = (1 - \theta)(r + \pi) = (1 - \theta)i$. With complete inflation indexation, $\theta_2 = 0$ and $i_N = (1 - \theta_1)r + \pi$; the net real rate of interest received by households is thus $r_N = i_N - \pi = (1 - \theta_1)r$.

The economy is characterized by an exogenously growing population:

$$N = N_0 e^{nt}. \tag{1}$$

The labor force is a constant fraction of the population. Production can be described by an aggregate production function with constant returns to scale. The relation between aggregate output per capita (y) and aggregate capital stock per capita (k) is

$$y = f(k), \tag{2}$$

with $f' > 0$ and $f'' < 0$. For simplicity, both technical progress and depreciation are ignored.

The Demand for Capital

The investment and financing behavior of firms is influenced by the corporate income tax. An important feature of the corporation tax is that the interest paid on corporate debt may be deducted by firms in calculating

2. In the more general model of Levhari and Patinkin (1968), the savings rate does depend on the rate of return but there are no corporate or personal income taxes.

taxable profits while dividends paid on corporate equity may not be deducted. Although the method of finance need not affect the analysis in models without a corporate income tax, it is necessary in the current model to identify the method of finance. Because the focus of this chapter is on the effect of inflation on the rate of interest, I will assume that all corporate investment is financed by issuing debt.[3] The tax deduction of interest payments may also be adjusted for inflation: let τ_1 be the tax rate at which the real component of interest payments is deducted and let τ_2 be the tax rate at which the inflation component can be deducted. The net rate of interest paid by firms is then $(1 - \tau_1)r + (1 - \tau_2)\pi$.[4]

In the absence of the corporation tax, the firm maximizes its profit by investing until the marginal product of capital is equal to the real rate of interest, $i - \pi$. Stated somewhat differently, the firm's capital stock is optimal when the marginal product of capital $[f'(k)]$ plus the nominal appreciation in the value of the capital stock per unit of capital (π) is equal to the nominal rate of interest:

$$f'(k) + \pi = i. \tag{3}$$

The effect of the corporation tax on this optimality condition depends on the way that depreciation is treated by the law. Consider first the simple case in which capital lasts forever, that is, in which there is no depreciation. The corporation tax then reduces the net-of-tax marginal product of capital to $(1 - \tau_1)f'(k)$. There is no tax on the unrealized appreciation of the capital stock. The firm maximizes profits by increasing the capital stock until the net nominal return on capital $(1 - \tau_1)f'(k) + \pi$ is equal to the net nominal rate of interest, $(1 - \tau_1)r + (1 - \tau_2)\pi$. The first-order optimum of Eq. (3) therefore becomes

$$f'(k) = r - \left(\frac{\tau_2}{1 - \tau_1}\right)\pi. \tag{4}$$

3. It would of course be desirable to have a more general model in which corporate debt and equity coexist. The exclusion of equity in the current analysis and the full deductibility of corporate interest payments imply that the present value of corporation taxes is zero. The present model might therefore be regarded as an approximation to a model in which equity profits are intramarginal and all marginal investments are financed by debt (see Joseph Stiglitz 1973). Dale Henderson and Thomas Sargent (1973) studied the effect of inflation in an economy in which firms finance all investment by issuing equity. Because they use a short-run analysis with no accumulation of capital, their conclusions cannot be compared to those of the current analysis. After this paper was accepted for publication, Jerry Green, Eytan Sheshinski, and I developed a more general extension of the current analysis in which firms use an optimal mix of equity and debt finance (Feldstein, Green, and Sheshinski 1978).

4. In steady-state growth with fully anticipated inflation there is no need to distinguish between short-term debt and long-term debt.

If the capital stock does depreciate, $f'(k)$ can be interpreted as the marginal product of capital net of the cost of replacing the capital that has been used up in production. If the corporation tax allows the deduction of the replacement cost of this depreciation, the net-of-tax marginal product of capital is again $(1 - \tau_1)f'(k)$, and Eq. (4) continues to hold. I will use this condition to describe the demand for capital.[5]

Liquidity Preference

The real value of household assets is the sum of the real values of outside money (M/p) and corporate bonds (B/p):

$$A = \frac{M}{p} + \frac{B}{p}. \tag{5}$$

Since outside money bears no interest, the ratio of money to bonds that households will hold is a decreasing function of the after-tax nominal rate of return on bonds, $i_N = (1 - \theta_1)r + (1 - \theta_2)\pi$. The real value of bonds (B/p) is also the real value of the capital stock (K). The liquidity preference relation can therefore be written in per capita terms as

$$\frac{m}{k} = L[(1 - \theta_1)r + (1 - \theta_2)\pi], \quad L' < 0, \tag{6}$$

where $m = M/pN$, the real money balances per capita. In steady state, m/k must remain constant. Equivalently, M/pK remains constant, that is, the rate of growth of M is equal to the rate of growth of pK or $\pi + n$. Thus[6]

$$\pi = \frac{DM}{M} - n. \tag{7}$$

---

5. The U.S. corporation tax does not allow replacement cost depreciation but partly offsets historic cost depreciation with accelerated depreciation schedules. An analysis of the effect of historic cost depreciation is presented in the paper by Feldstein, Green, and Sheshinski (1978).

6. Stein (1970) examined a more general Keynes-Wicksell model in which the adjustment of price to the excess demand for cash balances is not immediate. Fischer (1972) explained that in the long run a steady rate of increase of the money supply will come to be anticipated, causing the Keynes-Wicksell behavior to converge to the familiar neoclassical behavior of Eq. (7). All of the results of this chapter will therefore continue to hold in a Keynes-Wicksell version of the current model.

The Supply of Savings

In steady-state growth, the supply of savings (S) is proportional to the households' real disposable income (H). The savings propensity may of course depend on the real net return that savers receive:

$$S = \sigma(r_N) \cdot H. \tag{8}$$

Disposable income is equal to national income (Y) minus both the government's tax receipts (T) and the fall in the real value of the population's money balances ($\pi M/p$).[7] The total taxes are the sum of the corporate tax, the personal interest income tax, and a residual tax that may be regarded as a lump-sum or payroll tax. The government uses these tax receipts plus the increase in the money supply (DM/p) to finance its purchases of public consumption (G). Disposable income is therefore

$$H = Y - T - \frac{\pi M}{p} = Y - G + \frac{DM}{p} - \frac{\pi M}{p}. \tag{9}$$

Since $\pi = DM/M - n$,

$$H = Y - G + nM/p. \tag{10}$$

If public consumption is a constant fraction of real national income ($G = \gamma Y$), per capita disposable income is

$$h = y(1 - \gamma) + nm. \tag{11}$$

Per capita saving is therefore

$$s = \sigma(r_N) \cdot [y(1 - \gamma) + mn]. \tag{12}$$

Growth Equilibrium

All savings must be absorbed in either additional capital accumulation or additional real money balances:

$$S = DK + DM/p. \tag{13}$$

---

7. The capital loss on corporate bonds is just offset by the difference between the real and nominal interest rates paid by firms. There are no corporate retained earnings.

The constant ratio of capital to labor in steady-state growth implies that $DK = nK$. Similarly, the constancy of $m = M/pN$ implies that the rate of growth of (M/p) is nM/p. The requirement of equilibrium growth is therefore, in per capita terms,

$$s = nk + nm \tag{14}$$

or

$$\sigma(r_N) \cdot [(1 - \gamma)y + nm] = nk + nm. \tag{15}$$

This completes the specification of the model. It is useful to collect now the six equations that jointly determine y, h, k, m, r, and π:

$$y = f(k) \tag{2}$$

$$h = y(1 - \gamma) + nm \tag{11}$$

$$\sigma[(1 - \theta_1)r - \theta_2\pi] \cdot h = nk + nm \tag{15'}$$

$$f'(k) = r - \left(\frac{\tau_2}{1 - \tau_1}\right)\pi \tag{4}$$

$$m = L[(1 - \theta_1)r + (1 - \theta_2)\pi]k \tag{6}$$

$$\pi = \frac{DM}{M} - n \tag{7}$$

The exogenous variables are the rate of population growth n, and the government policy variables $\theta_1, \theta_2, \tau_1, \tau_2$, and DM/M.

Effects of Changes in the Rate of Inflation

The model of the previous section will now be used to study the effects of inflation on capital accumulation and interest rates. Although the rate of inflation is endogenous, the model can be decomposed to obtain π as the difference between the two exogenous variables, DM/M and n. The analysis can then proceed to use the remaining five equations with π regarded as predetermined.

By appropriate substitution for y, h, m, and r in Eq. (15'), the growth equilibrium provides the basic relation between the equilibrium capital intensity and the steady-state rate of inflation:

$$\sigma[(1 - \theta_1)(f' + \pi\tau_2/(1 - \tau_1)) - \theta_2\pi] \cdot [(1 - \gamma)f + nkL]$$
$$= nk(1 + L), \quad (16)$$

where the arguments of L in Eq. (6) are not explicitly specified. Total differentiation with respect to k and π yields

$$\frac{dk}{d\pi} =$$

$$\frac{(1 - \sigma)nk[(1 - \theta_1)\tau_2/(1 - \tau_1) + (1 - \theta_2)]L' - h[(1 - \theta_1)\tau_2/(1 - \tau_1) - \theta_2]\sigma'}{\sigma[(1 - \gamma)f' + nL] - n(1 + L) - (1 - \sigma)nkL'(1 - \theta_1)f'' + h'\sigma'(1 - \theta_1)f''} \cdot$$
$$(17)$$

The denominator can be shown to be unambiguously negative if the savings rate is a nondecreasing function of the real rate of return, $\sigma' \geq 0$.[8] With this condition, the denominator is clearly negative if $\sigma[(1 - \gamma)f' + nL] - n(1 + L) < 0$. To show that this inequality is true, multiply by k and substitute $m = kL$ to obtain the equivalent condition

$$\sigma[(1 - \gamma)kf' + nm] - (nk + nm) < 0.$$

From Eq. (15),

$$nk + nm = \sigma[(1 - \gamma)f + nm].$$

The required condition is therefore

$$\sigma[(1 - \gamma)kf' + nm] < \sigma[(1 - \gamma)f + nm]$$

or $kf' < f$ which clearly holds. The sign of $dk/d\pi$ is therefore the opposite of the sign of the numerator.

The first term of the numerator,

$$(1 - \sigma)nk[(1 - \theta_1)\tau_2/(1 - \tau_1) + (1 - \theta_2)]L',$$

---

8. This is equivalent to $\sigma(r_N) \geq 0$ in the asset demand equation (8). In a life-cycle model, this occurs if an increase in the real net rate of interest causes a postponement in consumption. In the simple two-period model in which all income is earned in the first period, $\sigma(r_N) \geq 0$ is equivalent to an elasticity of substitution of the two-period utility function that is greater than or equal to one. Although I will only discuss the implications of $\sigma' \geq 0$, the opposite may be true and its implications deserve examination.

is unambiguously negative because the demand for money is inversely related to the nominal rate of interest, $L' < 0$. If the savings rate is an increasing function of the real net rate of interest ($\sigma' > 0$), the sign of the second term and therefore of the entire numerator depends on the nature of taxation. In two important special cases, the second term is zero and therefore the numerator is negative:

1. *Full tax indexing:* There is full indexing of the taxation of interest income, that is, the personal income tax is on the real rate of interest only ($\theta_2 = 0$), and the corporation tax allows a deduction only for real interest payments ($\tau_2 = 0$).
2. *Equal tax rates:* There is no indexing of the taxation of interest income but the rate of corporation tax is the same as the rate of personal income tax, that is, $\theta_1 = \theta_2 = \tau_1 = \tau_2$.

In both these cases, $(1 - \theta_1)\tau_2/(1 - \tau_1) - \theta_2 = 0$ so that the second term is zero, the numerator is negative, and $dk/d\pi > 0$. In these cases the sensitivity of the savings rate to the net rate of interest (σ') influences the magnitude but not the direction of the impact of inflation on equilibrium capital intensity. The direction of the impact reflects the reduction in desired liquidity that results from the higher nominal rate of interest that accompanies inflation. A smaller ratio of real money balances to capital implies that a larger fraction of savings is channeled into real capital accumulation. The resulting increase in capital intensity lowers the real net rate of interest; if savings respond positively to this rate of interest, there is a reduction in the rate of savings that partly offsets the portfolio composition effect but that cannot reverse its sign. This dampening effect of the savings response appears as the term $h\sigma'(1 - \theta_1)f''$ that increases the absolute size of the denominator.

Neither of the two cases considered above corresponds to the current situation in the United States. There is no indexing of the taxation of interest payments. The real and inflation components of the nominal interest rate are treated in the same way by both the personal and corporate income taxes: $\theta_2 = \theta_1$ and $\tau_2 = \tau_1$. Because of the progressivity of the personal income tax, a simple comparison of the corporate and personal income tax rates is not possible.[9] I will therefore consider the implications of both $\theta < \tau$ and $\theta > \tau$ where the common rate of the income tax is denoted $\theta = \theta_1 = \theta_2$ and that of the corporate tax is denoted $\tau = \tau_1 = \tau_2$. The analysis will assume that the savings rate is an increasing function of

9. The actual problem of comparison is even more complex because individuals as well as corporations are borrowers.

the net rate of interest; the reader can easily discover the implications of reversing this assumption.

When the corporation tax rate exceeds the personal tax rate, inflation induces an increase in the savings rate that reinforces the reduction in liquidity. To understand the nature of this reinforcing effect, recall from Eq. (4) that

$$r = f'(k) + \left(\frac{\tau_2}{1 - \tau_1}\right)\pi. \tag{18}$$

With $\tau_2 = \tau_1$, the nominal rate of interest is

$$i = r + \pi = f'(k) + \frac{\pi}{1 - \tau}. \tag{19}$$

Since the personal income tax is levied at rate θ on this nominal rate of interest, the real net rate received by savers is

$$r_N = (1 - \theta)i - \pi = (1 - \theta)f'(k) + \left(\frac{\tau - \theta}{1 - \tau}\right)\pi. \tag{20}$$

At any given level of capital intensity, $f'(k)$ is a constant and the direct effect of an increase in π is to increase r_N whenever $\tau > \theta$. This increase in r_N induces a higher rate of saving and therefore greater capital accumulation. More formally, it is clear from Eq. (17) that increasing the value of τ causes an increase in $dk/d\pi$ whenever $\sigma' > 0$.

Equation (20) also shows that when the corporation tax rate is less than the personal tax rate, inflation induces a reduction in r_N and therefore in the savings rate. The net effect of inflation on capital intensity depends on the relative strength of the negative savings effect and the positive liquidity effect. There is no unambiguous a priori conclusion. Recall that inflation increases capital intensity if and only if the numerator of Eq. (17) is negative. With $\theta_1 = \theta_2 = \theta$ and $\tau_1 = \tau_2 = \tau$, this condition reduces to $dk/d\pi > 0$ if and only if

$$h(\theta - \tau)\sigma' + (1 - \sigma)nk(1 - \theta)L' < 0. \tag{21}$$

A series of substitutions and manipulations shows that this condition is equivalent to

$$\frac{\eta_L}{\eta_S} > \frac{a}{(1 - \sigma)m} \cdot \frac{\theta - \tau}{1 - \theta} \cdot \frac{i_N}{r_N}, \tag{22}$$

where $\eta_L = -i_N L'/L$, the elasticity of the demand for real money balances relative to capital with respect to the nominal net rate of interest, and $\eta_S = r_N \sigma'/\sigma$, the elasticity of the savings rate with respect to the real net rate of interest.[10] Recall that $a = k + m$, total wealth per person, and that $r_N = i_N - \pi$. Note that (22) shows that $dk/d\pi > 0$ is more likely when the demand for liquidity is interest-sensitive (η_L is large) and when savings behavior is not sensitive to the net yield (η_S is small). The required inequality is clearly satisfied in the cases that were previously considered: $\theta \leqslant \tau$ (or $\eta_S = 0$). But if $\theta > \tau$ and $\eta_S > 0$, the inequality in (22) may not be satisfied. When inequality (22) is false, an increase in the rate of inflation reduces equilibrium capital intensity. Consider, therefore, some plausible values for the right-hand side. At the end of 1974, total private wealth was approximately \$4 trillion. A useful empirical measure of the stock of outside money is the monetary base, the sum of currency in circulation and member bank reserves at the Federal Reserve Banks. At the end of 1974, the monetary base was approximately \$100 billion. With an average saving rate of $\sigma = 0.1$, the value of $a/(1 - \sigma)m$ is approximately 40.[11] If $\tau = 0.5$ and $\theta = 0.6$, (22) is equivalent to

$$\frac{\eta_L}{\eta_S} > 10\frac{i_N}{r_N}. \tag{23}$$

Starting from a situation in which there is no inflation (that is, $i_N = r_N$), the introduction of positive inflation will increase capital intensity only if $\eta_L > 10\eta_S$. With a substantial rate of inflation, the condition for $dk/d\pi > 0$ is even more difficult to satisfy. From Eqs. (19) and (20) we obtain

$$\frac{i_N}{r_N} = \frac{(1 - \theta)f'(k) + \left(\dfrac{1 - \theta}{1 - \tau}\right)\pi}{(1 - \theta)f'(k) + \left(\dfrac{\tau - \theta}{1 - \tau}\right)\pi}. \tag{24}$$

10. If $r_N < 0$, η_S is not well defined. The inequality (7) can instead be written

$$\frac{L'/L}{\sigma'/\sigma} > \frac{a}{(1 - \sigma)m} \cdot \frac{\theta - \tau}{1 - \theta}$$

whenever $\sigma' > 0$, even if $r_N < 0$.

11. Restricting attention to outside money ignores the role of private banks in creating liquidity. A broader measure of the money supply, defined as currency plus demand deposits, was \$285 billion at the end of 1974, implying $a/(1 - \sigma)m = 16$. However, most of the money supply measured in this was "inside money" and not appropriate to the current model.

If, for example, $\pi = f'(k) = 0.12$, Eq. (24) implies that $i_N/r_N = 0.144/0.024 = 6$. The inequality in (23) now implies that $dk/d\pi > 0$ only if $\eta_L > 60\eta_S$.[12]

The above examples are only illustrative. They nevertheless indicate that, in an economy with a relatively high rate of tax on interest income, an increase in the rate of inflation may decrease capital intensity. More generally, the presence of taxes may reduce or magnify a positive effect of inflation on capital intensity.

Effects of Inflation on Interest Rates

The relation of the interest rate to the rate of inflation is substantially influenced by the presence of the corporation and personal income tax. This is true even if inflation has no effect on the capital intensity of production. As a result, the real net rate of return earned by savers also generally depends on the rate of inflation.

The basic marginal productivity relation derived above,

$$r = f'(k) + \left(\frac{\tau_2}{1 - \tau_1}\right)\pi, \tag{25}$$

implies that the nominal rate of interest is

$$i = f'(k) + \left(\frac{1 + \tau_2 - \tau_1}{1 - \tau_1}\right)\pi \tag{26}$$

and the real rate of return is

$$r_N = (1 - \theta_1)f'(k) + \left[\frac{(1 - \theta_1)\tau_2 - (1 - \tau_1)\theta_2}{1 - \tau_1}\right]\pi. \tag{27}$$

Consider first the effect of inflation on the nominal rate of interest. Irving Fisher originally explained that the nominal interest rate would rise by the rate of inflation, thus leaving the real interest rate unchanged. The force of his argument rests on the equivalence of the real interest, the cost

---

12. There is substantial controversy about the magnitudes of η_L and η_S. In earlier econometric studies I found that $di/d\ln M$ was approximately 10, implying that η_L is approximately 0.01 (see Feldstein and Chamberlain 1973 and Feldstein and Eckstein 1970). The estimates of η_S range from negative to positive, but none of the estimates measures r_N correctly as the real net-of-tax rate of return. Obviously, even a very moderate positive value of η_S would exceed the η_L reported above.

of capital to the firm, and the real return to savers. Although all three would be equal in the absence of taxation, the current analysis has shown that this is not true in an economy with corporate and personal income taxes. Tobin's analysis (1965) modified Fisher's conclusion: because inflation reduces the demand for money balances, it increases capital intensity, lowers the real rate of return, and thus causes the nominal rate of interest to rise by less than the rate of inflation. Again this analysis ignores the effect of the personal and corporate income tax.[13]

In contrast, Eq. (26) implies that

$$\frac{di}{d\pi} = \frac{1 + \tau_2 - \tau_1}{1 - \tau_1} + \left(\frac{dk}{d\pi}\right)f''. \tag{28}$$

Fisher's conclusion that $di/d\pi = 1$ corresponds to the special case of no taxes and an interest-insensitive demand for real money balances.[14] In Tobin's analysis this is modified by the fall in the marginal product of capital, $df'/d\pi = (dk/d\pi)f'' < 0$, where $dk/d\pi$ reflects a portfolio composition effect but no savings effect. The magnitude of this portfolio composition effect is, however, very small. Even if the relevant money supply is defined to include inside money, the value of the money stock is less than 10 percent of the value of real assets. Thus, even if some rate of inflation would completely eliminate the demand for money, the equilibrium capital stock would rise by less than 10 percent. With a Cobb-Douglas technology, the marginal product of capital would fall by less than one-tenth of its previous value. It is difficult therefore to imagine that the absolute value of the portfolio effect, $(dk/d\pi)f''$, exceeds 0.01.

In the more general case in which taxes are recognized, the nominal rate of interest may rise by substantially more than the rate of inflation. With no tax indexing, $\tau_2 = \tau_1 = \tau$, and

$$\frac{di}{d\pi} = \frac{1}{1 - \tau} + \left(\frac{dk}{d\pi}\right)f''. \tag{29}$$

With no change in capital intensity, $di/d\pi = (1 - \tau)^{-1}$; a corporate tax rate of $\tau = 0.5$ implies that the nominal rate of interest rises by *twice* the rate of inflation. The analysis of the previous section shows that $dk/d\pi$

---

13. Bailey (1956) provides a similar analysis of the effect of inflation on the rate of interest through the change in money balances. His analysis is static and also ignores taxation.

14. Equation (17) shows that $\tau_1 = \tau_2 = \theta_1 = \theta_2 = 0$ and $L' = 0$ imply $dk/d\pi = 0$.

may be greater or less than zero. The nominal rate of interest may therefore rise by either more or less than *twice* the rate of inflation.[15]

With tax indexing, $\tau_2 = 0$, and

$$\frac{di}{d\pi} = 1 + \left(\frac{dk}{d\pi}\right)f''. \tag{30}$$

Here with no change in capital intensity the original Fisherian conclusion that $di/d\pi = 1$ obtains. The previous section also showed that with full tax indexing ($\theta_2 = \tau_2 = 0$), the sign of $dk/d\pi$ is determined by the portfolio composition effect and thus $(dk/d\pi)f'' < 0$. With full tax indexing of interest payments, the nominal interest rate will rise by slightly less than the rate of inflation.

Consider now the effect of inflation on the real net rate of interest received by savers. Equation (27) implies

$$\frac{dr_N}{d\pi} = \left[\frac{(1 - \theta_1)\tau_2 - (1 - \tau_1)\theta_2}{1 - \tau_1}\right] + (1 - \theta_1)\left(\frac{dk}{d\pi}\right)f''. \tag{31}$$

If there are no taxes and the demand for real balances is not sensitive to the rate of interest, Eq. (31) yields the Fisherian conclusion that the real return to savers is unaffected by inflation, $dr_N/d\pi = 0$. In two further special cases, the effect of inflation on the real net interest rate is limited to the relatively small portfolio composition effect: $(1 - \theta)(dk/d\pi)f'' < 0$. If there is full tax indexing ($\theta_2 = \tau_2 = 0$) or equal tax rates for corporations and households ($\theta_1 = \tau_1$ and $\theta_2 = \tau_2$), the first term of Eq. (31) is zero and the sign of $dk/d\pi$ depends only on the portfolio composition effect.[16]

More generally, however, inflation can have a substantial effect on the savers' real net rate of return. If there is no indexing, Eq. (31) reduces to

$$\frac{dr_N}{d\pi} = \left(\frac{\tau - \theta}{1 - \tau}\right) + (1 - \theta)\left(\frac{dk}{d\pi}\right)f''. \tag{32}$$

---

15. Recent empirical studies suggest that during the past decade the long-term corporate bond rate has increased by approximately the increase in the rate of inflation (see Feldstein and Chamberlain 1973, Feldstein and Eckstein 1970, and Gordon 1971). This is smaller than the steady-state increase suggested by the analyses above, especially since there was unlikely to have been any substantial induced change in capital intensity during so short a period. The difference reflects the failure of the above analysis to allow for equity financing, historic cost depreciation, and personal capital gains taxation. In addition, the estimated $di/d\pi$ in the studies noted above may differ from the value of $di/d\pi$ in a sustained inflation.

16. Recall that Eq. (17) and the discussion in the previous section established that either of these conditions makes $dk/d\pi > 0$.

If the corporate tax rate exceeds the personal tax rate, the first term is positive and the second term is negative.[17] The real net rate of return may either rise or fall. If the personal tax rate is higher than the corporate tax rate, the first term is negative. The previous section showed that in this case $dk/d\pi$ can be either positive or negative. If $dk/d\pi < 0$, an increase in the rate of inflation reduces the saver's real net return. If $dk/d\pi > 0$, the change in r_N depends on the balancing of the two effects.

The case in which $dk/d\pi = 0$ illustrates the potential magnitude of the effect of inflation on r_N when $\theta > \tau$. If the marginal product of capital is $f'(k) = 0.12$ and the personal tax rate is $\theta = 0.6$, the net rate of return in the absence of inflation is $r_N = (1 - \theta)f' = 0.048$. If the corporate tax rate is $\tau = 0.5$, a 12 percent rate of inflation reduces r_N by 0.024 to half of its previous value, $r_N = 0.024$.

This substantial sensitivity of r_N to inflation is a result of our tax system. Equations (32) and (17) show that without taxes ($\theta = \tau = 0$), r_N is unaffected by inflation except for the small liquidity effect on capital intensity.[18] A tax system in which the effective tax rate on capital income changes with the rate of inflation is arbitrary and inequitable.[19] If the definition of taxable interest income is altered to tax only the real interest ($\theta_1 > 0, \theta_2 = 0$) and to allow companies to deduct only the real component of interest payments ($\tau_1 > 0, \tau_2 = 0$), the return to savers will remain constant except for the liquidity effect; this is seen for $\tau_2 = \theta_2 = 0$ in Eqs. (31) and (17). Complete indexing in this way also keeps unchanged the ratio of the tax paid to the net return. The magnitude of the possible changes in effective tax rates and net yields under our current tax system indicates the importance of revising the definition of taxable income and expenses to neutralize the effects of inflation.

The Welfare Effects of Inflation

Studies of the welfare effects of anticipated inflation have focused on the distortion in the demand for money that results from inflation.[20] More recently, Edmund Phelps has pointed out that the revenue from inflation

17. The previous section showed that $\tau > 0$ implies $dk/d\pi > 0$.

18. With $L' = 0$, r_N is constant.

19. A number of recent discussions have emphasized that real tax liabilities should be independent of inflation. This has prompted proposals to adjust the income tax by the consumer price index so that the progressivity of the rate schedule does not cause inflation to increase real tax burdens. There have also been proposals to change the taxation of capital gains by adjusting the "cost" basis for changes in the consumer price index.

20. The analysis of this issue began with Friedman (1969) and Bailey (1956). Subsequent contributions are discussed in Clower (1971), Johnson (1971), and Phelps (1973).

permits a reduction in other distorting taxes so that some inflation is part of an optimal set of taxes when lump-sum taxation is not possible. These studies have been done with a basic model in which there are no interest income taxes. The current analysis suggests an additional important effect of inflation on economic welfare: inflation changes the distortion in saving that is due to the tax on interest income.

The corporation tax and the personal interest income tax introduce a differential between the marginal productivity of capital $[f'(k)]$ and the real net rate of return received by savers (r_N). Equation (27) implies that with no indexing this relation is

$$r_N = (1 - \theta)f'(k) + \left(\frac{\tau - \theta}{1 - \tau}\right)\pi. \tag{33}$$

The differential between r_N and $f'(k)$ depends on the tax rates and the rate of inflation. If $\tau > \theta$, a positive rate of inflation can reduce the distorting effect of taxation. With $\pi = [\theta(1 - \tau)/(\tau - \theta)]f'(k)$, the net rate of return to savers is equal to the marginal product of capital. If, however, $\tau < \theta$, a positive rate of inflation increases the differential between $f'(k)$ and r_N.

Phelps stressed that the increase in money that causes inflation is also a source of government revenue that permits a reduction in distortionary tax rates.[21] With a corporation tax and a personal interest income tax, the effect of inflation on government revenue is more complex. With no indexing of interest income, a rise in nominal interest payments increases revenues from the personal income tax but decreases revenues from the corporation tax. Total tax payments will rise with an increase in nominal interest payments if $\theta > \tau$ and will fall if $\theta < \tau$.

Since nominal interest payments per capita are ik, the net tax revenue on these payments is $(\theta - \tau)ik$. The change in net revenue from this source when inflation increases is therefore

$$\frac{d[(\theta - \tau)ik]}{d\pi} = \frac{\theta - \tau}{1 - \tau}\left\{k + [\pi + (1 - \tau) \cdot (f' + kf'')]\left(\frac{dk}{d\pi}\right)\right\}. \tag{34}$$

Since the sign of $f' + kf''$ depends on the form of the production function, the sign of the right-hand side of (34) cannot be unambiguously deter-

---

21. Phelps used a model in which the tax is levied on wage income and distorts the labor-leisure choice. The current model could easily be extended to include such a tax. Tax-induced changes in labor supply are equivalent to changes in the labor force participation rate and would not alter the effects of inflation on the capital intensity of production or the rate of interest. See Chapter 18.

mined without further restrictions. In the most plausible case,[22] $[\pi + (1 - \tau)(f' + kf'')] > 0$, so the change in net revenue is negative if $\tau > \theta$ and $dk/d\pi > 0$. The second section showed that $\tau > \theta$ does imply $dk/d\pi > 0$ and therefore that inflation reduces tax revenue. In the opposite case of $\theta > \tau$, an increase in inflation may increase revenue.[23]

The relation between the effect on revenue and the effect on the differential between $f'(k)$ and r_N should be noted. When $\tau > \theta$, a small positive rate of inflation reduces the differential between $f'(k)$ and r_N but also causes a reduction in tax revenue from this source. Although the distortion in the supply and demand for capital is reduced, the fall in net revenue requires an increase in tax rates that increases distortion elsewhere. Conversely, when $\tau < \theta$, a positive rate of inflation exacerbates the distortionary differential between $f'(k)$ and r_N but may yield an increase in tax revenue that permits a reduction in other distortionary taxes.

Of course, if the corporation tax and the personal income tax are fully adjusted so that they recognize only real interest payments, there is no effect of inflation on either the differential between $f'(k)$ and r_N or on the net tax revenue.[24] A more complete adjustment by the government would also provide interest-bearing money that would eliminate both the liquidity and revenue effects of inflation. But until such changes are made, determining the optimal steady-state rate of inflation requires balancing at least three effects of inflation on economic welfare: (1) the welfare loss that results from reduced liquidity; (2) the change in welfare that results from the increase or decrease in the differential between the marginal product of capital and individuals' marginal rate of substitution; and (3) the change in other distorting taxes that results from the increase or decrease in the net tax revenue in response to inflation. With this broader model of economic effects, it is no longer possible to conclude as Friedman did (1969) that the optimal rate of inflation is negative or as Phelps did (1973) that the optimal finance of government expenditures should include a heavy tax on liquidity through a high rate of inflation. A full evaluation of the optimal rate of inflation with our current tax rules is a subject for another study.

22. Note that kf''/f' is the elasticity of the marginal productivity of capital with respect to the capital intensity. With Cobb-Douglas technology, this is $\alpha - 1$ and $[\pi + (1 - \tau)(f' + kf'')]$ is unambiguously positive. Unless the elasticity of substitution is very great, the sign of $[\pi + (1 - \tau)(f' + kf'')]$ will be positive.

23. If $\theta > \tau$, net revenue will increase with inflation if $dk/d\pi > 0$. The second section showed that $\theta > \tau$ leaves the sign of $dk/d\pi$ uncertain. If the portfolio composition effect dominates the savings effect, $\theta > \tau$ does imply $dk/d\pi > 0$. In this case, an increase in inflation causes an increase in tax receipts.

24. There will be a small effect on tax revenue because of the increase in capital intensity that results from the change in portfolio composition.

Conclusion

This chapter has explored the impact of inflation in a growing economy. The presence of the corporate and personal income taxes substantially alters the effect of inflation on the capital intensity of production, the market rate of interest, and the real net return to savers. The existing theories of the optimal rate of anticipated inflation must be revised in light of these effects. The analysis also suggests that recent proposals to adjust the tax rules for inflation should be modified to include a specific adjustment for the inflation premium in the rate of interest.

There are several directions in which this research might usefully be extended. First, the model of financial behavior was highly simplified. It might be enriched to include corporate equity finance, household borrowing, and the use of inside money.[25] Second, this chapter focuses only on the steady-state effects of fully anticipated inflation. An analysis of the transition path would be valuable. Third, a model with two sectors would allow an analysis of the problems considered by Duncan Foley and Miguel Sidrauski (1971) as well as the issues raised by a tax that is limited to the corporate sector.

With a richer analytic structure, it would be both possible and necessary to introduce evidence with which to quantify the effects that have been discussed. The problem of inflation is likely to remain with us for a long time to come. It is important to improve our analytic understanding of its effects and to adjust our institutions accordingly.

25. A model with equity finance is presented in Feldstein, Green, and Sheshinski (1978).

REFERENCES

INDEX

References

Aaron, H. J. 1972. *Subsidies and Shelters: Who Benefits from Federal Housing Policies*. Washington, D.C.: Brookings Institution.

Abel, A. 1978. "Investment and the Value of Capital." Ph.D. dissertation, M.I.T.

Agarwala, R., and G. C. Goodson. 1969. "An Analysis of the Effects of Investment Incentives on Investment Behaviour in the British Economy." *Economica* 36 (November): 377–388.

Akerlof, G. 1970. "The Market for 'Lemons': Asymmetrical Information and Market Behavior." *Quarterly Journal of Economics* 84 (August): 488–500.

Almon, S. 1965. "The Distributed Lag between Capital Appropriations and Expenditures." *Econometrica* 33 (January): 178–196.

Amemiya, T., and W. Fuller. 1965. *A Comparative Study of Alternative Estimators in a Distributed-Lag Model*. Technical report no. 12, Stanford Institute for Mathematical Studies in the Social Sciences.

Ando, A., and F. Modigliani. 1963. "The 'Life Cycle' Hypothesis of Saving: Aggregate Implications and Tests." *American Economic Review* 53 (March): 55–84.

Andrews, W. D. 1974. "A Consumption-type or Cash Flow Personal Income Tax." *Harvard Law Review* 87 (6): 1113–1188.

——— 1969. *Federal Income Taxation, Cases, Problems and Notes*. Boston: Little, Brown.

Arena, J. J. 1964. "Capital Gains and the 'Life Cycle' Hypothesis of Saving." *American Economic Review* 54 (March): 107–111.

Arrow, K. J. 1965. *Aspects of the Theory of Risk Bearing*. The Yrjo Jahnsson Lectures. Helsinki: Yrjo Jahnsson Foundation.

——— 1964. "Optimal Capital Policy, the Cost of Capital, and Myopic Decision Rules." *Annals of the Institute of Statistical Mathematics*, vol. 16, nos. 1–2, Tokyo. Reprint no. 85, Stanford Institute for Mathematical Studies in the Social Sciences.

Arrow, K. J., H. Chenery, B. Minhas, and R. Solow. 1961. "Capital-Labor Substitution and Economic Efficiency." *Review of Economics and Statistics* 43 (August): 225–250.

Atkinson, T. R. 1956. *The Pattern of Financial Asset Ownership*. Princeton, N.J.: Princeton University Press.

Auerbach, A. J. 1979a. "Wealth Maximization and the Cost of Capital." *Quarterly Journal of Economics* 93 (August): 433–446.

——— 1979b. "Share Valuation and Corporate Equity Policy." *Journal of Public Economics* 11 (June): 291–305.

Bailey, M. J. 1957. "Saving and the Rate of Interest." *Journal of Political Economy* 65 (August): 279–305.

——— 1956. "Welfare Cost of Inflationary Finance." *Journal of Political Economy* 64 (April): 93–110.

Balinfante, A. 1972. "The Identification of Technical Change in the Electricity Generating Industry." In *Production Economics: A Dual Approach to Theory and Applications,* ed. M. Fuss and D. MacFadden. Amsterdam: North-Holland.

Balogh, T. 1958. "Differential Profits Tax." *Economic Journal* 68 (September): 528–532.

Balopoulos, E. T. 1967. *Fiscal Policy Models of the British Economy.* Amsterdam: North-Holland.

Barlow, R., H. E. Brazer, and J. N. Morgan. 1966. *Economic Behavior of the Affluent.* Washington, D.C.: Brookings Institution.

Barna, T. S. 1961. "On Measuring Capital." In *The Theory of Capital,* ed. F. A. Lutz and D. C. Hague. London: Macmillan.

Bhatia, K. B. 1971. "Capital Gains and the Aggregate Consumption Function." Research Report 7112, Department of Economics, University of Western Ontario, May 1971.

Bhattacharya, S. 1979. "Imperfect Information, Dividend Policy, and 'The Bird in the Hand' Fallacy." *The Bell Journal of Economics* 10 (Spring): 259–270.

Bischoff, C. W. 1971. "The Effect of Alternative Lag Distributions." In *Tax Incentives and Capital Spending,* ed. G. Fromm. Washington, D.C.: Brookings Institution. Pp. 61–130.

——— 1969. "Hypothesis Testing and the Demand for Capital Goods." *Review of Economics and Statistics* 51 (August): 354–368.

——— 1968. "Lags in Fiscal and Monetary Impacts on Investment in Producers' Durable Equipment." Cowles Foundation Discussion Paper no. 250, Cowles Foundation for Research in Economics, Yale University.

Black, J. 1959. "Investment Allowances, Initial Allowances and Cheap Loans as a Means of Encouraging Investment." *Review of Economic Studies* 27 (October): 44–49.

Blume, E., J. Crockett, and I. Friend. 1974. "Stockownership in the United States: Characteristics and Trends." *Survey of Current Business* 54 (November): 16–40.

Boskin, M. J. 1978. "Taxation, Saving and the Rate of Interest." *Journal of Political Economy* 86 (April): S3–S27.

Box, G. E. P., and G. M. Jenkins. 1970. *Time Series Analysis.* San Francisco: Holden Day.

Bradford, D. 1979. "The Incidence and Allocative Effects of a Tax on Corporate Distributions." NBER Working Paper no. 349, May 1979.

Branson, W. H., and A. K. Klevorick. 1969. "Money Illusion and the Aggregate Consumption Function." *American Economic Review* 59 (December): 832–849.

Break, G. F. 1969. "Integration of the Corporate and Personal Income Taxes." *National Tax Journal* 22 (March): 39–56.

Break, G. F., and J. A. Pechman. 1975. *Federal Tax Reform: The Impossible Dream?* Studies of Government Finance. Washington, D.C.: Brookings Institution.

Brechling, F. 1975. *Investment and Employment Decisions.* Manchester, England: Manchester University Press.

Brinner, R. 1973. "Inflation, Deferral and the Neutral Taxation of Capital Gains." *National Tax Journal* 26 (December): 565–573.

Brinner, R., and S. Brooks. 1979. "Taxation, Inflation and Equity Values: Is There a Rational Linkage?" In *Economic Effects of Taxation.* Washington, D.C.: Brookings Institution.

Brittain, J. A. 1966. *Corporate Dividend Policy.* Washington, D.C.: Brookings Institution.

Bruno, M., and J. Sachs. 1979. "Macroeconomic Adjustment with Import Price Shocks: Real and Monetary Aspects." NBER Working Paper no. 340, April 1979.

Butters, J., L. Thompson, and L. Ballinger. 1953. *Effects of Taxation: Investments by Individuals.* Boston: Harvard University Graduate School of Business Administration.

Cagan, P. 1971. "Measuring Quality Changes and the Purchasing Power of Money: An Exploratory Study of Automobiles." In *Price Indexes and Quality Change,* ed. Z. Griliches. Cambridge, Mass.: Harvard University Press. Pp. 215–239.

Cass, D., and J. Stiglitz. 1972. "Risk Aversion and Wealth Effects on Portfolios with Many Assets." *Review of Economic Studies* 39 (July): 331–354.

——— 1970. "The Structure of Investor Preferences and Asset Returns and Separability in Portfolio Allocation: A Contribution to the Pure Theory of Mutual Funds." *Journal of Economic Theory* 2 (June): 122–160.

Clark, P. K. 1979. "Investment in the 1970s: Theory, Performance, and Prediction." *Brookings Papers on Economic Activity* 1979:1, pp. 73–113.

Claycamp, H. J. 1963. *The Composition of Consumer Savings Portfolios.* Urbana, Ill.: Urbana Bureau of Economic and Business Research.

Clower, R. W. 1971. "Is There an Optimal Money Supply? II." In *Frontiers of Quantitative Economics,* ed. M. Intriligator. Amsterdam: North-Holland. Pp. 289–299.

Coen, R. M. 1971. "The Effect of Cash Flow on the Speed of Adjustment." In *Tax Incentives and Capital Spending,* ed. G. Fromm. Washington, D.C.: Brookings Institution. Pp. 131–196.

——— 1969. "Tax Policy and Investment Behavior: Comment." *American Economic Review* 59 (June): 370–379.

——— 1968. "Effects of Tax Policy on Investment in Manufacturing." *American Economic Review* 58 (May): 200–211.

Corner, D. C., and A. Williams. 1955. "The Sensitivity of Businesses to Initial and Investment Allowances." *Economica* 32 (February): 32–47.

Crockett, J., and I. Friend. 1967. "Consumer Investment Behavior." In *Determinants of Investment Behavior,* ed. R. Ferber. New York: Columbia University Press. Pp. 15–127.

Dalton, H. 1954. *Principles of Public Finance,* 4th ed. London: Routledge and Kegan Paul.

Darling, P. G. 1957. "The Influence of Expectations and Liquidity on Dividend Policy." *Journal of Political Economy* 65 (June): 209–224.

David, M. 1968. *Alternative Approaches to Capital Gains Taxation.* Washington, D.C.: Brookings Institution.

David, P., and L. Scadding. 1972. "What You Always Wanted to Know about 'Denison's Law' but Were Afraid to Ask." Mimeographed.

DeLeeuw, F. 1965. "A Model of Financial Behavior." In *The Brookings Quarterly Econometric Model of the United States,* ed. J. Duesenberry et al. Chicago: Rand McNally.

Denison, E. F. 1958. "A Note on Private Saving." *Review of Economics and Statistics* 40 (August): 261–267.

Dhrymes, P. J., and M. Kurz. 1967. "Investment Dividend and External Finance Behavior of Firms." In *Determinants of Investment Behavior,* ed. R. Ferber. New York: Columbia University Press. Pp. 427–467.

Diamond, P. A. 1975. "Inflation and the Comprehensive Tax Base." *Journal of Public Economics* 4 (August): 227–244.

———— 1970. "Incidence of an Interest Income Tax." *Journal of Economic Theory* 2 (September): 211–224.

Domar, E. D., and R. A. Musgrave. 1944. "Proportional Income Taxation and Risk-Taking." *Quarterly Journal of Economics* 58 (May): 388–422.

Duesenberry, J. S. 1958. *Business Cycles and Economic Growth.* New York: McGraw-Hill.

Economic Trends. 1962. "Income and Finance of Quoted Companies, 1949–60." No. 102 (April): 2–13.

Eisner, R. 1978. *Factors in Business Investment.* Cambridge, Mass.: National Bureau of Economic Research, General Series no. 102, Ballinger.

———— 1972. "Components of Capital Expenditure: Replacement and Modernization versus Expansion." *Review of Economics and Statistics* 54 (August): 297–305.

———— 1969. "Tax Policy and Investment Behavior: Comment." *American Economic Review* 59 (June): 379–388.

———— 1967. "A Permanent Income Theory for Investment." *American Economic Review* 57 (June): 363–390.

Eisner, R., and M. Nadiri. 1968. "Investment Behavior and the Neoclassical Theory." *Review of Economics and Statistics* 50 (August): 369–382.

Eisner, R., and R. H. Strotz. 1963. "Determinants of Business Investment." In *Impacts of Monetary Policy,* a series of research studies prepared for the Commission on Money and Credit. Englewood Cliffs, N.J.: Prentice-Hall. Pp. 60–192.

Enzer, H. 1966. "On a Useful Capital Growth Matrix." *Econometrica* 34 (January): 183–192.

Evans, M. K. 1969. *Macroeconometric Activity: Theory, Forecasting and Control; An Econometric Approach.* New York: Harper & Row.

Feenberg, D. 1981. "Does the Investment Interest Limitation Explain the Existence of Dividends?" *Journal of Financial Economics* 9 (Fall): 265–269.

Feldstein, M. S. 1982. "Inflation, Tax Rules and the Accumulation of Residential and Nonresidential Capital Stock." NBER Working Paper no. 753. *Scandinavian Journal of Economics* 84 (2).

————1980a. "Fiscal Policies, Inflation and Capital Formation." *American Economic Review* 70 (September): 636–650.

————1980b. "Inflation, Tax Rules and the Stock Market." *Journal of Monetary Economics* 6 (July): 309–332.

————1980c. "Inflation and the Stock Market." *American Economic Review* 70 (December): 839–847.

————1980d. "Tax Rules and the Mismanagement of Monetary Policy." *American Economic Review* 70 (May): 182–186.

————1979. "Taxes, Inflation and Capital Formation." *National Tax Journal* 32 (September): 347–349.

————1978a. "Inflation, Tax Rules, and the Long-Term Interest Rate." *Brookings Papers on Economic Activity* 1978:1, pp. 61–109.

————1978b. "The Welfare Cost of Capital Income Taxation." *Journal of Political Economy* 86 (April): S29–S51.

————1977. "Does the United States Save Too Little?" *American Economic Review* 67 (February): 116–121.

————1976. "Taxing Consumption." *The New Republic* 28 (February): 14–17.

————1975. "Corporate Tax Integration," a statement before the Senate Budget Committee, September 19, 1975, in *Encouraging Capital Formation through the Tax Code*. Washington, D.C.: U.S. Government Printing Office. Pp. 165–197.

————1974. "Social Security, Induced Retirement, and Aggregate Capital Accumulation." *Journal of Political Economy* 82 (September/October): 905–926.

————1970. "Inflation, Specification Bias and the Impact of Interest Rates." *Journal of Political Economy* 78 (November/December): 1325–1339.

————1969. "Mean Variance Analysis in the Theory of Portfolio Selection." *Review of Economic Studies* 36 (January): 5–11.

————1967a. "Alternative Methods of Estimating a CES Production Function for Britain." *Economica* 34 (November): 384–394.

————1967b. "The Effectiveness of the British Differential Profits Tax." *Economic Journal* 77 (December): 947–953.

Feldstein, M. S., and G. Chamberlain. 1973. "Multimarket Expectations and the Rate of Interest." *Journal of Money, Credit and Banking* 5 (November): 873–902.

Feldstein, M. S., and O. Eckstein. 1970. "The Fundamental Determinants of the Interest Rate." *Review of Economics and Statistics* 52 (November): 363–375.

Feldstein, M. S., and D. K. Foot. 1971. "The Other Half of Gross Investment: Replacement and Modernization Expenditures." *Review of Economics and Statistics* 53 (February): 49–58.

Feldstein, M. S., J. Green, and E. Sheshinski. 1978. "Inflation and Taxes in a Growing Economy with Debt and Equity Finance." *Journal of Political Economy* 86 (April): S53–S70.

Feldstein, M. S., and C. Horioka. 1980. "Domestic Saving and International Capital Flows." *The Economic Journal* 90 (June): 314–329.

Feldstein, M. S., and J. Slemrod. 1978. "Inflation and the Excess Taxation of Capital Gains on Corporate Stock." *National Tax Journal* 31 (June): 107–118.

Feldstein, M. S., and L. Summers. 1979. "Inflation and the Taxation of Capital Income in the Corporate Sector." *National Tax Journal* 32 (December): 445–470.

———1977. "Is the Rate of Profit Falling?" *Brookings Papers on Economic Activity* 1:1977, pp. 211–228.

———1976. "Efficiency Effects of Taxes on Income from Capital." In *Effects of the Corporation Income Tax,* ed. M. Kryzaniak. Detroit: Wayne State University Press.

Feldstein, M. S., and S. C. Tsiang. 1968. "The Interest Rate, Taxation and the Personal Savings Incentive." *Quarterly Journal of Economics* 82 (August): 419–434.

Ferber, J. F., H. Guthrie, and E. Maynes. 1969. "Validation of Consumer Financial Characteristics: Common Stock." *Journal of the American Statistical Association* 64 (June): 415–432.

Fischer, S. 1972. "Keynes-Wicksell and Neoclassical Models of Money and Growth." *American Economic Review* 62 (December): 880–890.

Fisher, F. 1971. "Discussion." In *Tax Incentives and Capital Spending,* ed. G. Fromm, papers presented at a conference of experts held November 3, 1967. Washington: Brookings Institution.

Fisher, I. 1954. *The Theory of Interest.* New York: Kelley and Millman (reprinted).

———1937. "Income in Theory and Income Taxation in Practice." *Econometrica* 5 (January): 1–55.

——— 1930. *The Theory of Interest.* New York: Macmillan.

———1896. *Appreciation and Interest.* New York: Macmillan.

Flemming, J. S. 1971. "Portfolio Choice and Taxation in Continuous-Time." Mimeographed.

Flemming, J. S., and I. M. D. Little. 1974. *Why We Need a Wealth Tax.* London: Methuen.

Foley, D., and M. Sidrauski. 1971. *Monetary and Fiscal Policy in a Growing Economy.* New York: Macmillan.

Foot, D. 1972. "Interactive Investment Behavior." Ph.D. dissertation, Harvard University.

Friedman, M. 1969. "The Optimum Supply of Money." In *The Optimum Supply of Money and Other Essays,* ed. M. Friedman. Chicago: Aldine.

———1959. "The Demand for Money: Some Theoretical and Empirical Results." *Journal of Political Economy* 67 (August): 327–351.

———1957. *A Theory of the Consumption Function.* Princeton, N.J.: Princeton University Press. (National Bureau of Economic Research, no. 63, General Series.)

———1953. "Discussion of the Inflationary Gap." Reprinted in M. Friedman, *Essays in Positive Economics.* Chicago: University of Chicago Press. Pp. 251–262.

Fromm, G., ed. 1970. *Effect of Investment Tax Credit and Accelerated Depreciation on the Level of Interest.* Washington, D.C.: Brookings Institution.

Goldsmith, R. W. 1956. *A Study of Saving in the United States.* Princeton, N.J.: Princeton University Press. (Vols. 1 and 2, 1955; vol. 3, 1956.)

Goode, R. 1964. *The Individual Income Tax.* Washington, D.C.: Brookings Institution.

———— 1951. *The Corporation Income Tax.* New York: Wiley.

Gordon, R. J. 1971. "Inflation in Recession and Recovery." *Brookings Papers on Economic Activity* 1:1971, pp. 105–158.

Gordon, R. H., and D. Bradford. 1979. "Stock Market Valuation of Dividends: Links to the Theory of the Firm and Empirical Estimates." Mimeographed.

Gordon, R. H., and B. Malkiel. 1979. "Corporate Financial Structure." Paper presented at Brookings Conference on Economic Effects of Federal Taxes, October 18–19, 1979.

Gordon, R. H., and D. W. Jorgenson. 1976. "The Investment Tax Credit and Counter-Cyclical Policy." In *Parameters and Policies in the U.S. Economy,* ed. O. Eckstein, Amsterdam: North-Holland, pp. 275–314.

Gould, J. 1968. "Adjustment Costs in the Theory of Investment of the Firm." *Review of Economic Studies* 35 (January): 47–56.

Granger, C. W. J., and P. Newbold. 1974. "Spurious Regressions in Econometrics." *Journal of Econometrics* 2 (July): 111–120.

Grant, E. L., and P. T. Norton. 1955. *Depreciation.* New York: Ronald Press.

Green, J. 1980. "Taxation and the Ex-Dividend Day Behavior of Common Stock Prices." Harvard Institute of Economic Research no. 772, June 1980.

Griliches, Z. 1970. "The Demand for a Durable Input: U.S. Farm Tractors, 1921–57." In *The Demand for Durable Goods,* ed. A. C. Harberger. Chicago: University of Chicago Press.

———— 1962. "Capital Stock and Investment Functions: Some Problems of Concept and Measurement." In *Measurement in Economics,* ed. C. Christ et al. Stanford: Stanford University Press.

———— 1961. "A Note on Serial Correlation Bias in Estimates of Distributed Lags." *Econometrica* 29 (January): 65–73.

Haavelmo, T. 1960. *A Study in the Theory of Investment.* Chicago: University of Chicago Press.

Hall, C. A., Jr. 1960. *Fiscal Policy for Stable Growth.* New York: Holt, Rinehart and Winston.

Hall, R. E. 1977. "Investment, Interest Rates, and the Effects of Stabilization Policies." *Brookings Papers on Economic Activity* 1: 61–122.

———— 1971. "The Measurement of Quality Change from Vintage Price Data." In *Price Indexes and Quality Change,* ed. Z. Griliches. Cambridge, Mass.: Harvard University Press. Pp. 240–271.

———— 1968a. "Technical Change and Capital from the Point of View of the Dual." *Review of Economic Studies* 35 (January): 35–46.

———— 1968b. "Consumption Taxes versus Income Taxes: Implications for Economic Growth." Proceedings of the Sixty-first National Tax Conference.

Hall, R. E., and D. W. Jorgenson. 1970. "The Quantitative Impact of Tax Policy on Investment Expenditures." In *Effect of Investment Tax Credit and Accelerated Depreciation on the Level of Interest,* ed. G. Fromm. Washington, D.C.: Brookings Institution.

———— 1969. "Tax Policy and Investment Behavior: Reply and Further Results." *American Economic Review* 59 (June): 388–400.

———— 1967. "Tax Policy and Investment Behavior." *American Economic Review* 57 (June): 391–414.

Hannan, E. J. 1960. *Time Series Analysis.* London: Methuen.

Harberger, A. C. 1966. "Efficiency Effects of Taxes on Income from Capital." In

Effects of the Corporation Income Tax, ed. M. Krzyzaniak. Detroit: Wayne State University Press. Pp. 107–117.

——— 1964. "Taxation, Resource Allocation and Welfare," In *The Role of Direct and Indirect Taxes in the Federal Revenue System,* ed. J. Due. Princeton, N.J.: Princeton University Press.

——— 1962. "The Incidence of the Corporate Income Tax." *Journal of Political Economy* 70 (June): 215–240.

——— 1959. "The Corporation Income Tax: An Empirical Appraisal." In *Tax Revision Compendium,* House Committee on Ways and Means, 1959.

Harrod, R. F. 1948. *Towards a Dynamic Economics.* London: Macmillan.

Hart, H., and D. F. Prusmann. 1963. "A Report of a Survey of Management Accounting Techniques in S. E. Hants Coastal Region." Mimeographed. Department of Commerce and Accountancy, University of Southampton.

Hartman, D. G. 1979. "Taxation and the Effects of Inflation on the Real Capital Stock in an Open Economy." *International Economic Review* 20 (June): 417–425.

Helliwell, J., and G. Glorieux. 1970. "Forward-Looking Investment Behaviour." *Review of Economic Studies* 37 (October): 499–516.

Henderson, D. W., and T. J. Sargent. 1973. "Monetary and Fiscal Policy in a Two-Sector Aggregative Model." *American Economic Review* 63 (June): 345–365.

Hicks, J. R. 1932. *The Theory of Wages.* London: Macmillan. (Reprinted 1963.)

Hirshleifer, J. 1965. "Investment Decision under Uncertainty: Choice-Theoretic Approaches." *Quarterly Journal of Economics* 79 (November): 509–536.

Holbrook, R., and F. Stafford. 1971. "The Propensity to Consume Separate Types of Income." *Econometrica* 39 (January): 1–22.

Holland, D., and S. Myers. 1979. "Trends in Corporate Profitability and Capital Costs." In *The Nation's Capital Needs: Three Studies,* ed. R. Lindsay. Washington, D.C.: Committee on Economic Development.

Holt, C., and J. Shelton. 1962. "The Lock-In Effect of the Capital Gains Tax." *National Tax Journal* 15 (December): 337–352.

Howard, R. A. 1960. *Dynamic Programming and Markov Processes.* Cambridge, Mass.: M.I.T. Press.

Internal Revenue Service, U.S. Department of the Treasury. 1967. "Personal Wealth, Statistics of Income 1962." Supplementary Report no. 482. Washington, D.C.: U.S. Government Printing Office.

Jakobsson, U. 1974. "Personal and Corporate Taxation and the Growing Firm." Mimeographed.

Jensen, M. C. 1972. "Capital Markets: Theory and Evidence." *Bell Journal of Economics and Management Science* 3 (Autumn): 357–398.

Johansen, L. 1959. "Substitution versus Fixed Production Coefficients in the Theory of Economic Growth: A Synthesis." *Econometrica* 27 (April): 157–176.

Johnson, H. G. 1971. "Is There an Optimal Money Supply?—I." In *Frontiers of Quantitative Economics,* ed. M. Intriligator. Amsterdam: North-Holland. Pp. 279–288.

——— 1956. "A Comment on the General Equilibrium Analysis of Excise Taxes." *American Economic Review* 46 (March): 151–156.

Jorgenson, D. 1973. "The Economic Theory of Replacement and Depreciation." In *Essays in Honor of Jan Tinbergen,* ed. W. Sellykaerts. New York: Macmillan.

———1966. "Rational Distributed Lag Functions." *Econometrica* 34 (January): 135–149.

———1965. "Anticipations and Investment Behaviour." In *The Brookings Quarterly Econometric Model of the United States,* ed. J. S. Duesenberry et al. Chicago: Rand McNally.

———1963. "Capital Theory and Investment Behavior." *American Economic Review* 53 (May): 247–259.

Jorgenson, D., J. Hunter, and M. Nadiri. 1970. "A Comparison of Alternative Econometric Models of Quarterly Investment Behavior." *Econometrica* 38 (March): 187–212.

Jorgenson, D., J. J. McCall, and R. Radner. 1967. *Optimal Replacement Policy.* Chicago: Rand McNally.

Jorgenson, D., and D. Siebert. 1968. "A Comparison of Alternative Theories of Corporate Investment Behavior." *American Economic Review* 58 (September): 681–712.

Jorgenson, D., and J. A. Stephenson. 1967a. "Investment Behavior in U.S. Manufacturing, 1947–60." *Econometrica* 35 (April): 169–220.

———1967b. "The Time Structure of Investment Behavior in United States Manufacturing, 1947–1960." *Review of Economics and Statistics* 49 (February): 16–27.

Kaldor, N. 1955. *An Expenditure Tax.* London: George Allen & Unwin.

Kelley, M. G. 1971. "Taxes, Depreciation and Capital Waste." *National Tax Journal* 24 (March): 31–37.

Kendrick, J. W., K. S. Lee, and J. Lomask. 1976. *The National Wealth of the United States, by Major Sector and Industry.* New York: The Conference Board.

Keynes, J. M. 1936. *The General Theory of Employment, Interest and Money.* London: Macmillan.

King, M. A. 1977. *Public Policy and the Corporation.* London: Chapman and Hall.

———1972. "Corporate Taxation and Dividend Behavior—A Further Comment." *Review of Economic Studies* 39 (April): 231–234.

———1971. "Corporate Taxation and Dividend Behavior—A Comment." *Review of Economic Studies* 38 (July): 377–380.

Klein, L. R., and A. S. Goldberger. 1955. *An Econometric Model of the United States, 1929–52.* Amsterdam: North-Holland.

Koyck, L. M. 1954. *Distributed Lags and Investment Analysis.* Amsterdam: North-Holland.

Krzyzaniak, M. 1970. "Factor Substitution and the General Tax on Profits." *Public Finance* 25 (4): 489–514.

———ed. 1966. *Incidence Effects of the Corporation Tax.* Detroit: Wayne State University Press.

Laidler, D. 1969. "Income Tax Incentives for Owner-Occupied Housing." In *The Taxation of Income From Capital,* ed. A. Harberger and M. Bailey. Washington, D.C.: Brookings Institution.

Lampman, R. 1962. *The Share of Top Wealth-Holders in National Wealth, 1922–56.* Princeton, N.J.: Princeton University Press.

Leamer, E. 1978. *Specification Searches.* New York: Wiley.

Leland, H. 1968. "Dynamic Portfolio Theory." Ph.D. dissertation, Harvard University.

Levhari, D., and D. Patinkin. 1968. "The Role of Money in a Simple Growth Model." *American Economic Review* 58 (September): 713–753.

Lintner, J. 1964. "Optimal Dividends and Corporate Growth under Uncertainty." *Quarterly Journal of Economics* 78 (February): 49–95.

—— 1956. "Distribution of Incomes of Corporations among Dividends, Retained Earnings and Taxes." *American Economic Association Papers and Proceedings* 46 (May): 97–113.

Little, I. M. D. 1962. "Fiscal Policy." In *The British Economy in the Nineteen-Fifties,* ed. G. D. N. Worswick and P. H. Ady. Oxford: Clarendon Press.

Liviatan, N. 1963. "Consistent Estimation of Distributed Lags." *International Economic Review* 4 (January): 44–52.

Lovell, M. 1978. "The Profits Picture: Trends and Cycles." *Brookings Papers on Economic Activity* 3: 1978, pp. 769–789.

Lucas, R. E., Jr. 1976. "Econometric Policy Evaluation: A Critique." In *The Phillips Curve and Labor Markets,* ed. K. Brunner and A. Meltzer. The Carnegie-Rochester Conferences on Public Policy, a supplement series to the *Journal of Monetary Economics,* I. Amsterdam: North-Holland.

Lutz, F. A., and V. Lutz. 1951. *The Theory of Investment of the Firm.* Princeton, N.J.: Princeton University Press.

Lydall, H. F. 1955. "The Life Cycle in Income, Saving, and Asset Ownership." *Econometrica* 23 (April): 131–150.

Maddala, G. S., and A. S. Rao. 1971. "Maximum Likelihood Estimation of Solow's and Jorgenson's Distributed Lag Models." *Review of Economics and Statistics* 53 (February): 80–88.

Malinvaud, E. 1966. *Statistical Methods of Econometrics.* Chicago: Rand McNally.

—— 1964. *Méthodes Statistiques de l'Économetrie.* Paris: Dunod.

—— 1961. "Estimation et Prévision dans les Modèles Économiques Autoregressifs." *Review of the International Institute of Statistics* 29 (2): 1–32.

Markowitz, H. 1959. *Portfolio Selection.* New York: Wiley.

Marris, R. L. 1964. *The Economic Theory of Managerial Capitalism.* London: Macmillan.

Marston, A., and T. R. Agg. 1936. *Engineering Valuation.* New York: McGraw-Hill.

McClung, N. 1966. "The Distribution of Capital Gain on Corporate Shares by Holding Time." *Review of Economics and Statistics* 48 (February): 40–50.

McLure, C. E. 1976. "Integration of the Income Taxes: Why and How." *Journal of Corporate Taxation* 2 (Winter): 429–463.

Meade, J. 1955. "The Effects of Indirect Taxation upon the Distribution of Income." In *Trade and Welfare* II, Mathematical Supplement. London: Oxford University Press.

Merton, R. C. 1969. "Lifetime Portfolio Selection under Uncertainty: The

Continuous-Time Case." *Review of Economics and Statistics* 51 (August): 247–257.

Meyer, J. R., and E. Kuh. 1957. *The Investment Decision.* Cambridge, Mass.: Harvard University Press.

Mieszkowski, P. 1969. "Tax Incidence Theory: The Effects of Taxes on the Distribution of Income." *Journal of Economic Literature* 7 (December): 1103–1124.

―――― 1967. "On the Theory of Tax Incidence." *Journal of Political Economy* 75 (June): 250–262.

Miller, M. H. 1977. "Debt and Taxes." *Journal of Finance* 32 (May): 261–276.

Miller, M., and M. Scholes. 1978. "Dividends and Taxes." *Journal of Financial Economics* (December).

Mitchell, W. 1951. *What Happens during Business Cycles.* New York: National Bureau of Economic Research.

―――― 1927. *Business Cycles: The Problem and Its Setting.* New York: National Bureau of Economic Research.

Modigliani, F. 1970. "The Life Cycle Hypothesis of Saving and Intercountry Differences in the Saving Ratio." In *Induction, Growth and Trade, Essays in Honour of Sir Roy Harrod,* ed. W. A. Eltis et al. Oxford: Clarendon Press.

Modigliani, F., and R. Brumberg. 1954. "Utility Analysis and the Consumption Function: An Interpretation of Cross-Section Data." In *Post Keynesian Economics,* ed. K. Kurihara. New Brunswick, N.J.: Rutgers University Press. P. 430.

Modigliani, F., and M. H. Miller. 1958. "The Cost of Capital, Corporation Finance and the Theory of Investment." *American Economic Review* 48 (June): 261–297.

Mossin, J. 1968. "Taxation and Risk-taking: An Expected Utility Approach." *Economics* 35 (February): 74–82.

Musgrave, R. A. 1959. *The Theory of Public Finance.* New York: McGraw-Hill.

Musgrave, R. A., and P. B. Musgrave. 1973. *Public Finance in Theory and Practice.* New York: McGraw-Hill.

―――― 1968. "Fiscal Policy." In *Britain's Economic Prospects,* ed. R. E. Caves et al. Washington, D.C.: Brookings Institution. Pp. 21–67.

Myers, S. C. 1977. "Determinants of Corporate Borrowing." *Journal of Financial Economics* 5 (November): 147–175.

Nerlove, M. 1972. "On Lags in Economic Behavior." *Econometrica* 40 (March): 221–251.

―――― 1968. "Factors Affecting Differences among Rates of Return on Investments in Individual Common Stocks." *Review of Economics and Statistics* 50 (August): 312.

Nerlove, M., and K. F. Wallis. 1966. "Use of the Durbin-Watson Statistic in Inappropriate Situations." *Econometrica* 34 (January): 235–238.

Netzer, D. 1973. "The Incidence of Property Tax Revisited." *National Tax Journal* 26 (December): 515–535.

Nickell, S. J. 1978. *The Investment Decision of Firms.* Cambridge Economic Handbooks. Cambridge: Cambridge University Press.

Nordhaus, W. D. 1974. "The Falling Share of Profits." *Brookings Papers on Economic Activity* 1974:1, pp. 169–208.

Orcutt, G. H., and D. Cochrane. 1949. "A Sampling Study of the Merits of Autoregressive and Reduced Form Transformations in Regression Analysis." *Journal of the American Statistical Association* 44: 356–372.

Paish, F. W. 1965. "Government Policy and Business Investment." Sir Ellis Hunter Memorial Lecture, York University, York, England.

Parkinson, J. R. 1957. "Ship Wastage Rates." *Journal of the Royal Statistical Society,* Series A, 120, pp. 71–83.

Penner, R. G. 1964. "A Note on Portfolio Selection and Taxation." *Review of Economic Studies* 31 (January): 83–86.

Phelps, E. S. 1973. "Inflation in the Theory of Public Finance." *Swedish Journal of Economics* 75 (March): 67–82.

———— 1963. "Substitution, Fixed Proportions, Growth and Distribution." *International Economic Review* 4 (September): 265–288.

Pigou, A. C. 1947. *A Study in Public Finance,* 3rd ed. London: Macmillan.

———— 1920. *The Economics of Welfare.* London: Macmillan.

Poterba, J. 1980. "Inflation, Income Taxes and Owner Occupied Housing." NBER Working Paper no. 553, September 1980.

Pratt, J. W. 1964. "Risk Aversion in the Small and in the Large." *Econometrica* 32 (January–April): 122–136.

Prentice-Hall 1972 Federal Tax Handbook. 1972. Englewood Cliffs, N.J.: Prentice-Hall.

Projector, D., and G. Weiss. 1966. *Survey of Financial Characteristics of Consumers.* Washington, D.C.: Board of Governors of the Federal Reserve System, Federal Reserve Technical Papers.

Ramm, W. 1971. "The Valuation and Estimation of Automobile Services, 1961–1968." Ph.D. dissertation, Northwestern University.

Revell, J., et al. 1967. *The Wealth of the Nation: The National Balance Sheet of the United Kingdom, 1957–61.* Cambridge: Cambridge University Press.

Ricardo, D. 1951. *On the Principles of Political Economy and Taxation,* ed. R. Sraffa. New York: Cambridge University Press.

Richter, M. K. 1960. "Cardinal Utility, Portfolio Selection and Taxation." *Review of Economic Studies* 27 (June): 152–166.

Ross, S. 1977. "The Determination of Financial Structures: The Incentive Signalling Approach." *Bell Journal of Economics* 8 (Spring): 23–40.

Rothschild, M. 1971. "On the Cost of Adjustment." *Quarterly Journal of Economics* 75 (November): 605–622.

Rowley, J. C. R., and P. K. Trivedi. 1975. *Econometrics of Investment.* London: Wiley.

Royal Commission on the Taxation of Profits and Income —Final Report. 1955. Cmd. 9474. London: Her Majesty's Stationery Office.

Rubner, A. 1964. "The Irrelevancy of the British Differential Profits Tax." *Economic Journal* 74 (June): 347–359.

Ruggles, R., and N. Ruggles. 1956. *National Income Accounts and Income Analysis.* New York: McGraw-Hill.

———— 1970. *The Design of Economic Accounts.* New York: National Bureau of Economic Research.

Samuelson, P. A. 1969. "Lifetime Portfolio Selection by Dynamic Stochastic Programming." *Review of Economics and Statistics* 51 (August): 239–246.

———1958. "An Exact Consumption-Loan Model of Interest with or without the Social Contrivance of Money." *Journal of Political Economy* 66 (December): 467–482.

Sandmo, A. 1969. "Capital Risk, Consumption, and Portfolio Choice." *Econometrica* 37 (October): 586–599.

Sargan, J. D. 1964. "Wages and Prices in the United Kingdom." In P. Hart et al., *Econometric Analysis for National Economic Planning*. London: Butterworth.

———1958. "Estimation of Economic Relationships Using Instrumental Variables." *Econometrica* 26 (July): 393–415.

Sargent, T. J. 1978. "Estimation of Dynamic Labor Demand Schedules under Rational Expectations." *Journal of Political Economy* 86 (December): 1009–1044.

Sato, K. 1967. "Taxation and Neoclassical Growth." *Public Finance* 22 (3): 346–370.

Sato, R. 1963. "Fiscal Policy in a Neoclassical Growth Model: An Analysis of Time Required for Equilibrating Adjustment." *Review of Economic Studies* 30 (February): 16–23.

Securities and Exchange Commission. 1977. *Statistical Bulletin,* June 1977.

Sen, A. K. 1961. "On Optimizing the Rate of Saving." *Economic Journal* 71 (September): 479–496.

Shephard, R. W. 1944. "A Mathematical Theory of the Incidence of Taxation." *Econometrica* 12 (January): 1–18.

Shove, G. 1933. "Review of J. R. Hicks, *The Theory of Wages*." *Economic Journal* 43 (September): 460–473.

Shoven, J. B. 1976. "The Incidence and Efficiency Effects of Taxes on Income from Capital." *Journal of Political Economy* 84 (December): 1261–1283.

Shoven, J. B., and J. Whalley. 1972. "A General Equilibrium Calculation of the Effects of Differential Taxation of Income from Capital in the U.S." *Journal of Public Economics* 1 (November): 281–321.

Sims, C. 1969. "The Role of Prior Restrictions in Distributed Lag Estimation." Harvard Institute of Economic Research, Discussion Paper no. 60.

Smith, V. L. 1963. "Tax Depreciation Policy and Investment Theory." *International Economic Review* 4 (January): 80–91.

———1961. *Investment and Production.* Cambridge, Mass: Harvard University Press.

———1957. "Economic Equipment Policies: An Evaluation." *Management Science* 4 (October): 20–37.

Solow, R. 1971. "Some Implications of Alternative Criteria for the Firm." In *The Corporate Economy,* ed. R. Marris and A. Wood. New York: Macmillan. Pp. 318–342.

———1960. "On a Family of Lag Distributions." *Econometrica* 28 (April): 393–406.

Solow, R., J. Tobin, C. C. von Weizsacker, and M. E. Yaari. 1966. "Neoclassical Growth with Fixed Factor Proportions." *Review of Economic Studies* 33 (April): 79–115.

Stein, J. 1970. "Monetary Growth Theory in Perspective." *American Economic Review* 60 (March): 85–106.

Stiglitz, J. E. 1976. "The Corporation Income Tax." *Journal of Public Economics* 5 (April–May): 303–311.

——— 1973. "Taxation, Corporate Financial Policy, and the Cost of Capital." *Journal of Public Economics* 2 (February): 1–34.

——— 1972. "Portfolio Allocation with Many Risky Assets." In *Mathematical Methods in Investment and Finance,* ed. T. Szego and K. Shell. Amsterdam: North-Holland.

——— 1969a. "Behavior toward Risk with Many Commodities." *Econometrica* 37 (October): 660–667.

——— 1969b. "The Effects of Income, Wealth, and Capital Gains Taxation on Risk-Taking." *Quarterly Journal of Economics* 83 (May): 263–283.

Streeten, P. 1960. "Tax Policy for Investment." *Revista Di Diritto Finanziario E. Scienza Delle Finanze* 19 (June): 117–137.

Suits, D. B. 1963. "The Determinants of Consumer Expenditure: A Review of Present Knowledge." In *Impacts of Monetary Policy,* a series of research studies prepared for the Commission on Money and Credit. Englewood Cliffs, N.J.: Prentice-Hall. Pp. 1–57.

Summers, L. H. 1981. "Taxation and Corporate Investment: A Q-Theory Approach." *Brookings Papers on Economic Activity* 1981:1, pp. 67–127.

Surrey, S., P. McDaniel, and J. Pechman. 1976. *Federal Tax Reform for 1976.* Washington, D.C.: Fund for Public Policy Research.

Swan, P. 1970. "Durability of Consumption Goods." *American Economic Review* 60 (December): 884–894.

Taylor, L. 1971. "Saving out of Different Types of Income." *Brookings Papers on Economic Activity* 1971:2, pp. 383–407.

Terborgh, G. 1954. *Realistic Depreciation Policy.* Chicago: *MAPI.*

Theil, H. 1961. *Economic Forecasts and Policy,* 2nd ed. Amsterdam: North-Holland.

Tobin, J. 1969. "What is Output? Problems of Concept and Measurement." In *Production and Productivity in the Service Industry,* ed. V. Fuchs. New York: Columbia University Press.

——— 1967a. "Comment on Crockett-Friend and Jorgenson." In *Determinants of Investment Behavior,* ed. R. Ferber. New York: Columbia University Press.

——— 1967b. "Life Cycle Saving and Balanced Growth." In *Ten Economic Studies in the Tradition of Irving Fisher.* New York: Wiley.

——— 1965a. "The Theory of Portfolio Selection." In *The Theory of Interest Rates,* ed. F. H. Holm and F. P. R. Breckling. London: Macmillan.

——— 1965b. "Money and Economic Growth." *Econometrica* 33 (October): 671–684.

——— 1958. "Liquidity Preference as Behavior towards Risk." *Review of Economic Studies* 25 (February): 65–86.

——— 1955. "A Dynamic Aggregate Model." *Journal of Political Economy* 23 (April): 103–115.

Treadway, A. B. 1969. "What is Output? Problems of Concept and Measurement." In *Production and Productivity in the Service Industry,* ed. V. Fuchs. New York: Columbia University Press.

Ture, N. B. 1967. *Accelerated Depreciation in the United States, 1954–60.* New

York: Columbia University Press for the National Bureau of Economic Research.

Uhler, R. S., and J. G. Cragg. 1971. "The Structure of the Asset Portfolios of Households." *Review of Economic Studies* 38 (July): 341–357.

U.S. Congress, Committee on Ways and Means. 1977. "Tax Policy and Capital Formation." Prepared for the use of the Task Force on Capital Formation, April 4, 1977. Washington, D.C.: U.S. Government Printing Office.

U.S. Department of Commerce, Office of Business Economics. 1976. *Survey of Current Business*, "U.S. National Income and Product Accounts, 1973 to Second Quarter 1976," July 1976. Section 8: Supplementary Tables, pp. 22–68. Washington, D.C.: U.S. Government Printing Office.

———1971. *Fixed Non-Residential Business Capital in the United States, 1925–1970.* Supplement to the *Survey of Current Business.* Washington, D.C.: U.S. Government Printing Office.

U.S. Department of the Treasury, Internal Revenue Service. 1976. "Preliminary Report, Statistics of Income—1973—Corporation Income Tax Returns." Washington, D.C.: U.S. Government Printing Office.

U.S. Senate, Committee on the Budget. 1976. "Tax Expenditures: Compendium of Background Material on Individual Provisions." Washington, D.C.: U.S. Government Printing Office.

Vinals, J. 1981. "Factor Price and Macroeconomic Activity." Ph.D. dissertation, Harvard University.

Von Furstenberg, G. M. 1977. "Corporate Investment: Does Market Valuation Matter in the Aggregate?" *Brookings Papers on Economic Activity* 1977:2, pp. 347–397.

Wales, T. 1966. "Estimation of an Accelerated Depreciation Learning Function." *Journal of the American Statistical Association* 61 (December): 995–1009.

Wallis, K. F. 1966. "Lagged Dependent Variables and Serially Correlated Errors: A Reappraisal of Three-Pass Least Squares." Cowles Foundation Paper no. 60727; shorter version published in *Review of Economics and Statistics* 49 (November 1967): 555–567.

Watts, H. W., and J. Tobin. 1967. "Consumer Expenditures and the Capital Account." In *Studies of Portfolio Behavior,* ed. D. Hester and J. Tobin. New York: Wiley.

Weber, W. E. 1970. "The Effect of Interest Rates on Aggregate Consumption." *American Economic Review* 60 (September): 491–600.

Wicksell, K. 1934. *Lectures on Political Economy,* vol. 1. London: George Routledge.

Williams, A. 1966. "Great Britain." In *Foreign Tax Policies and Economic Growth,* a conference report of the National Bureau of Economic Research and the Brookings Institution. New York: Columbia University Press. Pp. 397–467.

Winfrey, R. 1935. *Statistical Analyses of Industrial Property Retirements.* Bulletin 125, Iowa Engineering Experiment Station, December 1935.

Wright, C. 1969. "Saving and the Rate of Interest." In *The Taxation of Income from Capital,* ed. A. C. Harberger and M. J. Bailey. Washington, D.C.: Brookings Institution.

Wykoff, F. 1970. "Capital Depreciation in the Postwar Period: Automobiles." *Review of Economics and Statistics* 52 (May): 1968–1972.

Index